copy

Evalyn A Clark

Cambridge

1958

THE GERMAN *Idea* OF FREEDOM

LEONARD KRIEGER *is Associate Professor of History at Yale University.* During World War II he served as an OSS officer in Germany, and later as a civilian with the State Department. In 1956-57 he did research at the Center for Advanced Study in the Behavioral Sciences, Stanford, California.

THE GERMAN *Idea* OF FREEDOM

History of a Political Tradition

Leonard Krieger

BEACON PRESS *Beacon Hill* Boston

Contents

Preface   ix

First Section. THE TRADITION:
Liberty and Sovereignty in the
German Old Regime   1

1. Society and Politics   8

    Social and Political Structure of the Territorial State   9
    The Dualistic Principality   14
    The Transition: From Principality to State   19
    The Period of Enlightened Absolutism   21

2. Constitutional and Political Theory   46

    The Absolutists (1650-1750)   50
    The Constitutionalists (1750-1789)   71

Second Section. THE ASSUMPTIONS:
Reformers, Nationalists, and Radicals in the
Revolutionary Era (1789-1830)   81

3. The Philosophical Bases: Kant and Hegel   86

    Kant   86
    Hegel   125

4. The Politics of Reform (1806-1813)   139

    Stein   147
    Hardenberg   155
    Humboldt   166

v

5. National Liberation (1813-1815)   174

   The Intellectual Preparation: Fichte and Arndt   176
   Liberation Nationalism   196
   The Response   206

6. Post-Liberation Politics: Bureaucrats, Constitutionalists, and Radicals (1815-1830)   216

   The First Prussian Constitutional Conflict (1815-1823)   217
   Constitutional Dualism in Southern Germany (1815-1830)   229
      The Constitutions   231
      Karl Rotteck and the Theory of Political Dualism   242
      The Doctrine of the *Rechtsstaat*   252
   The German Student Unions (1815-1833)   261

Third Section. THE MOVEMENT:
The Struggle for a Liberal State (1830-1870)   273

7. The Rise of the Liberal Intellectuals (1830-1850)   278

   The Development   280
   The Conditions   287
   The Ideas   296
      The Moderates   303
      The Dualists   314
      The Radicals   322
   The Revolution   329

8. The Decline of the Liberal Intellectuals (1850-
   1870)   341

   The New Moderates   348
   The Old Moderates   358
   The New Radicals   371
   The Old Radicals   383
      The Converts to Conservatism   384
      The Doctrinaires   388
      The Middle-Class Radicals   393

9. The Rise and Decline of Institutional Liberalism (1859-1870) 398

  The Social Basis 398
  The Pressure Groups 407
    The Congress of German Economists 407
    The National Union 413
  The Parties 427
    The Progressive Party 429
    The National Liberal Party 438
    The German People's Party 450

Epilogue 458

Notes 471

Select Bibliography 529

Index 534

To My Father and Mother

Preface

This book is not designed to cover a section of history. It is designed, rather, to provide answers to a definite set of historical questions arising out of the "German problem." The questions are these: Did the Germans' failure to achieve, under their own power, a liberal democracy in the western sense mean simply the triumph of conservatism over generic liberalism in Germany or was a peculiar German attitude toward liberty involved in its defeat? If there was such an attitude, what were its ingredients? And finally, given the ingredients of a special German approach to the problems of political freedom, how did that strange historical development work which kept changing the conditions while leaving the ingredients themselves constant?

The first of these questions, on which the others hinge, is easily decided. Without minimizing in the slightest the conservative weight of German authoritarian institutions or the bitterness of the liberal opposition to them during the 19th century, an historical view into any period of modern German history must still acknowledge that the external posture of German liberalism has ever been qualified by its distinctive internal structure. The juxtaposition—indeed, even the connection—of one conception of liberty that could be realized only within the authoritarian state and of another that could be realized only in an absolute realm beyond all states is a commonly remarked German phenomenon. It has been traced back to Luther and up to Hitler. My problem is to show what the connection between these two apparently antithetical conceptions has been and how it has grown.

Both the scope and the method of the book are tailored to this problem. The kind of liberty or freedom which is relevant to it is the individual secular liberty familiar to the western political tradition. Unless otherwise qualified it is in this sense that these terms will be used and that the historical advocates of them will be selected. The time-span of the book covers the historical periods in which freedom in this sense was a central issue—roughly the era between the medieval type of corporativism and the contemporary type of collectivism, punctuated by the Protestant Reformation at one end and the national

ix

unification at the other. The first section—characterized by the
term "Old Regime" as a somewhat arbitrary short-hand for the
period from the Reformation to the French Revolution—and
the epilogue deal with the transitions into and out of the era
of individualism which furnishes the setting for the main drama.

The method should be adapted to the content of history. This
book is primarily intellectual history because the protagonists
of individual liberty in Germany were primarily intellectuals.
But still certain methodological issues have arisen because it
cannot be exclusively intellectual history. Ultimately it is the
analysis of the German ideas on freedom that provides the
answers to our questions, but such an analysis can proceed only
on the basis of the knowledge that these ideas were doubly conditioned: they were responses to a politically, economically, and
socially formed German situation, and they were themselves
formed under the particular social and political circumstances
attendant upon their liberal progenitors. Since all these factors
are relevant and since a complete research into them all would
prolong this investigation indefinitely into time and space, definite criteria of selection have been employed. First, original
sources have been used especially for the presentation of ideas
while the wealth of scholarly works has been exploited for the
economic, social, and political context. Secondly, within the
intellectual sphere I have chosen rather to give specific representative figures intensive analysis than to give extensive treatment to the whole galaxy of writers in any period. As a corollary
of this decision, the familiar creative thinkers are preferred to
the more obscure popularizers and publicists, because only in
the former do the theoretical depth and the logical coherence
of the argument permit the historian to penetrate beyond the
letter of the political tenet to its meaning. Finally, the book is
focused chiefly, albeit not entirely, upon the Prussian version
of the German problem, because this version portrayed the
dilemmas of freedom in their most categorical forms.

The continuous stream of communication which criss-crosses
academic life at once intensifies scholarly obligations and com-
plicates their characterization. Hajo Holborn's continuous sup-

ply of information and insights, his patient reading of my manuscript in its preliminary as well as its final stages, and his unfailingly perceptive judgments on it are the most identifiable but perhaps the least important of his gifts. In his work and in his person he has demonstrated to a whole generation of historians how humanism and humanity combine to make a scholar, and this is a gift which cannot be assayed.

With other benefactions, similarly, the listing of services that can be specified should be understood to include the more intangible boons of personal intercourse that can not. Felix Gilbert read the bulk of the draft manuscript and contributed generously of his time and thought to its improvement. For me as for so many others he mixed approbation, criticism, and suggestion in optimum proportions. Otto Kirchheimer commented helpfully on a large block of the manuscript and supplied encouragement at a time when it was sorely needed. Carl Schorske and the late Franz Neumann read portions of the manuscript in an earlier version. Sherman Kent fostered the notion that this should be a general book on the German problem.

The contribution of my wife exceeds even more any standard for measuring it. She performed admirably in all of several roles ranging from proofreader to reviewer of substance and she lent expert assistance in all questions touching on philosophy. But she has rendered one crucial service that remains above and beyond the call of conjugal duty. Her qualities of mind and of political conscience have made her the model of the reader for whom I write.

I should like to acknowledge the following permissions to reproduce extended quotations: in Chapter 2, from the Oxford University Press for Samuel Pufendorf, *De Jure Naturae et Gentium Libri Octo* (Oxford, 1934, Eng. tr. by C. H. and W. A. Oldfather), II, 1010-1011; in Chapter 3, from the Oxford University Press for Immanuel Kant, *Critique of Aesthetic Judgement* (Oxford, 1911, Eng. tr. by J. C. Meredith), p. 14; Immanuel Kant, *Critique of Teleological Judgement* (Oxford, 1928, Eng. tr. by J. C. Meredith), p. 124; and T. M. Knox, ed. and tr., *Hegel's Philosophy of Right* (Oxford, 1942), pp. 105, 259; from

The MacMillan Company for G. W. F. Hegel, *The Phenomenology of Mind* (2nd ed., New York, 1931, Eng. tr. by J. B. Baillie), pp. 519-520; from The Liberal Arts Press, Inc. for page 3 of Kant, *Critique of Practical Reason*, translated, with an introduction by Lewis White Beck (New York: The Library of Liberal Arts No. 52), reprinted by permission of the publishers, The Liberal Arts Press, Inc.; in Chapter 8, from the University of Nebraska Press for Eugene N. Anderson, *Social and Political Conflict in Prussia, 1859-1864* (Lincoln, 1954), p. 149.

LEONARD KRIEGER

Yale University

First Section. THE TRADITION:

Liberty and Sovereignty in the
German Old Regime

Liberty and Sovereignty in the
German Old Regime

The lasting social achievement of 19th century Europe was the reorganization of law and politics which produced in public institutions an operative respect for the rights of individual persons. In its fully developed forms this process comprehended three kinds of rights: freedom of the spirit, which included the right to hold and communicate beliefs and opinions; material liberties, which included rights of free economic initiative and exchange, of social mobility and juridical security; and finally the broad distribution of political powers which conferred control over public institutions upon representative sections of the governed. When combined, these various kinds of rights became organized into a consistent and total constitutional system which endowed them with a permanent form and guarantee.

Freedom in the sense of this system was integrally realized only in those nations of the west which can be loosely denominated as the Atlantic community, and here it has proved so stable that subsequent proliferations of liberty—confessional, collectivist, and nationalist—upon which liberal parties have split have not shaken their firm basis in constitutionally guaranteed private, civil, and political rights. In eastern Europe and in the colonial areas even further distant from the Atlantic group the pattern was equally simple: the constitutional issues associated with the emancipation of the individual from the traditional bonds of caste and despotism were scarcely even joined before they were engulfed by the transverse currents of socialist and anti-imperialist appeals to freedom. It is in the middle of Europe, and particularly in Germany, that the problem of freedom has proved to be most vexatious. The liberal spirit did affect German institutions and these institutions penetrated through the facade of professional politics to effect real changes in the life of the nation. But the process was incomplete and unintegrated. Not only was the capstone of political rights left wanting but spiritual and material liberties were never organized into a single system of rights, and consequently the half-finished structure

3

crumbled under the strain of later social and international conflicts.

The political divergence of Germany from the west during the
critical period of liberalization which stretched from the last
generation of the 18th century to the last generation of the 19th
has provided the occasion for classic analyses of contemporary
German culture in the large, for in it the explanation of the separation has been sought. Friedrich Meinecke established the
intellectual process by which the Germans developed a clear and
practical consciousness of their national individuality out of the
undifferentiated cosmopolitanism of the 18th century. Ernst
Troeltsch provided another unforgettable formulation of this
process when he analyzed the development of Germany away
from the west in terms of a distinctive German romanticism
which became a predominant national characteristic at the beginning of the 19th century, as opposed to the common tradition
of a rational natural law retained by the west. Hajo Holborn,
finally, has recently given the social underpinning to this analysis
by emphasizing the particular structure and orientation of the
German middle classes and Protestant churches which aided the
monopolization of moral and actual authority by the state.[1] In
their general explorations of the early 19th century German
divergence, these studies have uncovered the fundamental relationship which is the necessary starting-point for any consideration of "the German problem." The Germans' position half
within and half without the western community caused them to
participate genuinely in ideas and institutions of the western
type while imparting new connotations and new associations to
them. These categories of western thought and activity were far
more than a veneer or a set of techniques to be juxtaposed with
non-western values and traditions, but they were not so literally
absorbed that the variance from the political forms of the Atlantic nations seemed equivalent to the perversion of a common
ideal. In short, the Germans shared so much of and so internally
in western norms and practical arrangements that they named
their own values and actions in western terms and saw in their
divergence only their positive cultural creation within the common western pattern. Thus the limited efficacy of individual

rights in their political system during the 19th century was, for most Germans, an indication not of a defect in freedom but of a distinctive German dimension to freedom.

This cultural relationship between Germany and the Atlantic community opens up a new set of considerations. If the studies of the overt phase of the German separation from the west have revealed a process of obvious differentiation under the retention of common titles during the 19th century, then the question naturally follows whether the common titles of the putatively undifferentiated European culture during the earlier centuries of the modern period—from the 16th to the end of the 18th—. did not also cover an actual process of differentiation, however covert or obscure. Such a process can indeed be affirmed, and the consequent relocation of the origins of the German divergence has ramifications far beyond the mere discovery of historical precedents. When the point of separation is moved back into a period in which neither Germany as a whole nor its particular principalities had yet organized their states into absolute systems of authority, then it becomes clear that the peculiar 19th century version of political freedom was founded upon older national assumptions which made the idea of liberty not the polar antithesis but the historical associate of princely authority.

During the centuries from the Reformation to the Revolution a particular German tradition of liberty, conditioning both political action and thinking, was consolidated from medieval roots, and this tradition was to provide the basic forms into which the modern libertarian influences of the revolutionary era were to flow. The composition of the native tradition has been open to misconstruction. To be sure, the much-discussed influence of Lutheranism in politics, with its tendency toward the categorical separation of the Word and the Flesh, spirit and the world, freedom and action, contributed to the early elaboration of a particular German definition of freedom. But it was, as such, not the most prominent nor the most important influence. In general, the relationship between Lutheranism and politics seems to have been one in which Lutheranism was the passive rather than the active factor, more receptive than formative,[2] and certainly for the problem of political liberty it was not itself central. Lutheranism was part of a whole complex of social and constitutional institutions and ideas collected around the untranslatable concept of *Libertaet,* and it was this concept rather than German religiosity as such that indicated the primary framework molding the early German attitude toward freedom in this world. In its most literal sense, *Libertaet* referred simply to the rights of the German princes within the Holy Roman Empire, but it connoted much more than this. It held different overtones which for the princes extended it to cover their growing political authority and which for the people extended it to represent the political rights of the society as a whole. Involved in the concept was the process by which the special chartered liberties of medieval corporations were grafted, during the early modern period, onto the sovereign powers of those corporations which became territorial states. The internal connection, reflected in the notion of *Libertaet,* between the governing rights of the princes and the representative rights of the people was the first link in the development which was to associate freedom with the very authority of the state in Germany. The aristocratic liberty of the newly autonomous principality in the sense of *Libertaet* was to be a crucial assumption for the peculiar role which individualized freedom in the sense of *Freiheit* later played in the modern states of 19th century Germany.

In the Germany of the old regime the central core of political action was the territorial state which gradually developed out of the feudal lordship of the prince. Both as a reality and as an idea it absorbed the energies of social groupings and constitutional theorists into itself. Certainly the state was a cynosure throughout Europe in the early modern period, but the particular principalities of Germany occupied a special position. They not only embodied, like other states, a growing monopoly of the practical and moral instruments of authority; they also, unlike other states, continued to embody traditional and theoretical claims of rights against authority. The German principalities of the old regime took up a larger place in the life and thought of the society than elsewhere, despite their comparative weakness as states, precisely because they loomed as representative of both the general order and of men's chartered liberties within it. The process by which the German principalities acquired and maintained this rare attribute of a sovereignty defined by social claims upon sovereignty was a process both actual and theoretical. The actuality was a history in which the social structure was not, as elsewhere, subordinated to the control of a constitutional structure independent of it, but was integrally inter-woven with it. Because the German territorial states asserted their powers simultaneously *vis-à-vis* the social groups within them and the constitution of the Holy Roman Empire of the German Nation outside them, these states continued, down to the end of the old regime, to be not only established political institutions resisting the claims of social and individual right-holders, but also themselves claimant social corporations demanding analogous rights from the Empire. And on the theoretical level, similarly, the historical development of the German old regime was distinctive for the constancy with which, under changing terms, doctrines of sovereignty continued to be defined in terms of freedom.

1. Society and Politics

In general, the social structure of Europe during the early modern period comprehended two kinds of orders. It included, on the one hand, those groupings and arrangements, generally called "feudal," which had been carried down from the middle ages, losing most of their corresponding public functions en route, and, on the other, certain newer groupings seeking rearrangements to correspond with their novel needs and functions. The bulk of the hereditary landed nobility, the conservative tenure-holding peasantry, and the incorporated municipal oligarchies composed the first of these social types, while the merchants dealing in wholesale trade, international exchange, and domestic industrial production, their associates among the commercialized sectors of the agrarian aristocracy, the young bureaucracies, and the financiers whose political investments embodied the link between large-scale trade and royal administration made up the second. Within this general European structure the German old regime was distinguished by the unchallenged preponderance of the "feudal" over the commercial type of social order and by the consequent concentration of the weak social tendencies toward change in an estate of intellectuals whose close identification with the bureaucracy emphasized the primacy of the state over the citizen in all matters of reform. The result of this social imbalance was a cultural relationship in which the German society was dominated by the aristocratic weight of stagnation while the German princely states took over all responsibility for change. In the early separation of economic and social life on the one side from political and intellectual tendencies on the other lay the sociological root of the more notorious split between the German reality and the German spirit.

But if this schema provides the general framework in which the German problem had its origins, it raises issues which cannot be schematically resolved. First, the idea that enlightened princes, officials, and intellectuals foisted modernizing reforms upon an apathetic and retrograde society ignores the problem raised by the existence somewhere in that society of elements which received those reforms and gave some reality to paper decrees.[1]

Secondly, even if a case be made for princes and intellectuals operating in a kind of social vacuum, this can surely not hold for the German bureaucracy—and particularly for the higher bureaucracy of the 18th century. The officials—including the intellectuals among them—stemmed from typical groups in the society and maintained association with them. Thirdly, if the administrators and theorists are to be congratulated for their effective activity, then certainly the society upon which they acted must have undergone some change by the very dint of such activity, and it must subsequently have borne a mien very different from its original form.

The general sense of these objections is to indicate that the rifts within the German culture of the old regime were not so radical as they at first glance appear. The German princes never lost their intimate connections with the rest of the nobility nor their states an ineradicable remnant of aristocratic corporativism, and the German society in its turn did produce certain clear, if subordinate, impulses of a dynamic kind which progressive states could and did use. These modifications of the stark image of the Two Germanies do more than soften its outlines. They change the very nature of the problem. From this vantage-point the focus turns from Germany to the territorial states within it and the central theme from a static and categorical cultural dualism to the historical process by which the influential groups of the German society came to deposit their aspirations as well as their loyalty in them.

Social and Political Structure of the Territorial State

It can hardly be disputed that the landed aristocracy remained the dominant group in the German society from the beginning to the end of the old regime—i.e. from the Protestant Reformation to the French Revolution. This position was based economically upon the continuing quantitative superiority of agriculture[2] and socially upon the continuing qualitative inferiority of

a burgher estate sunk in commercial apathy since the middle of
the 16th century and a peasantry passive since their rebellion of
1525. Consequently, the social power which their legal status as
overlords conferred upon the nobles made them the most exclusive caste in the west. Unlike the English and French nobility,
which assimilated important sections of the commoner classes the
German aristocracy was able to maintain itself in comparative
purity.[3] Its social hegemony was expressed by its unchallenged
predominance among the territorial estates (*Landstaenden*),
which were not only organs of corporate self-administration
along traditional feudal lines but which were at the same time
the only basis of political representation in the new states. The
territorial diets (*Landtagen*), in which the estates assembled, were
organized by separate order, and hence the respective roles of the
various groups are easily discernible. The peasantry was rarely
recognized as an order at all for purposes of representation and
only in a very few places did it participate in the provincial, let
alone the territorial diets. Indeed, by Imperial court decision
the peasantry was "undiscoverable" as an estate in the German
constitution.[4] This public status was an expression of the dependence in which the great majority of German peasants were
held by their lords. Although the harshest aspects of serfdom
fell away during the 18th century, when almost all peasants were
granted legal personality in the sense that they were no longer
bought and sold and could bring suits at law, they remained in a
status of "hereditary subjection," bound to the soil and attended
from birth with all manner of personal and real obligations. The
degree of bondage varied greatly, to be sure, from the purely
private services due the land-leasing aristocracy of the west
(*Grundherrschaft*) to the combination of manorial and sovereign
local powers acquired by the estate-managing nobility of the
east, but the facts of social subjection and political apathy among
the peasantry were general in Germany after the 16th century.

Towns played a greater public role, for they retained both a
broad sphere of local autonomy and their own curia as a distinct
order in the diets. But burgher influence in the diets and generally in the state beyond the town walls had been definitely subordinated to that of the aristocracy ever since the victory of the

landed lords over the towns in the strife of the 16th and 17th centuries which had repelled the urban drive toward complete legal independence and toward expansion over the countryside.[5] The Imperial municipalities were hardly more significant than the territorial cities.[6] This public position of the towns correponded to an economic situation which was characterized not so much by absolute decay as by the failure to develop during an expanding era. The efflorescence of German commerce and finance during the 15th and early 16th centuries had been the equal of any nation's in volume, in capitalist institutions and motives, in the burghers' taste for freedom and for power. The decline in the German burgher class, which began to set in after 1550, was a decline in initiative, in expansiveness, and in the libertarian spirit. The actual volume of German trade kept up well—except for a break around the Thirty Years' War—because the relocation of the European economy from the Mediterranean to the Atlantic which undermined the German north-south commerce increased the importance of the east-west transit trade.[7] The decline of the Hansa as a whole was balanced by the prosperity of former members like Koenigsberg, Stettin, and Danzig in the 17th and early 18th centuries.[8] Hence the basis for a German urban development and burgher influence continued to exist, but the abstention from the characteristic activities of western European townsmen during the commercial era made for a social and political subordination which confirmed the contemporary power of the landed aristocracy and ensured that even the ultimate initiative toward development would come from outside the burgher group itself.

As a final guarantee of aristocratic primacy, a separate order of the clergy within the secular principalities was either nonexistent or, by reason of the system of aristocratic patronage, unimportant.[9] The post-Reformation churches in Germany did increase the administrative power of the prince, but their higher clergy remained a social component of a single aristocratic estate.

But at the same time as the German aristocracy was consolidating the social hegemony which guaranteed the perpetuation of their privileges in both private and public affairs the German princes were establishing the political superiority which subjected the aristocracy, together with the rest of the territorial society, to their overriding sovereign will. Indeed, the rise of the princes was the direct result of their victory over the traditional political autonomy of the powerful territorial nobility itself. This process took place in two main stages. By the middle of the 17th century the princes had successfully interposed themselves between the Empire and the nobility within their own territories and had made the territorial principality the preponderant unit in the constitutional hierachy. The tendency of the essentially non-political Reformation to increase this preponderance was originally a sign of how the balance of forces lay and subsequently an additional cause of further increase. Though primary, however, the princes were not yet, at this stage, absolute. Their states were not sovereign but dualistic, characterized by the competition between the princes on the one side and the aristocratic and burgess estates on the other. This competition was not for the possession of the state power itself—which was recognized as the princes'—but for the extension or limitation of the state power as such *vis-à-vis* other kinds of authorities and corporations. The second stage witnessed the completion of the process. By the early 18th century the claims to corporate autonomy and dual authority had been smashed in the name of princely absolutism within the sovereign state. The importation of an aristocratic court culture from France in a literal, and often absurd, imitation of the Versailles of Louis XIV and the conversion of an important section of the German aristocracy to this culture capped the development.[10]

In its general aspects the state-making process in the early modern era is familiar enough. In Europe as a whole during the old regime princely absolutism was grounded both in the leveling tendencies of the new military, bureaucratic, mercantilist state as the supreme organ of public law and in the continuing hierarchy of private relationships from feudal times. In Europe as a whole the aristocracy was both disenfranchised in politics and confirmed in its economic and social privileges, including prescriptive rights to office in the royal administrations and to the domination of local government. Not only did the German development share these general characteristics but even the economic and social relations which spurred the rise of kings in the western countries extended for a time to Germany, where they helped to elevate the territorial princes. Between the 14th and the 16th centuries Germany and the west alike participated in the growing insufficiency of the universal claims of Empire and Papacy, the economic and technological undermining of the local aristocracies, the great rise of commerce and of towns, and the consequent demands for an order that would be more general than that of the local authorities and more real than that of the universal moral authorities. But from the middle of the 16th century to the 18th, the distinctive problem arose in Germany which began to differentiate it perceptibly from the western nations. Where the monarchical states of western Europe completed their development toward internal sovereignty by holding aristocratic and burgher groups in balance and establishing their political authority as a kind of supra-social force above both, the German principalities completed their development toward sovereign statehood under conditions of an unchallenged aristocratic preponderance. The question arises, then: how was it possible for the princes to inflict political defeat upon the nobility in an aristocratic period?

The answer, obviously, is that the German territorial states absorbed a more definite aristocratic character than their counterparts elsewhere. The overt forms taken by this influence were of two kinds. In Brandenburg-Prussia the compromise between prince and nobility went beyond the standard division of labor between political power and social privilege to incorporate the aristocracy into the authoritative military and civil posts of the state itself. A second sign of the continuing aristocratic political influence in the new German states was the maintenance of territorial and local estates and diets, complete with their wonted representative functions, in several of the more important principalities through the 18th century.[11] Such forms, however, were but patent indications of a more general and a more fundamental, albeit a subtler, absorption of an ineradicable aristocratic attribute into the new absolute monarchical states. The German princes never ceased to feel themselves aristocrats as well as monarchs,[12] not only personally because of family origins and connections, not only socially because of their special dependence upon the nobility worked by the peculiarities of the German economic and social structure, but even institutionally, because the social and constitutional structures of Germany were so integrally intertwined that the very development of the German princes toward absolute sovereignty in their own territories was at the same time a development of their aristocratic rights in the German Empire. It was this institutional connection between sovereign power and aristocratic liberties that gave *Libertaet* its inimitable connotation of a traditional corporate freedom necessarily associated with absolute state authority and that made this kind of *Libertaet* the representative expression of German political liberty in the old regime.

The Dualistic Principality

The pattern of the dualistic or corporate principality which prevailed in Germany until the middle of the 17th century left a lasting heritage for the German territorial state. The relationships which tied the prince both to the Empire above and his aristocracy below him were appropriate to the period before Westphalia but they were perpetuated, primarily through the persistence of the Imperial connection, into the 18th and 19th centuries. The achievement of independent statehood against the Empire did not vitiate the continuing status of the principality as the possessor of aristocratic estatehood with the Empire. For the increasing concentration of the political center of gravity in the territorial princes did not make the Empire meaningless. Although powerless in political practice, it remained a subjective force. It was the official arbiter of the German social structure and a decisive unit in German jurisprudence down to the 19th century. In terms of social structure, which was thus measured by Imperial standards, the princes were recognized simply as one section of the larger German nobility. Although they tended to be segregated, within this caste, in the category of "high nobility," which became increasingly exclusive during the 17th and 18th centuries, and although the possession of sovereignty came to be frankly acknowledged as the definitive attribute of the Imperial high nobility, this acknowledgement constituted no break in the Imperial social structure. For Imperial law, it was but the final phase in the gradual development of aristocratic overlordship. Moreover, the distinction between "high" and "low" nobility was not carried through in such a way as to separate the princes from the main corpus of the German aristocracy as a body different in kind. The distinction between high and low nobility as a barrier between sovereigns and aristocracy was broken through by further distinctions which created intermediate categories and which consequently tended to create a common consciousness of caste over and above the political differentiation. The high nobility, which composed the Imperial Estates, was itself divided two ways—between the secular and the ecclesiastical princes and within the lay section among Electors, Imperial Princes, and Imperial Counts. Moreover, the ranks of the princes were broken into by the exceptional inclusion of a few old leading families who had lost their sovereign rights. The low nobility included not only the territorial aristocracy which was subject to the princes but also the Imperial Knights, who were recognized to be free of princely jurisdiction and directly subject to the Empire but to whom the attribute of sovereignty was denied. And to cap the continuity of this structure, the Emperor retained the exclusive power to create peers, both Imperial and territorial.

Sovereignty had become indeed a criterion of social hierarchy, but in its application to the German aristocratic society it became so graduated that its divisive power was blunted. The presence in the Imperial constitution of independent ecclesiastical states whose abbatial, episcopal, and archepiscopal heads were perforce elective and appointive rather than hereditary supplied a continuously renewed connection between the noble families who provided the candidates and the circle of sovereign rulers to which these candidates, as princes, subsequently belonged. Pufendorf noted that the Imperial abbots and bishops "often stem from the low nobility or from the baronage and the counts' estate, and they attain their princely rank only through election by their chapter; yet, in the Imperial Diet and elsewhere they have almost a higher rank than the worldly princes . . . [and]

they have the same jurisdiction and sovereignty over their subjects."[13] Even the legal distinction which was constructed to
attribute a lesser degree of sovereignty to the Imperial Counts
than that held by the Princes was less categorical than it seemed,
for actually the distinction was based upon the proportionate
scope of power rather than upon absolute prescription of law.[14]
The collective inclusion of the Counts in the Imperial Estates encouraged the Imperial Knights time and again to claim a similar
status.[15] Finally, even the low nobility within the principalities,
who were leveled to the status of subjects within the princely
state, retained something of the character of a public government.
The aristocratic estate and the diets which it dominated were, in
their origins, not the representatives of the subject inhabitants
but rather representative, together with the prince, of all autonomous authorities participant in the public power.[16]

Thus the rights of aristocracy in the community were inextricably confused with the exercise of political rulership. The continuum between noble subject and noble sovereign left its imprint upon the development of the territorial state, which was
established in a society for which the nobility remained the un-
disputed spokesman. Political sovereignty, as the concentration
of all the formerly dispersed authority in the area, developed as
the exercise of aristocratic freedom. The prince subdued the
claims of the Empire and of his own aristocracy by defining his
power as the synthesis of their liberties. As a contemporary discussion of "the freedom of the Estates" in the Empire put it, "the
German [Imperial] Estates deem the most important of their
rights to be their power to treat their subjects either wholly arbitrarily or according to the contracts between the subjects and
themselves."[17]

The primitive union of feudal aristocrat and new monarch in
the German princes was more than mere attitude. It was built
into the institutions and practices of the states which these
princes led. It was an outstanding feature in the dramatic events
which opened the old regime in Germany as well as in those
which immediately preceded its close.

The Peasants' Revolt of 1525 laid bare in a striking way the
early process in which the emergent rulers were creating their

states out of the materials of aristocratic overlordship. It is generally agreed now that the agrarian uprisings were spurred by the new burdens levied by rulers who were trying to convert their polyglot territories into uniformly administered states and that the ultimate goals of the revolts were more political than economic.[18] Equally important, however, and insufficiently emphasized are two qualifying facts. First, the peasants made no such distinctions. They viewed these novelties simply as an unwarranted extension of the economic and social obligations of their class to their superiors. Secondly, this subjective reaction had a real basis in the tendency of the rulers to use the private legal privileges accruing to them as land-owning nobility for administrative measures in the service of state-building. Thus the complaints of the rebellious peasants lumped together indiscriminately demands for relief from personal dues and services with the defense of their self-administration against the encroachments of the princely bailiffs and his courts.[19] This commingling of categories followed naturally from the princely employment of both kinds of measures to finance the new instruments of state and reduce the peasantry to a common level of political subjection. The political designs of the most radical sections of the peasant movement betrayed a similar confusion, for they began as projects for self-government against the incursions of the territorial rulers and then found the logical conclusion to be the destruction of all aristocracy.[20] Their tendency to attribute valid authority only to the Emperor underlined their identification of all intermediate levels of nobility, lord and prince alike, with aristocratic privilege. Nor did the activity of the rulers belie the position of the peasants. Not only did princes and nobility present a common front against the peasantry but the authorities themselves summarized calumny of "king electors, and princes" as "disobedience against the nobility." [21] If the revolt was limited to the south and particularly to the area of minuscule territories, the fact remains that the formation of the bureaucratic state was most advanced here and the component of feudal privilege in political sovereignty most in evidence.

By the end of the old regime the admixture of private aristocratic privilege of the feudal type in the practice and the con-

sciousness of domestic politics had indeed faded, but the persistence of its influence on the Imperial level was plainly evident in
the affair of the League of German Princes during 1785. The
initiative, to be sure, came from Frederick the Great, whose action now as always was dominated by consideration for the interests of the Prussian state as a European power and who had previously characterized the Imperial constitution as "this anachronistic and bizarre state-form" because of its incapacity to act as a
political unit under the Emperor.[22] Nevertheless, not only did
Frederick choose to exploit the relationships of this very state-
form as the most efficacious means of securing German support
against the offensive designs of Emperor Joseph but in his own
thinking he seemed to view himself as a German aristocrat as
well as a Prussian sovereign. Long before he developed the project for the League, Frederick was writing privately to Joseph
along lines in which the rights of the German territorial states
were explicitly associated with their feudally deprived liberties
as Imperial Estates. The actual issue, he wrote, is not the maintenance of peace "among the European powers" but "whether an
Emperor can dispose arbitrarily of the fiefs of the Empire." He
went on to maintain the opposition of this thesis "to the laws,
customs, and usages of the Roman Empire," to predict that
"every prince will call upon feudal law" against "the power of a
despot who will despoil him . . . of his immemorial posses-
sions," and to assert that for his own part he would, "as a member of the Empire," "maintain the immunities, liberties, and
rights of the Germanic community." [23]

Frederick's project for the League of German Princes, which
he drew up in October 1784, embodied this identification of sovereign interests with aristocratic freedom. He called for a revival
of the anti-Imperialist tradition, appealing to the Golden Bull
for authority and to a secularized Schmalkaldic League for a
model. He summarized the particularistic tradition as "the
rights and immunities of the German princes." [24] The actual
formation of the League of Princes, moreover, was initiated by
the separate agreement of three Electors (Brandenburg, Hanover,
Saxony) on conditions which recalled the old Electoral Unions.[25]

Even more revealing, perhaps, than the event itself was its reception in Germany. Despite what to retrospection appears to be a patently reactionary quality the League of Princes was a vital expression of the German nation for the sixteen princes who adhered to it and for the whole section of the politically interested German public to which Goethe later gave voice in his memoirs.[26] The extent to which the territorial sovereigns in Germany could still be viewed as a natural elite representing the society against a supervening absolute sovereignty became articulate in Duke Ernest of Gotha, who cited the American Revolution as analogous to the struggle of the German princes for the rights of humanity against despotism.[27]

The Transition: From Principality to State

The union in the person of the prince of state and estate, of the ruler's new general authority with the subject's old-style special liberties, established a basic pattern for the definition of government in terms of freedom. In this literal form, certainly, the union was unstable, for with the shift of the prince's primary interest, which became manifest in the second half of the 17th century, to the construction of the centralized administrative state, considerations of social hierarchy and special rights were subordinated to considerations of common system and uniform rule. During the long period of transition between the dualistic state of the 16th century in which the prince shared the public power with the traditional estates and the mature absolute state of the mid-18th century in which the alliance between prince and territorial nobility was recemented in a new form, commoners played an outstanding role in the actual process of state-building. Academically trained jurists of burgher origins were influential legal and administrative aides in the consolidation of the princely power, and they were instrumental in framing the ideas and the policies which minimized the aristocratic component of princedom and emphasized its representative status as exclusive head of a single body politic.[28]

The influence of this group in German politics was, however, both temporary and limited, for no progressive economic group of fellow-burghers existed to give them social connections and support. The notables in the towns tended rather to resist the authority of the state by reason of their exclusive concern with the defense of communal oligarchic privilege. The officials of burgher origin, consequently, not only remained numerically inferior to the nobles in state service but they tended themselves to be absorbed into the aristocracy, and by the middle of the 18th century the bureaucratic position of the academic middle class was decisively weakened. But it did contribute two permanent features to the territorial state in Germany. First, by virtue of their social isolation, the commoner-bureaucrats reinforced the facet of princely policy which tended to establish the state as a neutral controlling force above all groups alike in the society. Secondly, this uprooted bureaucracy strove to compensate for its isolation by conceiving itself as in some measure representative of the whole body social and its claims upon the state.[29] Here was the origin of the pattern which was to prove so characteristic of the state in Germany throughout its development, whereby the important issues between the state and the society were transplanted via the bureaucracy to an arena within the institutions of the state itself.

But if middle-class officials shared notably in the establishment of the new government they did little to modernize the institutions and practices of liberty. They participated, to be sure, in the negative work of destroying traditional corporate rights, but they performed this in the service and the name of effective authority. It was a crucial circumstance in the development of German political liberty that during the period of academic middle-class influence upon the government of the old regime the German middle classes at large pressed no new positive libertarian claims, and that when such needs began to be felt in the second half of the 18th century middle-class influence upon the state was a thing of the past.

The Period of Enlightened Absolutism

The sponsorship of liberal claims redounded to the aristocracy, which began from the middle of the 18th century to develop both a preponderant influence upon the centralized territorial governments and a positive economic interest in liberalism. It was under the social auspices of the German nobility itself, then, that a new pattern of freedom was grafted onto the traditional connection between princely rule and aristocratic rights. The continuity of the auspices made for a continuity in the connection. The shift from a privileged to an indiscriminate kind of liberty took a form which left 18th century liberal practice in Germany still a function of the relations between monarch and social hierarchy. The change meant not the attenuation of the aristocratic principle but rather its transformation, not a new definition of the state but rather its redefinition. On the one hand, the nobility was opened to modernization through its continuous participation in the apparatus of the new state, and the aristocratic principle was consequently given a form consistent with the rational standards of the political authority it now served. First the prince and then small but important sections of his territorial aristocracy began to recast their rights in the mold of the state and of the secular reasoning which accompanied its rise, and in this way feudal franchise tended to develop into claims for a modern kind of uniformly applicable liberty within the sovereign state. On the other hand, since its apparatus was now dominated by this aristocracy the princely state absorbed the new version of aristocratic freedom, translated it into the language of government, and reissued it in the form of an absolute monarchy which by its very nature had to pursue general liberal policies within a limited number of fields. Enlightened despotism, which represented the fully developed stage of this process, was thus not so much anti-aristocratic as anti-traditional. A polyglot collection of special charters and privileges, binding upon all kinds of public and private activities, had constituted the old aristocratic principle; these were now reorganized into a set of private and derived public rights within a single order of political authority, and in this form they constituted the new aristocratic principle within the absolute state.

The chief agency for the reciprocal influence of nobility and state in 18th-century Germany was the marriage of aristocracy and bureaucracy. The rise of new types of preparatory schools for the nobility with study plans designed to train it for work in the universities (Knights' Academies and *Gymnasia Illustra*) and the preference of its scions for precisely those universities which specialized in political science and represented the most modern tendencies in that field (Halle during the first half of the century and Goettingen during the second), were sign-posts of this integration. The kingdom of Prussia was in the van of this process which converted the feudal type of personal relationship within the prince's councils into the functional and technical type of objective relationship between the prince and all classes in his bureaucracy, and it was here that the full implications of the process were most evident and most consciously perceived. In the century between the accession of the Great Elector in 1640 and the death of Frederick William I in 1740 the Prussian monarchs had used aristocrats and burghers alike to destroy the prescriptive political and administrative rights of the nobility in the name of the order and authority of the state. After 1740 Frederick the Great turned deliberately to the nobles for his chief public agents and at the same time he began to define the purpose of the state in terms of liberty as well as of authority. Thereby Frederick fixed a permanent pattern of authoritarian alliance between aristocracy and monarch within the bureaucratic state, but he reformulated the traditional political values of the social hierarchy into the ideal of the freedom inherent in the modern state. It was in this form that the influence of enlightened despotism radiated out from Berlin into the courts of the Dukes Karl Friedrich of Baden, Karl August of Weimar, Karl Wilhelm Ferdinand of Brunswick, and the Emperor Joseph II of Austria. Frederick's influence was thus mediated through two channels. First, his personality and his practical policies became an institutional model for absorbing a whole society into a single political system of command while preserving its traditional hierarchy, through the assignment to each group of its due position in the state. Secondly, Frederick's political writings, despite their undoubted liberal distortion of his real policies, were largely designed for and actually circulated through his civil and military bureaucracy, with the result that a whole generation of aristocratic officials was inculcated with political conceptions that led them to look to the policies of state for the assertion of social rights.

The formal political principles which Frederick developed to guide and to justify his government revealed that the basic framework of his politics was set by the logical extreme of the leveling sovereign state, in which the relationship between ruler and subject was unambiguous, impersonal, rational, and hence eminently controllable. No consideration of tradition, hierarchy, or privilege should impede the comprehension and concentration of political power in a single system which brought all the citizens into an equally direct connection with the head of the state. Frederick's norm was a Hobbesian leviathan strengthened by a superstructure of social and moral motives which Hobbes neglected. The assumption that the acme of power lay in the rationality, the equality, and the immediacy of the political relationship reconciled for Frederick his inherently incompatible combination of "interests of state" [30] and contractual obligation as the criteria of authority. What both canons had in common was the exclusion of all extraneous elements from a clear, simple, and uniform definition of the political relationship. Thus on the one hand he placed little stock in hereditary prescription, including his own dynastic title to rule, which he considered to be non-functional in the state,[31] and on the other, he set limits to the activity of the state in order that the ruler might dispose the more fully and effectively over its proper sphere.

Frederick's adoption of natural-law principles was governed by such considerations. His selection among these principles made clear their function of establishing new supports for the unprecedented royal authority which the professionalized secular state now made possible. The "social pact," in which individual family heads contract to form a civil society and elect magistrates for their mutual protection, brings it about that "the sovereign is attached by indissoluble bonds to the body of the state," that "the sovereign represents the state," for "he and his peoples form but one body." [32] The result of this relationship —summed up in the dictum that the magistrate is "the first servant of the state" [33]—is twofold. First, the contractual limitation of the sovereign to legislate in the interests of "the whole community" actually magnifies his power, and Frederick proceeded to show that in matters of war, foreign policy, finance, agriculture, industry, and commerce the "active and upright" sovereign who governs with "all his energies" in the interest of his entire polity is the truly effective ruler.[34] Secondly—and this was Frederick's main point—the respect for equality and liberty in areas outside those in which government had a proper interest intensified the obedience and sacrifice of the citizens to the ruler in the spheres where he had genuine need of it. In his advocacy of religious tolerance Frederick declared that the stipulations of the social pact for the individual contractants assigned to the ruler "the maintenance of the laws we want to obey in order that we be governed wisely and defended," but "for the rest, we require of you that you respect our liberty." [35] Such fields were fitted for individual liberty, to Frederick, because they were beyond the proper competence of the state,[36] so that state intervention here aroused civil discord injurious to the state.[37]

Frederick's whole conception of government depended upon his assumption that the recognition of the popular origins of government, the removal of politically privileged intermediaries, and the exercise of rulership with due regard to the material welfare, the legal personality, and the spiritual freedom of all subjects would evoke an otherwise unobtainable reciprocation. Frederick's many homilies on the duties of sovereigns were counterbalanced by the several disquisitions on morality and patriotism in which he pounded unremittingly upon the necessity of the individual's total self-commitment to the community in which he enjoyed rights.[38] "Men attach themselves to what belongs to them," he wrote,[39] and upon this basis constructed his political ethic. This amounted to little more than an argument for political obedience, which extends to "whatever kind of government your country lives under." [40] Thus, through respect for the rights and needs of society, have kings ever acquired "the love of their people" and the basis for the "greatness" and the "prosperity" of their governments.[41] Patriotism was to unite sovereign directly to subject on the basis of a mutual and general recognition of rights, and it was thereby to make dispensable the divinely ordained hierarchy and the intermediary authorities it sanctioned, as the motivation for political obedience.

But within the framework of these systematic political principles Frederick filled in a content of frankly hierarchical social principles and policies. This relationship between political and social principles was reflected in the law code which Frederick inspired, for it juxtaposed the equal "general rights of man," grounded in his "natural freedom to seek his own good," with the unequal "particular rights and duties," grounded in his "estate," and made the state arbiter over both.[42] Frederick insisted upon the important gradations in the attachments of the subjects to the state: the masses are bound by a materially defined self-interest, the aristocracy by the higher self-interest of ambition, which sponsors an instinctive inclination to social virtue. This virtue and ambition are satisfied through active participation in the government of the state.[43] Hence, in Frederick's scheme the aristocracy took its place among the ruling bureaucrats under a prince who possessed its qualities in a merely intensified degree. Frederick's policy combined the preservation of aristocratic social privilege with the political transformation of the nobility. On the first count, Frederick acknowledged the necessity of maintaining, for the present at least, the admittedly unjust agrarian structure of serfdom and its relics, because of the state's interest in uninterrupted production and in the security of the noble beneficiaries.[44] On the second, Frederick retained the high civil and military posts in the state as an aristocratic preserve and gave special care to the civic education of the nobility who were to fill them. He sought to convince them that the criteria of "emulation" and "glory" lay in superior service to the fatherland rather than in private or corporate ambition.[45] The nobility were to turn in the rights and privileges based upon a special dispensation *sui generis* for the measure of freedom

based upon the rational and general standards of active membership in the bureaucratic state.

The Frederician state, then, was not so much an enlightened,
leveling absolutism, marred by concessions to social actuality as
it was the consolidation of the union between sovereign power
and aristocratic principle into a total system of government. In
this system the aristocracy became the common link between the
government whose authority was to be strengthened and the society which was to be reconciled. Just as the old aristocratic
principle had united political authority with chartered liberties,
so the new was to unite bureaucratic rule with liberal policy.
The sovereign state was thus penetrated with the aristocratic
virtues of service and patriarchal self-limitation. Frederick himself admitted the strong aristocratic influence in his state when
he declared, in a notable passage, that "good monarchies form
in our era a kind of government which is closer to oligarchy than
to despotism," for counsellors, administrators, officers, and the
provincial estates "all participate in the sovereign authority." [46]

Frederick did his job well—in one sense, indeed, too well.
His success in inculcating the rational standards of his service
state into the aristocracy can be measured by the modern liberal
form which the economic opposition to his policies among the
noble bureaucrats took during the latter stages of his reign. In
part this opposition was a reaction against the preponderance
of the absolutist over both the aristocrat and the liberal in Frederick's practical habits and policies. To this extent the violated
balance of his system was simply righting itself. The real meaning of the opposition, however, lay less in the mere fact of its
existence than in its peculiar structure. For whereas in modern
history economic opposition is wont to take an overt political
form, in this case the reverse was true: bureaucratic opposition
to Frederick, insofar as it partook of a liberal tendency, took
conscious form in the realm of economics. Not only was there resistance to the specific practice of Frederick's mercantilism but for
many officials this opposition began to find a theoretical formulation with the introduction of Adam Smith into Germany after
1776 through the Universities of Goettingen and Koenigsberg.[47]
Particularly noteworthy of this economic liberalism, which be-

came an influence upon policy after Frederick's death in 1786, was the co-existence in the same government of its advocates and of the political reactionaries who were inspiring the Censorship Edict of 1788 and conservative revisions of the projected legal code. The juxtaposition was indicative, for it revealed that a compartmentalized economic freedom was the first definite articulation of bureaucratic liberalism and that it developed while the political and constitutional aspects of the liberal approach were still inchoate.

The advocacy of economic liberty toward the end of the old regime was frequently the characteristic mode of expression of a more general liberalism.[48] At Hanover's University of Goettingen, where Adam Smith was first known and translated, it was contact with his economic doctrine that helped stimulate professors like A. L. von Schloezer and J. S. Puetter to a more far-reaching interest in public affairs and reforms. In the University of Koenigsberg, the friendship of the professors Immanuel Kant and Christian Jacob Kraus reflected the connection between an individualistic ethic with liberal political implications and an enthusiastic rendering of Adam Smith. The Prussian minister, Karl August von Struensee, who maintained his contacts with Koenigsberg, worked for free trade during the late 1780's and then developed his disposition for general reform to the point where he could tell the French ambassador in 1799 that "the revolution which you have made from below will be achieved by us from above." [49] A similar conjunction can be remarked in two of the important early influences which operated on both Stein and Hardenberg, the future Prussian reformers. Goettingen, with its Anglophilia and its emphasis upon the validity of aristocratic estates, and Friedrich Anton von Heinitz, the Prussian minister who fought for his free-trade views against Frederick II himself, both left indelible impressions upon the two young men.[50] Ultimately this connection fed a general social and political liberalism, but this stage was not developed beyond the point of academic possibility during the old regime in Germany. The characteristic form which the modern individualistic type of liberalism took in the German bureaucrats before 1789 remained economic. Both the force and the limits of this administrative liberalism in Germany were defined by the connection of bureaucracy with aristocracy. The higher officialdom which sponsored laissez-faire policies was composed chiefly by the nobility, and this bureaucratic nobility retained its ties with the landed aristocracy in the country.[51] Its connection with the absolute state helped to convert a part of the nobility's traditional bilateral claims which were incompatible with the uniformity of the new state into claims for policies of general economic individualism which were compatible. Its connection with the nobility at large, which made economic individualism into a prescriptive right of aristocracy, helped to convert contingent liberal policy of government into a permanent strand of administrative liberalism within the German state. This connection helped as well to limit official liberalism to measures compatible with the fundamentals of the existing social and political structure.

The influence which the aristocracy wielded within the public administrations was powerfully seconded by its development outside the bureaucracies as a pressure group rooted in the country at large. And here, more important in the long run than the resistance of large sections of the nobility to reform was the domination of the tendencies for liberal reform by other sections of this same nobility. The greatest progress toward a capitalistic system in 18th-century Germany took place in the field of agriculture and on the large estates of the nobility. Since the landed aristocracy was the main source of liberal pressure outside the state apparatus, it bestowed its imprint upon practical individualism and brought a strong social reinforcement to the officials who were tailoring liberalism to the pillars of existing authority.

From about the middle of the 18th century both the aims and the methods of German agriculture began to undergo a qualitative change. Certainly its over-all pattern down to the reforms of the early 19th century does not belie the usual textbook description of a static system based upon a bound peasantry, the three-field tradition, and a subsistence economy, indicating the continuity of the agrarian system since the days of Charlemagne and confirming the persistence of a feudal aristocracy in Germany down through the 18th century. The new kinds of activity which began to stir in the second half of the 18th century were not yet sufficient to transform the general character of the system, but they did betoken a leaven of commercialized enterprise and capitalistic spirit within the landed aristocracy. This proportion of stagnation and mobility was reflected in the rise of immediate claims to a greater economic freedom within the existing economic and social structure.

It is true that German agriculture had had commercial connections prior to this period, for grain exports had gone from central Germany through Hamburg to Holland, Sweden, and southern Europe since the 16th century. But this trade had become a part of a customary economic pattern, and, in conjunction with the dislocations of the Thirty Years' War, constituted no decisive spur to productive development. Around the middle of the 18th century, however, such spurs began to make themselves felt, with the expansion of the grain market in the western countries and the modest opening of a new internal market in western and southern Germany which followed upon population increase and industrial growth. Reflected in rising grain prices and land values from about 1760 on, this economic change displaced old market patterns and stimulated agricultural production: central Germany now supplied food for the rising population of the new German industrial centers, while East and West Prussia became the great grain-exporting region of the country.[52]

The pressure toward the capitalization of agriculture drove many German princes to identify the interests of state with the productivity and the rationalization of capitalistic enterprise. But the attitude of the absolute state to the liberal implications of capitalism was an ambiguous one, for the recognition of the economic strength derivative from expanding production was countered by the fear of unsettling the social foundations of the state and the practical necessity of preserving the static productive forces of the society. Thus the Prussia of Frederick II was governed by a sliding system of import and export prohibitions and a network of royal warehouses which effected an indirect but forceful control over agricultural prices. The aims of the system were mercantilistic self-sufficiency and equilibrium between the interests of agricultural producer and urban consumer.

Its effect was to protect traditional economic forms. Nevertheless, within the limits set by the military absolute monarchies of the 18th century liberal economic policies did get some application. Over and above the requirements of a balanced economy, Frederick encouraged free trade. Not only did he remove trade restrictions on the Elbe but he launched the Elbe Trading Company, a joint-stock enterprise with the estate-owners of the Elbe valley as its participants, as an explicitly free-trade rather than a monopolistic enterprise, to promote export trade in grain over and above the requirements of the Prussian state.[53] Moreover, the provinces of East and West Prussia, which had little industry to supply, were given an exceptional status in the monarchy and endowed with a free-trade regime. After Frederick's death, when the system through which he balanced all groups and interests in the state began to crumble, the strength of free-trade among the progressive nobility was demonstrated. The aristocratic bureaucrats who dominated the Prussian government under Frederick William II were inspired by their agricultural connections and their education in Adam Smith to institute a general system of low tariffs and free entry during the years from 1786 to 1790. As a system it had to be abandoned after 1790 and the advantages of free exchange were once more balanced off against the other considerations of state. Free trade entered into the German political tradition not as the absolute principle of economic freedom against the state but rather in the form of a conditioned part of the larger governmental policy for the state.

Equally limited were the liberal effects of the incipient capitalism of the German landed nobility. The shift in the character of agricultural literature from the so-called "patriarchal (*hausvaeterlich*)" to "scientific" schools, a shift which has been described as a development from the predominance of the idea of family life to the predominance of the idea of "net profit (*Reinertrag*),"[54] was produced, characteristically by the juncture of bureaucratic and private aristocratic tendencies. On the one hand the Cameralists, who represented in general the point of view of state mercantilism, sought to apply scientific principles to agriculture as an integral part of their "cameral science," which can be roughly defined as a transitional doctrine that grafted the rational principles of contemporary statecraft onto the patriarchal traditions of the German territories. On the other hand, practising estate-owners set themselves up as experimental agricultural economists and contributed importantly to the new literature both as individuals and through newly founded agricultural associations.[55] The ideas and techniques of a rational agriculture, sedulously developed from these two sides, were, to a limited extent, carried into practice in two corresponding arenas—on the princely domains and on large private estates. The role of the prince in the reform of agriculture was exercised not through direct regulation, in his capacity as the sovereign head of state, but rather by example and encouragement, in the half-private, half-public capacity which his position as largest estate-owner, largest banker, and supreme aristocratic magistrate gave him. Hence the conversion of most of the larger German princes to the cause of agricultural progress did not entail the reorganization of agrarian relations, for only comparatively small groups of territorial nobles followed the same course. Consequently, nobles who desired a general change of agrarian system looked toward the progressive policies of the princes rather than the corporate powers of their own peers as the embodiment of aristocratic interests.

The combination of princely and aristocratic motives in the movement for agricultural reform determined the peculiarly limited demand for individual freedom which it raised. The liberalization of the traditional lord-peasant relationship was the *sine qua non* for agricultural advance by both parties. Yet the peasantry hardly raised its voice for the dissolution of manorial bonds, and the princes and nobles who did call for their reform exalted the benefits not of emancipation as such but only of as much specific non-political and non-social relief as would redound to the higher ends of technical agricultural progress, monarchical state power, and the interests of privileged estate-owners. Princes in their public policy were restrained in their reforming zeal by the necessity of maintaining uninterrupted production. Private estate-owners—including the princes and their lessees on the royal domains—sought to free themselves from the

traditional bonds with little regard for the impact of such measures upon peasant freedom, save where a modicum of it was
inextricably involved in their own economic flexibility. Straight
dispossession of the peasants (*Bauernlegen*), the separation of
the lord's demesne out from the peasants' strips, the appointment
of bailiffs or the leasing of estates for the maximization of income, the conversion of traditionally indefinite tenure into terminal peasants' leases—all these measures marked the rise in the
nobility of a modern idea of property out of the older feudal
notion of possession.[56] But all of them marked too a growing
insecurity of peasant possession rather than a liberalization of
the peasant's position, for the bondage of the peasant to the
estate was independent of his tenure. The idea of a general liberation that would create homogeneous groups of large and small
property-owners was indeed known but almost nowhere realized.
The individual estate-owner was restrained by the hostility of his
caste and by lack of capital. The princes were less troubled by
such handicaps, but on their own demesnes they showed themselves susceptible to the same corporate limitations as other progressive landed nobles. The considerations of public policy
which drove them to enact model reforms on the royal domains
did lead the German princes of the 18th century to guarantee
hereditary tenure for their own peasants, but they stopped well
short of the establishment of peasant property and peasant emancipation.[57] Theirs was only in a very limited way a liberal policy.
Frederick William I of Prussia found it not incompatible with
his own declared desire "to support" the peasants "under the
arms like a loyal father of the people." Frederick II, moreover,
found no contradiction in seeking the extension of this guarantee to private estates, despite his acceptance at the same time of
institutions like compulsory labor and bondage to the soil in
private lord-peasant relations. Undeniably, however, the concern with hereditary tenure did carry with it certain overtones
of personal liberty, for there was some idea that the right to this
security was essential to the rights of a free man. Thus the
Prussian Civil Code (*Allgemeine Landrecht*), which was drafted
during the 1780's under Frederick the Great, combined in the
same paragraph the provision defining the peasants' hereditary

attachment to the estate, binding upon peasant and lord alike, with the peasants' general attribute as "free citizens of the state," able "to acquire property and rights and to defend them against anybody . . ." [58] Only a very few princes late in the century, like Frederick and Duke Karl Friedrich of Baden, carried their domainial reforms beyond security of tenure and conversion of services to a genuine liberation from obligations. Even here, however, the internal limitations upon the private policies of the princes were evident. The abolition was limited to personal services, and, in Frederick's case at least, the fact of personal freedom for domain peasants was established by implication and not in the name of personal freedom. The orders were so specific and disconnected that the subsequent personal independence of the domain peasants was ascribed to tradition rather than to the reforming edicts.[59] This peculiar ratio of impulse to restraint in the princes' private land reforms was repeated in their policy of encouraging the voluntary dissolution of commons and mixed farming strips into individual plots while yet refraining from the step beyond this technical arrangement to the creation of a regime of free property.

Yet the measures which the prince pursued in his capacity as aristocratic land-owner on his own estates were far more liberal than those which he could prosecute as sovereign head of state. In his latter capacity, the only effective activity of the 18th-century prince affecting royal and noble estate alike was oriented toward the policy of peasant protection (*Bauernschutz*), and this policy had little connection with liberal aims. It was concerned neither with personal freedom nor with freedom of property, but rather with the preservation of the existing quantity of peasant lands in peasant hands so that the level of population, i.e. labor power and military recruits, might be maintained. The aristocratic limitations upon peasant reform resided not only in the will of the prince but in the structure of his state. On the rare occasions when he attempted to liberalize by edict outside his own domains, either he had to make compliance voluntary—in which case it generally was not complied with—or his bureaucracy did not carry out the order and it remained sterile.

Acting primarily through their peers in the state service the

German nobles, led by their princes, gave both impetus and limitation to the increase of economic freedom. By its very nature this demand for greater mobility transcended the frame of traditional local rights, but its aristocratic sponsorship ensured that the general form it took was that of a subordinate princely policy within the established political and social system.

The position of the aristocracy in the territorial state of the 18th century was authoritative but not totally exclusive. The hierarchy of commoners was subordinate in all social and most public respects, and their political role was, aside from a small minority of legists and bureaucrats, a passive one. Still, the commoners had an indirect but important impact upon the state. The prince developed his territory into a sovereign state precisely by elevating all inhabitants to a status of common membership in the community. His capacity as sovereign head of state, consequently, was a function of his political representation of the subordinate commoners. If the aristocracy supplied the social content of the territorial state, the commoners were responsible, indirectly through the prince, for its political form. If the aristocracy supplied the basic principle that liberty is integrally joined to the exercise of public authority, the commoners were responsible, indirectly through the prince, for the general and rational form which this principle took in the notion that the state is the embodiment of human freedom. To the extent that the prince went beyond the aristocracy in acknowledging a general interest, in establishing right of citizenship, and in curtailing or generalizing the privileges of nobility, he was taking account of the commonalty. But the role of the commoner went beyond his status as an object of action. The prince succeeded in asserting his sovereign powers in part because his commoners— and particularly the burghers—were responsive to his direction. Although they lacked initiative, the German commoners had undergone, by the mid-18th century, sufficient economic and intellectual development to be accessible to governmental action.

Within the hierarchy of commoners the groups which were the prime objects of the state's innovating zeal were those belonging to what were later to be called the middle classes. In this period these groups were still recognized only as peasants and burghers (in the literal sense of citizens of towns) by constitutional law and as free peasants, peasants, cottagers, merchants, free masters, guild masters, members of the university faculties and of the state civil services, by functioning common law. Mixed in with this institutional structure, however, was a transverse tendency which created lines of class community among some of these groups. The consciousness of their coherence as middle classes was frequently articulated during the old regime. This consciousness had its roots in the old corporate municipal spirit which continued as a part of the new consciousness, but the modern element which developed in the 18th century was the sentiment for the integrity of a propertied and educated commoner class *vis-à-vis* both the aristocracy and the unpropertied mob.[60] It came, in part, from an increasing mobility within German society which blurred the traditional lines of division and created new lines of connection and distinction among the historical corporations. Although the older distinctions remained sufficiently vital for the newer tendency toward a middle class to retain a definitely burgher cast distinct from peasantry as well as landed aristocracy, the barrier between country and town was being undermined by the development of rural handicraft and domestic industry and by the small but significant movement of burghers into agriculture, both as private estate-owners and as lessees of the royal domains. Moreover, with the growth of more centralized forms of industry in 18th-century Germany, the traditional distinctions between town and country and between imperial towns and territorial towns were being bridged over and superseded by a distinction between the increasingly populous industrial and commercial cities, which were seats of capitalistic enterprise, and the smaller stagnant handicraft towns.[61] Scions from many ranks of the urban hierarchy went into the bureaucracy and into academic life, and in the 18th century they constituted more than another corporate association. They thought and acted as the representatives of the whole vast variegated congeries of rooted, propertied, untitled burghers, and they created a literature which was recognized as the highest expression of national life and became the pride and cement of the social groups from which it came and to which it was addressed.

In economic life, the extension of the putting-out system of domestic industry and the beginnings of the factory system undermined the meaning of older functional distinctions by raising a new kind of division between the merchant capitalist and the factory-owner on the one hand and many master-artisans as well as journeymen on the other. Moreover, by introducing the labor question, it brought to both merchants and masters the beginnings of common class interest.[62]

Clearly then, the existence of some kind of middle class in 18th-century Germany is hardly questionable, but clearly too the peculiar structure of this class, the rare amalgam which was both a simple mixture of pre-middle class with middle-class elements and a kind of chemical compound working the older influences into the very nature of the new middle class, makes the relationship of this class to politics a complex question indeed. What was the foundation in material life of the spiritual achievements of the German middle class, and why was this internalized realm so overwhelmingly the preferred arena for the assertion of their freedom?

The key to these problems lies in a kind of transvaluation of values, produced by the historical process which witnessed the birth of the German middle class and which like an ineradicable natal influence penetrated the very being of that class. The essence of this transvaluation consisted in the paradox which dissociated rights and liberties from self-government and associated them with the absolute state.

The wide-spread decline of German town life from the 16th century to the 18th effectively undermined the traditional basis for the assertion of burgher liberties. With both civic and private initiative falling off, the original connection between the chartered rights of the towns and the chartered liberties of their citizens was calcified into an association of municipal privilege within the state or Empire with oligarchic privilege within the municipality. The restriction of urban independence and influence by prince and landed aristocracy was accompanied by the "feudalization" of the great banking and merchant families into rentier groups living off a static economic system.[63] The result of this joint process was that in territorial and Imperial towns alike the municipal government tended to harden into a closed, co-optative corporation, dominated typically by allied patrician and feudalized merchant groups. Mixed constitutions continued in nominal operation, but the citizenry was represented in municipal assemblies of corporate delegates who either ineffectually resisted or positively collaborated with the ruling clique.[64] The guarantees of administrative municipal autonomy which had been procured from the princes as the price for political subordination within the state functioned under these conditions as safeguards of political oligarchy and economic monopoly within the towns. After the middle of the 18th century, when the princes began to turn their political title increasingly into administrative fact, the municipal legists reacted by reviving claims of inviolable prescriptive rights, but only externally for the relations of the town with higher authority. Despite the equally oppressive limitation of rights by the ruling families within the towns, the municipal legists discussed internal relations not in terms of rights but only in terms of means for perfecting the municipal police power.[65] The old language of town freedom had become a mode of expression for the preservation of the oligarchic system in urban politics and society. The paradox was established whereby liberties under the traditional municipal regime were increasingly defined as the right possessed by the bearers of these liberties to refrain from the free development of their own activities and to prevent others from developing theirs.

At the same time, however, the prevalence of this position was being challenged by changes which were starting to sponsor new attitudes of the German burghers to the problems of liberty. Two factors which were to become substantial agencies in German history helped work the change—the beginnings of industrial advance and the assumption by the state of real control over territorial towns and the industrial economy.

The initial impulse toward the development of capitalistic forms of commercial and industrial enterprise was given by emigres from western Europe. They had come into Germany as refugees and as invited colonists from the 16th century on, bringing with them an aggressive business attitude, advanced techniques of industrial production and management, and, occasionally, capital.[66] Scotch Catholics and Calvinists who fled to Germany during the 16th and 17th centuries and became prominent merchants along the Baltic littoral in the areas of what was to be East and West Prussia, and French Huguenots who escaped or were invited to Germany during the 17th and 18th centuries and founded much of capitalistic domestic industry, were the most numerous and important of these groups, but the Dutch and Jews, in lesser numbers, played their parts as well. It was around the beginning of the 18th century that the isolated endeavors of these immigrants reached the point at which they began to dominate whole branches of trade and industry. They created a new pattern of economic development into which native German entrepreneurs tended to be drawn as well. It is noteworthy that the chief centers of German trade and industry in the 18th century were places where the emigres had concentrated: Hamburg, Frankfurt am Main, Koenigsberg and Elbing for trade and banking, Berlin, Magdeburg, Krefeld, Vienna, and Electoral Saxony for industry. This economic advance, which established the domestic system and even witnessed the beginnings of a factory system in textiles, was furthered by a mercantilist policy of state. Governments encouraged and even established the newer forms of industrial enterprise. By substituting the positive canons of state regulation and state-wide markets for the stuffy confines of municipal regulations that aimed at preserving the monopoly of the local market in particular and the economic and social *status quo* in general, their measures actually expanded the horizons and increased the freedom of action of merchants and manufacturers.[67] The efficacy of these measures is apparent in the shift of industrial primacy from the Imperial cities to the territorial towns and in the introduction of rational economic calculation into certain sectors of private enterprise by princely regulation.[68] Even the young Baron vom Stein, sensitive as he was to the extension of bureaucratic control, favored the increase of governmental control over the mining industry for this progressive purpose.[69]

That the two factors of industrial advance and mercantilist policy were related is obvious, but the precise meaning of this relationship is not so evident. The main point is not the distinction between the roles of free initiative and government tutelage but rather the combination of the two types of activity. For this combination helped to change the relationship between the common individual and the state. The coupling of corporate municipal rights against the state with the apathetic submission of the individual within the town gave way to a new frame of reference in which the aggressive individual and the sovereign state rose together as the chief protagonists of social power and as the primary antagonists for its possession. Out of this development, which combined the seeds of independent individual initiative on the part of the common citizen with the reality of a compulsory governmental sponsorship of such initiative, came the practical strand of the "German problem." It set up the relationship between individuals and the authoritarian state in which the state was both favorable and necessary to the material side of personal freedom and in which the individual, consequently, was both beholden to the state and, to evade this dependence, withdrawn from it.

The general pattern of this relationship was common to all the European bureaucratic and mercantilistic states during the *ancien regime*. The peculiarity of the German situation, which forged what was elsewhere a passing phase into a permanent tradition, lay in a tempo of development that kept the growth of individual enterprise vital enough to encourage liberal governmental policy but limited enough to prevent its rejection in the name of individual independence. Both the autonomous economic growth and the state's domination of it were, in a sense, foreign importations into Germany. The role of the emigres in the capitalistic forms of commerce and industry and the competitive standards of commercial and economic power set for the princely states by the European powers were equally impositions from without which imposed new tendencies upon economic and social relationships not organically prepared for them.[70] Hence economic growth was never sufficient, during the old regime, to imbue the German society with a spontaneous vitality and an immanent pressure for movement and change. The development, like the stability, of the country remained under political control and aristocratic social predominance. Considerations of *raison d'état* were simply added to the traditional concern for the corporate structure of society as criteria for the rate and the extent of directed change.

The upshot of this constellation was a governmental policy which both sponsored and limited individual enterprise by the commoners and an urban citizenry which produced a small, politically uninfluential minority of dynamic businessmen and intellectuals out of a large majority of tradition-ridden burghers. Governments pursued simultaneous policies of opening up and detouring around the guilds on the one hand while conserving and revivifying the guild system as such on the other. Again, princes strove to establish an economically independent, aggressive, and competitive entrepreneurial class, and at the same time they imposed a whole network of import and export prohibitions, conditional grants of capital, equipment, and labor, and strict regulations on the whole process of production and marketing.[71] In Prussia particularly, the 18th century witnessed the development of industrial policy from an outright state capitalism to state aid for private capitalism within the permanent framework of a regulatory system.[72] The burgher estate manifested a corresponding duality. On the one hand, Mirabeau could claim that Prussia contained no rich merchants or manufacturers who could carry on an independent enterprise, and the publicist Justus Moeser could generalize this to the dictum that Germany as a whole lacked a third estate.[73] On the other hand, it has been estimated that in Electoral Saxony as much as one-third of the population was engaged in manufacture and handicraft by the end of the 18th century, while in Prussia the proportion of urban to rural population in the middle of the century was already the same as it was in 1867.[74] Beyond the quantitative growth of the urban sector, moreover, it must be recognized that an increasingly prosperous and capitalistic group of middle-class lessees of the royal domains and the capitalistic proprietors of domestic and factory industry played an important part in Germany's modest but perceptible economic development during the 18th century.[75] Indeed, in the closing decades of the century there were even signs that the vanguard of an economic middle class was beginning to press up against the absolutist and aristocratic limitations upon the liberalizing policies of government. Still fundamentally dependent upon the state and recognitory of its existing forms, a sector of the burgher group had yet developed sufficiently to protest against specific restrictions in government policy. The shift in the opposition to Prussian economic policies from the conservative resentment of merchants against the dislocation of traditional patterns of commerce to the liberal resistance of certain industrialists and bureaucrats against the extent of state controls over the economic process was paralleled by the shift in urban constitutional claims from the defense of municipal privilege against the sovereignty of the state to the assertion of municipal rights and influence within the accepted sovereignty of the state.[76]

The social background of German 18th-century culture was thus constituted by a burgher estate suspended in the early stages of the leap between traditional corporate stagnation and free individual activity and torn by a love-hate relationship to the Janus-faced state that was its bridge between the two worlds. The prime bearers of this culture were intellectuals of burgher origin, and the position of their class in social and political reality supplied the assumptions of their own attitude toward that reality. The much-remarked tendency of the great classical school of literature which flowered in the last third of the century to celebrate freedom as the highest spiritual value, and to avoid any consideration of its social and political applications, is best understood in the light of the similarity which this duality bears to the duality in the structure of the burgher estate. As scions of this estate, the intellectuals took up into their writing the anomaly of the burgher position in 18th-century Germany. The beginnings of the transition into a modern middle class opened the burghers and the writers to the more advanced currents from the Atlantic civilization, but the continuing isolation of the burgher estate from the rest of a German society that was rigidly organized and very unevenly affected by the Enlightenment, confined the operation of values for the burghers to the realm of private life and for the intellectuals to the realm of spiritual life.

Moreover, the structure of the German burgher estate produced a secondary isolation of the intellectuals from its main body. For the intellectuals were not simply a branch of the burgher estate with the function of developing and rationalizing its claims and attitudes. In large measure the educated commoners became a new autonomous estate with a specifically cultural function and with only the most general sense of community with their social forbears. Men passed into academic and literary careers as distinct callings, in part because mercantile profits in a preponderantly stagnant economy took a fluid form and tended not to be transmitted from generation to generation in the rooted institution of a permanent business. When the burgher became a rentier he was left free to pursue creative activities or to acquire status in another field.[77] The production of the intellectual out of the burgher testified in Germany rather to the immaturity of economic life than to its success, rather to a decision to leave it than a tendency to glorify it. Furthermore, a large proportion of the intellectuals were academicians or bureaucrats. In either case they were officials of the state, associated with its general functions in society and cut off from the social group of their origins.

The isolation of the burgher estate from the other social groups and of the intellectuals from the economically based burghers was not a new factor. This social fact and the etherealized German thinking which it helped to produce were persistent factors in Germany from the Reformation until the end of the old regime. Indeed, theology continued to be the favorite discipline of the middle-class intellectuals. What was new was the tension which appeared within this structure in the second half of the 18th century with the modest economic advances of a middle class in Germany and the efflorescence of liberal thinking and writing outside Germany. The response of the German writers to this tension was to develop ever more intensely the theme of the dignity and freedom of the individual human personality, but to embody them still in the insulated ethical and aesthetic patterns which were the traditional modes of expression for German ideals. The traditional structure of German life had channeled social energies, aside from the large sphere reserved to religion, primarily into two activities—cultural pursuits and state-building. The developments of the 18th century modernized these pursuits and associated the values of individual liberty with them but did not go beyond their orbit.

Undoubtedly the cultural achievements of the German burgher estate represented the best that was in it, but the social and political implications of these achievements are not the whole story of its political position. From about 1770, simultaneously with their non-political literary achievements, the German intellectuals developed an avowedly political wing. Moreover, unlike their previous role in politics, their characteristic field was no longer law or administration but journalism, and their chief function no longer buttressing the power of the sovereign ruler but criticizing his exercise of it. Nor was this reforming political journalism a negligible factor in burgher life. Between 1770 and 1790 some thirty to forty periodicals appeared that were devoted exclusively to political discussion and at least as many general journals with a political interest. Readership, moreover, was relatively extended in burgher circles: A. L. von Schloezer's *Correspondence* had about 4,000 subscribers at its height and Christian Schubart, one of the very few literary men to adopt journalism as a free profession, derived a comfortable living from the sales of his Chronicle.[78] The general reading public which had been developed by the Enlightenment was exposed for the first time to a group of intellectuals who applied the ideal of freedom and the idea of the rights of man as criteria for the behavior of princes, bureaucrats, and nobility.[79]

Actually, however, these beginnings of a middle-class politics did not bridge the gap between the values and the social practice of the German burgher estate. Rather did they confirm it, for the fundamental duality was simply repeated within the political wing of the estate. Not only was the extent of political interest limited by the concentration of activity in the writing of a small group of intellectuals and by the exclusively receptive posture of the audience, but the quality of the political interest itself tended simply to articulate the ambivalence of dependence and resentment in the burgher attitude toward the state. As in other countries, political criticism developed from the application of the rational standards of the Enlightenment to social affairs, but for Germany this meant the transfer into political attitudes of the moral and religious tone which had been the distinctive hallmark of the German Enlightenment. The intensity of the criticism from this higher ground was accompanied by its continued separation from political issues as such. It is hardly surprising, therefore, to find that the strictures on the princes were so specific, so diverse, and so moralistic that the writers were themselves unconscious of their political import.[80] Consequently, the political writers tended to express, in somewhat different terms, the same combination of elements that characterized their literary colleagues—a commitment to the fundamentals of the existing political system and a subscription to a transcendent ideal of freedom with which to judge it. If the classical literature of the age asserted the ideal in a realm outside of politics, the political writings came to a very similar end through an artful juxtaposition of anti-absolutism on the purely theoretical level and enlightened absolutism on the level of practical political discussion.

Thus the few economic bourgeois who wanted a larger economic liberty, the literary sections of the middle class who exalted liberty of the spirit, and the political writers who called for civil liberty reveal a single pattern. Out of the mass of German burghers an identifiable middle-class minority had emerged which, by the second half of the 18th century, was beginning to raise claims to a freer life within the existing system of absolute states. By elevating the ideal of liberty to the status of a disembodied moral principle and by dispersing the substance of liberty in a host of discrete demands for specific action by the authorities, this group assumed that the established state was compatible with and necessary for the exercise of the new principles of general liberty, but they assumed too that the established state, however necessary in practice, was but an imperfect embodiment of these principles themselves. At this point, when the German intellectuals were just beginning to be politicized, the essential continuity in the German attitude toward freedom dimly emerges. The combination of secular submission and spiritual independence which had been established by the German religious and philosophical tradition of the old regime in the face of a pluralistic society was in the process of turning into the political alternatives of practical accommodation and dogmatic radicalism, in proportion as the state expanded its powers and claims over its subjects. This cultural duality which became a political disjunction was, in either phase, a logical response to the central fact of a political system in which monarchs absorbed into their states, together with all public authority, the exclusive title to realize the public freedom. The German middle classes had either to accept or ignore the state which the aristocrats had been so influential in shaping.

Despite all the arbitrariness, the oppression, the burdensomeness, the venality, and often even the absurdity, of German princely rule during the *ancien regime,* the relationship of the princely states to the authoritative groups of the society which they governed remained a vital one. Even the more vigorous and assertive members of these groups were dependent in good measure upon the states for their very vigor, and they attributed to the nature of the state the qualities which they deemed most essential to a progressive society. The prince, who was part German aristocrat and part territorial sovereign of a public state, indeed possessed the social conservatism of the one and the authoritarianism of the other, but he also took from the aristocracy the traditional feudal claim to contractual liberties, and from the middle-class component of the bureaucracy the tendency to generalize this claim and to distribute it in some degree over all groups of his subjects. Thereby he built the feudal union of chartered liberties and magistracy in his own particular person into a modern union of liberal policy and absolute authority in the public state. This was the first stage of that remarkable process in which both the agents of political authoritarianism and the social hierarchy in Germany absorbed what was inevitable in innovation and adapted themselves to it in such wise as to leave the fundamental relationships of their position unimpaired.

2. Constitutional and Political
Theory

The development of the German political system from a group of autonomous aristocratic principalities to a set of monarchical sovereign states with limited liberal policies was paralleled in the realm of ideas. Through academically trained jurists associated with government through bureaucracy or the legal faculty of the universities, constitutional and political theory during the old regime absorbed the conditions of real political life and contributed both to their clarification and to their progress. For the role of theory in Germany was more than mere justification. In a country where men's values tended to take a conservative, private, or religious form jurisprudence and political doctrines had a genuine operative function in creating a realm of positive public values and in attracting public loyalties to the territorial state. These academic activities, moreover, were utilized by princes to rationalize their governments and to orient their policies in directions that would attract these loyalties. The course of theory, then, accompanied the course of politics, sometimes anticipating and sometimes ruminating, but in any case demonstrating the connections and the meaning of disparate events.

So it was that the intricate relationship between the prince as German aristocrat and the prince as particularist head-of-state found expression in the relationship between constitutional and political theory. For the constitutional theory of the German old regime was concerned primarily with the structure of the Empire, while genuine theories of politics began only with the recognition of the sovereignty of the territorial state and were addressed chiefly to it. Constitutional writings dominated the field as long as princes held to traditional conceptions of their own position, but around the middle of the 17th century, when the princes turned to a frank concentration upon the institutions of particular state-building, then, too, did political doctrines move to the fore-front of civil discussion. But the mark which the princes' wonted status as Imperial Estates left upon their new territorial states was given definition and substance in the influence which

German constitutional exegesis had upon the subsequent development of absolutist political theory. In constitutional writing as in constitutional practice the Imperial tradition died hard. In the 16th century the German jurisconsults applied the concepts and formulations of Roman law directly to Germany as the extension of the Roman Empire, and in the 18th century the German Empire still retained a juristic, albeit not a political, validity: not only Imperial historians like J. P. Ludewig, J. J. Maskov, and Justus Moeser but even the natural-law writers like G. A. Achenwall, J. S. Puetter, and A. L. Schloezer were still asserting the individuality of the German constitution as the guarantor of freedom.[1] The continuity of the tradition vouches for the continuing vitality of the framework which saw the German territorial states as constituent members of a greater whole, and thus it was that an approach which was most appropriate to an earlier period remained a constant condition upon the political thinking about the particularist sovereign state.

The period down to the middle of the 17th century was the heyday of this Imperial jurisprudence. To be sure, the legists of the princely states expounded and used a combination of Roman and natural legal principles which was generally applicable, but for constitutional questions the "German-Roman Empire," with its peculiar blend of definite structure and universal claims, seemed the appropriate field. This was all the more the case since the natural law component in legal thought, with its general political concepts and its corollary of state sovereignty, tended to be weaker in Germany than elsewhere during this period. The Imperial framework was one of the primary strands in the tradition that moderated and limited the application of natural law in Germany. Hermann Conring, the founder of German legal history, did not belong to the natural law school at all, while C. B. Besold tended to identify natural law with positive law in a justification of the *status quo*.[2] More typically, the categories of natural law were imposed upon the German constitution, but in the process the meaning of such political concepts as sovereignty was weakened by the necessity of adapting it to the division of authority between Emperor and the Imperial Estates and to the confusion of territorial sovereign and German

subject in the Imperial Estates.[3] The outstanding exception to
this pattern of ideas was Johannes Althusius, who sought to develop a genuine political theory of universal applicability
founded upon the explicit independence of "politics" as a discipline, the natural-law idea of contract, and the new doctrine of
indivisible sovereignty. Althusius, however, was scarcely representative, for his connections were primarily Dutch, his models
Swiss, his inspiration Calvinist, and his context the declining free
cities. But if his political principles were not typical of Germany
in the early 17th century his interpretation of the German constitution was in line with the national consensus: he identified
the Empire with the state and characterized the principalities
simply as its "provinces," albeit he conceded that they might take
a sovereign form.[4] In general, then, down to the middle of the
17th century German publicists took the Empire as their unit and
the question of its monarchical or aristocratic constitution as
their issue. In this universe of discourse, the cutting edge of the
political concepts which were taken over from the state-building
of the west was blunted. The dual position of the German
princes was recognized in the alternative attribution to them of a
representative character, as aristocratic or even popular spokesmen *vis-à-vis* the Emperor, and of governmental character, as
participant with the Emperor in the sovereign authority of the
Empire.[5]

With the Empire absorbing the discussion of constitutional
principles, the principality was subjected to traditional considerations in the political writings of the 16th and early 17th centuries. From Johann Oldendorp, a Lutheran jurist of the Reformation period, to V. L. von Seckendorf, a small-state councilor
after the Thirty Years' War, literature on the territorial level
took the old mirror-of-princes form, lumping the private and
public capacities of the prince together into the notion of the
just and patriarchal magistrate. This traditional pattern, which
was consonant with the place of the prince in the Imperial strand
of the tradition, was amended in one important particular during
this period. The Reformation had increased the ecclesiastical
powers of Lutheran and Catholic princes alike, a development
which received theoretical expression for Lutheran princes in

the doctrine of the *jus episcopale*. Ultimately both the fact and the doctrine, which conferred upon the prince the prime responsibility and the supreme power for the organization and maintenance of religion in his territories, were to contribute signally to the extension of authority which led to the organization of the sovereign state, but the contemporary effect of the *jus episcopale* was rather to reinforce the traditional aspects of the principality. Not only did it perpetuate the ideal of the Christian commonwealth as the framework of government and the policy of maintaining the divinely sanctioned historical order as its purpose,[6] but it re-emphasized the union in the prince of the rights accruing to society and the authority accruing to government. For the *jus episcopale* inhered not in the prince as head of state but in his person, so that he effected a purely personal identity of two distinct orders, the religious and the political. But this implied the familiar mixing of his private and public capacities, for if the independence of religion required that the prince be bishop not as a sovereign but only as *primus inter pares* within the church community, still it was undeniable that his clerical primacy stemmed in good part from his political magistracy. The impact of the Reformation, then, was to increase the powers of the prince and his government, but the forms which it took, in the midst of this increase, helped to make the territorial monarch the indispensable conjunction of the governed and the government in the new state: he was the agent of spiritual freedom for his society as well as of political power over it. Not until the Treaties of Westphalia was the *jus episcopale* legally recognized as an integral part of territorial sovereignty as such.

In that very period, then, when Bodin, James I, Grotius, and Hobbes were developing the doctrines of natural-law and divine-right sovereignty which helped to segregate the state and the individual as polar opposites in the western nations, the distinction was being limited in Germany by the vitality of the hierarchical concept and particularly by the mediating role of the territorial prince in constitutional and ecclesiastical theory. After the middle of the 17th century, consequently, when the most prominent German jurists turned their chief attention to the emergent territorial states and appropriated the fundamental concepts of western political thought in order to account for them, this characteristic amendment was carried over into the German version of the prevalent natural-law absolutism. In the form of "enlightened despotism" the doctrine was particularly appropriate to the Germans, and it is hardly coincidence that in the century of its dominion over European political thinking the Germans produced their main old-regime theorists of continental stature and supplied its most rigorous formulations. A tendency that in other countries proved to be inconsistent, unstable, or derivative from other considerations, enlightened absolutism was in Germany, from Pufendorf to the pre-revolutionary Kant, anchored securely in the tradition of state. The essence of enlightened absolutism was its translation of the reciprocal relationships between state and society into definitive attributes of rulership. When the Germans translated the historical Imperial and ecclesiastical connections of the princes into the rational language of territorial sovereignty after the Thirty Years' War they converted the external relations of the magistrate into the constituent conditions of absolute dominion. Through the logic of sovereignty the older particular corporate and religious claims were transformed into universals whose realization became part of the definition and purpose of the state.

The Absolutists (1650-1750)

The transition stands revealed in the work of Samuel Pufendorf. In him the break with the traditional constitutional theory derived from the particular nature of the Empire and the consequent turn to general political theory applicable to all territorial sovereigns were articulated in distinct steps, and the transfer of vital elements from the one stage to the other made apparent. He stood at the beginning of the unbroken line of political thinkers who adapted the essentials of the German constitutional and social structure to the conscience of the west. Pufendorf, Christian Thomasius—his most famous disciple—and Christian Wolff, the synthesizer of European natural law with the conservative Germanic influence of Leibniz, dominated the political speculation of the century 1650 to 1750 in Germany. They adopted the western assumptions which made individuals the primary units of society and individual rights the basis and the limitation of the state, but they interpreted these assumptions in a way compatible with the preservation of the peculiar German corporate rights and made the prince arbiter over all.

Pufendorf initiated the process when he broke with both the Empire and the constitutional theory which had been built upon it, in his *Concerning the Constitution of the German Empire* of 1667. But the rupture was a peculiar one, and neither the nature of Pufendorf's influence nor the character of subsequent German political theory can be understood without a grasp of its essential complexity. For it was not simply a rejection of the Imperial constitution as a fiction in favor of the reality of princely sovereignty. This kind of rupture had already been performed by the juristic generation of the Thirty Years' War. Bogislaw Chemnitz, writing under the pseudonym of Hippolytus a Lapide, had refuted the prevalent interpretation of the Empire as a mixed constitution and had asserted it to be a pure aristocracy, with the body of princes sovereign. Hermann Conring had gone even further. He had deprecated Empire and Emperor together as products of religious, moral, and natural-law considerations which were invalid for politics, and he had exalted in their stead the particular territorial principality as the real creation of the rational will of the ruler and as the valid exercise of his *Libertaet.*[7] But such extremes of particularism proved to be provocative rather than authoritative in Germany, where consideration for the traditional relationships binding upon the princes was still required. The influence of Chemnitz and Conring tended to be mediated through Pufendorf, who used their historical realism and their demonstration of princely power but who combined with these factors an appreciation of the moral, legal, and customary limitations upon that power. In his work on the German constitution Pufendorf's objections were directed against all previous tenets without exception, on the ground that every constitutional position—whether in favor of the Emperor's or the princes' sovereignty—falsified the German situation. His break was not simply with previous doctrines but with the very categories of thinking and acting. The fault of German jurists, Pufendorf insisted, was their legal and constitutional scholasticism and their ignorance of the "fundamental relationships and doctrines of *politics*," and the fault of the German statesmen lay in their strife-ridden attempts to enforce simple constitutional solutions.[8] What must now be recognized, he went on, is that the German Empire is "an irregular state-body, similar to a monster." [9] By this he meant both that it was not susceptible to rational treatment according to the Aristotelian "rules of politics" in theory and that the "irregular and monstrous" "form and conformation" of the parts manifested "disease" and weakness of the body politic in practice. Unlike the territorial states and city-states, which were readily classifiable into monarchies, aristocracies, and democracies, the Empire could be referred to no recognizable "state-form" nor even to a confederation of sovereign states, for it had too little concentration of power in any organ for the former and too much for the latter.[10] Here then lay the difficulty: the Empire conformed to no rational political consideration and everyone thought and acted as if it did. Indeed, within this Imperial universe of discourse Pufendorf himself could arrive at no tenable solution. Monarchy would be most desirable but is impossible "without violent convulsions," while a confederation of sovereign territorial states would be possible but is unfeasible because of Hapsburg power.[11] Nevertheless, the concrete proposals which he advanced to minimize present evils betrayed the kind of rationalization which he was making of the German situation. He suggested that the princes voluntarily direct themselves to policies of German alliance and religious toleration and that the Hapsburg Emperors voluntarily limit themselves to the existing scope of their power.[12] For Pufendorf, the solution which accounted for the new concentration of political authority and yet preserved traditional social and constitutional relationships was the sublimation of the heterogeneous contractual relations into a definite form of the ruler's political will.

Pufendorf's chief concern thus became the analysis of sovereignty in the territorial state, where the reality of sovereign power and the uniformity of its structure in the various states made it theoretically viable. But at the same time his chief problem became the transfer to the new system of the older limitations upon princely authority. Taking over from Hobbes the idea of an irrevocable contract between the people formed into a political society on the one hand and the ruler on the other and the consequent exhaustion of the sovereignty of the state by the absolute ruler, Pufendorf tried to show, in contradistinction to Hobbes, that this absolute sovereignty of state and ruler was limited. His solution of this apparent paradox lay in his crucial assumption that absolute rule consisted in free discretion undeterred by the will of others within the proper sphere of sovereignty and that this absolute rule could therefore be limited by its own nature, i.e. by the attributes which defined the functions of the sovereign. ". . . He who holds supreme sovereignty is not understood to be able to will anything but what sane reason can discover to be appropriate for that end." [13] Now in itself this kind of formulation was hardly distinctive in political thought. What made it distinctive was Pufendorf's specification of the moral, self-limiting nature of sovereignty in terms of individual rights, which he designed it to secure. Thus far more explicitly than Hobbes did Pufendorf develop, as the necessary foundation of the contract of rulership, the notion of a social contract whereby individuals in the state of nature formed themselves into a political society for the security of their natural rights, a function which was subsequently devolved upon the ruler. This anticipation of Locke defined the purpose of the state as the execution and application of natural law and admitted the existence of individual natural rights and even of constitutional limitations against government, but unlike Locke, Pufendorf refused to admit the existence of any organ to enforce these purposes, rights, or limitations on government. The attribution to the ruler of the full sovereignty of the state within the proper sphere of the state and the assertion of real but imperfectly guaranteed rights, both personal and constitutional, against the violation of this sphere had the effect of making the ruler responsible for exercise both of authority and of popular rights. Consequently authority and rights were equally included in the concept of the ruler's sovereignty. Given this internal character of the check upon power, it is hardly surprising that Pufendorf emphasized the necessity of strengthening the moral basis of natural law and sought to develop an ethic of duty.[14]

It was an extraordinarily difficult theoretical problem which Pufendorf set for himself, this attempt to work into a single system the absolute claims of a secular state sovereignty in the exclusive possession of the ruler and the propensity of natural and constitutional law to bind the ruler. Not only was he among the first to deal with the issues raised by the interpretation of natural law in terms of individual rights valid even in the condition of political society, but he was the first major European advocate of absolutism to deal theoretically with the issue of constitutional limitations upon the sovereign. The compulsion which he felt to formulate such a problem was a testimony to the insistent challenge posed by the hierarchical German society to the new theories of the sovereign public state, and Pufendorf's intricate response constituted the first characteristic German accounting for this structure in terms of modern political concepts.

The counterpart to Pufendorf's doctrine of natural and constitutional rights which in a sense did and in a sense did not bind sovereign power was his doctrine of society, which in a sense did and in a sense did not continue to exist as such after the foundation of government. On the one hand, Pufendorf followed Hobbes in asserting that the political rights of the society were extinguished in the contract of submission which set up the ruler, and that thereafter the ruler took over the entire public identity of the society, leaving only private rights outside his sphere. On the other hand, however, Pufendorf was careful to specify not only a prior social contract whereby political society came into existence as a public person, but also a constitutional statute, intermediate between the pacts of society and rulership, in which the political society laid down the fundamental laws for its future government. The assumption which made this dual relationship between the society and its ruler internally compatible was a complex notion about the nature of society which established it simultaneously as the aggregate of its component individuals and as an integral corporation above them. While Pufendorf did take over from Hobbes the doctrine that the sovereign ruler was the exclusive political representative of society, he amended it to make the act of representation complete the existence of a civil society rather than to constitute it—the establishment of rulership did not create the unitary will and the personality of the society but made it practical and gave it legal status. Where Hobbes brought the ruler into direct relationship with individuals by making society simply a function of this relationship, Pufendorf built upon his similar acceptance of the individual and contractual basis of organized society a superstructure which made society an autonomous link between individuals and government. Society converted the natural rights fed in by its members at the bottom into the legal powers distilled out by government at the top. Pufendorf's society was able to perform this alchemy by virtue of his key notion of "the moral person," for through this concept physical persons, together with their natural liberties, were transformed into the holders of stations, and society as the collectivity of physical individuals into the hierarchical support of the state. "A moral person is a person considered under that status which he has in communal life," while "otherwise . . . a person is said to be that which possesses a civil condition, that is, personal liberty." [15] Since "moral" in this context consisted for Pufendorf in the attributes imposed by human decision upon physical beings in order to provide the framework for "rights," "obligation," "authority," and in general the legal organization of society, his distinction between physical and moral persons had the effect of subordinating natural individuals to the prescriptions of the prevailing system of law and custom. Societies, as composite moral persons, attain dominion over their constituent individuals in the latter's capacity as simple moral persons. Not only does a society have "its special rights and goods which cannot be claimed by individuals as such" but the individual as a moral person becomes subject to hierarchical and corporate relationships of social status, like seniority, hereditary caste, callings as officials or servants, and the political category of governor and governed.[16] In this way Pufendorf made individuals the foundation of societies and yet absorbed the rights and claims of these constituent individuals into the traditional organic structure of society.

Pufendorf's purpose in this transmutation was to work the original rights of natural man into a social shape from which they could in turn be politically transposed into attributes of sovereign rulership in the state. "In general," wrote Pufendorf about freedom as a social status, "liberty denotes the status of those who serve merely the state and not another fellow-citizen in addition," a declaration which revealed his design to concentrate authority in the ruler and equate this authority with lawful freedom.[17] His doctrine of society could effect this relationship because it was founded upon individual rights and completed in the representation of those rights, now socially organized, by the ruler. In the case of the general civil society, this second stage by which it was completed is called the state.

> A state is a moral body which is understood to have one will. But since it is made up of many physical persons, each of whom has his own will and inclination, and since these wills cannot physically be compounded into one or combined in a perpetual harmony, it follows that the one will in a state is produced in the following fashion: all the persons in the state submit their will to that of one man, or of a council, in whom the supreme sovereignty has been vested.[18]

Pufendorf's state consists in the representation of the dispersed rights of independent natural individuals by a unitary sovereign, and the mediation between them is performed by the corporate institutions of a hierarchically-organized society. This society serves two concrete political functions. First, it funnels rights into authority so effectively that the sovereignty in the state is both indivisible—that is, the totality of it must be vested in one man or council—and "supreme" —that is, the sovereign ruler is above controversion by or even accountability to any human agency.[19] Secondly, however, the existence of the civil society apart from the ruler, although too imperfect to endow it with autonomous political rights in the state, is sufficient to impress a certain attribute upon the very essence of the governing power—that it be guided by the rule: "Let the safety of the people be the supreme law."[20] Now it is as a resultant of this twofold role of society, which both exalted and conditioned sovereign authority by associating it with the exercise of the socially organized freedom of individuals, that Pufendorf could endow the sovereign ruler with supreme powers subject to obligations that are "merely imperfect"—i.e. unenforceable.[21] The formula of imperfect obligation was particularly revealing, for it represented an artificial intermediate link in the theoretical process which converted the plurality of medieval political liberties into one internally conditioned authority. Pufendorf's ruler was under imperfect obligations of two kinds, constitutional and contractual, and both reinforced the attributes of sovereignty rather than the checks upon it. In accordance with the former kind of obligation, Pufendorf admitted a "limited" as well as an "absolute" type of "supreme sovereignty." In a limited sovereignty the will of the ruler is bound for certain specified matters to the observation of fundamental statutes and, usually, to the consent of a council or assembly in legislation on these matters. But Pufendorf was very explicit in asserting that this limitation meant no lessening of the ruler's powers in their proper sphere. ". . . There exists, in the strict sense of the word, an absolute sovereignty, at least in habit and theory if not always in practice, in every state," for supreme sovereignty everywhere involves the right of rulers "to decide by their own judgement about the means that look to the welfare of the state." [22] Constitutions creating limited sovereignty, then, restrict rulers simply "to a certain manner of procedure" [23] and are no derogation from their exclusive powers. The will of the ruler remains the "supreme" and exclusive expression of the will of the state, for "all the acts of sovereignty can be exercised as well in such a monarchy (i.e. limited) as in an absolute one"—the difference is only that some of them must be willed "under a certain condition." [24] To embody the political rights of the people in procedural conditions which did not affect the substance of the ruler's sovereignty was simply to confirm the internal character of that sovereignty. The assemblies that constitutionally "limit" the sovereign are called and dissolved by the ruler, pass resolutions that have effect only by the will of the ruler, and if need be can be negated by the ruler. For these constitutional "conditions and agreements" are intended "never to lead to the commission of anything which would prejudice the common safety of all, . . . or lead to the overthrow or dissolution of the state," and "in the event of such things happening . . . the king will be empowered carefully to correct pacts which are destined to lead to the destruction of the state." That Pufendorf could find these assemblies which represented all popular political rights not vested in the ruler compatible with an exclusive ruler's sovereignty was undoubtedly connected with his assumption of their organic nature. Pufendorf's assemblies were "orders"—either primary assemblies of family heads in small communities or "assemblies of the estates" for larger political units, but in any case corporate bodies which converted the natural freedom of individuals into the conscience of the ruling authority in the state.[25]

Nor were the original contractual stipulations binding upon rulers—absolute and limited alike—any more enforceable, save in the last extremity. The sovereign indeed violated the contract and exceeded his powers when he did things "repugnant to the safety of the state or opposed to natural laws," but the safety of the state itself required that the ruler be judge of what lay within these limits. "Therefore the supreme sovereign can rightfully force citizens to all things which he judges to be of any advantage to the public good." [26] Even a tyrant cannot be stripped of his sovereignty, "because such obscurity usually surrounds civil acts that the common sort cannot recognize their equity or necessity" and "there is always a presumption of justice on the part of the prince." [27] Both separately, as individuals, and collectively, as a people, the society retains rights that are not exhausted in the ruler's sovereignty and can be violated by him; but they are unenforceable as long as any shadow of public consideration can be advanced for the ruler's action. Yet there are extreme occasions upon which individuals and even the people are released from obedience and can "defend their safety" against the ruler, and the criterion which is common to the occasions enumerated by Pufendorf epitomized his political theory. Essentially, his prince could not be resisted as sovereign of the state; he could be opposed only when he does not act as sovereign. Thus the rights of subjects are violated and resistance justified not only through excess of power, when there is oppression "without any pretext of right or public good" and "upon the urge of no necessity," but also through the insufficiency of power, when the ruler does not exert his due authority.[28] For Pufendorf, then, the political rights of the society were exhausted in a properly defined sovereign authority which disposed over the appropriate adjustment of civil rights to public safety as part of its own inherent nature.

> For surely it is by no means repugnant to the nature of supreme sovereignty that it should direct the acts of all citizens to the public safety, and that it should hold the severest punishment before him who flaunts its decrees, without also having the power to slay anyone at its pleasure and allow him no degree of resistance.[29]

Pufendorf's main emphasis lay in his theory of sovereignty—that is, in his organization of the political rights of individuals and peoples into the supreme political authority of a sovereign ruler. His doctrine of a state whose power was wholly vested in an independent prince, whose justification was ultimately attributed to the rights of individuals, and whose basis was a traditionally-structured society was to have a notable career in Germany. But what Pufendorf mentioned and did not work out was the relationship between the political powers of the state and the rights of individuals and associations which were dedicated to other than political ends. Involved in this relationship was the crucial problem of providing an actual, rather than merely verbal, conciliation between the sphere of a constitutionally absolute monarchical sovereignty and the sphere of fundamental human rights which it was bound by its very nature to protect. Implicit in Pufendorf, this problem was taken up by his followers Thomasius and Wolff, who worked out the theoretical association of German political absolutism with the civil rights of man.

Christian Thomasius, Prussian jurist and philosopher whose career spanned the decades around the turn of the 17th century, based his work firmly on Pufendorf's fundamental tenets. But the progress of the Enlightenment, capsulated for him particularly in the influence of Locke, drove Thomasius to concentrate upon two related problems which had not been central for Pufendorf. Thomasius was vitally interested in the question of spiritual freedom, including here both academic freedom and freedom of conscience, and he was correspondingly concerned with the question of political obligation. For since Thomasius turned his attention primarily to those freedoms which were parts of individuals' natural rights existing prior to and outside the sphere of the state, the question—why and how far should the individual obey the state—became infinitely thornier than when the security afforded by the state to such rights was the foremost consideration.

The authenticity of Thomasius' advocacy of the freedom of the spirit is beyond doubt. In a letter to Elector Frederick III of Brandenburg, Thomasius wrote during 1692:

> Freedom! Indeed it is freedom which gives genuine life to all spirit and without which the human understanding, however many advantages it may otherwise have, appears to be almost dead. The understanding knows no master but God, and therefore the yoke which is imposed on it when a human authority is prescribed to it as a guide is intolerable. . . .[30]

He attributed Germany's lagging cultural position to the lack of it in academic life, and he insisted that religion cannot be a matter of constraint. True, the chief targets of his active literary campaign for these goods were not the princes but the scholastics and the orthodox Lutherans, but the fact remains that his theory was clear and strong in its assertion of the inviolability of these liberties from the state.[31] Thomasius formally justified these indefeasible liberties with the assertion that "whatever human action is subject to the will of no man is also not subject to the will of a prince." [32] But rights which were "subject to the will of no man" was precisely his definition of "inborn" or natural rights in general, and this raises the question of the reason for Thomasius' one-sided emphasis upon the spiritual liberties—a question all the more pertinent for his avid reading of and susceptibility to Locke, who certainly expressed no such partiality.[33] Thomasius even limited his precious spiritual liberties when they approached the realm of social practice. His general formula for individual rights was: "The action and inaction of subjects which can neither hinder nor further the common peace are not subject to the rights of the prince." [34] Since the common peace was implicitly defined as the established political order not only were the more concrete rights immediately limited but even religions which disturbed this peace—i.e. atheism, intolerant religions, and those more obedient to a man or college independent of the prince than to the prince himself—need not be tolerated by the prince.[35] Moreover, even if the prince does infringe the inviolable inborn rights of man, his subjects, though no longer obliged to obey him, must not resist him and must suffer the injustice.

From the externals of his theory, Thomasius (like Voltaire) would seem to have solved the problem of reconciling individual liberties with political absolutism simply by assigning the rights of man primarily to an ethereal sphere in which they could do little political harm. But measured against the German tradition of political thought even this modest step appears momentous. Although the tendency to internalize or spiritualize liberty was still evident in Thomasius, the line between the world of spirit and the world of flesh was far differently drawn than in the libertarian concepts of Luther or even Leibniz. Common to this traditional Protestant school was the postulation of an integral spiritual plane in which man could realize himself freely, either against or within the physical world as a whole, without raising political or social conflict. Thomasius preserved the realm of spirit as the prime abode of human liberty, but he secularized it and shifted its locus to a plane continuous with the actual political and social life of man. Thereby he created the German form of the problem of the state and civil liberties, for the change did not concretize freedom to the extent of challenging the foundations of political and social power but it did modernize these foundations by bringing the conditions of liberty within the purview of statecraft. Thus when Thomasius replaced the episcopal with the territorial theory of church-state relations and attributed to the prince simply the general powers of a political sovereign over the church as a non-political association, the substitution left the prince with a full complement of governmental authority over the churches but it also moved the profession of religion from the other-worldly invisible church into the sphere of civil liberty and made logical a state policy of toleration.

This shift in the context of freedom was articulated in Thomasius' own development.[36] The early Thomasius (of the *Institutiones Jurisprudentiae Divinae,* written in 1687) solved the problem of reconciling liberty and political obligation essentially along the older lines of weaving a divine ethic and political au-

thority into a seamless web which automatically insured that the
main force of human freedom would be exercised outside the
political and social realm. To be sure, he applied the categories
of natural law, but only to keep religion and the state separate,
for from their union he feared the undermining of secular authority, of liberty, and consequently of religion itself. But what he
dissociated directly he rejoined indirectly. He broke the direct
line of authority from God to prince to subject in order to allow
to each his due rights, but he reassembled these rights in a
hierarchical system which actually reknit the chain of command
he had meant to loosen. According to the early Thomasius, God
is not the immediate but the mediate founder of the state and its
sovereign. The state is actually founded by individual men, who
go into it out of their natural condition through the voluntary
conclusion of the successive contracts of society and of rulership.
Nevertheless, God's role is palpable, for while the natural law
through which he acts upon men is law as reason (*Recht*) this
rational law is itself the product of law as the command of a
superior (*Gesetz*). By rooting the rational prescriptions of the
law of nature in the coercive sanction of God's command, Thomasius brought God down again into the arena of men's political
affairs. This rational law worked through men's natural freedom
and their natural sociability; the necessity of remedying the
natural insecurity of the one and of fully realizing the other
manifested God's will to the state. But once within the state the
formal principle of natural law in its sense of the command of
God—obey God—was supplemented by the practical substantive
corollaries—obey the constituted ruler, and do all that is necessary to fulfil the purpose of civil society, i.e. moral and material
happiness. Thus the same natural law whose divine authorship
sanctified the rights of men likewise sanctified the political obligation of obedience to the sovereign ruler. The law which the
state was founded to apply was not only a political law but a
general moral law, and the purposes of the state itself were not
only to protect rights but also to help realize moral obligation.
But Thomasius did not at this time work out the problems inherent in this kind of synthesis of liberty and authority. While
insisting upon the reservation of individual rights—and par-

ticularly the right of religious liberty—from state action, Thomasius in this first stage of his development actually furnished the grounds for the disposition over these rights to be included in the purview of the sovereign.

Thomasius himself came to realize the implications of his theory.[37] In the course of his non-political writings of the 1690's he began to divest himself of his earlier assumptions.[38] First, he renounced metaphysical reason and pure knowledge in favor of a more pragmatic reason based on experience oriented toward active usefulness in life. Secondly, he worked himself away from the assumptions that the will of man is bad as against his reason which is good and that the love of others is a natural attribute of man, toward the ideas that the will of man is potentially good and that the love of others is the highest moral principle, whose destiny rests with the human will.

Thus the political theory of the later Thomasius (in his *Fundamenta Juris Naturae et Gentium e Sensu Communi Deducta* of 1705) was built upon foundations quite different from those of his earlier period. The titles of his works themselves betray the new approach: from natural law as divine jurisprudence to natural law as a deduction from common sense. This shift in the analysis of politics from the point of view of God's will for man to that of the empirical needs and capacities of human nature itself was dictated by more than the desire to carry through radically the secularization of the state. It signified Thomasius' renewed effort to reconcile inviolable liberties with ruler's sovereignty, this time by dissociating political authority from a divine ethic both externally and internally coercive, and reducing it to a definite place in men's unaided working out of a free, purely human ethic. While ruler's sovereignty within the political sphere was safeguarded by the maintenance in *positive* law of the distinction which made the legal system the product of the command of a superior (the production of *Recht* from *Gesetz*), Thomasius now scrapped this distinction in his concept of natural law, which became simply a "dictum of reason"—that is, "counsel" creating a moral internal duty but no coercive external obligation. This new formulation removed natural law from the sphere of compulsion which had intertwined it with politics and moved it into the sphere of the free moral conscience of man. But if sovereignty lost its ultimate moral foundation, by the same token did the individual rights contained in the natural law lose their coercive sanction. Consequently, Thomasius sought to develop a new ethical basis for both individual rights and political obligation out of a philosophy of human nature. By positing the inner sovereignty of the will over the other faculties within man, Thomasius asserted the ineluctable freedom of the individual, for the will was itself directly uncontrollable. By positing further, however, the possibility of indirectly controlling the activities of the will through man's autonomous judgment and capacity to curb his passions, Thomasius asserted the possibility of directing human actions, but only if this direction were worked through the individual and as an outgrowth of his original freedom.

Hence Thomasius now grounded the ultimate origins of the state not in a divine command but in the free determination of men to obtain the security of an objective norm amidst all the differing, conflicting individual wills. In order to build both authority and freedom into a state which harbored no higher sanction for either, Thomasius took the obvious course of simply placing them side by side in the structure and the purpose of the state. Since the norm for the organization of individual wills consisted essentially in the exercise of the understanding and the control of the passions, Thomasius divided the state into the wise men, who governed, and the fools, who were governed, and he distinguished, within the governors, between the teachers who enlightened the understanding and the princes who bound the passions. The teachers give moral counsel, which is of purely internal obligation, and the princes issue legal commands, which have external binding force; but both equally make up the authority of the state. Thus free moral guidance and legal compulsion were partners in the structure of government. The purpose of the state, for Thomasius, was similarly accordion in character. He distinguished between a broader and a narrower meaning of natural law, which the state was charged with executing. In the larger sense it included ethics, or the acquisition of internal peace of soul; politics, or the acquisition of external social peace; and law, or the avoidance of external breach of peace. In the narrow sense, it referred primarily to this third component. Thus again, a kind of continuum was established between the state's power to order externals and its capacity to create the conditions for moral freedom. In line with this he added a new element to the familiar formulation of the state's purpose as the guarantee of rights through the punishment of social depredations: the state was now also to guide the individual's exercise of his rights toward the social moral principle which was his earthly salvation.[39] Here, then, was an early expression of the important development which was to make the state, for Germans, a *Kulturstaat*—a state of culture or morality —as well as a *Rechtsstaat*—a state of law.

The unmistakable conclusion from the later Thomasius was that the individual would find his freedom increasingly in conformity with rather than in resistance to the power of the state, not only because the state as power limits itself to the sphere of the legally necessary but even more essentially because the state as the most perfect organization of the community embodies the social norm which, in the form of love, makes the individual morally free. With Thomasius modern individualism in the explicit sense of an emphasis upon the inviolable rights which men possessed as individuals entered into German political theory, and Thomasius' use of these rights to intensify rather than to challenge the power of the absolutely ruled state set a pattern which was to be characteristic of a whole school of future German liberal thought. The general basis of rulership was strengthened, for all kinds of concrete social and political action by the ruler were justified in the name of individual rights.

By equating the realm of spirit with the sphere of individual rights Thomasius brought a new tension into politics, but he also showed the way to its resolution. If the individual recesses of the spirit were now impervious to the state, individuals still were the means and spirit still was the authority for coercion by the state over all else, since in the state now the role of sovereign and the role of moral teacher fused. Thus did the political theory of Christian Thomasius domesticate the new tendencies toward natural-rights individualism in such a way as to throw into sharp relief the crucial mediating role of the German princes in the integration of emergent liberalism with the traditional structure of the German society.

If Thomasius broke ground in the association of individual liberties with the power of the sovereign ruler, Christian Wolff, the outstanding German philosopher between Leibniz and Kant, developed the doctrines on both sides of this association so radically and so fully that their union assumed classic proportions. In this unmistakable and striking form, then, the German political version of European individualism percolated down to the more popular levels of thought and expression.[40]

The theoretical difficulties of the combination were manifest in Wolff, for his political system was ultimately something of an anomaly: he carried the doctrine of individual natural rights to an unprecedented extreme for German theory, and yet he sanctioned an interventionist state of almost totalitarian proportions.[41] Where the problem had been in some measure eased for Thomasius by a kind of division of labor which assigned liberty primarily to the realm of spirit and political obligation primarily to the realm of action, Wolff seemed to ignore such a solution; he extended the area of individual rights to the realm of practical action and the area of sovereign power to the realm of the spirit. He defended explicitly the integrity of all the original rights of the individual not specifically conferred upon the state by contract, and he even associated with them the inviolability of acquired rights whose infringement would do injury to the essential nature of man.[42] Thus he admitted that private property may be founded in the state of nature and is compatible with the law of nature.[43] Upon occasion he advocated free-trade on the basis that the individual merchant is the best judge of his own interests.[44] He developed a right of association, which founded the autonomy of non-political societies and their authority over their members not upon delegations of power from the state but upon the inherent rights of such societies, contractually derived in turn from the original rights of its constituent individuals.[45] Moreover, Wolff even carried his concern for practical civil rights to a recognition of the possible validity of the people's political rights in the state. Not only did he pay his respects to democracy as the form of government in which "the people enjoy civil liberty . . . not only in relation to other nations but also in relation to itself," but he insisted upon the people's original possession of the public power in all civil societies, upon their right to bind rulers effectively through fundamental laws, upon their right to set up limited or mixed forms of government with a validity equal to the pure forms, upon the derivation of even hereditary monarchs from the will of the people.[46] And finally, Wolff asserted the right of passive resistance against the sovereign who violates natural law and the right of active resistance to the sovereign who violates constitutional or fundamental law—"if he usurps the rights which the people and the nobles have reserved to themselves." [47]

And yet the tendency of Wolff's theory was toward an absolutism that was even more of a leviathan than were the intellectual creations of Pufendorf and Thomasius. Despite his academic recognition of constitutional government, Wolff made it quite clear that his own preference was for absolute monarchy and most of his political writing assumed this form of government.[48] He declared that "he who exercises the civil power has the right to establish everything that appears to him to serve the public good"—the sovereign power is irresistible as such—and he attributed legislative, executive, judicial, and dispensing powers to him.[49] The legitimate scope of the sovereign's activities, moreover, were most comprehensive. He was responsible for his subjects' possessing the material necessities of life, and to this end he had complete regulatory and even operational authority over the economy, including the state organization of new industries, price- and wage-fixing, compulsory labor mobilization, compulsory savings, and state-poor relief. Wolff held moreover that to the sovereign accrued all the essential functions of public welfare—public and private health, education, public buildings, and entertainment. Even in the field of law, Wolff buttressed the ordinary punitive powers of the sovereign with the unconditional right of emergency decree and the exceptional right of torture. Nor did Wolff scruple to have his sovereign invade areas bordering on the realm of the spirit. He should not only punish acts against the natural law but positively aid his subjects to observe it, and he should see to it that they "fulfill their duties toward themselves, toward others, and toward God." Consequently, the sovereign disposes over education, over "external divine worship" —i.e. the building of churches, fixing of holidays, and appointment of ministers—over "vices," and over publications, both negatively through censorship and positively through the institution of state poets, musicians, and academies to secure the edification and systematization of knowledge for the use of the state.[50]

Wolff attempted to bridge the gulf between his doctrine of natural rights and his emphasis upon the authoritarian monarchical state in two ways. First, within the field of politics he compensated for his stress upon the inviolability of all that lay outside the proper sphere of sovereignty by extending the area of what properly lay within that sphere. He declared the purposes of individuals in forming the state to be not only the usual security from domestic and foreign invasion of rights but also "the acquisition of whatever is required for life—that is, an abundance of the things which serve the necessities, the comforts, and the pleasures of life and an abundance of the means of felicity." [51] Consequently, every individual in the civil society, and particularly the sovereign, was bound not simply to defend the rights of all but positively "to advance the common good as much as he can." [52] Under this exegesis of "the public safety" which "is the supreme law" all kinds of material welfare functions became legitimate activities for the ruler. Secondly, Wolff elaborated a social ethic which added a spiritual component to the idea of common good which bound the individual to the sovereign. The crucial assumption of this ethic derived the natural rights of individuals from their natural duties: primary in the moral constitution of man are his duties "to do what tends to the perfection of himself and his condition," and his inherent rights are what give him the freedom requisite to the fulfillment of these inherent obligations. "There would be no right if there were not obligation." [53] The natural duty to perfection and its derivative natural liberty have reference in the first instance to the original absolute independence of the individual, but because of the equally natural insufficiencies of individuals, this duty and this liberty come to include the obligation and right of individuals to work for the perfection of others and of the collective society—and this in the triple sense of "perfection of the soul, the body, and external condition." [54] Hence this obligation and this right were incumbent not only upon individuals but to an even greater extent upon their sovereign, for the quantity of duties and liberties varied with status.[55] The epitome of the prescriptive laws of nature—advance the internal and external perfection of the individual and the society—was addressed to individual and state alike.

Thus did Wolff make over into a political ethic the concept of "perfection" which Leibniz had designed to reconcile Christianity with the new scientific world, and it served the same synthetic function in its new setting as in its old. The goal of "perfection" united the spiritual and physical realms, with their individual and sovereign agents, into one embracing system. The state was at the same time an instrument of individuals for their own perfection and itself a higher social individuality which could achieve the moral and material perfection of society only by encouraging and enforcing the inner and outer perfection of its constituent individuals. Through the doctrine of perfection Wolff clearly transcended the traditional spiritual-worldly division of labor between the individual and the state. He did not, however, thereby abolish the division but rather replaced it with an end-means distinction—the actual striving toward perfection is the function of individuals and the role of the state is to furnish the means for its success.[56] The Lutheran doctrine of the two-sworded Christian state was continued, but in the new dress of the moral authority of the secularized state. The division between the inner life of the individual and the outer jurisdiction of the state was perpetuated, but in a form which joined them in one realm and created a harmonious continuum between them. This pattern of thought sponsored the peculiar but characteristic tendency in German political theory which extended the powers of the state in direct proportion with the increasing recognition of individual rights: the greater the individual's rights the larger his responsibility, and the larger therefore the role of the state as the guarantor of the rights and the objective incorporation of the responsibility.

This relationship was spelled out in the doctrine of the pre-established harmony, the complement of the concept of perfectibility in Leibniz. Wolff took it over explicitly into his philosophy of man[57] and implicitly into his political system. Devised to establish total unity and purpose in a universe which would yet permit human freedom, the doctrine furnished Wolff with the possibility of assuming an organic society which harmoniously dovetailed individual rights into sovereign power. From this assumption was derived not only the strong patriarchal tone which pervaded Wolff's treatment of natural-law kingship but also his illogical defense of mixed government and his admission of a hierarchy of legal "honors," "titles," and "privileges" for superior grades of service to "the common good." [58] This aristocracy was appointed with special rights for the particular performance of duties naturally incumbent upon every individual by the sovereign ruler who disposed over the duties and rights of all. Here was a characteristic embodiment of the internal union of freedom and power in Wolff's system.

The German theory of enlightened absolutism, which found its apogee in Wolff, contributed three basic principles to the permanent tradition of German political thinking. First, it filled the concept of sovereign political authority with a positive moral content, which could be summarized as the community of everybody's liberties. This authority enforced the external dimension of the fundamental laws which in their totality constituted the rule of moral freedom. The political authority is self-limited—limited by the essential qualities of its own moral being and not by any force outside itself. Secondly, the concept of the state was developed as the larger framework in which the common rights of its subjects were attached to sovereign authority. Replacing the older notion of the Christian commonwealth, with its distribution of functions over the divine chain of being, the idea of the state defined the supreme public power exclusively in terms of the rights of constituent individual citizens and hence was a short-hand expression for the reconciliation of monarchical absolutism with the new individualism. Thirdly, the assumption of an organic, hierarchical society infiltrated into the logical political structure of the state to convert the originally equal liberties of individuals into a social organization receptive to the activity of a unitary governmental authority.

The Constitutionalists (1750-1789)

The staying power of these tendencies in German political thinking was confirmed quickly. During the second half of the 18th century the ideal of enlightened despotism was undermined in the political theories of the Atlantic nations by the emphasis on an effective material individualism and an effective popular participation in government, but in Germany the ideal came through in far more integral shape. Until the outbreak of the French Revolution Germany produced no political thinker of stature. The natural-law absolutism of the Pufendorf-Wolff school held sway in the universities and, from the point of view of theory, writers and statesmen were concerned primarily with its popularization and application. But this persistence did not mean an entire absence of development, for German jurists and publicists proved to be thoroughly susceptible both to a native resentment against the practices of absolutism and to the liberal ideas from the west. Not only the obscurantism of the myriad of unenlightened German princes but even the ubiquitous, albeit enlightened, intervention of a Frederick the Great, which extended to censorship of the press and other media of communication, called forth an intellectual disposition toward reform. This disposition was being fed at the same time by the reading of Montesquieu, the British constitutionalists, the Encyclopedists, and by the intense concern with the constitutional conflicts in America, Britain, Sweden, and—with the accession of Joseph II— in the Empire itself. These influences found their way into political writing, and during the last third of the century the preoccupation with the rights and liberties of the subject was a constant theme in the literature on public affairs. But in Germany this theme did not inspire theoretical alternatives to enlightened absolutism. Indeed, the discussion of liberal rights contributed more in the long run to the persistence of the authoritarian tendency in German theory than the neglect of them would have done. By presenting these issues as problems of application—that is, of monarchical policy—the liberal intellectuals did increase the tensions within the artfully contrived theory of enlightened absolutism, but they also established the patterns of reconciling rather than resolving them in the face of new challenges.

The writers of the late 18th century exhibited two different patterns of reconciliation—by resignation and by adaptation. The first of these paths was taken by critics like J. J. Winckelman, Georg Hamann, and J. G. Herder, who abhorred enlightened despotism as the dictatorship of reason but who resigned themselves to political absolutism by locating their opposing ideal of a historically sanctioned, vitalistic, organic freedom in the non-political realms of aesthetics, religious pietism, or national folk-culture.[59] Only in Justus Moeser did this tendency take a political form, and here the comprehensive, moderating quality of the organic approach became evident. But the genuine political genre of the latter 18th century was the natural-law school, which defined freedom in terms of popular civil and political rights and which sought to adapt the reigning political system to them. The first of these claims—the sanctity of human rights against violation by government—was perfectly compatible with the system of monarchical sovereignty: the literature on this subject tended to single out specific abuses for correction and to assert general liberal norms morally binding upon government without doubting the competence of the sovereign rulers to fulfil these requirements. Friedrich Carl von Moser opened up this genre of political journalism in *The Lord and the Servant* (1759). He declared categorically that "the constitution of a . . . country may be good or bad—the crux comes down to the ruler himself"; that the ruler must act "systematically," in accordance with "fundamental principles"; that pursuant to these he should rule his subjects "as free men with understanding" by whose reason his acts should be judged; but that he was bound simply by "the voice of God and conscience." [60] This kind of criticism dominated the popular political journalism of the day, and it came to cover the championship of intellectual freedom, juridical security, and economic liberty as a principle. As the century wore on Moser's note of personal paternalism did tend to drop out, but even the doctrinaire strictures of a Schloezer or a Cotta did not carry freedom to the point where it seemed incompatible with the ruler's sovereignty. In 1786 Cotta declared indeed that "the good of the state depends not on the good will or the despotism of the prince but exclusively on the maintenance of the rights of every single citizen," but he immediately added that these rights were assigned by "Imperial or territorial norms" and only in their absence by "natural freedom." [61]

More difficult to integrate with theoretical absolutism was the second challenge—the acknowledgment of popular political rights in sovereignty. That the integration was somehow made is clear from the simultaneous prevalence of a political preference for enlightened, reforming monarchs and a constitutional preference for mixed government. So pervasive was this combination that it is even to be found in pronounced absolutists who scarcely participated in the liberal tendencies at all. J. H. G. von Justi, for example, best known for his Cameralism (a German version of mercantilism) and for his addiction to enlightened absolute monarchs, developed a juristic theory which not only admonished respect for the natural rights of individuals but validated permanent political rights for the people in the state and adjudged a mixed government with some kind of equilibrium of powers to be the best constitution.[62] D. Nettelbladt, Wolff's disciple and successor at the Prussian University of Halle, elaborated a similar blend: accepting the doctrine of exclusive ruler's sovereignty which was basic to enlightened absolutism, he gave it an alien context by distinguishing within the state between the "supreme power" which is the ruler's and the larger "civil power" which is shared by people, estates, and ruler alike and founds permanent political rights for all of them.[63] If such men could be tempted into adding constitutionalism to natural-law absolutism, it is readily understandable that such a tendency should be almost universal among liberals.

But how could men who professed a constitutional system that negated absolutism make their public mark as proponents of civil and social reforms within absolutism? In part, the combination was a result of external duress: a censorship that was remarkably lax about the abuses of other princes and the declaration of generalities helped direct publications to these kinds of expressions, and the absence of any social force able and willing to take up the demands of the writers helped channel appeals to the princes. But more interesting were the characteristics of the political literature itself which made possible the combination of absolutism and constitutionalism.

Fundamentally, the co-existence of the two doctrines was possible because constitutional theory in 18th-century Germany had its own orbit and led a life separate from politics and political ideas. This relationship was at its most obvious in the few republicans of the era, for their republican doctrines were extravagantly utopian and were connected less with political ideals than with a radical aesthetic or religious lyricism for which they were to furnish a context. Carl Friedrich Bahrdt, who has been characterized as a radical republican,[64] actually was not interested in politics at all.[65] His obsession was "natural religion," and it was in this sectarian interest that he wrote against the Prussian Censorship Edict of 1788 and came into the public limelight. And even then, Bahrdt summed up his political attitude in the tame formula: "Everything that does not injure the state can be freely spoken and written; but whatever directly and really injures the state . . . must be forbidden." He sought, indeed, to found a democratic "German Union," but this was only a non-political project for a national free-mason society directed against fanaticism and moral despotism." [66] Adam Weishaupt's republicanism was similarly an off-shoot from his Illuminist religious concern and was in any case conceived as a prelude to the ultimate disappearance of the state entirely. Friedrich von Stolberg found a utopian poem the appropriate vehicle for radical republican views and anticipated the establishment of a German republic in the 20th century.[67] Others even looked confidently to the princes to abolish themselves and set up the republic.[68] And what was caricature in republicanism was still characteristic in the more feasible and the more wide-spread doctrines of constitutional monarchy: its academic endorsement in Schloezer, Herder, Moeser was not brought into contact with their acceptance of monarchical absolutism and seemed to refer to quite a different order of being.

But the theoretical explanation of the paradox can be pushed even further, for the dual espousal of constitutionalism and monarchical absolutism without consciousness of friction was made possible by certain characteristics which were attributed to both. The German political writers thought of constitutional representation in the organic terms of the existing corporate estates and they thought of monarchical rule in the mechanical terms of the supreme direction and operation rather than the exclusive possession of the state power. The notion of representation by estates was designed to check only the unpolitical use of the ruler's political authority, and within the legitimate sphere of politics it organized the society in support of the self-restraining monarch.

The juxtaposition of a constitutional system compatible with royal supremacy and a monarchical loyalty compatible with constitutional "limitation" was the product of a serious theoretical dilemma. The German middle-class jurists and publicists of the late 18th century attacked two targets simultaneously—the arbitrary princes and the territorial aristocracy—only to find that in the absence of a third force these attacks tended to cancel each other out. To secure the leveling action of the prince against the nobility the liberal writers had to support the powers of the prince, since according to the natural-law theory to which they subscribed his function was precisely to enforce the natural equality of all men in the possession of rights through establishing an equality of citizenship in the state. But in order to secure the individual against the degeneration of monarchical into despotic rule these writers were also forced to support the position of the nobility.[69] They had acquired a consciousness of and belief in the people, i.e. the third estate, sufficient to demand for them the direct political representation of their rights in the state, but not sufficient to assign to them the leadership in the fulfilment of liberal aims, *vis-à-vis* either the prince or the aristocracy. Consequently, these aims were blunted by the interlocking attack upon and need for rulers and nobles. F. C. Moser, for example, admonished the princes to respect the decisions of their representative estates and yet castigated the whole political genus of estates for their general obstruction of the royal will.[70] The theoretical upshot of this dilemma was first, the maintenance of the principle of representation by estates rather than individuals, and secondly, the organic integration of this representation into the sphere of sovereign rulership under the supreme direction of the prince. Thus was it envisaged that the aristocracy could play its political role checked by the third estate from below and the prince from above, while the prince maintained the unified leadership of the political structure. The organic principle was transferred from society to the political sovereign itself. This transfer left society with the principle of individualism as its basis. The state itself now became a continuous organic hierarchy with no clear lines of division within itself and through it the princely power could impose itself directly upon the individuals in the society. A juristic doctrine which became prevalent in Germany emphasized the undivided participation of several organs in sovereignty,[71] and this expressed perfectly a political theory which expanded the sovereign to include all the vital forces in the society, but which so organized them that their functions and hence the precise limits which they set to the prince's authority remained undefined. Thus the Frederician officials of Prussia could declare that the submission of the Civil Law Code (*Allgemeines Landrecht*) to the provincial Estates for their comments and suggestions was proof that Prussia was a constitutional monarchy. The cautious absorption of an aristocratically dominated society into the state thus ended by giving a theoretical constitutional buttress to the power of the prince; it worked simply as an additional moral sanction to guarantee a just and liberal policy by the prince. So it was that the belief in the principles of constitutional monarchy remained academic and proved no bar to an emphasis upon the policies of the factually absolute princes.

This pattern appears in both August Ludwig von Schloezer and Justus Moeser—representatives of the two divergent patterns of German anti-absolutist thinking.

Schloezer, spokesman for the natural-law school, was by all odds the outstanding liberal in Germany during the period preceding the French Revolution. Journalistic gad-fly of the nation, popular professor of political science at the University of Goettingen, Schloezer was most articulate in his opposition to existing conditions in Germany. Yet the two sides of his career did not seem to hang together. As a journalist he appeared (and has been judged) an advocate of enlightened absolutism; as a political theorist his devotion to the British constitution and to the cause of constitutional monarchy in general was unquestionable. This split political personality can be attributed in part to the general obscurity, vacillation, and instability which characterized the immature German liberal thinking in general during this period.[72] But there was also a political logic in the split, for it reappeared within his formal theory of constitutional monarchy itself. Through this theory there ran a double line: Schloezer emphasized equally the necessity for a strong ruler and the necessity for realizing the natural rights of man and the political powers of the society. Thus on the one hand the sovereign must be unitary, indivisible, and "irresistible"; he combines in himself the legislative, executive, judicial, punitive, and even—since he is the "deputy of the whole people"—the "representative" power; indeed, special contractual stipulations aside, the ruler is the "leader who directs everything" and commands anything that "benefits all, or some, or one without hurting others." [73] "If this unlimited power is called despotism, then every form of government and every state . . . is despotic." [74] On the other hand, the state has its ultimate basis in the original rights of its contractant individuals and it must preserve "all their prior human and civil rights, particularly full freedom in their actions, less only the small part required by the new rights of the state"; the "people," moreover, have the right of resistance, deposition, and punishment of "usurpers and tyrants." [75] Schloezer's solution was expressed in his categorical advocacy of "mixed government" —i.e. constitutional monarchy. This was a kind of artificial *deus ex machina* which permitted him to solve his problem by juxtaposing the incompatible elements and calling them "counterweights." [76]

This solution was possible for him only on the ground of certain definite assumptions. First, "the state is a machine." [77] On this basis Schloezer could conceive the sovereign "ruler" of the state as a composite, integrated set of organs in which the monarch exercised the dominant authority and was checked by the other parts of the machine only in some entirely unspecified way ("such sovereign rights should be reserved from him without which he cannot misuse the others").[78] Thus Schloezer could attribute unity, indivisibility, and irresistibility to the sovereign power of the state as a whole and yet could credit the princely operator of this powerful machine with only a partial and limited authority in his own name. Schloezer's second main assumption which lay behind his espousal of constitutional monarchy was the attribution of an organic and hierarchical structure to civil society and the absorption of individuals into it. He inserted between man's natural condition and the creation of the state an autonomous stage of "civil society" in which a "natural nobility" —propertied, honorary, service, and hereditary—had already given permanent institutional form to the social inequality of men.[79] Political rights, moreover, inhered not in individuals but in corporate "estates," hereditary and electoral, and the right of resistance to oppression could be exercised neither by individuals nor "the people as a mass" but only by the constituted representative organs.[80] Schloezer's third and final assumption, which seemed to seal his doctrine into a closed system, made the representative corporations of the people functioning parts of the sovereign authority within the state. Here was the main theoretical development produced by the liberal writers of the late 18th century over the previous attempts by the school of enlightened absolutism to limit the ruler. Whereas previously the prince was assigned the whole of the sovereign authority and the limitations upon him were derived from its definition by rights of individuals and society lying outside the sovereign power, a part of these rights were now moved within the structure of sovereign government and thus made literal the internal association of sovereignty and freedom. In Schloezer this development took a particularly transparent form, for he extended the sovereign machine which was dominated by the prince down to include not only regular organs of political representation but also "the general civil right" of individual citizens to interest themselves as "voluntary estates" in public affairs.[81] And it was Schloezer himself who showed how this wholesale transfer of the political rights of the people into the sovereign power could be used to justify the established order in the name of liberty, for he explicitly adjudged the existing "state constitutions" of Germany, with their actual princely supremacy and politically impotent, oligarchic estates, to be the best application of his principles.[82]

Justus Moeser brought a very different attitude to the discussion of political problems. He foreshadowed the departure from rational natural law and the preference for the historical and concrete integrity of customs and institutions which was to characterize German Idealism and dominate much of German intellectual life for half a century. Rejecting the doctrine of sovereignty and the theoretical individualism of the Enlightenment, he yearned for the corporate liberties and the organic national unity of the German tribal community.[83] He viewed the original —and ideal—German constitution as an organic democracy in which men, acting in their corporate capacities (e.g. as landed property-owners), participated directly in a state whose functions were kept to the barest minimum. In this context the rise of the sovereign territorial state marked the degeneration of the good constitution. And yet, such was the force of contemporary political and social relationships in Germany that Moeser joined his natural-law colleagues in accepting the established system of territorial states as the best possible guarantee of liberty. For him the "happy" emergence of the sovereign princes was the only tolerable solution for a situation in which the decline of all other estates—particularly the third estate—undermined property, liberties, and order and blocked all other possibilities.[84] He followed the tendency of his age when he emphasized the limitation of the princes by the Empire above and their territorial estates below and bridged his interest in popular rights and his acceptance of monarchical authority with the magical concept of constitutional monarchy. But he was typical too in conceiving this in a way that was compatible with the actual powers of the German rulers: the state, he said, is like a pyramid in which "the lowest part [i.e. the people] supports the highest [i.e. the prince] completely but with the least possible burden" and the aristocracy represents the people to the prince.[85]

Moeser appropriated from the natural-law tradition the derivation of the state from a social contract of property-holders and the concentration of political authority in a ruler, and he merged these ideas into his lively sense of the corporate and Imperial tradition in Germany. Thereby he recapitulated the work of some two and a half centuries of German theoretical development, which built the doctrine of rulership defined by natural rights upon the tradition of princely representative rights in the Empire to produce finally a firm association of individual and social liberties with the governing power of the state. The pattern of the theoretical history during these centuries, moreover, anticipated the pattern of actual history during the 19th: spiritual, material, and constitutional rights were built seriatim into the unquestioned structure of aristocratic monarchy, so that one was absorbed before the others challenged, and the combined force of men's many-sided aspirations toward freedom was never brought into focus against the established order. By the time the French Revolution broke out and changed the face of the whole European world of politics a fundamental character had been consolidated in the German old regime and projected into the future as a national tradition and context: the monarchical state was the central core of public life, the agency of freedom as well as of order. Men who wanted to increase the measure of their liberty would be driven either to compromise with the existing authorities as the only possible advocates of their claims or to move toward radical renunciation or revolution as the only possible forms of freedom not already claimed by the state.

Second Section. THE ASSUMPTIONS:

Reformers, Nationalists, and
Radicals in the Revolutionary Era
(1789-1830)

Reformers, Nationalists, and
Radicals in the Revolutionary Era
(1789-1830)

Across the ramshackle structure of political Germany the flame
of the French Revolution threw a brilliant light, illuminating the
old pile before the roaring fires actually leaped the frontier. So
it was that even prior to the convulsion of Germany by invasion
and occupation the German intellectuals discerned, in the glow
of the neighboring revolution, the seams and patchwork with
which they had joined the older system of power to the newer
doctrines of liberty. The first significant impact of the French
Revolution on Germany, then, was theoretical: it compelled the
direct confrontation of issues which the political theory of the
ancien regime had been able to gloss over.

If this theoretical problem was primary, for our purposes, it
was not, of course, exclusive. The general response in Germany
to the French Revolution was broad-gauged and varied: it ranged
from the temperamental approval or disapproval of the literati
through the coffee-house plotting of the clubs of Rhenish intellectuals to the sporadic uprisings of Saxon peasants and Silesian
weavers. The full analysis of this reaction—political, social, and
atmospheric—has been made too often and too well to bear
repetition here.[1] Its main lines emerge clearly enough. They
show a temporal pattern in which original enthusiasm gave way,
with the radicalization of the Revolution, to disillusionment and
repudiation. The social spectrum varied from intellectuals absorbed in the problems of the Revolution, through middle classes
interested as distant spectators but at home still disposed to
reform within traditional institutions or to political indifference, to the peasants and the urban "common citizens (*ge-
meine Buerger*)" uncaring in their lethargy or blind and even
reactionary in their futile risings. The governmental response
was equally diverse: it included concession in Baden, repression
in the Rhenish archbishoprics, and self-justification in the minister Hertzberg's propaganda on the liberality of the Prussian

state. The uncertainty of this political and social reaction was repeated among the intellectuals: the fundamental distinction lay between the bulk of them who made no attempt to apply ideal to reality and the few revolutionaries who found no social support in their sporadic attempts at application. This division was cut across by the further substantive variegation of revolutionary interpreters into political radicals, liberals, moral individualists, historical empiricists, and political romantics.[2]

Undoubtedly many of the ideas and experiences gleaned by the Germans from this historical situation fed ultimately into the later rise of an organized liberal movement. But for the most part the channels of transmission were both porous and devious. The revolution in France did not take root in Germany. It inspired no contemporary organization of any permanence. Even the political theorizing on the new situation took no classic form. Hence the legacy of the French revolution in Germany was quickly dissipated; it lost its specific identity and was refracted into a number of separate and subordinate stimuli which simply pushed theorists and authorities to expand the established order of thought and action until it neutralized the challenge through piecemeal absorption. These stimuli typified, in an incipient form, the issues which were to confront the German state-system during the greater part of the 19th century, and the positive responses to them in the period down to 1830 set the mold for future political thinking and action. Through all the confusion induced by the external pressure from France and the social isolation of the reformers at home, the experience of this revolutionary era called forth, successively, the three types of reaction which were to harden into assumptions and constitute alternative solutions for the coming generations. First came the attempt to associate the state directly and actually with a far-reaching individual freedom through the enactment of individualistic social and civil reforms by the existing governments of Prussia and the Rhenish Confederation. This "Era of Reform" was followed by the "Era of Liberation," in which a second set of assumptions was created: a kind of political dualism emerged when a new faith in the "people" rose to match the weakened but still vital loyalty to the ruler, and political nationalism was born as the higher synthesis of both. And finally, during the postwar period of disillusionment, disappointment with the monarchical states' exercise of their monopoly for the establishment of secular liberty helped spawn the third type of liberal politics. The traditional radical renunciation of politics in the name of freedom began now to take on the politicized form of a revolutionary radicalism against the state and all its works.

The future impact of these early patterns was secured by their embodiment in traditions—of bureaucracy, of war legend, and of student unions (*Burschenschaften*). But their projection was most striking, most overt, and most comprehensible in the theoretical form which they took through the political philosophies of Kant and Hegel. Characteristically for the German politics of the age, the three main types of responses to the revolutionary challenge had their first expression in these theories, which thereby became forerunners in their own period and models in the next.

3. The Philosophical Bases:
Kant and Hegel

The political ideas of Kant and Hegel were exceptions to the instability and the anonymity that became the historical destiny of the German political writing which tried to deal with the contemporary fact of the French Revolution. It was not that the revolutionary doctrines were integrally reformed in Kant and Hegel, but rather that both of them, in different ways, recapitulated the German experience at large by subordinating the politics to the established canons of their philosophies and by giving their ideas of political freedom identities only as parts of general metaphysical and moral systems. Precisely because of the rudimentary form of their political thinking, Kant and Hegel could become consciously employed authorities for the great bulk of German liberals in the first two-thirds of the 19th century, for the sturdy philosophical frameworks gave an illusion of political stability while the diffraction of political ideas through these frameworks permitted the two philosophers to combine and justify all the disperse German approaches to the problem of freedom in polymorphic systems. It was to the vogue of Kant and Hegel above all that the conversion of the political patterns of the revolutionary era into theoretical assumptions conditioning future political action was due.

Kant

Perhaps more than any other single man Immanuel Kant is the representative figure of German liberalism. In him its peculiar problems and its general mode of solution are made manifest. An ethics separated from politics and a politics ultimately based upon ethics; an ethics of duty and a politics of rights; the supremacy of a universal absolute standard of reason and the doctrine of individual consent; the primacy of the general will and rejection of democracy in favor of mixed government; the emphasis upon the inviolable liberty and equality of all individuals,

and the equal emphasis upon the necessity of a superior authority and of a measure of inequality for human progress; the necessity of popular representation as part of a genuine division of
powers and the rejection of revolution or resistance against the
unjust monarch: these were Kantian formulations which were to
become familiar in German liberalism under the unifying concept of the sovereignty of law. That these ideas added up to a
very moderate kind of liberal doctrine is clear, and that they
perpetuated the traditional German confusion about the relationship between morals and politics is likewise clear,[1] but what
their influence was beyond these generalities is not so evident. Of
the Germans who were influenced by Kant's politics, some took
him to furnish a moral basis for political obedience, some to
furnish a moral basis for political liberty, and some absorbed
and continued his apparent dualism between the ethical and
political spheres. Thus did the problem of Kant pass unresolved
into German liberalism, and the answer to this problem becomes
the first step in unraveling the enigma of the movement in Germany. A whole generation of liberals after the beginnings of the
movement around 1830 followed Kant in intermingling the categories of philosophy and politics, and they did this not in blind
imitation of Kant but because they were driven by something
akin to the motivation which lay behind Kant's political thinking, with all its inconsistencies. The question, then, concerns not
so much the implications of Kant's political theory but its fundamental presuppositions.

It has been adjudged that what lay behind the Kantian political dualism was the discrepancy between the ideal and the
actual within his theory.[2] To the extent that this was true Kant
joined the line of German theorists who drew a radical distinction between the world of the spirit and the world of the flesh.
But the judgment is only partially true. For Kant not only subjected these worlds to a re-examination but he concentrated on
the boundary lines, the border areas, where they met. In a well-
known statement Kant confessed that Rousseau had converted
him from the anti-social Wolffian intellectualism which had made
him "despise the mob, who know nothing," to a respect for men
and to the use of academic inquiry for the purpose of "establish-

ing the rights of humanity." [3] From this point on, the *leitmotiv* of the beginning, the middle, and the end of Kant's critical philosophy, as Cassirer says, was the gospel of human freedom.[4] In the course of the development of this message Kant redefined the old dualism and brought its elements close to a dialectical relationship: he thought still in terms of two realms, a realm of nature which was the sensible world and a realm of freedom which was the intelligible world, but since the first of these realms was organized by the human understanding in accordance with principles of knowledge and the second of these worlds was defined by the human will in accordance with the principles of action the realization of freedom in actuality became a crucial problem. For in this redefinition not only were the two realms connected by the common denominator of humanity but they underwent a peculiar inversion which made them necessary to each other: with the exclusion of metaphysics in both its theological and secular forms and the denial of the sufficiency of empiricism, knowledge, traditionally the avenue of absolute spirit, now became the basis of the contingent world of sense, and practice, traditionally contingent upon knowledge, became the principle of the unconditioned intelligible world. And with this commingling these qualities became incomplete: the world of concrete experience was governed by universal rules which referred it beyond itself, and the world of the practical absolute pressed continuously for the realization of its law in experience. Thus the social and political organization of the necessitous natural world was compatible with some degree of human freedom, while the supreme prescription of the absolute moral law of freedom—"I should never act in such a way that I could not will that my maxim should be a universal law"—[5] assumed a society of men as part of the noumenal realm in a form which looked to its connection with the phenomenal political and social organizations of the realm of necessity. The tendency to extend moral liberty to civil and political liberty was present in Kant even before the French Revolution kindled his political interest.

But if the realms of nature and of freedom both contained men as individuals and as societies and if the empirical men and societies stood in some kind of relationship to moral men and societies, the fact remained that within the general framework of Kant's philosophy this relationship was indeterminate. How much and what kind of tangible liberty emerged depended on the degree to which Kant worked the possibility of this relationship into a definite part of his system, and this took time. Because of the "Copernican revolution" which Kant claimed to have brought about in philosophy he was faced first with the need to establish the integrity, the coherence, and the universal validity of each of his realms, and only then, when purely human reason had arrived at absolute certainty in the principles and limits of knowledge and absolute autonomy in the authority of its own laws of action, was a secure framework created within which Kant could proceed to demonstrate the internal relationship between the realms and therewith the place of freedom in the sensible world of nature. The watershed of this development fell in the years 1789-1790. Certainly the outbreak of the French Revolution did not cause Kant's transition from one stage of his thought to the next, for the first phase was concluded in any case with the publication in 1788 of the *Critique of Practical Reason,* but the Revolution did insure that when Kant turned in the 90's to integrating freedom into the phenomenal world political and civil liberty would be the primary and characteristic components of this freedom. Kant's political theory is usually treated as a static whole and explicated by reference to the main doctrines of his ethics, but while this procedure suffices for the presentation of his political ideas, the fundamental questions about Kant's politics can only be answered from an analysis of the tendency of its own development and from a comprehension of its changing place in the development of his general philosophy.

During the first stage of Kant's critical philosophy, a period lasting roughly from 1770 to 1790, the external evidences of his political position showed scarcely any difference from that of the average German intellectual of the period. Not only did politics occupy a subordinate place in his philosophical interests but the political pronouncements in which he did indulge marked him a devotee of enlightened absolutism. Kant was taken up in the 70's with the epistemological investigations which were to be embodied in the *Critique of Pure Reason* (1781), and in the 80's with ethics. The sparse political writings of his pre-revolutionary phase were published around the middle of this second decade.[6] They came, then, at a time when the realm of nature had been delineated and the realm of freedom was in process of formulation. This setting is important, for if his political ideas at this stage added up to a moderate absolutism their rationale manifested an ambiguity and instability explicable only in terms of Kant's general position at the time.

Kant's reconciliation of his expressed concern for civil liberty with his complete acceptance of monarchical absolutism as a political system in many ways followed well-worn paths during this period. The idea that "those natural faculties which aim at the use of reason shall be fully developed in the species, not in the individual,"[7] the observation that this can be achieved only through "a civil society which administers law generally,"[8] and the insistence that "man is an animal who . . . needs a master who can break man's will and compel him to obey a general will under which every man could be free,"[9] seemed to reiterate the usual anthropological foundation for the transfer of political power in the name of liberty. The corollary which Kant accepted as a maxim of policy—"argue as much as you will, and about what you will, only obey!";[10] its specification in terms of the emphasis upon spiritual freedom; the greater conformity of such freedom with a strong monarchy than with a republic (in Kantian usage, a constitutional state);[11] and the necessity of such freedom for the power of the monarchy:[12] these tenets are all equally familiar. Finally, in the polemical argument that unless human reason subjects itself to the limiting laws of pure reason it will call in political authorities who will destroy freedom of thought to prevent civil disorder, Kant seemed to bring his philosophy into line with the requirements of the absolutist state.[13]

But despite the apparent symmetry of this political position, its theoretical underpinnings, as Kant set them forth in the same writings, were so dualistically formulated that the decisive questions were left open and the resultant political attitude deprived of any logical rigor. In the sphere of political theory proper Kant asserted four ideas which did not jibe with his

espousal of enlightened absolutism and implicitly threw its validity into jeopardy. First, the plan of nature is for man to develop
his faculties, his happiness, and his perfection solely through
the efforts of his own reason.[14] Now, even if it be assumed with
Kant that this work requires a combination of the greatest possible freedom with the most precise possible limitations of that
freedom under external law[15] and that the process of enlightenment—"the release" of man's reason from its "self-incurred tutelage" [16]—which is the chief vehicle for realizing this plan of
nature involves an initial spiritual operation that is compatible
with political absolutism, still an implicit question remains un-
answered: if man's destiny is rational self-control of all his works,
then what is the essential position of the master who has to break
man's will for the sake of the general will? Kant did not raise
this problem. Even when he explicitly recognized its urgency in
a preliminary form, to wit, that since the master is a man he "is
in turn an animal who needs a master," he refused to face it as
a political question: he lumped hereditary monarch and elected
bodies together in the concept of "master" and indicated that the
problem simply showed the artificial character of all human government, the inherence of control over one's destiny in the future of the species rather than the present life of the individual,
and the general difficulty of establishing a just civil constitution.[17]

Secondly, Kant reversed the usual formulations of spiritual
liberty: instead of assigning private opinions to individual freedom and their public expression to restriction by social authority
Kant insisted that "the public use of one's reason must always be
free," while "the private use of reason, on the other hand, may
often be very narrowly restricted without particularly hindering
the progress of enlightenment." [18] In such public use of reason
Kant included not only religious liberty but specifically freedom
to criticize existing laws and proposals for legislative improve-
ments.[19] With the sphere of freedom so defined, the acceptance
of the existing monarchical order becomes at least problematical
for the writer who can proclaim that "in freedom there is not the
least cause for concern about public peace and the stability of
the community." [20] Thirdly, Kant exacerbated this problem on

occasion by casually expanding his defense of the freedom of thought to include a freedom of action which he then assumed, without further examination, to be equally compatible with the existing political order.[21] Thus he held that as the freedom of thought worked back upon the character of the people they became "capable of managing freedom" and made it to the "advantage" of government "to treat men, who are now more than machines, in accordance with their dignity." [22] Fourthly, if Kant clung to the customary natural-law justification of the ruler—that "his law-giving authority rests on his uniting the general public will in his own" [23]—he seemed to give unconscious recognition to the strain which his emphasis upon the rational self-direction of man had placed upon this doctrine by adding a hypothetical qualification. "The touchstone of everything that can be concluded as a law for a people lies in the question whether the people could have imposed such a law on itself. . . . And what a people may not decree for itself can even less be decreed for them by a monarch." [24] This early use of the subjunctive, which was to play such an important role in Kant's later political theory, was the first direct indication of the presence of Kant's two philosophical realms within his politics.

The equal emphases upon monarchical authority and civil freedom which we may call Kant's political antinomy was certainly not felt to be such by Kant at this stage. The implicit conflict was hidden beneath the superficial application of two covering formulas. First, Kant's tendency to think of the political aspects of freedom in the general terms of mankind as a whole rather than in specific terms of individuals caused him to view government simply as a human arrangement for the acquisition of genuine liberty and to neglect the issues which could arise between men and their governments. Secondly, his concentration upon the destiny of "the species," a term which for him meant man taken in his future potential, and upon the process of enlightenment as the road to that destiny enabled him to assume a kind of temporal division of labor, whereby the citizen's intellectual freedom and political discipline could be combined for contemporary politics while the general and challenging elements of freedom in his system would be an ultimate result which need not yet be politically accounted for.

But however satisfactory such formulas may have been to Kant's casual political interest of the 80's they did not resolve his political antinomy. Indeed, they could not, for the antinomy had its roots outside politics, in a philosophical realm where the chasm between compulsion and freedom was Kant's primary emphasis. The connection, during the 80's, between Kant's political problem and his philosophical dualism was provided by his anthropology, which was equivalent at this time to his philosophy of history. For it was here that he elaborated on the relationship between the individual and the species—a relationship which he simply assumed in his politics to be a compatible one—until he subsumed it under the fundamental categories of morality and nature. Only then do the assumptions which made possible the compatibility of individual and species, civil liberty and political absolutism, lie revealed.

In his early anthropology Kant showed himself to be already aware of an inherent conflict between the destiny of the individual and the destiny of the species. Not only did he maintain that the infinite destiny of man could be fulfilled only by the infinite totality of the human race and not by finite individuals,[25] but he even associated the individual primarily with the realm of freedom and the species primarily with the realm of nature.[26] Consequently, they operate under different laws—the natural history of the species is inevitable progress, the history of individual freedom is not. But what he had here disjoined Kant immediately proceeded to rejoin—the individual and the species, moral freedom and nature. Individuals must use their freedom to raise themselves above nature but yet to conform to it—the moral destiny of man is that his works, when perfect, must become nature.[27] The basis of this conjunction, for Kant, would seem to have rested on an assumption that nature was ultimately moral, and it was at this point that his early politics, with their assumption that monarchical authority was ultimately beneficent for men's liberty, took off. Human history, he summarized in his *Idea for a Universal History,* "could be viewed on the whole as the realization of a hidden plan of nature," in which nature guides the manifold diversity of man's varied propensities and antagonisms in the course of time to the rational end of a just civil constitution, as the final and exclusive condition for the self-development of man's natural faculties.[28] This presumptive system of natural history, moreover, produces not only its natural end but also the transformation of "the raw natural faculty of moral discrimination into definite practical principles," "the *pathologically* enforced coordination of society. . . . into a *moral* whole,"—a transformation worked by the development of culture and enlightenment from the interplay between the original human inclinations of asociability and sociability.[29]

It becomes apparent, then, that Kant could find nature and freedom compatible in his philosophy of history, despite his recognition of their philosophical divorce, simply because at this stage he assumed the primacy of nature in the social and political affairs of men and etherealized freedom to the point where it was compatible with this primacy. The subject-matter of history, he wrote, is the record of "the phenomenal appearances of the will, i.e. human actions"; it belongs to the world of nature and is "determined by general laws of nature like any other event of nature." He recognized, indeed, the freedom of the human will which produces these actions, but as products of freedom they are "complicated and accidental in individuals" and not susceptible to rational knowledge.[30] Hence, if Kant admitted that history was both the play of the freedom of the human will "in the large" and the knowledge of the lawful sequence of nature, these approaches were not now of equal value in his treatment of human society. He threw history into the realm of nature and turned human freedom into a mere basis for purposefulness within that part of nature reserved to human history. This decision signified Kant's refusal at this time to work out the connection from the world of moral freedom to the world of natural experience. The world of moral freedom is real and plays its part in experience, but what this world of freedom is and how it plays its role in the empirical world Kant did not now ask.[31] He simply excluded the moral realm as such and approached it only through its empirical effects; and since its direct manifestations in the actions of individuals were so disperse and fortuitous as to render it unknowable in this form, it becomes knowable in the indirect form of a system of nature which gives an external regulative organization to the internally unplanned activities of the whole species. In sum, Kant's attitude toward human history made it more a source of natural knowledge than an arena for men's moral action.

Behind these social views of the mid-80's lay the general position which Kant had reached at this stage of his philosophical career. He was in process of drawing a radical distinction between knowledge and action, between the natural world of what is and the moral world of what ought to be, and in the course of this process he had temporarily tipped the balance in the scales of man's temporal destiny, toward knowledge and nature over action and freedom. Kant's procedure to this end was to set up morality in an absolutely autonomous sphere by restricting the validity of knowledge exclusively to the contingent world of experience, and this meant an emphasis upon the independence of the moral realm from experience and upon the certainty and adequacy of the principles of knowledge for experience. By the mid-80's, when he wrote his anthropological essays, Kant had brought the analysis of the empirical world of nature to its limits, but he had not yet finished with the similar constitution of an independent moral realm.

The first of these tasks Kant had performed in the *Critique of Pure Reason,* published in 1781. His main purpose was to draw a sharp line between knowledge and action, experience and things-in-themselves, nature and freedom, the theoretical and the practical employments of reason, but he did this in a special way. His point of view was from the first terms of these disjunctions; the second terms operated more as limits to the empirical world than as an independent world of beings. The prevalence of this attitude in the *Critique of Pure Reason* indicated that Kant was interested not only in establishing the mutual independence of appearance and reality but also in pressing the structure of sensory experience so hard against its own frontiers that the empirical realm seemed not incompatible with the reality of the realm of moral essences.[32] The inherent need of reason for unity is such, for Kant, that it rises pyramid-fashion above the manifold of sense-impressions until in its higher reaches it borrows from what is later to be the moral world the hypothetical ideas according to which the world of experience can be ordered and known. The key doctrine here was what Kant called "the regulative principles of reason" in which he included "the transcendental ideas of reason," and to these "ideas" the entire second half of the *Critique* was devoted. These ideas had super-sensible objects, not derived from nature and consequently unknowable. When reason sought to prove the reality of these objects it became involved in antinomies, but the transcendental ideas could be validly employed as heuristic principles. Taking these ideas as purely hypothetical unities, that is, proceeding "as if" these unifying ideas were the real, unconditioned bases of experience, men can validly use such ideas as tools for the organization of experience into its greatest possible unity. Finally, at the pinnacle of the structure of knowledge, even "further removed from objective reality" than the transcendental ideas, is the transcendental ideal, which is the transcendental idea unified in an individual thing, the type unified as archetype. Still hypothetical, the transcendental ideas and ideals have "practical power" as regulative principles; though without objective reality, they supply reason with an indispensable moral standard and "form the basis of the possible perfection of certain *actions*." [33]

At this point, the structure of knowledge designed to unify the empirical world reached the border of the moral and the intelligible. Kant even indicated cautiously that the transcendental ideas of reason "may perhaps make possible a transition from the concepts of nature to the practical concepts, and in that way may give support to the moral ideas themselves, bringing them into connection with the speculative knowledge of reason." [34] Reason's search for ultimate unity makes it "evident that the ultimate intention of nature in her wise provision for us has indeed, in the constitution of our reason, been directed to moral interests alone." [35] Thus the regulative principles of reason were a kind of bridge over the crucial middle ground between the natural world of experience proper and the moral realm of things-in-themselves, but this meant that the decisive middle ground was dominated by the world of nature, for the regulative principle indeed "does not in any way debar us from recognizing that the whole [empirical] series may rest upon some intelligible being that is free from all empirical conditions," [36] but it can never assert its reality and it "never in any way" proceeds "counter to the laws of its empirical employment." [37] The regulative ideas systematize knowledge in such a way as to indicate the susceptibility of experience to purposive action, but their validity remains bound to the empirical facts for which they supply the necessary unity, and hence they can provide no authority for action. Thus when Kant resolved the famous Third Antinomy— the antinomy of causality—by turning freedom into a regulative (transcendental) idea he warned that he did not and could not prove "the reality of freedom" nor even the "possibility of freedom," but he felt that he had proved that "causality through freedom is at least *not incompatible with* nature." [38]

After Kant had developed the systematic unity of experience to the limit at which the regulative principles revealed reason's simultaneous need and incapacity to provide for an absolute grounding of phenomena, he turned to "the only other path which still remains open to it, that of its *practical* employment." [39] In other words, he planted himself squarely in a world of noumena, of things-in-themselves, of freedom, constituted by practical reason's timeless laws of moral action. In the brief consideration which he devoted to this realm at the end of the *Critique of Pure Reason* he seemed to promise to approach this world through the intermediate area between morality and experience, which he would enter now from the moral side. By providing absolutely valid ends, made real by action, for the regulative ideas he seemed about to create a genuine synthesis between nature and freedom, knowledge and action. He did not embark on such an attempt directly in the *Critique of Pure Reason* itself, for here he led the moral realm back into a synthesis with nature only on the celestial level of theology: for this purpose among the moral postulates he emphasized God and immortality more than freedom, and from these postulates of the moral world developed the necessary synthesis of morality and happiness in a future life and the necessary synthesis of the unity of ends in the moral world and the unity of things in the natural world, "of the practical with the speculative reason," based on the "supreme original good" that is God.[40] However, Kant did leave signposts which pointed to a more direct relationship based primarily upon freedom. Not only did he assert bluntly that "[the fact of] practical freedom can be proved through experience,"[41] but he explicitly explained that although the moral world—i.e. the world as it ought to be according to the necessary laws of morality—is "so far thought . . . as a mere idea," because he has left out of account its conditions and its difficulties in the sensible world, it is "at the same time a practical idea, which really can have, as it also ought to have, an influence upon the sensible world, to bring that world, so far as may be possible, into conformity with the idea. The idea of a moral world has, therefore, objective reality, . . . as referring to the sensible world, viewed, however, as being an object of pure reason in its practical employment, that is, as a *corpus mysticum* of the rational beings in it, so far as the free will of each being is, under moral laws, in complete systematic unity with itself and with the freedom of every other."[42] In this isolated statement the ethical potentialities of the Kantian philosophy became visible: the old distinction between the world of spirit and the world of flesh still subsists, but since the world of spirit is now thought of as pure act it can transform the flesh and realize itself in existence. Moreover, in another parenthetical passage,[43] which contained what was clearly the political analog of this ethical position, the possible implications of such a position for politics were foreshadowed in general terms. Here Kant assigned the idea of a free civil constitution—"A constitution allowing *the greatest possible human freedom* in accordance with laws by which *the freedom of each is made to be consistent with that of all others*"— to the moral realm and hence endowed it with the absolute, unconditional validity of moral ideas. It "must be taken as fundamental not only in first projecting a constitution but in all its laws." The validity of this idea of a free and perfect constitution cannot be impugned by the claim of its impracticability, since— and this is Kant's main point here—no one can know how great or how small the limitations on man's capacity to realize his ideas may be. "For the issue depends upon freedom; and it is in the power of freedom to pass beyond any and every specified limit."

The crucial fact for the understanding of Kant's political thinking during the 1780's is that neither in the *Critique of Pure Reason* nor in the ethical writings of the 80's did Kant take up and develop the relationship between the realms of morality and experience to which he momentarily had here referred. It is hardly surprising, then, that the political analog, which made civil liberty an absolute value by aligning it under moral freedom and which called for concrete action in this world of time and space to realize itself, was also left in abeyance. Indeed, Kant's chief ethical works of the decade contain no political discussion whatever. For Kant's chief preoccupation during this decade was not to work out the relationship of morality and experience but rather to cut morality radically off from experience. He was concerned with elaborating the character of the moral realm, and because the very identity of this realm depended upon its absolute antithesis to every form of experience and independence from the forms of theoretical knowledge the connection with the empirical world was neglected for the a priori development and insulation of the moral world proper. In the preface to the *Foundations of the Metaphysics of Morals* (1785) Kant justified the work in terms which expressed clearly the break between it and the approach promised by the *Critique of Pure Reason.* "A careful separation," Kant wrote in the preface of the *Foundations,* "of the rational from the empirical part" of ethics must be made; the rational, or metaphysical, part of ethics is "morals proper," the empirical part merely "practical anthropology"; the metaphysics of morals is the "prior" science, and hence the question which Kant posed for himself in this work was: "Is it not of the utmost necessity to construct a pure moral philosophy which is completely freed from everything which may be only empirical and thus belong to anthropology?" For "not only are moral laws together with their principles essentially different from all practical knowledge in which there is anything empirical," but "morals themselves remain subject to all kinds of corruption so long as the guide and supreme norm of their correct estimation is lacking." [44] This procedure was a far cry from the *Critique of Pure Reason* which seemed to project the application of the pure forms of morals to the empirical nature of man.[45] When Kant did broach this problem in his ethical works of the pre-revolutionary period it was always from the point of view of its reflection upon the validity of the pure moral law and not the impact of the moral law upon the actual lives of men. Both the natural world proper and even the intermediate area of man's social and political affairs were left to natural laws and regulative ideas.

But if Kant neglected the important problem of the action of moral ideas upon the world of events, he did utilize the philosophical independence of the moral realm which he had withdrawn from contact with the external world to construct a moral system whose values were actually independent of those of his own external world. For Kant took up the idea of freedom and made it the core of his ethics.[46] He sought to give it the greatest possible scope and the greatest possible validity. For the one, he placed it within the reach of every individual human; for the other, he made freedom its own authority. To satisfy both requirements Kant found a form for freedom which made it a principle of individuality and yet which secured the universality and necessity needful for its absolute autonomy; for unless freedom created an order for itself, the integrity of the individual personality would be split by the heteronomous pull of other ordering principles and consequently deprived of the capacity for self-movement essential to freedom. Kant therefore defined freedom negatively as independence of the sensible world, since in this world man as an active being was dissolved and his components placed under laws of mechanical necessity. He defined freedom positively as the obedience of the will to the moral laws of practical reason, which the will gives to itself.[47] The meaning of this apparent paradox that obedience equals positive freedom is crucial to Kant's ethics and ultimately to his politics. The will, the active faculty of desire in man standing between his reason and his natural inclinations, is the principle of his integration, his individuality. Reason is the universal principle in man, for it can exercise itself only through necessary, universal laws. Reason in its practical, or moral, employment, is the faculty which bridges individuality and universality in man: as resident in every man and as addressed to the will it is an integral part of the individual's personality, while as the prescriber of moral laws of inherent, unconditioned validity it elevates man to the universal ground of all being. But this mediating role which reason and law (which expresses reason) play between the individual and the universal had two concentric meanings for Kant. First, the law of reason could be taken to mediate between the individual man and that which is universal *in him.* The moral law here obliges the individual to obey the absolutely unconditioned precepts which his practical reason presents to his will, and this obedience constitutes freedom because the universal and unconditioned precepts of action embodied in the moral law and produced by pure reason liberate man from the compulsions of the sensible world and positively make the will of man self-legislating, i.e. "a law to itself." [48] But secondly, Kant also took the mediating role of reason and its moral law to mean the relating of the individual to a universal that was *both in him and outside him,* that is, to a universal realm including all humanity, of which each individual is an equal member. Here the universal becomes in a sense horizontal as well as vertical for the individual, and the moral law provides the bridge whereby the individual participates in an order which secures the equal and mutual recognition of individual personality by all men. Obedience to the moral law in this sense constitutes freedom because only such conformity enables the individual to project himself into a universal order which includes others as well as himself and yet in which his will may find itself.

This twofold synthesizing function of the moral law which related both individual and social duty to the freedom of the individual personality gave to the concepts "law" and "reason" (for general purposes they were used interchangeably) a crucial, if curiously flexible, place in Kant's ethics (and later in his politics as well). In the 80's, when Kant was building a self-contained realm of morals on an a priori basis apart from the world of experience and practical politics, he developed both these implications of moral law in a form that was to be important for later application, but his emphasis during this decade was definitely upon the direct relationship of the law to the individual. In his *Foundations of the Metaphysics of Morals* he analyzed the sub-

stantive precept of the categorical imperative—"Act only according to that maxim by which you can at the same time will that it
should become a universal law" [49]—into two further principles
which he derived from this precept. It is not clear whether Kant
meant these principles as rigorous implications of the categorical
imperative, but in any case he used them to sketch the framework
of a noumenological civil society. They were: "Act so that you
treat humanity, whether in your own person or in that of
another, always as an end and never as a means only," [50] and
become through your maxims a legislative member of a possible
realm of ends.[51] This "realm of ends" for Kant was a moral
society composed of rational beings systematically united by the
common law which prescribes that each rational being should
treat himself and all others as ends in themselves. Moreover,
Kant furnished this realm with a kind of constitution when he
distinguished between "the members" and "the sovereign" of
this realm, defined the members as those rational beings who
legislate the universal laws to which they are subject, and the
sovereign as the rational being who likewise legislates the universal laws but who is subject to the will of no other because by
his very nature his maxims inevitably conform to the law and
render him a completely independent being (though not expressly stated, the divinity of the sovereign is clearly implied).[52]
The binding quality of the law upon the members is even expressed in the political-sounding formulation: "This principle
of humanity and of every rational creature as an end in itself is
the supreme limiting condition on freedom of the actions of each
man." [53]

Now this sketch did seem to furnish an ethical model for a
political constitution, and indeed it was a most indicative exercise in the social implications of Kant's conception of the moral
law, with its combination of civil and democratic liberty at once
required and limited by the necessary adherence to an absolute
standard of action. But Kant, in his writings of the 80's, did not
design it as a social model. The context of Kant's discussion of
the realm of ends shows clearly that it was designed as a kind of
figure of speech, with the purpose of spelling out how the individual human, located partially in the natural world, could be

governed in his moral maxims by the a priori universal law produced by pure reason in him. In the development of these principles out of the fundamental law of the categorical imperative, Kant explained, he "intended to bring an idea of reason closer to intuition (by means of a certain analogy) and thus nearer to feeling." [54] Kant conceived the realm of ends in "analogy" to the realm of nature simply to clarify it. The analogy was a portrait of the moral law in the familiar setting of man's experience with the laws of nature. It is hardly surprising, then, that scarcely a trace of the social "realm of ends" is to be found in the *Critique of Practical Reason*. Even when Kant developed the *Foundations'* casual idea of the "analogy" to the realm of nature into the *Critique's* precise doctrine of "the typic of pure practical reason," he expounded it simply in the general form of a means to present the moral law "as a symbol," for the purely ethical purposes of making judgments upon its applicability to concrete maxims for possible action and thus of guarding against both "the empiricism" and "the mysticism" of false morality.[55]

Thus in the segregated realm of freedom which Kant worked out in his ethical writings during the decade preceding the French Revolution he developed a moral theory which made individual personality the bearer of the reality created by action. This active moral individualism formed a strict counterpoise to the general, external, classificatory operation of understanding in the world of nature which Kant had elaborated previously. But, whereas Kant had built the structure of transcendental reason out from the world of nature into that intermediate area between nature and freedom where the social and political relationships of man have their home, he did not in the 80's build a corresponding span out from the side of the noumenal world of freedom.

Such is the philosophical context against which Kant's political ideas of the pre-revolutionary period must be set. The ambiguities in these ideas herewith become explicable. Kant's plan of nature, which unified the history of man under the point of view of its climax in a just civil constitution, was clearly a regulative idea of theoretical reason, and Kant's political ideal consequently suffered from the same ambiguity with which he deliberately invested regulative principles in his philosophy. The actual regime of political compulsion was primary as part of the realm of necessitous nature; the ideal of the free civil constitution was only a hypothetical end which imported the shadow of ethical freedom to organize the world of phenomenal political experience. Hence the ideal of individual freedom could become a standard for the existing political system of absolutism and could even provide inconsistencies in his scheme of a liberal absolutism, but it had not the absolute authority or power in Kant's theory to shake this system. Because politics, at this stage of his thought, belonged more to the realm of nature than to the realm of freedom it could aim at no more than the conditions for man's development of his *natural* faculties. Since nothing that was based on experience, however indirectly, could be a source or condition for moral action, the free constitution as the end of a plan of nature could not call forth the determinate action of autonomous moral individuals. The free constitution, moreover, as a regulative principle of the world of political experience was more appropriate to knowledge than to political action from moral principles, and this helps explain Kant's greater emphasis upon culture than reform. And finally, the *deus ex machina* of Kant's philosophy of history—the unexplained "transformation of a *pathologically* enforced coordination of society . . . into a *moral* whole" [56]— finds a rationale in Kant's version of the philosophical process: through the enlightenment and culture which is the result of the pathological coordination of society reason discovers the limitations of knowledge and turns "to the only path that remains open to it, that of its practical employment," that is, to the absolute laws of moral action.[57]

For Kant the French Revolution marked the great break in this dualistic structure, for the event and more particularly the "participation" of observers everywhere in the event, breached the barriers between the realm of nature and the realm of morals. "For such a phenomenon in human history can never be forgotten, because it has revealed a trait and a capacity in human nature which no statesman could have gleaned from the previous course of things and which alone unites nature and freedom according to internal principles of law in human history. . . ." [58]

The twofold essence of this event, which was at the same time a "phenomenon" and "something moral in principle," was strictly political: "the right that a people must not be hindered by alien forces from giving itself the civil constitution it deems good for itself," and the acceptance as "lawful and morally good" only of a "republican constitution"—the only kind whose principles abhor aggressive war.[59] Thanks to the Revolution, politics became for Kant the chief arena wherein he sought the "historical signs" which were the effects in experience of man's conversion to morality.[60] Throughout the 90's the fundamental constitutional achievements of the Revolution kept him a partisan despite his acknowledgment of its "misery and atrocities," and his interest in the Revolution soon led him to politics in general as the leading concern of his reading and his writing.[61] "The critical philosopher . . . became the publicist." [62] But Kant's enthusiasm for the revolution in France and his conversion to liberal constitutionalism did not make him a revolutionary, either against the reigning political system in Germany or against his own former political ideas. In his own person he knuckled down to the Prussian censorship, promising "as your Royal Majesty's most loyal subject" to keep silence on the controversial subject of religion and professing only to seek "a corner of the earth" where he could end his life "free from anxiety." [63] In his writings he insisted that revolution against the head of the state was unjustifiable and that reform is a duty "not of the citizens but of the head of the state" and must come "not from below up but from above down." [64] Kant's liberalism of the 90's did not explode the framework of German thought and politics. What it did do was to merge moral with material liberties and constitutional with civil rights in the central concept of political freedom, to recognize political freedom frankly as the chief problem of human culture, and to initiate the modern German pattern of reconciling it with the established political structure.

The essential context for Kant's political ideas of the 90's, no less than those of the 80's, was furnished by the unfolding of his philosophical system. The French Revolution, which meant to Kant the breaching of the world of experience by a tremendous moral act, coincided with just that point in his philosophical development when he was linking the realm of freedom to the realm of nature by means of a comprehensive and vital synthesis. This synthesis was embodied in the *Critique of Judgment* (1790). Here the basic intellectual framework was set up within which was brewed the peculiar blend of morals and politics characteristic of Kant's subsequent minor works. This final stage of Kant's political development was climaxed in 1797 and 1798. *The Metaphysics of Morals* (1797), which itself combined "The Metaphysical Elements of Jurisprudence" and "The Metaphysical Elements of Ethics" in a single whole, had as its sequel the *Anthropology, Pragmatically Considered* (1798). These works revealed Kant's intense desire to unite the realms of morals and of social experience in one system, while his *Conflict of the Faculties* (1798) amounted to an application of this system to his contemporary situation.

The *Critique of Judgment* is important for Kant's political theory not only because it provided the philosophical basis for the operation of his liberal ethic in the temporal sphere of politics, but even more because it provided the fundamental explanation for the special role which freedom would have in Kant's idea of a just political order. That the faculty of judgment "forms a middle term between understanding and reason" [65] and that art and teleology, the twin realms of its application, are intermediate between nature and freedom[66] showed Kant's intention in this third *Critique* to crossbreed the strains whose purity he had developed for two decades. But even more significant than the fact of Kant's bridging of nature and freedom was the manner of it.

Albeit, then, between the realm of the natural concept, as the sensible, and the realm of the concept of freedom, as the super-sensible, there is a great gulf fixed, so that it is not possible to pass from the former to the latter (by means of the theoretical employment of reason), just as if they were so many separate worlds, the first of which is powerless to exercise influence on the second: still the latter is *meant* to influence the former—that is to say, the concept of freedom is meant to actualize in the sensible world the end proposed by its laws; and nature must consequently also be capable of being regarded in such a way that in the conformity of law to its form it at least harmonizes with the possibility of the ends to be effectuated in it according to the laws of freedom.[67]

Thus Kant announced his readiness to re-examine the realms of being from a point of view far different from that of his earlier work. What had there been muted and subordinate he now advanced to the front of his philosophical stage. He had admitted that an interrelationship between the realms was not impossible but he had left this motif untended while he developed the separate integrity of the two worlds. Now, however, at the start of the 90's Kant not only took up the interrelationship as his main concern but specified at once (what had certainly been implicit in his earlier thought) that the character of the interrelationship was essentially the influencing of nature by freedom, of the principles of knowledge by the laws of action. His first step, consequently, was to review the realm of experience in the light of this influence, and his instrument for this purpose was the faculty of judgment and its concept of "a *finality* of nature"—"a concept that makes possible the transition from the pure theoretical . . . to the pure practical. . . . For through that concept we cognize the possibility of the final end that can only be actualized in nature and in harmony with its laws." [68] This reassessment of experience from the standpoint of morality was the preparation for his return to the moral sphere later in the 90's, when his main concern became precisely the demonstration of how this possible relationship could be actualized.

It is clear that at this stage in Kant's thinking judgment replaced theoretical reason's transcendental ideas in the governance of the border area of knowable experience.[69] But herein lies the crucial problem. Reflective judgment—that form of judgment which adds to knowledge by organizing experience under a unifying concept which is not derived or known from experience—is, like the transcendental idea, a regulative principle. Consequently, like the transcendental idea, the reflective judgment organizes experience under concepts whose objects are supersensible and have no objective reality, which are purely hypothetical, and which find their validity not in themselves but in their functional success in advancing the systematic knowledge of the world of experience.[70] Where, then, was the advance over the *Critique of Pure Reason?* Where was the new principle of mediation between nature and freedom?

The answer to these questions yields the key to Kant's liberal political theory of the Revolutionary period, for the new element in his concept of reflective judgment was freedom in a form appropriate to the world of time and space. For judgment "thinks the particular in terms of the universal," [71] while theoretical reason thinks the general in terms of the universal. When, therefore, the universal goes beyond the understanding's laws of the empirical world and becomes unknowable—when, that is, judgment becomes reflective and the ideas of reason transcendental— the universals which they posit must be of different kinds. The hypothetical universal which is the object of the transcendental idea is designed only to go behind the general classifications of empirical nature and to furnish an unconditioned law under which these contingent laws may be unified; but this universal must be of the same type of law as the laws of nature—that is, it must be classificatory and external, explaining the general possibility of a being but never its individual existence. The hypothetical universals of reflective judgment, on the other hand, are designed to explain precisely this individuality, or particularity, of natural beings which neither the natural laws of the understanding nor the transcendental ideas of speculative reason can make comprehensible to the human mind. For knowledge of such modes of being to be possible, a principle that will order these manifold particulars as such, internally, into a system must operate side by side with the laws of nature and of theoretical reason which afford a typology of their external relations.

This principle is given by reflective judgment, which hypothesizes a universal causality as analogous to the production of individual actions by an intelligent being like man; the individuality of irreducible natural relationships thus receives an explanation satisfactory to men's minds on the deliberately assumed hypothesis that such relationships were produced in nature analogically to the way which men produce their individual actions, as components in a series directed to a certain end. Whereas the transcendental ideas are for reason simply hypotheses to which the generalizing external kind of knowledge is driven as its absolute limit, the teleological hypotheses of the reflective judgment are definite analogies whose basic principle links the particular in man's natural experience with the individual in his moral action and consciously attempts to organize man's knowledge of the natural world on the standards of the moral world, thereby preparing experience for the reception of his freedom. But because this work of preparation remains a mere "subjective" hypothesis of satisfactory explanation and confers no reality on the process that is thus explained, physical teleology brings no authority to the end which it posits and consequently it neither supersedes nor subsumes the mechanism of real natural laws.[72] What it does do is to indicate that in nature, in addition to mechanical causality, there is the possibility of a causality analogous to that of men in their moral actions. There can never be, in this life, a graduation from the world of nature and its limitations into a world of freedom, but on the other hand the possibility of natural teleology means that when action comes independently out of the pure moral realm of freedom there is place for its effectuation in actual experience.[73] In other words, the two realms of nature and freedom continue as integral wholes, under their respective laws, but the effective passage of free actions into natural experience is now made possible by systematizing experience according to a moral analogy and thus joining it up with the articulation of freedom according to a natural analogy.[74] In this intermediate area, narrowly bounded on the one side by the requirements of morality for its own independence and on the other by the over-all dominion of natural law in experience, men could give temporal form to the moral maxims of their free wills.

But what did this anomalous interrelationship mean to Kant concretely? Overtly, nothing. For the whole tenor of his discussion in the *Critique of Judgment,* like the argument in the *Critique of Pure Reason* was designed to refer the final synthesis of nature and freedom to the necessary existence of God. But the *Critique of Judgment,* consonant with its moral emphasis, made man the nodal figure astride both worlds. Consequently, the implications of the interrelationship for humanity made up a constant theme in the third critique. Most striking, perhaps, was the analysis of man's place in nature, for it was at this point that Kant's development was most graphically revealed. Kant summarized, with little change, his argument in the *Idea for a Uni-*

versal History on nature's plan for man, but then added a new climax which transformed the total meaning of the whole conception. In the earlier work the end to which nature strove in its plan for mankind was a condition in which men could develop their own natural faculties, an end which still envisaged man as a part of nature and which kept the whole plan in the realm of nature. In the *Critique of Judgment,* this end, under the title of "culture," still subsisted as the "ultimate end" of nature, but this was now deemed insufficient. We now see "nature striving on purposive lines to give us that education that opens the door to higher ends than it can itself afford"; the arts and sciences of culture simply "prepare man for a sovereignty in which reason alone shall have sway." [75] The ultimate end of nature, then, is merely preparatory to a higher "final end." This final end is still indeed man, but it is "man regarded as noumenon, . . . man considered as a moral agent." [76] Thus man is the final end of nature insofar as he sets himself moral goals independent of nature—"in the *freedom* of his faculty of desire, and not as a link in the chain of nature" [77]—and only on this basis can nature be regarded as having any plan or ends at all. Without man as a moral being, "the whole of creation would be a wilderness, a thing in vain." [78] Only because man is a being in the natural world who yet sets himself necessary ends independent of it, can there be "a rational ground to explain why nature, when regarded as an absolute whole according to principles of ends, must be in accord with the conditions of his happiness." [79] The status of the plan of nature, then, changed for Kant from a regulative idea which brought system into the knowledge of human history to a concept of reflective judgment which organized human experience so as to show the possibility of effecting his freedom in it through action.

Although Kant did not, in the *Critique of Judgment,* expatiate on the precise forms which human freedom could take in the temporal world, their general pattern was implicit throughout. If the world, as viewed through natural laws, was composed of lifeless, interchangeable, physical entities, moving mechanically through time in an irreversible sequence imposed upon it by external compulsion, the role of freedom was to feed a spark of dynamism into certain of these entities, imparting to them the capacity for self-movement, an element of intentionality, and a vital relationship of parts which made for the irreducible integrity of the whole. This pattern was expressed clearly in Kant's conception of the "organism," the only kind of natural being to which in itself a physical end could be ascribed: the parts and the whole produce each other and consequently must be considered as both ends and means in relation to each other. But more important, the organized being has "a self-propagating formative power, which cannot be explained by the capacity of movement alone, that is to say, by mechanism," and which it can impart to the material—itself devoid of such power—that it organizes.[80] Kant himself pointed out the political implication of this idea, for it was within the framework of his discussion of organism that he wrote the parenthetical footnote which was the only important political reference in the book. He asserted the validity of using the organism as an "analogy" to throw light on an ideal civil constitution, and, applying the analogy to the *de facto* French constitution of 1789—"a complete transformation, recently undertaken, of a great people into a state"—he approved of the term "organization" as descriptive of the constitution of the state. "For in a whole of this kind certainly no member should be a mere means, but should also be an end, and, seeing that he contributes to the possibility of the entire body, should have his position and function in turn defined by the idea of the whole." [81] Here, then, was the pattern which Kant was to follow in the political theory which he elaborated in the subsequent years: the freedom of individuals could not create a world after its own image within the temporal political realm, but it could supply the dynamic and cohesive element within and among the natural political entities. This element of freedom would make these entities, or states, genuine denizens of the border area between nature and freedom which would afford to individuals not the means but the possibility of realizing their moral sovereignty.

The relevance of Kant's philosophical framework to his politics was confirmed by the repetition of the developmental scheme of his general philosophy in the unfolding of his political system after 1790. At least some of the difficulties in Kant's political doc-

trine can be unraveled when it is analyzed in an evolutionary
context: in his first political writings of the 90's he worked out
separately the principles of the moral world in its natural analogy
and of the political world in its moral analogy, in preparation
for their synthesis in his final political works.

In his *Religion Within the Limits of Reason Alone* and the
"Contra Hobbes" section of his *Theory and Practice,* both published in 1793, Kant took up the ideas of the moral realm of
ends and the natural civil constitution which he had broached
during the 80's and developed them toward each other.

In the *Religion Within the Limits of Reason Alone* Kant
stated frankly that "the sovereignty of the good principle is attainable, as far as men can work toward it, only through the
establishment and spread of a society in accordance with and for
the sake of the laws of virtue, a society whose task and duty it is
rationally to impress these laws in all their scope upon the entire
human race." [82] It follows that "the species of rational beings
is objectively, through the idea of reason, destined for a social
goal, namely, the promotion of the highest good as a social
good." [83] Starting from the chronic inability of the individual
to follow the universal moral law prescribed by his own higher
being, Kant seemed at first to use the concept of an ethical society
of all humanity which would be based upon this same law simply
as the indispensable means of demonstrating its universal validity. Indeed, Kant was careful to distinguish between such an
ethical society and a political society by emphasizing the distinction between ethics as obedience to law by intention, which could
not be forced, and politics as obedience to the law in external
action, which could be compelled. Yet he went on to insist that
the ethical society of men could achieve its necessary moral unity
only by developing into "an ethical state" or "ethical commonwealth." Moreover, in developing this concept of a civil constitution of the moral world Kant deliberately pursued "a certain
analogy" to the political commonwealth, replete with an ethical
state of nature, ethical original contract, a public lawgiver, and
separate ethical civil societies *vis-à-vis* one another in a state of
nature.[84] In this moral realm, however, the crucial problem of
the relationship between the individual and the society did not

really develop, since compulsion was by definition excluded. The basic principle of the ethical commonwealth required that its public laws be indeed the commands of a common lawgiver but that this lawgiver be neither the people as a people nor a superior being legislating through his statutory will: this lawgiver could only be a God who was an hypostatization of individual freedom, and the common laws legislated by Him could only be the laws of virtue which every individual in the society as a rational individual gave to himself.[85] Thus Kant began his serious political writings of the revolutionary period with the idea of an ethical commonwealth which, however far removed from the visible churches of this world, manifested his conviction that even in the realm of moral maxims—even prior, that is, to the problem of realizing morality by concrete action in the world of sense—a social organization of man was necessary. He manifested, too, his ideal that the sovereign law of reason would not be a social authority above the individual but the expression, in the clear form of a universally valid authority, of that which was truly free within the individual.

After thus projecting an ethical commonwealth in general analogy with a political society but not yet in contact with this area of experience, Kant then turned about and proceeded to erect a theoretical political structure out from the realm of political experience without directly touching morality. In his *Theory and Practice* Kant indeed decried the derivation of the principles of constitutional law from political experience and insisted upon a constitutional theory based upon principles of a priori validity, but he did not connect these principles in any overt way with morality. He was careful to write only of "external laws," "external rights," and "freedom in the external relations of human beings to each other," and consistently with this terminology he defined individual freedom within the state in the sensuous terms of the pursuit of happiness in one's own way.[86] Yet the parallels, both formal and substantive, between Kant's constitutional and moral principles were patent. Constitutional principles could not be drawn from empirical experience, such as men's desire for happiness, because such experience was deemed too manifold to provide the common basis necessary for law; consequently, such principles must be "willed by pure a priori legislating reason" and have "objective practical validity without our considering what good or ill may result." [87]   Hence both laws and rights, despite their externality in this context, "have nothing at all to do" with men's natural purposes but are of a priori and universal validity. According to these definitions, "right is the limitation of every man's freedom so that it harmonizes with the freedom of every other man insofar as harmonization is possible according to a general law," and law is this general coercive rule which makes such harmony possible.[88]   From these concepts three a priori principles, "the only principles according to which a state could be constituted" rationally, followed: "1. The freedom of each member of society as a man. 2. The equality of each member with every other as a subject. 3. The autonomy of each member of a commonwealth as a citizen." [89]

Clearly these are precise counterparts of the three principles in the moral realm of ends which Kant derived from the categorical imperative in the *Foundations of the Metaphysics of Morals*,[90]   but throughout this constitutional section of his *Theory and Practice* Kant made no serious reference to this moral basis. The freedom, equality, and autonomy of the members of the state, like the concept of law from which they were derived, had no other basis than the necessary workings of an external legislative reason, a peculiar intermediate concept which was itself related to nothing more fundamental. It hung suspended between heaven and earth, tied to neither, but indeed closer to the world of sense than to the other since Kant justified it in terms of the earthly experience for which it provided a general standard. The character of this framework had a decisive effect upon the status which Kant assigned to individual liberty in civil society: the canons of liberty were normative for political actuality but they did not really enter into it. This effect was manifested in two stages, during the course of which the force of liberty was attenuated as it approached present political experience. First, even in the original civil contract of society, where the three principles of the freedom, equality, and autonomy of men were real and active factors, they were defined and essentially limited by experience. Freedom was the right of the individual to seek happiness apart from the paternalistic interference by the state; equality was the equal "right of coercion" of each against all, with the head of the state completely exempt; autonomy was expounded in its negative aspect which denied equality in the right to legislate on the original contract to those who were not economically independent.[91] But secondly, in an existing constitution this original contract which was the product of these principles was to be construed not as an actual historical fact bequeathing actual political principles, but as "a mere idea of reason" which obliges the judgment of present laws on the criterion of whether "they *could* have originated" in such an original contract and according to such principles.[92] Thus "the inalienable rights" which the people have against the head of the state "cannot be coercive," and the limitations which these principles set for the head of the state are "evidently valid only for the judgment of the legislator, not for that of the subject."[93] Thus, once the civil constitution was established, the autonomous political right of citizens to legislate the laws to which they were subject was transformed into a hypothetical "as if,"[94] and simply becomes part of the rational norm of freedom and equality to which the head of the state is to adjust his laws. In the final analysis, then, "people are never entitled to use force against the head of the state or to obstruct him in work or deed."[95]

What Kant tried to do in his *Theory and Practice* is both clear and instructive. He raised a constitutional structure whose independence was patterned on a moral analogy but whose reference was solely to the world of experience. His main purpose was to show that an a priori legislating reason embodying principles of liberty was compatible with the order established by the natural laws of political experience.[96]

So Kant had constructed the theories of two states, an ethical state in which the sovereign law of reason brought society to the moral service of the individual and a juridical state in which the sovereign law of reason brought the individual to service of the civil society. But by their very structure each of these states was incomplete and required each other for fulfilment: the moral state required the possibility of realizing its maxims in concrete action and the juridical state required a moral basis for its external law of reason. It was in his last political works—the *Perpetual Peace,* the *Metaphysics of Morals,* and the *Conflict of the Faculties*—that Kant welded them into a single system of politics.

The starting-point of Kant's political synthesis was the emphasis upon the actuation of morality in experience which was a result of his philosophical synthesis. "The result of the moral improvement of man," he wrote now, "can be posited not in an ever-growing quantity of moral conviction but only in the increase of the products of their legality through dutiful actions, whatever the motives by which they are inspired. . . ." [97] "There can be no conflict of politics, as a practical doctrine of right, with ethics, as a theoretical doctrine of right. . . . Thus true politics can never take a step without rendering homage to morality. . . . One cannot compromise here and seek the middle course of a pragmatic conditional law between the morally right and the expedient. All politics must bend the knee before the right." [98] Politics, for Kant, now had its locus in that crucial intermediate realm that connected morality with the temporal world. It was the chief means for converting freedom into a form not incompatible with the laws of nature. Kant underlined this fundamental new role of politics by appending a revised version of his philosophy of history as the basis for it. Applying the philosophical system which he had developed in the *Critique of Judgment* Kant took up again his old idea of the plan of nature with its end in the just civil constitution but changed its whole meaning by adding the organization of men into a moral realm of ends as the final goal of the natural process. He reiterated his idea that nature may be viewed as necessity (destiny) or as design (providence), but now he stated frankly that when viewed as the latter "the mechanism of nature may be employed" to the moral end whose reality is well established by practical reason. Nature favors "man's moral purpose"; she guarantees "(by compulsion and without prejudice to his freedom) that he shall do that which he ought to but does not do under the laws of freedom." Specifically, Kant repeated the argument that nature acted upon the selfish natural inclinations of men to pit them against one another, make them cancel each other out, and thereby produce good government, but now he insisted that such government was inadequate and that it served only as a necessary preparation for the moral constitution which would be adequate. By accustoming men to obey coercive laws and by disciplining men's unlawful inclinations, nature "actually facilitates the development of the moral disposition to a direct respect for the law." This moral development is necessary, for nature gives the opportunity but not the assurance that men's true end will be achieved. Nature does not guarantee this end "with sufficient certainty for us to predict the future in any theoretical sense, but adequately from a practical point of view, making it our duty to work toward this end, which is not just a chimerical one." Thus the mechanism of nature, according to Kant, could not only be used by statesmen to prepare men for morality through government, but it could then be used by the moral will "to make the concept of law effective." Between these two steps—both now possible in the realm of experience—a genuine accession to morality could be required, for the essential characteristic of the just state was the ethical trait of deriving its political maxims from the a priori moral law of reason, independent of all natural inclinations and experience in politics.[99]

With this integration of politics and morality, the role of the just state has shifted in Kant's political thinking. His former idea, expressed in both the *Idea for a Universal History* and the *Theory and Practice,* viewed the just civil constitution as the climax of nature but still within its plan: the civil constitution was an institution in which the dominance of the compulsory mechanism of nature was expressed in the sovereignty of a ruler governing in accordance with principles which would ultimately prepare for the rise of morality independent of nature and outside of politics. But now this constitution became only penultimate, a training ground for the new just state in which the mechanism of nature and the effecting of morality were to be synthesized.

With the context of Kant's politics moved from the realm of nature into an autonomous intermediate realm between nature and morality, the content of his politics underwent a corresponding change. The new connection between politics and morality

was manifested in the new role attributed to the active principle
of freedom in politics. Kant explicitly associated morality in
politics with political freedom when he attributed to the individual not only the character of *"homo phaenomenon"* in his capacity as a subject of the state but also the character of *"homo
noumenon"* in his capacity as co-legislator.[100] Kant now asserted
categorically that the rational constitution makes "freedom its
principle—makes it indeed the condition of all compulsion"—
and he derived the validity of man's inborn, inalienable rights in
the state to his possession of these same rights in the moral realm
of ends.[101] Moreover, the activation of freedom in the realm of
politics made for an emphasis upon a new kind of liberty: Kant
now rearranged his hierarchy of freedom so that his former preference for "civil equality" and "civil liberty" (the rights of individuals to life and livelihood against violation by other individuals and by government) gave way now to his insistence
upon "legislative freedom" (the right of the individual "to obey
no other law then that to which he has given his consent") as
the characteristic form of liberty in the state. Civil liberty and
equality are rooted only in "natural liberty and equality" and
make men "passive parts of the state"; only political liberty
constitutes "the citizen" and capacitates him "to deal with the
state as an active member." [102] With this new emphasis Kant's
former subjunctive qualification to legislative freedom—the right
to obey only laws "to which I *could have given* consent"—did not
entirely disappear, but it was minimized and often replaced by
the simple declarative. Thus the achievement of world peace,
for which Kant had looked to the plan of nature, he now based
upon the constitutional necessity of the actual, not the putative,
consent of the people to a declaration of war.[103] Hence Kant
subscribed openly, in his mature political works of the 90's, to the
doctrine of popular sovereignty: The legislative power—or "sovereignty"—"can only belong to the united will of the people";
the ruler or prince exercises only the executive power and, like
the judiciary, are simply "agents" or "representatives" of the
people.[104] All valid government, then, must be "a representative
system of the people." [105]

But if the realm of moral freedom infiltrated into politics in the form of a new validity for the political rights of the people Kant still had to fit it into the continuing requirements of the political realm of nature. For politics, as the sphere where freedom and nature met, had to take account of man as a phenomenal as well as a noumenal being. As a phenomenal being man is errant, and hence the ideal of the people as legislators of their own government "is limited in practice by the condition that its existing means must coincide with morality." [106] The characteristic political expression of the realm of nature, for Kant, was the authority of a higher power. He abhorred democracy because in it "everyone wishes to be master," and if he similarly rejected political despotism as part of "the mere mechanism of nature" he still believed that an independent authority was required even "to rule autocratically" for the purpose of controlling men's passions and improving "the phenomena of the ethical disposition of humanity." [107] Clearly, Kant's attempt to work popular sovereignty, as the political expression of freedom, into the authoritarian political structure which he continued to endorse was beset with difficulties. These he tackled on two levels, and on both he established patterns which were followed in later German political thought and behavior.

First, within the sphere of his political theory proper Kant developed the doctrine of constitutional monarchy until it became the seminal concept of politics, supplying the answers to the fundamental questions of political obligation. "The republic," which for Kant meant "the political principle of the separation of the executive power (the administration) from the legislative" —i.e. a mixed constitution—is "the only constitution which derives from the idea of the original compact and on which all juridical legislation of a people must be based." [108] The constitutional doctrine of the separation of powers thus became Kant's central political idea, and he proceeded to employ it as the framework in which the political rights of the people could be institutionalized without challenging the irresistibility of monarchical power. For this republican constitution is both "the only one entirely fitting to the rights of man" and a technically "good organization of the state" which balances men's natural "selfish inclinations" off against one another.[109] Kant accomplished this junction by imposing a deliberate ambiguity upon the nodal concepts of "legislation," "representation," and "law," an ambiguity which stemmed from his attribution of both ideal and phenomenal meanings to them. As "a pure idea," the three powers of the state—legislative, executive, judicial—are simply internal relationships of "the a priori rational will of the people," but as phenomena they are attributed to different persons.[110] Hence the original legislative sovereignty of the people, which as an ideal makes all governmental authorities merely the people's "deputies," in political experience simply legitimates the established legislator or sovereign, whoever he may be. "The currently existing legislative power is to be obeyed, whatever its origins." [111] Thus, by making "legislation" mean both constitution-framing as an idea of reason and ordinary statutory enactment as a present phenomenon Kant could carry the connotation of political freedom which inhered in the constitutional legislation over into the independent authority who was the civil legislator. And similarly with the doctrine of "representation." In its ideal sense "the representative system" which Kant espoused meant that all authorities were simply agents of the united popular will. In its applied form, however, Kant refracted this meaning into a whole spectrum of concrete meanings which ranged from a faithful translation of the ideal of popular accountability at one end to an indirect and obscure kind of "representation" at the other. Thus Kant began with the representation of the political rights of all subjects by the political rights of the economically and socially independent individuals who were the "active citizens"; he discussed the people's "deputies," or "representatives," in parliament, and called them "trustees" of the people's "freedom and rights"; but having thus asserted the applicability of the original meaning of representation, Kant then indicated the insufficiency of these particular forms and carried their popular connotation over into the "representation" of the people by an irresponsible, irresistible ruler. "When the empirical head of the state (be it king, aristocracy, or democratic union of the people) allows itself to represent, the united people . . . is the sovereign itself." [112] The power of the ruler is still supported by the ideal of direct popular representation but Kant now made this mean that the existing will of the ruler represents the normative legislative will of the people and is consequently supreme over the people's existing will. This sliding scale with which Kant sought to synthesize the ultimate freedom of individuals with the absolute validity of an objective authority was capped in his politics as in his ethics by the doctrine of the sovereignty of law. For law was the rule of reason which straddled all realms, and in politics it gave the ideal of freedom the phenomenal form of the ruler's authority. As a norm (*Recht*) law postulated the political right of man to will the rule he obeyed, but it took effect in experience as a fact (*Gesetz*) only when it was expressed through one sovereign will to which the will of the people had subjected itself. Law, then, was the unifying, validating, and perpetuating force in the republican— i.e. divided—constitution. The ruler cannot change the form of the state unilaterally because of the ideal component of popular will in the law; the people can neither change the form of the state nor resist the sovereign ruler in any way because of the physical embodiment of law in the person of the ruler.[113]

Secondly, Kant used his doctrine of the republican constitution—i.e. constitutional monarchy—not only to solve the problem of the relationship between liberty and authority within the sphere of politics but also to solve the problem of the relationship of politics as a sphere to the philosophical realms of freedom and necessity. He had declared politics to be intermediate between morality and nature, but his general formulations of this position had tended to obviate the synthesis by rediscovering the larger antinomy within politics itself. Kant was forced to admit that his ideal of a self-legislating sovereign people, composed of free and equal individuals, was "only an idea," a "Platonic ideal," a political *"Ding an sich* itself . . . for which there is no object adequately existent in experience." [114] "It is sweet to spin out constitutions which correspond to the demands of reason (particularly from the point of view of fundamental law), but it is presumptuous to propose them and punishable to arouse the people to the overthrow of the presently established order." [115] Nor can rulers transfer political sovereignty to the people or educate them to the moral maturity which it would require.

Even the philosophers, whose devotion to the service of reason liberates them from the tutelage of the state and gives them the prime responsibility for the public education of the people, cannot go beyond enlightenment in the sense of "merely natural and common-sense rights," and these do not touch the moral realm of ends to which popular sovereignty gives political expression. Thus Kant's political framework now included a politicized version of moral principle which constituted a "duty" for citizens —particularly for monarchs—and which consequently functioned as a binding "eternal norm" for all existing civil societies, but he could find no direct way short of "Providence" to apply it.[116] It was precisely at this point that Kant fitted in his "republican constitution," as the only possible means of getting his moral ideal physically applied. Such a constitution, as Kant envisaged it, was the final step in the political synthesizing of morality and nature. Politics as a realm brought morality and nature into mutual relations, but it took the republican constitution to organize these into a working relationship. It was "the portrayal of the *respublica noumenon* according to the laws of freedom through an example in experience (*respublica phenomenon*)." [117]

The separation of powers which was the heart of Kant's republic thus represented the crucial mediation between the ideal sovereignty of the people and the existent sovereignty of the ruler. To buttress this compromise with the established order philosophically Kant developed special constitutional implications of the law of reason and of freedom which would be appropriate to what was empirically possible. Unlimited obedience to the existing ruler became now not only a fact but an a priori "concept of practical reason"; the "juridical (and hence external) freedom" which was the corollary of practical reason in this context became the subjunctive "privilege to lend assent to no external laws except those to which I could have given consent." [118] Kant's republic thus was not a literal constitution with separated physical powers: it maintained the political freedom of the people as a spiritual entity in order to identify it in the physical sovereignty of the prince which it justified. The republican constitution was simply a spirit or "mode of government" binding upon all rulers in all kinds of states alike. Kant summarized his authoritarian solution to the problem of freedom bluntly: monarchs must "rule autocratically and administer republicanly [sic] —that is, in the spirit of republicanism . . . analogically to the statutes which a people would give itself according to the principles of fundamental law." [119] With this translation of freedom and of law into the hypothetical attributes of enlightened absolutism Kant seemed to return to his own position of the 80's and to the main tradition of German political thinking. But there was an essential difference. Kant now acknowledged absolute monarchy, with its administration of a hypothetical political freedom of the people, to be "provisional" and he looked forward to the literal application of the separation of powers in which the people would be the actual legislators of their freedom. Kant continued to acknowledge that the moral basis of human actions was unchangeable, that politics could contribute only "negative wisdom"—i.e. removal of the hindrance, war—to morality, and that consequently the ruler's initiative and the separation of powers must mark the final pattern of earthly human freedom. But at the same time Kant's new emphasis was not upon the admitted ultimate limitations of man's moral disposition, with its authoritarian political consequences, but upon the possibility of securing more temporal results from this stable moral disposition.[120] The agency which was to give direct external realization to man's ideal freedom was the constitutional legislative liberty of the citizens. It was to function as the moral motor of the natural political machine.

It has been asserted that Kant had no glorified notion of the state and that he attributed to it no organic character.[121] In general these judgments are valid, for he rejected morality and welfare as political objectives, and hierarchy as a social structure. He limited the function of the state to the external realization of a priori principles of right and he deliberately destroyed the foundations of an organic society by his blanket rejection of the autonomy of corporate bodies and his explicit opposition, in the name of equality, to the very existence of an hereditary aristocracy.[122] But actually, the second of these achievements undermined the first: Kant's abhorrence of social hierarchy left civil society with no center for the administration of its values but the sovereign power of the state. By making constitutional liberty the dynamic moral factor within a state which retained the function of natural compulsion, Kant enclosed the expansive power of political liberty at the same time as its presence moralized the traditional organs of state power. The state became an instrument for the realization of moral freedom through the external compulsion which, in the name of the inner moral law, it exerted against men's immoral and unfree natural acts. Moreover, this state partook of a moral character not only because its functions were defined or limited by a moral purpose—for this was nothing new in German political thought—but because the introduction of legislative rights as the external form of individual freedom translated moral freedom into political as well as civil liberty within the state. In Kant political liberty became the dynamic and cohesive factor within the state which justified its natural mechanism of coercion in terms of liberty itself.

This Kantian pattern of political thinking exercised a remarkable influence upon future German liberals. The frank recognition of politics as the crucial arena for working out the problems of both the spirit and the flesh terminated the traditional categorical distinction between these two realms, and the emphasis upon active political liberties as essential to the moral and material well-being of man initiated the era of liberalism in Germany. At the same time the reappearance of the distinction between ideal and existence within the world of the state in the form of the necessary co-existence of individual freedom with the independent authority of the monarch even when this freedom included political rights funnelled the German cultural tradition into 19th-century politics. But the Kantian influence upon German liberalism was not limited to the conscious pattern of this thought. The net result of his political considerations was similarly anticipatory. For Kant ended in a condition of virtual political paralysis. The rational individualism which forced him to deny all corporate, national, or organic mediation between the collectivity of free persons and the monarch left him with no means of proceeding, within the "republican" constitution, from the enlightened absolutism which he accepted to the balanced government which he desired. He rejected action toward this end by people, prince, and intellectuals alike as unlawful and unfeasible. All that remained was his counsel to accept, after they had succeeded, the revolutions which one must oppose in their origins and their course.[123] And even so were the German liberals to act in the revolutions of 1848 and 1918.

Hegel

If the acceptance of Kant's political legacy was to be testimony to the complex and compromising character of German liberalism, the influence of Hegel's betokened its instability. In the political as in the other fields of thought Hegel took up the delicate balances in Kant's philosophy as uncompleted midwaystations on the path to truth, used them as his starting-points, and drove them to monistic resolutions. Because he dealt with the problems of individual freedom and its authority which had been Kant's concern, his procedure bequeathed instruments which could be subsequently employed by liberals in search of a more dynamic and assertive theory than Kant's. But at the same time because Hegel applied these instruments to the ultimate construction of a synthesis that was all-inclusive rather than selective, his own political system was not a liberal one. When he put together what Kant had torn apart he tightened Kant's loose organic metaphor into a resurrected political ideal of a completely integral organic totality which became the necessary expression of individual freedom and which consequently could be justified in terms of it. Moreover, if Hegel's synthesis could not hold a balance between liberty and authority, no more could his liberal disciples'. His own system anticipated the instability of the liberal doctrines that were constructed under his influence during the first generation of the liberal movement—an instability which developed after 1848 into the split between a conservative acceptance and a socialist rejection of the existing structure of state and society as a whole.

Hegel's political system did not, then, in itself contribute to the origins of German liberalism, but two aspects of it did exert considerable influence and illuminate what were to be the inner workings of that movement. In the first place it provided a tool, a method, for radical political analysis, for it made freedom the product of incessant change. Secondly, its substantive definition of freedom explicitly associated liberty with authoritarianism not only as a fact but as an ideal, and it showed how the national idea could be used to reconcile the extremes.

Of the manifold facets in Hegel's general philosophy, two were to make a particular appeal to liberal intellectuals as useful theoretical weapons for the assertion of their political and social goals: the attribution of an essentially critical and dynamic power to sovereign reason and the insistence upon the necessary relationship and ultimate identity of mind and nature, ontology and history, the universals of ideas and the particulars of experience.[124] Moreover, the striking power of these weapons was reinforced by their own internal unity. They were as two heads of a single hammer: the critical function of reason was constituted by the relationship between ideas and facts and hence was oriented to the supersession not only of beliefs and opinions but of the whole of existing reality; conversely, the relationship between ideas and facts was constituted by the operation of critical reason and hence was both dynamic and progressive. Hegel seemed to offer a means to the solution of a deep-seated and century-old problem for German intellectuals—the integration of ideals and concrete reality by a cement other than the passive acquiescence in the traditional political and social order, for he placed spirit both within and without the existential world and thus emphasized the possibility of living existence in accordance with spirit while yet maintaining the absolute validity of the ideals posed by spirit. He wove logic, history, and ontology into a system which expressed a single principle; not only were the structures of thought, of existence, and of being entirely homologous processes within themselves but they constituted a process among themselves which made them mutually dependent. Thought can know itself only through the realization of its process in existence; the truth of existence lies not in the bare given fact but in this fact plus its inherent underlying possibility of becoming something other than it is, and it requires thought for the recognition and the actualization of this possibility; the structure of being, finally, depends upon the interaction of the other two processes—upon the actualization of the logical process and the rationalization of the historical process. Thus for Hegel the rational spirit, which was the absolute principle unifying the whole system, both retained its a priori validity and received the power to immerse itself in and transform concrete ability.

Moreover, Hegel himself established the applicability of this standard of a critical and dynamic rational spirit to the social and the political life of man. The key to this application lay in Hegel's definition of the process of spirit as a process of freedom; *"the final cause of the World at large,* we allege to be the *consciousness* of its own freedom on the part of Spirit, and, *ipso facto,* the *reality* of that freedom."*[125]* The crucial mediation performed by freedom in the Hegelian system stemmed from its position at the precise point of fruitful conjunction between the ideal and the temporal aspects of life. Metaphysical freedom consisted in the spirit's recognition of its universal self in particular facts; moral freedom consisted in the finite human will's conscious recognition of universal spirit in its particular acts: but in any case "the concrete mean and union" of the "merely general and abstract" idea of Spirit and "the activity of man," which produces actuality, is "Liberty, under the conditions of morality in a State." [126]

For Hegel, then, the problem of finding a theoretical place for freedom in the sphere of politics—the problem which had plagued Kant—was scarcely a problem at all. The definition of freedom, in Hegel, not as one of two distinct realms above experience but as the synthesis of two principles in experience established the idea of liberty in the intermediate sphere, inhabited by both natural necessity and moral ideals, wherein politics has always dwelled. Indeed, early in his career Hegel attacked Kant and Fichte (whom he considered a Kantian disciple) on these very points, and in the course of his refutation he made clear his own basic position, which he was to hold throughout his life. Hegel railed against what to his mind was Kant's moral formalism, which he attributed to the latter's radical separation of the moral absolute from reality,[127] and in this false separation Hegel saw the root of the equally false distinctions between the

individual and the general freedom, between morality and legality, and consequently between the individual and the state.[128]
The consequence of this disjunctive way of thinking, Hegel
judged, was to make polar abstractions of these concepts and to
leave open no path of mediation between the individual basis
and the valid universal ends of action save that of naked, futile,
and uncontrolled force, which led politically either to a stagnant
equilibrium of powers or to despotism.[129] So long as internal
ideals are kept isolated in principle from external actions, morality must remain individualized with no chance of realization and
politics must remain in a real realm of compulsion and necessity.
This kind of politics administers a law which has no moral content but only a negative form addressed to the realization of
morality; hence it justifies either oppressive action in the name of
the general freedom or totally destructive revolution in the name
of the freedom of all individuals as such.[130]

Hegel replaced this approach with the concept of "the absolute ethical order," in which freedom, as the identity of the ideal
and the real, worked itself out through a dialectical interplay
between the individual and the universal, the moral and the
legal; these distinctions he considered as merely negative, posited
for the actualization of freedom but ultimately returning to a
positive identity under "ethical totality." Thus the state as well
as the individual was subjected to the standards of the ethical
order; juridical compulsion as well as private voluntary choice
was included in the area of freedom. Hegel affirmed that the
individual was the necessary basis of the ethical order, but he
insisted both that this individual principle be viewed simply as
a particular determination of the universal rather than absolute
in itself and that even within this relative validity the individual be viewed as a negative determination *vis-à-vis* freedom's positive determination in natural law. Natural law, then, was not
for Hegel derived from the rights of individuals but was a direct
manifestation of the universality of the absolute ethical order
in a general system of legislation. Law was the crucial mediating
form assumed by the absolute ethic when it proceeded to give a
moral organization to inorganic nature.[131] "The system of right
is the realm of freedom made actual, the world of mind brought

forth out of itself like a second nature." [132]   The sphere of politics was thus in Hegel himself a significant arena for the restless activity of dialectical reason, which crystallized itself both in the universal standards of law and in individual consciousness and through their interplay progressed to the ever greater actualization of the absolute. His early emphasis upon the constant need for modernizing civil laws and institutions to bring them into a living relationship with the ever-advancing mores (natural law) and purposes (consciousness) of the people was a model for the later liberal application of the Hegelian dialectic to politics.[133]

But in what way, then, did this philosophical instrument prove unstable for liberal purposes? The disciples themselves were to deny that the instrument itself was unreliable, and they were simply to point out a development from the early to the later Hegel wherein Hegel, on personal grounds, became illogical and untrue to his own principles. That some such development did take place in Hegel is generally agreed, whether the change be characterized in an overt political form as the arbitrary cessation of the dialectic at the final realization of Spirit in the contemporary Prussian state, or in the more philosophical form of the shift from the progressive unity of thought and action to a one-sided emphasis upon thought—religion and philosophical truth —as the ultimate realm of freedom.[134] But the liberal intellectuals rejected Hegel's later phase in both these senses, and consequently what is important for Hegelian legacy was not his own political instability but the diverse implications of his doctrine as such. For if this theory supplied the critical instruments for attack upon the contemporary order, these same instruments when applied to the positive ordering of a liberal doctrine led ultimately outside the framework of liberalism. In the young Hegel as well as the old the idea of freedom was associated with concepts of collective bodies in a way which took account of individualistic considerations but subordinated them to higher principles—the principles embodied in the nation, the corporation, and the state.

The political integration of the individual into supra-individual principles was grounded in the very core of Hegel's philosophy, and hence this side of Hegel's political thought was just as fundamental as his critical approach to political institutions through dialectical reason. For if these institutions sacrificed their authority when they lost contact with the progressing consciousness of their subjects, this consciousness on the other hand retained no validity without subordination to an objective universal standard. And just as absolute spirit crossed over into the sphere of phenomenal reality to guide changes in existing institutions, so too it sanctified institutions when they had been brought into accord with the stage reached in the objectification of spirit. Thus what in Hegel's logic were the basic terms of the particular and the universal were translated for politics into the individual and the state, and Hegel's dialectical logic which insisted upon the necessary movement and interrelationship of those basic terms had its political counterpart in his population of the realm between the person and the state with a host of organic forms uniting the individual and the universal. Individualism was hereby denied in favor of "individuality." This concept expressed the particular insofar as it was united with the universal; consequently it separated the value of particularity (i.e. the realization of the universal) from actual living individual humans and bestowed such value on those societal forms which mediated between such individual humans and the universal ideas of reason.[135]

Equally in his earlier and his later writings Hegel emphasized that the prime individuality was the nation (*Volk*).[136] The nation was "the moral individual" which crystallized what was universal in individual men, a crystallization which these individuals could not perform separately. Here then in Hegel was the first clear and fundamental philosophical grounding of the intermediary role of the nation in reconciling the freedom of the individual to the authority of the state. Moreover, Hegel himself revealed the possibilities of this association by developing in an extreme form the subordination of the individual and the independence of state power which it permitted. Individuals, the relations among individuals, and the rights and liberties resulting therefrom were all assigned to "civil society," an inferior realm within the nation which Hegel called "the world of ethical appearance." [137] But even within this inferior realm the role of the individual was limited. The principle of the civil society was indeed the "concrete person" and its ostensible aim the care for individual interests, but the means to this lay through a formal universal which ordered interpersonal relationships toward this goal and subsumed individual persons under supra-personal entities even within the civil society. It is true that for Hegel the universal in civil society was law and that law embodied the general recognition of individual rights, but since that which was common to a myriad of private wills must be of a formal and abstract order the principle of civil society was really not the concrete person as such but his property. "The universality of freedom" protected by law in civil society was simply the right of property.[138] But if individuals, organized in a national civil society, participated in the universal only through their property relations, they did not participate in it as individuals. Early in his career Hegel had laid down the principle that "self-consciousness within the life of a nation descends from the universal only down as far as specific particularity," but not down to the single individual, and this dictum was explicitly spelled out to mean that the individual was part of the nation only insofar as he acted not in terms of himself but in terms of "the laws and customs of his class or station." [139] When Hegel came later to develop this principle he sought to show that even in the sphere of civil society, which was based upon individuals and their particular interests, the identification of individual rights and interests with material rights and interests meant that individuals shared in a legal order only as members of an economic class.[140] Moreover, the only integral union (though only partial in scope) of universal and particular within the civil society was via the corporation: the corporation, which is "especially appropriate" to "the business class" (i.e. the middle class) as the class most concentrated upon individual interests, brings to its members the consciousness of the universal connections of their interests, thereby introduces ethical principles within civil society, and becomes the immediate social basis of the state.[141]

Hegel's treatment of civil society betrayed his constant preference for "totalities" over their constituent individuals in the dialectical interplay between universally valid authority and personal freedom. Not only could individuals within civil society enter into this interplay only as members of such totalities (however restricted in scope) but the realm of civil society itself, as the arena of individual, subjective freedom, was characterized by the necessary alienation of the individual from the true universal and hence from his actual self. The state, on the other hand, as the arena of objective freedom, was not characterized by an analogous alienation: it was both the seat of the universal and the unity of the universal with the individual.[142] Thus while the individual was denied the possibility of creating his own moral authority through his liberty, the state was given the capacity to incorporate the liberty of the individual. In Hegel's treatment the modern state was the core of the realized spirit of the nation not so much because it embodied the universal authority of reason but because it embodied it in a form which at the same time actualized individual freedom as well. "The state-power is . . . the achievement of all, the absolutely accomplished fact, wherein individuals find their essential nature expressed, and where their particular existence is simply and solely a consciousness of their own universality. It is likewise the achievement and the simple result from which the sense of its having been their doing has vanished; it stands as the absolute basis of all their action . . ."[143] The state is "that form of reality in which the individual has and enjoys his freedom; but on the condition of his recognizing, believing in, and willing that which is common to the Whole." Not that "the subjective will of the social unit attained its gratification and enjoyment through that common Will," or that "the individual, in his relation to other individuals, thus limited his freedom, in order that this universal limitation—the mutual constraint of all—might secure a small space of liberty for each," but rather "are Law, Morality, Government, and they alone, the positive reality and completion of Freedom."[144]

Hegel's basic point of view was that freedom—the capacity of men self-consciously to create a reality in accord with their ideas —could be realized only in the nation. Freedom had indeed to make its appearance through the actions of the individuals composing the nation but the realization of freedom was beyond the capacities of individual nationals as such and must find its agent in the state, which organized the nation into "an individual totality" on the basis of the universal values of reason.[145] "The essence of the modern state is that the universal be bound up with the complete freedom of its particular members and with private well-being," and "its strength lies in the unity of its own universal end and aim with the particular interest of individuals," [146] but for Hegel this relationship was essentially one-sided. The fulfilment of individual freedom, rights, interests depended upon the individual's conscious adoption of the universal order manifested in the state as the standard of their measurement. ". . . What the state demands from us as a duty is *eo ipso* our right as individuals, since the state is nothing but the articulation of the concept of freedom. The determinations of the individual will are given an objective embodiment through the state and thereby they attain their truth and their actualization for the first time. The state is the one and only prerequisite of the attainment of particular ends and welfare." [147]

This fundamental relationship between the individual and the state was faithfully articulated in Hegel's analysis of the constitution of the state. He explicitly denied that the constitution could be founded upon individual consent,[148] but insisted rather that the state comprehended the individual principle in such manner that this principle endowed it with security and strength. Hegel could assert that the stability of the state depended upon the identity of "public and private ends" and upon the satisfaction of the "subjective aims" of the citizens because in his doctrine these private ends and citizens' subjective aims were asserted in the constitution not by individuals but by social institutions like corporations. Such institutions are "the pillars of public freedom since in them particular freedom is realized and rational" and the firm foundation of "the citizen's trust in . . . and sentiment towards" the state.[149] For these institutions not only produce a consciousness of the national community but as organs of the state produce "patriotism" in the form of "political sentiment," the internal attachment of the individual subject to the objective reality of the state.[150]

Thus the Hegelian state was frankly "an organism," and "this organism is the constitution of the state." [151] The form which the constitution takes in the final historical period when the state becomes the realized freedom of all is that of a constitutional monarchy. But Hegel's peculiar version of constitutional monarchy became visible in his bold application of his dialectical logic to the organs of state power: the legislature was the universal principle, the executive (more precisely, the administrative) the particular principle, and "the Crown" the principle of individuality—the higher synthesis of both.[152] From this pattern Hegel drew two important inferences. First, just as the movement of the dialectic was a movement from unconscious unity through separation to conscious unity, the political separation of powers could not be taken in the usual sense of the independence of the powers from one another and the resulting balance of powers. Rather was it the self-differentiation of the state in which its organs effected "a living unity" and constituted the concept of the state as a whole.[153] Secondly, as the individuality in which the self-conscious unity of the whole was realized, the Crown contained all the differentiated functions of the state in itself under its "power of ultimate decision." Thus "the absolute self-determination" "to which everything else reverts and from which everything else derives"—that is, the "sovereignty of the state" in virtue of which alone "is the State *one*"—was the "distinctive principle of the power of the Crown as such." Moreover, not only was the Crown the unifying power in the political embodiment of objective spirit but it was also the political realization of individual subjective personality. The Crown "is not individuality in general, but a single individual, the monarch," for "it is only as a person, the monarch, that the personality of the state is actual" and fulfils its function of realizing "the basic moment of personality" in general.[154]

Since for Hegel the monarch was the supreme active unity of universally valid authority and individual personality, the role of the representative body in the state was of necessity the subordinate one of contributing a mere aspect to the synthesis in the monarch. But this body was only an inferior part of the legislature: it furnished to the Crown's legislative power of decision the knowledge of what in particular the state's power needed. Its function in the constitution as a whole was indeed the representation in the state of the private judgments, wills, and liberties of men in civil society, but since even in their universalized form of a "public consciousness" these judgments, wills, and liberties remained but "empirical" and "subjective," their representative body has to deal "not with the essential elements in the organism of the state"—which were the realization of rational rather than mere empirical freedom—"but only with rather specialized and trifling matters. . . ." [155] The real role of this body, then, was that of "a mediating organ," "a middle term," standing between the government in general on the one hand and the nation broken up into particulars . . . on the other." [156] In general terms this meant that through the representative body "the state enters the subjective consciousness of the people and . . . the people begin to participate in the state," [157] but Hegel betrayed one of the cardinal practical concerns behind the organic idea when he emphasized that representative bodies "prevent individuals from having the appearance of a mass or an aggregate and so from acquiring an unorganized opinion and volition and from crystallizing into a powerful *bloc* in opposition to the organized state." [158]

This function required a certain kind of representative body, and it is hardly surprising to find that Hegel flatly rejected an assembly representing individuals and accepted only Estates representing classes.[159] The assembly based on the individual principle would be based on "The Many . . . connected only as an aggregate, a formless mass whose commotion and activity could therefore only be elementary, irrational, barbarous, and frightful." [160] Considered politically, the individual could be taken into consideration "only as a member . . . of a social class," for the individual could have political recognition only insofar as he acted through the forms compatible with the order of the state. Hegel even justified the social existence and the political privileges of the aristocratic estate as the class essentially fitted for the task of political mediation.[161]

Hegel's political system was important for future German theory, including liberal theory, because it took cognizance of the new political principles clustered around the idea of freedom and yet marked out the path through which they could lead back to a rejuvenated system of traditional authority. Where German theorists of the old regime had tacitly utilized the presence of a hierarchical, organic society to transfer the exercise of an abstract conception of liberty from the individual to the state, Hegel utilized the conception of liberty to construct an organic state which justified the continued existence of the hierarchical society.

Hegel himself began the application of this achievement to German conditions. In his early essay on the German constitution he analyzed the older German idea of freedom, asserted its anomalous character, and sketched out the lines of its renovation.[162] The theme of the essay was precisely the relationship between the two stages of German freedom. The first stage was the freedom associated with traditional German particularism, and in his discussion here Hegel came to grips with it in both its concrete and its theoretical forms. He asserted frankly what had been vital but often only implicit in the tradition: that freedom in Germany was the freedom of the independent German states;[163] that it was an expression of the inherent German passion for autonomy;[164] that its embodiment in the separate sovereign princes was a development from an original basis of freedom in every individual;[165] that this princely freedom was subsequently founded upon the prince's representation of his people—and their liberty—in the government of the German Empire;[166] that this freedom was consequently founded upon the commingling of the princely positions of Imperial Estates and independent sovereigns and upon the confusion of their private civil rights and their sovereign state powers.[167] But after having given this kind of freedom its full due, Hegel proclaimed that it had become a false freedom, and herewith he broke with the old ways of justifying authority in the name of liberty and pointed the way to a new. Freedom *from,* he said in effect, must be transformed into the freedom *to.* The old kind of particularistic freedom had proved illusory, not only in principle, since it rejected the valid universal standards of law and was left dependent upon caprice, but in fact, since the German people had become mere passive stakes in the capricious play of the foreign policies of the great powers and had become subject to the arbitrary will of their own princes.[168] This kind of freedom must therefore give way to a new genuine kind of freedom which was to come from participation in a national state based upon law.[169] Thus Hegel seemed to break with the old particularistic conservatism which justified itself by associating freedom with the German principalities. Actually, however, he simply modernized it into a national conservatism, by using the new individualistic principles of liberty to convert the historical association of freedom with princes into a rational association of freedom with a national German Emperor.

The new freedom, then, consisted no longer in the negative liberty of the princes but rather in the positive liberty of the people within the national state. Three different aspects of this positive liberty can be distinguished in Hegel's analysis: first, the freedom of the citizens to order, through their associations and corporations, all those of their affairs which were not necessary to the existence of the state-power;[170] secondly, the "cooperation" of the people, through their deputies, with the head of the state for those general affairs necessary to the existence of the state;[171] finally, the guarantee of the freedom of the citizens by the concentration of the supreme state-power in one center—the monarch.[172] Now, of these three elements of the new idea of freedom, the third was for Hegel the most fundamental; it was, indeed, both the condition and the measure for the existence of the others. Only the crystallization of the ultimate factors of power in the hands of an independent, hereditary monarch could assure the authority of general law on which rational freedom was based and could guarantee the internal and external security within which freedom could be afforded.[173] Thus the liberty of citizens over all matters not absolutely requisite to the power of the state must be "conceded (*ueberlassen*)" by the government, not only because such freedom is "sacred in itself" but because a state power which allows its people a free hand "in the more subordinate public activity" is "infinitely strong" through its "support by the freer, unpedantic spirit of its people." [174] It followed that the participation of the people in the lawmaking power of the national government must not only take the general organic form of the "cooperation" of members with the head of the state but must specifically take the form of representation by Estates—a representative body which had not the right of legislative co-determination but only the right of limiting the sovereign will of the monarch by the granting or withholding of monies.[175]

In Hegel, then, the pattern of what has proved peculiar to the modern German idea of liberty was laid down. Retained from the older tradition was the conviction that liberty could achieve a general existence only by becoming an attribute of state power itself and by taking a compatible form within the structure of authority. Added now was a recognition of the more prominent role which must be accorded to the individual in the control over his destinies, but in a form that harmonized with the basic relationships of the traditional conception. Individual rights were recognized, but they were absorbed into corporations and the national framework which were also expressions of the moral power of the state. In the final analysis, Hegel's system was a model for the binding of individualism. Hegel himself anticipated the historical destiny of German moderate creeds based on this bondage when he predicted that the liberty which he deemed necessary to the modern national state would not be used by the people to establish that state. It could come not from a rational act of the citizens' freedom but only from the physical force of a conqueror's gift.[176]

4. The Politics of Reform
(1806-1813)

The French Revolution had more than an intellectual impact upon Germany. In its ultimate effects it seemed to inspire a whole new integration of German politics upon a liberal basis. If the revolution in France exercised the theoretical influence of reorienting the German intellectuals to a more concrete approach to the problem of liberty, the attempted export of the revolution to Germany by force of arms exercised a practical influence in liberalizing German institutions. From 1794 to 1814 the French were in occupation of some part or another of Germany. Both in emulation and reaction the realities of German life were adapted to the requirements imposed by the physical presence of representatives from the new revolutionized society of France. German politics was impregnated with a spirit which brought it into an apparently integral relationship with the politically oriented German intellectuals. Now it is undoubtedly true that in both spheres of life the Germans had been slowly developing in these directions on their own for at least half a century before the French made such development a question of life or death: the German intellectuals had been tending toward a political formulation of human freedom and German institutions had increasingly been reshaped according to standards of civil liberty and general law. Nevertheless, this final invasion of Germany by western European liberalism, in the insistent shape of a revolutionary model and a crusading army, was to be of decisive importance for Germany, with ramifications infinitely more far-reaching than its immediate impact.

The real meaning of this invasion transcends the old historiographical conflict between the view which credited the French revolution and occupation with implanting the seeds of a genuine liberal nationalism and that which adjudged it merely a stimulant of an indigenous German movement already at work. Its meaning consists rather in its enforced acceleration of liberal and national tendencies—whatever their origins—to a premature synthesis of theory and practice that proved to be a topheavy burden upon a materially undeveloped German society. A chapter of political action was indeed written into the German intellectual tradition, and a liberal element was grafted on to the political institutions of the German states. But despite this advance the integration achieved during this period was actually both transitory and incomplete. When the extraordinary pressures of imminent world revolution, world empire, and total war were lifted, the synthesis of liberal doctrine and political institutions fell apart once more. The German states were left to absorb this new liberal dosage into their historical framework of aristocratic absolutism, while the liberal spirit, modernized by the taste and the promise of realization, withdrew again to the world of the intellectuals to resume its development as doctrine. In part, this discontinuation of reform liberalism was the work of a powerful opposition outside it, but in part too it was the product of an internal dissolution. The reform movement had the peculiar structure of "a revolution from above" and it had a peculiar approach. It was an inclusive, conjunctive movement which rejected the either-or in favor of the both-and; it added liberal arrangements to the existing state and society, asserted the the inherent compatibility of these and indeed of all political principles and interests with one another, and thus attempted to institutionalize the organic unity of individual, state and nation which was being explicated in German political theory. The movement was too eclectic to take firm root in the society before it foundered, but it lasted long enough to present the themes of future conflict and to establish the tradition of governmental initiative in the practical liberalization of society.

It is hardly fortuitous that the historiography of the Age of Reform has been, in terms of quality, overwhelmingly weighted on the side of biography. By the common consent of the historians who have written the classic works on this period, the historical factors which were decisive for its characteristic structure and movement did constitute a kind of liberalism, but it was a liberalism embodied not so much in the German society itself as in the personalities of individual statesmen. The clear implication of this historiography is that reform liberalism, like the partial recognition of the principle of personal freedom by the enlightened monarchs of the 18th century, was imposed by philosopher-politicians who fed the advanced standards of European culture into the top echelons of the German states and then sought by the instrumentality of these states to galvanize a retrograde society. Little had transpired in the economic sphere even by the end of the reform era to spur a mass or even a class movement for liberal goals.[1] Yet the liberal reformers at the beginning of the 19th century differed from their forbears of the German Enlightenment precisely in the conscious and systematic extension of liberal principles to concrete economic, social, and political institutions and practices. How is this development to be explained?

Undoubtedly the main factor in this change was the obvious combination of the intellectual impact in Germany of revolutionary practice in France and the actual necessity of creating institutions wherewith to meet the popularly sustained French power in the field. But a social element indigenous to Germany was also involved. The Germany upon which the reformers impressed their policy was not an entirely stagnant economic and social body. The reformers themselves were not only disciples of liberal intellectuals and officials of a state bureaucracy. They were also members of the German aristocracy,[2] and what small social pressure for liberal reforms did exist in Prussia stemmed from a section of the nobility. This identifiable aristocratic factor in the state liberalism of the reform period would seem to indicate some kind of development in the material foundations of the German nation, and indeed within the fundamentally persistent economic and social structure a change of pattern is discernible. To call this change an economic and social "crisis" would be to overstate it.[3] Rather was it a partial dislocation of certain traditional economic relationships and long-established social customs which marked more the loosening of an old system than its dissolution by a new one.[4] Consequently, this change did not give rise to strong forces for change, but rather fostered a limited disposition and an equally limited possibility for reform from above.

The outer signs of the dislocation, which set in perceptibly around 1790, were correspondingly modest. A rupture in the economic pattern was indicated by the sizeable rise in grain exports which was the natural response to the growing industrialization of England, the expanding stock of precious metals in Germany with its concomitant inflationary effect upon the price level, and the spread of speculation in land values. Simultaneously, the older social routine was broken by a marked rise in population, unemployment of artisans in the towns, the movement of peasants from the land and their increasing vagabondage in the countryside, spontaneous local risings by both groups, protests by responsible local spokesmen against the abuses of princely and aristocratic dominance, the growing surplus of middle-class intellectuals over and above the posts available to them either in the civil service or the free professions, and an important extension of the tendency toward the capitalization of agriculture on the large estates.[5] To the extent that these developments worked their way into social consciousness their impact tended naturally to be centered upon the aristocracy, not only because it was land that was most immediately affected by the changes, but also because a liberalized aristocracy was the appropriate agent of influences which touched the society but were not decisive enough to challenge its fundamentals. It is hardly surprising, then, to find that the leading economist of the period was the scientific agriculturalist Albrecht Thaer, who preached the gospel of production for profit, taught the application of scientific methods to agriculture in the service of economic efficiency, and asserted the necessity of large estates based upon free economic relationships as requisite for a rationally operated enterprise. Moreover, the one liberal pressure group with a modicum of cohesion was an East Prussian circle of officials, landowners, and merchants in which the aristocrats Theodor von Schoen and Friedrich von Schroetter played the leading roles.[6] Here the increasingly important commercial connection with England and the increasing adaptation of grain production to it provided a material basis for the extraordinary position of the province within the Prussian monarchy—the comparative fluidity between the noble and the middle classes and the extension of an economic emphasis upon free-trade to the adoption of a general albeit moderate liberal point of view under Kantian auspices.[7]

But if the economic and social situation in Germany became more conducive to the rise of an aristocratic liberalism it was not sufficient to endow this liberalism with an independent social power. Even in East Prussia, not only were the nobles who took the initiative in the activity of the liberal group important provincial officials of the Prussian state, but as long as they operated through parliamentary discussion within the provincial estates and without benefit of compulsion by the state power, they were unable to get their chief plank, peasant emancipation, through against the resistance of the rest of the nobility and the weak indifference of the rest of the burghers.[8] The social basis of the reform era gave an aristocratic impress to the liberal policies of this age and provided it with its titled bearers, but the drive that led not merely to the application but even to the articulation of liberal principles as a policy was propelled by the requirements of state.

The respective shares of monarchical and aristocratic interests in liberal reform varied from state to state in Germany, and this difference gave rise to the two main types of political pattern in the reform era. The first type was constituted by the southern and western territories of the Rhenish Confederation. Here the primary goal of reform was the consolidation of monarchical absolutism, the instrument was the centralized bureaucracy, and the decisive weight behind it the direct external pressure of the French rather than any internal social force of consequence.[9] In these states the great bulk of the population, including the notables, remained passive. The few liberal-minded men at first associated themselves entirely with the official reforms of the satellite royal and ducal courts, and even when they later came to resent the military and financial oppression of the new absolutism they simply retreated to the reactionary claims of the traditional estates.[10] Thus the extent of liberal change was directly proportional to the intensity of French interest in the area—greatest in the annexed Rhineland, tangible in the model kingdom of Westphalia and the neighboring Grand Duchy of Baden, and somewhat more tenuous in the kingdoms of Wuerttemberg and Bavaria—and it never exceeded the quality of liberalization characteristic of the Napoleonic regime. Hence the policies of the Rhenish states were simply an extension of traditional enlightened despotism, with French influence permitting a more radical execution of its egalitarian implications against the local notables and requiring a more radical justification of monarchy by the general principles of liberty and equality.

The general rule of reform was the extension of monarchical authority by destroying the remnants of aristocratic political and administrative autonomy, by establishing the equality of all citizens before the royal law, and by conceding an economic and social mobility which would undermine local and provincial attachments. Consequently, the characteristic legislation of the Rhenish states reorganized the administration into a centralized bureaucracy; abolished or weakened the patrimonial police powers of the nobility; adopted or adapted the whole or parts of the Code Napoleon—abolition of serfdom, religious toleration, the abolition or diminution of exemption from taxation, the loosening of the guilds' stranglehold on trade and industry. The rulers also promulgated constitutions, in Westphalia and Bavaria, which proclaimed the principles of general civil liberty—personal freedom, legal equality, security of person and property, freedom of conscience and of press—to be fundamental law, but set up a plutocratic and impotent representative organ to insure their purely academic character. These policies broke new ground for southwestern Germany but chiefly in a political rather than a social direction: they rooted the tradition of a liberal enlightened absolutism in the south and west but did not change or mobilize the society that lived under it. Like their enlightened predecessors of the old regime, the Rhenish princes stopped their reforms short of fundamental alterations in social relations: the notables whose diets they destroyed they absorbed into their administrations; to the lords whose serfs they freed they preserved the traditional real dues and compulsory services accruing to lordship; for the guilds which they reformed they maintained the old corporate jurisdiction and compulsion.[11]

Thus the contribution of the confederated Rhenish states to the reform era was a moderate liberal monarchism, sponsored by individual noble-bureaucrats like Montgelas of Bavaria and Reitzenstein of Baden, but in general limited rather than spurred by the aristocratic interest. This type of liberal reform betrayed the ultimate political bankruptcy of the south German aristocracy under conditions of 19th-century politics and prepared the way for middle-class primacy in south German political movements, but foreign duress was too strong, native participation too weak, and the reforms too restricted for the bureaucratic liberalism of the Rhine to do more than bring this region abreast of the sovereign state-building in the east.

It was the Prussian type of reform that introduced a new era in German history. The characteristic feature here was the active cooperation between a section of the German nobility and the Prussian monarchy in a definitely liberal enterprise. The net results of the Prussian reforms were not greatly at variance from those of the Rhenish states, but the conscious formulation of the principles behind the policies and the enthusiastic participation of a whole aristocratic party in the modernization of state and society combined to make the Prussian contribution to the era a new chapter in the political and social history of Germany. For here was cemented the marriage of monarchy and aristocracy in Germany to cope positively with the challenge of a dynamic Atlantic society. In the century of alliance between these two forces during the old regime they had collaborated in the simultaneous assertion and limitation of a principle of liberty which could mobilize but not fundamentally change the traditional structure either of politics or of society.[12] Now, however, under the pressures engendered by the British market, the French Revolution and the French occupation, the mutual limitations which had contributed so heavily to this *modus vivendi* were broken down. The progressive section of the aristocracy expanded their platform to include political liberties, while the monarch, under severe military and financial requirements, was forced to legislate the equality necessary to call up all possible support for the state. In Prussia, as in the Rhenish states, the pressure of foreign ideas and soldiers lent urgency to liberal issues before the great bulk of the society was ready to support them. The great-power tradition of Prussia, however, and the strength of its aristocracy combined to exclude a natural gravitation toward the Napoleonic model such as took place in the south and west.

This pattern was indeed tested in Prussia during the "pre-reform" period (1797 to 1806), when the middle-class cabinet counsellors Beyme and Mencken, with the compliance of the king, Frederick William III, tried to drive through reforms dedicated to peasant liberation, tax equalization, economic mobility, and popularization of the army. The Prussian minister Carl August von Struensee characterized the spirit of these measures as the French Revolution from above. "The King is a democrat in his way: he works constantly for the limitation of the nobles' privileges. . . . In a few years there will be no more privileged class in Prussia." [13] But despite the constructive importance of these attempts in preparing the ground for the reform era proper, this attempt at egalitarian reform by interpreters of the Frederician tradition failed to progress much beyond the discussion stage.[14] The sequel showed that the opening of an effective reform period in Prussia required not only the stunning defeat of the old state at Jena but the accession of a determined group of progressive nobles to power.

But if the Napoleonic type of monarchy was frustrated in Prussia, the alternative of a Whig aristocratic liberalism was equally avoided. Forced to reform under external duress, neither monarch nor liberal aristocracy could find a necessary internal ally save in each other. Consequently, at the very time when the disappearance of the German Empire had wiped out the last justification of the older, particularistic liberty (*Libertaet*) which had helped bind princes and territorial nobility together, monarch and aristocracy reforged their alliance on a new level by cooperating in a formulation and application of the new individualistic liberty with which both could agree. Appropriate to this combination, the liberal policies in Prussia after 1806 were undertaken by German noblemen in the Prussian bureaucracy. The liberalization of Prussian institutions initiated under these joint auspices was the first step in ushering the old state and the old society into the new age: as aristocrats, these liberal leaders endowed the revolutionary idea of popular freedom with a hierarchical social context that they insisted was compatible with a strong, authoritarian state; as officials of the state, they limited this idea of freedom by considerations of *raison d'état* which could not countenance the smashing of the aristocratic order of society.

Stein and Hardenberg, the two heads of the Prussian government during the reform period and authors of the general programs under which it operated, were both in themselves and *vis-à-vis* each other striking exemplars of this combination of social types which gave the first practical form to German ideas of political liberty. For Stein was primarily a liberal aristocrat who in this period hitched his goals to the power of the Prussian state; Hardenberg was primarily an enlightened bureaucrat who ultimately sought to buttress his state by an aristocratic constitution: they were conscious of the gulf between their respective outlooks, which was clearly visible in their specific policies, and yet in the last analysis their work was not only complementary but in a sense homogeneous.

Stein

Baron Karl vom Stein was in no sense a political thinker. Not only did he not give genuine theoretical expression to his political ideas but he did not derive them from the doctrines of political thinkers. The bent of his mind was practical, and his ideas developed only gradually as deposits left by his actual political experience after it had been screened through personal feelings and values.[15] The adoption of a liberal program and the sponsorship of liberal measures by such a man were sure signs that the extension of tangible individual liberty had become a concrete issue in the very fabric of German politics. That his measures and program took on a quality very similar to the characteristic forms of German liberal theory indicated the presence of a real social constellation behind the apparent involutions of that theory. Thus Stein, with all his aversion to theory (particularly to the natural-law theory of the Enlightenment) and with all his openness to the concrete realities of German experience, still wound up in the difficult syncretic position familiar to German political thinkers. He too thought in terms of the both-and. He set up both a broad social freedom and a strong state power as two independent poles of political endeavor, valid in themselves and necessary to each other. By his origins as an Imperial Knight and by his continued addiction to Whig constitutional principles, Stein was predisposed to the moderate, historically-conditioned, aristocratic liberalism espoused by his Goettingen friends Brandes and Rehberg. What came increasingly to distinguish him from them were the considerations of German patriotism and the appreciation of a strong, authoritative state power which Stein added to the Anglophilic liberal tenets of his early years in what has been called "quite a unique combination of political ideas." [16] Stein's activity thenceforward has had to be characterized conjunctively, to denote his simultaneous concern for real individual liberties and heightened state power: his liberal reforms were undertaken both for their own sake and to strengthen Prussia against the occupant; he was possessed both of an aversion to bureaucracy and of the conviction that it must be reinforced.[17]

Now this kind of approach meant more than the mere acceptance of successive aristocratic and bureaucratic experiences by an empirical mind open to the varied elements in the German situation. For it was deep-seated in Stein: it ran through his most fundamental social and political attitudes and seemed inseparable from the very process of his thinking. He defined the purpose of social reform variously as establishing "the possibility that every individual can develop his forces freely in a moral direction," [18] as the "free development and ennoblement of the particular nature of every nationality (*Voelkerstamm*)," [19] and as imposing "the obligation upon the people of so loving king and fatherland that they will gladly sacrifice property and life for them," [20] without divining the possibility of an internal conflict among these ends. He accepted the principle of social equality,[21] but still he continued to think of society in terms of estates and even to indicate the necessity of a preferred position for one estate or another, according to the occasion.[22] At times his interest in peasant liberation seemed limited to the mercantilistic purpose of increasing productivity of a capitalistic agriculture;[23] at others he called the emancipation "the first fundamental law of our state, our Habeas-Corpus Act," in line with "the original and inalienable rights of humanity." [24] Moreover, this was but one instance of his general position on civil liberties, in which he typically and repeatedly juxtaposed the sanctity of personal freedom apart from governmental intervention with the desirability of a unified and powerful governmental administration.[25]

Even Stein's much-heralded idea of self-administration did not so much resolve these problems as repeat them. Certainly his oft-stated constitutional aim—that the whole nation must be called to run its own affairs[26]—and his interpretation of his Municipal Ordinance of 1808 as having actually turned over "the undivided administration" of the towns to the citizenry[27] appear clear enough on the surface. Even these assertions, however, were complicated by the qualification that the nation must be gradually "habituated" to govern itself[28] and by the distinction between municipal self-administration and self-government which was implicit in the reservation of all police powers to the exclusive competence of the state.[29] The essential complexity of Stein's constitutional position was confirmed by his alternative reference of it to both English and Napoleonic models[30] and by his insistence upon both the general necessity of peaceful legal action by the people[31] and their violent insurrection against Napoleon and even against the satellite German princes.[32] He praised the 18th-century German constitution as a genuine guarantor of civil liberty and yet demanded its replacement by one buttressed with popular institutions.[33]

Nor was Stein's attitude toward self-administration proper entirely unambiguous, for his thoughts on the subject were honeycombed with distinctions. He drew a sharp distinction in kind between self-administration on the local level and that on the national and provincial levels. He distinguished, in his definition of self-administration, between the appointment from the ranks of Prussian society of administrative counsellors who would act as state officials rather than representatives and the participation of frankly representative bodies in the administration. Finally, he distinguished between the endowment of such bodies with merely consultative functions and their exercise of real legislative and administrative powers.

The puzzle in Stein lies in the fact that he made these distinctions and then proceeded to adopt every one of the disjunctions which he had thereby created. On the one hand he defended his policies as *de facto* Prussian prime minister in terms of their restriction of self-administration to local government. He pointed out that on the provincial level the citizens who would join the administration would assume an official rather than a representative capacity while the provincial representative would be excluded entirely from state affairs.[34] Again in his plans for a general Prussian representative assembly he explicitly restricted the initial functions of such a body to consultative functions on subordinate interests.[35] On the other hand, his ultimate constitutional projects stipulated the necessity of representative bodies with genuine legislative powers from the national German level through the particular states and on down to the localities.[36]

Two explanations lie behind this difficult position of Stein's. The first factor is that of Stein's own development. In general his cautious attitude stems from the period of Prussian reform, which for him ended in 1808; thereafter he entered into the preparation for national liberation and foreshadowed its more pressing liberal demands. Whereas in the first of these stages he was primarily concerned with the structure and the order of the state which he headed, in the latter he was striving to give a popular foundation to the new German state which was to be created. But this point should not be stretched to break the continuity in Stein's ideas, for despite the shift in emphasis he did insist upon the necessity of civil liberties during the reform and upon strong state authority—whether of an Emperor or a Prussian-Austrian hegemony—during the liberation. Hence the second factor which explains Stein's ambivalence is a complex set of assumptions which embraces the whole range of his evolution. For Stein the decisive impulse to the good society lay neither in governmental authority as such nor in popular rights but in an integral unity of both. Given the present condition of "culture," exclusive authority degenerates into despotism or impotence (or both, as in the case of the princes of the Confederation of the Rhine), while the people, when isolated from government, are diverted to selfish interests of the lowest material kind. Hence authority and liberty must be connected, yet remain independent, and the only possible framework for such a relationship is the structure of the state. In the different periods of his activity Stein could tip the balance toward one pole or the other of this structure, but what remained constant was the attribution of the moral education of society, including its monarchical governments, to the state. The state, therefore, became the arena in which governmental power and political liberties acted as dialectically related principles, at once autonomous and associated.

During the first period of his mature political activity—the Prussian reform era—Stein took the existing political order, i.e. the existing Prussian state, as his starting-point and sought to work the necessary transformation of society in it and through it. Government was to be strengthened by its expansion to include society and society was to be morally disciplined by its participation in a preestablished governmental authority. It is this conception of the dual nature of the state, taken from the initial point of view of the existing structure of the state, that explains many of the problems in Stein's reforms. These problems may be summed up in the apparent paradox that government was to direct men to be free and how to be free. This idea was not only implied in the actual reforms enacted from above but it was frankly acknowledged by Stein in several different contexts. Government should publicize its tax measures so as at once to take into account and to direct public opinion on these measures.[37] The city ordinance is designed to rouse public opinion but government should ignore bad public opinion about the city ordinance. The nation should be *given* a share in the administration "under certain limitations and provisions." [38] The nation should be *inculcated* with ideas of self-help, sacrifice, and insurrection against Napoleon, and the resulting popular spirit can then be used by government.[39] Peasant emancipation is justified because when cultural conditions change and bring friction within the society "the ruler" must change the institutions.[40] And finally, "if the greater part of the nation is in a condition of crudity and low sensuality, . . . if freedom and property is the lot only of the upper privileged classes, then must the government lead, instruct, encourage, through laws, rewards, educational institutions, subsidies, travels." [41]

During the reform period, consequently, Stein's primary concern was with the increase of governmental power as the chief agency in the revitalization of the Prussian state. The free activity of individuals, while essential, was contributory to this agency: it must strengthen the established political authority, take a form compatible with it, and submit to being moralized by it. This emphasis was visible in the general dictum of Stein's "Political Testament" that "the immovable pillar of every throne is the will of free men." [42] Moreover, his whole approach to Prussian problems was conditioned by it. He declared the chief issue to be a reform not of state but of government, and consequently he limited the participation of the citizens in the state primarily to activity within the cadre of the official administration, where they could be politically educated toward a later legislative representation.[43] Stein now characterized the purpose of self-administration to be the fostering of "civic spirit (Gemeingeist)," which was to intensify loyalty and channel the strength of the society to the royal government by revealing the needs of the nation, contributing local knowledge and experience, and explaining governmental measures to the people.[44] Thus would the people be bound by conviction to the Fatherland, the state, and the monarchy.[45]

Only those of Stein's policies which were in accord with this emphasis were actually institutionalized in Prussia. Peasant emancipation, equal economic liberty for all classes, municipal self-administration, rationalization of central and provincial administrations[46]—these were the lasting reforms of Stein, and they were perfectly in harmony with the idea of social liberty as a constituent of rather than a check upon the power of the state.[47] Indeed, Stein's municipal reform afforded the striking spectacle of a liberalization that was imposed in the interests of the state upon the apathy of the citizenry to whom the freedom was being granted, and that resulted in the strengthening of their loyalty to the monarchical state but not in an active and independent utilization of the new civil and self-administrative rights.[48] Thus was individual liberty given a form eminently compatible with an authoritarian political order and in this form built into the permanent practice of the Prussian state.

But despite Stein's concentration upon it and despite its practical ramifications this administrative liberalism made up but one side of Stein's general policy even during the reform era. His constitutional plans, although unenacted, are important not only for their later influence but for the light they throw upon the intent of the measures that were enacted. For Stein was never a mere bureaucratic liberal and his edicts were never designed— whatever their effects—merely to create a modern individualistic society under a traditional absolute government. Moreover, even the modest self-administration which he promulgated as an immediate measure could not ultimately fulfil the demands set by his fundamental requirement of a simultaneous balance and union of nation and government. Indeed, as his prime ministership wore on, the combination of an increasingly active cabal against him at the court and the increasingly patent inability of the Prussian government to meet the political and economic challenge imposed by the French occupation, reawakened his doubts about not only bureaucratic but absolute government as such. Hence, in February, 1808, he actually convened a provincial diet of the East Prussian estates, which he projected to be a regular institution, and he came to moot plans for a representative constitution which only a short time previously he had characterized as premature. But the peculiar form which his constitutional ideas took rendered them complements rather than amendments to his administrative activity. For he did not think in the simple terms of a mixed constitution with divided powers. His basic conception was rather a polar one: on the one hand, the king is "master," endowed with "the supreme power," and his "unlimited" rights are "sacred"; on the other, the fate of the state depends upon the realization of the right of every active citizen to representation.[49] How these two poles were to be reconciled in a constitutional system was the crucial German problem, and Stein went beyond such techniques as the concession of merely consultative powers to provide a fundamental social solution in

which the future trend of German development was foreshadowed. The mediation from the free individual to the sovereign
monarch was to be performed by a flexibly-structured society
which combined elements of modern individualism and traditional hierarchy and embodied this combination in representative assemblies of Estates. Such a society was capable of this
mediating role because, for Stein, its very being as an organized
society was a product of its participation in the political order.
Thus public opinion is sought in vain from individuals and
associations—but it can be found in representative bodies of the
estates.[50] Without some kind of popular constitution the people
"appear as a mere passive mass." [51]

Because Stein's basic framework was political, his social ideas
and policies were molded by the requirements of his constitutional system. This system demanded a broadening of the political base of the monarchy through the establishment of representative bodies which brought a greater mass support and yet
did not break down the principle of representation by estates as
such, and Stein's corresponding social goal was of a nation composed of personally free individuals who were yet organized in
an hierarchical order. This flexible concept of society was expressed in policies which aimed at the moral reformation of the
aristocracy through the removal of their exclusive legal privileges,
and at the liberation of the burghers and the peasantry through
the removal of legal and economic trammels. Yet these groups
would be maintained as distinct social entities. Stein thought
to work this social synthesis between social reform and preservation by making the ownership and operation of landed property
the canon of social power and to extend it into a political synthesis by making the same criterion the basis of political rights
as well.

The connection between the society and the political order
was given for Stein in the estates. The anomaly of unprivileged
social estates in a nation of legally free and equal individuals was
paralleled by the anomaly of political diets elected by estates but
sitting together and voting by head.[52] The justification of both
—aside from Stein's general claims for the moral benefits of corporate institutions—was epitomized in the political function

which Stein assigned to the nobility: it would be represented in a projected popular chamber as well as in a projected house of lords, for the Crown shared with the nobility "the honorary right to certain privileges" and hence through the nobility would acquire a secure position in the popular organ.[53] Here the ultimate tendency of Stein's thought and his Prussian reforms lies revealed. Through liberal social legislation the traditional position of the nobles as subordinate public authorities under the king was undermined. To this extent the aristocracy became a component of a homogeneous society, and the basis of its power became its share in property rather than its exclusive privileges of birth. At the same time, however, the maintenance of the estate principle, the traditional expression of the solidarity of princely and aristocratic public powers, continued the former function of the nobility in a new form. The fundamental interdependence of monarchy and aristocracy was reaffirmed, but with the nobility no longer participating directly in the exercise of public power over the society but now leading the society to political action in support of the monarchical order.

Hardenberg

If Stein was led to his views and policies concerning the state from modernized aristocratic social convictions, Prince Karl August von Hardenberg traveled in a reverse direction from a starting-point in the absolute monarchical state toward the attribution of an implicit though unintended aristocratic character to this state. The remarkable consequence followed that two statesmen as divergent in temperament, general outlook, and political ideas as were Stein and Hardenberg legislated reforms which not only were continuous and complementary but frequently ensued from the explicit approval and cooperation of both men.[54] This combination testified to the power of the actual pressures which were forcing the German states to face up to the liberalization of their political and social systems as a practical problem and to the definition of reform in Prussia by a progressive interpretation of both royal and aristocratic interests. The fundamental posi-

tion which Stein and Hardenberg shared was the explicit conviction that no essential part of the old order in Germany was
inherently wrong or evil and that this order had simply to be
adapted to the changing conditions of a transitional age, together
with the implicit corollary that the essential parts were to be
modified and preserved in it.[55] Consequently, the differences in
their ultimate aims and ideas scarcely disturbed the basic homogeneity of their practical policies.

But the figure of Hardenberg raises questions of quite another
order than the Stein problem, and consequently it illuminates
the German situation of the reform period from a different angle.
Whereas Stein took up the various elements of this situation into
his conscious thought and sought to anchor them in a complicated, balanced system, Hardenberg sought to take a single line
and yet was forced to adjust to the antithetical factors, both by
unconsciously absorbing assumptions alien to his original political absolutism and by the specific concessions which he was forced
to make before he could make real contact with existing groups
and circumstances.[56]

There is general agreement that Hardenberg was a political
monist and that his fundamental political attitude revealed a
simple consistency from the beginning to the end of his career.
Hardenberg was and remained a liberal bureaucrat out of the
18th-century school of enlightened despotism. He was oriented
primarily toward foreign policy and its demands, and he defined
the purpose of the state, consequently, in terms of power, its
means in terms of the rational considerations of *raison d'état,*
and its structure in terms of the unified leadership afforded by
the undiluted absolutism of the monarch and his administration.
Trained in the French Enlightenment, open to the lessons of the
French revolution and its Napoleonic sequel, he developed his
original conception of the welfare state to its logical conclusion
in an atomized society whose individuals stood in an immediate
relationship to the absolute government through their unmediated political dependence upon it and their unmediated material
and civic support of it.[57]

Thus the governmental rationalization and the exclusion of
the traditional estates from all essential fields of legislation and

administration, reforms which even before the Revolution he deemed essential to the diplomatic and military power of the state,[58] developed through his appreciation of the material and military strength of the French revolutionary state into an endorsement of a thorough-going economic and social individualism. This development coincided with Hardenberg's entrance into Prussian service and the great world of European politics, and his attitude was consequently articulated in analogous foreign and domestic policies. The characteristic note in these policies was the attempt to utilize the achievements of the revolution for the reinforcement of the fundamental pillars and objectives of the established monarchy and within the limitations posed by its requirements. In foreign policy this meant using the revolution for traditional Prussian expansion in northern Germany through a policy of neutrality which would accept the new France without breaking with the conservative powers.[59] In his German policy it meant the advocacy of a more centralized German constitution which would deprive the smaller princes of sovereignty in military matters, but this reorganization would not go beyond the traditional structure of Germany as a federation of princes rather than peoples, and it would simply serve the end of Prussian hegemony over northern Germany.[60] In his domestic policy, Hardenberg's approach similarly rejected revolution—the "French so-called freedom"—as such and sponsored the realization of a "true freedom" which consisted in "opening free competition to talent and merit in all classes," in equal application of the laws, in equal distribution of burdens, in "complete security of property and person," and in the internal connection with "religion and civil order, without which it cannot exist." [61]

The Prussian collapse at Jena seemed at first to activate rather than change Hardenberg's policies. The famous Riga Memorandum of September 1807, drawn up in collaboration with von Altenstein and completed by Hardenberg, projected a reform program which simply systematized his ideas for a mobile, egalitarian society under a centralized bureaucratic monarchy. Postulating the basic principle that Prussia must expand or die, Hardenberg insisted that the Prussian state must "seize the true spirit of the age" if it was to survive, and he frankly admitted that this spirit, in terms of which the state "must undergo a complete rebirth," was the one created by the principles of the French Revolution. For "the power of these principles is so great, they are so generally recognized and wide-spread," that the state which does not accept them must expect either its decline or the enforced acceptance of them.[62] Noting, moreover, that these principles had given to the French "a whole new surge" by awakening "all sleeping forces" and destroying the weak and the outmoded, Hardenberg emphatically justified the liberalization of Prussia by its beneficial effects on the power of the state. Consequently, he proposed as the proper model not the Revolution itself but Napoleon's exploitation of it. The proper form for this "revolution in the good sense" would be "democratic principles in a monarchical government," introduced by "the wisdom of the government." [63] This amalgam of political ideas Hardenberg expressed bluntly as the obligation of "a monarchical state" to "limit the natural freedom and equality of the citizens no more than the stage of their culture and their own welfare require." [64]

Accordingly, the specific planks in Hardenberg's program were directed primarily to the removal of caste distinctions and to the enactment of a general free mobility in material concerns. He proposed to retain only the titles of an hereditary aristocracy—and this to take advantage of the tradition which emphasized its service to the state—but in general he advocated the procedure of purely honorary ennoblement as a reward for merit in any individual and recognized no substantive aristocratic privilege.[65] Later, in another context, he made the categorical suggestion that distinctions of estate should be dropped entirely.[66] Likewise in the spheres of tax and army reforms his emphasis was upon the equalization of burden and opportunity rather than popular participation.[67]

But it was in Hardenberg's proposals for the enactment of civil liberties that the proportions of continuity and change between the old regime and reformed Germany came to their clearest expression. Like the more liberal prerevolutionary publicists, Hardenberg was interested in retaining the absolutely ruled state while associating it with the advantages of individual liberty, but he tended to reverse their means: he proposed an almost unlimited freedom in practical activities but great caution in spiritual affairs. Under the heading "The Creation of the Freest Possible Use of the Forces of Subjects of all Classes," which was designed to realize "natural freedom," he included only measures of economic emancipation.[68] He came out sharply for complete liberation of the peasant both in person and property, without reference to any protective measures, for freedom of trade and industry with the explicit rejection of tariffs and guilds, and full liberty in the ownership and disposition of property of all kinds.[69] He declared indeed that the same liberal principle applied to the arts and sciences, but his specific policy on academic freedom and liberty of the press was much more limited than his categorical endorsement of the mundane activities of individuals. The former "should be extended as far as circumstances permit," the decision on the circumstances to be determined by the administration.[70]

Hardenberg's emphasis upon the association of material rather than theoretical liberties with the absolute state betokened a new evaluation of the usefulness of economic energies and the dangers of spiritual autonomy for the existing order. This change was the result of the politicization of spirit worked by the Revolution, and Hardenberg's wariness of intellectual freedom was part of his fear of political rights. He declared that if the king came to depend upon the support of the nation it could well cost him his throne.[71] He did indeed accept into his Riga Memorandum, through Altenstein, Stein's idea of building a representative element into the Prussian state, but he accepted it without the ultimate constitutional design which was the final goal of Stein's thought. He subsumed it entirely under the head of the "connection of the nation and the state administration," limited the activity of the representatives exclusively to functions within the several official administrative bureaus among which they were distributed in restricted numbers, and expressly stipulated that they should "form no special constitutive corporation, no authority of their own," lest they be taken for "dangerous national assemblies." [72] Hardenberg's ultimate purpose in projecting this institution of representation became visible in his conviction that "influence upon their constituents" constituted a key function of the representatives, equal to that of deliberation.[73] Clearly, the form which Hardenberg gave to popular political rights made them as compatible as possible with his essential authoritarian framework, yet the compulsion which he felt to adopt such an idea at all into his fundamental political planning was the first indication of his recognition that absolute government and individualistic society did not automatically complement each other and that some kind of intermediary might be necessary.

The legislation which Hardenberg, from his re-entry into office during June 1810 to the end of the reform period in 1813, built into the Prussian state was consistent with this main tendency of his political ideas: further centralization of the administration;[74] equalization of tax burdens; complete industrial freedom (with a few exceptions for special industries); secularization of Catholic and Protestant church estates; the beginnings of the civil emancipation of the Jews; a domestic service ordinance which placed the servant relationship on the basis of private contract; a regularization edict and a land act which prescribed the commutation of the natural dues and services incumbent upon the holdings of peasants with bound holdings (Lassites and tenant farmers) and aimed at the creation of free, modern property relationships both on the large estates and on the peasant plots.

It was in the process of applying these reforms that elements alien to Hardenberg's original design of a purely bureaucratic liberalism began to appear in his policies as practically necessary conditions of their execution. The most striking instance was the provisional national representation which Hardenberg instituted in 1811 as an adjunct to his financial reforms and which sat intermittently until 1815.[75] For what he set up was not a system of isolated groupings of representatives within the state administration but rather a plenary body to deal not only with the budget but with all manner of financial affairs. To be sure, both the occasion of and the ideas behind this institution bore witness to an inspiration of Hardenberg's which was by and large not inconsistent with the general tendencies of his political thinking. Napoleon's exactions and the recalcitrance of the nobles in traditional provincial estates to underwrite the extraordinary measures required by the financial crisis impelled Hardenberg to think in terms of a representative system, which would bring to the state private funds hitherto independent of the state through a new kind of organ politically dependent upon the government and divorced from the traditional estates with their political demands for a feudal revival.[76] The announcement of a popular representation (and of industrial freedom and the liberation of peasant property as well) within the context of a financial project calling for the uniform extension of indirect taxes over all groups and for the enactment of an extraordinary general land tax set the tone for Hardenberg's elaborations of the purpose of the new institution. It was to concentrate the unity of Prussia over and above the old provincial and social distinctions; it was to stimulate private initiative in the direction of increased productivity and contributions to the state, and it was to mold public opinion in support of governmental measures.[77] The interim "Assembly of Notables" which Hardenberg convoked in 1811 was appointed by the king and was designed to represent all classes, independent of the electoral principles of the traditional aristocratically dominated provincial estates. Hardenberg admonished them to consider the king a wise father who requires both obedience and initiative from his children, to give counsel on the means of executing the financial edict rather than on the edict itself (which was already law), to convince themselves of its necessity, to spread this conviction in the provinces, and to assist in the application of the law.[78] The Assembly of Notables was to initiate the transition to a regular, elected, but still consultative representation of the nation, and the standards which Hardenberg applied to the Assembly he hoped to transmit to the later constitutional body. Thus when in 1812 he moved one step further along the transition and convoked the first elected all-Prussian body—the so-called "Interimistic Representation"—as the successor to the Notables, he not only prescribed a strong bureaucratic influence upon the elections but in general continued to treat it as a purely advisory body by which he was in no way bound.[79]

Hardenberg's attempt to broaden and strengthen the basis of Prussian absolutism by grounding it directly in a society of free and equal individuals enjoyed a partial success, but in many ways its application to the actual Prussian society with its aristocratic predominance imported into the final results a distortion from the original theoretical intent. Not only did the so-called Gendarmerie Edict of 1812, in which Hardenberg sought to realize his idea of substituting a state subprefect system for the prevalent aristocratic control of the county administrations, prove completely impossible to execute, but under the pressure of the nobility both the regularization of peasant property and the tax laws were transformed from their original purposes. The land acts came to have the effect of favoring the consolidation of the large estates on a capitalistic basis and their engrossment of peasant properties rather than the creation of a large mass of free peasant property-owners.[80] The tax laws did succeed in breaking down the old distinctions between town and countryside and between province and province, as well as in subjecting the nobility to personal levies, but the purported equality of taxation—and particularly a uniform land tax—was in effect dropped.[81]

But it was especially in the matter of the national representation that Hardenberg, despite his principle of the representative equality of the estates, came face to face with the realities of the Prussian social structure and saw his ideal of a unifying connection between authoritarian government and liberal society frustrated. The alterations which the land and the tax laws underwent were the results of pressures which were channeled through the Assembly of Notables and the Interimistic Representation.[82] In both the appointed and the elected bodies the nobility emerged with the preponderant voice, in the earlier organ because of the natural weight of the nobility among the appointed "notables" of the realm, and in the later because Hardenberg preferred to transact specific economic concessions with the aristocrats rather than to entertain the demands of the third estate for the constitutional regularization and the expansion of powers of the Interimistic Representation.

Hardenberg accepted these modifications because of the subordinate but constant presence of aristocratic predispositions beneath the bureaucratic and leveling tendencies in his own make-up.[83] In the prerevolutionary Hardenberg this counterpoint was patent. His memorandum of 1787 which defended the exclusive rights of the Duke of Brunswick over the schools acknowledged that the rights of the estates were founded upon a legal basis independent of princely rights, and that they included not only the right to be consulted on some matters but also the right of legislative co-determination on others. To be sure, Hardenberg's main argument was a particular and historical one, to the effect that these representative rights varied with the specific constitutional development of the country concerned, but he grounded the validity of such independent rights, whatever their scope, both in Imperial law and in "general principles." [84] Now certainly Hardenberg did not retain this traditional principle of privileged representation by estates, but the attitude which this principle bespoke was not entirely crushed under the pressure of the change wrought in him by the ideas of the Revolution. Several minor points kept cropping up to mar his picture of society as a level plain composed around a single promontory which gave it form and life. He was personally averse to the abolition of the patrimonial police powers of the landed aristocracy: he declared bluntly not only that it was impossible to abolish them but that he himself as an estate owner would not tolerate it.[85] Again, he was reluctant to tax landed estates which had been hitherto exempt from taxation—which meant primarily the lands of the nobility—on the grounds that the exemption formed part of their property value and that taxation would consequently be a violation of property rights.[86] This feeling, combined with his hostility toward direct taxation in general and Stein's proposals for an income tax in particular, helped to bring about his surrender of the uniform land tax and to adopt, under extreme financial pressure, a general property tax and a classified personal tax (*Klassensteuer*—a kind of income tax, but classified by estates rather than individuals) only on the condition that they be a war tax, limited to the period of emergency.[87]

These policies were clearly flaws in his egalitarian escutcheon which could not be patched by his justification that with the abolition of restrictions in the ownership of estates such privileges would not redound to the exclusive benefit of any one class. For given the actual economic and social constitution of Prussia at the beginning of the 19th century this policy could and did mean a new kind of preference for the nobility, equipping it for continued vitality in the new mobile society of individualized property relations. Thus, despite Hardenberg's acknowledgement of the advantages of free peasant proprietorship, his preference for large agricultural units[88] influenced the framing of his land laws in such a way as to make possible the advantage which the Prussian nobility took of them. These discrepancies, subordinate as they were in themselves for Hardenberg's total scheme of things, build up to the great enigma in Hardenberg's career—his insistence upon an organ of national representation. Despite his conception of it in a form compatible with his basic political ideas, i.e. a means by which an absolute government could control and be supported by the activity of a nation of free and equal individuals, and despite the stringent limitations which he imposed upon its powers of initiative and decision on the Napoleonic model, his repeated recurrence to the scheme after repeated setbacks remains something of a paradox in view of Hardenberg's notorious tactical shiftiness. He tried it in 1811 after the unpleasant experience of the preceding Dohna-Altenstein ministry with the provincial estates. He attempted it once more in 1812 after the Assembly of Notables had proved recalcitrant. And after the Interimistic Representation had petered out in 1815, in part because of his own refusal to regularize it, he was to devote the bulk of his energies during the remainder of his career, in the midst of a black reaction, to the introduction of this kind of representative constitution. Moreover, despite his opposition in principle to the distinctions between estates and despite his actual organization of the representative organs without regard to such distinctions, he did not concern himself either with preventing elections by estates or even with preventing aristocratic pluralities.

The Hardenberg problem affords an important insight into the whole German development of the reform period. When he came to rejuvenate the bases of the Prussian state his thought tended naturally to assume forms which would retain for the aristocracy, albeit in new terms, its influence and power within the dawning competitive society. His opposition to the aristocracy as an estate was grounded in his aversion to the historical independence of their traditional political privileges from the omnipotence of the state and to the nobles' leadership of the old society against his liberalization by the state. But precisely because it was a question of liberalizing such a traditionally structured society from above, the aristocracy remained the chief social point of cohesion for the state in a new society organized by individuals. Whether directly, as in his advocacy of the patrimonial powers of the local aristocracy, or indirectly, as in his advocacy of encouragements to consolidated large estates, Hardenberg's view that the power of the state lay in the equalization of individual opportunity stopped short at the point where the new principles of social organization threatened to engulf the nobility. From this point of view, his preoccupation with the question of national representation can be seen as an attempt to re-create a political hierarchy between government and society that would be both subordinate to government and appropriate to the new social organization, and in the given German social conditions this meant the translation of aristocratic influence to the new stage.

The project foundered because the attempted enactment of a constitutional representation, following so closely upon the legalization of a modern individual property system, could not yet produce the loyal social hierarchy of property-owners which was desired. Indeed, it may be said in general that where the checks within Hardenberg failed, those in the Prussian constellation outside him operated to permit only that degree of liberalization in the reform period which would accrue to the power of the state without undermining the chances of the nobility in the new world of the 19th century. Whether one starts from the liberalized aristocratic conceptions of Stein or the democratized political absolutism of Hardenberg the results of the Prussian reform were to modernize the connotations of liberty associated with the monarchical state and simultaneously to modernize the economic and social position of the aristocracy which served it as a buttress against the political consequences of that liberty.

Humboldt

Stein and Hardenberg were the outstanding figures of the German reform era because they held positions which forced them to develop general principles for the comprehensive reorganization of a characteristic section of German society. Precisely on this account, however, they were not representative figures, for the typical liberal reformer in the Germany of this period combined a vagueness of political principle with a concentration upon specific reforms in particular fields. Without the pressure of all-around responsibility which the French focused upon the heads of state and their first ministers, progressive-minded Germans could not yet find in the economic and social relationships of their country the compelling need to make a political connection between their ideals of cultural and moral freedom on the one side and their perception of individual abuses and oppression on the other.

The weakness of the reform era in appropriate political ideas was perhaps best exemplified by Friedrich von Coelln, leader of a circle of radical young Prussian bureaucrats and himself a doctrinaire radical by temperament who yet could not find his way to a radical political doctrine. Starting from the familiar precept that man's destiny consists in his striving for spiritual and moral perfection, Coelln's fervor for the social realization of this destiny was exhausted in hypercriticism within the established political regime. The fundamental and authoritative law of nature, for Coelln, was the law of equality—"reason knows no other law but what is grounded on equality . . . from which alone freedom can come" [89]—and his emphasis was upon social and legal reform according to this principle by the monarchical state. "All have equal rights and equal duties *vis-à-vis* the state —all obey the same laws." [90] He demanded a return to his anti-aristocratic version of the absolutist tradition of Frederick the Great, the "genuine Prussian state-system"—unity of administration, abolition of tax exemptions, office-holding on the basis of merit, personal and real emancipation of the peasants, abolition of patrimonial police powers.[91] On the relations of monarch to people, Coelln paid lip service to the academic ideal of a representative constitution but for practical purposes resigned himself to an ultimate friction between the individual, who desires his own happiness, and the state, which directs the individual to the destiny of the human species. He assigned the realization of the natural rights of the people to the ruler, through the self-limitation of his own power. "The example from the throne works mightily, and a limit which the ruler himself honors will soon be sacred to every individual." [92] The essentially unpolitical character of this radicalism was betrayed by Coelln's fellow agitator, H. H. von Held, who soon repented of his intra-official criticism, left the secret society, and summed up its radicalism as simply an admonition to the ruthless use of power by the authorities: hate something or love something—but in any case become a despot or a tyrant for the sake of the good.[93]

Nor were the political principles of the officials who worked in collaborative or subordinate capacities upon the separate items of reform more consistent. When such men of the "reform party" attempted to work out general programs on their own the results tended to be sketchy, uncrystallized, or imitative.[94] Even such a figure as Theodor von Schoen, who was more politically-minded than the rest, mixed advocacy of undivided political authority, rigid laissez-faire, and self-administration in a compost of political ethics which has been justifiably characterized as "arbitrary." [95]

Hence the representative reformer of the pre-liberation era held his general political ideas in the peculiar form of a cross between vague inferences from his philosophical, religious, or aesthetic ideals and the specific requirements of his own special field of reform. Wilhelm von Humboldt, the Prussian educational reformer, was the "prototype" of this German liberal cultural tradition in its first encounter with the concrete realities of political life.[96] Certainly in his early years Humboldt measured up fully to the classic picture of the unpolitical German intellectual.. He had adhered emphatically to the cult of the spiritual sovereignty of the individual who realizes his highest values through intellectual and aesthetic contemplation,[97] and he had recapitulated the history of this cult by moving from the positive acceptance of the existing absolute welfare state in the 1780's to the rejection of the state and of politics in general in the 1790's. If he seemed to transgress the pattern by expressing this second attitude in a treatise which apparently cast his individualism in the political mold of classic western liberalism,[98] his refusal to publish the work[99] and a closer examination of its foundations indicate the illusory nature of this appearance. His concern was not to liberalize the political life of men but to accept the existing political system as the highest embodiment of the state and then to exclude it from all possible spheres of human activity, on the grounds that politics was pernicious to the development of the human spirit.

What drove this traditional polarity of power and spirit to an extreme in Humboldt was his overlay of the further polarity of collectivity and individuality upon it. For his fundamental unit was the individual and his fundamental value the free development of his spiritual forces by the individual.[100] Wherever the state impinges upon the individual it lays the hand of death upon this highest value.[101] Consequently, Humboldt professed to be concerned only with limiting the competence of all states and to be unconcerned with the form or constitution of the state. At many points, however, he betrayed the implications of his position by indicating his preference for monarchical absolutism, on the grounds that the individual will cannot be politically represented and that any influence which connects the citizen positively with the body politic distorts his free development.[102]

Now the anti-political tendency of all this is clear enough, and Humboldt was consistent with it when he accounted for his own doctrine as "principles of pure theory," when he insisted that its application could come only from the gradual, organic growth of the forces of self-development within the spirit of men and when he consequently rejected political revolutions both from below and above.[103] But these conclusions sat insecurely upon a fundamental and unresolved problem in the very core of his position. He had started from the accepted tenet of the primacy of the individual spirit but then had extended its benefits to cover the inviolability of individual activity in the outer world, thereby confusing the traditional basic categories of spirit and flesh and requiring liberating action by the absolute state in fields where he denied its competence. For if he justified his idea of individual freedom by reference to the requirements of the human spirit, yet he defined it in the general terms of the individual's "highest and most proportionate development of his forces to a whole." [104] This implied not only the obvious hostility of state-imposed external arrangements to the individual spirit, but also the positive necessity of freedom in these external arrangements for the freedom of the spirit.[105] Moreover, if Humboldt in general limited action by the state to what was absolutely necessary to maintain existence—which meant ultimately to security abroad and justice at home in their narrowest possible scope—he did assign to the state the unspecified duty of "influencing the spirit and the character of men, . . . of giving it a direction which will no longer be appropriate" to the present form of things, although this present form of things itself must not be touched by the state.[106]

Two tenets, held by Humboldt in rudimentary form before the reform era, were ultimately to help resolve these difficulties which arose from his insistence upon the practical realization of his non-political individualism. The first was his idea of a social connection among individuals, that on the spiritual side would supply the desired many-sidedness to the inevitably one-sided development of the isolated individual, and on the practical side would supply the "unity of arrangement" that was necessary for the achievement of any purpose.[107] In the *Ideas* this concept of non-political association took the institutional form of a series of small, voluntary, contractual societies which would exercise state-administered functions, but in its general form it was a harbinger of the role which nationalism was to play in Humboldt. His second saving tenet lay in his recourse to the idea of "necessity" as the ultimate canon of state action.[108] By opposing it to "usefulness" as a canon he meant to restrict the competence of the state, but he also relied on it to introduce an element of flexibility in situations where men were not yet ripe for free self-development. This was a harbinger of the considerable role which he was later to engross for the state in his practical work as a reformer. Neither of these ideas was worked out, and at this time Humboldt used them to exclude rather than to integrate politics into his value system. But their ambivalence revealed Humboldt's basic problem: the reconciliation of a thoroughgoing individualism in both intellectual and practical activities with political absolutism. During the 90's the problem did not press him because he concentrated upon the cultivation of the spirit and so could dismiss all political systems. But when he was himself called to reorder society through the mechanism of the state it became inescapable.

It is generally agreed that when, in February 1809, Humboldt accepted the commission to become Chief of the Section for Education and Religion in the Prussian Ministry of the Interior he committed a decisive break in his career with which his ideas only very gradually and never completely caught up.[109] Both in his assumption of the important administrative post, and in his actual exercise of it, he committed himself to a course of positive state activity while the theoretical bases of this activity, although now only peripherally expressed, continued to negate the validity of it. He attempted to justify his new position in terms of the expanded scope it afforded to his own individuality and ideas, in terms of the necessity of political action at that critical juncture, and in terms of his membership in the Prussian reform party, which seemed to guarantee that the state would be reformed in line with his own standards.[110] But these grounds had meaning only within the larger framework of two basic assumptions.

First, he was led to the conviction that it was now necessary for him to express himself in the Prussian state through his recognition of the German nation as the fundamental social unit to which he, as an individual, was inevitably committed.[111] Secondly—and more importantly for the reform period—he evaded the problem by remaining essentially non-political even during his tenure of office. This non-political assumption involved more than a contradiction between theory and practice.[112] It involved more even than the idea that his activity was pedagogical rather than political, and more than its corollary that he was educating the German nation for spiritual survival even if the state should collapse.[113] The ultimate meaning of this assumption was that it permitted Humboldt to set up the principle of freedom as the measure of both the spiritual activity and the practical organization of society, without the concomitant necessity of drawing the general line between those matters which must be inviolable from action by the state and those which were susceptible to ordering by the state as the instrument of freedom. Thus Humboldt could avoid the necessity of working out the implications of this principle of freedom for the political structure itself. His political ideas during the reform period formed no system but tended rather to be *ad hoc* generalizations from the specific functions of his office.[114] Occasionally he seemed to revert to the old distinction between the inner spirit which was to be free of state control and the outer organization which was subject to it,[115] but actually he mixed principles of freedom and intervention as the occasion seemed to require. He declared that "unlimited freedom from censorship" was the only right principle, which "one must ever approach more and more with time," [116] but this did not prevent him from acting on the conviction that neither the situation of the Prussian state abroad nor the self-discipline of its citizens at home could warrant the application of such a principle: consequently, he accepted the position of supervising all Prussian censorship,[117] endorsed and applied its restrictive provisions,[118] and limited his project for its reform to the rationalization of administrative authorities and procedures.[119]

Humboldt's reorganization of the Prussian educational system[120] was dominated by a similar mixture of principles, for he applied simultaneously the ultimate goals of free inquiry into truth, with its concomitant requirement of the general humanistic education of all individuals to equip them for such inquiry, and the immediate means of increased state powers in this sphere both to guarantee these goals against the retrogressive influences within the society and to direct them toward the strengthening of the state itself. Both in the results and in the motivations of the reforms the proportion of state regulation to freedom diminished as the hierarchy from elementary schools to the universities and academies was ascended, but still a combination of both elements penetrated all levels. Humboldt expressly rejected the idea of elementary education by individual caste and aimed "at furthering that development of human forces which is equally necessary to all estates," but he aimed also at "maintaining the inclination to obey the laws, adhere to the ruler (*Landesherrn*) with inviolable loyal love, to be moderate, moral, religious, and diligent toward their callings in private life." [121] To the secondary schools Humboldt gave their 19th-century gymnasial constitution, based upon a course of study which emphasized the humanistic universality of knowledge and upon an organization which did away with the old local rights of patronage in favor of the examination and appointment of teachers by the state, general supervision by the state, and a modest measure of academic self-administration within this framework. Humboldt's university policy, embodied in his organization of the first royal Prussian university at Berlin in 1810, gave greater weight to the principles both of academic freedom and of corporate self-administration, but on this level too these principles were integrated into a system of state control, expressed particularly in its power over appointments.

In the 1790's Humboldt had denied to the state any role whatsoever in the educational process,[122] and even now, in the reform period, he insisted that the "idea" of the university and even more of the academy was that "insight into pure truth (*Wissenschaft*)" which "man can find only in and through himself," through "solitude," "freedom," and "an unbroken, self-vitalizing, but unforced and undirected cooperation" with one another; on the other hand, he now also conceded to the state not only the "direction of youth" as "a practical need of the state" but the maintenance of the pursuit of truth "ever in its most active and strongest vitality." [123] He attempted to rationalize the role of the state by characterizing its function as the supply of academic endeavor with "the external forms and means" which "must exist in positive society for any widespread effect," but ultimately he had to admit that the familiar association between outer compulsion and inner freedom was invalid. The state "does not and cannot really affect" academic endeavor, but rather "it is always a hindrance when it intervenes, . . . the business would go infinitely better without it," and "the very fact of the existence of such outer forms and means is something wholly alien, always works disadvantageously by necessity, and draws the Spiritual and the High down into the material and lower reality." [124]

From this impasse Humboldt saw no logical way out. For practical purposes he bridged the gap with two notions, loosely conceived in themselves and loosely connected. With the first notion Humboldt simply brought intellectual individualism into line with the traditional Germanic conception of the existing state as the embodiment of liberty, but in a form that avoided consideration of the political implications of this association. The Prussian state, in its educational policy, not only should take into account its practical need to train subjects for good citizenship, but should also take the higher principle of free inquiry into truth for its own sake as a canon of action regardless of practical consequences.[125] He felt that the absorption of this higher standard would bring a moral strength and even a moral primacy of the Prussian state over other states, but he remained uncertain at this stage about the political implications of this moral force: he vacillated between the suggestion that it would reinforce the political power of the state[126] and the assertion that it would replace the political power of the state.[127] If this first notion of Humboldt's had reference to an older political standard, his second notion gave an intimation of a future one: the idea of nationalism. Like Fichte, Humboldt believed in the superiority of the German disciplines over those of other nations precisely on the score of the Germans' greater dedication to the unrestricted universality of knowledge. The Prussian state should positively foster academic freedom both because of the general prestige to be acquired in the service of a cosmopolitan principle and more particularly because of the "intellectual and moral" influence over Germany which would accrue to Prussia as the center and protector of free German inquiry into truth.[128] This was not yet a political notion, but it gave an early indication of the nature of the impulse which was to galvanize German political thinking into new resolutions of the problem arising from the association of the old absolute state with the modern doctrines of civil liberty.

5. National Liberation (1813-1815)

During the period of reform, ideas and practices of economic and personal liberty were built into the political absolutism of the German particular states. During the war of national liberation a second tradition was forged. Now the attempt was made to recognize the independent value of popular rights and still to establish their compatibility with the equally independent values of traditional social and political authority: German nationalism gained the historical stage as a political force, holding forth a supreme value in terms of which the freedom of states and of individuals coincided so that the settlement between the principles of authority and of liberty could be extended from the social to the political structure without the sacrifice of either principle.

Now it is certainly true that the consciousness of German nationality had long been in existence and that it had been expressed not only in cultural forms but even in the political institutions of the German Empire. It is true too that the nationalism of the liberation period was still in an early stage of development. It was still mixed with particularistic, cosmopolitan, and purely cultural elements, and in general it failed to achieve the status of a clear, full-fledged doctrine of political unification.[1] Nevertheless, it was during this period that the idea of a national cohesion, undeveloped as it was, became for the first time a relevant and crucial political factor. It supplied to 19th-century German politics the assumption of a larger whole, at once popular and ordered, which comprehended states and individuals and gave a homogeneous structure to their apparently conflicting relationships. It even presaged the dichotomy of its own possible authoritarian or revolutionary consequences in the event that individuals or states, respectively, proved to be recalcitrant participants in the national synthesis.

The undeveloped and uncrystallized quality of this nationalism was important not so much because it allowed particularism and universalism to remain as obstacles to its effectiveness, but rather because it affected the character of the nationalism itself. As a political factor this nationalism was premature, in the sense that a popular war hastened its birth before intellectual and material conditions in Germany had ripened sufficiently to give it a broad and independent basis in the society. Its practical political implications were not worked out, and, despite the undoubted presentiment of its revolutionary possibilities, recourse had ultimately to be taken to existing political authorities for the execution of nationalistic aims. Thus the first stage of political nationalism in Germany ended by establishing a pattern in which the new synthesis between political authority and the citizen was weighted on the side of the former.

The war of national liberation was not a spontaneous mass uprising. Both the policy of a national war and the participation of the populace in it were initiated by a small group of patriots —almost all of whom were employed in official capacities. The popular response was limited to compliance with governmental edicts, and activity within officially established institutions was geographically circumscribed. Often it required special compulsion.[2] Yet the spirit and the success of the popular participation within these limitations signified a mass activity in a public cause unprecedented in Germany since the Reformation.[3] The picture which emerged was that of a people loyally rising under their princes to free both their states and themselves from the invader under the banner of a national German appeal. The appeals which evoked this popular response furnish a clue to the generally accepted character of nationalism in this era. They promised the reconstitution of Germany as a political entity and they promised an admixture of representative institutions, but this concession to the popular element in nationalism was combined with a traditional emphasis upon the legitimacy of the particular states and the general spiritual values of Christendom to produce a program of the vaguest political character.

Even where citizens seemed to take the initiative these limits were not exceeded. The East Prussian Diet approved the formation of a national guard (*Landwehr*) and a local militia (*Landsturm*) in February 1813, before the Prussian government had declared war on France; however, not only were both the convocation of the Diet and its agenda produced by the orders of Stein, in the commission of the invading Russian Czar, but a formula invoking the interests of the Prussian state and saving the authority of its king had to be found before the Diet could be opened.[4] Again, the officer posts of the Prussian national guard were, by the royal decree of March 1813, to be filled first by nominees of civilian county commissions and later by election, but the results of these popular procedures showed that far from its later role as the stronghold of the liberal and nationally minded middle classes, the national guard was now run by officers who were composed overwhelmingly of the traditional notables: professional military men, civil officials, and estate-owners.[5]

The Intellectual Preparation: Fichte and Arndt

The political nationalism that went into the war of liberation, then, was injected for the most part by the small group of statesmen who were responsible for the national appeals to which a larger section of the German society then responded. The policies of the leaders gave a political form to the mixture of monarchical loyalty, national patriotism, and general moral convictions characteristic of the community-at-large. For they were not entirely isolated from the German society upon which they acted. The connection between them and it was embodied in a diffuse group of intellectuals who, during the years immediately preceding the war of liberation, were a kind of two-way channel of communication through whom a growing awareness of national values within the society was impressed upon the statesmen and the statesmen's readiness to apply these values politically was communicated back to the society.

Intellectual nationalism, before the government spokesmen seized upon it, was essentially non-political. Even after 1806, when the termination of the Empire, the ubiquitous presence of the French, the Austrian war of 1809, and the Prussian resurgence brought political overtones to the expression of national consciousness in German literature, this literature remained culturally-oriented and politically colorless. In all parts of Germany the pride in German academic research, philosophy, arts, and letters which had been growing since the 17th century assumed first the defense of the national contributions to western culture in these fields against the French version of cosmopolitanism, and then turned to the idea of a national political defense of these contributions when the French, with their cultural claims, became a political factor in the country. But despite this measure of politicization the intellectuals' idea of a German political unity was both subordinated to and infiltrated by the blend of national and universal cultural values, and because they reacted against the politics of the French Revolution from an essentially cultural point of view their own national politics had no definite direction and brought forth a nationalism that was as often conservative as liberal in its implications.[6] These qualities were common to that complex of classical idealism and romanticism which made up the dominant intellectual tendency of the age.[7] Both movements shared the development from an unbridled, unpolitical individualism through the extension of the idea of individuality in an organic national super-person to the intimation of an ideal political form for this national unit which would serve a religious or cultural universal cause and somehow harmonize the frictions arising from the unavoidable encounter of the individualized spirit with the collective political reality.

One form which this development took was the inclination to glorify the ideal of a purified, revitalized German Empire, with both its old universal and its new national connotations.[8] Friedrich Schlegel's nationalism developed in step with the rooting of his originally anarchic individualism in religious and political authority. Although his exaltation of the German Empire represented a stride toward the national state beyond his former purely cultural conception of the nation, the result was to give a modern foundation to traditional Catholic universalism and a new fillip to political and social conservatism.[9] Similarly, the rise of a strong nationalistic motif in the Prussian theologian Friedrich Schleiermacher after the collapse of 1806-1807 was, from a political point of view, an attempt to rejuvenate the monarchical conservatism of German Protestant tradition. He would educate the individual to a free personality and endow him with a modicum of civil liberty, but he would then place him in a divinely ordained corporate state through the organic unity of the nation.[10] It is scarcely to be wondered at, then, that Schleiermacher's idea of patriotism was a flexible mold which stretched indeterminately from a Prussian to a German nationalism.[11] Heinrich von Kleist continued to serve an aesthetic and moral absolute even when he developed, after 1807, a politically oriented nationalism out of his search for a fitting relationship between the sovereign creative individual and the group to which he was necessarily attached. He went beyond most of his fellow writers in his addiction to patriotic pamphleteering, his plans for a national uprising, his delineation of a future German nation-state, and in his demand for individual freedom within this state, but in the last analysis his chief preoccupation with the society lay in the opportunity which it could provide for "the individual members of a nation to perfect culture as far as humanly possible," and alongside this preoccupation his political proposals were "meager." [12] Consequently, his interest in liberalizing politics was limited to establishing the external conditions for free cultural activity: he defined freedom as the voluntary love and trust which should cement society. He embodied these principles in the ideal of a nation which would sublimate both the social relationship of castes and the patriarchal relationships of monarch and subject into institutions of liberty.[13]

In but two intellectuals of stature—the philosopher J. G. Fichte and the publicist E. M. Arndt—did the new nationalism incorporate definite liberal tendencies, and consequently it was through these writers that the reciprocal influence between the politics of the Prussian reformers and the cultural nationalism awakening within sections of the German society was directly expressed. Like most of the reforming statesmen Fichte and Arndt were non-Prussians who ultimately attached themselves to the Prussian state, but unlike most of the reformers they came out of the unprivileged social orders.[14] Hence they brought to political thinking and to national consciousness the egalitarian element which was to serve as a prime link between the two.

Fichte's development affords a striking case-study of the function performed by nationalism in the liberal intellectual who sought to adapt his political ideas to German conditions. It grew gradually, in direct connection with his step-by-step attempt to evolve the doctrine of a strong state out of an original radical individualism.[15] Fichte sought to begin where Kant stopped, not only in a general philosophical sense by asserting the free creativity of the ego in the sensory as well as the moral realm, but also in a political sense by dealing directly with the problem of the just constitution and the realization of freedom for men in society.[16] In his last formal political works, moreover—the *System of Jurisprudence* of 1812 and the *Political Theory* of 1813—these were still his ultimate aims.[17] But this nominal fidelity to the liberal ideal served only to underline the remarkable changes in its context which intervened between the initial and the terminal points in the development of Fichte's political system, for in the interim an appreciation of power in the state and of value in the nation were associated with the ultimate libertarian goal and profoundly altered its meaning.

Fichte's earliest political writings[18] were aggressively individualistic. In them the typical German intellectual approach of segregating the superior realm of spirit from the antipathetic sphere of politics was combined with the contractual doctrine of natural law to form a political theory which severely delimited the scope of the state by a broad definition of the sacred rights of man. To be sure, a large dose of German tradition remained a component of this theory. Hovering over it, in the background, was the philosophical concept of an integral world of spirit which, as the abode of the transcendental ego in its undifferentiated totality, supplied the universal forms and values binding upon all real individuals. The destiny of these real individuals was essentially the moral one of approaching this world by working for their own "perfection," so that politically "worthiness of freedom must come from below up, but liberation can, without disorder, only come from above down";[19] the primary right of man, the guarantor of human progress for which all other civil rights could be sacrificed, was freedom of thought, "this celestial palladium of humanity." [20] But the context in which Fichte set these old ideas transformed them into a liberal doctrine. He relegated the

philosophical concept of transcendental totality wholly to the
background and emphasized the necessity of its self-conscious
realization by the real individual egos into which the transcendental ego was differentiated within the world of sense. The supreme freedom of individual men to work for their own moral
perfection not only characterized the realm of spirit but involved
"culture toward freedom" in the sense of creative activity upon
the external world to bring it into conformity with the requirements of moral spirit.[21] If the basic inalienable right of men
was derived directly from this a priori unrestricted freedom to
obey the moral law, this freedom founded inalienable rights in
the realm of sense as well as spirit, and it even dictated that the
sphere of alienable rights, which included all other aspects of
human activity, remain subject to the "free choice (*Willkuer*)"
of individuals, that such rights might indeed be partially alienated but never totally or irrevocably, and that individuals never
lose the opportunity to apply them in the service of the inalienable rights with which they were integrally connected.[22] Thus
did Fichte extend the scope of the inalienable rights inviolable
by the state from the freedom of thought obviously necessary for
the spiritual basis of moral perfectibility to its unrestricted
physical communication[23] and even to the rights of private property and of amending or seceding from the civil polity.[24] This
aggressive doctrine of natural rights, in conjunction with Fichte's
characterization of all monarchical states as tending toward "unlimited and exclusive domination in internal policy and universal
monarchy in foreign policy," [25] gave the theoretical foundation for
his passionate anti-absolutism which was so emphatically negative
in its approach that the narrow positive function of the state—
the protection of the material rights of man—was given only
passing mention.[26]

But despite the logical pretensions and the dogmatic tone of
Fichte's argument it was essentially inconsistent and uncertain.
There was a discrepancy between the complexity of its elements
and the simplicity of its conclusions. Now, it is clear that at this
stage in his thought Fichte's primary motive in positing a theoretical separation between the inviolable sphere of the moral law
and the negotiable sphere of empirical free choice was to insure

the primacy of the former, but this duality was at the same time a device to account for the political institutions which were binding upon man, despite their dissonance with the liberal requirements of the moral law. Fichte's theory left entirely intact the structure of the existing absolutism: by withdrawing it from the field of the moral law he drastically curtailed the exercise of its power, but by basing it upon individual consent—i.e. empirical free choice—he validated it, within its due sphere, and made its existence compatible with the moral law.

Fichte at this time did not work out the distinctions in the dualistic foundations of his argument. His ability to blur them through his overwhelming emphasis upon the inalienable rights associated with the moral law was accountable to one basic—and as it turned out, temporary—assumption: real individuals are capable, by their own efforts, of regulating their thought and activity and so of creating a world which would realize morality; the sphere of the state, then, is rather unimportant.[27] Now it is certainly true that Fichte appeared even in these early writings to build a bridge between the moral and the political elements of his thought through his concept of society, which, like his later concept of the nation, he designed to be the intermediary between the free individual and the compulsory state. But his emphasis upon society as an association of free individuals placed it among the permanent ends of man and opposed it to the state which was only a subordinate means condemned to wither away in the course of time.[28] Society, like the sphere of man's alienable rights, was thus weighted toward the sanctity of the individual's pursuit of the moral law, but this overemphasis obscured rather than resolved the problem of justifying political authority in terms of freedom. For it gave only a verbal cover to the actual institutions which Fichte accepted: his recognition of functional —albeit unprivileged—estates,[29] his gratuitous anti-Semitism,[30] and his acknowledgement of an undivided monarchical constitution pointed up the duality which was to spur the development of his political ideas.

It can scarcely be surprising, then, that when, after the first flush of his reforming enthusiasm, Fichte organized his political views into a logical system, this implicit dualism emerged starkly.

In his *Foundations of Natural Law According to the Principles of Science* of 1796 and *The Closed Commercial State* of 1800 (which Fichte thought of as an "appendix" to the *Foundations*) he retained the inalienable rights of the individual soul and the indefinite liberal postulates for the individual's practical efficacy, but he developed the area of external alienable rights into a valid sphere for the broad activity of a strong authoritarian state. If in his initial period Fichte was guilty of distorting the elements of his own thought by overextending the claims of individual morality into the external world he now strained his ideas in an opposite direction by slighting the connection between the moral and the sensory worlds, and emerging with a theory quite in line with the traditional separation of a spiritual realm reserved to the individual and an actual realm surrendered to the state. Fichte was to enter into the first decade of the 19th century and the period of his nationalism with two partially contradictory and unresolved political systems, one based upon the inviolable requirements of individual morality and the other based upon the necessary material demands of the state.

Fichte began his *Foundations of Natural Law* with the autonomous requirements of the sensory realm, and save for his peroration he kept within this famework during the whole course of this work and its economic "appendix." He asserted unequivocally that the natural law, together with its derivative civil, family, and international law, "has nothing to do with the moral law," [31] and in conformity with this principle Fichte's entire deduction of the basic concepts of law and the associated ideas of individual rights and of the state was developed in the simple context of concrete rational beings active in the external world of sense without reference to their moral or spiritual nature and destiny.[32] Consistent with his earlier postulate Fichte started from the finite rational individual who by his very being is free, not in a moral sense but in the sense of his possession of an original free choice (*Willkuer*) which permitted the self-determination of his actions in the external world.[33] From this exclusively empirical point of view, however, the political realm took on a value very different indeed from his earlier depreciation of it. Fichte now drove his argument inexorably from the impossibility of isolated individual life through the insufficiency of apolitical social life until he finally found rest in the state as the primary unit of human organization in the sensory world.

To balance his initial assumption that the freedom of individual humans in the realm of sense was ultimately rooted in the moral authority of the transcendental ego, Fichte insisted that in this realm the idea of man was unthinkable save in society.[34] In conformity with this bipartite conception, Fichte on the one hand attributed only to individuals "the fundamental right (*Urrecht*) . . . to be . . . a cause in the sensory world," and he accorded it a valid role in political theory. On the other hand he declared that such a fundamental right was for political reality a mere "fiction" since only the mutually limiting rights of men in society could be actual.[35] What Fichte was trying to do in this complex initial argument was evidently this: to make an externalized, watered-down version of his moral individualism the fundamental normative principle of the sensory world but to prove at the same time that the operative principles in this world, while authorized by and oriented toward this individualistic norm, were themselves supra-individualistic relationships which were at once necessary and problematic for personal freedom.

But this procedure redounded to the benefit of the state rather than to purely social relationships. Society for Fichte now became a mere transitional stage between the individual and the state. Indeed society all but disintegrated under his pen between the sum of individuals that composed it and the state which it founded. It is true that Fichte attributed the fundamental proposition of natural law—everyone must limit his freedom so as to permit the freedom of others—to the social relationship as a community of free rational beings, but he immediately proceeded to show that the authority of this social relationship was merely "hypothetical"—that is, it could not be absolutely grounded in the nature of man.[36] The authority of the law, then, could not be derived from the society but depended upon the presence of a mutual trust and confidence in the reciprocal respect of freedom by the constituent individuals which could only be brought about through the voluntary transfer of their right to enforce such respect to a third party—that is, to the state.[37] Thus for Fichte, far from a free society grounding the natural law governing political relations, this law on the one hand was "deduced from the concept of the individual," [38] and on the other had itself to be actualized by the state in order to realize the hypothesis of the free society which was its authority. Fichte thought in terms of two kinds of rights, the fundamental right (*Urrecht*) and the compulsory right (*Zwangsrecht*) which enforced the observation of one's fundamental right by other men; the fundamental right pertained exclusively to individuals, the compulsory right was transferred entirely to the state, and society was thereby reduced to the status of a kind of matrix, setting the conditions for the activities of both individual and state and connecting them, but with little essential positive function of its own.[39] Hence the series of contracts which had been for Fichte in his earliest period purely social contracts were now all telescoped into sections of the civil contract, and the "common will" of society led but a momentary existence between Fichte's emphases upon the free self-determination of the individual wills that went into it and upon its embodiment in the state which ensued from it.[40] Once the state was formed the common will was represented as an operative force only in the sovereign ruler. The only rights outside the purview of the state were those of individuals,[41] while the common will of the society, as a party to the final contract, was entirely invested in the state and was thereby excluded, in the ordinary course of events, from the exercise of either non-political or political rights.[42] The political operations of society were exceptional: the sole agency of the community in the state was the "ephorate," an institution expressly denied any exercise of political or administrative power and designed to call upon society to reconstitute the state only upon the occasion of the governmental violation of the civil contract.[43]

It was not until Fichte came to the consideration of the state itself, that he reached what was for him the primary effective organ in the sensory world, and it was only at this point that the radical separation of the structure and functions of this organ from its individualistic and social bases became clear. Despite Fichte's dictum that the form of government must depend upon empirical circumstances rather than any pretended absolute scale of preference, the general qualifications which he required of the structure of all just governments emphasized the exclusive and unified concentration of governmental power in the sovereign, who was independent of both individuals and the community within his allotted sphere of competence.[44] Thus Fichte denied the possibility of the division of powers, and, characteristically for his insistence upon the autonomous forcefulness of government, he made legislation and judicature attributes of the overriding "executive power," which was synonymous with sovereignty.[45] The limitations upon this power lay, in Fichte's view, in the category not of structure but of function, for even the ephorate, the only public institution independent of the sovereign, existed outside of government and came into operation only when the state itself was called into question through the unconstitutional transgression of its functions. Fichte's general formulation of these functions seemed at first glance to adhere to the liberal doctrine of the severely limited state, for he summed them up in the familiar slogan of the protection of the rights of man.[46] But as he developed this slogan it took on an unwonted flexibility until it ended by conferring upon the state what amounted to full powers over the whole sensory realm of man's existence. In the course of this argument he redefined the concept of "protection" to mean a positive and active guarantee of security[47] by the state and the concept of "property"—used in the Lockean sense of the sensory summary of human rights—to mean the absolutely inalienable "right to live," also administrable by the state.[48]

Already embodied in his *Foundations of Natural Law*, these redefinitions became the basis for the all-embracing economic and social competence of the state in his *Closed Commercial State*, which must thus be considered continuous with this political theory. The right to live from one's labor is, according to Fichte, "the highest and general purpose of all free activity," the condition for the existence of the person and for his freedom; it is the individual's real purpose in the conclusion of the civil contract and consequently its positive protection is likewise the real purpose of the state, which "must set up institutions for it." [49] It is the state which first gives to man his property, and it is the state which thereafter protects him in it by licensing all economic activity and subjecting it and the social groupings formed around it to a strict control with the view to the equal distribution of all available means of subsistence among the individual citizens.[50] In this analysis Fichte's initially postulated sphere of individual rights apart from the state tended to disappear as such.[51] They became a part of the definition of the state through the stipulation that it direct its positive activity to the active securing of the individual's fundamental right to existence, and the only remnant of their original independence lay in the implicit authority which they furnished for holding the state to this definition. It was hardly surprising, then, that ultimately for Fichte not only did the state come to dominate the whole realm of external human relations, but he developed its efficacy right up to the borders of the moral world. Not only "does the state itself become the natural condition of man and its laws . . . realized natural law," [52] but the abstract association of individuals in society becomes in the state "a real whole, . . . a totality," which prepares individuals in the sensory world for participation in the absolute moral totality of humanity.[53] Only in an indefinite sphere connected with morality and outside the state, do individuals retain their freedom.[54] In its applied form, this principle meant the distinction between the material activities of men, which were subject to control by the state, and the spiritual activities of the arts and sciences, which were left to individual freedom.[55] But this division of function violated Fichte's original demand for a genuine integration of the external world into the moral lives of individuals. In his effort to set up the supremacy of the state in the sensory world, he had drawn it so far from individual morality that he neglected or refused to work out the relationship between them. He referred to the moral educative function of the state, but he did not develop the point at this stage. Indeed, his reluctance to face the implications of synthesizing the two realms was such that on one occasion he withdrew from his position that the state was a real totality and characterized it as "nothing but an abstract concept," while "only the citizens are real persons." [56]

The illumination which Fichte sheds upon the political function of German nationalism appears here. It was at this very
point, where the attempt to justify both the fact of the authoritarian state and the value of individual freedom by defining each
in terms of the other threatened to founder on the practical need
to procure a political channel for men's free energies, that the
idea of the nation, as a real value and a possible fact, was given
the political status of mediating between the two polar principles.
For Fichte's first serious reference to nationalism came toward
the close of his *Closed Commercial State*,[57] in the very context
of his distinction between free spiritual and controlled material
activity. It was only a brief reference, a foreshadowing of future
possibilities, but in his indication that the state, through a rigid
system of economic and social control, would create the conditions for the rise of a genuine nation and "a sharply defined
national character" which would ultimately make such control
superfluous, Fichte gave a first hint of the synthetic role of
nationalism.

In the years between 1800 and 1807 Fichte's basic assumptions
underwent a reorientation as he struggled to account for the gulf
between the moral and sensory worlds, to work out the relationship between them, and to lay the groundwork for their reunion.
This general development prepared the way for and revealed the
function of the national idea in his thinking, for as the shift in
the philosophical bases progressed so did the early external
adjunct of nationalism gradually strike stronger roots into his
system.[58] The reorientation followed two interrelated lines. In
the first place, reinforced by a growing religiosity, the transcendental character of Fichte's idealism became intensified in a
way that stressed not only the totality of being in the moral
world but also its immediate immanence as totality in the world
of sense, thereby casting into the background the earlier emphasis
upon the sensory differentiation of the moral totality into individual persons. Secondly, he came increasingly to characterize the
contemporary scene as the dominion of a materialistic, selfish,
and anarchic individualism which was indeed a stage in the
world-plan of history, but in which nonetheless man's arbitrary
emphasis upon his exclusive individuality cut him off from the

moral order now possible of realization.[59] Together, these emphases provided the foundation for the direct embodiment of the moral unity in supra-personal institutions of this world, which were endowed with the fundamental authority to coerce individuals not merely toward their moral freedom but in the name of moral freedom itself. In his transitional essays, *Patriotism and its Opposite* (1806) and *On Machiavelli as a Writer* (early 1807), Fichte haltingly groped his way toward the political application of his revamped approach. Although his ideas were far from ordered and his nationalism far from developed, the tendencies of this application were already visible. The former claims of both individual and state receded in the face of a new prominence of the nation as the this-worldly embodiment of moral totality. Moreover, the emphasis upon the unity of the nation tipped the balance of individual and state within the nation slightly but unmistakably in favor of the state.

Fichte asserted that for political purposes individuals must be assumed to be essentially evil and that while the principles of the rights of man must be observed they are not sufficient for the establishment or the administration of states.[60] Nor did he find the state's own claims to obedience to be adequate in themselves; he insisted that the pretensions of the state to an exclusive loyalty *vis-à-vis* the nation were "artificial," since the state merely provided the sphere of "efficacy" in which the individual could work for the fundamental values of his nation (and thereby for humanity).[61] Thus individuals and governments are bound to each other and reciprocally limited only through their mutual participation in the supreme good of the nation.[62] But then Fichte proceeded to attribute the primary responsibility for the realization of national values in general to the state and in particular to the reigning prince: "his nation's whole destiny in the eternal counsels of the Divine has been placed in his hands." [63] Moreover, the divine sanction of the nation directs the citizen's concern to the order and security of his state[64] and authorizes the external expansion of the state.[65]

But it was not until the extension of French power after Jena provided the impulse to integrate state and individual under a larger conception of freedom that Fichte's *Addresses to the Ger-*

man Nation of 1807-1808 raised nationalism to its predominant role in his political system. Fichte started with the point which he had intimated previously—that the direct bonds between individuals and states were too weak to hold them together and that they must be transformed into the total commitment to a national whole which included both[66]—but now he anchored this position in his philosophy and developed its implications. The primary metaphysical and moral reality which underlay this world of appearances and which could alone support the permanent bonds of the social order embodied itself most immediately neither in the individual nor in the state but in the nation. Fichte emphasized that this primary reality was a divinely unified totality of being; while it was still differentiated on earth into finite individuals this manifestation was now only indirect and subordinate to the immediate embodiment of the metaphysical moral totality in an earthly moral totality.[67]

Thus Fichte no longer defined freedom in individual terms, as a necessary postulate of the individual's activity, but now distinguished between a "lower" and a "higher" sense of freedom, declaring that despite the possession of free choice, i.e. its lower sense, the individual was free in the higher sense only if he conformed to the true divine being.[68] The absolute still appeared in the essence of each individual, but its seat was now in a being also extending beyond him rather than in the law within him. Now Fichte's individual had to undergo not simply a social cultivation of his finite nature which would permit him to raise himself to moral freedom, but he was to be educated from without to "pure morality" itself, a moral education which would "completely destroy the freedom of the will and produce strict necessity of decisions . . . in the will." [69] But the state in itself cannot furnish the authority for such an education, for its functions are derived from a "mere clear concept" and despite the inclusion of the maintenance of "the personal freedom, life, and well-being of all" as well as the protection of property in its ordinary purposes, this concept has in itself no contact with the moral force fundamental to life.[70] Not only must the self-conscious nation be at the basis of the "perfect state" [71] but unless the state is "only the means, condition, and tool" of the external purpose of the nation, unless patriotism "rules the state itself as its highest, final, and independent authority," both the government's "rights of sovereignty" and indeed the actual substance of genuine governing are lacking.[72] Thus the relationship of individuals and of states to fundamental reality and thereby to each other can be consummated only through the nation. The nation, as *the* earthly embodiment of the eternal,[73] is the form of human society which comprehends and establishes the order of both. The individual is integrated into the nation by the dependence of his own seed of eternal moral being upon the national totality of eternal moral being,[74] and the state is encompassed by the nation by receiving the fundamental sanction and direction of its power therefrom. Politically, this meant for Fichte an integration of individual and state in which the nation secured to the individual his only real guarantee of liberty in the state.[75] At the same time, by virtue of its natural encompassment and moral tutelage of individuals, the nation directed the state toward liberal policies and enhanced its competence to compel the realization of moral freedom.[76]

The basis for this solidarity of princely governments and peoples in the authoritarian state lay not only in Fichte's idea of the internal spiritual synthesis worked by nationalism, but also in his idea that princely and popular freedom were externally and practically united when they asserted the national freedom against the foreigner. It was thus under the pressure of the French occupation that national independence seemed to reconcile the liberties of individuals with the authority of native governments. The prime quality of the nation was, for Fichte, its particularity, and its prime practical requirement was that it remain free from "intrusion and corruption by anything alien." [77] Against the context of this external practical emphasis the domestic implications of Fichte's nationalism receded into a spiritual realm, redefining the relationship between individuals and government in terms of a reorientation of attitude which bred creative loyalty on the one side and the official dedication to moral liberty on the other. So spiritual, indeed, was Fichte's internal nationalism that far from demanding its investment in a German nation-state he felt it to be perfectly compatible with the existing particularistic state-system, which he not only accepted but praised as a basis for German patriotism.[78] At the root of this astonishing judgment lay the key to the fundamental historical function which political nationalism fulfilled in Germany during the first two decades of the 19th century. Fichte exalted particularism to the status of a German "republican constitution," [79] and he characterized the particular states as bearers of liberty, competing fruitfully in the dispensation of freedom within the framework and for the service of the nation.[80] This hearkening back to the formulas of the *ancien regime* betrayed the political function of Fichte's nationalism to be the rejuvenation of the traditional association between the traditional liberty of subjects and the power of princes. Nationalism replaced the defunct Empire as the frame of reference for this association, and it rooted the connection in the new age by making emphatic what had only been implicit in the Imperial confederation of sovereign authorities— the inclusion of the free individual citizen and his values in the nationally sanctioned claim of the state to be the highest earthly organ of human freedom.

When Fichte came in his last years to reformulate his systematic political theory[81] he continued to make the individual's moral freedom and derivative civil rights his points of departure and of terminus,[82] but now he utilized the idea of the nation as the means to merge individual rights into an organic conception of the "rights of all" [83] and thence into the state.[84] Moreover, he could now frankly uncover the corollaries of this state which was authoritarian in the very name of liberty. He denied the validity of natural law outside the state.[85] He recognized the law of the state as the necessary condition for morality.[86] He attributed to the state not only its negative compulsory rights against unjust acts but a positive compulsory right to educate its citizens to moral freedom.[87] He assigned this power to a single sovereign authority in the state.[88] Fichte explicitly avowed that the union of spirit and nature in the state itself leaves the society with no need for the actual institution of an ephorate,[89] leaves the individual with no inalienable rights save that of the attitude which he brings to his necessary obedience,[90] forbids popular political action against all existing constitutions and sovereigns,[91] and relegates political change to the intervention of Providence in the indefinite future.[92] And to fit his practice to his theory Fichte announced, in his final address, that the duty of the moral individual to withdraw himself from an immoral world and to work spiritually upon it was cancelled only when government initiated the struggle for national freedom. He announced his own intention of descending into the political arena to contribute his moral force to the national effort of the Prussian government against the alien oppressor.[93]

As Fichte represented the liberal intellectual who was politicized, under the auspices of nationalism, in a conservative direction Arndt provided the complementary embodiment of essentially conservative tendencies for which nationalism opened the way to a moderate political liberalism. Only this combination uncovers the full implications of the synthetic function of nationalism, as the mediator at once between the ideal and the actual and between the individual and the political powers, in the liberation period: it harnessed the unpolitical spiritual tradition, as typified in Fichte, to the existing political system in the name of liberty and it vitalized the historically-grounded acceptance of a German cultural nationality and its attendant political system, as typified in Arndt, with an individualistic ideal in the name of order. This role of nationalism as a common denominator which linked the desire for real roots in the concrete present with revolutionary aspirations by providing a larger framework as the meeting-point between the two goes a long way toward explaining its cohesive force in the German liberal movement.

An heir of Moeser and Herder, Arndt stood in the geneology of that line of the German intellectual tradition which rejected conceptual for immediate reality, asserted the existence and the value of a German cultural nationality as a concrete historical fact, and accepted, implicitly or explicitly, the fundamental structure of the political order in which it had historically expressed itself. But into this tradition, which actually occupied a middle ground between the ultimate individualism which it intentionally eschewed and the concrete reality which it unintentionally skirted, Arndt fed elements from both extremes: the current ideal of humanitarian individualism on the one hand and an "earthy," practical, activistic appreciation of and demand for the political realization of the cultural nation on the other.[94] Thus Arndt simultaneously introduced a liberal goal and a potential national benediction of established political authority,[95] and it was this expansion of the older cultural tradition in both of these opposite directions that endowed the new political nationalism with its internal vagueness and its magnetic power.

In Arndt the nation was the starting-point rather than the resultant of his development,[96] and the political ideas which he founded upon it had the strength and the incoherence of immediately felt convictions rather than the rigor of a logical system. For him the nation was at once the basic reality and the agent of the supreme values upon earth, the sole unit of human life which gave it meaning. Deeply concerned by the "apparent" dualities between heaven and earth, spirit and actuality, freedom and necessity, unity and diversity, Arndt found in the nation the real unity of these forces in man.[97] Only in the nation did that synthesis of heaven and earth take place which embodied meaningful unity in human history and independence in human action while not violating the vitality of manifold nature.[98] The nation, then, is the expression of God in the world of time,[99] and "to be a nation, to have one feeling for one cause; to come together with the bloody sword of revenge, is the religion of our times." [100] Thus the nation represents the highest earthy sanction, but it has such an authority in the name of freedom.[101] It legitimizes both the freedom of individuals and the authority of states, and it reigns supreme over them. On the one hand Arndt signified the foundation of the nation upon the mass of its constituent individuals by his constant use of the term "people (*Volk*)" as its synonym, by his insistence that the realization of national values depended upon the free activity of moral individuals,[102] and by his acknowledgement that the ultimate goal was "a higher humanity" for all individuals.[103] On the other hand, however, he emphasized not only that to be a "free citizen" of a nation was a necessary condition to becoming a "free man" [104] but even that "the individual man, the individual deed and event, however extraordinary and sensational they may be, are nothing and produce nothing—the link should move in the chain, the man with his activity should integrate himself into the long series of generations." [105]

But however clear Arndt's conviction was that the dualistic form taken by the fundamental forces of the world necessitated the embodiment of the individual's values in the saving unity of the supra-personal nation, what remained uncertain in this circular relationship between individual and nation was the problem of which was to realize which. Here Arndt inserted his ideas on the state to resolve this uncertainty and therewith transplanted the problem into the sphere of politics. On the one hand hand he accepted established political authority without question,[106] assigning to it the function of creating free citizens for the nation and promising intensified loyalty and obedience from this creation.[107] On the other hand, however, Arndt cast even this apparently stable fulcrum of his political thinking into uncertainty when he identified the divine right of rulers with a fundamental "law of politics" which made the maintenance of the nation the basis of their sovereignty,[108] which made the princes "everything through the nation and . . . nothing without the nation," [109] and which, in the event of the princes' defection from this duty, appealed to the conscious members of the nation as the "kings and heroes," the bearers of the "invisible majesty" of the nation, for the fulfilment of this function.[110] Indeed, Arndt himself admitted that the ideas of "state, people, freedom, nation," constituted a "divine circle." [111] His political solution of the problem, which thus threatened an infinite regress, was twofold. First, the steady purpose of his political thinking was ever the destruction of the French oppression, and this then became the constant *point d'appui* permitting an external definition of liberty in terms of the free nation in which individuals and governments were alike comprehended.[112] Secondly, Arndt sought to synthesize internal freedom and authority in a project for a German national state in which the inclusive unity of the nation founded an expanded political order allowing room equally for legitimate monarchical rule, political and social hierarchy, and popular liberty.[113]

Arndt's peculiar combination of severe stricture upon princely absolutism and aristocratic privilege on the one side[114] and his equally passionate disavowal of radical or revolutionary intent upon the other[115] corresponded precisely to the natural structure of his political nationalism in which "the old" should be "shaped into the form of the new spirit" [116] and should "embody itself and dissolve itself in it." [117] "Therefore be armed," he admonished the Germans, "not to disobedience against the princes but to obedience toward the nation." [118]

Arndt had, in this period before the experiences of the war of liberation itself, no definite scheme for the German constitution which would satisfy these requirements,[119] but he did indicate certain general lines of preference which revealed the political implications of his thinking. Traditional political authority should be guaranteed by the investment of German sovereignty in the hereditary Emperorship of the House of Hapsburg and by the support to be vouchsafed the Emperor in the attribution of hegemony over nothern Germany to the Prussian Hohenzollerns.[120] Civic liberty should be guaranteed by the institution of representation from the people organized as estates.[121] These two elements would themselves be bound together on the side of the sovereign through his limitation by the nation which constituted the basis of his power and on the side of the people through the deliberate foundation of their political representation upon one-sided, functional, corporate interests which were to find unity only in the sovereign. General liberty was to be guaranteed not by the possession of political power, but by the freedom of the press and by the harmony between sovereign and people which would be vested in the political and social hierarchy between them.[122] This was to stretch from the larger ex-princes, who would be at once princes of the blood and peers of the Empire and would "represent at the same time the majesty of the Emperor and of the people," [123] through the smaller Imperial princes and lords and the larger territorial nobility whose claim to aristocracy would be based upon property and who would form "a kind of advisory body or upper house within the people," [124] to the younger sons of this new nobility and the less-landed members of the old who would join "the middle class of the people." [125]

Thus did Arndt strive with the measure of his nationalism to rework the German political tradition along the lines of the liberal requirements of his age. He adhered to the idea of intellectual freedom as "the palladium" of human rights and to it he added a new version of the old German *Libertaet,* which had associated the particular states with the assertion of specific liberties. Rejecting now the old forms which attributed to all the princes equal parts of sovereignty and aristocratic rights within a politically abstract Empire,[126] he looked to the larger framework of a real national Empire which would permit a division of function between the two greatest princes who would possess sovereignty and the rest to whom would redound the aristocratic protection of the freedom of the society. Such an Empire could afford a representative constitution which would both stimulate and harness the popular energies of the nation.

Liberation Nationalism

Intellectuals like Fichte and Arndt articulated the national feeling that was being forced to consciousness by external duress in the German society, but they represented too its reference of political initiative to governments. As a real political factor rather than a half-conscious welter of emotions or the shape of an ethical ideal, German nationalism originated in the minds and measures of high public officials. Since the moderate implications of the popular nationalism corresponded to the needs and desires of the liberal aristocrats in the bureaucracy, it is hardly surprising to find that the governmental proponents of the new political nationalism found their chief spokesmen in members of the reform party who occupied the upper administrative echelons of the Prussian state. Stein, Gneisenau, Clausewitz, Scharnhorst and Boyen—those familiar figures were primarily responsible for the official appeals and policies that focused national consciousness into a political force. Like the unofficial nationalists, the political nationalism of these leaders was a gradual growth, becoming emphatically and consciously political only after 1807, when the hostility to the French inspired the national *deus ex machina* which seemed to solve their problem of combining a measure of popular freedom with the structure of the traditional state. But the statesmen were forced beyond the politically un-crystallized nationalism of the society at large by urgent practical problems weighing upon states that were competing in the advanced western community of nations. The physical and moral inadequacy of a particularistic liberalism for the fight against Napoleon drove a group of the Prussian reformers to formulate their policies on a national basis, where their requirements for a state that would produce the maximum of material and spiritual power by harmoniously balancing the unity of monarchical direction and the dynamism of popular liberty seemed to find satisfaction.

This development of an official nationalism out of the concrete needs of the state was demonstrated by the central role which army men took in the movement. The military necessity to consider the totality of actual and potential forces in the state drove them beyond their specific occupational concerns to general considerations of power which opened the way from the state to the nation. These men indeed remained ever tied to the undeveloped assumptions of their 18th-century background, which juxtaposed a political orientation to the particular German states with a moral orientation to humanity at large, and they never worked them into a synthesis on the intermediate grounds of the self-conscious nation.[127] All the more striking, then, were the accomplishments which they did make, from the unguided interplay of their assumptions and their practical requirements, in this direction: first, they raised their measures and plans from the level of reforming military policy within the existing structure of the Prussian state to the level of fundamental political reforms which would permit participation of the Prussian nation in the state; and secondly, they pushed a short distance beyond this to indicate, however unclearly, the comprehension of the Prussian in a German political nationalism.

The gradual progress from purely military to social to political ideas of reform which has been remarked for Gneisenau[128] was characteristic of the whole military group. The collapse of the Prussian army at Jena in 1806 stimulated the formulation of general principles of military reform and the perception of the social postulates of these principles, but not until members of the military group began during 1808 to think in terms of a liberating war and to ponder the implications of nationalism did their planning begin to lose its specialized administrative character and take on a general political scope. Between 1806 and 1808 the primary motive of the army reformers was to rebuild the Prussian army under conditions which excluded foreign recruitment and which demanded the greatest possible strategical mobility and concentration of fire-power.[129] This aim had as its social corollary the desideratum that personal dignity, individual initiative, and leadership by ability be sponsored within the army so as to tighten its bonds and activate its loyalty to the country as a whole.

The reforms of this era, which stressed changes in army organization, arms, and training, the rationalization of channels of command, the emphasis upon honor as the canon of military discipline, and the introduction of procedures to favor promotion by merit, did not go beyond these military concerns. Even the policy of unversal conscription, which was ultimately to lead military into political considerations, was not clearly formulated until 1808, and even then only under the exigency imposed by Napoleon's prohibition of a Prussian militia.[130] Behind this concentration upon limited military problems was the restriction of the military reformers' purpose at this time to the integration of specific new elements into a completely accepted political structure. They wanted simply to call forth new movement and force in the social connections that supported the traditional political institutions. Gneisenau's envious analysis in 1807 of the achievements of the French Revolution was oriented toward the military power created by its social changes, and his aim was to convince the old states of the necessity of similar reforms if they were to maintain their international and internal integrity.[131] Even more striking for the narrow political assumptions of the military reform party before 1808 was Clausewitz' celebration of German individualism and freedom, not in connection with human persons, but rather in the traditional style of associating these values with the variety and independence of the particular states *vis-à-vis* an Imperial government.[132]

Only the challenge of an imminent war and the inherent order of an organic nationalism carried a group of the military reform party beyond the established political framework into projects for political change. The political function of their nationalism was spelled out in their emphasis upon a Prussian rather than a German nationalism as the aegis under which they conceived their military and constitutional reforms from 1808 to 1814. They viewed the Prussian nation as the social organization of citizens upon which the state rested, and they recommended that it be summoned by the royal government to constitutional participation in the state. This recognition of the ultimate dependence of the strength of the state upon the forces of its citizenry was the point of union between their military and their political planning, for with their idea that the army must be strengthened by an intimate relationship with the civil society, taking from it the virtues of civic freedom and in turn penetrating the society with disciplinary and sacrificial virtues, they were led from martial to constitutional policies. But if this genesis of the general political projects of the military reformers explains their liberal character it also indicates their limitations. They thought of the Prussian society in the form of a nation, because this form implied for them the recognition of a public role for the free activity of the individual citizen, but only within the framework of a natural organization headed and controlled by the established sovereign.

This implication in their definition of the nation was clearly revealed in the extreme case of Clausewitz. He was an emphatic advocate of the *levee en masse* but he denied that a constitutional reform was required or even immediately advisable for it.[133] He declared that the whole people must participate militarily in the state for their freedom,[134] but he then insisted that "the honor of the king and the government is one with the honor of the people and the only palladium of its good," [135] since the king represents not only "the moral person of the state but the nationality of the whole people." [136] Consequently, his view was that the people were capable of asserting their freedom within the internal order against an external enemy, but that they must be led to it and even rigorously compelled to it by the constituted government, which as representative of the nation must "force the people so to act and so to be as it thinks wise." [137]

The main body of the military reform party did not indeed go so far in this direction. Gneisenau's memoranda in the summer of 1808, urging the king to wage war against Napoleon with the support of a popular uprising, coupled with it the grant of "a free constitution" which would include municipal self-government and a national assembly of "all Estates" with financial powers, on the ground that "it is both fair and shrewd for the people to be given a Fatherland if they are to defend a Fatherland powerfully." [138] Moreover, in October 1808 the bulk of the military patriots, including Scharnhorst, Gneisenau, Boyen, and Grolmann, submitted a joint petition urging as an alternative to the royal ratification of the Prussian convention with Napoleon the convocation of a Prussian national assembly of all estates, the submission of the French demands to it, and Prussian leadership of the inevitable subsequent national uprising against the French. The memorandum even warned that the insurrection would take place without the king and would turn against him if he did not take the initiative.[139] Yet these constitutionalists among the patriots fundamentally shared with Clausewitz the idea that the king was the natural head of the nation and that the civic participation of the nation should take place in a political hierarchy, whose traditional form should be modified only to the extent required by its extension to include the entire nation. In the joint memorandum the patriots expressed their conviction that it was infinitely desirable that the whole nation should have a single cause with its head and emphasized the tactical importance of a Prussian national assembly as permitting a delay which the king could use in his conduct of policy.[140] Even the comparatively radical Gneisenau endorsed this view, arguing that "a good constitution, coming from the throne and envied by other peoples, will increase the loyalty to the king, and neither ambition nor egoism can fight against a government which makes its aim the prosperity, enlightenment, morality, and civic freedom of the nation." [141] The same quality of fitting popular institutions into the pre-existing structure defined the reformers' later military legislation which set up universal military service in Prussia.[142] Indeed, here the integration was literal, weaving together the royal instrument of the standing army, the national guard (*Landwehr*) based upon the estates, and the local militia (*Landsturm*) based upon democratic election.[143] When this integration was formalized in the definitive army law of 1814, the standing army, recruited by conscription for three years of active service and two years in the reserve, was characterized as the core of the whole armed force and the school of all the martial institutions of the nation; the national guard was divided into two levies, each for seven years' service, for the precise purpose of permitting one to be absorbed into the field army under regular army officers during war-time while the second maintained its local officers and the visible connection of army and nation; the militia, comprehending the mass of the nation who had either aged out of military training or had never been submitted to it, was now vouchsafed the symbolic status of a vague existence, officially unconfirmed and unorganized.[144]

But if a man like Boyen was entirely content with this kind of Prussian patriotism, and if Scharnhorst scarcely ventured beyond it in any articulate way, Gneisenau and Clausewitz clearly felt its insufficiency and gave indication that it must ultimately be referred to a German nationalism as its fount. In Clausewitz, with his disinclination toward discussion of political reform, this tendency took the overt shape of a confused attribution of the concept and values of the "nation" to both Germany and Prussia, but implicit in this lack of discrimination was a habitual assignment of the fundamental values of cultural nationality to Germany and the operative values of political nationality to Prussia. Germany thus became the repository of the strength which the Prussian king should seek in his people and the seat of values for which the Prussian people should fight.[145] In Gneisenau this relationship took a more explicitly political form. For him too the Prussian state furnished the political framework essential to the civil vitalization of the nation, but he could not find in the Prussian nation an adequately firm foundation for the union of king and people. Hence he went beyond it to the idea of a German nation which would become a political reality by attaching itself to Prussia. Starting with the practical aim of attracting as many forces as possible to the Prussian standard for the projected war against France, Gneisenau went beyond the proposal for a Prussian constitution that would bring a popular interest and contribution in the struggle, and he advanced the project of appealing to the German nation, through this constitution, for political union with the Prussian state.[146] In coincidence with his practical requirements, Gneisenau found in the German nation the ultimate ground for his constitutional plans. Adopting the principle that the German nationality was the sacred fount of freedom in its political as well as its spiritual aspects[147] and, concentrating his political radicalism upon this nation, he demanded that the German princes who oppose the war of liberation be deposed and that "their subjects elect more worthy rulers in their stead." [148] Thus he made of Germany an absolute source for the popular principle which must be added to the Prussian state as the permanent and harmonious counterweight to its monarchical and martial authority.

It was, however, in Stein, who remained close to the military group and supplied much of its political inspiration, that the nationalist development of the reforming statesmen was most articulately spelled out. During his last months in office he tended to combine a rising animus against Napoleon with an increasing insistence on a representative constitution for Prussia, and after November 1808, when he was forced from office and into exile, his obsession with the overthrow of the French system led the liberal bureaucrat beyond this particularistic constitutional planning into the broader arena of the liberal nationalist. The constant backdrop to this growth was his characterization of the Napoleonic domination as destructive at once of the European state-system and of individual freedom, and consequently he saw in an integral union of rulers and peoples the natural alliance for the defense of an ordered moral liberty, which he deemed the fundamental quality of the age, against the common foe.[149] At first he sought to realize this end by reiterating his demand for a Prussian constitution, which he now openly connected with the policy of *levee en masse* and total war against the French.[150] But he soon came to realize that the Prussian government would not grant such a constitution or embark upon such a policy[151] any more than the smaller princes would,[152] and that the people would not realize true moral freedom, i.e. national independence, without "the Richelieu policy" by which governmental authority would not only educate but compel this "barbarized, unbridled nation" to preserve their state and thereby to return to "more liberal principles." [153]

Confronted by this stalemate on the level of the particular state and abetted by the occupational demands of the posts which he occupied with the Austrian government in 1809 and the Russian government from 1812 to 1815, Stein raised the German national consciousness which had been growing within him since his departure from Prussia to the status of a primary political principle. Gradually but perceptibly his indiscriminate use of the terms "nation" and "fatherland" to refer both to the political organization of society within the particular states and to the general cultural and historical coherence of Germans shifted to the concentration of both meanings upon an imminent German nation-state.[154] He declared that the Napoleonic rule in Germany had dissolved the bonds between subjects and princes and that "thence arises the general wish for a constitution based on nationality, unity, and force, and any great man who would be capable of establishing it would be welcome to the nation, which turns away from the powers of mediocrity." [155]

This reliance upon a "great man," a role which he later assigned verbally to the Tsar and actually to himself, betrayed the political function of his nationalism. In the name of the nation, that was to be accomplished which could not be accomplished in the name of the particular states: a power was to be created above the existing relationships of governments and peoples which could dispose sovereignly of both, mixing the elements of traditional authority and popular participation in their due proportions and realizing the union of authoritative moral sanctions and libertarian ends characteristic of the national ideal.

In 1809 and again in 1812-14 Stein sought to use the power of the God of War himself as the required *deus ex machina*. He proposed a dictatorial occupation authority, governing in the name of the German nation, endowed with "a lawful basis and form" (on the earlier occasion as the agency of a new German confederation to be set up under a Hapsburg German Emperor and on the later as the agency of the Allied occupying powers), and using its supreme authority to control, reorganize, and replace governments for the purpose of achieving the greatest possible power and exploiting the greatest possible popular participation in the national war for German independence.[156] The neat balancing of political liberty for the society and independent political power for the traditional monarchical state which such a sovereign national authority made possible was apparent in Stein's combination of an appeal for a mass national uprising —even against the German princes, if need be—[157] and a policy of calling representative bodies to participate in legislation and its administration.[158] But he excepted the heads of the Austrian and Prussian states from overthrow;[159] he provided a place for them in the supreme occupying authority;[160] and he rejected a spontaneous national revolution in favor of an officially sanctioned, controlled, and compelled popular movement.[161]

The Central Administrative Council which was created after the outbreak of the war in 1812, with Stein as its moving force, failed to assume the national political prerogatives he had planned for it, for the legitimate Allied governments represented in the Council proved to be solidary with the German princes. As if in compensation for this setback, Stein then turned increasingly to developing his principles for a permanent German settlement into detailed projects for a German constitution. And with this shift the pattern of his policy changed. Whereas he originally thought in terms of a national structure which would be imposed from without and would overthrow the petty despotism of the particular princes, in favor of a union of national monarch and people,[162] he had now to think in terms of a federal constitution created by the consent of the princes. Accordingly, he transferred the guarantee of liberty from its absolute recognition in the nation-state to the older idea of a complex constitutional balance between rulers and representative estates within the particular German territories.[163]

Thus Stein was forced by the persistence of the historical

German state-system to spell out the implications of his policy. His final position in the liberation period acknowledged the condition of permanent conflict, irreconcilable in itself, between the principles of liberty and authority within the traditional states of Germany. A national political authority became the literal resolver of the dilemma. His late constitutional drafts and comments gave an unwonted emphasis to the freedom of person and property against the prince, to the large measure of legislative and administrative power to be granted the representative territorial estates independent of the prince, and to the probability of a running conflict both between the princes and their estates and between the princes and the liberties of the individual.[164] The task of resolving these conflicts and of protecting individual rights against the princes was vested in the national authority,[165] which now appeared in the traditional German dress of a governmental power at once independent of the individual citizens and yet by its very nature the agent of their liberties. Thus, as against his rigorous insistence upon constitutional guarantees of the political and civil rights of the subjects against the princely governments, Stein was at first indifferent whether the sweeping governmental powers of a German emperor should be exercised with or without a parliament.[166] When he had to adapt his plans to a federally-constituted national authority, with its princely influence, he then called for a German parliament endowed with legislative powers and representing the territorial estates as well as governments, but he explicitly based their necessity upon the federal nature of the constitution. He envisaged no sharp distinction of powers or possible opposition between the popular representation and the national executive run by the expanded Prussian and Austrian states.[167]

This development of Stein's, the man who more than any other single individual was responsible for the official national appeals to the German people during the war of liberation, furnished the first example of nationalism as a systematic policy of government and as a possible addition to the German tradition of the state. Liberal statesmen of the Stein school pursued a national policy as a higher synthesis of governmental authority and constitutional freedom which strengthened the power of the state and renewed its association with the liberty of the governed. Through new political devices they made fruitful contact during this period with those sections of German society—particularly its middle-class academic circles—which were ready for a freer activity on the public stage, on condition that they would be led to it.

The Response

The practical success of the national appeal made by the liberal German statesmen was reflected not only in the victories of the new mass armies but in the promulgation by a large proportion of the German middle-class intellectuals of a claim for popular participation in political power. In the widespread political pamphleteering of the period from 1813 to 1815 the great bulk of German political writers for the first time raised a common standard for constitutional guarantees of civil and political liberties, and if this standard was made up of diverse colors and fuzzy patterns the fact remains that as a whole they expressed the response of an important group in the German society to the official call for a greater popular contribution to the shaping of the nation's earthly destinies.[168] That the ideas of these articulate intellectuals manifested more than their own disembodied desires and ideals is clear from the accuracy with which in general they reflected the basic alignments in the existing situation. Their political nationalism was more implicit than self-conscious. They continued, even in their constitutional drafts, to attribute political initiative to the reigning sovereigns and worked their liberal and representative principles into the existing system. They held to the estate principle as the hierarchical basis of society and its political representation. In all this their ideas ran a course very similar to those of the official nationalists, and this general acceptance underlined the propriety and the force, in this liberation period, of the attitude which sought to renovate the old association of the German state-system with the ideal of liberty by reviving the constitutional structure of the German nation. In one major respect, however, the two groups diverged, and in this divergence lay the seeds of future liberal division. The difference characterized not their results but their starting points. Where the reformers had started before the war from the point of view of the states which had been the initial locus of liberal measures and which were to be strengthened by nationalization, the intellectuals began their political nationalism only during the war, from the point of view of "the people," whose response persuaded them of its political maturity and capacity for free constitutions.

The very vagueness[169] of the intellectuals' projects betrayed their embarkation from a newly accredited civil society which had accepted a place in the area of politics but which had not yet developed its own political direction. The middle-class intellectuals did not, during this period, carry ideas of liberal reform to the point of challenging the fundamentals of the existing system. They deemed the German populace ripe for a larger initiative in their civil existence and for some share in their political governance but not for a thoroughgoing regime of freedom and the opposition to the old powers which this involved. Not only was the political nationalism implicit in the common demand for some kind of effective German federation covered over by the tribute paid to German particularism and European balance of power but the domestic proposals were correspondingly conditioned by the requirement that liberal reforms be instituted in union with the governments and that they function so as to support rather than oppose the princes. Thus the prevalent concept of liberty placed it within rather than against the state and made the civil freedom of the individual simply a part and consequence of the larger external independence binding all elements of the state against foreign oppression. The emphasis in the discussion of the civil and political rights which should be granted to the citizens was upon their usefulness to the prince in increasing the power of the state.[170] Popular freedom and princely power were coupled as "internally bound concepts": not only was the possibility of a conflict between the prince and the representatives of the people usually not even considered but it was generally agreed that no earthly power, including the people, was above the prince.[171] Corresponding to this vague constitutional balance between new and old forces, the current ideas on the structure of society showed a similarly uncertain attempt to jam the new recognition of the common people into the old hierarchically ordered framework. The distinction between the political representation of society in parliaments, based upon the electoral voice of the individual citizen, and its expression in assemblies of estates based upon traditional or functional corporations, was scarcely made at all. The general tendency was to expand and loosen the old caste system by granting the right of political representation to all estates and to the bulk of the property-owners within each estate and by insisting that the deputies represent the whole community rather than their own estates, but still to retain the system.[172] This juxtaposition of popular rights and traditional institutions in both politics and society postulated the synthetic notion of the state as the ordering framework of these heterogeneous elements, and several of the pamphleteers during this period did refer to the state as the sovereign sanction of rights and duties incumbent upon both peoples and princes.[173]

The tacit assumptions on which the bulk of this pamphleteering was based were worked out more openly in the three figures whose writing wrestled explicitly with the impact of a populism born in the war of liberation upon the non-political or historical acceptance of the established order. Wilhelm von Humboldt, Arndt, and Josef Goerres—the aristocratic liberal, the plebeian Prussian patriot, and the middle-class west German progressive —represented the application of three different strands of the German intellectual tradition to this problem.

The emergence of "the people" as a focus of politics was most strikingly evident in Humboldt, who occupied a peculiar intermediate position between the official reformers and the intellectuals. The first stage in the anchorage of this uprooted aristocrat in political reality had been reached in 1809 with his reluctant acceptance of a policy-making post in the administration of the Prussian state, but it was the second stage of this attachment around the middle of 1813 that betokened an integral "conversion." [174] The force that broke through to work this conversion was not simply the convulsive experience of a national war but his impression of the sacred power of the people as the bulwark of the nation.[175] "There are only two good and beneficent potencies in the world, God and the people. That which lies in the middle is worth nothing and we ourselves have value only insofar as we place ourselves close to the people. . . . All force, all life, . . . all vitality of the nation can lie only in the people. But still more does one need, to act right and to avoid perverted action, its sense and its spirit." [176] This revelation stimulated Humboldt to transcend his former tacit acceptance of the existing state and to draft plan after plan for a politically unified German nation which would be a higher synthesis of state and people. For his recognition of the role of the people did not annul his previously formed commitments to the historical state and to an hierarchical order of society.

Prussia was now for him the concrete totality in which the people were incarnate,[177] and society was a stratified organic unit in which an aristocratic elite of cultured individuals and the mass of the people stood in intimate connection, the one giving direction and the other giving vital force, but each maintaining its respective position.[178] Humboldt institutionalized this union between the traditional state and society on the one hand and the newly validated function of the people on the other in a national constitution. Germany was "One Nation, One People, One State," by the authority of the natural order of things which made the nation the fundamental entity where "the individual who is nothing in himself and the species which has validity only in the individual"˙ met and penetrated each other and which made the state the guarantor of the national development in defending the nation against foreign oppression and in maintaining the dignity and "the spirit from which all internal blessings flow." [179] Starting from the two poles of state and people, Humboldt's constitutional design for Germany combined without integrating them. The upper reaches of his design were reserved exclusively to the existing states; the national government was to be a confederation of the particular sovereigns, led by the allied Austrian and Prussian monarchs as the basis of national power, including the lesser princes as the embodiment of traditional Germanic *Libertaet,* and excluding any kind of popular representation.[180] The lower reaches of the design were assigned to the people through the guarantee both of the inviolable personal and civil liberties of every individual *vis-à-vis* his prince and of the right of the people to participate through representative estates in the exercise of political power within the particular states.[181] The structure was held together only by the assumption that collective political power and individual freedom were merged in the nation, and consequently by basing the individual's rights upon his Germanhood [182] Humboldt expected the protection of them by the princely delegates assembled on the national level.[183] Humboldt was half-statesman and half-intellectual, and the loose joints in his constitutional edifice reflected the persistence of the duality between state and people in the liberation era.

Arndt, who had already exalted a normative idea of the people in the martial appeals which he had addressed to it, believed his ideal to have been realized by the popular participation in the war of liberation. He exaggerated this role, particularly in Prussia, into a rising of "the whole people," [184] which thereby "has become a real state," [185] and he attributed the Prussian military success primarily, among earthly things, to the "freedom of spirit" which had been conferred upon and utilized by the Prussian people.[186] The political consequence of this view was Arndt's emphasis upon a representative constitution for Germans,[187] based upon man's fundamental God-given right "to be ruled as noble and free men, that is, to help to rule ourselves." [188] Moreover, he now asserted that the French Revolution had produced many valid and useful ideas,[189] proposed a German parliament elected by the territorial representative assemblies which themselves were to have "the deliberative and co-governing power" in their states,[190] and boldly characterized his constitution as "democratic." [191] To be sure, in his distinction between democracy as "rule for and by the people" and ochlocracy as "rule by and with the mob" [192] he provided for the continued hierarchical order of the people in traditional estates replete with entails and guilds,[193] but still he insisted that man's secular emancipation from clerical tutelage was proof of the maturation

of society's capacity for freedom.[194] The state must now be constituted by public representation "from all classes of the inhabitants," and particularly from "the peasants and the burghers,
this greatest and most honorable part of every people," whose
participation must inevitably infect the other estates and give
a truly popular impress to the whole state.[195]

The development of Goerres' nationalism into a liberal constitutionalism under a distinctly populist inspiration during the
war of liberation was similar, but in him it had a particular importance. Not only did he exercise a powerful influence as
editor, and to a large extent author, of "the most celebrated
German newspaper of the 19th century," [196] the *Rhenish Mercury* (1814-1816), but he was the first non-Prussian—either by
origins or attachment—among the politically-minded liberal intellectuals to rise to national stature in Germany during this
first crowded decade and a half of the new century. The tendencies which he typified foreshadowed the jump which south-
western German liberalism was to have on the other regional
branches of the movement in the next generation. For although
Goerres went through the familiar cycle of pro-revolutionary
cosmopolitan republicanism, disillusionment, and the awakening
of cultural national consciousness he was not particularly struck
or politicized either by the collapse or the reform of the Prussian
state. He made his way to a conception of national politics directly through his growing appreciation of the German people.
This development reached its fruition in concrete political agitation only during 1814 with the experience of the popular
participation in the national war, but the mold into which this
experience was poured had already been prepared in his *Reflec-
tions on the Fall of Germany and its Rebirth,* written in 1810
at a revealing midway point in his evolution. This essay, which
marked Goerres' return to political problems after a decade of
preoccupation with the arts and sciences, dealt with postulates
on the periphery of politics rather than with rights within a
political system, but it illuminated his political drift. He posed
the crucial question of how an ethically and culturally superior
nation like Germany was to achieve the real power required for
the assertion of its values.[197] His reply dismissed government as

the saving agent on the ground that "the general knowledge of the nation cannot be transferred and the nation itself exercises it according to the standard of its natural sense of justice and injustice in secret or, where there is freedom, publicly." [198] His solution was the creation of a definite public opinion by and in the people.[199] Thus Goerres identified the key agency in the portage of the ideal into the real with the citizenry of the nation.

At this stage Goerres restricted the political role of this popular public opinion to the open praise or censure of governmental measures,[200] as appropriate to his ideal concept of the people, but as soon as it had to his mind actually manifested itself in reality he went on to insist upon a concrete constitutional power for it in the state. This manifestation had taken place, for Goerres, by 1814, and from the opening number of the *Rhenish Mercury* he insisted that the event which "surprisingly, admirably, astoundingly, will be the basis of the form of the world and the destiny of the species for many generations" was the uprising of "the German people," indeed of "the mass of the people," who had clung to their nationality despite all the political machinations which went on over their heads.[201] Backed by this interpretation of contemporary reality, Goerres proceeded, through the columns of his periodical, to predict the total replacement of standing armies by the militia system[202] and to agitate for a representative German constitution. In this constitution the people were to be at once the cement and the foundation. What was to hold the princes together in national union was their essential position as the national "representatives of their peoples,"[203] so that in the assembled princes "the spirit of the whole people rests upon them" and threatens any display of exclusive sovereignty not only with its moral anger but with actual deposition.[204] Moreover, this position of the princes as the voice of the people in the nation was to be buttressed by the real participation of the people in the government of the princely states through representative assemblies endowed with an effective share in political power.[205] To these assemblies Goerres attributed the central function of "the pendulum" in the state, correcting, balancing, and maintaining "the free action and reaction which vitalizes the otherwise dead mass."[206] He adopted

indeed the older views of an hierarchical social structure and consequently of political assemblies organized by estates and functioning as "the mediators between the people and the government," but he gave them a new setting in his assignment of these
crucial organs not to a neutral concept of the nation which comprehended both government and people but to the people itself.
Though formed from three estates, each assembly is "a single
corporation" which "represents the whole people"; it comes from
"the bosom of the people," and through it "the people is granted
its fair share in its own government," as part of its civil freedom.[207] And consistently with this position, Goerres' conception
of society not only provided for free mobility among the estates
but made them functional divisions of the people rather than the
usual spectrum leading from the masses to the government: the
nobility became "The Protective Estate (*Wehrstand*)" whose
place was "in the midst" of the armed people; the clergy became
"The Teaching Estate (*Lehrstand*)," mixed in with the secular
intellectuals and bearing "public opinion" to the throne; the
masses of the people became "The Nutritive Estate (*Naehr-
stand*)," "the vital blood which in them is formed for the nourish-
ment, the vitalization, and the strengthening of the whole body
of the state" and which must be granted the freedom necessary
to this activity.[208]

But even for Arndt and Goerres, who were so intensely impressed by what they interpreted as the rising of the nation, the
populist emphasis led into but not beyond a genuine political
dualism between governments and peoples. Despite Arndt's
acceptance of the development of the people toward the autonomous assertion of their rights, he still drew a sharp distinction
between the civic patriotism in which this development was
manifest and the readiness for complete political self-government
as a further stage which had not yet been reached. Hence Arndt
could characterize the contemporary scene as a transitional point
in which the capacity of the German people for freedom had
been proved but the will to realize it politically had not, since
they had not yet shown themselves prepared to erect out of
themselves the ultimate framework of law and order that was
absolutely requisite to real liberty.[209] The constitutional counter-

part, for Arndt, of this transitional point in the national development was a system in which the new capacities of the people toward autonomy were indeed irrevocably recognized through the legislative functions of their representative assemblies, but only within a structure whose pillars were the traditional hierarchy of kings and nobles. "The law-giver . . . must create out of the elements which exist," [210] and amongst these historical elements in German life of which account must be taken are the nobles "who stood and stand with definite duties and rights in definite relationships" and the prince, "the supreme appearance in human affairs, the supreme form of majesty and justice on earth." [211] Moreover, they not only must but should be maintained, for the increase in the popular capacity for freedom requires liberal institutions to be sure but also, by this very token, "stricter regulations [and] firmer laws." [212] If popular representative organs are necessary to maintain "the equilibrium" of social and political forces, the prince and the nobles are equally necessary, the one as the "power which could compel obedience to justice," [213] the other as the bridge between people and prince and consequently the embodiment of "the divine splendor of the state." [214] Once the people had been granted their due and proper place in this organic political and social structure, Arndt looked to the lineup of prince, aristocracy, and peasantry as the "earthly" powers which were the real basis of the state to throw their predominant weight on the side of political constancy against the urban and intellectual drive towards incessant change.[215]

But it was in Goerres that the ultimate meaning of the political experiences of the liberation period found its most overt expression. For as emphatic as was his championship of popular rights he used them not as a weapon against the old regime but as an addition which would provide an institutional as well as a spiritual guarantee that the princes would actually fill the role, which traditional German constitutional theory assigned to them, of the natural aristocratic representatives of the people within a larger national state. Thus Goerres fixed as the primary requirement for a German constitution "internal firmness and unified conduct toward the outside world," [216] and to achieve this he aimed at the institution of a national authority which would "lead the whole from the top down, . . . protect the individual in his integrity," and effect unity "even by command." [217] Consequently he did not question the established rule of the princes nor their right to predominance in the government of the nation.[218] He admitted that "the freedom of the peoples finds its limit in the freedom of the princes," [219] and when he asserted that the converse was equally true his emphasis was not so much upon the limitation of monarchical power as such but rather upon the bonds which made the monarch a part of the people and directed his power to their ends. For Goerres the proof that the German particular sovereigns were within the body of the German people and that princely powers were a political expression of popular rights was found in the fact that the Imperial constitutional grouping of the German states into spiritual princes, secular princes, and Imperial cities were really the political representation of the social grouping of the people into Teaching, Protective, and Nutritive Estates.[220] The chief function of the institutionalization of popular rights in the form of representative assemblies and civil liberties would be to give the princes a visible reminder of their coherence with the people and thus to assure that they exercise their powers not as independent sovereigns but as national estates.[221]

In this way Goerres typified the crucial link that was forged at this crossroads of German history between the problem of national unification and the problem of personal freedom. He raised the political standard of a German nation which rested upon the support of its people but was organized according to the traditional system of particularistic monarchies on the ground that they were the historical creations of the people itself. His justification of this system bound the old *Libertaet* to the new freedom.

Thus did there emerge the beginnings of a liberal tradition which viewed particular states and individuals as naturally complementary forces for the achievement of the higher synthesis of authority and freedom in the German nation.

6. Post-Liberation Politics:
Bureaucrats, Constitutionalists,
and Radicals (1815-1830)

With the coming of the postwar period Arndt and Goerres gradually dropped out of the liberal limelight, and nothing reveals as graphically as this the sharp break which the years after 1815 brought to the incipient movement. It was not only that the external conditions which had seemed to favor the synthetic mode of political thinking characteristic of these Liberation nationalists were gone, nor was it only the Prussian censorship which cut deeply into the effectiveness of their writing. The nature of the German liberal endeavor itself changed and now passed them by. This change was even reflected in the post-liberation writings of the two men, for where they had formerly harmonized nation, state, and people in an organic integration of all the fundamental forces in Germany and had castigated particularistic despotism and popular revolution as equally alien products of French influence, they had now to recognize not only conservative reaction but also particularism and radicalism as dominant tendencies within Germany itself which afforded little support to their ideas.[1]

The failure of the Congress of Vienna and the young German Confederation to enact the Liberation synthesis of traditional authority and popular liberties led, during the postwar era, to the dissolution of the synthesis. Its constituent elements, now dissociated, tended to fall into the pattern of a political spectrum. The spectrum ranged from the renewed attempts of officials to liberalize their particular states wholly by governmental fiat, through the outbreak of indecisive conflict between sovereign and popular assembly in the particular states which had actually granted modern-style liberal constitutions, to the union of democracy and nationalism in a small group of idealistic intellectuals who would unleash an unprecedented revolutionary movement against the whole system of particular states. The first of these positions was represented primarily by Prussia, where the monarch recoiled so far from the spirit of the Liberation that the absorption of a popular representation into the constitutional structure of the state was, despite war-time promises, ultimately rejected and the reform tradition was channelled into a non-political bureaucratic liberalism. The intermediate position in the spectrum was occupied by the states of the south-west, where the failure of the new constitutions either to modernize or dissolve the traditional association between particular princeship and German *Libertaet* led to an outright political dualism. On the extreme left of the postwar spectrum the German Student Unions (*Burschenschaften*) became the locus of the unwonted struggle to dispense with the initiative of the traditional political and social agencies in the creation of a new Germany.

These three tendencies did not found movements, for they drew their motive power from the turbulent era of occupation, reform, and liberation which was in process of vanishing and they ran down during the pacification of the 1820's. They did, however, insert into the institutions of post-Vienna Germany the three alternative solutions which the disruption of the liberation synthesis bequeathed to the problem of freedom in the 19th century: the official liberalism which depoliticized the liberal challenge and absorbed it piecemeal; the moderate liberalism which hung suspended between its faith in and its doubts about the capacity of the traditional authorities to associate themselves with the new demands of an individualized society; and a radical liberalism that would realize the western libertarian ideal absolutely by destroying the whole constituted structure of German politics and society.

The First Prussian Constitutional Conflict (1815-1823)

"Freedom depends much more on administration than on constitution." [2] Thus, in 1815, did the Prussian historian and official, B. G. Niebuhr, interpret the meaning of the Prussian reforms. This characterization foreshadowed the direction into which the manifold seeds and tendencies of the Prussian Reform period were to develop during the postwar era. During this era the attempt to develop the beginnings of the political reorganization of the Prussian state into a permanent constitutional form was filtered through a growing network of political reaction and emerged in the clear, thin tradition of a narrow bureaucratic liberalism. Thereby the autocratic Prussian institutions were consolidated in such wise that they remained unchallenged down to the eve of the revolution of 1848. Their prior assimilation of a limited liberalism, moreover, conferred on them an organic adaptability toward even the subsequent convulsions.

The period from 1815 to 1823 which established this political framework cannot, then, be described in the simple formula of the struggle between constitutionalism and absolutism. Rather was it a complex process in which the projects for a liberal aristocratic constitution were time after time nullified by opposite projects for a feudal aristocratic constitution and in which the ever-diminishing circle of liberal political possibilities led their protagonists to concentrate more and more upon the more innocuous and less disputed creation of liberal facets within the structure of the absolute state itself. The pattern of history during this period reveals a gradual, inexorable process of constriction. It started at the Congress of Vienna with the exclusion of the nation from participation in the political reorganization of Germany. It progressed successively to the exclusion of the Prussian society from participation in the political reorganization of the Prussian state and to the unsuccessful projects of the liberal wing of the Prussian government for the inclusion of popular elements in a constitution that was reorganized by fiat from above. And it ended in an administrative reorganization which was designed in part as a tactical detour toward the desired constitution through the politically neutral ground of governmental efficiency, but which characteristically remained as the permanent achievement of the period. The governmental liberals were driven by conservative opposition and permitted by their own assumptions to initiate the pattern whereby the struggle for a liberalized state was transferred from the social arena into the monarchical administration itself. During this process Prussia made social and economic policy rather than political rights or spiritual function the liberal aspect of the authoritarian state, and thereby showed how its traditional association with corporate privileges could be gradually extended to include the necessary measure of individual freedom without structural injury to itself.

The details of this first Prussian constitutional conflict need no repetition here.[3] Certain of its general features, however, must be remarked, for they show the political and social logic of the process which strained the broad but temporary projects and measures of liberation vintage into the narrow but permanent bureaucratic liberalism which was to dominate 19th-century Germany.

The meeting of the sovereigns at Vienna in 1815 witnessed the two successive decisions which set the stage for the following struggle within Prussia. The defeat of the projects for a German representative constitution in favor of a confederation of sovereigns was followed by Frederick William III's refusal to enact the representative constitution for Prussia which Hardenberg hoped to activate immediately upon his return from Vienna. Hardenberg could secure only the famous royal promise of May 22, 1815, which promised that "a representation of the people is to be formed" but which looked to the traditional provincial estates, existing or restored, as its basis and limited its powers to "consultation" on matters affecting the personal and property rights of the citizens.[4] These decisions meant that neither the German nor the Prussian people were to collaborate in the reorganization of the Prussian state and that the liberal cause had to be entrusted to the bureaucratic wing of the movement. Moreover, the ambiguous terms of the decree of May 22nd gave aid and comfort to feudal as well as liberal circles of aristocrats around the court. It insured that a fierce political conflict would be waged over the constitutional issue, that the stake would be the soul of a king rather than the soul of a people, and that the struggle would be contained within the halls of government. This localization of the conflict in the royal councils, which was projected by the initial decisions, was abetted during the course of the struggle by the overwhelming preponderance of aristocratic conservatism in the articulate public opinion of the country at large.[5] The

strength of the feudal party in the Prussian society not only reinforced the bureaucratic character of Prussian constitutionalism
by showing the absence of a popular party to support liberal
demands, but its corporate opposition to both liberalism and
centralization helped to forge a working alliance between bureaucratic liberals and bureaucratic absolutists for administrative
policies at once individualistic and unitarian.

As a result of this constellation the bureaucratic liberals led
by Hardenberg pursued two simultaneous tacks. On the one
hand, together with reformers like Humboldt and Gneisenau
they persisted in direct attempts to get a constitution approved
and legislated by the king. On the other hand, together with
such bureaucratic specialists as Karl von Maassen and Friedrich
von Motz they sought to build the policies which were being
blocked in the constitution into the administrative structure of
the state. If a constitutional Prussia was not to produce the
reorganization of the Prussian state, then the reorganization of
the state might still produce a constitutional Prussia. The conscious adoption of this line of reasoning was revealed by Hardenberg in 1817, when he wrote:

> It is indeed the constant purpose of the government to set up a repre-
> sentation appropriate to the nation, but we have believed that we must
> allow the organization of the administrative authorities to precede it
> and that given the great variety of the provinces—in part entirely new
> —constituting the Prussian monarchy we must approach the problem
> deliberately and cautiously.[6]

The important point about this relationship between the constitutional and administrative facets of the liberal program was
that it was not only tactical but internal. With all due regard to
Hardenberg's noted diplomatic flexibility—"the art of governing consists not in clinging blindly to arbitrary and uniform
maxims but in adapting them to the events, the circumstances,
the opinion, and the real needs of the people" [7]—his political
mentality reveals a more fundamental historical necessity in the
channeling of Prussian constitutional into administrative liberalism. Having decided upon the necessity of a representative constitution as a preservative of state power required by the needs
of the times,[8] Hardenberg was confronted with the problem of

admitting into the political structure of Prussia a society which
was being polarized into feudal reaction and intellectual revolution. Consequently, his reliance upon administrative reform was
more than a tactical detour in the face of overwhelming opposition. It was the product of his conviction that the administrative
structure of the Prussian state was the only secure instrument for
the constitutional guidance of the society from the fetters of traditional corporate privilege to the strength of free individual initiative without reactionary or radical revolution. Not only, then,
were the administrative reforms to prepare the social ground for
loyal popular participation in a socially progressive monarchical
constitution, but Hardenberg tended to consider the constitution
as a kind of branch of the administration. What he sought
ultimately was the establishment of a kind of constitutional department within the government which would offer the necessary
concessions and encouragements to all social units and groups,
new and old, with the purpose of allaying unrest and attracting
the positive and concrete support of the nation to the state. Because the function of this constitutional department was social
attraction, concessions in all directions—both to a hierarchical
system of representation by estates and to the principle that "we
have nothing but free property-owners"—were precisely its business. But if flexible tactics both in the constitutional and the
social spheres thus became an administrative principle, what remained constant was the fundamental maintenance of royal authority over this as over other departments of government. The
reservation of legislative initiative exclusively to the Crown, the
finality of the royal veto, the king's power of dissolution—these
ultimate sources of control over what might be called a special
ministry of social concessions were never questioned. Such a
ministry would, in Hardenberg's plans, never be able to threaten
the royal prerogative, but would rather serve to divert the political pressure from foreign affairs, army, and police—preserves
which Hardenberg always assigned to the unlimited will of the
king.[9]

The administrative connotation which Hardenberg gave to his
constitutionalism illuminates the thorny problem of his conflict
with Humboldt, who was appointed minister for corporate and

communal affairs in January 1819. To be sure, personal dislike and a purely bureaucratic squabble on the respective powers of the chancellor and his ministers were crucial in the controversy, but their sharp opposition on the issue of the Carlsbad Decrees, which Humboldt disapproved, and Hardenberg's sincere belief that Humboldt was abetting the revolutionary party refer the feud to a more fundamental ground. What this ground was, however, is not easy to determine, for their substantive constitutional ideas were very similar. Indeed, Humboldt's long and analytical memorandum of October 1819 proposing a constitution for Prussia seemed simply to provide a rationale for the position which Hardenberg asserted, but did not discuss. That the statesman, who had his roots in the enlightened bureaucratic absolutism of the old regime, and the intellectual, who was spawned in the non-political individualism of German cultural idealism, should agree upon the principles of a constitutional system which would blend corporate organs and popular rights in an amalgam most compatible with governmental authority was a clear sign of the inescapable conditions imposed by the continuing vitality of crown and aristocracy upon the thinking, as well as the actions, of those who would modernize them. But Humboldt drew a distinction between government and state that went beyond Hardenberg. Where Hardenberg assumed their equivalence and recommended a combination of liberal and corporate policies as instrumental to the strength of state and government indiscriminately, Humboldt insisted that individual liberty and social hierarchy must indeed be compatible with government but that they were, along with it, autonomous participants in the nature of the state. A state "can live only through its education of the people to intelligent action," and this education, in turn, can be worked "only by institutions which assign a free arena to the activity of the individual" and "join people's interests to the particular civic units existent in the state . . . and thus allow it to rise gradually to general points of view"—i.e. to "the people's vital and appropriate share in their own affairs." [10] For Humboldt, the monarchical government was indeed to guide this process, but through the medium of an interaction with individual rights and corporate forms that was infinitely more reciprocal than was the material and administrative connotation that Hardenberg gave to interests of state. Humboldt opposed the Carlsbad Decrees because he felt that they violated the nature and endangered the sovereignty of the Prussian state.[11] Hardenberg enforced them because he feared for the security of his government.

Even the divergent forms in which the two men clothed their constitutional drafts were relevant to this difference in political approach. Humboldt's intensive analysis expressed the urgency which he felt to settle all the essential relationships between crown, corporations, and people in the constitutional law that would condition them all equally, and the synthetic pattern of his thinking expressed his desire to include all three actively in his solutions. Hardenberg's curt sketches of bare constitutional proposals and the deliberate indecision with which his drafts explicitly postponed crucial issues to post-constitutional legislation were evidence of his assumption that the government should be the caretaker of the constitution. It should be the active and constant determinant of the relations between the social hierarchy, the people, and the state, on the empirical criteria of the loyalty and the support brought by the various combinations of these elements to the government. Behind all the personalia of the Hardenberg-Humboldt vendetta lay the conflict within the official Prussian aristocratic liberalism between those who would retain the bureaucratic administration at the heart of the constitution and those who would retain it as one of a number of autonomous organs in an organically integrated state. With the defeat of Humboldt and his party in 1819, the chances for a liberal constitution in Prussia were narrowed down to the possibility of working it through the administrative structure of the state.

Hence when Hardenberg's own frontal assault upon the constitutional issue failed in 1819 his shift to administrative reform was a move internally consistent with his governmental approach to constitutionalism. The state administration was to him a politically neutral instrument whose liberal orientation could prepare the social ground for the acceptance of a constitution. Even more, as the heart of any future constitution it could itself be a constitutional microcosm. Hardenberg's administrative reforms were not substitutes for a constitution but represented simply a relocation of it, and this fact was to contribute mightily to the renewed association of liberal values with the authoritarian Prussian state. Indeed, at the beginning of 1820 Hardenberg plotted his program so as to make a representative constitution the logical as well as chronological culmination of the series of administrative edicts: finance decree, local ordinance, national Prussian constitution.[12] The administration was to be fitted out as the secure framework for a constitution; the state-supporting function of the constitution was to be made literal by rooting it in the very structure of the financial and administrative organs of the government.

The finance edicts of 1820 were, in the long run, a successful application of this technique. Not only did many officials who were opposed in general to a representative constitution—including the king—accept representative institutions within the framework of the finance administration,[13] but this constitutional seed bore ultimate, albeit belated, fruit in the United Diet of 1847 which spelled the end of absolute monarchy in Prussia. Behind the edicts lay Hardenberg's coupling of economic liberty with political conformity. He advocated "as much as possible the removal of all hindrances" to commerce as "a new system" of trade necessary to avoid "the destruction of loyalty and love for the Prussian government." [14] An industrial economy could be, by its very nature, susceptible only in an inessential degree to action by the state. The success of the economy depends on "the spirit which informs the business class," and this spirit is developed through competition and free experience rather than by "the power and wisdom of government." [15] But economic liberty required representative institutions as the only practical means of channeling its advantages to the state. Financial administration was acknowledged to require more than the usual technical reforms in the direction of uniformity and rationality. Built into the financial structure now was the acknowledgment that government required from the society an assistance which could not be taken but had to be given. Thus the decree on the state debt was designed obviously to restore the public credit, but public credit was now defined in terms of the investing groups of the nation, and its soundness predicated on the assumption that new loans would have to be approved and debt administration supervised by national representative estates (*Reichsstaende*). Again, the tax reform of 1820 was dominated by the need for increased revenue, and to this end the customary local dues were replaced by a unified tax-system on a statewide basis. This administrative need, however, was used both to justify a further equalization of tax burdens[16] and to employ a reorganized system of provincial estates in the allocation of the land tax.

The second line of administrative reform which Hardenberg took up during 1820 in pursuit of the elusive Prussian constitution consisted in a projected communal and county ordinance. The connection between this project and an imminent constitution was no secret, for two successive constitutional commissions of the Council of State—the third and fourth since 1817—were given the responsibility for preparing the local government bill. The third commission was packed with officials of the Hardenberg party led by Friese, the pro-bourgeois head of the Prussian Bank, and the results of its deliberations show very well the substantive purpose of the measure. If the political emphasis in the finance acts was to provide for representation within the governmental structure, the aim of the communal and county reform went beyond this to ensure that the basis of this representation would be such as to support both constitution and state. The whole tendency of these draft bills on local government ran directly counter to the moderate, concessive spirit which had characterized Hardenberg's constitutional proposals since 1815. Whereas he had been careful, and would be again, to bring the organic and corporate elements into his constitutional plans, the projected local government reform which Hardenberg backed combined self-administrative and bureaucratic features whose only point of compatibility was their mutual hostility to such elements. In general, the provisions for the communal ordinance stressed self-government based on representation of individuals while the proposed county ordinance stressed the centralistic and bureaucratic elements. The former would extend the competence of popularly elected local administration *vis-à-vis* both aristocracy and bureaucracy, while the latter would divest the nobility of its former strongholds in favor of the central administration.

The relationship of the proposed administrative reorganization to the ultimate constitution was frankly admitted by the commission. Since the government was, through its imminent national constitution, in process of "giving away a part of its total power" to a genuine popular representation, it could assert its exclusive rights over those officials who had previously taken on a kind of unofficial prescriptive representative character.[17] In the minds of the Prussian liberal officials, governmental unity was clearly the necessary concomitant of modern constitutionalism, and their local government project was to establish at the very basis of the constitutional pyramid the pattern of government in which the administration would be purged of all extraneous aristocratic influence, and could safely admit a rationalized representative system for limited functions within the governing process. The hard core of the royal administration was to remain intact and to dispose the heterogeneous elements of the constitution to the purposes of government.

Despite Hardenberg's attempt to balance the rigor of the local government bill with a draft constitution of October 1820, which went to the opposite extreme in its concessions to the corporate aristocratic principle for the representative diets,[18] both nobility and king reacted violently. Stein set the tone by castigating the local government bill as a work of "bureaucratism and liberalism," [19] and even Hardenberg's resolution in favor of the royal power of all the constitutional issues which his previous drafts left open could not dissuade the king from rejecting both the local government bill and the constitution which was based upon it. The provincial reorganization which was enacted after Hardenberg's death under conservative auspices in 1823 resurrected the cooperation of bureaucracy and aristocracy. Provincial diets were reestablished or newly established "in the spirit of the old German constitutions"—i.e. with organization by estate and an emphatic predominance of the nobility—and their powers were local, consultative, and administrative, under the overriding controls of the bureaucratic monarchy. But if Hardenberg's official constitutionalism remained unrealized, it helped to create in the Prussian civil service the tradition which imbued it with the notion that it was the political representative of the country as a whole against special interests. The espousal of constitutionalism by the bureaucracy against the resistance of the bulk of the nobility and the apathy of the people confirmed the Prussian pattern of imposing free institutions by fiat from above in the small doses compatible with the perpetuation of an authoritarian political system.

The characteristic sphere for the application of this pattern was Prussian commercial policy, which presented the rare phenomenon of having its liberal principles not merely preserved but expanded during the reactionary decade of the 1820's. The development from the Prussian tariff of 1818 into the German Customs Union of 1834 was not the result of conscious planning, but the criterion of Prussian state interest which guided the specific economic decisions tended increasingly to consist in the expansion of the area of free exchange.[20] As long as Prussian policy aimed merely at the inclusion within a single customs system of enclaves and principalities which separated the eastern and western halves of the state, such expansion could be viewed as purely instrumental and subordinate to normal bureaucratic considerations of administrative unit. But when in 1828, a customs union was concluded with Hesse-Darmstadt despite obvious geographical, administrative, and financial disadvantages for Prussia it was clear that the advocacy of commercial liberty was not so much derivative from as definitive of *raison d'état*.

The Prussian minister who made this deliberate political decision out of a long-standing official economic attitude was Friedrich von Motz, an official whose development recapitulated the convertibility of constitutional and bureaucratic liberalism in early 19th-century Prussia. Motz laid down the bases of his policies in a series of memoranda to Hardenberg during the years 1817 and 1818.[21] A native of Hesse-Kassel in Prussian service, Motz started from a resentment at the divisions and impotence of Germany under the Confederation set up in 1815 and looked to the concentration of power in Prussia for its remedy. The German problem was modulated, in Motz' thinking, into a Prussian problem through his conviction that the first stage in the national program must be the assertion of Prussian hegemony over northern Germany, and that the physical separation of the western and eastern sections of Prussia made policies which aimed at the unification of the Prussian state the simultaneous instruments of north German unity. With these larger horizons for his Prussian activities, Motz propounded a brand of constitutionalism akin to Hardenberg's as an indispensable force for cohesion in the structure of the Prussian state. For Motz, too, the development of a special legislative area for the participation of the society in the state had to be balanced by the countervailing development of strict centralization in the area of bureaucracy.[22] The victory of the reaction drove the constitutional program from Motz' politics, but the general attitude of mind betokened by such a program remained unchanged. Motz continued to think of the strengthening of Prussia in terms of the dynamic support to be supplied by autonomous forces in the society, but now he gradually evolved the policy of integration through freedom of trade to replace the bankrupt one of integration through freedom of suffrage. His famous memorandum of June 1829[23] revealed strikingly how literal was this translation of policy. Just as Motz had begun in 1817 with the deficiencies of the German Confederation in political matters, so he now began with its economic failures; and just as he had recommended military agreements and a representative constitution to weld together Germans, new Prussians, and old Prussians, so he now anticipated the centripetal effects of an expanded free market.

> If it is a truth of political science that tariffs are only a consequence of the political division of different states, then it must also be a truth that the union of these states in a customs and trade association means at the same time also union into one and the same political system. . . . In this connection, which rests upon equal interests and a natural basis and which must necessarily spread into the center of Germany, will there once more come to existence a truly confederated Germany, stable and free internally and externally under the protection of Prussia.[24]

The policy and, after 1834, the practice of the German Customs Union embodied the politically innocuous residue of the impulses which had been sifted through the constitutional conflict. It was primarily through the material form of free economic enterprise that the traditional political and social structure of Germany began to absorb and to acclimatize itself to the dynamism of the advanced western societies.

Constitutional Dualism in Southern Germany (1815-1830)

At the same time as postwar Prussia was struggling over the dimensions of bureaucratic liberalism, the southern German states were developing a constitutional dualism between the independent authority of government and the autonomous political rights of the active citizenry as a second possible response to the challenge posed by the individualized societies of the west. Of the several constitutions or constitutional statutes promulgated after 1815, those of Bavaria (May 1818), Baden (August 1818), and Wuerttemberg (September 1819) were the most important in the establishment of this pattern; in nothern states like Hanover and Brunswick the charters effected only nominal changes in the old institutions while in states like Hesse-Darmstadt, Nassau, and Saxe-Weimar they were either imitative or they affected principalities too small to seem generally applicable. In the three southern middle-sized states, however, the new constitutional life acted as a cynosure to politically interested men all over Germany, and despite its stagnation under the pressure of monarchical reaction after 1823, the constitutional institutions and the memory of their active use remained to condition the political views of the succeeding generation. The direction of this influence was set by the general uniformity in the political experience of these states during the postwar years. In each case the voluntary decision of the prince to confer a representative constitution for the purpose of unifying his realm was followed by divisive struggles among the government, the social corporations, and the doctrinaire liberals which disturbed the traditional equilibrium of society and introduced a deep-seated duel for power within the state in the form of conflicts between prince and representative diet. These conflicts contributed ultimately to the acceptance by the particular governments of the repressive measures enacted by the German Confederation and hence to the bankruptcy of the whole post-liberation pattern of monarchically inspired liberal politics, but not before they had spawned two political doctrines which, in different ways, perpetuated the pattern for the edification of future German politicians. It was here that Karl Rotteck's categorical political dualism took its rise as the consistent expression of southern constitutionalism, and it was here in the south, too, that the theory of the *Rechtsstaat*— the state defined by law—which was to have such a notable career all over Germany was first formulated as a conscious application to constitutional dualism of the familiar pattern formerly applied to the problems of religious and personal freedom—the assignment of the ideal of liberalization to the reality of the established authorities.

But if the southern stalemate between government and assembly within an actual constitution contributed an alternative different in kind from the Prussian intrabureaucratic policy-making towards a presumptive constitution, yet the two patterns were connected. The constitutional dualism of the south foreshadowed the assumptions of the moderate liberal movement in Germany, but it foreshadowed as well the assumptions behind the moderates' union with the official Prussian liberalism of Bismarck. Despite the common prejudices on the uniqueness of the Prussian mission and the contrasting western liberality of the south Germans, the two sections were joined in a long-standing congruence of politics which furnished a background for the unifying nationalism of the future. A political geography which opened them to competition and hence to stimuli from the more advanced western nations; a political chronology which protracted the process of state-making until monarchical unification could be completed only during the liberal era of the 19th century; an intermediate economic condition that was beginning to feel the effects of western capitalism while still sheltering traditional forms of economic and social organization; the resultant princely initiative in constitutional change; a still vital political tradition which was building the corporate liberties of an Imperial estate into the modern sovereignty of the territorial state

—these factors were common to most German governments of the age and helped to create a certain conjunction in the postwar politics of the various principalities which made Prussia representative in its problems albeit individual in its solution. Southern constitutionalism, then, was not a simple categorical alternative to the conservative solution. It was rather the first actual attempt to work the dimension of constitutional liberty into the traditional structure of state and society. Consequently, the southern constitutions composed a spectrum, with Bavaria on the conservative extreme, Baden on the dualistic extreme, and Wuerttemberg intermediate between them. It was against this background that the Badener Rotteck exhibited the dualistic implications of constitutionalism in all their rigor, and that Robert von Mohl gave definitive form to the *Rechtsstaat* doctrine out of his Wuerttembergian and Bavarian experience, as the means of aborting these dualistic implications and turning them into the southern contribution to the modernization of princely authority in Germany.

The Constitutions

The Bavarian constitution of May 26, 1818, was in its main lineaments closest to the projected Prussian charter, and it represented a balance of political and social forces just one stage to the left of the Prussian constellation. The most firmly rooted of the southern states, the least shaken by the experience of the Rhenish Confederation, liberation, and pacification, the Bavarian monarchy established a constitutional system which was the product of free royal decision and which broke least with the principle and practice of corporate estates. As in Prussia, the deliberations on the enactment of the constitution took place entirely within the councils of the government and were free from popular pressure.[25] As in Prussia, too, the constitutional issue came as the apparent climax of a whole series of administrative and social reforms which went a long way to create an individualistic social system governed by a centralized bureaucratic state. And finally, in the person of Count Maximilian von Montgelas, Bavaria possessed a leading minister whose longevity

of leadership (1799 to 1817) and addiction to enlightened despotism of the Napoleonic type made him in many ways the
counterpart of Hardenberg. Such factors indicate the stability of
the Bavarian state which helped to moderate the provisions of its
constitution of 1818.

Yet the Bavarian monarchy did go beyond the Prussian pattern
when it promulgated and set into actual operation a written constitution which involved a real if partial alienation of sovereignty.
The character of this constitution was conditioned by the situation which it was designed to meet. No more than in Prussia was
there a popular liberal movement to be placated, nor were the
bureaucratic considerations—imminent bankruptcy and the need
for attaching newly annexed territories—more pressing than
elsewhere. Indeed, as late as January 1817 Montgelas was insisting that constitutionalism of the western type was not applicable. "Everybody needs civil freedom, but how few men there
are in a state who can enjoy—indeed who can even understand—
the rights of political freedom." [26] The crucial factor would seem
to have been the position of the Bavarian aristocracy, whose
political and legal *points d'appui* in the structure of government
had been completely leveled in the bureaucratic centralization
of the Napoleonic period, but whose economic and social privileges, now without political guarantees, had been left largely
intact. The power of the aristocracy, then, lay somewhere between that of the Prussian, which had retained its place in the
political structure, and those of the other southern states, whose
corporate force had been decisively weakened. Thus it was the
conservative, clerical, historically oriented Crown Prince Louis
who cooperated with the liberal bureaucrats Georg von Zehntner
and Baron Alexander von Lerchenfeld to get enacted a constitutional system in which the restoration of aristocratic influence
and the tapping of new middle-class energies could be satisfied
together. This constellation of forces established the seeds of
constitutional dualism by throwing the weight of aristocracy as
well as commonalty into a representative legislature that would
be separate from the strictly bureaucratic administration under
the personal identity of the king, but at the same time it raised an
organic cover over this dualism by establishing an aristocratic

predominance within the legislature that made for its internal harmony with the monarch.

This melange of absolutist, parliamentary, and corporate factors found a precise embodiment in the Bavarian constitution.[27] The king reserved to himself "all rights of the state-power," including exclusive responsibility for the constitution, the possession of the executive power, and the rights of legislative initiative, veto, and dissolution. The Diet was granted an organization into two chambers on the western model, and genuine legislative powers over the state debt, new taxes, alienation of state property, and everything affecting personal liberty and property. The aristocracy was granted "special rights and privileges"—election by corporate estate, numerical predominance in the elective chamber, the right of both mediatized and territorial peers to individual seats in the upper house, and the guarantee of restoration of a whole set of social privileges ranging from patrimonial jurisdiction to the old monopoly of notarial rights. The common citizens were granted a list of constitutional "principles"—freedom of conscience, equality before the law, and membership in a political estate. By endowing the aristocracy with a social position which made it a loyal support of monarchical authority and by simultaneously endowing it with a political position which made it the chief but not exclusive representative of popular rights, postwar Bavaria showed how a hierarchically organized constitution might join bureaucratic government as twin supports of state power. It was characteristic of this constitution that the progressive officials accepted it as a preservative of governmental authority, the middle-of-the-road aristocrats welcomed it as the cooperation of ruler and nation through the union of traditional privilege and modern parliamentary liberties, and middle-class liberals viewed it as a contract between ruler and people establishing the dualistic independence of the popular legislature *vis-à-vis* the king.[28]

The second of the southern constitutions to be granted occupied the other extreme of the spectrum, for if the king of Bavaria succeeded best in preserving the rights of his nobility the Grand Duke of Baden was impelled to give the most recognition in his charter to the liberal, in the sense of the individualistic, motif. Indeed, it was precisely here in Baden, which was to become "the real school" of 19th-century German liberalism,[29] that the practical transition from the older to the modern institutions and principles of liberty, was most clearly depicted. More than any other a state of recent Napoleonic vintage, Baden now encompassed prominently a host of the newly mediatized nobility and knighthood who had proudly borne the combination of aristocratic liberties and public authority down into the 19th century.[30] Even the old margraviate which was the core of the grand duchy and supplied it with its name and its prince was not far removed from this relationship so characteristic of the Imperial Estates in Germany. The absence of a strong principality upon which to hang the agglomeration of new territories made the new Baden the most artificial and unstable of the middle states in Germany. Not only the bureaucracy, as in Prussia and Bavaria, but also elements of the Badenese society, including aristocratic tradition, participated in the process of making the liberal constitution. An important force in the pressure which finally forced a constitution from the reluctant and procrastinating Grand Duke Charles was made up of the agitation and petitions arising within segments of all groups of the population. Although the action took place within each social class independently, the most energetic movement—and the most impressive to the government—came undoubtedly from the aristocracy, and the activists in this group were the mediatized aristocracy which demanded, naturally enough, the guarantee of the rights and privileges which they had enjoyed as autonomous subjects of the Empire. But unlike the bulk of the Prussian nobility, which had deposited its tradition of special liberties with the state long before, the response of the new Baden nobility to the rationalizing discipline of enclosure in a modern state was to translate their demands for privilege into the inherently strange language of modern constitutionalism.[31] Here, then, was a clear case of the contribution which the forms of aristocratic liberties in the tradition of the German old regime made to the beginnings of German modern liberal institutions.

But the popular pressure in Baden, remarkable though it was for German politics, was not nearly sufficient to translate itself directly into constitutional results. The activity of the nobility as well as the lesser impact of the unrest among the commoners of town and countryside had effect only insofar as it was taken into account by the free decisions of the princely absolute government. Thus the movement among the populace achieved its climax during the latter part of 1815 and early 1816, while the constitution was not enacted until the second half of 1818. The immediate response of the government to the postwar agitation for a constitution was to reaffirm traditional absolutism. It rejected the petitions, refused to honor its promise to call an assembly of estates, and returned to the nobility some of the material privileges which they had lost, such as an alleviation of direct taxation, patronage rights over ecclesiastical benefices, and guardianship over local records. Thus did the Archduke Charles (1811-1818) attempt to renew the old social hierarchy of prince and aristocracy within the general political framework of a modern state which linked all subjects directly to the prince. The rationale behind this policy was supplied by the government official, Wilhelm Reinhard. He insisted equally upon the legal equality of all individuals as the necessary basis of the state and upon the preservation of aristocratic privilege as the necessary adjunct of princely power.[32] Thus were the historic liberties of the Imperial aristocracy translated into attributes of sovereignty.

But the next step of the Baden sovereign was to issue a charter of liberties in a form that broke with the corporate tradition and approached western constitutionalism. Considerations of state dictated a change in the nature of the freedom conferred. Internal unrest abated after 1816 but foreign pressure did not, and the hankering of Austria, Bavaria, and Prussia for parts of Baden's recently acquired territories exerted upon the princely government of Baden a force for constitutionalism which the internal movement did not possess. It was the desperate need of the government for internal cohesion against the foreign danger that produced the decision for a constitution, and it was the weakness of the traditional social supports for the state that filled the substance of the constitution with unprecedented liberal innovations. The historical autonomy of the mediatized Imperial aristocracy which had been forcibly integrated into Baden cast doubts upon their loyalty, and the conversion of their political rights into social privileges cast doubts upon the extent of their influence upon the Baden society at large. Hence the Grand Duke consented to go beyond the association of the state with the institutions of aristocratic liberty and to base his constitution primarily upon the common rights and duties of all citizens of the state.

Such was the context for the singular Baden Constitution of August 1818.[33] The dual emphases upon the prince as the source of the constitution and the sovereign possessor of the entire state power and upon the equal rights of all citizens to be guaranteed by their popular assembly were not mediated by an organic corporate structure. *Vis-à-vis* the Grand Duke, who was equipped with the full panoply of governmental rights—including the rights of legislative initiative, veto, and dissolution—stood a "second chamber," for which both electoral and membership rights were based exclusively upon geographical districts and property and age qualifications. The criteria of representation, in short, were by individuals and not by estates, for which there was no provision whatever in the lower chamber. Unlike all other German states, in Baden the universities, clergy, and whole landed aristocracy were represented in the upper chamber alone.[34] Not only, then, was the homogeneity of the upper chamber weakened—the liberal Karl Rotteck agitated there for years as member for the University of Freiburg—but its moderating influence upon the lower house was minimized. The further provisions specifying legal immunity for deputies and full publicity of debates emphasized the Diet's role as popular tribune rather than as instrument of government.

The internal connection between the interests of state and its calculated risk of an outright political dualism was made manifest in the person of Carl Nebenius, the finance expert who wrote the constitution. Nebenius' development from liberal bureaucrat to the far broader principles of the liberal constitutionalist was predicated on the complete unviability of the historic finance and tax systems which came with the polyglot collection of territories that composed the new Baden. Since the government could not draw upon custom for the satisfaction of its material requirements Nebenius turned to uniform representation as its source. Hence the rejection of estates in favor of individuals as the basis of the suffrage, and the preference for towns over countryside in the drawing of electoral districts for the lower house, were connected with the provisions basing representation upon tax payments and patterning the electoral districts upon the areas of tax administration. The dependence of the liberal provisions of the Baden constitution upon the diplomatic and financial authority of the government showed how a German monarchical state could be forced to associate its power with modern forms of constitutional freedom when the counterweight of a reliable aristocracy was lacking.

The postwar history of Wuerttemberg climaxed the movement toward dualistic constitutions in the south. It was a climax both in the logical sense that the results amounted to a synthesis of the Bavarian and the Baden constitutions and in the dramatic sense that the opposition between the government and the social powers which had been absent from the process of constitution-making in the first case and abortive in the second broke out in the full fury of open conflict in the third. The crystallization, in Wuerttemberg, of tendencies into active political groupings with identifiable social connections, specific issues, and concrete appeals for the practical support of public opinion did not prevent these groupings from falling into a familiar mold. Thus the protagonists were the king and a section of the bureaucracy, representing absolute government; the estates, dominated by corporate interests who pressed for a traditional revival; and a modern liberal group led by intellectuals and organized around a political journal. And thus, too, the bitter four-year struggle over the constitution went through a confusing, tortuous course in which these groups moved with constant intensity and determination in and out of almost every possible line-up of the three forces. The chameleonic course of this wrangling showed clearly that the social basis for a clearcut political conflict was simply not at hand in Germany, for even here in the "advanced" west the traditional organs of princely government and corporate diet remained the political channels for social claims. The agents of the new liberal individualism, without sufficient footing in the society to create their own organs of combat, were constricted into dependence upon one or the other of the two historic institutions. But conversely, the two age-old antagonists both felt the need of the new liberal elements, sought them out, and tried to adjust themselves to them. From 1815 to 1819 the constitutional conflict was waged by the king on the one side and a kind of constituent corporate Diet on the other, but each side acted and reacted not only in terms of the other but also in terms of the putative sources of strength which were symbolized by the existence of the small liberal group.

The Wuerttemberg conflict is an impressive case-study of how ideas and institutions pertinent to the freedom of individuals came to be fitted into a pre-established political and social framework pertinent to the authority of prince and corporations and how the resulting constitutional dualism remained resoluble by agreement of the traditional powers. The setting of the conflict brought the relations among the three forces of prince, estates, and liberals out into the open. Wuerttemberg had been the only important German state to maintain a vital system of political estates and an effective division of powers between prince and diet throughout the old regime. Hence, whereas in other German states, the traditional alliance between prince and aristocracy gave to the opposition an appearance of independent liberalism, in Wuerttemberg the initial opposition between an absolutist leveling king and a reactionary but anti-absolutist set of political corporations made obvious the conservative sponsorship of liberal ideas. This sponsorship was embodied in the character of the main actors in the Wuerttemberg drama. King William I, who succeeded the bureaucratic despot Frederick I to the throne in October 1816, had been a popular and accessible Crown Prince who was to try all kinds of combinations in the service of the royal prerogative. His chief rivals, the old Wuerttemberg estates, had a peculiar social composition which manifested the profound hold of corporate organization upon German society, beyond its usual association with the landed aristocracy, and which made possible the assumption of a liberal posture by out-and-out reactionaries who aimed at a simple restoration of their political, administrative, and social privileges. For the traditional estates still had their stronghold in the old Duchy of Wuerttemberg, where the landed nobility was weak. Despite the accession of mediatized nobility from the newly annexed sections of the state to the corporate party, control remained vested in the burghers, the village officials, and the clergy who had always dominated the estates. This party fought for the restoration of their corporate rights under the appropriate banner of "the good old law," but the non-noble status of this aristocracy aided it in appropriating the verbiage of the new liberalism as an instrument in this struggle. It fought in the name of "freedom," artfully mixing the various vintages of the concept for maximum effect: the participation by important members of this party in the war of liberation against the French helped them to join the modern national connotations of "German liberty" to the old rights which they claimed to have been guaranteed by the German Empire.[35]

But the force of the pattern that mixed conservative with liberal principles was manifested even outside the king and estates who were the chief antagonists. The loose coterie of liberals for whose support the conservative parties strove was characterized by an analogous blend. Organized around political periodicals in overlapping circles of which "The Friends of the People" was the outstanding group and the young Friedrich List the outstanding contributor, the liberal party had connections both in the government through the progressive Baron Karl von Wangenheim and in the Diet through the publisher Baron Johann Cotta von Cottendorf. The liberals opposed both political absolutism and exclusive corporate privilege, but in their positive program they sought to combine such ill-assorted elements as natural law with historic law,[36] equal individual rights with a corporate structure of political society,[37] the principle of popular sovereignty with the assignment of full governmental power to the prince.[38] List, native of the mediatized town of Reutlingen, modernized the combination of chartered freedom and sovereignty in the old Imperial city when he insisted on the general freedom of corporations—and particularly municipal freedom—as the necessary link between the freedom of the individual and the power of government in the modern state.[39]

The "organism" of society—i.e. the hierarchy of corporations resting on the commune and including the representative diet— was for him the means by which "all the individuals in the people," who are "the source of power" in a "naturally organized state," get their rights embodied in "the supreme power in the hands of the ruler," who is "that point into which the force of all the individual parts flows together." [40]

Given the political flexibility of all three parties, it is hardly surprising to find the course of the Wuerttemberg constitutional crisis characterized by a bewildering series of combinations and counter-combinations. When the process is viewed as a whole, however, it falls into a pattern which epitomizes the trend of the 19th-century German political history. The first stage of the struggle, which was pursued through most of 1815, was dominated by the opposition between the royal government on the one hand and the alliance of corporate oligarchs and liberals on the other. The second stage, which was initiated by the king's fear of insurrection and lasted into 1817, was characterized by the alliance of government and liberals against the oligarchs. The third stage, which covered to the end of 1817, witnessed the dissolution of all alliances and the unstable isolation of all three parties. The definitive resolution of the conflict followed only when the king struck up a connection with the conservative corporate party, and the constitution of 1819 was written under their joint auspices.

The constitution was essentially a working agreement between an independent king and his autonomous estates which included the modicum of liberal constitutionalism required to reconcile the divergent claims of a ruler who demanded the uniform subjection of his citizens and an oligarchy which demanded the guarantee of its rights within the unified political system. Hence the constitution was built upon an old-fashioned dualism, bridged by the new-fangled language of liberalism.[41] The charter was grounded explicitly upon agreement of king and estates and upon the greatest approximation to "the former contractual and lawful rights and liberties of our old state," but "adapted to present conditions." To the king went "all the rights of the state power," including legislative initiative, dissolution, and veto. The diet was possessed of the general competence to "assert the rights of the country" *vis-à-vis* the ruler, and this was applied in the preservation of such traditional privileges as the "class" (i.e. estate) organization of elections, the standing watchdog committee of the estates, their own treasury and administration of tax monies, and the corporate integrity of the old electoral bailiwicks. But added now to this traditional duality of absolutism and conservatism was the attribution to "all Wuerttembergers" of "equal civil rights," the rearrangement of the estates into a two-chambered parliamentary system, provision for voting by head, publicity of proceedings, and inclusion of all tax-paying citizens in the lower electoral estates. These liberal amendments to the hallowed division between prince and estates tended to replace the centrifugal claims of absolute authority and independent privilege with a single framework of reciprocal rights and duties. The untouchable public rights of the estates were converted into operative constitutional functions in which the king had a legitimate claim to control.

The character of this constitution was revealed in the immediate reactions which each of the participants in the long drama had to it. The king used it immediately to oppose Metternich and to reject what he felt to be the encroachments of the Carlsbad decrees upon his sovereignty. The aristocracy which dominated the estates welcomed the constitution by taking over the government under it.[42] They accomplished their "restoration" through government rather than against it, thereby testifying to the development which had changed a pluralistic principality into a constitutional state. Finally, the liberals revealed the balance of forces expressed in the constitution by their uncertainties about it: their relief at the achievement of some constitutional form for rights was balanced by their disgust at the oligarchic substance of the rights thus secured, which they deemed detrimental to "king and people" alike.[43]

By and large the constitution proved appropriate to Wuerttemberg. None of the bitter struggle that was enlivening constitutional Baden was to extend into Wuerttemberg after 1819. If it was conflict under the constitution that was to produce the political dualism of the Badener Karl Rotteck, it was the resolution of conflict by the constitution that was to produce the *Rechtsstaat* doctrine of the Wuerttemberger Robert von Mohl.

Karl Rotteck and the Theory of Political Dualism

Between 1819 and 1824 the constitutional organs of government and diet in the state of Baden worked out a pattern of politics which attracted the attention of all Germany and contributed a significant strand to the national political experience. Whereas the struggle for a constitution had become a familiar process after the war, the conflict in Baden within a commonly-accepted constitution appeared new and fundamental in German political life. The weakness of the Baden aristocracy and the basis of representation in propertied individuals rather than in traditional corporations undermined the organic connections which the German constitutions of the day inserted between the independence of the princely governments and the autonomy of the representative assemblies. Consequently, the constitutional dualism that was implicit elsewhere became overt in Baden. For the government, the constitution was an instrument for attracting the support it could not otherwise requisition, and it called upon the chambers to vote the proposed budgets and adjourn. For the diet—and particularly the popular lower chamber—the constitution provided the means for the publication of the principles of individual freedom and for the reform of the political and social system in line with them; hence it refused to vote the requested monies until the government would embody its motions for such things as separation of justice and administration, jury courts, free press, public trials, militia army, economic liberty, and abolition of manorial tithes and dues in draft legislation. The Baden diet became an open forum in which for the first time not only constitutional principles but all manner of public issues were discussed in the fundamental terms of governmental prerogatives and human rights.

But if the struggle in Baden introduced a politically unlettered German public into the great issues of 19th-century European politics, yet these issues remained enclosed in the narrow constitutional dualism which was their mold. The preeminent role of the constitutional issue between government and assembly made all other rights, however fundamental in discussion, actually dependent upon the respective organs of the state for their realization. The issue of freedom had broken out of the closed circle of government but it did not penetrate beyond the restricted arena of the state. The conflict over the valid extent of individual liberties flowed into the preestablished channels of the constitutional dualism between government and assembly, where it seemed to become simply a question of the proper organization of the authorities operating the constitutionalized state. Thus, not only were leading liberal parliamentary leaders like Ludwig von Liebenstein and Ludwig Winter themselves state officials but the struggle over the most far-reaching issues was gradually but inexorably forced into a legalistic debate over constitutional interpretation. Whether it was the dispute over the freedom of the press, over nobiliary privileges, or over the relations of army and society, the pattern was uniform: the conflict began with the ringing proclamation of universal natural rights which must not be violated and ended with a specific defense of the rights of the diet under the constitution and of the priority of the constitution to confederate decree.[44] In none of these cases was the issue itself resolved. Once reduced to a question of constitutional exegesis it fed the dualism between ministry and chamber and became part of the problem of organizing the state.

This was the experience from which the political ideas of Karl Rotteck, professor at Freiburg and member of the Baden diet, took their rise. His writings, which were to be source-books for the liberal opposition all over Germany in the 19th century, actually immortalized the constitutional experience of the south for the whole nation.[45] Despite the superficial simplicity of his rationalistic method and his natural-law individualism Rotteck's political position was actually a composite one. Through him the remnants of German corporate dualism were metamorphosed into standard constitutional dualism for 19th-century moderate liberals. The gap between the radical monism of Rotteck's theoretical foundations and the moderate dualism of his results[46] is explicable as much by the actual influence of south German conditions as by the dialectical logic of the natural-law school. For Rotteck was a practising politician with a flair for generalization equally as much as he was a political philosopher,[47] and consequently the paralyzing duality between the requirements of practise and the implications of theory entered into the very substance of his political writing. His experience in constitutional Baden supplied this duality with its political dimension, and in turn he gave to southern constitutionalism a form which aligned it with the traditional division between the flesh and the spirit in German intellectual life.

The framework for Rotteck's political theory had been set well before the promulgation of the Baden Constitution in 1818. In his youth his native Austrian Breisgau had witnessed the influence of the French cultural Enlightenment institutionalized in the forms of Josephinian radical absolutism, and its later integration into Baden had brought French Revolutionary ideas and Napoleonic practice. This conditioning was reflected in the earliest and most influential of his major works, his *General History,* which began to appear from 1812. Here he insisted upon the fundamental distinction between the postulates of the "philosophers" and the actual events of history. Rotteck's early dedication to a "general" or "world" history, which he carefully defined as intermediary between the a priori idealism of "history of humanity" on the one hand and the meaningless purely empirical data of "universal history" on the other, impressed upon him the necessary looseness in the relationship between the singularity of system and the multiplicity of actual occurrences in human history.[48] It is hardly surprising, then, to find him explicitly dependent at this stage upon Kant and Montesquieu,[49] both of whom were so obviously plagued with the same kind of problem, or to see him specifying the lesson by claiming for monarchy on historical grounds the primacy which he thought the contract theory postulated for democracy.[50]

When, under the influence of his parliamentary experience, Rotteck came to formulate his political system this framework helped to translate the actual conflict into the memorable terms of an absolute political dualism. He made continuous use of Kant's desperately unified political philosophy and of the logical unity in French natural-rights thinking—particularly Rousseau's general will—but his inclination was ever the reverse of his models': he persisted in emphasizing disjunctions where they had achieved system. His set toward political actuality urged him in every case to pose the duality of practice against the monism of the ideal. Rotteck accepted the abstract monism of a cosmic law of freedom. Under it, however, he redrew the general distinctions between speculative and practical reason, the external and inner worlds, laws of nature and morality, which Kant had made in philosophy, and he moved these polarities wholly into experience. Thus where Kant had sought to establish law (*Recht*) as the synthesis in experience of the separate worlds of morality and nature Rotteck blurred the sharpness of the metaphysical distinctions only to etch them the more vividly in the concept and the realm of law (*Recht*) itself. He explicitly redefined Kant's idea of moral freedom so as to bring it out of the insulated realm of the unconditioned into an essential relationship with actual freedom of choice,[51] and after attenuating the distinction between morality and law he interned the polar relationships between norms and facts within the sphere of law.[52] He saw the dichotomy between ideal and existential components running through every field of law,[53] and he climaxed this kind of analysis with his finding that the law of the state consisted in both the ultimately absolute private law of individuals and the ultimately conditioned public law of political society.[54]

It followed from these philosophical assumptions that when Rotteck came to treat of politics proper, he rejected every convention commonly employed by constitutional dualists to compromise, moderate, or synthesize their antitheses. His abhorrence of the middle way was such that he stridently refused to associate himself with the reformist tendency which actually occupied a position in the political spectrum similar to his own, for the simple but basic reason that he mistrusted conciliation as a method of politics.[55] Consistently with this judgment Rotteck excluded from his politics every social force or institution that had traditionally served or could possibly serve to mediate the conflicting claims of individual rights and governmental power: a political aristocracy would not mediate between people and government, for it would simply form "part of the government," "united" with the prince "against the people";[56] in general, the historically autonomous "corporations" were rejected in favor of "societies," and since the latter were founded upon precisely the same contractual basis as the state, itself merely a civil society, they shared its antinomies;[57] nationality, finally, found no political or social role in Rotteck's formal thought, and even in his practical politics he used it merely as a variable accessory, a derivative from the fortuitous circumstances of the natural rights constitutionalism which remained ever primary to him.[58]

But all this was a build-up to the most striking manifestation of the dualism which was the final effect of Rotteck's political thinking: his open and emphatic denial that "the state power" can have an actual unity. Not only did Rotteck dismiss the application of the organic analogy to the state as utterly inappropriate,[59] but he expressly affirmed the necessity and the desirability of dividing the state power irrevocably between government and parliament and of relegating the unity of the state to the realm of abstract ideals.[60]

Rotteck's positive political theory was founded upon his tendency to diffuse an original unity in its concrete application. The system of absolute rational principles upon which all states rested was given the revealing label of "State Metaphysics," and only after it had been sifted through "State Physics"—"the empirically given conditions, forces, needs, influences and counter-influences" which work on the state—does "the merely ideal nature or abstract essence of the states established in the State Metaphysics" obtain "its more definite, material content" and does the application of fundamental law (*Recht*) to the actual life of the state become possible.[61] Hence it was hardly fortuitous that the problems connected with Rotteck's political doctrine appear in the third section, on operative theory, for the monism of his political metaphysics became constitutional dualism after it was refracted through the "physics," or more accurately the typology of the circumstances of politics.

The substance of this logical development is the story of the realization of the "general will (*Gesammtwille*)." Rotteck's first step was to establish the general will as the metaphysical unity behind all states. It arose out of the social contract into which autonomous individuals freely entered, and thereby it inherited the authority pertinent to the absolute original rights of all men to an equal freedom; but it was not simply the sum of these rights, for Rotteck's general will was an attribute of the integral "personality" of civil society, whose function consisted not only in the mechanical legal organization of individual rights but also in the direct contribution, from its own nature, to the development of man's physical and moral capacities.[62] The general will served as a unifying concept whereby the individualistic justification of the negative liberal state was joined to the far-reaching power of the positive moral state. The explicit duality of purpose with which Rotteck equipped his theoretical state[63] revealed his appreciation of the social benefits of independent political authority as well as of guaranteed individual rights, and yet the abstract principle which he selected to unify this juxtaposition of conservative and liberal goals was not a compromise synthesis but the radical dogma of popular sovereignty which was expressed in the general will.

When Rotteck applied his political metaphysics to the various kinds of geographical, economic, and sociological circumstances which help to mold actual states, the duality which had been merged in the theoretical unity of the general will reasserted itself in the form of an out-and-out dualism in constitutional doctrine. The radicalism which characterized his natural-rights philosophy of absolute freedom and equality was moderated in its effects but not in its approach, for the actual expression of the general will in a power independent of its logical democratic expression operated to neutralize democracy while the simultaneous retention of the metaphysically radical general will as a ubiquitous "ideal" for governments preserved Rotteck's radicalism of attitude even in political practice.[64] The result was a constitutional system in which the logic of democracy butted continually against the necessities of contemporary circumstance and bowed reluctantly before them.

Thus Rotteck validated two separate and mutually independent organs of government, the "natural" and the "artificial (kuenstlich)." By the "natural" power Rotteck meant the representative assembly, by the "artificial" power the specific personality (whether singular or collective) invested with the chief governing authority of the state. But, as the labels indicate, this was not the usual doctrine of the balanced constitution. The validity of the artificial power, and consequently of the mixed state, was founded in the requirements of practice rather than principle, in convenience rather than natural law. Provision for its establishment was to be found neither in the social contract which authorized civil society nor in a rulership contract, whose existence Rotteck denied.[65] And it was not to be found in such fundamental charters precisely because Rotteck viewed this separation of powers as simply a contingent determination of the general will that was not "identical" with the "essence" or the purpose of the state but was only a "means deemed advisable for its attainment." [66] Democracy, then, Rotteck admitted, is the "most natural" and indeed, the original form of every state, since it is the immediate expression of the authoritative general will;[67] moreover, it is still the fitting form for small states:[68] only the circumstances of contemporary political societies, such as size, which demand special instrumentalities of government, make its supersession feasible.[69] Yet the dualism which Rotteck justified so contingently was a perfectly genuine one for him. He condemned democracy along traditional lines for concentrating undivided power in the hands of a temporary majority and tending ineluctably toward despotism or anarchy,[70] and he wound up with the liberal theorists' traditional identification of the mixed constitution with "the true republic." [71] He insisted not only upon the independence of the artificial organ from the people as a condition of its validity but also upon a distribution of powers which equipped it with an authority equal to that of the natural organ.[72]

Clearly, the simultaneous insistence upon the logical primacy of a unitary democracy and the actual primacy of a mixed state posed difficulties. Rotteck's resolution of them was embodied in his deliberately ambiguous concept of the "natural" power of the state. In this cultivated ambiguity lay the key to much of Rotteck's thinking and the liberal politics that stemmed from him. Rotteck shifted artfully between the employment of the natural, or representative, organ as the direct institutional expression of the ideal general will and its use as one of two empirical, fallible, balanced agencies of government. Thus the fundamental function of the natural organ lay in its disposition over the rights which the general will of the people reserved to itself, and yet this same organ had not only to be checked by an independent government in the exercise of this power but could even be considered as a part of this "artificial" power itself.[73] By means of this very elastic concept of the natural organ Rotteck introduced a curious flexibility into the state. When the natural organ was brought near the general will of the people and treated as its immediate representative in the actual constitution, the resulting propinquity of the ideal general will to real politics authorized both a decisive spirit of critical opposition to established "artificial" government and the infinite expansibility of the scope of the state power as a whole.[74] When, however, the unitary and ideal general will was placed far above the actual practice of both artificial and natural organs, it led naturally to the emphasis upon the mutually checking duality of the governing powers, and it became the legal authority for the radical curtailment of the activities of the state as such.[75] This broad range of possibilities was encompassed by a set of malleable formulas whose function was essentially to supply the looseness of logical framework required for Rotteck's desiderata of a state potentially strong but actually weak. The political function of this approach was exemplified in Rotteck's distinction between the distribution of powers which he did advocate and the classic separation of powers which he did not. He denied that each power in the state (i.e. the legislative and the administrative) should have its own distinct organ and favored rather the participation by each organ in both powers, because this principle provided the necessary flexibility for the preponderance of ruler or diet according to circumstances, and because as against the finality of the formal separation of powers it provided both present division and potential unity.[76]

Precisely the same kind of thinking, in which a unitary ideal became half of a dualistic real situation, was visible in Rotteck's proposals on the constitution of the representative diet. Equality

of rights is essential to—indeed, "identical with"—the fundamental natural law and with freedom, and free individuals participate equally in the contractual establishment of the general
will.[77] In his description of the physical circumstances of actual
states, however, Rotteck recognized the existence of "classes" of
inhabitants—physical, functional, and even social—which are unknown to "the abstract concept of the state" but are "natural,
almost inevitable" formations and necessary objects of consideration for theorist and politician alike who want to "think about
reality rather than a Utopia." [78] This conflict between theory and
practice had its particular constitutional embodiment in the
apportionment of political rights, since civil rights remained
private and therefore equal by definition. Rotteck divided the
operative electoral system into two sections and assigned a different principle to each—equality to the passive suffrage, class distinctions to the active.[79] The overt rationale behind this division
consisted in Rotteck's idea that natural law was appropriate to
the passive suffrage while "The question of active suffrage is more
of a political [i.e. instrumental] than of a strictly legal nature." [80]
Behind this formal argument, in turn, lay a more revealing
ground to which Rotteck unwittingly referred when he insisted
upon group rather than individual qualifications to the active
suffrage.[81] The prime realities of Rotteck's ideal world were
individuals, those of the actual world groups and institutions:
deputies were inescapably individuals and consequently to them
the ideal of equality applied; voters and electors were a mass,
and to them therefore the necessary limitations and diversifica-
tions of empirical life were "naturally" applicable. Literal representation of the people was forsaken for a pragmatically "true"
representation, by whatever system of active suffrage this result
was reached, and correspondingly the collective ideal of a political
"nation" was rejected as a "fiction," in favor of the "natural"
representation of particular local interests and districts.[82] The
rare spectacle of a corporate electoral system recommended as a
practical offshoot of "the democratic principle" and an individualistic theory of natural law—to such oddities was Rotteck
driven in his accommodation of his political system to the con-

temporary German reality in order that at least a minimum program might be actually achieved.[83]

Even when he confronted the ultimate question of all politics —the limits of civil obedience—Rotteck could not rise to a categorical resolution. He sought to ground political obligation upon a combination of the classic doctrine of consent from Rousseau and the equally classic doctrine of inalienable individual rights which had been immortalized by Locke. In Rotteck's abstract musings the sphere of the general will left the private rights of the individual inviolate and there was no conflict, but when he came down to cases the wonted rift appeared. The right of revolution which Rousseau and Locke had both affirmed was lost in Rotteck, for he tended in practice to stand paralyzed between their positions. On the one hand the state, together with all its organs, was sacred, since it was founded on the general will;[84] on the other hand, its sphere of action was limited by equally sacred natural and social rights. Within its proper sphere government cannot be rightfully resisted.[85] Outside this sphere, however, Rotteck found the conflict of the two sanctities logically insoluble, for there could be no rightful obedience to an unlawful command of ruler or majority but neither could there be rightful resistance to agencies which were, however temporarily aberrant, essentially organs of the holy general will. Characteristically, he took refuge in the purely amoral and a-legal world of "fact" and strife. The individual has undertaken the solemn obligation that he will "apply no self-help and suffer all the privation and injustice which flows inevitably from the nature or the faulty institutions of the community." [86] The majority were told either to complain "in an orderly way" through a constitutionally established organ, or, if there were none such, to understand that any further decision—whether in favor of submission to injustice or for unlawful resistance—was wholly *"de facto (faktisch),"* had nothing whatsoever to do with rights, obligation, or law, and was subject to purely expediential considerations of which the horrors of civil war were the most outstanding.[87]

The paralysis which Rotteck's political ethics suffered in the final practical issue posed by man's life in society furnished eloquent testimony to the pulverizing impact which the limiting conditions in the German environment exercised upon political ideals. Karl Rotteck was the archetype of what was to become one of the most remarked tendencies in the left wing of the German 19th-century liberalism: the transformation of the energy harbored within the categorical simplicity of radical theory into the negative opposition of one organ of a dualistic system against the other in radical practice.

The Doctrine of the *Rechtsstaat*

The south rejuvenated constitutional dualism in a liberal form, but it also provided the key for its transcendence. The need for securing unity among the organs of the state and between the governors and the governed, a need which even Rotteck had sensed and feebly tried to fill with his admittedly abstract "idea of the state," was most seriously tackled in Germany through the doctrine of the *Rechtsstaat,* the state of law. This concept was to become the focal point in the standard German theories of political freedom and in the due course of time it came to mean all things to all men,[88] but its original bent reveals its essential function in German political thinking—the practical reconciliation of new liberties with old authorities.

In its origins the doctrine of the *Rechtsstaat* was simply the southern version of that familiar modernization of the state which was being attempted under frankly authoritarian auspices in the north of Germany. The powerful unity which the institutions of the Prussian state supplied had to be supplanted in the south by doctrine. The liberal policy which in Prussia seemed to require only another governmental department sponsored in the south a political dualism which required a strenuous new doctrinal effort for its resolution. The *Rechtsstaat* doctrine which came out of these circumstances between 1815 and 1830 attempted to rationalize the combination of individualism in state purpose with traditionalism in state structure. In the subsequent history of the doctrine, one or the other of these factors was emphasized in accordance with the temper of the times, but the idea never entirely escaped from the dictates of its initial function. Thus the appropriation of the doctrine by the progressives who, after 1830, turned it into an antonym of police state and a synonym for decisive liberalism was compensated by its diversion after mid-century from its prescription of the purposes to its prescription of the outer forms of state action. These two later stages in the development of the *Rechtsstaat* doctrine, in which it appeared first as a full-blown political theory and then as an hermeneutic principle of jurisprudence, were equally derivative from its initial usage. It was originally, during the first third of the century, a descriptive category applicable to all modern states which used general laws to harmonize the sovereign concentration of political power with liberal policy.

Before the *Rechtsstaat* became a doctrine during the post-Liberation period it had a prenatal history as a term of political reference in which two of its later salient characteristics were already apparent. The *Rechtsstaat* was not univocally liberal; and it was concerned more with the redefinition than with the limitation of the state.

The first employments of the word [89] have been traced to the reactionary Adam Mueller, in his Berlin lectures of 1808,[90] and to the liberal Karl Theodor Welcker, professor at Giessen Hesse-Darmstadt), in his book *The Foundations of Law, State, and Penalty*, published in 1813. Despite the patent divergences in their fundamental political orientation the respective functions to which they applied the concept *Rechtsstaat* showed remarkable similarities. For both men it was a category of philosophical politics through which the raw material of the new political reality uncovered by the French Revolution was ordered. For both men then it was at least as much a unifying as a discriminating principle. It was oriented toward the recently realized facts of individual liberties, and it distinguished the kind of states that did from the kind of states that did not account for them. But in their usage of *Rechtsstaat* both writers proceeded to go well beyond the mere recognition of such facts. They adjusted the traditional cosmos so as to include them in its system. The state *qua Rechtsstaat* was definitely excluded from certain areas, particularly in Welcker's application of the concept, but in the last analysis it was difficult to say whether the scope of the state had actually been diminished or merely defined along a new plane.

The key to this primitive function of the *Rechtsstaat* as a concept in political thought would seem to lie in the opening problem which by a striking coincidence was posed almost identically by Mueller and Welcker. The issue was the contradiction between theory and practice, and both men undertook to pose it and to solve it from the point of view of practice.[91] Common to both men was the conviction that the multiformity of reality could no longer be encompassed by the prevalent absolute systems of deductive reason and in all its variegated specificity must be the irrefragable touchstone of a new political philosophy. But neither man was willing—for opposite reasons—to surrender the field to an unbridled positivism, since this would validate revolutionary achievements unwelcome to the one and capricious princely actions hateful to the other. Their task was consequently not to abolish but to reconstruct along a new dimension the relationship between theory and practice, norm and act, unity and diversity. The *Rechtsstaat* was a product of this reconstruction. Despite all divergences in content, its weight for both writers lay definitely on the unifying side of these disjunctions; its function was to restore order in the shuffled social cosmos.

When Mueller declared the state to be "the totality of human affairs, their merger into a vital whole," [92] and the idea of law (*Recht*) to be the principle of "unity (*Einheit*)" in this totality,[93] he was obviously seeking to restore authority over a fragmented reality. Requiring the process of individuation for the rejection of the system of natural law, and yet fearing its consequences, Mueller set up the *Rechtsstaat* as a dialectical idea which established a general control over particular objects, while it remained internally related to their specificity and to the requirements of their existence. The *Rechtsstaat* did not, in this usage, signify a new kind of state but a new way of looking at the old state; it was the name given the traditional political authority whose justification had now to rest upon its conscious organization of the "freedom of the individual citizen" and "the freedom of the people." [94] The best constitution remained an aristocratic monarchy, governed by "the law of the unity of power," and in effect absolute.[95]

Welcker was far more interested in carving out a realm of inviolate freedom for the individual. Yet in the last analysis the term functioned for him, too, as much to limit as to guarantee such a realm. For Welcker the *"Rechtsstaat"* was the "state of reason," or a fundamental type of the state characteristic of the modern period in the history of humanity.[96] Welcker's abstract dictum that the foundation of both law and state was vested in the consent of all was elaborated to mean not popular sovereignty but a conservative indifference to the actual constitutional distribution of political power and a formal sanction of consent in the rights of petition and emigration only.[97] These rights were the substantive "points" of the good constitution. They clearly lumped together the acceptance of traditional rulership and the recognition of the undeniable claims of individual rights in an indigestible mixture. Their leaven consisted in "the primary condition of every *Rechtsstaat*" which cut across these substantive "points"—the necessary observation by both ruler and individual citizen of the "form of objective law" [98]—and with this formulation the crux of the problem passed from the distribution to the nature of the state's power. But here the formal emphasis in the *Rechtsstaat* stood revealed. For the administration of *Recht* was not the sole purpose of the *Rechtsstaat,* Welcker admitted frankly, "As . . . the idea of the absolute good should be reflected in all of men's actions so should it even in their activity in the state and in the activity of the state itself." [99] "The final goal of the state is: the greatest possible attainment of the virtue and humanity and thus of the happiness [*Glueckseligkeit*] of all, through and in the form of objective law." [100] Thus for Welcker the absolute subjective moral rights of the free individual and the traditional moral controls by the ruler over the individual in such fields as education, religion, and culture were equally valid. The function of the *Rechtsstaat* was not to exclude this vital area from the compulsory scope of the state but rather to organize the variegated substance of both individual and sovereign claims. And this, as Welcker confessed, was possible only if the *Rechtsstaat* was conceived as a formative or ordering principle rather than a terminal idea. "The enactment of fundamental law (*Rechtsgesetz*) prescribes only the outer form for spiritual and moral activity, just as the physical organism is the form for the expression and activity of the soul. A state without positive moral inspiration would be like a marriage, a family, in legal form but without love." [101]

The formalistic element in the *Rechtsstaat* doctrine, which became predominant after mid-century thus assisted at the very birth of the *Rechtsstaat* as a liberal concept. Welcker's argument bears a striking similarity to that of Friedrich Julius Stahl, the Bavarian whose transplantation to Prussia after 1840 led him to renew Adam Mueller's conservative exegesis of the *Rechtsstaat* and whose classic statement is usually credited [102] with having first formalized the doctrine.[103] The similarity establishes the continuity, but between Welcker's emphasis upon the *Rechtsstaat* as "form" and Stahl's definition of it as "method" lay Robert von Mohl's elaboration of it as "purpose."

It was Robert von Mohl who developed the idea of the *Rechtsstaat* from a descriptive category into a doctrine and who thereby raised it to prominence in German political theory. The halcyon days of its doctrinal influence came indeed only after 1830 during the pre-March period, but its first characteristic appearance in Mohl had its roots in the conditions of the 20's. Himself a Wuerttemberger, he elaborated it in the first volume of his treatise on the constitutional law of the kingdom of Wuerttemberg, published in 1829. Moreover, the political dualism which took its rise in the south during the Restoration period seems to have been the decisive if unwitting circumstance in Mohl's elevation of the *Rechtsstaat* to the level of a self-conscious political doctrine.

In 1829, before he began reading the concept back into the whole natural-law tradition, Mohl recognized as his particular predecessors in the development of the *Rechtsstaat* as a political theory, two Restoration political writers whose peculiar contribution consisted precisely in an attempted practical adaptation of the familiar Kantian tradition to contemporary conditions. Neither the Saxon Karl Poelitz nor the Bavarian-born and trained Sylvester Jordan[104] actually used the term *"Rechtsstaat"* but they set the stage for its elevation into a key doctrine.[105] They unwittingly demonstrated that Kant's abstract principle of the state as a mere instrument of natural law (*Recht*) for the simple regulation of conflicting relationships among absolutely free individuals could have no precise or consistent application to the constitutional states of post-1815 Germany. Their inability to find a familiar political system that could fit or direct their analysis of post-liberation Germany prepared the ground for the new doctrine of the *Rechtsstaat*.

Both men started from the absolute moral freedom of every individual and followed the already broken logical trail to natural law (*Recht*) as the order which made possible the realization of morality by securing external freedom for individuals in actual society and for the state as the institution which enforced this law.[106] If the *Rechtsstaat* connoted only this substantive limitation of the state to the enforcement of the law of mutual freedom among its citizens and against other states its meaning would be relatively simple. But the real meaning of the concept for German political thinking actually hinged on the further development of the argument in Poelitz and Jordan. Both were intensely concerned with the thorny problem of applying the principle to the "actual states" around them,[107] and in the process of this application the literal *Rechtsstaat* in the pure Kantian sense—the definition of the state in terms of the enforcement of natural law as its exclusive purpose—was distorted into something much more complicated. Where the literal conception of the German classical philosophers had been designed to characterize the free state by its inherent nature whatever its constitution, the Restoration political writers, in seeking to make it practical for their times, modified this simple structure in two related ways. First, they recognized the necessity of a constitution which permitted the participation of the people or its representatives in the governing power of the state. This amendment was most striking in Jordan, who maintained frankly that in principle the governing power of the state was absolute and unconditioned since its sole function was the execution of an absolute and unconditioned fundamental law, but that in actual practice the ruler required the support, the assent, and the participation of the people for the validity of its measures. Secondly, their categorical assertions that the purpose of the state consists entirely in establishing "the rule of fundamental law (*Recht*)" [108] could not stand proof against their recognition of the moral and social functions actually pursued by the German states. Whether by logical legerdemain or by bare-faced contradiction, both men added these purposes to the putative exclusive legal nature of the state.[109]

The result of these modifications was a curiously loose theoretical structure. The classical norm of *Recht* was itself amorphous enough, even in principle, since it united what Jordan admitted to be two incompatibles—the most extreme possible freedom of individuals with the absolute rule of law and of the "state power" that administered it—[110] and the acknowledgment that the state had secondary purposes that went beyond the administration of *Recht* put an intolerable strain upon the theory of the state. Similarly, their practical endorsement of representative constitutionalism undermined their fundamental principle that the primacy of *Recht* dictated a pragmatic test for constitutions and hence a complete constitutional relativism.[111] In a sense, these two dilemmas were mutually compensatory, for with the loss of the rigid limitation upon the sphere of valid state action the individual freedom protected by the law needed the new guarantee of participation in the state power.

But under what general concept was this potpourri of principle and concession to be held together? For both Poelitz and Jordan the unifying formula was the time-worn device of the "organic" state[112] in which the popular role in government was somehow meshed with the absolute indivisibility of the state power, and the dominant role of the ruler with the inviolable rights of the citizen.[113] Robert von Mohl, however, came forward in this situation with a new unifying formula in the explicit doctrine of the *Rechtsstaat*.

The early works in which Mohl first developed the *Rechtsstaat* as a central concept in political theory started with the problems which had beset Poelitz and Jordan and these became the theoretical cradle of the doctrine. Mohl's ostensible concern was with the purpose rather than the structure of the state, and yet he could not keep himself from the constitutional problems posed by the politics of his day. He declared the essential point in modern statecraft to lie in the "tasks" of the state, to which any form of government could in due circumstances be most appropriate,[114] but his first published work dealt exclusively with the problem of representative government[115] and even in his mature writings he required some kind of "participation in public business" as an unconditioned right of the qualified citizen.[116] Moreover, Mohl raised the second great theoretical problem of his age when he gave an elastic definition to the purpose of the state, however constituted. On the one hand he was categorical in his assertion that the very nature of the modern state, "with all its institutions," "is intended exclusively to protect and make possible" "the freedom of the citizen," [117] and he insisted upon the negative formulation of the state's function in terms of "the removal of hindrances" and its abstention from all activities which could be undertaken by individuals and their free associations.[118] On the other hand, however, Mohl was equally adamant in rejecting the implication in this definition that the *Rechtsstaat* was simply a law-enforcing institution *vis-à-vis* transgressors.[119] The legal activity of the state made up but half its function, and he deemed this half perhaps superior in value but certainly inferior in extent to the "removal of hindrances which stand in the way of the general rational development of humanity." [120] This removal Mohl acknowledged to be equivalent to "positive action" by the state in supporting and supplementing man's efforts to achieve his life's goals.[121]

At this point, however, Mohl separated himself from the other political publicists whose thinking had revolved around the same problems. He rejected the outright dualism of Rotteck and he ignored the evasive organicism of Poelitz and Jordan. Mohl attempted to retain the constitutional alternatives and the flexibility of state purpose required by German conditions and yet to obliterate the line drawn by his predecessors between ideals and existences, form and content, principles and concessions. His design was to homogenize all these into a single order of "political science." This was the context for his introduction of the *Rechtsstaat* as a central concept in German politics. Its function was to merge the norm of individual freedom with the further-reaching facts of political authority. The union of the notion of "fundamental law (*Recht*)" with "state" was appropriate to this end because it synthesized the dual meaning of law in the development of modern politics: the guarantees which theory assigned to it for personal liberties and the instrument which jurisprudence recognized in it for the expression of sovereign will. Thus Mohl's *Rechtsstaat* stood at one and the same time for the particular theory of state which prescribed the protection and support of individual rights as its purpose and for the general historical category of all "modern" statehood.[122] Later Mohl was himself to acknowledge the tension in this merger when he admitted that the concept of the *Rechtsstaat* was perhaps too narrow for the reality to which he was applying it,[123] but he applied it nonetheless. He grafted individualism in purpose upon lawfulness in form as essential requisites of all modern states, and thereby he made the liberal state a matter not of constitution but of definition, guaranteed by "the laws of thought" which made a functioning political system of any other kind inconceivable.[124] Mohl's *Rechtsstaat* doctrine thus required a strong and independent political authority for the realization of the individuals' goals in society. The doctrine of the *Rechtsstaat* became the means of integrating individual freedom as an operative policy into the larger order of existing states; personal and civil rights became an end product toward which a strong and independent political authority could work under varying constitutional conditions and with manifold legislative means. It is hardly surprising, therefore, to find that Mohl's first systematic development of the *Rechtsstaat* idea was designed to defend rather than to combat the positive welfare activities of the state in terms of individual liberty.[125]

This inter-locking of *Rechtsstaat* and individualism brought to the latter a new applicability in Germany and to the former a doctrinal content. From a descriptive category signifying the historical appearance of states which operated through general laws, the *Rechtsstaat* was now to become the central tenet of a political theory which validated any kind of rulership so long as it governed through the generic type of modern state, which by its very nature operated upon all its citizens according to general laws and with the ultimate aim of their emancipation within the laws. The theoretical motive behind Mohl's *Rechtsstaat* was carried on in his endorsement of "social science," with which he supplemented it after the failure of political moderation in 1848. The origin which he assigned to social science applied equally to the *Rechtsstaat*—that it came from "the necessity of interposing a new sphere between the doctrine of the state power and its organism on the one side and the doctrine of the civil rights and duties of individuals on the other." [126] Growing out of the political experience of the constitutional south after 1815, the doctrine of the *Rechtsstaat* represented the classic attempt to by-pass constitutional conflict and to bind all political authorities, traditional and representative alike, in the common service of civil freedom. The *Rechtsstaat* was born and remained an idea of conservation as well as liberalization.

The German Student Unions (1815-1833)

In addition to the bureaucratic liberalism within absolute governments like the Prussian and the institutional liberalism within constitutional states like the southern, the political stimulus of national liberation generated still a third type of postwar movement for reform. The unsettling pressure of the occupation and the war reached beyond governments and assemblies to trigger the political mobilization of a section of the governed society itself. With this first crystallization of private individuals into a popular political organization the third liberal possibility was planted in the seedling bed of modern German history.

This third alternative consisted in a combination of two distinct factors, one sociological and the other theoretical. It included, first, a social institution which rooted an unofficial political program in a permanent, sizeable, and influential group in the country, and secondly, a political program which looked to the "people" rather than to the traditional organs of authority for the agency which would execute the desired reorganization of the nation. Neither autonomous pressure organizations nor revolutionary political ideas were overly rare after 1815, but only the German Student Unions (*Burschenschaften*) combined both.[127] Mirrored in the complex relationship between the Student Unions as social institutions and the Student Unions as political organizations was the whole tension between social capacities and political claims which was to dog the future development of German liberalism.[128]

The leaders of the movement for Student Unions conceived of them both as reformed vocational connections of the traditional type and as microcosms of the entire national society.[129] The two views were sufficiently agreed upon to make possible the famous Wartburg Festival of October 1817 and the formation of a national cover organization, the General German Student Union, in October 1818, but a difference in emphasis persisted between those who would make the program of reforming student corporations an end in itself, and those who would treat the reformed associations as cells for the reorganization of the nation.[130] An important sociological meaning was lent to this difference by the coincidence of the first group with the students who were working for reform from within the specific traditional associations[131] and the coincidence of the second with those who eschewed these associations to create new ones.[132] Thus, the degree of entanglement with the historic social structure of Germany helped to determine whether the Student Unions as social institutions were simply reformed functional corporations or free associations with general social and political goals. It is hardly surprising, then, to find the political activists in the early stages of the movement concentrated around the student union known as "The Blacks (*die Schwarzen*)" at Giessen, where student reformers were most influenced by political professors and least embroiled with the traditional student corporations.

In one sense, the movement as a whole can be characterized as political, for its ultimate aim was the "unity and freedom" of Germany.[133] But the disparity in the social views of the organization led its different sections to very different kinds of politics. The Student Unions were divided, in the characterization of a contemporary unionist,[134] between a party that "thought only of a spiritual rising of the people" and one that thought of a political rising like "the revolutions in Spain, Italy, and Greece." The first of these parties considered the Student Unions as the seat of an ideal national unity, whence the moral and patriotic training of young men would slowly percolate through the nation at large to bring about the desired political changes in the due course of time; the second of these parties would use the Unions directly as part of the mobilization of the whole German society for mass action in favor of a united Germany on a liberal constitutional base. This political line-up, like the concern with politics in general, corresponded to the social distinctions within the movement. The more conservative political wing was roughly identical with the group that was most preoccupied with the reform of the old student corporations as such. The political radicals in the movement could be identified correspondingly with those who were most emancipated from the traditional associations.

The intensification of reaction in Germany after 1815 favored the development of radical predominance. During the formative period of the Student Union organization, from its origins in 1815 to the enactment of the Carlsbad decrees in 1819, all the variegated tendencies—social and political alike—were harmoniously juxtaposed, if not composed, under the flexible shield of liberation nationalism. Indeed, the cohesive force of nationalism, its capacity to absorb the abrasions and frictions of ill-mated and illogical components, could hardly have had a more convincing demonstration. Thus the first general meeting of student unionists, in April 1818, produced a prospectus in which the "quick and violent" introduction of "innovation . . . by individuals" and the gradual influence to be exercised "from above down" by the future "servants of church and state" were listed as equally permissible public goals of student activity.[135] This latitudinarianism represented a kind of *modus vivendi* in which the vague notion of a national German spirit seemed to harmonize the narrowly functional reform of the traditional students' corporations with the civic reform of the general community. Only the extremes of complete corporate insularity and of the immediate political action by the unions as such "upon the shaping . . . of our Fatherland" were excluded from the accepted formulas of the period.[136]

In the second phase of the movement, which ran from the suppression of open organizations in 1819 to the suppression of secret organizations in 1826 the primary concerns of the Student Unions were definitely oriented away from corporate student interests toward politics, and within politics from non-partisanship to radicalism. The organs of this development were the secret political cells which grew up within the camouflaged Student Unions after the outlawing of public political discussion by the Carlsbad decrees. In the confusion and embitterment aroused by these edicts the leadership of the remaining associations fell to the cells.[137] The more secret and highly organized the cells, the more they dominated the parent bodies and the more politically extreme were the goals of their domination. Just as a network of "narrower associations," with a program of liberal constitutionalism, tended to control the public unions, so the "Youth League (*Juenglingsbund*)," with a belief in popular sovereignty, tended to direct the association. The democratic revolutionary junta around Karl Follen in Switzerland supplied, in turn, the organizing force behind the politically more inchoate branches of the League in Germany. Certainly this organization was of the loosest kind, since all varieties of social and political views continued to characterize the students, and since the Student Unions were a convenient framework for the political training of their individuals rather than themselves units in a political party or conspiracy. But still, the result was that in the student movement there was no point of political focus short of radical dogma.

The final phase of the Student Unions as an organized movement, from the political prosecutions of 1826 to the general dissolution of 1833, witnessed the unravelling of the strands which had been harmonized by the indefinite nationalism of the first stage and held in suspension by the political resentment of the second. The political suppression of 1824-1826 smashed hard at the political cells—particularly the Youth League—but left the rest of student union institutions relatively unscathed. The reorientation of the movement which began in 1827, consequently, went along two diametrically opposed lines. On the one hand, the Arminians revived the program of the moral, organizational, and social reform of student life, but now overwhelmingly within the non-political functional framework of the students' corporation. The Germanists (*Germanen*), on the other hand, drew from their losses at the hands of the governments the lesson only that the student unions had been insufficiently politicized. Now they sought to impart to the unions themselves "a practical-political tendency" [138]—which meant the transformation of the student unions into political clubs.[19] The Arminians were liberal reformers in student business and conservatives in politics; the Germanists were radical politicians and conservative students.[140] This confusion of positions was actually quite reasonable: the Arminians were social reformers within the limits of the German corporative society and politically indifferent beyond it, while the Germanists, essentially political reformers, were heedless of corporative concerns. Consequently the first accepted the established political framework in order not to endanger or divert their liberal reorganization of student groupings, while the second of these parties tended to accept the external forms of the traditional student associations because of their own unconcern for student affairs and their great concern to adapt the student unions to political conspiracy. And so it was that in the final stages of the Student Union movement its implications for German history were worked up into the overt levels of its own actual development. Attachment to the kind of social grouping which typified the traditional structure of the German people meant ultimate submission to the political authority which traditionally controlled it, however liberal the localized program of reform might be. The birth of an autonomous popular movement for constitutional freedom was conditioned by emancipation from the historic social forms. For intellectuals this social emancipation left them with no anchor short of revolutionary faith.

Hence revolutionary radicalism became, in the post-liberation period, the characteristic political attitude of the Student Unions. "The path of revolution is the only one that should be pursued for the present," the Stuttgart meeting of the Germanists resolved categorically in 1832.[141] Despite the secessions which the resolution occasioned and the constant numerical preponderance of political moderation in all unionist groups the unremitting drift of the movement into the radicals' sphere of influence was unmistakable. The nature of this development, so difficult to chart in an organization as amorphous as the Student Unions, was graphically delineated in the ontogeny of the figure who fathered the revolutionary strand of the movement. The origins of political radicalism in modern Germany can be traced in the career of Karl Follen.

Karl Follen's contribution to the post-liberation era appears as something of an anomaly, for it combined two historically incompatible tenets.[142] Follen was primarily responsible both for the conversion of part of the Student Union into a revolutionary society for the realization of extreme natural-rights democracy, and for the introduction into the Student Union of the strong Christian emphasis which came to operate as a politically conservative, obfuscating, or pacifying force in this period. But the key to early German radicalism lay precisely in this combination. And this in two ways. First, the strong religious motif represented a theoretical root in German tradition to compensate for the social disembodiment of the radical intellectual, and to this extent it meant a kind of adaptation to historic German conditions for those who completely rejected the actual survivals of the corporate society. Secondly, the addition of a religious dimension to the revolutionary political thought of the west enhanced the dogmatism of radical doctrine and provided its first principles with the security of an absolute ground.

The Christian idea, as part of a program of corporate reform, was the midwife of Follen's radicalism. Foreshadowing the main trends in the history of the Student Unions in the large, Follen moved from an unpolitical nationalism in 1813 to revolutionary republicanism in 1817 through an intermediate period of Student Union activity characterized by a strong religious emphasis. The religious emphasis of Follen and his "Giessen Blacks" served the reform functions of breaking down social and provincial distinctions within the student estate. Hence their slogans constantly associated the members' capacities "as Christian, as Germans, and as students" and the purposes of their union "for faith, freedom, and Fatherland." [143] "Between non-Christians and non-Germans scarcely any distinction can be drawn, because devout [and] national striving are internally one . . . In the activation of patriotism the love of God finds expression." [144] For Follen and his friends, clearly, the religious emphasis was the bridge between the divided, corporately-structured nation in which they lived and the united but still politically undefined nation in which they wanted to live. Less bound up with the traditional student orders than were the new unions elsewhere and more intensely nationalistic than the others at this time, the Giessen Blacks singled out the Christian rather than the corporate strand in the German social tradition as the most flexible and mobile agent for the translation of the national dreams of the future into the unreformed existing present.

But no more than national liberation did this incarnation of the ideal in a combination of patriotic sermons and local student reform provide an anchorage for Follen and his disciples. From 1815 on they drifted ever more rapidly away from the organic grouping of student association, church, and nation into the uncharted waters of general politics. By mid-1817 the Giessen Blacks were participating, under Follen's leadership, in the popular agitation for a representative constitution in Hesse-Darmstadt. By the end of 1817 the Blacks had lost all interest in the student movement as such, and under the aegis of the political principles now systematically enunciated by Karl Follen and his brother August, they became a minuscule political organization for the revolutionary achievement of a radical democracy in Germany. August Follen's draft of a federal and democratic constitution for a monarchical Germany, elaborated during the winter of 1817-1818, was already left behind by the summer of 1818, when brother Karl insisted upon a unitary democratic republic.

The process of continuous radicalization seemed overtly to consist simply in the progressive drawing of ever more categorical inferences from the western theories of absolute natural rights, contractual basis of government, and popular sovereignty.[145] But in two different ways the political development of the Follen circle possessed an individual character which marked it off from the well-worn type of logical evolution from the model of Voltaire to that of Rousseau.

In the first place, the critical motif remained a predominant factor even in the constructive process of working out a positive democratic system. The persistence of a strongly negative approach denoted the exclusive sponsorship of political radicalism by socially uprooted intellectuals, whose characteristic political expression consisted precisely in universal criticism rather than concrete engagement. The general criticism of society involved, for this group, the specific revulsion against the state as such. Thus Robert Wesselhoeft, a prominent member of Karl Follen's youth movement, admitted frankly that "great bitterness against the state possessed me and I held myself absolved from all duties toward the state since it had violated its obligations toward me." [146] Karl Follen converted this anti-state attitude into the first proposition of his political theory: "Man, apart from any and every State, can never and may never, as a rational being, deny the goal of the development of his spiritual powers which is prescribed to him by his very existence." [147] This categorical rejection of the whole political system, which found expression in essentially negative programs like tyrannicide and mass emigration, was evidence of the tendency to identify the state with the existing form of the state and consequently to find no rest short of the revolutionary extreme.

Secondly, however, the conversion of temperamental extremism into an actionable radical doctrine of politics required some kind of positive grounding, and this was found only in religion. The religious derivation of their ultimate presuppositions provided, in Follen and his group, the kind of footing for revolutionary ideas which the German intellectuals could not find at this time for other forms of decisive political opposition. The basis for the political thinking and acting of Follen's group was "The Principle (der Grundsatz)," a religiously derived ethical proposition propounded by Follen from mid-1818. Hence they called themselves "The Unconditionals (die Unbedingten)," to show their uncompromising adherence to "The Principle." The two epithets underlined the intellectual process which lay behind this initial espousal of democratic revolution in Germany, for both referred to the moral point of transfer between the absolute categorical validity of transcendent religious truth and the uncompromising dogmatism of radical politics. "The Principle" asserted that "wherever a moral necessity exists, all means are permitted for those who are convinced of this necessity"—a formulation which summarized Follen's view of the unlimited practical obligation imposed by "moral necessity." [148] "Unconditional" was a logical designation for those holding to such a principle, but even more revealing was the range of interpretations which the Unconditionals themselves gave to their name. For beyond the obvious ethical application that "all means are equivalent" in reference to moral necessity,[149] the title was also applied to an even more practical political program—to an unconditional loyalty in the service of the Fatherland,[150] to the unconditional advocacy of "the republican form of state," [151] and to the unconditional sacrifice of all, including "the heart's blood of a friend," in the interest of the organization with this political and moral dedication.[152] Thus did the rigor of the moral imperative take on as its natural consequence the categorical simplicity of a revolutionary republican movement.

The ideas and the behavior of the Unconditionals show that if it was a combination of concrete disappointments, frustrations, and resentments at the existing governmental order of things which sparked the decisive transition from moral prescription to political action,[153] still it was the rejuvenated vitality of religious faith that supplied the authority for a definite system of such action.[154] Christianity provided the ultimate ground, goal, and inspiration for political institutions designed along humanist lines. Thus when toward the end of 1818 Karl Follen came to enshrine his cherished revolutionary ideals in a political lyric— "The Great Song"—he delivered it in a church and concluded it by taking Holy Communion. The appeal was to man and the ideal was that of the free secular state, but they were intertwined with a sanction that was God's. Thus:

> Only the equality of man, the will of the people, is
> Sovereign by grace of God.

> Up, up, my people, God created you free,
> Call yourself from slavery's wasteland
> To the haven of freedom. . . .
>
> One realm of free citizens,
> One God, One People, One Will should be,
> Yet only the humanity in the people creates the bond.[154]

Religion provided more than the ultimate ground of Follen's political system; it performed a crucial function within it. Follen's Christianity, with which he remained all his life, was a practice-oriented religion. ". . . All our various duties, our civil and religious obligations, are connected by an intimate and indissoluble bond, and . . . this is essentially a moral bond." [156] Religion did not occupy a sphere apart. Essentially it was the faith that "all things in the world are constituted and directed" to permit of man's moral fulfilment; it was "the germ of infinity" in man's activity; it was "the mightiest agent in human affairs." [157] Follen's Christianity, consequently, was an otherworldly dimension in man's worldly action; it penetrated his ethics and it penetrated his politics. Hence Follen's adoption of the familiar secular doctrines of natural rights, social contract, and popular sovereignty was complicated by the running Christian accompaniment which played along with them. The political difficulties inherent in democratic theories which sought to harmonize the civil rights of individuals with the political rights of majorities were thereby broadened into cosmic antinomies of secular life in general.

Follen started familiarly enough with the absolute and equal rights held in the state of nature by rational individuals who voluntarily contract into a civil state which will guarantee their freedom against "hindrances" and "arbitrary action." [158] But ultimately he drove a broad wedge into this apparently seamless web of political logic not simply through the dualism which assigned individual freedom to the realm of absolute morality and the state to the realm of law but even more divisively through the condemnation of the law and the state to an essential incompatibility with moral freedom. "Even in the most perfect possible state constitution, the general principle of the state can and will come into conflict with the individual who acts according to conviction." [159] To this antinomy between individual liberty and even a democratic state Follen added the further distinction between the guarantees of the general freedom which constitutes the "abstract" and "eternal purpose" of the state and the local adaptations to time, place, and circumstances which go into the various concrete versions of its "temporal purpose." [160] Once again this distinction meant, for Follen, a deprecation which rendered it the more profound: not only is representative democracy reduced to an imperfect necessary "temporal" substitute for the "eternal" and impracticable direct democracy but the whole category of actual, temporal states, together with their laws, "must be viewed as nothing good in itself but only as a smaller evil for the avoidance of a greater." [161]

Now, given this system which was so riddled with moral and political antinomies, the role of religion becomes clear: just as it deepened political into cosmic problems, so it supplied the transcendental unity which could resolve these problems and leave intact the threatened radical political principles. For Follen himself recognized the disintegration which he had sewn into his theory and he used religious values to overcome it. Since the individuals who create the state should and must rebel when the government violates its purpose of protecting the general freedom, and since Follen's depreciation of political actuality made such violation inevitable, he admitted that "according to this principle no particular state could justly exist and every state must find itself in a condition of revolution from the very start." [162] But all these objections disappear and "everything becomes harmony" if the state is viewed "from a higher, general point of view." [163] This "higher" vision opened the gates to religion, which could dispose individuals to accept democratic government and could dispose democratic governments to respect individual rights. The first of these functions was worked through the introduction of "love" into the theory as a political value equivalent to freedom. Love prescribes that individuals suffer voluntarily, for the sake of the generality of men, the necessary sacrifice of their rights which the imperfections of the temporal state require. But it prescribes too, as a corollary, that the state be controlled by this generality for the sacrifice to be necessary.[164] The meaning of this crucial intrusion of "love" becomes clear in the light of Follen's definition of it in his "Great Song": through love man develops his own humanity, but in such a way that God "remains goal and reproach to us." [165] Follen modified his democratic doctrine further along the same lines when he made participation in the Holy Communion one of the two qualifications of his demand for universal male suffrage.[166] And finally, Follen projected an official state Christian Church to which he would attribute the authoritative unity he refused to the sovereign individual and sovereign state alike. This church would furnish the dogma for "freedom, truth, and love"; would be "in accord with the whole nature of humanity"; and would consequently tolerate no other religions or sects, since they would breed division in a Christian doctrine that is "only one and entirely clear in itself." [167] The startling and obvious opposition between his religious authoritarianism and the libertarian emphasis of his political principles reveals the different levels upon which Follen conceived them and intended them to operate: the transcendent unity of religious dogma, inculcated equally into all the citizens of the state, was to guarantee the co-existence of a radical secular individualism with a radical secular democratic state.

Follen's attempt to use the student unions as the core of a revolutionary political society was frustrated by the suppression following upon the Carlsbad decrees, and his subsequent effort to organize Germany for revolution from his Swiss exile through a general political society—"the League of Men (*Maennerbund*)" —of which the youth movement would only be an auxiliary came equally to naught. The center of political thinking and planning remained back in the student unions, where he had helped to implant it. It was from such historic social corporations that the third possibility of rooting political liberty in Germany was to grow— the development of a popular movement that would force it out of the governments. This was the possibility that was to occupy the center of the political stage for the generation that followed upon the July revolution of 1830.

Third Section. THE MOVEMENT:

The Struggle for a Liberal State
(1830-1870)

The Struggle for a Liberal State
(1830-1870)

The middle third of the 19th century witnessed both the decisive conflict and the denouement in the history of the modern state in Germany. During this period the initiative for the reorganization of political and social institutions in line with the ever-increasing mobility and individuation of western society was displaced outside the official organs of state and came from the ranks of the governed themselves. The advocacy of political liberties graduated out of the melange of reforming bureaucrats, constitutional diets, and isolated cells of the preceding era into a gradually expanding popular movement, which took over the primary sponsorship of the cause *vis-à-vis* official authorities. And yet the traditional patterns of German politics remained operative, only now transplanted within the popular movement itself. The three types of relationship between freedom and the state which had become manifest in German political reality during the previous generation now reappeared as distinct tendencies within the liberal movement proper. Across all the confusing heterogeneity and changing modes of organization which the liberals experienced after 1830, one familiar set of distinctions continued to constitute the fundamental divisions within the movement down to 1870 and beyond. These distinctions were between those who looked to the existing authorities of state, those who hovered uncertainly between dependence upon the established powers and appeal to popular rights, and those who dogmatically demanded a radical break with the whole system of existing politics.

Behind this persistence of political pattern was a combination of factors. Outside the liberal movement but continuously influencing it, the authoritarian structure of the German states and societies retained and indeed reinforced its traditional claims and connotations of freedom. The maintenance and the modernization of these connections took not only the obvious form of the extension of constitutionalism among the German states after 1830, but also the more spectacular policies which Prussia, in particular, periodically espoused toward the same end—from the formation of the German Customs Union in 1834 through the national Union attempt of 1849-1850 to the Bismarckian *coup* of 1866. The enduring vitality of this association between monarchical authority and popular liberties drove constant wedges between the moderate, dualistic, and radical tendencies in liberal politics.

But beyond this pressure the process of historical change itself worked to prolong the ingrained habits and attitudes. Such a combination of ideal and material forces for reform as might have conjointly overwhelmed the slow pace of official auto-liberalization never quite came into being in Germany. The failure of the liberal movement to overcome the traditional German pattern of politics both without and within its own ranks was accountable in large measure to the time differential which dispersed the respective maximum effects of ideological and economic individualism over two distinct political generations. To this extent the destiny of the struggle for a liberal state in Germany was decided in the process of history which brought the dominant intellectual liberalism of the pre-March (i.e. pre-1848) period into decline when it was reorganized during the 1850's into the economically conditioned liberalism of the crucial 1860's.

The stage for this drama tended gradually to expand from the political arena of the particular state to the political arena of the German nation. The expanding network of material and technological interests, the continuous pressure of the advanced nations to the west, and the increasing conviction of the political rigidity and unviability of the old territorial states helped to focus the struggle for liberal states in Germany until it became primarily the fight for a single German state. Accompanying the growing centrality of the national issue was the growth of nationalism as a political doctrine. The conflict over the unification of Germany was at the same time a conflict over the political direction of German national feeling. In the era of liberation German nationalism had been not only sporadic but politically colorless. As it developed into an emotional bond which absorbed the continuing loyalty of increasing numbers of individual Germans the political function of this new force became a crucial issue. Until the decade of the 1860's, consequently, nationalism was more the target than the source of political action; political groups tended rather to direct nationalism toward their own respective programs than to be directed by it toward any specific political orientation. Since nationalism had reference to a German nation-state that did not yet exist it became the vehicle of wish-fulfillment. From 1830 on the liberals of various shades sought to mold nationalism in their own image, and from 1849 on this effort was increasingly challenged by a conservative interpretation of the national bond. The ultimate victory of the authoritarian over the liberal party in 19th-century German politics was mediated through the triumph of the conservative version of nationalism—a triumph which represents the final stage in the association of liberty with traditional authority in Germany. For with the conservative initiative in the actual political unification of Germany the interests, the connections, and the loyalties that had been built up within the politically uncrystallized national ideal were separated from the liberal principle with which they had been loosely joined and were turned into supports of the governing powers which had given the direct satisfaction craved by these elemental strivings. With the removal of the national issue, not only did the last sphere of flexibility go out of German politics but nationalism became a definite political force internally allied with the authoritarian state.

7. The Rise of the Liberal Intellectuals (1830-1850)

The French Revolution of 1830 set off in Germany the popular movement which was to spawn the protagonists of political freedom in Germany for two generations. But if the relocation of the liberal impulse from official institutions into citizen groups was the undoubted positive accomplishment of the new departure, "movement" is a misleading term if it is taken to imply unity or organization in any but the most tenuous sense. Indeed, the extraordinary variegation was its most characteristic quality. It exhibited neither a central organizational core, nor a coherent line of development nor a community of substantive political theory.

The liberal organizations were essentially local in scope, forging only the most slender and discontinuous of connections outside the town or province of their residence. Moreover, even these local units themselves were often loosely or fortuitously associated groups rather than organizations in any real sense. The consequence was such a dissimilarity of structure as to render the relationship among them incongruous and indeed almost incommensurable by any criterion. Thus certain of the "groups" were simply labels for a number of individual notables who had little or no direct contact with one another but sponsored the same general line of thought or policy; others were composed of publicists grouped around a journal; still others were gathered around a recognized social or political institution, like a church or a diet. Again, along another line, certain of the groups were composed exclusively of free intellectuals, others of intellectuals in association with an economic or social elite, and still others of intellectuals with a latent or even with an active mass support. Finally, not only were all shades of moderate and radical opinion represented among these groups but the particular group and even the individual liberal himself often exhibited a similar instability by undergoing striking dissolutions or transformations of political tendency during a comparatively short span of years.

Amid this kaleidoscope of individuals, groups, and institutions which appeared, flourished, faded, or led a peculiar shadow-life on the border between the coincidence of convivial academic opinions and a corporate existence for a political purpose, some seven ill-assorted groupings can be singled out as making up the organized sector of the liberal movement. A south-German constitutional liberal group which looked particularly to Rotteck and Welcker of the Baden diet; a north-west "classical" liberalism crystallized first around the diets of Hesse-Kasse and Hanover and then in the theory of Goettingen's Friedrich Dahlmann; a Rhenish and an East Prussian movement within the state of Prussia, each using its provincial estates as its point of focus but drawing its real force from the industrial and commercial capitalism characteristic of these regions; church organizations which swung their masses behind the liberal political requirements of their clerical position—orthodox Catholicism in the Rhineland, the dissident "German Catholic" and Protestant Illuminati movements in central Germany: these were the chief liberal groups connected with considerable interests or numbers in German society. Young Germans and Young Hegelians were two purely intellectual groups whose historical importance lies less in their organization and their social impact—which were equally minimal—than in their dramatic expression of the new tendencies in the German intellectual life after 1830. They embodied the powerful drive of the age for the application of ideals to practical activity, and they illustrated its tendency to merge individual theories into scholastic doctrines. Between these seven more or less stable historical personalities and the anonymous bulk of society with its capricious alternation between stagnation and sporadic activity lay a whole scale of evanescent assemblages, journals, and individuals who rose periodically to the political surface on the wave of popular explosions, spontaneous or induced. They ranged from the documented republican agitation of the Palatines J. A. Wirth and P. J. Siebenpfeiffer through the political poetry of Georg Herwegh to the obscure radical unrest of Berlin during the hungry 1840's.

The Development

The historical evolution of the pre-March liberal movement was as disjointed as its organizations. The three types of reform which had been initiated by the first political generation of the 19th century were all reinforced in their separateness in the brief outburst of political activity immediately after 1830. The spread of popular unrest outward from Paris after the July Revolution furnished indeed a common matrix for the revival of all three tendencies, but the tendencies themselves remained different in kind and unconnected. Thus the mass demonstrations were channeled first into the path of constitutional dualism by timely concessions on the part of the governments: Brunswick, Hanover, Saxony, and Hesse-Kasse were granted constitutions on the south German model, while in Baden the shift to a liberal ministry, free elections, and far-reaching civil reforms[1] directed the popular movement to support of a rejuvenated diet. Next, an attempt was made to organize the unrest directly into independent political action by the governed. The "Patriotic Press Association," an *ad hoc* association of democratic journalists in the Bavarian Palatinate, first set up the series of mass meetings which was climaxed in the famous Hambach Festival of 1832, and then worked with the radical student unions to sponsor the popular revolution which fizzled in the conspiratorial Frankfurt putsch of 1833. At the same time a purely intellectual version of the popular movement arose in response to the same conditions but independent of this ephemeral mass action. The school of literati who looked to Heinrich Heine and Ludwig Boerne in Paris and was grouped under the collective name of "Young Germany" was definitely converted to radical politics by the July Revolution and in this guise secured literary predominance among educated circles in Germany. Finally, the force of bureaucratic liberalism, the third in the triad of libertarian possibilities in 19th-century Germany, likewise was strengthened in this situation, but in a way even less connected with the other two types than they were with each other. The popular unrest which underlay both the extension of constitutions and the organization for direct action was indeed relevant to governmental liberalism as well, for the economic sources and claims of this unrest, which emphasized the miseries and the inequities wrought by local and territorial customs barriers, had some connection with the formation during 1833 of the German Customs Union which was the prime achievement of the progressive bureaucrats.[2] But the connection was tenuous, for the malcontents were in the main opposed to the project of the customs union as the answer to their complaints. Actually, then, the policies which led to the German Customs Union were sponsored and carried through exclusively by regular officials of the princely governments. The demonstrations after 1830 furnished them with an additional indication of the need for action, but they were moved essentially by the more orthodox fiscal and commercial reasons of state which spurred the launching of the movement toward customs unification as early as the mid-20's. The extension of the area of free exchange, and the adherence to the Prussian moderate free-trade system which were involved in the German Customs Union, were the work of a bureaucratic liberalism which continued an established pattern in its separation of economic liberty from civil and political freedom. Civil and political rights were rejected, but the principles of free enterprise were enforced against the opposition of unwilling material interests.[3]

None of these forms of liberalism, however, had a continuous development after 1833. The constitutions, the Young German radical journalism, the Customs Union, did indeed maintain life but they stagnated in their isolation, while the flare-up of popular direct action was squelched completely by the renewal of suppression via the German Confederation. The line of growth was diverted into still different channels. From action the emphasis in the quiet middle and late 30's came to be upon preparation, and correspondingly the center of gravity shifted from organization to intellect. The main events of this period were the publication of the *Political Dictionary*, edited by Karl Rotteck and Karl Theodor Welcker seriatim from 1834, and *The Politics* of Friedrich Christian Dahlmann in 1835. These were easily the most influential political writings to appear in Germany during the first half of the 19th century, and their coincidence in this otherwise uneventful period between two phases of frenetic activity symbolized the basically intellectual character of whatever continuity there was in the liberal movement. Indeed, the only noteworthy event of these years—the case of the Goettingen Seven in 1837—was not only concerned exclusively with professors but was limited in its impact to groups of intellectuals.[4] But characteristically, even the two works which contributed so markedly to the political maturation of the educated middle classes were divergent in their lessons: the *Political Dictionary* propagated the individualism and the natural-rights rationalism appropriate to the Francophilic constitutional tradition of southern Germany, while Dahlmann gave unforgettable expression to the organic "classical" liberalism which was to be absorbed in whole or part by so many of the intellectuals of the north. Consequently, this quiet political education ripened but did not yet unify the articulate groups in the German society.

When, around 1840, the liberal movement took new life from the impetus given it by the accession of a new king in Prussia, by the accelerated tempo of life accompanying the beginnings of industrialization, and by the social dislocations of an agrarian crisis, the centers of growth were again several. Not until the decade had worn its way along almost into the revolution which climaxed it, did these heterogeneous centers begin to find a common ground in the realm of politics and on this basis to assume the vague outlines of a single movement.

The opening signal for the resumption of the liberal development was sounded in Prussia, where the accession of the young Frederick William IV in 1840 brought promising initial reforms —the alleviation of the censorship, the convocation of a united committee from the provincial diets, and the revival of constitutional discussions. These reforms stimulated the revival of constitutional claims by the capitalistically inspired notables in the East Prussian and Rhenish provincial estates, the conversion of young theologians and philosophers into a politically oriented Young Hegelian group of intellectual journalists known in Berlin as "The Free (*die Freien*)," and the resumption of Prussian bureaucratic reform in the passage of the individualistic business ordinance of 1845. If Prussia gave the initial governmental inspiration, it was Baden again that furnished the constitutional core of the liberal revival. Spurred by the Confederation's confirmation of the Hanoverian absolutist coup d'état, the members of the opposition in the south-western and central German state diets began to confer together annually from 1839. This practice gave the Baden parliamentary liberals, who revived their decisive anti-governmental policies in the lower chamber soon after 1840, a channel to the larger German arena, but it was characteristic of the essential heterogeneity of the political movement in Germany that such an organizational connection bore no fruit until 1847, when other kinds of factors brought about this integration. For just as the particular manifestations which had been stimulated in Prussia during 1840 continued only in the Rhineland after the government's retreat to a policy of repression in 1843, so was the revival of political interest aroused by the case of the Goettingen Seven in the rest of the nation ultimately localized in Baden.

The liberal movement was carried on, but the primary agents of its development in the middle years of the decade were other than those of its revival at the beginning. Whereas the first years revived the familiar trio of bearers—government, constitutional estates, and intellectuals—the period from 1844 to 1847 witnessed the unprecedented transmission of the liberal movement to anonymous masses of the German people. What had been a local and limited phenomenon in the Palatinate of 1830-1833 now became the central and indeed the decisive force in German political development. Where the mid-30's had been characterized by the intellectual influence of Rotteck, Welcker, and Dahlmann, the mid-40's were dominated by the social influence of a changing economy. The famous rising of the Silesian rural weavers in 1844 was but the dramatic opening of a whole series of riots and demonstrations which, spurred by the impact of the potato famine upon longer-standing discontents, left scarcely an area of Germany unaffected. They even developed into bloody clashes with the military arm of monarchy in Leipzig and Berlin (April 1847). The importance of these events and the more general dislocation of which they were manifestations was not simply their preparation of the ground for the first active participation of large sections of the German people in politics since the Peasants' War, but also the relationship which they initiated between social unrest and the predominantly intellectual liberal movement. The movement now underwent an expansion to include for the first time organizations with intellectual leadership, a mass base, and a more than local scope. From around 1844 both the German-Catholic sects and the free church movement of the Protestant Illuminati (*Lichtfreunde*) began to find adherents numbering in the thousands among the burgher and more particularly petty burgher groups and to develop a consciousness of the liberal political implications in their clerical dissent.[5] At the same time the larger towns throughout Germany began to develop similar if unconnected political movements as economic crisis opened both burghers and artisans to the complaints and demands of liberal political journalists: particularly in Berlin, where the mass unrest was politicized into a primitive natural-rights radicalism by writers like Adolf Glassbrenner and Friedrich Held,[6] and in Mannheim, where the politicians Friedrich Hecker and Gustav Struve played a similar role,[7] did the unprecedented activation of the unprivileged and the unpropertied majority become visible.

The social developments of the mid-40's also made an essential qualitative contribution to the liberal movement. They provided a kind of matrix which made possible its integration. There was perhaps no single fact more fateful to the political destinies of the German people in the 19th century than the condition which made the relationship between the anonymous mass and the liberal notables the determinant for the relationship among the notables themselves. The surge of broad sections of society into an obscure and unorganized movement of protest or resentment during the mid-40's became the context of the growing connections among the diverse liberal groupings, just as the falling away of the popular supporting movement was to be the signal for the renewed predominance of divisions within the liberal camp during the revolutions of 1848. In the centripetal phase of this development, Young Germans, Young Hegelians, and "classical" liberals all found common ground in the anti-clericalism and the broad theological rationalism of the popular Illuminati organization.[8] Radical Young Hegelians like Karl Marx collaborated with representatives of the prosperous Rhenish bourgeoisie like Gustav Mevissen on the editorial board of the *Rhenish Gazette* (*Rheinische Zeitung*) in the attempt to combine speculative philosophy and practical economic interests into a single liberal organ of the Rhenish middle classes.[9] The popular aspects of these developments—whether religious or academic—provided a common ground on which the more sophisticated diversities of the intellectuals found a measure of conciliation. Equally important in this respect, was the rise of the intense awareness among the middle classes of what later came to be known as "the social problem." [10] The growing consciousness of the misery and privation endemic among the masses of working inhabitants in town and country bred in many property-owning burghers a great fear of social cataclysm and in some a determination to find economic and social remedies. This social awareness was an important force making for common action on the part of the propertied and the educated middle classes, whether the final aim of such action was to ward off or to alleviate the social ferment. Thus the Association for the Welfare of the Working Classes, which was formed in Prussia during 1844, brought into one organization bureaucrats and town oligarchs who were working for social conservation and radicals who sought to use the institution for the organization of the working masses.[11] The primitive mass movements of the mid-1840's confronted the politically conscious liberal intellectuals as a condition related but external to them. The shopkeepers, the artisans, and the peasants who were the chief agents of the turmoil had as the appropriate framework of their striving the traditional fields of religious spirituality and corporate security, and if the mobilization of these groups bestowed upon the liberal opposition a support, a unity, and a possibility of political activity hitherto lacking, it was at a price. The liberal intellectuals secured strength and harmony only by continuing to emphasize the religious and the social interests that tied them to the rest of the German society and by limiting the political program which they derived from western individualism to the specific concrete demands which would be generally understood.

The final phase of the pre-March period witnessed the amalgamation of intellectuals on a national scale around precisely such traditional foci and liberal demands. In 1847 and early 1848 the association of various stripes of liberal notables within particular regional or functional organizations, which had characterized the preceding years, grew into connections among liberals from all parts of Germany around institutions with old functional roots but new political claims. Academicians' conventions turned to questions of nationality and legal reform with the Germanists' Conference of September 1846.[12] The negotiations among south German, Rhenish, and East Prussian liberals during the first half of 1847 centered around the founding of a journal—that time-honored device of the intellectual. The *German News* (*Deutsche Zeitung*) aimed at organizing the whole weight of the propertied and educated middle classes under its moderate academic representatives in behalf of a program for a constitutional national state.[13] The Prussian United Diet of April 1847 laid claims to a role as a permanent organ. The informal annual conferences of the opposition deputies from the south German diets split into the Offenburg assembly of radicals which adopted a formal democratic program in September and the Heppenheim assembly of moderates which adopted a formal program of constitutional monarchy in October.

Such was the rising crescendo of liberal political organization on the eve of the February revolution in France. These activities of the last phase of the pre-March period featured once again the characteristic domination of the liberal movement by the intellectuals, and with it the incipient re-emergence of divisions. Thus it was that the mass eruption which accompanied the news of the Paris events of February created a unity which was but a temporary bridge over two profound sets of continuing divisions: the liberal groups which the popular uprising found in being remained associations of intellectual and social notables structurally isolated from the mass movement which they provisionally directed; and secondly, within the liberal intellectual circle itself essential differences of political tendency were only temporarily leveled by the homogenizing pressure of the German masses in action.

The Conditions

The sporadic social connections which bred both the isolation of the intellectuals as the bearer of the liberal movement and their dependence upon stronger but essentially unpolitical groups in the society was the product of a larger set of political and social circumstances. These circumstances, which were characteristic of German life in general during the second quarter of the 19th century, pressed in upon the liberal movement and molded its structure as well as its effectiveness.

Most obvious was the role of the external political conditions imposed by absolute or quasi-absolute governments in fostering the chameleonic pattern of pre-March liberalism. Practices like the ubiquitous censorship, the prohibitions upon political assemblies and associations, and the absence or insufficiency of representative organs not only inhibited the formation of political societies which would bring leaders and mass followings into a continuing contact, but even within the leadership made impossible the establishment of an arena in which political ideas could be exchanged, agreements boiled down to common formulas, conflicts sharpened to essential differences, and claims upon reality coalesced into common programs for action. Indeed, these conditions militated against organized political thinking, let alone genuine political parties, and until late in the period buttressed the original diversity of the liberal groupings.

But far more profound than this political conditioning was the impact of economic and social conditions upon the structure of the liberal movement. The peculiarities of the movement were those of the German social structure in general and of the particular role of the intellectuals in it. Germany in the pre-March period was pervaded by the structural stresses attendant upon a traditionally bound society which was just starting to move itself, and it was the intellectuals who translated this social geology into political liberalism.

The economic pattern of pre-March Germany was a prime determinant of the uneasy combination of conservation and dissolution in the social structure, for it was itself composed by a parallel combination of stagnation and development. The predominant tendency was undoubtedly stagnation. The basic forms and relationships of German economic life scarcely changed during the first half of the 19th century. The predominance of agriculture over industry and countryside over towns, the primitive intermingling of farming and industrial pursuits, the prevalence of handicraft or domestic modes of industrial production, were features as descriptive of 1850 as of 1800.[14] Not only did Germany lag relatively behind the western nations, but even by absolute standards its predominant economic attribute during the entire first half of the century was "a lame-hearted clinging to old forms" that "contributed little to the development of a capitalistic spirit."[15] The rate of interest tended to fall until the late 1840's and German savings were invested abroad. No regular economic cycle could be discerned until the 1850's. When machines were introduced during the 40's both the idea and the machines themselves were taken from England.[16] Measures of economic freedom had still to be forced by government upon a reluctant society. The Prussian bureaucracy led the way in fostering competition, based on moderate tariffs, against stiff industrial opposition during the 40's, and its initial relegation of railroad-building to private capital had to give way late in the decade to state enterprise because the concessions were not being taken up. Freedom of industrial enterprise was recognized in principle by the legislation of almost all German states, but in practice, the pressure of industrial groups forced the retention of all kinds of specific corporate arrangements.[17] Even in agriculture, the only branch of economic activity to show significant institutional change, such change was limited to the eastern sections of Prussia. Germany was a nation still composed overwhelmingly of peasants, aristocracy, artisans, and merchants, all supplying a local market and attached to customary methods and authorities. The economic basis for a numerous and powerful middle class that would be attached by both material interest and accompanying temperament to a practical political movement for the re-

moval of barriers and that would raise a supporting mass of uprooted and similarly-minded working men in its wake did not
exist in pre-March Germany.

And yet, within the confines of these fundamentally persistent
relations certain definite if limited factors of economic development can be discerned, making either for changes of quantity
within the traditional forms of production and exchange or for
minor outcroppings of qualitative change in particular cases
which disturbed but did not rearrange the old pattern. If the
basic *Gestalt* of German economic and social life was transformed
only with the rise of industrial capitalism after 1850 many of the
conditions which then helped make the new system had begun to
make perceptible breaks into the crust of custom from around
1840. Amongst the factors of general quantitative growth which
placed gradually increasing strain upon the complex of traditional
institutions within which they operated the most important was
undoubtedly the considerable increase in both population and
production. Between 1820 and 1850 the population of Germany
(1871 frontiers) rose by about one third, from 26.3 to 35.4 mil-
lions.[18] Between 1831 and 1849 production of sixteen basic com-
modities has been calculated to have increased by about one-
fourth per head of Prussian population.[19] Both these advances
betokened a development of demand, of labor supply, and of
accumulated wealth which prepared the ground for the later
change in the forms of economic production. The extension of
the effective free market through the operation of the German
Customs Union after 1834, and the notable advance in the internal means of communication, particularly in railroad-building
during the 40's, worked in the same direction.[20]

Of the limited qualitative changes in German economic development the alterations in the structure of German agriculture
were particularly outstanding. These alterations derived from
the combined effects of British industrialization and the peasant
liberation enacted during the early years of the century. The
clearest signs of the change were first the rise of capitalistic forms
of agriculture to predominance in Prussia and secondly the
general recession of the three-field system in favor of more rational methods of cultivation.[21] And yet agriculture manifested

in microcosm the mottled state of the German economy as a whole in the partiality and the unevenness of the change. For the development had constructive effects primarily upon Prussia, and within Prussia it affected the large-estate owners particularly, the prosperous peasants to a lesser extent, and the rest of the rural population not at all. Except in Prussia, peasant emancipation had meant primarily personal liberation and the transfer of tenure into property, but, since no provision was made for redemption of real dues, it did not mean free disposition over the soil or a structural change in agriculture. In Prussia such provision was made, but in such wise that down to 1850 the small peasants were dispossessed, the prosperous peasants had legal title to their land but not free disposition over it, and only the large-estate owners were furnished with the full property title which enabled them to rationalize and capitalize in response to the new market conditions.

The second chief qualitative development comprised the mechanization of certain sectors of industry in certain sections of the country. The opening of deep-pit coal mining in the Rhenish-Westphalian basin in the late 1830's, and the suddenly heightened demand for railroad materials at about the same time provoked, during the 40's, the application of coke to metallurgy and a concomitant conversion to the factory system. This conversion, however, was of modest proportions *vis-à-vis* the retention of handicraft and domestic industry; it was restricted almost entirely to mining and metallurgical industries and hence to the Rhineland and the central German (Silesian and Saxon) industrial basin. A breakdown of the familiar figures on the increase in the use of steam machines in Prussia (from 419 in 1837 to 2,001 in 1849)[22] shows that the terminal item was still very low in comparison with the achievements of the succeeding decade (8,166 machines for 1861); that fully one third of the increase during the 40's was accountable to the new transportation industry rather than a conversion of older forms; that one-third again of the increase was accountable to the extractive and metal industries; that the final 500 additional machines were so dispersed over various kinds of industry as to constitute isolated cases rather than centers of change; and that the machine-tool industry, which spells the difference between an economy with factories and a factory system, was negligible in scope and importance. Hence the direct influence that this kind of economic development exercised upon pre-March Germany was definitely limited both in extent and in intensity. Its general impact tended rather to be indirect, partial, and negative: it contributed to the mobilization and consequently to the dislocation of the older sectors of the economy which were in any case already being shaken by the new industrial system in the form of competitive British imports.

The impact of a limited economic development upon an over-all system of economic continuity was sufficient to spur all social groups into unwonted activity during the pre-March period, but it was not sufficient to exercise a homogeneous influence upon this activity. As the German economy was poised between old and new, just so was the German society which lived from it. Three different kinds of social movement can be identified during this era.

In the first place there developed small groups of industrialists, bankers, merchants, and estate-owners, organized chiefly around Rhenish industry and East Prussian commercialized agriculture and driven by the new capitalistic spirit. They perceived clearly both the immediate practical policies which their interests required of government and the general reforms of state and society which would be requisite to guarantee the uninterrupted expansion of their activities.

Secondly, the dislocation of the older sectors of the economy had as its consequence the uprooting and consequent activation of large masses of little people who had been ejected from the comparative security of decadent corporate institutions. At once mistrusting and regretting these institutions, the artisans and the peasants, who made up the bulk of the older social groups thus affected, erupted in a rare blend of radical turbulence in means toward a reactionary social restoration in ends. The famines of the hungry 40's stimulated these classes to responses that went beyond the blind reflex riots customary in such situations. The ephemeral misery seemed now to point up a more fundamental economic insecurity. It was not simply the new competition from cheap machine-made imports or from other German goods in the

free market created by the Customs Union that was squeezing out
the urban and rural artisan, but rather the increase of population—and hence of labor supply—and the advances which had
been made in the enactment of industrial and agrarian freedom
in most German states. These factors did not yet have their ultimate effect of concentrating large masses of men in the factories
and towns of a new industrial society. Their effect during the
pre-March period was rather to uproot them from their particular
places but still leave them adrift within the institutions of the
old society. Thus the immediate consequence for the artisans was
a surprising increase in the numbers of both masters and journeymen and concomitantly a diminution of handicraft enterprises
and a rise of artisan unemployment.[23] Similarly on the land
both the rising population, which was not yet being drained off,
and the alienation of peasant holdings fed social unrest not so
much in the form of a rural proletariat as in the activation of
that large group of poor peasants with holdings too small and
obligations too great to maintain life.[24] These were the groups
which influenced the liberal movement from without during the
40's, either through their desperate demonstrations throughout
town and countryside or through their support of an obscure
political radicalism in the larger cities.

The third—and for liberal politics the crucial—social effect of
the pre-March German economic pattern consisted in the growing
self-consciousness and mobilization of large and influential intermediate groups. Their roots were in the traditional structure of
society, but they inhabited the more mobile sectors of that structure and were beginning to develop beyond it. These groups
were composed of those members of the older middle classes who
grew with the quantitative development of the German economy
until they reached the point of feeling hemmed in by aspects of a
system to which they were still committed. These were the people
who entered into the liberal movement and composed its popular
following in those regions where it had mass support, and it was
the ambivalent status of these groups in the German economy
and society that helped to determine the complex forms of pre-
March liberalism. They included such callings as the port merchants, who acted through their city councils[25] or, as in East Prus-

sia, through the provincial diet; the small manufacturing masters
of southern Germany who combined the support of constitutional liberalism in the state diets with support of traditional
particularism and protection;[26] the viable and even prosperous
peasantry and rural middle classes, who in central Germany
thronged into the liberal religious sects of both Catholic and
Protestant persuasion and who were to lead the rural revolutionary movement in 1848.[27] These men had in common certain
specific grievances against the aristocratically dominated bureaucratic states—such as the capricious intrusiveness of officialdom
in their affairs and the remnants of feudal dues and privileges—
but at the same time they adhered to traditional institutions and
customs like the local estates and the network of functional social
corporations. Hence the authoritative role of this group in the
social underpinning of the liberal movement before 1848 contributed to the peculiar circumvention of politics which characterized the movement. Moreover, what there was of political initiative within pre-March liberalism lay with the intellectual estate
which in terms of social structure formed a section of this third
intermediary group.

It is generally agreed that pre-March political liberalism was
predominantly an intellectual movement and pre-eminently a
movement of intellectuals.[28] The German economic and social
structure goes far to explain not only the fact of this intellectual
primacy but its character. The fact is easily explained by Germany's ambiguous position in Europe as at once a retrograde
country cousin in the level and tempo of its material and social
life and a full member of the European republic of letters. Hence
whereas the economically bound social groups in Germany held
back from the political interests which were becoming the cynosure of social life in western Europe, the German intellectuals
participated fully in the political and social thinking of the
British and the French. Indeed, it has been said that in this
realm of the intellect the Germans borrowed so completely
from the west that they asserted little that was new or creative.[29]
This negative relationship between the mass of the German
society and the liberal movement indicates the important gap
which lay between them, but the temporal parallel between the

rising pace of economic change and the rising pace of the liberal movement during the 40's and the geographical parallel between the leading centers of economic development in the Rhineland, East Prussia, and the Silesian-Saxon industrial complex and the popular support of liberal organizations in the same regions show some positive connection between social structure and liberal politics. Insofar as economically based social groups were concerned, this connection was sporadic, as in the mass demonstrations outside the liberal circles, or indirect, as in the stimulus worked by the effects of academic and social change upon the intellectuals. Thus neither urban nor rural proletariat had much to do with liberal politics but the ideas of such writers as Karl Marx, Gustav Mevissen, and Arnold Ruge were decisively affected by their existence.

The more telling connection between social structure and liberal politics lay in the social status of the group that dominated the liberal movement—that is, of the intellectuals themselves. The intellectuals belonged sociologically to that large group of propertied commoners who stood in Germany midway between an estate of burghers and a middle class, and who were therefore at once dependent upon and galled by existing social and political institutions. While certain leading figures, like Mevissen and Hansemann, gave intellectual form to the small but dynamic new industrial group, and others, like the Young Germans, stemmed largely from the declining lower middle class,[30] the bulk of the intellectuals actually came out of the intermediate ranks of the historic German bourgeoisie. Arnold Ruge, for example, was the son of a middle-class bailiff, and he remained conscious of this honorable social status.[31]

Common to the group of liberal intellectuals as a whole, consequently, were both the desire for modern liberal reforms in state and society and the continuing attachment to the habits or institutions of a politically undeveloped country. Thus on the one extreme, administrative reformers made up part of the liberal opposition, while on the other even the most socially unbound, floating intellectuals were limited in their radical politics by the persistence of their primary concern with traditional issues of philosophy, theology, or aesthetics that lay beyond politics. This balance between political opposition and adhesion to prescriptive institutions or mores goes far to explain the general acceptance of the intellectuals' leadership. Their liberal movement could attract, from time to time, such antithetical groups as corporate-minded petty bourgeoisie and progressive, individualistic high bourgeoisie because the intellectuals themselves manifested both tendencies.

Within this ubiquitous combination, however, the proportions of traditionalism and modernity varied with the particular liberal organization, and the permutations of these two attributes provide a thread of coherence in the pell-mell confusion of parochial liberal groupings which flourished during this period.

At one end of the spectrum were those liberal organs which remained primarily rooted in their states or corporations, like the academic conferences, the progressives of the provincial diets and self-administering municipalities in Prussia, and the "classical" liberals who looked to historic institutions in general. At the other end were the journals and the philosophical or literary groups which led evanescent lives based consciously upon floating principle rather than stable institution. And in the middle reaches of the spectrum was to be found that myriad of religious sects, southern diets, and economic pressure groups whose intellectual representatives exhibited a continuous inner tension between the institution which was the focus and the convictions which were the leaven of liberal politics. The educated elite which dominated these organizations were correspondingly strung out on a curve running from its original status as an estate of lay clerks, through its intermediate function as vanguard of the middle classes, to its ultimate destiny as the classless society of free intellectuals. Thus the three main occupational categories into which this group of academically trained liberals fell were government officials at one extreme, free-lance journalists, men of letters, exiles, and cashiered civil servants at the other, and the professors and the lawyers—careers which in Germany involved both government service and a special autonomous tradition—in the middle. Certainly all individuals did not act according to type. Karl Mathy, who was both an exile and a free-lance writer, became one of the most prominent of the

Baden moderates, while the government official Adam von Itz-stein led the radicals in Baden for years. By and large, however, the three categories of intellectuals were typically the agents of the three corresponding kinds of liberal organizations. Officials like the Prussian administrator Georg von Vincke and the Baden prime minister Ludwig Winter sought to work upon government from within traditional institutions of government. The journalists and free-lancers of Young Germany and Young Hegelianism like Georg Buechner and Karl Marx denied their attachment to any existing institution. Between these two wings the old professions—half official and half independent—produced such representative figures as Karl Rotteck, Robert Blum, and Johann Jacoby, who helped to endow the Baden diet, German Catholicism, and East Prussian commercial capital-ism respectively with their dualistic blend of adherence to old institutions and accessibility to radical ideas.

Through its academic and governmental occupations, through its international connections, and through its membership in an awakening bourgeoisie, the intellectual estate became the political class *par excellence*. Through its participation in a preponderantly traditional society its political activity remained largely theoretical and its theories largely philosophical. The intellectuals founded the liberal movement and yet remained bound by the inherited relationships of the state and society they would transform.

The Ideas

The conviction that they represented a potential popular movement did more than turn the intellectuals toward political activity. It created a new dimension in their political thinking. To the older concerns with the definition and limitation of the state's power was now added the awareness of the indefeasibility of popular political rights. The chief problem for political theory was the alignment of this new factor amidst the tradi-tional mental habits of German intellectuals.

The multiplicity of liberal organizations had its counterpart in the variety of theoretical approaches to the problems of politics. The different liberal groupings were clustered around intellectual tendencies of the most varied description. The divergent philosophies of Kant and Hegel, the literary tradition of German classicism, the ethical and theological postulates of Enlightenment rationalism, the French emphasis upon natural rights, the English theory of the organic, balanced constitution, Baron Stein's legacy of the modernized corporate state—these heterogeneous sources bred misunderstanding and even mistrust. The hostility of the Young Hegelians toward the southern constitutionalists,[32] their dissatisfaction with the classical liberals,[33] the impatience of the Young Germans with all other breeds of German intellectual,[34] the break between the nationalist Friedrich List and the southern liberals Rotteck and Welcker in the planning of the famous *Political Dictionary* (*Staatslexikon*)[35]—these were examples of the sporadic and petty quarrels which expressed a relationship not so much of direct opposition as of heterogeneity. The issues of conflict were not defined; they ranged over a broad field from the relationship of ethical precept and practice, through the validity of natural law, to the desirability of Prussian hegemony. Moreover, the line-up of groups kept shifting with the question under discussion, since the issues themselves were often matters of arbitrary interest rather than consistent items in a single urgent problem.

And yet, behind this welter of ideas the persistence of pre-liberal intellectual categories in the liberal political thinking of the pre-March period produced three general characteristics that were common, by and large, to the whole galaxy.

First, liberal thought in the pre-March period tended to be derivative rather than originally political. Liberal politics was often an outgrowth of conflict in another field. The ubiquitous influence of Kant and Hegel pointed up the persistent necessity to search in an absolute, super-terrestrial realm the source of authority which could not be discovered in a fragmented German society. Young Hegelians like the Bauer brothers (Bruno and Edgar), Max Stirner, Arnold Ruge, and Karl Marx came to political opposition on the shoulders of their colleagues D. F. Strauss, and Ludwig Feuerbach, whose break was essentially with religious orthodoxy and its ethical implications, and they turned their attention to political liberalism only when the Prussian state of Frederick William IV associated itself with their clerical and philosophical antagonists.[36] The Protestant Illuminati similarly were concerned in the first instance with the recasting of dogma according to the simple and reasonable principles of a commonsense natural law and began to apply these principles against established authority in the secular state only when monarchical governments supported the pietism prevalent in the established churches.[37] Convinced Catholics in Germany remained, by and large, politically disinterested and insofar as they did assert themselves in politics gave their support to the established monarchical order.[38] Where small Catholic groups did join the liberal movement they contributed no characteristic political ideas or doctrine, for they were moved only by the specific and necessary practical requirements of their clericalism. Whether in the orthodox form of the liberal Rhenish Catholicism represented by the brothers Reichensperger or in the sectarian form of the German Catholic movement pioneered by Johann Ronge, the origins were religious[39] and the political liberalism defined by the endorsement of the limited constitutionalism needed by a church in a hostile state.[40] The Young Germans, finally, put the radical political ideas which Boerne and Heine took from revolutionary Paris during 1830 in the service of a more general purpose, part moral and part aesthetic. Their political declarations inevitably reached beyond the borders of politics into asseverations upon the social and the cosmic order. Thus when Heine described his ideal society he specified that "we fight not for the natural rights of the people but for the divine rights of man; we wish to be no *sansculottes,* no frugal burghers, no cheap presidents, but rather we are setting up a democracy of equally glorious, equally holy, equally blessed gods." [41] The firebrand Georg Buechner, who confounded the political cause of anti-absolutism with the social cause of poverty in his revolutionary pamphlet *The Hessian Messenger* (1824), wound up similarly with a "prayer" in which the coming revolutionary society was equated with the kingdom of God.[42]

A second characteristic common to the whole range of liberal writers was their conscious and desperate striving to bridge the gap between ideal and reality, theory and practice, project and execution. The consciousness of this ancient abyss and the active determination to destroy it through self-help testified to the new fact of a spontaneous political movement within the German society, but the painful iteration and reiteration of appeals and reproaches about the necessity of a procedure that elsewhere was implicit in the actual doing testified to the presence of old restrictions upon the new movement. The Young Hegelian Arnold Ruge gave the most direct expression to the self-conscious demand for the practical execution of ideas, but even he did protest too much and betrayed the inherent limitations upon such demands. His influential article, "The Self-criticism of German Liberalism," published in the *German Annals* of January 1843, was designed precisely to inveigh against the abstract character of "liberalism" as the expression of the non-political character of the Germans and to urge concrete political activity as the avenue to contact with reality.[43] But despite Ruge's undoubted conversion at this time to the primacy of politics and the necessity of working practically with the "people," [44] this apparent integration remained incomplete. He defined "the reality of freedom" as "the internality and dissemination of philosophy." [45] Moreover, he accepted the "bureaucratic and police state" as the necessary outer framework of politics and insisted that the main step in a "radical reform" is "to do with self-consciousness what previous politics has done only without consciousness." [46] Ruge's call for the integration of theory and practice meant not a surrender of his essential metaphysical framework but a search for new instruments of pressure to hasten the state in its accomplishment of the work of Reason.

Ruge was perhaps the most articulate example of the deliberate attempt of German intellectuals to seize reality by awakening a popular political movement without surrendering their philosophical idealism, but his was not an isolated case. Even more striking was the development of men like Moses Hess, Karl Marx, and Lorenz Stein, whose passion for contact with the concrete interests of humanity drove them beyond middle-class liberalism, but still did not dismantle the Hegelian framework of their thinking. Heine was attracted to Saint Simon, but only to translate his social doctrines into the "Hellenic" philosophy of the spiritualization of matter.[47] Mevissen consciously exploited his dual position as Hegelian and industrialist to mediate between a priori principles and economic realities, and he developed the idea of the state as the incarnation of morality with the function of stimulating and directing the economic interests and groupings of society to ethical ends.[48] The publicist Paul Pfizer announced the theme of his popular *Correspondence between Two Germans* to be precisely "the unresolved opposition of the theoretical and the practical," and although he too appealed to the necessity of their reconciliation he candidly declared his aim to be simply the presentation of both sides in their uncompromising integrity.[49] Gustav von Struve insisted similarly "that the task of our times consists essentially in filling the great gulf which lies between theory and practice," but this did not prevent him from espousing the side of the doctrinaire "Wholes" against the compromising "Halfs." [50]

Finally, pre-March liberalism was generally characterized by an apparent anomaly whereby agreement in specific political demands was juxtaposed with profound theoretical discord. Freedom of the press, limitation of bureaucracy, separation of justice from administration, trial by jury and public procedure, local self-administration, some form of popular representation, liberation of the soil from the remnants of manorial bonds, and the integration of the nobility into the regular system of local government—the demand for such immediate reforms was common to all kinds of liberal groupings. In part, this consensus was accountable to the uniformity of political conditions which stymied activity in the same way for all groups. The establishment of legal guarantees against the repressions of governments at once pro-absolutist and pro-particularist became a commonly agreed means for the prosecution of variously defined goals. But in part, too, the consensus was accountable to an important internal quality of the movement. The main lines of political thinking were still so flexible and ill-defined that the most various kinds of ideas were intertwined in each formulation.[51] Hence political theories were not yet so systematized as to involve dogmatically rigid practical programs as their necessary consequence, and groups that were opposed in their ultimate tendencies could be quite in accord upon immediate concrete demands. The trend toward concretion and consequently toward harmony increased as the period wore on and discontented masses of Germans put their weight behind direct action and a popular latitudinarianism in doctrine. German liberal doctrine was weak precisely in that vital theoretical middle ground between metaphysical or ethical preconceptions and practical consequences which makes for clear and firm political systems.

Hence in the pre-March period Germany did not exhibit the line-up within the progressive camp, so familiar in the political history of the western nations, which distinguished "liberals" from "democrats" in both political ideal and immediate action. The German progressives did not attain such integral political positions until after the outbreak of revolution in 1848.[52] Fundamental issues of political theory proper, which elsewhere inspired internecine struggle, were scarcely joined before 1847. Popular sovereignty, the form of the state, the extent of the suffrage, the legitimacy of revolution—these crucial questions were in general not raised to prominence. When they were discussed they tended to be settled on the moderate basis of the least common denominator. Ultimate republicans settled for the mixed sovereignty of constitutional monarchy; there was general agreement on indirect elections with voting rights based upon property qualifications; the possibility of revolution was soft-pedalled in favor of demands for fulfillment or extension of constitutional promises. Rotteck's trimming of an abstract popular sovereignty became standard in southern Germany. Gustav von Struve, leader of the Baden democrats in 1848 and 1849, plumped in his writings of the early 40's simply for the execution of the constitutional provisions of the Federal Act of 1815.[53] The Young Hegelians pleaded with the Prussian king as late as 1841 for liberal measures in the spirit of Frederick the Great and the Era of Reform.[54] The term "democrat" was used, but it had no specific meaning until just before the revolution. It tended to be appropriated by all those who believed in popular sovereignty as the theoretical basis and the ultimate culmination of the political process, but it included all varieties of analyses and proposals for the contemporary situation.[55]

A similar haziness hovered around the concept of representation.[56] A general consensus did exist among liberals on certain implications of the concept: it involved the representation of all citizens rather than of privileged corporations; it implied the care for the interests of the citizens as a whole rather than of discrete private groups; and it meant some participation of the people in sovereignty. But equally noteworthy were the confusions attached to the concept: the idea of a corporate (*staendisch*) basis of political organization continued to be applied to this newer as to the old aristocratic type of representation; the concept of representation was variously interpreted to comprehend only the people or the people and prince together in the sovereign power; it was identified with a flexible system of constitutional monarchy and rarely, even among radicals, was it worked out to the logical doctrinal conclusion of a parliamentary system. It followed that liberalism was not driven to develop its own implications into a particular political theory *vis-à-vis* democracy. Down to the eve of the revolution, liberalism remained the generic characterization of the whole progressive movement.

Thus the divisions within liberalism tended to be ethical rather than strictly political. The issue of moderate versus radical approach became the fundamental division in the liberal camp. To analyze it as a struggle between liberalism and democracy is to over-politicize the movement and to impute to it a clarity of political concepts which it did not possess.[57] The distinction between the moderates and the radicals refers not so much to political ideas as such, which were scarcely in issue, but to the preconceptions which the intellectuals took from their lofty religious, philosophical, or moral principles when they began to approach the terrestrial reality of politics. This vital distinction cut through the whole complex of diverse metaphysical and political ideas. It drew a simple line between those who would work with given existence and infiltrate the ideal into it, and those who would categorically displace and replace the given forms of existence at the behest of an uncompromising ideal and its requirement of an absolutely conformable reality. The primacy of this kind of distinction marked a level of thinking that was at once more specific than religion or philosophy and less specific than politics. Because this thinking was more concrete than it had been it began to appeal to non-academic groups in the nation, but in the measure that it still lacked political concretion its appeal was both indiscriminate and impermanent. Hence the support which the liberal intellectuals attained came from a sporadic coalition of the materially antagonistic groups of bourgeois and artisans, aristocrats and peasants which made up the transitional German society.

The ideas, like the structure, of pre-March liberalism are classifiable into three general positions along the line between moderation and radicalism. Rhenish and "classical" liberals, who justified the attachment to what they deemed to be the essentials in the institutions of historical order, were perhaps the most articulate representatives of the moderates' approach. The theoretical dualism of the southern liberals dominated by Rotteck clearly spoke for those intermediate groups in whom tendencies toward radical emancipation remained in an even—and often incompatible—balance with a cautious acceptance of established institutions. The categorical extremism which characterized the approach, albeit not the substantive political program, of the free-lance writers and the exiles among the Young Hegelians in the North and the doctrinaire natural-rights adherents in the south-west were representative of German radicalism after 1840.

The Moderates

The moderates' approach to politics stemmed from the fundamental attitude that the realization of ethical ideals demanded consideration for and the gradual reform of existing institutions and relationships. The moderates were the modernists, in the sense that they cherished the deep-seated respect for brute facts and forces which was to characterize the 19th century. They were influenced decisively by the rise of the empirical disciplines which respected the particular datum and of the new economy which lived on measuring and exploiting it. The moderates were disposed to attribute great value to existing institutions, which were deemed both worthy and secure vehicles for the realization of ideals. Thus both the classical liberals, who were dominated particularly by the new history most brilliantly pioneered by Hegel, Ranke, and the school of historical law, and the liberal patricians who were becoming conscious of the connections between the political order and the requirements of the budding industrial and commercial capitalism of the Rhineland, looked primarily to the libertarian traditions of the state, in which they had a vested moral and material interest, for the enactment of reforms.

The classical school shared with other liberal intellectuals the philosophical idealism which demanded real changes in the social environment as the necessary condition of personal moral perfection, but it was distinctive in its decisive affirmation that the transcendent ideal was already operative in actual human agencies and that this union of reason and reality was vested essentially in the supra-personal organs hallowed by history. This classical group went beyond their forbears in German aristocratic liberalism by attributing to individuals the ultimate embodiment of morality both in spirit and in realization, but they returned to their antecedents in their reliance upon established authorities for the force to lever individuals into the desired activity. They would ensure progress against both stagnation and social disintegration by utilizing existing corporate institutions as the firm mold for released individual endeavor. Where the radicals tended to think away all intermediaries between universal values and the individual, these moderates held a more organic view and took cognizance of the family, church, state, nation, and society as the essential transmitters which converted principles into potencies and bore them into the lives of concrete persons. This pattern was applied particularly to the state, the institution which above all others had inherited the ethical mission of the church.[58] Attracted to the notion of the state—and particularly of the Prussian state—by the connection which the territorial sovereigns in Germany had built up successively with the concepts of aristocratic rights, spiritual freedom, and economic liberty, the classical group of intellectuals now sought to rationalize this accumulation into a coherent concept by adding political rights to it and converting these heterogeneous associations into the conscious and consistent moral relationships inherent in the constitutional state. But this final step in the merger of the idea of individual liberty (*Freiheit*) with that of the territorial state's own freedom of action (*Libertaet*) implied a shift in the conditions required for each. For if the state was now endowed in all its parts with an individualistic ethic, individual liberty became in turn associated with and dependent upon the interests of the state which bore it. With the attempt to come to terms with established institutions by imbuing them with ideal values, the moderates shifted their focus of interest from the individual to the state and their values became inevitably entangled with the traditional amoral necessities of the state.

It was Friedrich Dahlmann who first gave a concrete political application to the moderate approach. His main work, appropriately entitled *Politics, Reduced to the Ground and Measure of Existing Conditions*,[59] became the classic authority for this branch of pre-March liberalism. Dahlmann, the most prominent of the Goettingen Seven who had been removed from professorships for maintaining the inviolability of the Hanoverian constitution against the Duke, manifested both in the theory and in the practice of his politics the combination of the absolute moral principles which aligned him with the rest of the liberals and the embodiment of them in established institutions which was the distinctive hallmark of the moderates. In his political theory Dahlmann chose the state to be the actual meeting-ground for this combination. He sought to develop ideas of the state's essence and its institutions which would at once justify traditional relationships and subject them to the meliorative influence of an overriding ideal.

Thus Dahlmann started from the state as his primary, irreducible unit—"an original order, a necessary condition, a capacity of man, . . . a corporeally and spiritually unified personality"[60]—and saw his initial problem to lie in relating it to the moral realm. The state was a part of the "worldly order" and could not even be considered without its real historical bases in the past and without the circumstances of "our present, our region, our people." [61] There was, however, a "higher order," which is "superior to every individual state and to all states collectively" and endows them with their "final purpose" and their "power." This moral order remains ever distinct from its servant, the state, for "the state as such can never represent the divine order with its demand for unconditional compliance." [62] The reconciliation of the state in its historical, existent forms with the requirements of an absolute ethical realm consisted for Dahlmann in the elevation of the state to the highest of earthly organs—"nothing on earth stands so close to the divine order as the state order"—and in the elevation of the ideal apart from the state almost—but not quite—clean out of political relevance. Dahlmann recognized that the individual was the agent of the divine order insofar as this order related to purely internal and ethical considerations; for "external arrangements" toward human perfection the state was the agent. "The individual true to his higher destiny brings to the state every sacrifice of his person and his property but the sacrifice of this higher destiny itself." [63] Consequently, while the state remained for Dahlmann the prime temporal agent of morality it had to make provision for the moral agency of individuals as well.

The pattern of Dahlmann's thought is familiar. It falls into the whole tradition of German legal and political writers stretching back into the 18th century, who had striven to reconcile a strong and independent governing power with some measure of secure freedom for the individual. Particularly orthodox in this respect was Dahlmann's attribution of "sovereignty" to the ruler. His will was unrestricted within the requirement of general laws set by the very nature of the "state," and he could be joined by a representative body that would not exercise any governing power but would simply, through its consent to laws, confirm the proper conditions for the free royal legislation.[64] Where Dahlmann advanced beyond this tradition, however, and underlined the distinctive demand of pre-March liberalism was in his elevation of the subjects' representation from its former status as a particular privilege inherent in certain traditional corporations or as a simple expedient to assure consent between governor and governed into a new position of fundamental right. In no state, according to Dahlmann, could constitutional laws be properly amended without the consent of "all the estates or branches of the people," and in the best states "civil freedom" is guaranteed by "the higher principle of political freedom"—the right to participate in the passage of all laws.[65]

Having established this a priori balance between the rights of authority and the rights of the subjects Dahlmann found the resolution of the implicit conflict not in a theoretical system but in the rule that the concrete application of these formal requirements accommodate itself as much as possible to the realities of the established order, including the reality of a social hierarchy which mediated between political opposites. "To persist, the form of government of a large state must be built out of materials that are not uniform but diversified and that are as little as possible artificial and as much as possible really existing." On the basis of this empiricism Dahlmann opted the conservative alternatives of hereditary rather than elective ruler, peerage rather than senate, and a representative body "based upon actual conditions" rather than a popular assembly based upon "indiscriminate individuals." [66] As he freely admitted, the fundamental assumption upon which this kind of association of the ideal with the real rested was the principle that "freedom has often come out of order, but never order out of freedom." [67]

To insure, however, that freedom would indeed develop from order Dahlmann modified tradition to equip it with the capacity for the necessary mediation between the actual pillars of the existing order and the libertarian goal of the spirit. He rejected as standards both "the old" and "the new," proposing rather as an intermediate principle of selection "the constant and the vital or the to-be-revitalized." [68] The political analog of this intermediate principle he found in the state, which he conceived concretely as the regulator of historic institutions in this sense. Kingship should remain hereditary as the permanent bulwark of order but must recognize the necessity of the evolution from "patrimonial kings" to "state kings," whose reason for being lies

in their governance of and for a general political community
and who, albeit still personally irresponsible as the source of
political authority, must now become responsible through their
ministers to the community for its exercise.[69] Similarly, Dahlmann required the continued legitimation of a peerage, but its
basis was to shift from the original superiority of blood or function to the requirement of state that the conservative influence
of an upper legislative chamber have an appropriate source in
the society. Correspondingly, it would include both the scions
of the old hereditary nobility and new accretions based upon the
possession of honorific office or the performance of service for
the state.[70] Perhaps most characteristic, finally, of this flexible
attachment to existing institutions was Dahlmann's injection of
the political estates with such an indefinite dosage of individualism that he was unable himself to decide whether his idea of a
proper representative body was corporate or popular.[71] He insisted that the old rigid division of society by estates had been
undermined by the process of historical change but he insisted,
too, that this change had not reached the point of completely
equalizing individuals. The ultimate units of society were still
"estates" based upon the diversity of "callings." [72] The relative
proportions of corporate and individualistic elements in the diet
would depend upon "what really supports the state." [73] The
state requires "intermediate links" so urgently that it must even
take "a leap" to create them when they are lacking; but it also
requires the subordination of corporate special rights to "the
active position of the individual" in the political order of the
whole society. Thus Dahlmann attributed political rights to a
social base which faithfully reflected the actual social structure
of Germany in its melange of estates and individuals.[74]

The balance which Dahlmann sought to strike between the
ideal and the real state was clearly one in which traditional political and social institutions would maintain their integrity but
would become flexible and mobile. This balance, weighted on
the side of moderation, received its most graphic illustration in
Dahlmann's treatment of the ultimate questions of the nature
and the limits of political obligation. The object of his loyalty
was neither the ruler as such nor a set of absolute political

principles as such, but rather the particular fundamental constitution of the state. The constitution meant for Dahlmann the relationship amongst the vital powers of government and society that integrated them into the general community of the state. Consequently he would not obey governing organs that transgressed it nor did he look beyond it for abstract values which could convulse it. Dahlmann exhibited this courageous but limited kind of political devotion not only in his political writing[75] but even more strikingly in his political action. His behavior after his expulsion from Goettingen was dominated by nothing more or less than the conviction of the sanctity of the moderate Hanoverian constitution: he insisted that there could be no concession to the ruler on this score and he insisted too that nothing but the maintenance of the constitution should be striven for.[76] Theory and practice coincided, moreover, in his ideas on the limits of obedience. His theory rejected and his practice did not look for active resistance to established authority, but in both capacities he recommended constitutional means of resistance to unjust government—notably tax evasion.[77] Beyond this characteristically median remedy he refused to go, and he justified his refusal with the epitome of the moderate approach to politics. The revolutionary, he wrote, is not rooted in concrete reality but hovers above the world, striving to transform the whole. Moral freedom, on the other hand, can be realized in society only if it is already embodied in some existing local institution. Therefore, he concluded, even under despotism the problem of liberty requires not revolution but withdrawal into one's own family, which thereby becomes the seat of "an inviolable realm of freedom" and "a model of the good state." [78]

Corresponding to the contribution which the political professors made to moderate liberalism through this kind of idealization of the historical fact was the support brought to it by the Rhenish progressives' frank veneration of the economic fact. The connection was made actual by Dahlmann's influence in the Rhineland after his appointment to the University of Bonn in 1843. The most striking tribute to the essential dependence of the moderates upon established public powers, and to their exaltation of the state as the organization of these powers into a libertarian posture, was furnished by the practical men who led the Rhenish bourgeoisie into an idealization of the Prussian state as the guarantor of their interests. This combination was literal in men like Gustav Mevissen and Ludolf Camphausen, for their new awareness of the individualistic reforms required by an expanding capitalistic economy and their intellectual commitment to a wonted cultural idealism were two distinct spurs to their public activity. To the consciousness that "industry is becoming a power conscious of itself" [79] Mevissen added the Hegelian ethical notion of the state as the organ of justice destined to direct the essentially egoistic interests in the society toward the general good. Mediating between these strands which tended on the one hand to spontaneous social freedom and on the other to state capitalism and the welfare state was Mevissen's Janus-faced emphasis upon the "free and mutually independent individuals in all circles of society" which it was "the role of the state . . . to create"—a merger of state and liberty which would have as its constitutional application the retention of the traditional authorities and the addition to them of "free corporate forms historically peculiar to the German nation." [80] In Camphausen the blend of new bourgeois aggressiveness and old burgher values was even more obvious, for despite his decisive sponsorship of free-trade, railroads, and the joint-stock company, his internal commitments to the traditional merchant's outlook inspired a moral loyalty to the existing order of state and society. The resultant was an open-minded Prussian patriotism. His, then, was the deliberate and recognized voice of compromise. The harmonization of Rhenish with Prussian governmental interests, the sponsorship of the German Customs Union as the meeting of free-trade interests with the extension of Prussian power, the assumption of the leadership in the Prussian ministry of conciliation after the first flush of the Revolution of 1848—these were the hall-marks of Camphausen's politics.

Even in David Hansemann, a self-made business man who lacked formal education in and taste for the German idealist tradition, did the championship of capitalistic material interests find its way, through the power of objective circumstances, to practical dependence upon and moral investment in the characteristic organs of the Prussian monarchy. Hansemann expressed his views, characteristically, through memoranda addressed to the King of Prussia.[81] Respect for established political authority, social class-consciousness, and the consciousness of the connection between the two, were probably more sharply defined in Hansemann than in any other liberal leader. He advocated as valid ends "the strength necessary to government," "the power of the state, and therewith of the monarch," on the ground that "the first principle of states is life and the continuous increase in force," and "the power of the king cannot be thought to be other than identical with the welfare and the power of the state." [82] The life-principle of the state lies now in the new social forces of "public opinion" and of the combined "property and knowledge" which have become "the common possession of a mass of citizens" and particularly of "the middle class," the "respectable merchants and manufacturers" who are the agents of the new equalizing changes in the society and which have become essential to the power of the state.[83] Hansemann proposed an alliance of crown and middle class, which was thus in large measure practical and utilitarian in its basis. Negatively, an interest common to both was the danger of revolution from "the lower classes," or "the mob," with its consequence of anarchy destructive of both the political and the economic order. Positively, the Prussian state, whose goal must be the achievement of power to assure its independence, must attach the new social means of power to itself if only to keep pace with the western nations which had already done so.[84] The merchants and industrialists would benefit externally through the employment of Prussian power for the expansion of their markets and internally through the stimulation of their initiative and enterprise by dint of their active participation in public affairs.[85]

But however emphatic, this identity of interests between crown and bourgeoisie was not sufficient for Hansemann. The very force of his class-consciousness impelled him to insist upon the dissolution of the traditional corporate bonds of the Prussian society for political purposes in favor of the indiscriminate mathematical criteria of property and geography. The palpable result of this insistence was to level the society down to the middle class and to leave the hereditary monarch with no visible means of social support for his prerogative. And to compound the problem, Hansemann's view of the prevalent political "apathy" of the German middle class left him dependent not simply upon the king's acceptance of his program but upon the crown's active initiation of it.[86] Despite Hansemann's repeated analysis of the conservative tendency of middle-class interests he patently continued to feel uneasy about this problem. He tried to solve it verbally by calling up the connotations of the past and characterizing "my system" as "essentially aristocratic and monarchical," seeking thereby to equate his propertied elite with the traditional hierarchical social basis of monarchy.[87] But ultimately Hansemann could escape his difficulty only by transcending it. He could reconcile a constitutional system dominated by the middle class with the strong and independent monarchical authority only by departing from the presumptive identity of interests and appealing to a "moral force" which was rather alien to him, but which returned him to the familiar main line of German moderate political thinking. The compulsion which Hansemann labored under to add a moral dimension to his view of the state was directly connected with his problem of adding a conservative dimension to his argument for liberal institutions under the state.

He admitted that the Prussian state had long possessed the civil liberties of both a material and intellectual type which the absolute monarch had already deemed feasible to confer. He insisted, however, that this kind of freedom was insufficient, that "no fundamental freedom, no elevating consciousness of freedom, is possible in the people if a participation in legislation is not granted it." [88] It was at this point that Hansemann abandoned his practical arguments and sought to justify this sharing of political authority by substituting the moral notion of "freedom" for the material notion of common interests as the basis of the state. While Hansemann theoretically conceived of freedom as including civil and political components alike, he arranged them in a hierarchy where civil liberty meant "the free movement of the individual in his own sphere" and political liberty "the striving for a higher sphere." [89] Consequently, it was to ground the grant of active political rights to the middle class by superior and more powerful authority that Hansemann clothed them in the mantle of a moral freedom and reverted to the traditional association of this ethical quality with the state. "The confirmation of freedom" in a representative constitution would bring the ennoblement of the people's character; "what the royal power would thus sacrifice would be regained and exceeded by the consolidation of conservative forces and the enhancement of the state power." [90] Royal power plus freedom equals state power —a time-honored equation in the German political algebra.

Inherent in the moderate approach was the tension between the established powers as the necessary agents of politics and the ideal which required their movement toward liberal reform, and in no respect was the problem more clearly manifest than in the moderate position on nationalism. Hansemann had a definite national program,[91] but this was as singular as his bourgeois class-consciousness, and indeed these two distinctive traits were internally related. Hansemann's recourse to political nationalism was specially motivated by his unimpeded view of expansive industrial interests and by his need to replace the organic structure which he had rejected within the Prussian state. Other moderates, not so exceptionally motivated and generally more favorable toward corporate institutions, were correspondingly less dependent upon the idea of a politically unified Germany in which princes and peoples could be harmoniously integrated as equally valid components of the nation. Fundamentally, the problem of the moderates vis-à-vis nationalism was that their historical approach prevented them from going very far beyond the particularistic institutions and rudimentary national relationships of their age. Consequently, the moderates, apart from Hansemann, had little conception of a national political program until the decade of the 40's. Dahlmann was conscious of Germany as a cultural and even a racial nation and he even viewed the German Confederation as the institutional expression of this nation,[92] but he was much too preoccupied with setting up an organic working relationship between the institutions actually in being within existing states to fabricate designs for a national state which did not yet exist. Dahlmann conceded that as a matter of convenient chance racial and cultural national homogeneity might ease the development of a state, but he insisted that as a matter of principle the state is "composite" and "has become something else than merely the form of the nation." "A whole nation need not be included in the same state . . . ; nor does . . . history tolerate that the state should grow out of one racial people, or, if once so grown, should continue undiluted." [93]

During the 1840's the moderates participated in the growing movement toward political nationalism and they contributed their characteristic practical emphasis to it. The Rhinelander Hermann Beckerath recognized that "it is material interest—a peculiar thing in a people so profoundly philosophical and moral —which is to become the bond among our state, otherwise so divided. . . . The economic activity of the nation bears it toward the idea of unity." [94] The historian J. G. Droysen, despite his full recognition of the state as the embodiment of Justice and the bearer of freedom, adjudged the modern state to possess "unlimited power" and justified the national mission of Prussia in terms of its increase.[95]

In the final analysis, however, this contribution of the moderates to political nationalism must be qualified by the *caveat* that they were adapters rather than initiators of it. Only after it had been pioneered by others and had become a practical issue reconcilable with real interests did the moderates tend to commit themselves actively to it.

The Dualists

To the left of the moderates in the liberal spectrum were the theorists and publicists who can loosely be classified as the dualists. This group was centered largely in southern Germany, where constitutional conditions stimulated an eclectic kind of political thinking. This comprehensive quality went far to give the southern liberals the predominant role which they played in the German pre-March political movement. They combined opposites so as to achieve an equilibrium between dedication to a transcendent ideal and investment in existing institutions—an equilibrium which reflected perfectly the interaction between progressive intellectual goal and lagging social condition in pre-

March Germany. This typical character of southern dualism was confirmed practically by the national attention which the southern chambers drew upon themselves through their blending of constitutional loyalism and decisive parliamentary opposition. It was confirmed theoretically by its assumption of doctrinal initiative in both of the two main lines of the progressive movement. Southern dualism pioneered both an active political liberalism and a genuine political nationalism.

The most influential organ of political liberalism in pre-March Germany was the *Political Dictionary* (*Staatslexikon*), and this organ was dominated by the dualistic doctrines of Rotteck and Welcker. Despite the fundamental differences in the philosophical preconceptions of these men, their practical experiences in Baden parliamentary politics after 1830 brought them to a similar balancing of the absolute rights of individuals and governments. While the essential structure of their dualistic systems remained unchanged from their initial formulations during the liberation and post-liberation periods, both Rotteck and Welcker shifted the locus of these systems after 1830 from the constitution of the state to the distribution of rights and obligations in the political society at large. With this alteration of approach from the implications of the just state to the implications of the popular movement Rotteck and Welcker intensified their antinomies by broadening their constitutional dualism within the state to a political dualism within the society.

In his preface to the *Dictionary* Rotteck admitted that the middle ground which he had sought between revolutions and reaction was disintegrating under his feet and that what had been a discussion of better or worse kinds of representative constitutions under a monarchical head was degenerating into "a battle of life and death between throne and freedom, absolutism and republic, suppression and revolution, sultanism and demagogy." [96] The remedy lay, for Rotteck, in neither the philosophy nor the jurisprudence of the state, but in a free discussion based on "the clearest possible view of the actual situation" and addressed to "all classes of the society." All rational citizens must be given the knowledge and the political ideas wherewith to exercise rights and duties in the state, for they must be equipped to decide in case of an irreconcilable break between government and assembly.[97] This education of a general public opinion was for Rotteck the ultimate purpose of the *Political Dictionary* but his delineation of its more direct aims showed that he was thereby broadening his dualism and not going over to radicalism. For he admitted frankly that the more special appeal of the *Dictionary* was directed at "the unimpassioned, moderate, thoughtful liberals," [98] and its political line was still, like Rotteck's position during the 1820's, the idea of constitutional monarchy—"the internal harmony of the true rights and interests of governments, and thus primarily of the throne, with those of the peoples" [99] —as "a right mean" that was, however, not a *"juste milieu"* with its detestable principle of compromise.[100] Hence the prefatory statement of goals foreshadowed the characteristic pattern of the *Political Dictionary*—a radical approach to moderate solutions.

This pattern was most clearly manifest in Rotteck's own articles.[101] He repeated his formal constitutional doctrines of the 20's,[102] but he added to them the new popular emphasis of the 30's. The result was a change of stress and a certain imbalance in several of Rotteck's positions. His argument against radical republicanism in Germany stressed much more than formerly its tactical unfeasibility under German political conditions and much less the distinction between the norms and the actuality of man's moral nature.[103] He now bluntly defended popular political rights with the authority of "the democratic principle." Although defined in a sense compatible with monarchy and short of full popular sovereignty, democracy authorized not only the anti-aristocratic "tendency toward the equal participation of all in the political rights accruing to the whole people and in the civil and human rights to be guaranteed to it" but also the actual independent powers of representative bodies and a free press which make the democratic principle "belong to the essence of the state" as neither monarchy nor aristocracy do.[104] Moreover, Rotteck tended now to make the people the final judge of questions concerning the limits on governmental power and of conflicts between government and diets.[105] And finally, Rotteck now asserted that "the freer and more republican a constitution is, the farther reaches the sphere of its competence," [106] and he thereby made popular political rights the fundamental practical criterion in the crucial relationship between political authority and individual liberties.

The added weight which Rotteck thus attributed to the role of the people in politics did not overturn his constitutional dualism but it did increase the tension between its constituent elements, particularly since Rotteck still retained the aversion to organic and national institutions which were for so many of his colleagues the counterweights to the recognition of an independent political role for the people in the state.[107] Hence the abstract "concept" of "the unity of the state power," which could serve Rotteck as his sole unifying principle so long as his concern was primarily with the balancing of constitutional organs, was no longer sufficient to hold his political structure together. Consequently, he now appropriated the concept of the *Rechtsstaat,* associated it with the liberal constitutional state, and thus helped to endow this chameleonic idea with the politically liberal connotation which has adhered to it through all its changes in actual meaning.[108] But this connotation, genuine as it was for Rotteck and for the pre-March period in general, should not obscure the function of the concept: it remained a theoretical device whereby traditional political authority and urgent popular rights could be clamped together as compatible parts of a single political system. What Welcker and Mohl had done with the concept in a period when civil liberties required integration into the monarchical system Rotteck now sought to do when the birth of a popular movement for political liberties seemed to stretch his constitutional dualism into an explosive antinomy.

Rotteck's explicit anti-national attitude and the general concentration of the southern liberals upon the constitutional issues of their particular states should not obscure the fact that it was from similar tendencies toward a political dualism that pre-March political nationalism received its chief impetus. The meaning of the national appeal during this period is ascertainable from its integral connection with the same kind of south German political thinking that produced Rotteck's and Welcker's liberal amalgam. Paul Pfizer's pioneer *Correspondence between Two Germans* of 1831 and 1832 expressed a national insistence shared by his fellow Wuerttembergians, Ludwig Uhland and Friedrich Vischer. The first organization dedicated to the goal of German political unification was similarly initiated by southern constitutionalists: the *German News* of 1847-1850 was founded and run by a group of Badeners which included moderates but in which Welcker, Georg Gervinus, and Karl Mathy, men at this time somewhat to the left of the moderates, took a leading role. This nationalism expressed the balance of real and theoretical elements characteristic of the intermediate tendency in the liberal camp by projecting a united Germany which would be at once a mere extension of existing cultural and material interests and a new embodiment of hitherto unrealized ideals.

Paul Pfizer supplied the initiative for the discussion of German political unification in the liberal camp, and in working out this historical prologue he anticipated the process through which the liberals were gradually to arrive at the appropriation of political nationalism as the indispensable framework of their constitutional program. The antagonists in his *Correspondence between Two Germans* were intended indeed to be extremists, but Pfizer deliberately drew them to be not the stock representatives of revolution and reaction, the disjunction so common to his age, but rather the representatives of radical and moderate tendencies within the liberal movement proper.[109] Moreover, Pfizer's portraits were not straw horses; they incorporated many of the distinctive features actually characteristic of the German progressives of his day. His radical was not a political revolutionary but rather a firm believer in the categorical primacy of ideas or "spirit" over existence as the indispensable ground of freedom and in the necessity of transforming actuality entirely in the light of philosophy.[110] His moderate espoused the primacy of tangible historical actuality as the indispensable starting-point of all action and found in the organic structure of reality the justification for proceeding from living existence to the ideas and the freedom immanent and bound in it.[111] The political deductions from these philosophical positions simply continued, in translation, the decisive opposition between them. For the radical, "the representative system," based on "the constitutional principle," was "the task and the gospel of the age," not only because it was the chief goal of the people but because "constitutional freedom," was the contemporary expression of that fundamental freedom which, as "the true life" and "the first law of all creatures," "has become a moral necessity and a duty of conscience." [112] For the moderate, the essence of politics revolved around the state as "a vital organism," composed of "organic forms . . . which have become natural and necessary through long custom" and held together by "the reciprocity of rights and obligations" among all the elements of the "state organism." In accordance with these criteria, the moderate proposed the institution by "the organs of power" of a political system in which "the people" was raised beside "the prince" as "an almost equal . . . half of a whole" but remained inferior to him "in all doubtful cases" and subordinated to him when their rights collided.[113]

Now the decisive point of the *Correspondence* is that Pfizer, having deliberately developed this conflict "in all its sharpness," led it ultimately to the discussion of German unification as the field of possible harmony between the two approaches. It was in this capacity that the problem of political nationalism became the focus and the climax of the whole book. For both sides agreed on the necessity of a German nation-state, and in terms of this agreement their differences became negotiable. The radical endorsed national unification basically because the nation appeared to him as the prime intermediary through which idea could become actuality. "A people becomes a state through conscious intelligence and reflective calculation, but it becomes a nation . . . only through nature, through an independent development which pursues necessary laws and is not disturbed by chance: in the genuine life of the people, state, and nation, intelligence and necessity must coincide. True political wisdom would recognize that the German people is robbed of its best property and is deprived of its most sacred right so long as . . . there is no German nation and our spiritual unity in customs, language, and mode of thought finds no external recognition." [114] The transformation of the cultural nation into the political nation is the only means through which Germans can have "the honor of working themselves" for the principles of progress, knowledge, justice, and freedom, which are the spiritual values of their nationhood.[115] In the realm of politics, "the civil liberty of the individual collapses, hollow and vain, without a secured national existence, and . . . the participation of the people in the direction of state affairs loses all meaning as soon as the state, bereft of its external prestige and effect, has nothing . . . to direct." [116]

Pfizer developed the position of his moderate spokesman equally to a demand for national unification. For the moderate, the nation was an empirically given, organic fact of nature, binding individuals with princes. "Nationality is the personality of peoples," and "the rights of nations are . . . as sacred and as inalienable as the right of personal freedom of the individual and of not less divine origins than the majesty of kings." [117] The emphasis in his nationalism was correspondingly not upon spirit but upon "force" and upon Germany's "demanding and securing her place in world history" against other nations.[118] The united Germany must have "a constitutional system" since it is "an unavoidable demand of the times," but this consideration is "not now the main point." It is subordinate to the overriding rule that the achievement of a great work like German unity requires "not only will but power" and that the future Germany be strong enough "to take its due place in the ranks of the European powers." [119]

Thus the diversity in theory between radical and moderate found an area of harmony in their practical application to the nation. The sole difference which remained between the two approaches was a matter of degree and of means, and hence the two positions were now commensurable. For the moderate, Germany must become "first united and then free"; for the radical, Germany must "first become free" and then "expect its unification from the . . . spirit of constitutional freedom." [120] The corollary of this difference was that the means consisted for the moderate in the power of the Prussian monarchical state and for the radical in the progress of constitutional freedom and the federative union of the constitutionally ruled states.[121]

In his *Correspondence* Pfizer carried the argument no further. Having indicated the role of nationalism in resolving the conflict within the liberal camp he left unresolved the remaining opposition on the national issue itself. In 1832, however, he appended to the second edition of the *Correspondence* a treatise on *The Aim and Tasks of German Liberalism,* and here he did try to present his own solution to the problem which he had brought to a soluble stage. In this answer Pfizer showed the mediating character of his nationalism, for he took its ingredients from both moderate and radical demands. To the moderate view he granted that "with the mere principles of civil freedom, as meritorious and necessary as their spread may be, Germany has for long not been helped. With all the drive of the individual for freedom The Germans will always play a wretched role . . . as long as they do not wish freedom as a nation." [122] He conceded even that "whether greater personal freedom in the German constitutional states will lead us to unity is doubtful, but it is not to be doubted that once unity exists, freedom, the most sacred possession of peoples, but which never has stability without the force of unity, cannot remain wanting." [123] From the radicals, however, he took the definition of German unity as an ideal "German freedom," and he espoused as the ideal means toward national unity the agitation for a German national assembly by "liberalism"—that is, the constitutional states of southern Germany.[124] On the principle that the ideal must be adapted to make possible the reconciliation of "justice (*Recht*) with power (*Macht*)," since "the right of the stronger is also a right," [125] Pfizer settled for a practical solution which seemed to rest precisely between moderate and radical requirements and to harmonize both—"a league of constitutional German Princes" which would be anchored in the representative institutions of its peoples. Thus "the material forces" of liberalism would be "concentrated into a unity," and the liberals would acquire a confederated seat of power within the larger German Confederation.[126] Pfizer conceded that Prussia might assume leadership of the movement at some later time, when the monarchy would have joined the constitutional states, but for the present his national program appealed to legitimacy only in the form of constitutional monarchies whose action toward German unity would be a genuine synthesis of actual institutions with the ideal goals of personal and political freedom.

The synthetic function of political nationalism was rooted in the characteristic doctrines of dualistic political theory. Pfizer's own principles manifested a duality of absolute natural rights and empirical "natural necessity" which were reconciled only in nationalism.[127] Pfizer thus operated out of a doctrinal system that was very similar to Rotteck's, but he resolved its problems in a dissimilar manner. Where Rotteck simply translated them into a political dualism Pfizer resorted to nationalism as the field of synthesis. He admitted frankly that the constitutional problem in Germany could be settled only on the level of the nation.[128]

What appeared as intransigent dualism in the narrow confines of the existing states could be idealized to an organic harmony in the broad spaces of a projected nation-state. The prospectus for the *German News* (*Deutsche Zeitung*), which was founded in 1847 to propagandize for German unity, made a settled policy out of the dualists' use of nationalism as a means for uniting their own split personalities and the liberal movement as a whole:

> Amidst the various regimes into which we are divided, the very different stages and view-points of political development in Germany, . . . the diverse concepts associated with the usual terms of position and opposition, liberalism and conservatism, progress and reaction, . . . our basic tendency should be to maintain and strengthen the feeling of the community and unity of the German nation.[129]

The Radicals

The German radicals of the pre-March period were spurred on, far more than the other liberal groups, by the consciousness of the abyss between theoretical ideal and practical action and by the intensity of their striving to overcome it. They retained a faith in absolute and inflexible principles of reason that required the greatest effort for coming to grips with existing things. The combination of this belief in undefiled transcendent ideals with the insistence that they find realization produced the characteristic radical goal: the sweeping reorganization of existence until it conformed with the undiluted requirements of reason as the only possible means of spanning theory and practice. Marx's emphasis in the last of his *Theses on Feuerbach*—"The philosophers have *interpreted* the world in various ways; the point however is to *change* it" [130]—was characteristic of the radical school in general. The problem of applying ideals to an actual world of appearances from whose influence they would yet maintain these ideas inviolate led radicals like Arnold Ruge to the one-way regimentation of actuality by reason.

> The truth is: everything irrational is rational and everything rational is irrational. But this means one thing in theory and quite another in practice. The theory which finds everything irrational is wrong, for it is itself then in the irrational "everything" and thus no longer has a criterion; but the practice that does not mean to break with all of history once a radical step to a new principle has actually been made would make no progress at all. Theory comes back to humanity; but in order to lead the world back to this its ground it must be totally renovated. It would be incapable of reforming itself if it did not maintain its basis, Reason, in the abstract, even in the midst of rotten existence.[131]

The pattern of change which he foresaw as necessary to the reconciliation of theory and practice could only be one of "great" and "wholly extraordinary convulsions" of the existential world.[132]

The chosen realm of the radicals for this reconciliation was the realm of politics, and the vehicle was the concept of freedom, which was extended for this purpose from an absolute moral freedom to the equal civil and political liberty of all. For the radical, then, liberty was not, in the first instance, the political expression of lower middle class or proletarian claims, nor was it even the logical working out of the libertarian political ideals as such. Rather was liberty rooted in a cosmic principle of freedom— Hegel's dialectical reason, Kant's moral reason, or the reasonable natural law of the French tradition—and the radical's emphasis was not so much upon concrete liberty, with absolute freedom as its ground and justification, but upon the absolute principle of freedom, with concrete liberty the locus for its rigorous and integral application. Georg Herwegh, the revolutionary political poet, defined "liberalism" as "rational knowledge applied to our existing conditions. Since Liberalism is the tendency of spirit in which we judge existence wholly abstracted from everything historical and according to the exclusive standard of the Rational, . . . everything which arises in history comes before the forum of reason. By its very nature Liberalism must be emancipated, because it is free . . . from the inevitable dependence characteristic of the historical; for freedom and reason are the same." [133] This sovereign knowledge must then be translated into "deed"; "spiritual freedom" and "social freedom" stand and fall together.[134]

Behind the rise of the radical wing in pre-March German liberalism lay the growing conviction that the literal and uncompromising realization of principle was not only necessary but possible. The distinctiveness of the radicals consisted indeed far more in this approach than in their specific political ideas. Thus the Baden radical, Gustav von Struve,[135] developed a formal political doctrine in which he seemed to differ hardly at all from his more moderate liberal colleagues. He deliberately organized his theory to begin with the frankly abstract "Essence of the State" and to proceed by easy stages down through the intermediate "Forms of the State" to the "Actions of the State." His theoretical sections made much of the usual distinction between the actual conditions and the lawful basis of political power. He rejected the contractual origins of the state in favor of the Aristotelian conception of the natural organic community founded upon the family;[136] he made fundamental law the criterion rather than the basis of government; he defined this criterion of the state by the flexible "harmonious development of the totality of the forces entrusted to it" and consequently placed his emphasis upon the purpose rather than the social composition of the state power.[137]

But if this dualistic structure of the theory was scarcely distinguishable from more moderate doctrines, Struve departed decidedly from the fold when he went on to develop the concrete application of the theory. For as he approached the level of political actuality his position became not more accommodating but more radical. His theoretical duality between the norm and the conditions of existence was still in evidence, but in the realm of political practice he placed greater and greater emphasis upon the absolute requirements of the norm in order to maintain its integrity. Accepting the relativizing organic analogy of the life-cycle of mankind and accepting, too, the moderating necessity of the separation of powers,[138] Struve yet spurned the tendency toward "the middle way" and came out flatly in favor of "popular sovereignty" and "democracy" as the necessary external complement of "inner freedom"—that is, "virtue." He insisted that "freedom in its purity . . . is developed only in a democracy," and in the light of this insistence he gave a practical radical resolution to his theoretical dualism by equating the present with the age of full human maturity and by requiring the unquestioned predominance of the democratic element in the necessarily mixed state.[139] Whatever the right combination might be for other states, Struve maintained that in the concrete case of Germany, the existing alliance of monarchy and aristocracy as exclusive possessors of state power left no alternative, if any freedom whatsoever was to be realized, but for the popular force which was developing outside the state to take over the hegemonial role within it in the name of democracy.[140]

When he came to write of immediate policy, Struve carried through this radical slanting of prevalent doctrine. Accepting the arena of the constitutional state with its divided powers, Struve insisted that the role of the popular representation was essentially that of "opposition" against the monarchical governments, an opposition that was "primarily negative, resistant, censorious" and that was led not by men of "moderation" and "half-measures" but by men of "unshakable firmness of character." [141] And as the ultimate practical recourse of such opposition Struve did not hesitate to recommend "the eternal and inalienable right of resistance to unjust power," as the guarantee "without which all other rights of the people become nothing." [142]

In general, the substantive reforms desired by the radicals seem originally to have differed but little in scope from the civil and social liberalization called for by the other progressives; they were simply more impatient and more thorough-going in these demands. Consequently, they were not initially committed to any specific agent of reform and during the early 40's they could look, like the Young Hegelians, to the Prussian king or, like Struve, to the parliamentary liberals in Baden. When these agents proved too refractory or lethargic for the restless radicals, they cast about them to find another vehicle for their absolute principles. The articles of men like Herwegh and Johann Jacoby testified to their disappointment and to the alternative upon which the radicals settled—"the people." [143] Thus the radical student Karl Brueggemann, riding the crest of the popular agitation in the southwest, made quite explicit this transfer of moral agency in a speech of 1831:

> "All these blessings [popular religion, civic courage, development of individuality, sanctity of family life] . . . will grow of themselves if only the existing political relationships, which cannot allow anything good and least of all humanity and courage to bloom, are destroyed. Turn your eyes not to impotent diets, still less to perjured princes, and least of all to foreign liberators. Our destiny must be the work of our youth, our freedom must come from our blood . . ." [144]

The radicals of the mid-40's thought similarly in terms of inculcating "energy into the masses," [145] for they were now convinced that "individuals . . . can show the way but cannot drag the people to it. The people goes its own way . . . but does not desert its vanguard on the road to freedom; it stands up for them, makes common cause with them, and proves by deed that the hour of freedom has struck." [146]

It was by the unusual process of going from an agent to a doctrine that the radicals, who thus began to look to the people as the agents of a philosophically, morally, and religiously conceived reform began finally to develop the foundations of what was to become a democratic doctrine out of their need to provide this people with a framework for political action.

The first stage of this process consisted in the self-conscious delimitation from moderatism on the one side and communism on the other. Edgar Bauer, in his radical phase—broke openly with the southern constitutionalists on the ground that the principle of freedom was the New Truth, a dynamic, critical force which could live only by the complete destruction of existing forms and by its own political establishment in the extreme form of absolutely equal liberty for all.[147] Ruge broke with Marx and the communists because of their neglect of both the individual and the state. It is real men—individuals—who make history, and "communism wants to realize the general as such and abstracts it from its realization in the individual." [148] The ordering principle through which ideal individual freedom can be realized is embodied in the state. "The dissolution of the category 'state'—that is, of the common will of associated persons—is insane, for every society which acts as a society . . . must have and express a common will . . . All civilization, or the inter-related labor of variously occupied men, can never be superseded but can only be ordered differently according to a higher princi-ple." [149] "An actual political and practical freedom, a sovereign and really existing people" [150]—this was the limit beyond which radical liberals in general refused to go.

The second stage in the working out of a radical politics came only with the elaboration of a positive democratic program on the very eve of the revolution. In September 1847 the deputies from the extreme left of the south German diets met in Offenburg and produced resolutions calling for universal suffrage, abolition of all privilege, and equalization of economic and social condi-tions within the individual property system. [151]

But until then the German radicals blended a community of approach with a diffusion of content. This was particularly marked in their position on the national question. The basic tendency of radicalism worked against an internal commitment to German nationalism, for it recognized no essential intermediary between universal principles and the human individuals who thought them. But concretely, this orientation led the radicals not to one but to two positions on the national issue: some of them reacted violently against the nation because of the exis-tential and emotional elements in it; others—and these consti-tuted the bulk of the group—adopted a pro-national view by emphasizing the ideal elements in it.

The cosmopolitan wing of the radical movement found their most emphatic spokesmen among the Young Hegelians. Ruge set forth the unmistakably transcendental basis of their hostility to nationalism. "Without the overthrow of patriotism," he wrote categorically, "Germany can never be won for freedom." The reason is that "philosophy has no fatherland, as little as freedom and thought is a national prerogative." [152] For "nationalities are only *existences* of freedom, . . . and to make them into its principle is to commit a brutality. Not my genus but my reason is the principle of the general world of men, and individuality,

. . . the movement of one existence against the others, is the character of the brutal world of animals." [153] Hence for Ruge "the true fatherland" was embodied not in the actual nation, with its elements of "barbarity," but in "the party of men seeking freedom," a party which cuts through all nations. "A free Frenchman is dearer to me than a German reactionary, because he belongs to my party and pursues the same idea toward which I strive. How simple! How necessary! How can you cling only to patriotism, the bait of reaction . . . ?" [154]

And yet the bulk of the radicals contributed to the nationalist agitation sponsored by pre-March liberalism. This contribution was particularly striking in the southwest German revolutionary movement of 1830-1833, in which the national appeal was stronger than the democratic. The proclamation of the Hambach Festival of 1832 called: "Rise, you German men and youth of every estate in whose breast the holy spark of Fatherland and freedom still glows!" [155] Siebenpfeiffer, whose speech at Hambach approached most nearly a recommendation of active revolution, tended to subordinate his castigation of oppression to his castigation of national division. The princes, he argued, are responsible for the disunity of Germany, while the German people cry, "No, the shame of the Fatherland is our shame and no free man can bear it." His vision of the future utopia was likewise nationally framed. "The day will come when a common German fatherland will arise which greets all sons as citizens and includes all citizens with equal love and protection." [156] J. A. Wirth, who shared with Siebenpfeiffer the leadership of the Festival went even further in sketching the national qualifications of the libertarian movement, for he refused to acknowledge an internal freedom that was not acquired through purely Germans means.

> Even freedom may not be bought at the cost of the integrity of our territory; the struggle for our fatherland and our freedom must be waged from within with our own forces and without foreign intervention. At the moment when foreign intervention takes place, patriots must suspend opposition against the internal traitors and call the whole people to arms against the foreign enemy.[157]

How is this rabid nationalism to be explained, among radicals with whom universalism was not only an a priori axiom but, in the form of a cosmopolitan appeal for the liberation of all peoples, an article of political faith? [158] The nationalistic emphasis of the radicals had little reference to the actual institutions of nationality; it was simply a convenient cultural frame, which was put to political use in default of a developed political theory for the purpose of providing the sovereign "people" with an organization and a justification of their collective rights. Wirth's *Political Reform of Germany* saw as the crucial problem the resistance not of princes but of the people itself to liberty.[159] Hence Wirth was confronted with the challenge of activating the masses upon whom he counted for the application of the ideal freedom. Now this activation meant for Wirth essentially a spiritual and a moral activation, for, as he wrote in another connection, "it is a law of nature that no material power can withstand the agreed and tested opinion of a people." [160] He could find the moral lever for radical political action by the people only in nationalism. He rejected the possibility of realizing "freedom" within the existing framework of "the provinces" and called upon patriotism to aid in the struggle of freedom against the "rule of the princes." "The interests of all the German peoples are, by virtue of the order of nature, necessarily the same and can be placed in jeopardy only by the selfish and ambitious purposes of princely families." [161]

Where the moderates projected into the future national state their concern with frustrated German economic interests and political power, and the dualists the synthetic solution of their constitutional dilemma, the radicals made it the contact-point of their dream world of revolution. Small wonder, then, that in 1848 the whole movement joined in setting up a united Germany and broke apart in the mode of applying it.

The Revolution

The German revolution of 1848 was driven by the changing relationships among three distinct protagonists.[162] The recent social emphasis in revolutionary historiography makes it clear that in addition to the conservatives who gathered around the beleaguered monarchs and the liberals who populated the revolutionary parliaments the mass activity of anonymous or unofficial citizens must be accounted an independent force. From this point of view the revolution no longer looks like a simple political struggle between reactionaries and liberals with changing quantities of mass support. It would seem now to be a much more involved process, at once political and social. The intellectual liberals sought to realize their pre-March mission of drawing government and people together as the real agents of their ideals, were progressively isolated from both of these powers, and were subsequently themselves torn apart into their three generic divisions as they fell into dependence upon divergent real interests or remained impotently suspended above them. The rationale behind this development can be best understood in terms of the three successive phases through which the revolution passed between 1848 and 1850.

The first phase, which pervaded the halcyon spring of 1848, was dominated by the dovetailing of the popular and the liberal movements in a joint uprising against the existing authorities. The relationship between the two movements is not entirely clear, but its main features seem certain enough. The mass uprisings and the liberal political assemblies were independent in their origins and their ultimate ends, but they coincided in their immediate aims and offered each other mutual support. Behind the popular demonstrations lay a decade of economic dislocation, and it is noteworthy that most prominent among the rioters were precisely the socially conservative peasant and artisan groups who had felt the dislocation most keenly. Southwest Germany—most notably the state of Baden—was the region where the revolutionary disorder was most violent, and it was the region, too, that was particularly characterized by such groups.

What these groups wanted essentially was the satisfaction of their economic ills, and they thought in the reactionary terms of restoring their old corporate security as the best remedy. Peasant rioters, exposed to the effects of the agrarian crisis by the personal emancipation of the liberation period, reacted violently against the remaining real manorial dues, which now seemed an unjustifiable burden, but they reacted in the name of their good old communal rights.[163] The analogous motivation of their urban counterparts was even more directly manifested, for a "Preparatory Congress" of guild representatives which met at Hamburg early in June emphasized their categorical opposition to the regime of economic freedom and demanded for their corporations full competence over industrial and social matters.[164]

The signal for the open rising of these groups, which had settled down after the sporadic unrest of 1847, was the news of the February revolution in France. The political revolution, on the other hand, had its roots in the pre-March movement of progressive intellectuals, who had begun to intensify their pressure and organize into larger units before the outbreak in Paris.[165] The aims of this latter movement were overwhelmingly political and liberal—constitutional reform in the Confederation and in its constituent states for the purpose of establishing the legal bases of individualism—and the great majority of the progressives soon showed their independence of the popular revolution. Everywhere the moderate liberals moved into the princely ministries and took measures against all attempts to press for reforms through direct mass action. In certain areas like the Rhineland and Berlin, where the March risings took on proletarian socialist tendencies, the liberal opposition to them took on the appearance of a class struggle.[166] In other sections, like Baden, it took the aspect of a political defense of constitutionalism against republican democracy. In general, however, the opposition within the revolutionary camp was not yet definitely joined. It was a matter rather of the inevitable gulf between two movements of profoundly different origins and orientations.

What lay behind these differences was indicated in extreme form by David Friedrich Strauss, the intellectual rebel of the pre-March period, when he wrote on April 3: "The element in which we liked best to move is coming to an end . . . For our element was theory, i.e. free activity not directed toward utility and need. This is now hardly possible any longer . . . For the principle of equality is as hostile to spiritual as to material preeminence." [167] This conviction that the popular revolution posed a utilitarian danger for ideal freedom was commonly held in a more concrete form. The characteristic internecine issue was the one which dominated the Frankfurt Pre-parliament during May: reform through national assembly built on top of existing authorities or reform through revolutionary committee and direct action. A fear of communism and resistance against the republican extremism of the Baden radicals were certainly involved in this issue, but more fundamental was the commonly held distinction between the political sovereignty of the law of reason and the dependence upon the empirical vagaries of the mob. With the problem taken in this form, the great bulk of moderates and democrats alike joined in the decision for the national assembly against a small extremist fringe led by Struve and Hecker.

But despite the consciousness that the mass and the liberal movements were different in kind and even potentially opposed, the prevailing relationship between them during the first phase of the revolution was one of cooperation. The political demands for limitations upon absolutist rule and for popular participation in the state were the common denominator which bound both movements in a *de facto* coalition. The mass endorsement of liberal political claims was attributable to their currency in the pre-March period as the standard expression of opposition, to their transmission through the popular journals and clubs of radical intellectuals in the towns, to the intermediary role played by the students in the actual uprisings, to the direct exploitation of the risings in some areas by the liberals for their own purposes, to the initial participation of prosperous burgher elements in the revolts, and to the consequent obscuring of the material aims of the mass movement. The demonstrators often exhibited an imperfect understanding of the liberal planks which they mouthed and the endorsement usually went along with a monarchical loyalty which fed the growth of popular conservative societies, but the liberals' insistence upon some kind of change and their demand for political organs through which social pressure could be exercised helped to channel the initial force of the popular unrest behind them. Thus the Hamburg congress of artisans proposed to present the work of their "social parliament" to the Frankfurt national assembly for legal enactment.[168]   Moreover, whatever the internal relationships between the two the uniform results of the first phase of the revolution throughout Germany were the appointment under popular duress of liberals to the ministries of the particular states and the election of the intellectual middle class—including the notables of the pre-March period—to the majority of seats in the Frankfurt assembly.

On the liberals' side, similarly, the political realm afforded a secure field for alliance with the popular movement. The liberals mistrusted this movement in the same way that they mistrusted monarchy—as a pure fact of self-directed social power. But when they had translated the activity of these powers into political terms and harnessed them into a constitution of state which would direct them to the realization of fundamental law, the liberals felt that "the people" like "the princes" would be the organs of the good society. Consequently, the same liberal movement that feared the mob and forced itself upon the rulers accepted a democratic suffrage and set out to secure the agreement of the princes. By the time the Frankfurt Parliament met in May of 1848 the general consensus had come so far as to recognize its powers as constituent, by the revolutionary authority of popular sovereignty, but this acknowledgement of the connection between the Parliament and the popular revolution was predicated upon a purely political and instrumental idea of "the people." According to Heinrich von Gagern, President of the National Assembly, this sovereignty became operative only because of the impossibility of securing a free constitution for Germany in any other way, and for him as for the liberal movement as a whole the popular will was totally embodied in the elected constituent parliaments. The task of the assemblies was to draft the desired constitutions and to direct both the people and the princely governments toward the acceptance and the operation of them.[169]

The second phase of the revolution ran from summer of 1848 into the spring of 1849. Its chief development consisted in the separation of the political liberal movement from its real supports in the society. The growing gulf between the two movements was manifested not only in the actual popular lethargy and in the shift toward the resurgent conservative powers but in the striking dissimilarity of pattern between the liberal and the social movements. For at the same time that moderates and radicals within the various constituent assemblies were achieving formulas of political cooperation in the drafting of constitutions, the constituent elements of the German society were being fragmented under a new consciousness of material group interest. Perhaps no feature of the revolution gives so clear an impression of the persistent intellectual basis of its liberalism as this insulation of the parliamentarians from the recoil and the disruption of the social groups originally behind the revolution. It is true that the practical issues involved in making constitutions and running governments crystallized the highly individualized intellectuals of the pre-March era into genuinely political groupings that roughly paralleled the spectrum of political clubs in the country at large. It is true, too, that the politicized liberals in the parliaments and the governments dealt with a multitude of economic and social problems in terms that revealed their pre-eminently bourgeois roots in the society. And yet the main tendencies within the liberal camp were directly opposed to the developments within the society. For the liberals, material interests took the form of constitutional and legal principles. Politics remained primary because it seemed to supply the vital mediation which permitted the ideals of freedom actually to meet with the forces of social reality and yet to control them. Thus the moderates' undoubted concern with middle-class property interests came out as a political emphasis upon the individualistic legal system and a balanced constitution, while the radicals' interest in the social question emerged primarily as part of their overriding insistence upon political democracy.[170] When transmuted into these political forms the issues between the parties proved susceptible to agreement, and despite the virulence of the debate between constitutionalists and democrats, federalists and unitarians, *Kleindeutschen* and *Grossdeutschen,* the record of political liberalism down into the spring of 1849 was primarily one of compromise and cooperation. In Frankfurt, not only were "the Fundamental Rights of the German People" hammered out in a series of accommodations between moderate and radical proposals,[171] but the German Constitution of March 1849 as a whole was produced by a compromise between the radicals who prescribed a democratic suffrage and parliamentary supremacy and the moderates who secured the provisions for a federal structure, agreement with the princely governments, and a Prussian Emperor. Moreover, even the more tumultuous Austrian national assembly succeeded in drafting its constitution of March 1849.

During this very phase of coalition among the political liberals the society which they would integrate in their political system evaporated out from under them. It evaporated both in the physical sense that it fell away from their support and in the more figurative sense that the kind of social unity upon which the liberal political activity was predicated ceased to exist. For the remarkable feature about the development of the popular movement during the summer and early fall of 1848 was that its disintegration into mutually hostile social groups left these groups equally disaffected from the political liberals. This process took place in two stages.

First, through momentum and disappointment activists among the artisans and the workers became conscious of their particular economic and social interests and worked to radicalize the revolution. The local liberal governments met the economic crisis, which the revolutionary spring had deepened, with administrative palliatives,[172] while in Frankfurt the peasant agitation for the relief from dues on the land, the demands of the artisans' parliament for a corporate charter of industry, and the organization of a proletarian workers' "Brotherhood" with a permanent central committee in Leipzig, were answered by the National Assembly's preservation of the property obligations on peasant land in an unspecified redeemable form and its defense of the freedom of individual industrial enterprise.[173] In conjunction with the natural momentum of revolutions, these indications of a new middle-class order helped to spawn, between June and October, the growth of "democratic" and "workers'" clubs through which the activists among the urban dispossessed pressed against the princely governments and upon the Frankfurt liberals for the radical overthrow of the political order as the preliminary of a vaguely defined social reorganization. From this movement came the rising of June 14 against the Berlin armory, the September revolts in Baden and Frankfurt against the national assembly, the second revolution in Vienna, and the radical "Counter-parliament" in Berlin during October.

At the same time, the social dimension of this radical movement stimulated the bourgeoisie to an intensified consciousness of its own property interests and to resistance against further progress of the revolution. Organized in their "constitutional" clubs and in the civil guards, the burghers strove to defend the political compromise with the old authorities against the threat to the social order. The Berlin civil guard successfully opposed the June 14th rising, and during the summer the rift between bourgeois and worker guards in Vienna ripened into open hostility.[174]

Between October of 1848 and May of 1849 the second step in this development was played out. During these months the suspicion which workers and bourgeoisie had evinced toward each other was now turned by both toward political liberalism, which, as a synthesis of democratic and moderate constitutional tendencies, now seemed to each group the representative of the other. The resumption of monarchical initiative in Berlin and the subsequent dissolutions of the Prussian and the Austrian constituent assemblies (in December and March respectively) were consummated without significant resistance from either social group, and the ground was prepared for the large-scale apathy which greeted the monarchical rejection of the Frankfurt constitution in April 1849. It must be emphasized that this was not a matter of opposition to the liberals but of withdrawal from them. There was plenty of abstract approval for the constitutional product of the liberals but only a sporadic disposition to act upon it and commit oneself wholly for a cause whose total victory might redound to the advantage of somebody else. The main division during this decisive phase of the revolution was not a class division which penetrated both society and politics but rather the gulf between the liberal political synthesis and the essentially unsynthesized juxtaposition of old and new societies.

Thus the withdrawal of the popular movement during the second phase of the revolution was but part of a more general withdrawal of real social supports from the political liberals. The monarchs' resumption of their political independence must be considered as a factor in the same process. The much-discussed failure of the political liberals to take over the instruments of power was a natural result of their general approach, which was to integrate the existing forces of the society, popular and princely alike, into a comprehensive system of law. The initial acquiescence of the governments had thus furnished the liberals with a pole of support which they welcomed and needed in order to avoid commitment to any partial social factor and to maintain the detachment required for an ideal synthesis. Hence the meaning of the monarchical resurgence in Austria and Prussia during the fall of 1848 was not that it opposed positive political reaction to the liberals but rather that it removed an essential social agency from the liberal constitutional system. The Prussian constitution which the king promulgated unilaterally on December 6, 1848, was a genuinely liberal charter on the Belgian model, complete with declaration of rights, constitutional army, legislative assembly, and universal (albeit indirect) suffrage. This was followed up in January by the abolition of patrimonial jurisdiction and special courts for aristocracy and bureaucracy and by the establishment of public trial by jury. Even in Austria, the dissolution of the constituent national assembly on March 7, 1849, was preceded by the Imperial grant of the March 4th constitution, which seemed at the time to be only temporarily suspended. The monarchical, like the popular, movement did not at this stage so much oppose the political liberals as become independent of their system, which was predicated upon the instrumental use of both people and prince.

The third and final phase of the revolution which covered the period from the revolts of May 1849 to the "humiliation" of Oelmutz in November 1850, witnessed the complete transfer of political initiative from the liberals to autonomous masses and to monarchs, the shift of the liberals from a controlling to a dependent relationship with these forces, and the consequent disintegration of independent intellectual liberalism. The crucial feature of these developments was the employment of characteristic liberal devices as means for the advancement of interests whose goals lay far beyond a legal and political system of free individuals. The short-lived revival of the popular movement in the risings which flared up in Baden, the Palatinate, Saxony, and the Ruhr during May 1849 was characterized precisely by the combination of an unprecedented intense social motivation[175] and an immediate-action platform which simply defended the liberal Frankfurt Constitution. The identifiable role of the workers in these revolts was proportionally greater than ever before—particularly in Saxony, where the central committee of the workers' Brotherhood was prominent in the insurrection—but only where their vague socialism found the Frankfurt Constitution an apt instrument or where—as in Baden and the Palatinate—artisans and peasants continued to find in political liberalism the only possible avenue to their goals did verbal loyalty to the Constitution become decisive action.

The Prussian monarchy played a similar constitutional line to advance its own power. Frederick William IV's rejection of the Frankfurt Constitution in April 1849 was followed by the conservative revision of the Prussian Constitution which, as formally enacted on January 31, 1850, provided for a three-class voting system, independence of the army from the constitution, and a weakening of the tax powers of the diet. But once freed from the liberal system the Prussian government embarked upon a program which would secure the loyalty of Prussian people and the adherence of the German people by absorbing constitutionalism into the traditional monarchical system. Under the administration of Otto von Manteuffel and the influence of Josef von Radowitz Prussia resumed the line of bureaucratic liberalism à la Hardenberg and organic nationalism à la Stein. To the conservative revision of the constitution and the equally conservative tightening up of the guild system during 1849 the Manteuffel ministry added libertarian reforms in the form of the definitive establishment of small peasant property and a more egalitarian system of rural self-administration against conservative aristocratic opposition during early 1850.[176] On the level of German national politics the rejection of the Frankfurt Constitution was followed by the project of Prussian Union, which was based initially upon a monarchical sponsorship of the Frankfurt draft in revised form. Despite the successive conservative amendments which came out of the Three Kings' Alliance of May 1849 (Prussia, Hanover, Saxony) and the Erfurt Parliament of April 1850 (representatives elected by the three-class suffrage from Prussia, the north German small states, and Baden), the official Prussian attempt at the unification of Germany remained focussed around the voluntary acceptance of a representative constitution which still provided for a popularly-elected national legislative chamber and a declaration of "the fundamental rights of the German people." [177]

The liberal posture taken by both the remnants of the popular movement and the rejuvenated Prussian monarchy had a magnetic effect on political liberalism. Bereft of their channels to social and political reality and attracted by the apparent sympathies of their former agents, the liberals were torn apart by the revival of both monarchy and revolution. A tiny radical fringe—intellectuals like Gustav Struve, Karl Schurz, Gottfried Kinkel, Ludwig Bamberger—went over to the sporadic local risings of May and June 1849. More important, the great majority of the moderate liberals withdrew from Frankfurt on the orders of their governments and passed across to the Prussian Union scheme. One hundred and forty-eight of this group, led by Gagern, Dahlmann, and Mathy, held a congress in Gotha at the end of June 1849, to endorse the Prussian plan by formal resolution. The moderates followed this up by supporting the Manteuffel ministry in the Prussian chamber and by participating in the officially convoked Erfurt Parliament—from which the more radical liberals abstained—for the acceptance of the government-sponsored Union constitution.[178] And finally, the large group of liberals intermediate between the moderate and radical extremes remained in suspension between the diverging popular and monarchical movements, unable or unwilling to surrender the fruit of their ideals to the interests of either and counselling, in consequence, an orderly, negative, and doctrinaire opposition to the enveloping hostility. Included in this group was the Stuttgart rump of the Frankfurt Parliament who would neither disband on royal order nor direct the popular risings in their favor.[179] Included, too, was the dominant party of the Prussian National Assembly, who, torn between their commitments to the Prussian state and to the common liberal cause, would not go beyond passive resistance and abstention. The polarization of the revolution had left the traditional states in renewed possession of the constitutional field and relegated the opposition once more to the choice of revulsion, compromise, or the paralysis of Buridan's ass.

The dissolution of intellectual liberalism under the solvent of conscious self-interest in its agents did not bring the definitive defeat of liberalism. It did, however, mean the beginning of the end for the philosophical approach to politics. Not only the disruption of the liberal movement proper, but the failure of either the popular revolts or the Prussian Union to attain their goals under the banner of political and constitutional freedom, introduced the general reorientation toward the frank and direct appreciation of interests and power which the revolution had shown to be decisive in German society and politics.

8. The Decline of the Liberal
Intellectuals (1850-1870)

In the generation that followed the Revolution of 1848 the lessons of the revolution were confirmed by the development of the material factors of power into a position of overt predominance in German life. The emergence of a Napoleonic France, an aggressive Austria, and an unsatisfied Russia loosened the interests of state from its association with the principle of conservative concert, while the massive growth of industrial capitalism riveted men's attention on the benefits of economic activity and the possibilities of economic power. For liberalism, such developments made possible the acquisition of what it had so sorely lacked—a broad social basis, gathered around a progressive middle class, interested in a free society for vital material reasons—and the revived liberal movement of the 60's was founded upon definite organizations which utilized this new support. But yet the traditional scissors pattern of German culture persisted. For the activity of the 60's was preceded by a decade of fundamental reorientation in approach which undermined the comprehensive appeal of the liberal political ethic. Whereas the pre-1848 liberalism had been characterized by the demands of a politicized ideal beyond the executable power of its available economic and social backing, the post-1850 movement was characterized by a strongly individualized society without the former power of absolute political principles to pull it together. The combined effects of revolutionary defeat, political reaction, and capitalistic growth during the 50's fostered a political positivism which weakened the subsequent liberal offensive from within. It was now the intellectual decline of German liberalism that diminished the force of the assault upon the prevailing state-system in Germany and broke the assaulting forces up once more into the three wonted types of divided and impotent response to the overwhelming fact of the renewed association of empirical freedom with the authoritarian state under Bismarck.

In terms of organized political activity the decade of the

1850's were years of stagnation, but they were crucial for both the conditions under which such activity would take place and for the inner development of the individuals who would lead it. Indeed, the political and economic conditions of the 50's were precisely such as to discourage aggressive liberal politics in the mass but to encourage its reassessment by individuals.

The common characterization of the period as one of "reaction" must be taken only in a qualified sense. Reaction prevailed in the fundamentals of politics: the sovereign power which had passed back into the hands of the princes and their bureaucracies in the first instance and under the influence of the aristocracies in the second was safeguarded by a whole series of constitutional revisions, laws, prosecutions, and police measures designed to undo the revolutionary transfers of and limitations upon political authority. The formal repeal, by the German Confederation, of the Frankfurt Parliament's declaration of fundamental rights and the establishment by the same body of the so-called "Reaction Commitee" led the work of unifying and enforcing the conservative standards of institutional regression among the several states. If its pressure was necessary in cases like the two Hesses and Hanover similar measures were undertaken spontaneously in most of the other German states. The general effect of these measures was to limit the suffrage, to favor the estate principle with its corollary of aristocratic preference in elections and local administration, to restore political initiative and decision to the governments, and to exclude liberal organizations and decisive liberals in any form from the political arena. But within this political framework the reaction was far from uniform and complete. Unlike the post-1815 pattern, the re-established authorities now recognized certain politically innocuous liberal achievements as necessary parts of their regular system of government. This was particularly notable in the fields of economic and administrative policies. The long step toward the completion of peasant emancipation which was taken during the revolutionary era was maintained even in Austria and Prussia. Moreover, the relocation of the Austro-Prussian political rivalry to the commercial plane of the German Customs Union was a striking acknowledgement of the connection between an expanded free-exchange area and the interests of state. For Austria, the offensive to force entry into the German system was but part of a general policy which actually established free trade within the Austrian Empire and aimed at the creation of a single market over all of central Europe as the bastion of Austrian hegemony. The architect of the plan was Karl Bruck, Austrian Minister of Trade and founder of the Austrian Lloyd shipping line, who consciously linked this Austrian customs policy with a program of economic liberalism designed to stimulate Austrian trade and industry by opening it to wider markets and more advanced competition.[1] The sponsorship of these policies by the absolutist Chancellor, Prince Felix Schwarzenberg, placed the official seal upon the new awareness of the relevance of a freer economic development to the maintenance of political power. Prussia was generally on the defensive in the struggle, but even here the decade brought not only the expansion of the Customs Union to include Hanover and Oldenburg but also the confirmation in Prussian policy, through the cooperation between the bureaucratic prime minister Manteuffel and the free-trading official Rudolf von Delbrueck against the Austrian sallies, of the government's vital interest in free trade within Germany and moderate tariffs in international commerce. The Prussian government of the "Reaction" may even have intended to appeal, by the intransigence of its stand against the protectionist southern states, to the pro-Union public opinion over the heads of the governments.[2] Certainly, this was the effect, and one of the most revealing events of the 50's was the continued adherence of the reluctant south to the Customs Union in conscious response to the demands of progressive industrial and commercial circles.[3]

The impact of the reaction upon the administrative structure within the revised constitutions was more uneven. In Austria and Prussia, the revolutionary advances in self-administration were stamped out, but even in these states the work of revision included changes testifying to the preponderance of bureaucratic over aristocratic considerations.[4] In Saxony and Hanover the restoration of the pre-March constitutions brought the alliance of bureaucracy and aristocracy to the helm once more, but in both cases with changed forms of local government. The traditional patrimonial rights of the nobility gave way in Saxony to a system consciously patterned after the English institution of Justices of the Peace, and in Hanover to a system which retained the bases of elective self-government enacted by the moderate liberal Johann Stueve during the revolution. Finally, in Bavaria and in Luebeck the reaction made scarcely any inroads at all; in the largest southern state the minister Ludwig von der Pfordten resisted reactionary intervention by the German Confederation and extended the structure of local self-government even beyond the revolutionary achievement, while the compromise constitution between the patriciate and the citizenry which the Hanseatic city-state had attained in the revolution was maintained afterward.[5]

Perhaps the most important of the limitations upon reaction during the 50's was the emergence of the written constitution—however conservative—as the standard form of monarchical rule. To be sure, most of the German states had already possessed such constitutions before 1848, but charters were given a new importance after 1850 by the significant addition of Prussia to the ranks of the constitutional states, the frank espousal of constitutional monarchy by Duke Ernest II of Saxony-Coburg-Gotha, and the continuous use which moderate liberals now made of representative organs. The effect of this development was minimal in Prussia, where the constitution had little more than a nominal existence down to 1859, and a mere handful of Old Liberal notables from the extreme right-wing of the liberal spectrum together with a minority of Union-minded conservatives (*Wochenblattspartei*) scarcely checked the compliant governmental majorities in the diet, but Prussia was not typical. In Bavaria, Baden, Hanover, and Hesse-Kasse moderate liberals in the diets waged a defensive but often effective struggle against the reactionary tendencies of their governments.

The net effect of political conditions during the decade of reaction, then, was to stop the further development of liberalism as an organized movement, but to allow it certain precarious and dispersed handholds in public life which offered both the possibility of further advance and the spur to take advantage of it. From subordinate places, like business associations and journals, municipal governments, the non-political level of the bureaucracies, and the parliamentary opposition in the state diets, moderates felt concretely the frustrating impact of arbitrary bureaucratic intervention and aristocratic privilege and worked against it within their own bailiwicks. Cut off by their previous failure from the arena of general politics but possessed of new points of entry into it, liberals of all stripes began quietly to reassess their political approach.

If the reaction of the 50's provided the political framework, the qualitative economic changes of the same decade supplied the new social context for the liberal reassessment. In the words of Werner Sombart, "the 1850's were the first great speculative period which Germany has experienced. In them modern capitalism was definitively made the basis of the national economy." [6] This was the great age for the founding and organization of industrial enterprise, while the following decade represented rather an extension of the previous accomplishment.[7] Not only did the 50's witness a tremendous increase in industrial production, the mechanization of such key industries as mining, metallurgy, and textiles, the creation of banks, industrial plants, and new railways, but it was also the era in which the characteristic institutions of large-scale capitalism took their rise. The system of capitalization banks, which was to be the key institution in the German concentrated industrial structure, was initiated with the founding of the Darmstadt Bank for Industry and Trade in 1853.[8] The corresponding industrial form, the joint-stock company, began to play a notable role in the economy at about the same time. Of the 800 million *Taler* worth of shares issued in Prussia between 1850 and 1870 one-half were emitted in the period 1853-1857, while in Baden during the 50's joint-stock companies were observed to be springing up "like mushrooms." [9] Moreover, the attention of contemporaries was focused on these developments by the internal roots and ramifications of the economic crisis of 1857, which marked the entry of Germany into the cyclical rhythm of modern capitalism.

The sudden leap into a dynamic society dominated by industrial capitalism was of such startling dimensions as to present an unmistakably transformed situation to contemporary liberals. It signified an obvious shift in the basis and the means of men's striving for freedom. The marked rise in the urban share of population, the growth in numbers and confidence of an aggressive entrepreneurial group, the conversion of the peasantry into trade-minded property-owners, all helped to create a strong social backing for liberal reforms[10] and to reorient political attitudes toward the forces which could realize them. This shift was perfectly clear by 1856 to the liberals who published the Berlin *National Gazette:*

> In the feeling of dissatisfaction over the defeated liberal aims, in the despair concerning the defeated ideal strivings, the intelligent and material force of the people has been concentrated on the sphere of business, and the present is the proof of what the concentrated force of peoples can do when intelligence and physical labor join in working toward one goal. What idealistic efforts strove in vain to do materialism has accomplished in a few months: the transformation of all the conditions of life, the dislocation of the centers and the relationships of power in the social organism, the rule of aspiration and ambition almost in all minds, and the straining of an unprecedented energy, a direct search for constant activity in all nerves, muscles, and sinews.[11]

That this apparent diversion from politics required not a surrender of liberalism but simply a new practical approach to it was self-evident to the spokesmen for free enterprise associated with the *Bremen Trade Journal:*

> The governments would easily give a patent to anyone who knew how to isolate the entire economic area as a contented idyll in which land and people would quietly and obediently carry on their material progress and would bear in their hearts exclusively the political feeling of gratitude toward the high officials, the furtherers of their fortune. . . . Whoever looks at the situation without prejudice and fear will recognize immediately the intimate connection especially in Germany of the national economic with the national political problem, this Alpha and Omega of German politics.[12]

The tendency which the political and economic environment of the 1850's gave to the concretization of liberal thinking was abetted by the change in intellectual climate which affected all Europe after mid-century. The great metaphysical systems lost their appeal, and the specific disciplines which had been maturing under their cover blossomed out into independent empirical sciences. In Germany not only did history and the natural sciences throw off the assumptions imposed by the philosophies of Hegel, Schelling, and cosmic natural law, but the inductive and specialized fields of social science, historical and social economy, and administrative science, began to separate out from their parent political science and political economy.[13] The origins of these developments antedated the revolution of 1848, but it was only after that event that their consonance with conditions in other fields of life made them an effective influence in turning men's attention directly to the particular, tangible, concrete objects existing in nature.

The impact of the post-revolutionary world upon the liberal intellectuals and students who had experienced the upheaval of 1848 was not, however, a simple conversion to political realism. Their receptivity to the new influences was countered by their desperate clinging to the ideal systems on which they had been raised. The meeting produced a profound *crise de conscience* from which there emerged a whole spectrum of combinations adding the material divisions of the future to the doctrinal divisions of the past. The liberalism which emerged from this inward crisis to wage the renewed political conflict of the 1860's manifested the continuity with its past by drawing its leadership from the same kind of middle-class intellectual notables as in its pre-March and revolutionary period,[14] but the political situation of these notables was now different, some because they had changed their approach to politics and others because their retained approach had a changed effect in the new conditions. With the shift of the liberal center of gravity toward empirical politics the older absolute principles lost their synthetic power and what had been negotiable intellectual tendencies became hardened into rigid doctrinaire positions on behalf of diverse material concerns. The emergence of political realists alongside the old idealists within both the moderate and radical wings of the liberal movement transplanted the age-old relationship between the transcendental notion of freedom cherished by the intellectuals and the authoritarian world of existences outside them into the very souls of the liberals themselves. With the

resulting duality within both moderate and radical camps the
traditional pattern of German liberty had infiltrated its opposition and disarmed it: within the liberal movement as outside it
the recognition of the power of the amoral existent fact reduced
the ideal of individual freedom to the status of a formal political
doctrine. The ideal was transformed into an impersonal teleology immanent in the facts of political and economic power.

The New Moderates

The moderate tendency within German liberalism had ever
been receptive to the accommodation of brute reality, and it is
scarcely surprising to find that the positivism of the 50's redounded primarily to its advantage. A whole galaxy of figures
who were to occupy prominent places in the National Liberal
politics of the 60's found their way from a pre-March doctrinaire
radicalism to it through the sobering observations and reflec-
tions of the intervening period. This group embodied the meeting of the rising empiricism with the declining idealism in this
generation of German politics, for they sought still to enclose
their new-found appreciation of political power and of practical
interests in a framework of absolute liberal principle. In this
tenuous balance the new moderates betrayed the respective
functioning of the two elements; according as they placed the
stress upon the older ideal or the new realism the various members of this school went ultimately into the left or right wing of
the National Liberal Party. Eduard Lasker, Ludwig Bamberger,
and H. B. Oppenheim became outstanding politicians on the
left, A. L. von Rochau, Rudolf von Bennigsen, and Johannes
Miquel, publicists and leaders on the right of the party. The
former group represented a tendency that was to vacillate for
almost half a century between the moderate and radical liberal
parties, and the latter a tendency that was to bring an important
section of the liberal movement into uneasy dependence upon
the traditional powers. The new moderates thus played the crucial historical role of carrying on the division between the dualists
and the compromisers into the second half of the 19th century.

Karl Twesten was probably the purest embodiment of the new moderate movement. He stood midway between its two wings, and it was characteristic of the movement that his syncretic position left him a political lone wolf who could find a home in neither group. But precisely because the equilibrium between empirical and ideal factors was most nearly perfect in him, he remains the outstanding theoretical champion of the new moderates. As a youth of the 1840's he had traveled the well-worn path which led from Feuerbach's religion of humanity through the Illuminati to radical republicanism in 1848.[15] The failure of the revolution caused a disappointment so deep that it led to a reassessment of values culminating in the rejection of Feuerbach and the adoption of Comtean positivism. Politically this meant opposition to the application of metaphysics to politics and emphasis rather on the role of industry and the positive disciplines, notably history. The typicality of this development was reflected in the enthusiastic reception accorded his pamphlets at the end of the reaction, for they were regarded as the classic expression of German liberalism at this time.

In his *What Is Fitting for Us* (1859), Twesten started from the frank declaration that the spirit of the times, the *Zeitgeist,* has turned from abstract doctrines and universally valid principles of state to the basis of facts, i.e. the relativity of the State to the existing material and spiritual conditions—and particularly the social relationships—of the society.[16] He insisted that a political program be pragmatic. Since it could only hasten or retard already existing social tendencies it must be derived from a historical and psychological estimation of the social situation and must prove itself concretely in this situation. For the contemporary German scene he proposed a combination of progress and order which would establish the conditions for individual liberty within the existing framework of state and society. His definition of the constituents of progress and order showed that despite his protestations the older ethical emphasis was not dead but that it had become involved in a necessary relationship with the existential political and social situation. He tackled this relationship from both sides, and on either tack he arrived at an equilibrium of the two elements. In *What Is Fitting for Us*

Twesten's emphasis was upon the principles of liberty, but he developed them in such a way as to show their necessary consistency with the interests and the established authorities of the state. His definition of the *Rechtsstaat* as a state of law equipped with an administration "inviolably respecting the rights and freedom of the individual and the collectivity of citizens" and supported by "the participation of the people in an important part of its own affairs . . . as a regular and constantly working part of the state organism" would preserve the values of general moral principles in politics but only in conjunction with national diplomatic and industrial interests. He posed his individualism not in abstract, absolute terms but as a necessary attribute of a state purposively organized toward its own greatest strength. The state limited itself through law, permitted the exercise of individual initiative, and called for the active participation of the citizens in order to arouse the moral and industrial forces of the people which now formed the chief basis of state power. In his subsequent *What Can Still Save Us* (1861) Twesten took the reverse path and ended with a similar balance. Here he started from the primacy of foreign policy as the standard toward which "everything else must be directed," from the necessity of rapid and forceful diplomatic action as the supreme immediate goal of politics, and from the acknowledgement of political initiative "from above," in "those who have power and authority." [17] Hence he explicitly rejected the notion of a "liberal" foreign policy as irrelevant to the supreme criterion of seeking "that which benefits our power position according to impartial judgment." But Twesten then proceeded to show that this criterion required liberal principles at home and in Germany, "because only a liberal policy is today capable of conferring the force and *élan* to confront events." From this requirement he then deduced a whole chain of necessary liberal measures, beginning with the obviously pertinent freedom of industrial expansion and moving logically to the fundamental reform of bureaucratic administration, the Prussian House of Lords, and the king's personal government.[18]

Twesten's persistence in returning to an equal emphasis upon liberal principle and actual power relations is reminiscent of the duality which reached back in the German liberal tradition at least to the era of reform and liberation, but this continuity sets off into bold relief the changed framework in which his equilibrium was set. Whereas total systems of freedom were formerly expanded to include actual conditions Twesten inserted liberal values as part of his primary actual conditions. He insisted that the progress of civilization had made the moral as well as the material interests of peoples the palpable basis of actual power in states, and he explicitly spelled this out to mean that "material interests," for which governments are primarily responsible, must be adjusted to the inevitable action of "the Ideal"—admittedly "something revolutionary"—alongside them as an integral part of a dynamic reality.[19] Even in the midst of the critical conflict between the Prussian monarchy and the liberal chamber of the diet, Twesten found the bureaucracy oppressive because it no longer responded to contemporary conditions and had lost its vitality, and he looked to the *"Rechtsstaat"* not as the embodiment of an ideal but as an "objective legal order" which would serve the pragmatic end of making the practice of states reflect the balance of real social forces as faithfully as their constitutions did only potentially.[20]

> Abstract popular right, parliamentary forms, and impeachment of ministers help constitutionalism to no reality so long as . . . the public law is established only *in abstracto* by legislation and *in concreto* by the administrative authorities.[21]

Thus did Twesten epitomize the fateful development which planted the liberal principle in the shifting ground of relative circumstance. The note of baffled pessimism which was to inform Twesten's correspondence during the 60's was an expression of his ultimate insecurity.

To the left of Twesten was the loose grouping of young men whose evolution from a marked radicalism during the revolution to a reconciliation with the existing order in the person of Bismarck was to stop at an uneasy alliance for the limited and specific purposes of German unity, economic liberty, and a constitutional framework for further liberal agitation. Connected by participation in the *German Annals for Politics and Literature* which H. B. Oppenheim edited between 1860 and

1864, these men remained dedicated to decisive liberal principles
but developed during the 50's towards new means, new forms,
and new fields for their expression. Eduard Lasker, who had
been active in the journalism of 1848 as a democrat with socialist leanings, put the experience of this group clearly and simply
in 1851 when he characterized the revolutionary period as "the
frontier—both an end and a beginning—of a section of life." [22]
His later political intimate, Ludwig Bamberger—known as the
"red Bamberger" during the revolution when he led the Democratic Society in Mainz and participated in the Palatinate revolt
of May 1849—likewise turned to private concerns during the
50's and summed up the impact of the banking business upon
his own mentality: "I wrote from life and not from books." [23]
But for neither was the break to be as complete as they thought.
Not only did they both return to journalism and politics after
1860, but they carried over their determined adherence to
individual rights into their new appreciation of the practical issues of politics.

The articles on Prussian politics which Lasker wrote during
the early 1860's revealed this pattern.[24] On the one hand, he
passed over theoretical and even constitutional issues and concentrated upon the concrete evils of the "police state." His
main target was the ubiquitous intervention of the bureaucracy,
not simply for its monopoly of "public affairs" but even more
for its power over "the larger and more important section of
private rights"—a power which vitiates "the pillars of a prosperous economy and of civil freedom." Particularly important
in this for Lasker was "the freedom of property," which "is the
basis of all state order." [25] Within this delimited sphere of concern, on the other hand, Lasker sought to establish the absolute
validity of individual rights. If he did not derive them from
fundamental notions of sovereignty he would not entrust them
to the discretion of administrative policy. The resultant was the
containment of such rights within the fundamental order of the
state and the categorical insistence that within these limits they
be absolutely respected. His former radicalism in the scope of
rights became transmuted into an intensity for their application
within a restricted scope. Hence he recurred to the idea of the

Rechtsstaat as the reconciliation of independent authority and individual liberties and then raised this compromise into an absolute dogma.

> Rule of law and rule of police are two different ways to which history points, two methods of development between which peoples must choose and have chosen. . . . The true man is the independent citizen. Every citizen should and must be independent, for each has to see to his own welfare. He has no other claim on the state than protection from injurious force; for this he has to sacrifice nothing to the state but his desire to attack the rights of others. To this alone are the laws and the ordering of the *Rechtsstaat* directed. . . . In the *Rechtsstaat* the violation of law is the worst evil; it may be suffered at no time from any side. The highest task of the state is to abolish it wherever it appears.[26]

Like Twesten, Lasker located the genius of the state in the concrete tendency of its laws, but, unlike Twesten, Lasker's liberal definition of this tendency had an absolute rather than a relative validity. Ultimately, Lasker's position was an unstable one, for he desired the best of both worlds. "The division of material and spiritual needs is a scholastic phrase," he said, "for it is impossible to permit such a division in any kind of state."

> I grant for myself that the core of my life will always be the spirit which the year 1848 called forth. . . . It has been this spirit which led us at least into the ranks of the constitutional, i.e., rationally governed states. . . . Yet I grant that it was a grave mistake, to a certain extent an excess of idealism to have dwelt so long on fundamental rights and during this labor not to have brought the other, material, elements into equal consideration.[27]

It is scarcely surprising that Lasker became the leading spokesman for those new moderates who could stay put neither in the party of compromise nor in the party of doctrinaire opposition.

On the right wing of the new moderate school the appreciation of material interests and power went beyond the acceptance of a new basis for liberal politics to the frank recognition of the contingent status to which it was thereby condemned. Such a status implied a two-fold limitation upon political freedom— its general subordination to the amoral practical requirements of the moment and its specific localization within the framework of the established political order—and in August Ludwig von

Rochau and Rudolf Gneist these emphases found their respective spokesmen.

Rochau was a Badener who had been a radical in his youth but who had repented before the revolution of 1848. Exiled after his participation in an uprising in 1833, he had fled to France, where he had been temporarily influenced by socialist ideas. Soon, however, his enthusiasm cooled down to a moderate constitutionalism, and when he returned to Berlin in a journalistic capacity during the revolution he directed his fire against the Prussian left from the right-centrist position. But it was not until 1853 that he published a systematic formulation of a new approach toward moderate politics. His *Principles of Practical Politics* (*Realpolitik*) conceded more to brute power than his political kinsmen would themselves admit, but the work was well received and indirectly was even endorsed with Rochau's appointment to the editorship of the weekly organ of the liberal *National Union* in 1859. Thus the term *Realpolitik* was first circulated as general political currency by a liberal and with a value appropriate to its later usage. For Rochau defined it in the sense of establishing force and interests as the standards of political action:

> The discussion of the question, what *should* rule, whether justice (*Recht*), wisdom, virtue, whether an individual, many, or few—this question belongs in the realm of philosophical speculation; practical politics has to do first of all with the simple fact that it is power alone that can rule. To rule means to exercise power and only he who possesses power can exercise power. This direct connection of power and rule forms the fundamental truth of all politics and the key to all history.[28]

He proceeded, moreover, to attack directly the traditional liberal veneration of the concept of *Recht:*

> The existence of the state is independent of the political consciousness of its members; but this consciousness is the essential assumption of public law (*Recht*). So it can be said: the state precedes *Recht*. . . . *Recht* is related to power as the idea is to fact. This purely conceptual relationship becomes real only when and insofar as the idea of *Recht* incorporates itself in public power or power is transfigured into the idea of *Recht*. Therefore *Recht* is completely independent of power in

its existence but it is essentially conditioned and sharply limited in its efficacy by the measure of power which is at its command.[29]

Consequently, continued Rochau, constitutions simply represent the relations of the social forces within the state. "Every social force has a claim to an influence in the state corresponding to its extent, and the force of the state consists simply of the sum of social forces which the state has embodied within itself." [30] Constitutions must not be judged in terms of principles but on the standard of whether they permit social forces to assume their due position in the state. Rochau frankly connected constitutional liberty with the claims of the bourgeoisie and validated these claims on the basis of their material power: landed property recedes every day in importance before the onset of mobile wealth; correspondingly, the aristocracy loses political force while "younger social forces" gain; the latter are accompanied by the rise of public opinion, which exercises a power in the state according to the strength and constancy of its convictions and not according to their rightness or reasonableness; the state must rule in concord with this public opinion and consequently in harmony with the concept of nationality which unites this new public under the state.[31] Its participation in the power of the ordered nation-state calls not for a parliamentary but for a "representative" system, for representation depends not on rights but on force. "If the representation is not the precise expression of the social forces, the representative system becomes necessarily a lie, for real life will always be victorious over a formula which contradicts it. . . ." Representation need not be based on the majority principle, for organization is stronger than mere majorities and "sovereignty is a power concept, not a legal concept." Representation must rather be based upon three factors—"wealth, opinion, and intelligence"—and the processes by which they get their representation are unimportant so long as they get it.[32] These attributes are politically worthless as individual qualities; they must be characteristics of a class, and as such they become "for one class of the people after the other the bridge to political power." The "people" do not constitute an undifferentiated whole; political influence must be measured by "the difference in forces and capacities among the various classes of the people," and "where political ability is found, there it must be applied in the appropriate way." [33] Concretely, this meant, for Rochau, that "the middle class is and remains the most indispensable and the most valuable stuff for the German state structure." [34] Rochau's assertion of the claims of the middle class on the basis of its economic power, within the framework of the existing state, and under the criterion of the strength of that state was to become the dominant tendency in moderate liberalism.

Like Rochau, Rudolf Gneist represented the new tendencies in their extreme purity, and yet the outstanding influence which he exercised both as publicist and as liberal party leader testified to the responsive chord which he struck among large sections of the educated middle classes.[35] His well-known doctrine of the *Rechtsstaat,* which in systematic form was to express most faithfully the attitude of the compliant bourgeoisie toward the Second Empire, was already developed in its main lines by the early 60's. The essential tendency of this new departure was to mark out the precise institutional outlines of the sphere within the state in which the exercise of a popular political freedom would suffice to secure private life from specific arbitrary bureaucratic invasions and yet not weaken the supreme force of a unified monarchical political authority. This sphere he found to lie pre-eminently in practical administration and, within this activity, in the local, dispersed sectors of it. Such an emphasis was reminiscent of bureaucratic liberalism, and indeed Gneist represents the transposition of this tendency into the liberal camp. A Berliner reared in the tradition of progressive officialdom, the young Gneist exhibited his practical and limited temper in politics even before the revolution by coming to an early interest in self-administration through his concern for judicial reforms. During the revolution he revealed himself to be a constitutionalist as well, but by 1849 he was already defining his own political realism, *vis-à-vis* the doctrinaire revolutionaries, in terms of the practical work of local government. The years of reaction pushed Gneist in two opposed directions at once: the feudal revival and the irregularity of the administration confirmed him in his constitutionalism, while his intensified concern with actual possibilities impelled him to scientific study of self-government within the administration of the authoritarian state. Hence he entered the ranks of the liberal movement but he carried with him into it the notion that freedom was guaranteed by the objective, self-limiting laws enacted under monarchical and bureaucratic leadership within the existing constitution and by the subordinate participation of the society in the local application of these laws.

Under the pressure of the Prussian internal conflict during the early 60's, in which Gneist was a prominent member of the liberal opposition, he found a general political formulation for these constitutional notions. Convinced that the monarchy was violating the self-imposed laws which defined its own essential nature Gneist sought to describe the precise fields of freedom required by the fundamental laws of the state. He distinguished "social freedom" and "legal or personal freedom" on the one hand from "political freedom" on the other.[36] "Social freedom" he defined as "freedom in property and acquisition, freedom in the whole economic being, . . . the free rise into the higher classes," and asserted that it was demanded by "the numerous classes of the continent who feel themselves chained by the remnants of feudalism, by guilds, monopolies, by strict limitations of free movement, or by protective tariffs and labor police." "Personal or legal freedom" he defined as participation in public affairs of any kind unhindered by the irresponsible police system of an omnipotent state. "Political freedom" is "participation of the people in the government of the state."[37] The degree in which these freedoms should be established, Gneist concluded, varies with their place on the scale running from private to public affairs. Social freedom, which is related to private interest, will be easily established everywhere, for the very instinct to self-preservation will destroy the remnants of the old "structure by estates." The more public liberties of personal and political freedom must be measured on a different standard, since the age of absolutism has separated state from society, duties from interests, so that society must be trained and forced to public duties from below in local self-administration and from above by state action. Personal freedom then can be granted only to those

people who have been habituated to exercise positions of authority by their activity in communes. Political freedom, finally, can
come only from a series of pre-conditions "for which the initiative
stems only from the state and not from the society and its customs.
Neither the enthusiasm of the individual, nor the embittered
struggle of social classes, nor the written letter of a constitution,
nor the suspicious separation of powers, and least of all the servile
imitation of a foreign model" can found political freedom, but
rather only "lasting institutions" founded by the state. For "freedom is order, freedom is power." [38]

Thus Gneist, and the group of moderates for which he spoke,
continued during the conflict to call for a powerful state, strengthened by its extension to national frontiers, which would derive its
force through the permission and the protection of the free
initiative and the social predominance of the leading groups in
the new economy. Gneist's *Rechtsstaat* was an attempt to make
the self-limiting forms of general law the precise constitutional
expression of the actual proportions of political force in monarchical government and civil society.

The Old Moderates

Alongside the new political realism a moderate liberal strand
of pre-revolutionary vintage retained sufficient vitality during
the decade and a half of reorientation to pass as an identifiable
element into the permanent national liberal settlement of 1867.
But if a philosophical and ethical framework for politics was thus
perpetuated, its place in the total political picture was vastly
different from what it had been. Not only did the "political professors" who were its chief agents lose much of their popularity
and their influence after 1848, but their intellectual systems were
stretched and strained in the effort to moralize the alien new
factors of power. The net result was to cast an ethical mantle
over a state that was admittedly outside the liberals' moral control.

The transmission of the old moderate tradition was primarily
the work of the "classical liberals," that group of intellectuals

which already in the pre-March period had sought to localize their ideal in living historical institutions. They had demonstrated their capacity for adaptation during the revolution itself, when they had elevated the tactic of agreement with the established governments into the status of a fundamental political principle, and when they had become the intellectual spokesmen for the moderates of the Gotha Congress of May 1849 who endorsed the official Prussian Union. However, in the rationale of Rudolf Haym, one of the original classical liberals, this compromise was purely tactical: the liberals want to do something in politics; to do something power is needed; the liberals lacked this power at Frankfurt and lack it still; the Prussian government has this power and consequently the liberals' only chance to contribute to German unity is to support this government.[39]

The development of the classical liberals during the 50's and 60's was essentially the process of working the independent initiative of governmental and material forces to which they had accorded reluctant *de facto* recognition into the very structure of their political systems.

The violent dislocation which the revolution and its failure brought to the settled proportions between actual institutions and ideal system in the political thinking of the old moderates was at its most articulate in the contemporary political articles of the historian J. G. Droysen. Whereas he had previously opposed the just state to the power-state and rejected naked power as the basis of either foreign or internal policy, his experience in the Frankfurt Parliament led him to recognize frankly the triumph of realities over ideals, of interests over doctrines, of foreign policy demands over internal policy desiderata, as the fundamental character not only of the recent events but of all modern history.[40] This was not, then, simply an external lesson which would require an adaptation of tactics but a new stage in historical development which must be comprehended in any system of politics. As early as August 1849 Droysen was acknowledging the necessity of a basic revision in the approach to the German problem. "It is not as if questions of internal political development are not relevant. They are, with as much importance and energy as ever. But to become finally soluble they demand decisions of another kind. International problems . . . are those which must be solved. Prussia's existence depends on their solution." "Not by freedom, not by national resolutions was the unity of Germany to be created. It needed a power against the other powers, to break opposition and to ward off their selfishness from us." [41] By 1854 Droysen was describing the new necessities as the marks of a profound crisis in the whole of western civilization.

> The old forms of the state as of society are destroyed in their assumptions and in their bases, not through doctrine but as the consequence of given facts, which doctrine only expressed and to which it gave imperfect foundation . . . As large-scale machine industry absorbs small handicraft more and more, so the state, as a summary of existing social and legal conditions, changes into an institution for the production and exercise of power . . .[42]

The "explosive forces" of modern European life have subordinated the state to the considerations of the "money economy" and spiritual life to the utilitarian considerations of practical science. These contemporary forces attempt to "extinguish the freedom of spiritual life and to make way for positivism, i.e. authority." [43]

The only possible resolution of the crisis, for Droysen, could come from a reliance upon forces still more elemental—upon the desires and hatreds of a frustrated nationalism and upon the "power which rests on those natural bases, those immediate impulses and passions, and which therefore has the force, when overturned, to raise itself all the stronger." [44] For the agencies of this power Droysen now looked to "the strong-willed personality . . . in the decisive office" and to "the old healthy center of power which has been planted and raised in Prussia." [45] Hence he dropped his pre-revolutionary idealistic appeal for the dissolution of Prussia in the Germany which that state was to unify by moral means; he plumped instead for the consolidation of Prussian strength and the subordination of the other German states to it. But this new emphasis upon power-politics did not mean for Droysen, as it did mean for the new moderates, the renunciation of the ideal framework. Rather did he attenuate it, in order that it might still cover the new autonomy of material interest and force in German and Prussian politics. "Only the

Protestant spirit has the inner freedom and the compelling force to do what is necessary," and only "the German spirit" that is its prime bearer can, "if anything healthy, genuine, or promising is to come out of the incalculable convulsions . . . that shake Europe and if any continuity in the development . . . of historical epochs and of the human race is to be saved, transmit past experience and achievements to the future." [46]

Hence Droysen justified the elemental in German nationalism by making it the bearer of the contemporary realistic revolution into the teleological system of history. For the internal politics of Prussia this meant the frank acceptance of a liberty tailored to this mission. The primary goal for the Prussian state was that it regain its "inner and individualizing vitality" by stimulating public interest in every citizen, and this could come not from "the superstition of dry abstractions" characteristic of pre-March liberalism but only from "the vital understanding of existing reality." To this end even the post-revolutionary reaction was salutary, for it had disciplined individuals into the right kind of free activity —that is, into concern with the "thousand forgotten and lost facets of real life" and the "local interests" which are the "authoritative pre-conditions" for the revitalizing of the stagnant institutions of state and society.[47]

Droysen's response sets into bold relief the tendency of the influences which began to act upon the old moderates from 1849 on, but the suddenness of it was not typical. For the bulk of this school the adaptation of political ideal to the post-revolutionary realism was a gradual process which was not concluded until 1866. The chief focus of this process was the group organized around the journal *Prussian Annals,* which was founded in 1857 by the leading academicians of the Gotha party, Max Duncker and Rudolf Haym, and a more decisively liberal group led by the historian Theodor Mommsen.[48]

For Rudolf Haym, editor of the *Annals* from its first issue in January 1858 until the middle of 1863, the tortuous inner struggle was waged literally in the name of political freedom. During the 50's his recognition that his party of moderate constitutionalists would have to take a path different from "the former way with its old expansiveness and its old simple confidence" meant not a change in fundamental attitude but the self-conscious adoption of the point of view of "the practical politician" *vis-à-vis* the theoretician. He still held the ideal of complete republican freedom as "the further goal of contemporary historical development" but claimed that his attention must henceforward be riveted upon the present means toward this goal, with all the concomitant "incessant laboring from purpose to purpose and from compromise to compromise." Translated into programmatic terms, this meant the endorsement of constitutionalism under the existing monarchies—a constitutionalism which would be neither "merely" empirical nor doctrinaire but which would "make possible the purification of democracy." [49] By 1861 Haym was spelling out this program to include both divergent tendencies: on the one hand, the primacy of the national over the liberal question and of foreign over internal policy; on the other, "the most thorough-going possible liberalism in Prussia" for the sake of the national mission, "although not for its sake alone." He insisted that he had "as much democracy—in the ideal sense of the word—in my blood as anyone could ask for" and that he agreed with the Prussian Democrats in their demand for "decisive progress" internally," but his emphasis upon "our real national and liberal interests" *vis-à-vis* their "unpolitical politics of principles" led him to endorse the Prussian army reorganization in the confidence that the government intended it to found a German state or that, even in the absence of such intention, it must "with inner necessity" tend toward this end.[50]

Ultimately it was just this idea, so characteristic for the classical liberals, of a transcendent moral process of history which Haym used to justify the support of Bismarck's national policy. In his private correspondence Haym continued to discern the disjunction between "the ideal Prussia of the past and the future" in which "the moral justification of annexation" must be sought and the "unmitigated energists, brutalists, and militaristic Junkers" who ran the Bismarckian government. He continued, too, to have "the painful feeling that the liberal ideas are too good to be used simply as a means to an end," as Bismarck was using them in his German policy.[51] But these doubts did not prevent Haym from penning the public "Declaration" of April 26, 1866, in which the

Halle "Old Liberals" initiated the submission of the bulk of the liberal movement to the Bismarckian order in Prussia and Germany. The chain of reasoning in the "Declaration" furnished eloquent testimony of the intellectual process which permitted the old moderates to overcome their reservations without giving up their wonted framework of thought. The "right of the German nation" is superior to the "right of self-determination" of its parts and to the character of the means applied by government for its realization; this national "right" is represented by "the state-power of Prussia"; in the present situation, moreover, a further identification must be made between "the interest of our state and that of its present government"; "existing relationships," therefore, require that "the power question" be resolved "before the freedom question." The signatories led by Haym announced their support of the Bismarckian regime "in profound trust" that "the power of the national idea" will guide "the power interests of Prussia" to German unity and that the royal pledge of a German parliament will, "through its own moral power," make possible a subsequent liberal nation-state.[52] Thus did Haym manage once more to make the self-limitation of the monarchical state the center of his ideal system of freedom and to convert liberal politics into a teleology of state. The state, he concluded during the electoral campaign of June 1866, must indeed expand through "moral conquests" based upon its guarantee of freedom to its citizens, but the secure "existence" of the state and the loyalty of the citizens must be the prior condition of this moral mission. And to develop the state from the stage of "blood and iron" to the stage of "law and freedom" the liberals can work only indirectly, by making Bismarck "our ally" and "identifying ourselves with the necessity of things" which he must take into account.[53]

While Haym spoke for the first generation of classical liberals who spanned the revolutionary era, academicians like Heinrich Treitschke exemplified the younger generation whose political formation came primarily out of the experience of the 50's and the 60's. Both generations subscribed to the tradition which would integrate a recognition of political actualities into a system of historical idealism, but the difference in vintage brought with it an important difference in the form which the problem took. Whereas the older group carried over a pre-established system which they modified to fit the new circumstances, the younger constructed their systems in the midst of these new relationships and formed their ideals in direct correspondence to them. It was through this group, then, that the old moderate tradition assumed the shape which it was to take in the new Empire after 1870: the conversion of the liberal principle into an absolute national ideal which conferred the moral blessing of freedom upon superior political power.

For the young historian Heinrich Treitschke, editor of the *Prussian Annals* from 1863, nationalism became the source rather than the resolution of political values. Unlike his forbears, Treitschke did not undergo any startling development in his political ideas until after the formation of the Empire in 1870. The sobering experiences which shocked the older group into a realistic elaboration of their theoretical framework were the natal conditions of Treitschke's, and consequently he started from points to which they had ultimate recourse.

The profound disjunction between the requirements of absolute systems and the force of concrete facts—a disjunction that remained a conscious and critical problem for the older generation—was so much and so early a part of Treitschke that he scarcely noticed it and tended to build upon rather than resolve it. Certainly both sides were present in him. Thus on the one hand Treitschke consciously based his world view upon the attraction to him of "the heterogeneity and the changing stream of real conditions"; upon the impossibility of "grasping any phenomenon in its totality"; upon the necessity of starting from the "facts" and deriving historical laws, without preconception, from them.[54] On the other hand Treitschke was also a poet who applied the aesthetic ideal of the essential unity of form and substance and would "work with all my might as part of a greater whole"; he was also a stern moralist in the Student Union tradition who applied the ethical standard of inner "conviction" to actions. Treitschke was an historical critic who could censure Gervinus' *Introduction to the History of the 19th Century* for tailoring facts to fit a system and yet "think it right that he applies such an ideal standard." He was an historian who could reject Hegel for "shackling our rich life" within the laws of the dialectic but could adopt his metaphysical notion of the "divine reason" which governed the collective life of man.[55] That this diversity was the product of two irresistible but unadjusted influences rather than a well-considered dualism was clear from one of Treitschke's rare flashes of self-recognition:

> I fear reasonably sure about the theory and yet I cannot wholly free myself in practise from the point of view which I have rejected. However often I tell myself that the concepts of morality, mores, etc., are only relative and vary with conditions and even with individuals, the idea of an absolute Good, in which I was reared, breaks through time and again, and I often cannot avoid wishing conditions to be different— or as we say euphemistically, "better"—although I fully realize their necessity.[56]

In Treitschke's politics this juxtaposition of impulses had the effect of making him always sound more radical than he actually was. Even as an adolescent observer of the Revolution of 1848 his subscription to the ideal that "the republic is unconditionally the most beautiful form of state" did not prevent him from rejecting any idea of its introduction into Germany as "the destruction of order and legality" and from passionately espousing the cause of the Saxon moderates against the radicals.[57] Treitschke's political growth during the 50's altered the terms but not the pattern of his beliefs. On the one hand, he became a passionate opponent of the existing regime, on the basis of his "moral conviction that no power in the world, no pope and no king, can command sin or release from duty" and that the contemporary rulers were openly doing just this. He rejected the "half-way conduct" of the moderate liberals in the diets and even took under consideration a popular revolution on the "principle" of "immediate self-help against every injustice from above." [58] On the other hand, he continued to count himself a partisan of the moderate Gotha party, and he would ground politics in the empirical relativism which dominated the decade.

> As long as there have been states . . . politics have ever been questions of power and not of law (Recht). What is called constitutional law (Staatsrecht) is in my view only a euphemism; it is simply the

statistical calculation and grouping of the political relationships of power existing in a state. This sounds like the right of the strongest but is not really so bad, for I understand by power not only crude force but any political capacity. A positive constitutional law is good then when it makes dominant by law those social forces which possess most political capacity.

The German problem, when taken in these terms, is "a pure question of power"—it is a matter of taking political power from the princes and nobility, who have no longer any capacity, and assigning it to those "social groups" which through education and wealth do. The separation of the people into the rulers and the ruled is not bad in itself or in principle; it is simply no longer appropriate to the present capacities of the people.[59]

Now the crucial point about the co-existence of these two strands in Treitschke's approach is that they remained unresolved on the issues of individual freedom but did achieve integration on the level of the nation state. As against the "dead principle" of pure individual freedom he insisted that "the state is an institution that is rooted completely in the nature of every man."[60] It must not absorb the whole individual, but neither must it be viewed as a burden upon the individual. "Under healthy conditions the state must be the heart of the life of the people and must be in constant connection with all its strivings."[61] And if the state was a necessary natural institution which influenced individuals toward freedom and morality, its guidance in this direction came from the principle of nationality, which, for Treitschke, inhabited the realm of the unconditioned ideal. "In the struggle which we young people fight every hour with the thousand mysteries of existence, there are only two things which have remained for me undoubted and upon which I depend with undivided enthusiasm —art and the Fatherland."[62] By putting nation and state together Treitschke could be categorical in his approach and moderate in his application to the problem of freedom. "Primarily," he wrote as early as 1854, "I am a completely radical unitarian [i.e. for a unitary Germany]. I hold freedom, etc., to be mere phrases so long as no nation exists, for it is the only basis for any development of the state. The path that leads most quickly to this national unification is the one most cherished by me, even if it should be despotism." Consequently, he explained, despite his inclination toward republicanism *vis-à-vis* the "monarchical ideas" of the Gotha party he adhered to this moderate group because they had the most "national enthusiasm" while the democrats were stymied in negation and pessimism.[63] It was this radical nationalism, connected with the essential reality of the state, that finally allowed Treitschke to endorse the political validity of a doctrinaire constitutional "dogma" which he admitted to be abstract and therefore philosophically invalid.[64]

These assumptions which came out of the 50's lay behind Treitschke's peculiar political course during the 60's, in which a systematic idealism in doctrine developed side by side with an equally systematic practise of compromise with events. The centrality of the nation-state concept, with its roots in both the ideal and the empirical realms, enabled him to cast a retroactive ethical validity over happenings for which his doctrine had not prepared. Moreover, it enabled him to do this without even feeling the need to adjust the doctrine to them. "It is false to start in morality from the individual instead of the human species and its laws of development," he wrote during 1865[65] and in his two chief political essays of the decade he showed how his collective absolutes could authorize a wide variety of actions taken in their name.

Treitschke's article, *Freedom* (1861), occasioned by John Stuart Mill's *On Liberty* and Edouard Laboulaye's *l'Etat et ses limites*, may stand as the classic exposition of the German liberalism of compromise. It was here that the distinction between western and German concepts of freedom received its standard formulation: "Whoever sees the state as only a means for the ends of the citizens must logically demand . . . freedom from the state, not freedom in the state." [66] Treitschke argued for "freedom in the state." The main thesis of the work opposed the idea of the state as "an end in itself . . . which leads as real a life as any of its citizens" to the idea of the state as a necessary evil. But the remarkable thing about the essay was its far-reaching recognition of individual rights apart from the state and claims upon the state. "Everything new that this 19th century has created is an effect of liberalism," proclaimed Treitschke, and he proceeded to substantiate the validity of the claims for the inviolability of "personal" and "social" freedom ("free movement in faith and knowledge, in trade and travel") from the state and for the application of "political freedom" ("government by consent") to the state.[67] Indeed, Treitschke summed up his position as complete agreement with Mill and Laboulaye in the demand for the greatest possible measure of personal freedom and disagreement only with the idea that the state was hostile to such freedom.[68]

The decisive assumption behind Treitschke's argument was a necessary relationship between the autonomous ideal of personal freedom and the autonomous validity of the state which made his categorical emphasis upon the former intensify the necessity of the latter. For Treitschke's theoretical assertion of a precise reciprocation and "mutual dependence" between the citizen who demands the greatest measure of personal freedom from the state for his own purposes and the state that bestows such freedom upon its citizens for its own purposes—i.e. as a necessary condition for its own freedom of action—was worked out concretely to mean the absorption of personal liberty into the state. The increasing measure of personal and social rights required an increase in the independent power of the state not only as a counterweight but as its fulfillment. As a counterweight this increased power was necessary because the spread of social freedom brings the threat of the tyranny of society over the individual and the reign of mediocrity over individuality. "So we come to the final and highest demand of personal freedom: that the state and public opinion must grant to the individual the development of his own character in thought and action." [69] But even more fundamental was Treitschke's assumption that the strong state was the ultimate fulfillment of individual liberty. The connecting link in this assumption was Treitschke's ambivalent concept of "political freedom." He used it to signify two distinct things: first, the political rights of individuals to participate in the state up to and including parliamentary government, and secondly, the freedom of the state as such, which was rooted in a moral and historical ground different from personal freedom—i.e. in "the historical imperative that humanity establish good and beautiful states" and that these states acquire international "honor." [70] Political freedom in the first sense was necessary to the full blooming of personal freedom, but primarily as a means for integrating it, through the inculcation of moral civic duty, into the autonomous political freedom of state in the second sense. And so the cardinal issue of political freedom was, for Treitschke, not that of self-government—which he insisted was already generally recognized and assured—but that of "the national differentiation of states." For Treitschke, then, "inner freedom . . . forms the firm basis upon which a free national state will be raised." [71] His newly articulated consciousness of individual liberty as a moral value ended by feeding his idealization of the nation state.

It is hardly to be wondered at, then, that Treitschke's most important political work of the 60's—his *Federal State and Unitary State* of 1864—was both doctrinaire and radical, but in a nationalist rather than a liberal dimension. The theme of the essay was the categorical demonstration that a federal state was appropriate only to democracies and that a unitary state which dissolved all principalities under the king of Prussia was the only possible national form for an incorrigibly monarchical nation like Germany.[72] The ostensible ground of this doctrine was the tendency of actual history, but behind Treitschke's apparent historical empiricism were assumptions determined by a whole metaphysical system, drawn primarily from Hegel and complete with "divine reason," "historical necessity," and "the spirit of history" which gave a priori determination to historical reality.[73] But the radical politics sponsored by this transcendental rationalism applied not to the absolute value of freedom as such but to the nation-state which incorporated it in history.[74] Treitschke explicitly rejected political freedom both in its traditional corporate form of the "German *Libertaet*" of the princes and in the extreme individualistic form of democracy so that he could concentrate his loyalty upon the monarchical state of Prussia, which for him embodied the valid elements of both. The roots of the Prussian dynasty in German tradition and the high promise of modern Prussian constitutionalism were both essential elements in this loyalty, but dynasty and constitution alike became political values only as ingredients in a Prussian state which was fulfilling the mission of German unification through "the continuous progress of the expansion of this state" as "the law of its own life." [75] Treitschke's revolutionary proposal for the destruction of the princely dynasties was thus balanced by his injunction that the liberals realize the necessary connection between the "freedom of the people" and the "state power" of royal Prussia.[76] The union in Prussia of the princely liberty of the past with the individual liberty of the future made it for Treitschke *the* German state, a rational reality upon which both kinds of freedom depended for their existence.

Treitschke's total investment of his political ethic in an historical state had the result of justifying completely all the national activities of that state. Treitschke's conception of nationality was one which abstractly put a premium upon national self-determination, and yet he approved wholeheartedly the annexation of both Schleswig-Holstein and of Alsace-Lorraine, against the admitted resistance of the inhabitants, in the name of the overriding "rights of the German nation." [77] In themselves, neither this approval nor the shift from liberal opposition to government support which accompanied it was distinctive, but his unabashed extension of his doctrinaire political system to cover them was indeed remarkable. Unlike old moderates like Haym and Hermann Baumgarten,[78] Treitschke did not need to relativize his political thinking in order to bring it into line with a surprising reality. On the morrow of the German unification Treitschke admitted frankly that it had come "through purely empirical means, in conscious opposition to all system" and then blandly proceeded to endow it with a systematic ethical sanction. He preached absolute loyalty to this "German kingdom" in the name of "German unity"—the political idea which "forces every other idea of the age into its service" and guarantees the future development of both the unitary state and of "parliamentary freedom." [79] Liberal doctrine had turned a full circle: as in the natural law doctrines of the old regime the existing state was acknowledged as the *de jure* seat of political liberty.

The New Radicals

The new power of material interests prepared a compromise mentality in many liberals, but this was not its necessary effect. The inherent presuppositions of the moderate approach did prescribe a selection from these new influences which generally tended in a conservative direction, but the examples of G. G. Gervinus and Robert von Mohl—though isolated—[80] at least show that even for the old moderates themselves other interpretations of the new possibilities were at least thinkable.

Gervinus was converted into a republican by the same revolutionary failures of 1848 and 1849 that turned his fellow constitutionalists toward concessions. He now characterized the moderates as "so principled, so conscientious, so doctrinaire, . . . so moral," and so unpolitical, because they did not realize that to attain their ends they must depend upon "the masses" as the concentrated physical force of the nation rather than upon the moral suasion of princes. Hence political realism requires that "we set up the banner of the republic" as the practical means of mobilizing "three quarters of the German people" in the cause of a free Germany. It requires even the possible resort to revolution as the only course through which a people like the German can acquire "political maturity and independence." [81] For Gervinus, then, radical republicanism meant the union of "the spiritual forces" with "the physical" in Germany, and where the moderates looked to industrialism and the Prussian state he looked to the common people as the real bearers of the political ideal of freedom in history.[82]

Mohl did not go nearly so far, for he continued to be a decisive opponent of both republicanism and democracy, but his heightened realism during the 50's did drive him to develop previously uncrystallized notions about society and the English constitution into full-blown programs for social science and parliamentary government. The two programs were internally related in Mohl, for he saw both as inferences from real facts and both as solvents of the old doctrinal dualism between the rights of the individual and the rights of the state.

Social science, according to Mohl, arises from an unprejudiced examination of "the facts" of the age, which show that the old confrontation of the individual and the state is being transcended by men's growing interest in questions of society—that is, in the "natural" relationships grounded in the crystallizations of particular interests. The interest-organizations which arise from this preoccupation form a social area of life which lies between the individual personalities of their members and the over-all unity of the state. It fills the gap "between the doctrine of the state power . . . and the doctrine of the civil rights and duties of individuals" by absorbing intrusive functions from the former and creating subordinate unities of the latter; thus it can resolve the traditional opposition between the two antipodes of politics.[83]

The constitutional expression of this mediating function, for Mohl, was "parliamentary government"—i.e. ministerial responsibility to the majority in the representative diet—which he deemed primarily to be "a way of making such a division between government and representative assembly impossible in practice." [84] The connection of this political program with Mohl's new attention to social interests was embodied in the reform of the representative diets which he insisted must accompany the introduction of a parliamentary system: representation must be given only to "every particular social group"; "the rights of the whole people and those pertaining to individuals require no representation on their own account." [85] Clearly, Mohl's political principles remained moderate. He insisted that "the prince would still be the possessor of the state power" and that his formal constitutional rights of government would suffer no change. The function of the representative assembly would still be simply to ensure that he define his independent right of government according to the prescriptions of positive laws and the principles of the *Rechtsstaat*.[86] But Mohl had ultimately to admit that the prince would have to limit his will by that of the parliamentary majority. This admission was the product not of principle but of Mohl's perception that the factual rise of conscious social interests made the

corruption of the state the only alternative to the political satisfaction of these interests.[87]

But in the cacophony of the transitional decades between the
revolution and the Bismarckian Empire, the strain that led from
an awareness of the new material powers in society to a radical
political liberalism was a muted one indeed. Those intellectuals
who were struck more by the social implications of the new
economy for the anonymous masses than by its national implications for the middle classes did evolve a clearly defined radicalism,
but this evolution went toward a social radicalism that carried
them out of the liberal camp entirely. Their social awareness
had fed an uncrystallized political liberalism before 1848, but
then it began to develop into a conscious socialism which declared
its independence from the ideal of political freedom during the
60's and thus divided the radical forms before free institutions
had been achieved.

All three of the founding fathers of the German Social Democracy—Ferdinand Lassalle, Wilhelm Liebknecht, and August
Bebel—worked in the radical wing of the liberal movement
before they took the fateful step of moving themselves and the
politically interested working class out of it. Although this liberal
stop-over was in many respects merely tactical and its duration
inevitably limited, yet in each case the ultimate socialism was
tempered by genuine liberal considerations which were over-
ridden only by the quick acceleration of class consciousness.[88]

Of the three, only Lassalle was an intellectual and only he
enshrined this experience in theory. Through him the traditional
German pattern of disjunction between the requirements of
theory and practice which had ever plagued German intellectuals
in their application of libertarian ideals to a conservative political
reality was carried over into the German social democracy. The
terms indeed were different. For the socialist the ultimate ideal
was collectivism, and existent reality included a liberal capitalistic
society as well as the monarchical-aristocratic state. But just as
the liberals were confused by the notion of an immanent order
in the ideal of freedom and by the authoritarian state's appropriation of liberal values, so were the relations of theory and practice

muddied for the socialist Lassalle by the material basis of the socialist ideal and the doctrinaire idealism of an unfulfilled bourgeois liberalism. This liberalism, consequently, acquired something of an autonomous status for Lassalle, for it provided not only the opportunity for practical political action but also a theoretical basis in principle which scientific socialism seemed to need. This internal relationship between the practice and the theory of liberalism was decisive for Lassalle's development. It made his early political radicalism more deep-seated than a mere tactic on the road to socialism, but by this very token when he then moved with his times to the subordination of freedom as an ideal under the triumphant facts of social interests and political power his disillusionment with liberal theory carried with it his fateful rejection of liberal practice. Thus did Lassalle come to initiate the break between socialism and liberalism even before their common target, the hierarchical and oppressive institutions of the conservative state, had been overthrown.

The starting-point of Lasalle's development was his uncritical acceptance of both liberalism and socialism, during the Revolution of 1848, as integral, interpenetrating, and complementary stages in a single, uninterrupted historical process. He adopted the Marxist theory of history and the Marxist program of agitating for democracy in Germany, but he used these ideas to justify him in working wholeheartedly for liberalism now and socialism later.

> It is true that my party and I look above all to social reform; the highest expression of our convictions is the social republic. But this is not the moment to realize our theories; their realization belongs to the future. The proletariat demands for now nothing more than to help protect your liberties, your rights, your laws.[89]

The first phase in Lassalle's development out of this simple and optimistic position began with the failure of the revolution. From 1849 on he became ever more conscious of the particular identities of liberalism and socialism, but during the 50's the divorce which he pronounced between them did not prevent him from retaining a strong commitment to both movements separately. On the one hand, then, he came to the realization that "no struggle can succeed any longer in Europe which is not from the beginning definitely a purely socialist one; no struggle can succeed which bears the social question within itself merely as an obscure element, an insolated background, and takes the overt form of a national rising or of bourgeois republicanism." [90] For a constituent assembly can never revolutionize society; it can only "sanction the revolution which has already been completed outside it." [91] He interpreted the workers' political apathy under the reaction as a growing independence from bourgeois interests and as "an introversion into themselves" which heightens their specific "class concept" and makes them a "more compact and conscious material" for revolution.[92] On the other hand, however, Lassalle continued to cherish his connection with the intellectual liberal tradition. "I have always been much attached," he wrote to Marx anent the forthcoming publication of his work on Heraclitus in 1857, "to classical, theoretical, and philosophical culture. . . . It is spiritual freedom and consequently the root and source of all other kinds. . . . The humanities and politics are neither opposites nor—in the profoundest sense—independent of each other. We Germans have produced our concept of freedom in this way—one that indeed may still lack vitality but is all the deeper for that." [93] At the same time Lassalle was composing his drama, *Franz von Sickingen,* which earned the censure of Marx and Engels for its subordination of the social class conflict. The theme of the plan was the inherently tragic relationship between the theoretical ideals of the revolutionary and the practical means which he must either use—and thereby compromise his ideals—or reject—and thereby surrender any chance for their realization. The ideals concerned in this conflict were primarily those of spiritual liberty and German unity—a choice which revealed Lassalle's continuing concern with the problem of political freedom, in its wonted form of an absolute principle to be practically applied.[94]

In the second phase of Lassalle's development, which began with the revival of political life in 1859, he emerged from his internal division of the 50's as a self-conscious political liberal. He joined the middle-class Prussian Progressive Party after its foundation in 1860 and worked within its ranks for a democratic and national revolution on the unitary basis of an expanded Prussia. He remained, of course, a socialist as well, but he now looked to liberalism for both the practical means and the reinforcing ideal of present socialist endeavor. Behind this twofold emphasis upon liberalism lay Lassalle's conviction that his "revolution-playing" with the workers during the 50's had yielded neither "practical" nor "theoretical" results. It "serves for nothing but to awaken only too often their worst appetites, . . . to make them interchange the general with their personal cause, and while they cry exploitation to become exploiters themselves." [95] In the face of this immaturity and this egoism Lassalle turned to radical liberalism for moral support as well as for the material assistance of the middle-class democratic parties. The prime characteristic of this phase, then, was the balance of practical means and final ends in Lassalle's conception of liberal politics. Nationality as international power and principle; law (*Recht*) as juristic power and principle; democracy as revolutionary power and principle: these were the themes on which Lassalle played between 1859 and 1862.

In his pamphlet on the Austro-Italian crisis of 1859 Lassalle emphasized the necessity of a national policy as the necessary expression of democratic principle and particularly advocated support for the Italian cause on the grounds of democratic solidarity. But he also argued along the lines of *Realpolitik*. He proposed publicly that Prussia should seize the opportunity to annex Schleswig-Holstein, and in his letters he claimed his real intention to be the use of the national idea simply to discredit the Prussian government.[96]

Lassalle's long treatise on *The System of Acquired Rights* applied an analogous intermingling of intrinsic and instrumental criteria to liberal jurisprudence. His main argument, that by their very nature the acquired rights of individuals could be validly abridged or even canceled without compensation by subsequent "legislation (*Gesetz*)" of the state, was certainly appropriate to use as a simple juristic rationale for a socialist revolution,[97] but equally revealing for Lassalle's political mentality was his insistence upon the liberal notion of fundamental law as the authority for this rationale. It was not only his emphasis upon the uniform extension of rights to all individuals within a given legal system *vis-à-vis* the spokesmen and institutions of special privileged rights or the general absence of the socialist *motif* in his discussion that bespoke Lassalle's preoccupation with his liberal framework.[98] More important was the grounding of the main argument itself, which went beyond the requirement of politic concessions to a popular front in its assertion of the validity of the liberal ideal. Casting his whole discussion in the individualistic form of the competence of retroactive legislation *vis-à-vis* personal rights, Lassalle insisted repeatedly that the only solution to the problem of rights must come from "the idea of law (*Recht*) itself." He sought to make "the concept" of individual freedom itself authorize the abridgement of individual rights. He argued that the acquired rights of the individual were grounded ultimately in "the concept of the subjective freedom of the spirit," since they arose through free actions of the rationally informed will of individuals. But this individual spirit necessarily and actually recognizes, as the tacit condition of the rights which it makes its own, the definition of their objective validity and extent by "legislation"—i.e. the "general spirit" or the "common consciousness of the whole people." [99] The abridgement or abolition of acquired rights is consequently not the limitation but the "realization of the concept of freedom," for "in the state every individual through his life, thought, and social activity is a co-producer of the general spirit, or at least must be viewed as such." [100]

Now, with this frankly Hegelian notion of an historically progressing spirit, manifested in the species and providing a continually changing "legal substance" for the subjective freedom of the individual, Lassalle might ultimately construct, as he claimed in a private letter, "a scientific legal system for revolution and socialism," [101] but in the meanwhile it showed that his alliance with liberalism was an internal one of principles as well as an external one of techniques. In this phase Lassalle obviously thought of socialism as the logical extension of the fundamental liberal principle of law (*Recht*). He insisted to Marx that "we must maintain the *identity* just as much as the distinction of our social revolutionary position" *vis-à-vis* the political democrats until "they have conquered." [102] By this time Engels was attributing to Lassalle a commitment to the traditional idea of absolute law, and the socially minded Lothar Bucher was coming independently to the similar conclusion that Lassalle was more concerned with the realization of the Idea in history than with the actual class struggle.[103]

The third stage of Lassalle's intellectual development, which lasted through most of the year 1862, witnessed his rejection of the political validity of the liberals' absolute principle but his retention of the liberal framework as an efficacious means of political practice. He deliberately ruptured his former balance between liberalism as an ideal and liberalism as an instrument, to the advantage of the latter. Starting from the disillusionment of his hopes in the liberals' application of absolute *Recht* to a democratic revolution, Lassalle dissolved the autonomous notion of *Recht* in favor of the primacy of material power and began to agitate openly for a democratic form of liberalism that would actually harness the raw power of the masses and their social claims to forceful action against the Prussian monarchy.

Lassalle opened this phase in April, 1862, when he began to shift emphases in his attempt to drive the bourgeois liberals to a new democratic revolution. Operating still within the framework of the Prussian Progressive Party, Lassalle now stressed liberalism as power rather than ideal and started to construct an ethic of social solidarity as the new ideal appropriate to proletarian interests. In a speech before a predominantly lower middle-class audience in Berlin, Lassalle anchored his appeal for political radicalism in a frank empiricism. His device for accomplishing this was to tear into shreds the *Rechtsstaat* doctrine through which the moderates and the radicals within the Progressive Party were held in balance. A constitution, said Lassalle, is a fundamental law, and a fundamental law is a force which imposes upon all other laws and legal institutions. Only one such force can exist and that is "the actual power relationships which exist in a given society." [104] A king with his army, a noble with influence at the court, a factory-owner with his power over the existence of his workers—these are pieces of the constitution.

These actual power relationships are written down on a piece of paper, written expression is given them, and when they have been written down they are no longer mere actual power relationships but now they have become law (*Recht*), legal institutions, and whoever goes against them is punished.[105]

Turning to the Prussian constitution, Lassalle, who continually addressed his audience as "petty bourgeois and workers (*Kleinbuerger und Arbeiter*)," explained it as a confirmation of the power of the king and the rich, a power which could be asserted against the greater social strength of the people only because of the organization of the former and the indifference of the latter to political liberty. There has been a change in the power relationships with the rise of the bourgeoisie, but in 1848 the bourgeoisie did not break the organized power of the king and consequently its written constitution was worthless. A written constitution is good "only in the one case . . . when it corresponds to the real constitution, the real power relationships which exist in the country." [106] The Progressives fearfully call for maintenance of the present constitution and this appeal in itself shows that this constitution no longer corresponds to the real power relationships, that it is inevitably doomed. It can be changed from the right, by the organized power of society, or from the left, by the unorganized social power if it rises, but in any case the present constitution is untenable. "Constitutional questions are primarily not questions of *Recht* but questions of power." [107]

The counterpart to this dissolution of the liberal ethic was Lassalle's new overt emphasis upon working-class interests. Speaking to a labor audience in Berlin on the contemporary position of the working class, he proclaimed that the period of social domination by the bourgeois ideal of capital was drawing to a close. "It is now the fourth estate . . . which wants to raise its principle to the ruling principle of society and to penetrate all social institutions with it." [108] Despite his class analysis of history, Lassalle still remained within the framework of political democracy. For he was careful to speak always not of the class but of the "idea" of the class that was achieving dominance. He insisted that his conception did not make for social cleavage but that it was "a cry of reconciliation, a cry which includes the whole society, a cry for the harmonization of all conflicts in the social groups, a cry of unification in which all should agree who do not want the superiority over and the suppression of the people by privileged classes, a cry of love which, since it has risen for the first time from the heart of the people, must remain forever the true cry of the people . . ." [109] And to emphasize the classless idea: "We are all workers, insofar as we just have the will to make ourselves useful to human society in some way." [110] Consonant with this line, Lassalle proclaimed the "idea of the working class" to be not socialism but universal suffrage, the ethical renovation of society, and the embodiment of the ethic of "solidarity," or "community" in the state. He attacked the negative conception of the state held by the bourgeoisie in its concern with the protection of the isolated individual, and he assigned to the state "the education and development of the human race to freedom." Through positive action, the state would bring "the destiny of man, i.e., the culture of which the human race is capable, to real existence." [111] At this point, then, Lassalle was still holding his rising commitment to the working class and to the Prussian state within a weakening loyalty to a liberal framework.

The decisive break came at the end of 1862. The constitutional crisis evoked by Bismarck's defiance of the Prussian diet impelled Lassalle to present the liberals with an ultimatum for strong action. Speaking in November to a lower middle-class meeting in Berlin as an avowed member of "the party of pure and decisive democracy," Lassalle called upon the Progressives to assert the supreme social power of the bourgeoisie by declaring that "the Prussian constitution . . . is a lie" and by suspending the activity of the diet until the government surrendered. If the government held out, the whole bourgeoisie and the whole society would organize against it, and by virtue of their social power their victory would be inevitable. Lassalle ultimately justified his proposal on the basis that all successful action must be "an expression of what is," and he criticized the Progressive Party because it "follows a system which consists in precisely nothing other than the expression of what is not," i.e.

the claim that the government is constitutional. He appealed over the head of the Party to "public opinion"; he called for popular agitation to exercise pressure upon the deputies in favor of his policy which he summed up as the demand for "parliamentary government." [112]

But because liberalism had been valued by Lassalle precisely for the moral force which it conferred upon contemporary political practice, his disillusionment with the absolute pattern of its ideal removed its practical usefulness for him as well. When the Progressive Party press answered his strictures with renewed appeals to the precedence of *Recht* over power, Lassalle rebutted brusquely that "in reality power always precedes *Recht* . . . until *Recht* gathers a sufficient force behind it to smash the power of *Unrecht*" and broke with the Progressives.[113] This rejection of liberalism even as a tactic, in February 1863, initiated the fourth and final stage of Lassalle's political development, in which Lassalle derived his ideal from the social interests of the working class, and his means from a combination of a labor party with the traditional instruments of state power. Of his democratic liberalism only a shadow remained—the technique of universal suffrage.

Lassalle launched himself upon this final phase of his career on March 1, 1863, with his epochal *Open Answer to the Central Committee for the Convocation of a General German Workers' Union in Leipzig*. The manifesto for an independent working-class movement in Germany castigated the Progressives not only along familiar lines for their failure "to bring about even the smallest real development of the interests of freedom," but more fundamentally for their inherent incapacity to work for anything more than "the maintenance of the privileged position of the bourgeoisie." Lassalle insisted that "the worker can expect the fulfilment of his legitimate interests only from political freedom," but this "political freedom" was for him purely and simply a system of universal suffrage derivative from the needs of the working class. Hence he declared that "the working class must constitute itself as an independent political party and make general, equal, and direct suffrage the principle and the gospel of this party. The representation of the working class in the legislative bodies of Germany—this alone can satisfy its legitimate interests in politics." [114] Lassalle then turned to the social question and showed how the goals of political action must henceforward be conceived in terms of specific economic and social interests. He scorned the previous concern of the workers' movement with the question of economic liberty. He rejected the liberals' cooperative movement on the grounds that it failed to touch the working class, which had no capital, and that its only effect upon the artisans at whom it aimed was to prolong the misery of their doomed struggle with large-scale industry.[115] Lassalle insisted that "nothing was further removed from so-called socialism and communism" than his program, which was based upon free productive associations with capital supplied by the state, but this was only to underscore its political realism the more. "The state belongs to you, gentlemen, the needy classes, not to us, the higher estates, for it consists of you! What is the state, I asked, and you see now . . . the answer: the great association of you, the poorer classes, that is the state. And why should your great association not work to promote and fructify your smaller circles of association?" [116]

Thus did Lassalle dissolve the unity of liberal ideal and practice in favor of the collective units of the social movement and the state. Precisely from this period on Lassalle articulated ever more strongly his view of politics as "actual, contemporary efficacy" and acknowledged his own drive for the possession of power, "for without supreme power nothing can be done." [117] From this point of view he turned against liberals and liberalism indiscriminately. "It is the special fate of Germany for the bourgeoisie to strive for domination not at the time of its own maturity, as the bourgeoisie did in France and England, but at a time when this maturity is already internally corrupted by the whole process of historical development." [118] He abhorred "the restless, cavilling liberal individualism, the great sickness of our age," which is rooted in "the oligarchical ground . . . of our liberal bourgeoisie and its subjective, selfish search for personality." [119] The union of political metaphysics and practice which Lassalle had sought in liberalism he now sought in the combination of state and working class, and on both levels he now found liberalism his chief enemy.

Lassalle's failure to find in the middle ground of liberalism a compatible blend of values and means led him to separate them so radically that he ended by seeking an alliance with Bismarck as a tactic toward social revolution. "The working class," he wrote the Prussian Prime Minister, "feels itself instinctively inclined to dictatorship if it can be justifiably convinced that this will be exercised in its interests, and . . . it would be inclined, despite its republican convictions—or more precisely on the basis of them—to see in the Crown the natural bearer of social dictatorship, in contrast to the egoism of bourgeois society if the Crown could resolve to take the improbable step of . . . transforming itself from a kingdom of the privileged estates into a social and revolutionary kingdom of the people." [120] Lassalle's mediate instrument for his ultimate revolutionary goal was no longer the liberal *Recht* but the collective state. He no longer considered democracy to be the logical extension of liberalism. It was now "the spirit of the masses" as against the spirit of individualism, and in the form of the technique of universal suffrage it became "the fundamental condition of all social help, . . . the only means of improving the situation of the working class" and "an immense means of power—the real 'moral' conquest of Germany." [121] Through the attachment of democracy to the state, freedom took on a "mass" form through which it became united with "authority" and conferred a moral blessing upon the coalition of social interest and political power.[122]

The Old Radicals

The radicalism of pre-March and revolutionary vintage was the liberal school which was most drastically undercut by the new generation of politics. The failure of the revolution of 1848 was ultimately a failure of political radicalism, and the empirical emphasis of the 50's redoubled the spiritual crisis of those who had sought to raise the world on the lever of absolute principle. The accumulation of hostile influences broke the old political radicalism into three distinct tendencies—even apart from the new socialist radicalism. The conversion of some to official conservatism; the isolation of those few who retained their old beliefs in the new age; the addition of a material middle-class dimension to the old universal principles: these were the chief evidences of the refraction which dispersed the striking power of the democratic parties during the crucial two decades before the founding of the Empire.

The Converts to Conservatism

Most striking for the destruction wrought upon the old radicalism in these years was the impressive list of left-oriented forty-eighters who took the iron of the new social and international issues into their souls in such quantity that they found their way to a general political conservatism or even into Prussian or Austrian service. Of these, Karl Rodbertus and Lothar Bucher are particularly representative, for they show the cooperation of the new social interest and the new emphasis on national power in their combined attack upon the old democratic faith. The force of the peculiar development from democracy to the support of Bismarck is revealed in the fact that both men went through it independently; although they were in close contact during the 60's, this communication was a product rather than a cause of their similar evolution.

Karl Rodbertus, collectivistic economist and progressive landowner, joined social interest to liberal politics during the Revolution of 1848. His politics were moderate in substance, but he was driven into the radical Left Center of the Prussian National Assembly under the force of his conviction that a permanent representation must propel the state to social action in behalf of the submerged classes. Influenced by French intellectual socialism Rodbertus saw in democracy the wave of the future which would be realized by the progress of society.[123] But however derivative, Rodbertus' constitutional liberalism during the Revolution was wholehearted and determined. Holding firmly to the ideal of a Prussian constitution which would be the product of "agreement" between Crown and people, he interpreted this ideal as conferring inviolable rights upon the people and their representatives to participate as an independent factor in the drafting of the constitution and of all legislation, to control taxes and budget, to require the guarantee of personal and civil liberties, and to enforce ministerial responsibility upon the government. In line with these principles, he resisted publicly the translation of the Prussian National Assembly from Berlin to Potsdam during November 1848 and refused to accept the granted constitution of December 5.[124]

During the 50's, however, Rodbertus' political and social concerns began to separate. He retained an academic belief in the ultimate triumph of democracy, but he turned his attention to the economic basis of his social doctrine and to the international problem of German hegemony over central Europe. He even looked to Napoleon III as the model of a Caesarism which could possibly concentrate state power for external expansion and the resolution of the social problem.[125] When Rodbertus resumed political agitation at the start of the 60's he had decided to work for a new party which would include political conservatives and democrats alike, under the higher goals of a progressive social policy at home and an aggressive Great German program abroad.

In this campaign he was joined by Lothar Bucher, an old colleague of the Prussian Left Center who stopped momentarily at this position on his way to employment under Bismarck in 1864. Where Rodbertus' shift had been primarily one of intellectual emphasis Bucher's was the result of a profound crisis of conscience, and where Rodbertus was increasingly dominated by economic considerations Bucher developed a fundamental skepticism about the parliamentary and revolutionary principles of the old radicalism, which stopped short only at his continuing concern for the social interests of the working classes and his belief in the national state as the only effective agent of foreign policy. "The State is an end-in-itself; its mission is to maintain and perfect itself." [126] Together with an old political friend, Philipp von Berg, Rodbertus and Bucher published a series of pamphlets during 1861 which were designed as a platform for a

Great German party. Scorning "principles," "sympathies," and "doctrines" in favor of "interest-politics," they rejected "the nationality principle" in favor of a "patriotism" which would be a "healthy egoism" pushing for the realization of the central European federation dominated by Germany and required by German practical necessities.[127] They asserted, too, the ultimate necessity of a democratic suffrage and constitutional reform in Prussia, but they deliberately played these ends down as "old goals" for which "new means" and much preparation must first be sought, and they subordinated them explicitly to the national issue. And even their demand for a powerful German state, buttressed by a representative assembly, was mellowed by their assertion that it was "attainable without the application of violence from above or below." [128]

The appeal evoked no response, and after a brief political flirtation with Lassalle, Rodbertus and Bucher went their separate ways into the Bismarckian camp. For Bucher, with his emphasis upon the primacy of foreign policy and his revulsion against the liberals, the transition was rapid and wholehearted. For Rodbertus, however, whose thinking was more genuinely socialistic and whose politics was more persistently democratic, the road was more tortuous. He attempted once more, as in 1848, to give a liberal form to the combination by joining the Progressive Party, but his membership was merely nominal and he soon recognized the incompatibility of his social aims with this middle-class group. As early as 1863 he was advising the German Workers' Union in Leipzig against both the liberal cooperative movement and the Progressive Party. Insisting that the iron law of wages was bringing about the impoverishment of the working class and a widening economic gulf between the classes, Rodbertus declared that the laissez-faire social policy of the liberal progressives was "diametrically opposed" to the social interests of the workers, which required the direct action of the state to redistribute the produce of the economy. He admitted that "as a politician or a democrat" he still believed in universal suffrage, but he deemed more pertinent his view "as a socialist" that political liberty was not necessary to social reform, since "for me social questions precede the political." [129] Consequently, he called for the workers to form a purely "social party" and to work with "social friends" from whatever political camp they came.[130]

Rodbertus' recognition that for him political values were secondary was a preparation for the acceptance of Bismarckian conservatism. Bismarck's triumphs in foreign policy convinced him that the same kind of political realism which could solve the national issue could also be applied to the social issue. He revived his project of a great democratic party—social, monarchical, loyal to the state power. He sought to convince the Progressives to form "the trunk of a monarchical democratic party which can later be used to bring the 'state-idea' again to account while it acts for the strength of the governmental power, absolutely necessary under the present circumstances, as for the social demands of the working classes, and which pursues not Rotteckian theory but *Realpolitik*." [131] Of the two great German needs, unity and freedom, Rodbertus recommended: "So let a mighty state power first create unity for you, and then later with united German forces you can proceed to the development of freedom." [132] For "the German question . . . has been pushed far into the foreground," and "whoever does not recognize . . . that no present parliament would be able to solve the question in this form [i.e. greater unity] from its parliamentary power alone has forgotten everything since 1848 and learned nothing." The independent bodies of Germany can form a unity only by being "hammered by 'iron' and knit by 'blood'." [133]

Rodbertus' conversion, however, was not unreserved. It is important to realize that for him, as for other old radicals of his ilk—like Bucher and Lorenz von Stein—the endorsement of the conservative state meant not the surrender of democracy but its only possible actualization. For Rodbertus monarchical authoritarianism and political democracy were equally necessary to his social program. Rodbertus was a socialist in his promulgation of the iron law of wages, a theory of surplus value, and the necessity of redistributing the surplus product, but he drew up short of proletarian socialism in his preservation of private property in the means of production, his fear of popular revolution lest it destroy "true property," and his insistence that the required social reform could come not through "one class" but only "with the agreement of all the rest of the classes." [134] The redistribution of the net product over the various factors of production, whose validity Rodbertus maintained, must therefore be the work of an independent political authority, above the classes, but at the same time there must be opportunity for pressure from the exploited working masses upon the monarchical power to insure that such redistribution is actually made. Rodbertus even welcomed the advent of the Social Democratic Party so long as it would remain "purely economic" and in 1874 thought of standing for the *Reichstag* as a socialist candidate.[135] Through the kind of thinking exemplified in Rodbertus the democratic impulse could be transformed into the attributes "social" and "national," and as such it was integrated into the monarchical state.

The Doctrinaires

A second group of old radicals bore their principles of 1848 unchanged into the political conflict of the 60's and emerged from it isolated and impotent. This group was composed almost exclusively of intellectuals who had been formed by the absolute moral categories of the pre-March period, and nothing shows better than their political tragedy how the subsequent generation of German politics extirpated this kind of approach from all possible influence. Most of these men were political democrats by conviction; some—like Friedrich Theodor Vischer— were not. Common to all, however, was the categorical assertion of principle—whatever its political content—*qua* principle against concessions to circumstance or power. The persistence of this old radical attitude pervaded the correspondence of a man like Vischer, who, undismayed by the reaction, continued in those dark years to insist upon the necessity of political discussion and agitation, and to speak of politics in terms of "the Rational," "ethical hatred," and the "appeal from the empirical to the ideal public." [136] Even to Bismarck's triumph over Austria Vischer responded in the old style. "The leaders of Prussia

. . . justify violence and so waive justice (*Recht*). . . . A fact is created through violence from which possibly good—i.e. a united Germany and later acceptable internal conditions—may later come, but a citizen may never approve of violence, because he thereby gives up what is sacred, the rights and honor of humanity." [137]

With the resumption of political action in the 60's the old radical die-hards tended to separate into two different camps: some adopted the line of radical opposition within the system of constitutional monarchy; others rejected the whole established political system in favor of a positive radical program of democracy.

Representative of the former tactic was Benedikt Waldeck, who led the left wing of the liberal Progressive Party in the Prussian diet. Waldeck's radicalism did not express itself in extreme political views; it consisted rather in the rigid and categorical emphasis upon the safeguarding of popular rights within the monarchical system. Both personally and politically Waldeck was the very personification of the monistic principle of fundamental law (*Recht*), floating free of empirical conditions and even of ultimate political goals. Republicanism, national feeling, the social question—all these lay essentially beyond the circle of his political thinking. A firm believer in the "little people"—he was known as "the peasant king"—yet he had little actual contact with them outside of electoral campaigns.[138] A faithful adherent of popular sovereignty, communal democracy, and the equal natural rights of all individuals, Waldeck saw these principles as the potencies of existing institutions rather than as the sanctions for a new state. He accepted the monarchy and stressed only the parliamentary assertion of popular rights against governmental violation according to the law of the constitution. These views, already developed in 1848, were to remain constant thenceforward.[139]

Waldeck's political views were appropriate to the policy of alliance with the moderates against the government which he adopted upon his re-entry into political life in 1861, for there was little in his substantive political ideas to alarm the propertied bourgeoisie. Hence Waldeck could assume the leadership of the moderate-radical coalition which made up the Progressive Party in the Prussian Lower House, after the appointment of Bismarck and the outbreak of the constitutional conflict in 1862 made radical opposition the order of the day even for the most cautious of liberals. The moderates continued, to be sure, to mistrust Waldeck for his "radical doctrinairism," but this referred to his political temperament—his "dogmatism" and his "pure formalism"—rather than his political program.[140] Waldeck's radicalism remained, like the pre-1848 vintage from which it came, a radicalism of approach rather than of theory. The political mood in Prussia became ever more radical after 1862, but Waldeck did not. From the beginning to the end of the conflict he scarcely varied in his demands: his democratic instincts and his trust in the common people were funnelled into the civil liberties and the representative rights of the dualistic Prussian constitution of 1850 which Waldeck asked only to see applied.

But the radicalism that he failed to develop in the way of a democratic or a parliamentary program he did develop in the way of an ever more uncompromising emphasis upon the absolute validity of constitutional principle. In Waldeck the philosophical proposition that the ideal is absolute sovereign over material interests and power became an actual political program. The conflict became for him the struggle between such an ideal, which he identified with internal constitutional freedom, and the compromise of it through the blackmail of economic interests or external success in the national question. Against the first of these dangers he declared, in May 1865, that "the economy . . . cannot claim to solve by arithmetical problems and numbers the question of politics, the question of military service, or the question of the constitution." [141] Against the temptations of nationalism his so-called "Great Prussianism" stood proof: he believed in a unitary Germany that could be created only by the inexorable expansion of a radicalized Prussia over the eager people of the whole nation; for this a liberal solution of the constitutional crisis was the absolute condition and the unification itself only the contingent result. Waldeck opposed the Danish War of 1864, the Austrian War of 1866, and the constitution of the

North German Confederation of 1867, on the grounds that any other course would mean the compromise of principle with power and success. With the unification itself he had no quarrel, but he insisted that "the seat of power" which created it must be "consecrated by making the constitution truly constitutional." At the basis of Waldeck's argument in his closing chapter of his political career was still his preoccupation with the ultimate moral question. He found the representation of interests—"this customs, telegraph, and postal parliament," as he scornfully called the North German *Reichstag*—compatible with absolutism. "Constitutional rights," by which he meant particularly the budget right of the parliament, belonged in a different realm. They were the only means of fulfilling the categorical demands of *Recht*.[142]

> Above all, the federal state must be constitutional. If it is not, . . . it is not worth the effort we make for it. . . . We have not wearied in six years of asserting our *Recht,* despite the lack of prospects for immediate success; we have not wearied of asserting this *Recht* under any conditions . . . To give it up, to give it up now—that is not good, that is absolutely impossible.[143]

This was the swan song of the old radicalism. Under Waldeck's leadership the Progressives lost the elections of July 1866, broke apart in September, and fumed impotently at the enactment of the North German Constitution. After 1867 the issues both of German politics in the large and of German radicalism in the small passed from the ken of the Waldecks forever.

To the left of the radical constitutionalists led by Waldeck were the radical democrats. Their strength lay primarily among the anti-Prussian populists of southern Germany but their outstanding theorist was the veteran East Prussian liberal, Johann Jacoby. Emphasizing the egalitarian component in liberty, Jacoby and his friends represented the last great attempt to attract the working class into the liberal camp through a comprehensive program of social reform. Jacoby's own development, during this decade, which ended in a theoretical position at once isolated and unstable, expressed the impotence of the party which responded to the national and the social challenge of the 60's with the pure ideal of a federal and classless democracy.

Jacoby's evolution reveals the essential character of this democracy. He resumed his political activity in 1858 where he had left it at the end of the revolution, as a determined proponent of personal, civil, and constitutional freedom. He was a political democrat because he thought the masses the best potential executor of this freedom, but he was also a constitutionalist because he wanted to secure a united front with the bourgeoisie.[144] In 1861, he joined the Progressive Party which had just been formed in Prussia to effect such a front, and he fought within its ranks in the Prussian Chamber of Deputies for "the Prussian *Rechtsstaat*" against the government. It was not until 1866, when Bismarck defeated Austria abroad and the Progressives at home, that Jacoby struck up connections with the preponderantly southern and outspokenly democratic German People's Party and tried to convert the Progressive Party to the populist appeal of full democracy. His fundamental attitude remained the same—the refusal "to sacrifice constitutional right and freedom for the illusion of national power and honor" [145]—but he began now his move to the left in the effort to find a political instrument for it. This was the context for his break with the Progressives in January 1868, and for his new emphasis upon social reform. Both departures were stimulated by the need to call the masses into the political lists. Jacoby accused the Progressives of betraying their principles by their refusal to declare for universal suffrage, and he called for economic and social equality as the only means of insuring the participation of the working class in the struggle for political freedom.[146] Jacoby's social theory meant not so much a fundamental change in his attitude as a simple extension of his natural-rights radicalism to cover a social dimension. Calling for the "transformation of existing political and social relations in the direction of freedom, based on the equality of all mankind," Jacoby could appeal to "all the social classes concerned" to participate in the mission. And if, by the end of the decade, he came to feel that this emancipation required the replacement of the wage system by a system of "associated labor"—i.e. state-supported producers' cooperatives—he still thought of such a social change in the old moral terms: the addition of the universal to the individual component in society and of equality to liberty in the state.[147]

Jacoby's attempt to hold political and social democracy in parity through the hegemony of liberal principle over both found no followers. His projected Prussian People's Party never got off the ground. The radical groups on which he worked went either to the Lassallean socialists or to the petty bourgeois Progressives, and Jacoby himself, completely isolated, went over to proletarian socialism in 1872. The social appeal had grown in Jacoby precisely in the measure that government pre-empted the national appeal; it became his primary political means to the achievement of the liberal state for which he fought his whole life long. Hence the growth of Jacoby's social sense did not amend the judgments on his political dogmatism which more adaptable liberals showered on him—that he was "the archetype of the abstract, unpractical, south-German, stateless, pre-March liberalism whose religion was opposition—and indeed, opposition on principle." [148] The ideal of an undifferentiated democracy, which was offered as the logical consequence of the old moral principle of absolute freedom, had few takers in the Germany of the 1860's.

The Middle-Class Radicals

The post-revolutionary generation did produce one brand of political radicalism with a future. Doctrinaire politicians of the left who cast about them for a practical emphasis that would be appropriate to the new age and yet consistent with their absolute ideal of liberty found it in the policies of voluntary cooperation and the principles of laissez-faire. The two key figures in this transition between the liberal radicalism of the Revolution and the liberal radicalism of the Second Empire were Hermann Schulze-Delitzsch and his disciple Eugen Richter.

Schulze-Delitzsch represents the transfer-point between the classless political ideal of the intellectual radical and the self-conscious social values of the middle-class trustee. In the Revolution of 1848 Schulze-Delitzsch became—and remained—a poli-

tical democrat. In the 50's he became—and remained—the or-
ganizer and theorist of a system of consumers', producers', and
credit cooperatives. In the 60's he became—and remained—
the liberals' chief contact man with the urban masses. As a result
of these experiences he represented liberalism on the turn. In all
aspects of his thinking—the relationship between ideals and
interests, politics and society, liberalism and the people, constitutional freedom and national unity—the pattern was similar:
he maintained the categorical validity of the liberal ideal but at
the cost of acknowledging its middle-class function.

In his general approach Schulze-Delitzsch insisted upon the
primacy of "the higher ideal element in the life of the individual
as in the collective life of the people"—an element which he
specified as "our sense of freedom and of justice (Recht)"—but
he admitted that only on the "real basis" of "material interests,
. . . the predominant trait and tendency of our age" can this
"higher cultural life develop soundly and truly." [149] When
applied to politics, this combination meant the primacy of political freedom as a value and the primacy of the social problem
as an issue. He maintained that "the function of fundamental
rights" in a constitution was to express the content of society—
"human, individual development and its possibility for all"—
but he conceded that this political goal could not be attained
until economic questions are solved, because "through the social
question the political movement of the people has been led
astray." [150] Schulze-Delitzsch's work with cooperatives, consequently, was dedicated to building a mass support for political
liberalism. To attract this mass support he argued that while
the individual and society were mutually conditioning, the primary relationship consisted in society's "guarantee of the possibility of individual development and activity." The obligation
of the individual to society must be fulfilled through voluntary
association.[151] Schulze-Delitzsch's answer to the social question,
then, was a populist's version of laissez-faire. Since the mission
of society was to educate the individual to freedom, Schulze-
Delitzsch aligned cooperatives based on the self-help principle
alongside the traditional demands of classless constitutional
liberalism—"complete civil and economic liberty, the realiza-

tion of the constitutional *Rechtsstaat* with the equality of all before the law and with general, equal suffrage a chief demand, the greatest possible self-government in state and commune: that is, what the great liberal party strives for throughout Germany and what the workers need as much as all the other classes." [152]

But just as Schulze-Delitzsch filled his ideal with a material content, his politics with a social issue, and his individualism with a collective means, so did his ideal of the people absorb a class dimension. In his early work—both organizational and theoretical—on cooperatives, Schulze-Delitzsch had made little distinction among the urban masses but had treated "artisans and workers" indiscriminately as groups which were to associate and educate themselves to greater productivity through self-help.[153] When, however, in October 1862 workers' groups began to agitate spontaneously for universal suffrage, a general workers' congress, and admission into liberal political organizations— notably the National Union—the social class content that was implicit in his position was driven increasingly to the fore. In the violence with which he now turned against any form of state aid to the cooperatives it became clear that the group which he really had in mind was the petty bourgeois artisans, for the adaptation of the classical political economy which he espoused—self-help cooperatives designed to organize saving and capital-formation for competition in a free economy—was appropriate to the class of labor already possessed of some capital rather than to the unpropertied proletariat.[154] At the same time, moreover, he began to draw a fundamental distinction between the middle class in its broadest sense—"*Mittelstand*"—and the "workers." Although he continued to favor universal suffrage and their joint participation in the liberal political movement, he now insisted that the middle class must lead and the working class must support. "The development of the true German nature depends upon the German middle class. Because we must have a middle class in Germany . . . we must have a working class that is secured in its existence." [155] The workers have neither the time nor the education to concern themselves actively with public affairs, and they should look to the middle class as the chief bearer of the liberal and national cause. Consequently, he supported the restriction of the National Union to middle-class membership.[156] Although Schulze-Delitzsch persisted in the formal view that all groups were in a sense working members of a classless society, he had drawn an ineradicable line between the upper and lower middle classes on the one side and the proletarian working class on the other. By 1867 he was publicly defending universal suffrage not only as a fundamental political right but as "a social principle" which would guarantee the system of "free labor" against the dangers of socialism.[157]

The pattern of Schulze-Delitzsch's thinking carried through into his policies on the national question. His ultimate position on this was that "freedom" was the prime ingredient of "the national idea" and that even national unity could not justify "the surrender of the fundamental rights, the constitutional life of the Prussian and the German people." [158] Yet he maintained that the national issue—like the social—had to be solved before the constitutional; that "the power question cannot be separated from national unification"; that "we Germans have not pursued *Realpolitik* enough"; that the national party must choose Prussian hegemony because it must "limit itself to the attainable." [159] In the final balance, however, Schulze-Delitzsch did not accept the Prussian solution in 1867 any more than he had accepted the proletarian solution in 1863. Indeed, the two problems were explicitly connected, for he looked to the labor movement as to the Prussian state as means toward a free and united Germany. In the social as in the national issue he decided in favor of the absolute requirements of the liberal principle, but only after he had weakened its universality by associating it with material interests from which it could henceforward never wholly escape.

The consequence of this association was the rise of Eugen Richter to leadership of the political radicals in the Second Empire.[160] For Richter had neither the background of revolution nor the disposition of the intellectual which, in his radical forbears, had preserved the sovereignty of the political ideal over the temptations of practical interests. Associated with Schulze-Delitzsch in the 60's, he perpetuated the doctrinaire temper and the economic preoccupation, but he could no longer share the comprehensiveness or the moral drive of the transcendent liberal principle. Radical liberalism in him tended to be wholly absorbed in the dogma of economic freedom. He cut his political eye-teeth on the defense of economic individualism against the Lassalle group in the German workers' movement, and this was but the beginning of an incessant public castigation of social democracy.[161] As leader and publicist of the Progressive Party from 1875 on, Richter's role was almost exclusively that of a hostile critic, turned equally against the government on the right and the workers' movement on the left. In each case his criterion was individual liberty, defined primarily in a practical or economic sense. His principled negation of both aristocracy and proletariat appealed to the petty bourgeoisie of the large towns, and his principled affirmation of laissez-faire appealed to the commercial bourgeoisie. The rise of Eugen Richter to political predominance foreshadowed the decline of political radicalism to the furious but limited defense of these minority groups.

9. The Rise and Decline of Institutional Liberalism (1859-1870)

During the decade of the 1860's the declining curve of intellectual idealism met the rising curve of middle-class self-consciousness, and from this juncture there issued forth the whole crop of active liberal organizations that fought the last critical battle for individualism against the authoritarian political system in Germany. These organizations were composed on the one hand of the older intellectually oriented leadership—primarily liberal land-owners and progressive officials—and on the other of a new accretion from the economic bourgeoisie.[1] Both in the structure of these institutions and in their history the ultimate preponderance of the middle-class interest over the intellectual tradition and its claims to speak for the whole society goes far to explain the break-up of political liberalism against the magnetic rock of a liberalized conservatism.

The Social Basis

The myriad of liberal societies and parties that sprang up around 1860 against the background of the previous gulf between a developed intellectual politics and an underdeveloped economy undertook the function of integrating the social groups which were coming to political awareness into the philosophically formed tradition of political liberalism. The structure of these organizations shows that they fulfilled this function sufficiently to acquire a significant proportion of long-range mass support for political liberalism but insufficiently to make it a genuinely popular movement. The liberal associations were organizations of notables. The educated elite co-opted leading lights in the practical life of the communities and appealed successfully to even broader social groups, but the social range of their institutions remained limited nonetheless. Even the interested partisans varied directly with their position on the economic scale. The statistics drawn from the Prussian three-class voting system, in which the principle of division was property-ownership (technically the amount of direct taxes paid), furnish a convenient comparative index of the groups attracted to political life even in the modest role of supporters: in 1861, the percentage of participation among electors of the first class was 55.8%, among those of the second class 42.5%, and of the third class only 23.1%.[2] While this signified an increased political interest on the part of the Prussian petty bourgeoisie and workers from the 12.7% and the 18.5% which had voted in the elections of 1855 and 1858 respectively, the fact remains that the great bulk of the masses stood outside party life, including liberal party life. Aside from the isolated cases of a very few cities like Berlin, Koenigsberg, and Leipzig, radical leaders had scant followings.[3]

Participation in the liberal organs was by and large limited to a restricted number of active amateurs. Organization in any formal sense was almost non-existent. Central committees or boards were indeed created, but only exceptionally did they have regional or local branches. Even liberal parties set up local election committees only on an *ad hoc basis* for each campaign. The Progressive Party in Prussia founded its first regular local electoral association only in 1867—and this, significantly, in radical Berlin. Organizational work on the local level was performed by small groups of influential individuals who addressed themselves to somewhat larger groups of the same kind. Even the democratic south German People's Party lacked a genuine structure. Local branches were founded where local leaders existed and the general outlook appeared favorable, and delegates from these popular societies met in regional conventions. Between this level and the central headquarters of the party, however, the lines were loosely drawn, and policy was established through the connections and conflicts of a limited number of radical leaders who claimed to speak for the petty bourgeoisie and the working class.[4] The absence of organization in the liberal bodies was indicative of the absence of masses to be organized.

The upshot was a continuation, in some degree, of the old isolation of political life. The political leaders constituted a self-contained club, bound by personal as well as by party ties. In their frequent exchanges of correspondence the public and its opinion were often speculated upon and discussed as an instrument of political action, but always as an outside, almost unknown factor with no direct relationship to themselves. They liked to think—and indeed they based their policy upon the supposition —that they represented public opinion in the fight against reaction,[5] but this was a political abstraction and in concrete cases they felt with the Progressive leader, Leopold von Hoverbeck, when he wrote:

> But I fear very much that this whole opinion of our moral successes is only illusion. Those circles of the people who read newspapers and concern themselves with politics have long since taken their stand on this question and have remained true to it even today . . . On the great mass of the people, however, on the third and in part on the second electoral class all our deliberations have no influence, since they experience nothing of it. . . .[6]

Thus, whereas Sybel could write to Baumgarten, that he should "warn the middle classes not to be frightened, warn them against Utopian ideals," [7] and could speak with precise knowledge of the wishes of the "Krefeld notables," [8] he had to report the uncertainties of the Progressives on their ability to organize successful mass deputations.[9] In similar vein did Twesten write helplessly of the uncontrollable movement of the masses toward revolution.[10]

But while German political life continued to be segregated from a widely based popular participation, it was with the significant modification that the upper sections of the economic bourgeoisie had grown into it. The political leaders who had sought to reconstitute society along liberal lines from ideal ethical motives now tended to become a part of the group of notables who spoke for the rising captains of industry, banking, and commerce. The liberal movement had passed quickly, under the impress of an intense economic development combined with the fatal political hiatus during the 50's, from an undeveloped position in which the masses were politically apathetic because they were economically underdeveloped to a class position in which the masses were politically apathetic because the movement no longer represented their already deviating social demands. Decisive liberal action was hindered not only negatively by the absence of mass backing but positively by the growing fear, on the part of the political leadership, of these masses which remained beyond organizational control. It was this fact which gave predominance, during the early 60's when monarchical recalcitrance drove liberalism to seek popular support, to those few left-wing leaders who were presumed to have authority with the lower middle and working classes. Thus Schulze-Delitzsch, although anti-revolutionary, claimed and welcomed the support of these groups in critical moments of political conflict,[11] while Waldeck's influence with the feared masses was candidly advanced as the sole reason for tolerating his leadership in the Prussian diet by the other liberal chiefs, who resented him mightily.[12]

The continued presence in the 60's of radical political leaders within the new liberal institutions revealed the transitional status of that age. These men were the outstanding manifestations of the older classless intellectual liberal tradition still active in the new liberal organizations during their early, uncrystallized phase. The left-wing group sought to use these predominantly bourgeois organizations as the instruments for the mobilization of all non-aristocratic social groups in the fight for liberal ideals. The most important of these organizations were actually founded by left-wingers, who adapted their program to the desires of the section of the bourgeoisie which sought to use liberal principles for the acquisition of political power. Hence the liberal institutions of the early 60's embodied a contradiction in their very structure. The dominant factor in their leadership was an informal coalition of political notables composed of radicals who aimed at a democratic society through radically executed liberal principles for all classes and of bourgeois intellectuals who saw in such principles and such general support the only possibility for the realization of vital interests. The dominant factor in their following was a bourgeoisie whose concern lay in pursuing the interests against both the government over them and the classes under them.

The composition of organized liberalism during the 60's threw its political leaders into increasing dependence upon the economic bourgeoisie, and consequently the character of this class became decisive for the destiny of the movement. The German middle class was marked, during this period, by the fateful conjuncture of two opposed attributes: it reached the apex of its progressive influence, but at the same time its self-assertion began to take direct practical forms. By virtue of the first trait, liberalism became a powerful political force; by virtue of the second, it failed of its objective—the creation of a liberal state in Germany.

Toward the end of the 1850's the manifold strands of an industrial capitalism at which increasing numbers of German bourgeois had been quietly working since the Revolution reached the point at which they began to cross and form a network. A new economic pattern was created which penetrated the consciousness of the bourgeoisie and operated with direct effect upon the social and political structure of the nation. The economic crisis of 1857 marked the transformation.[13] The short depression which the financial crash of 1857 introduced was an eye-opener, for it revealed with startling clarity the new relationships and interdependencies which had been forged in the economic rise of the previous two decades. It signalized the fundamental transition from the phase of early capitalism to the phase of high capitalism,[14] the period in which free enterprise began to dominate all the values of the nation and in which the entrepreneurs, becoming class-conscious, began to press, as a group, for social and political action in their interests. "These men of the 'liberalism of practice'," whose spokesmen were the politically articulate men of the intelligentsia, now began to come into their own.[15] For the bourgeoisie this was a transitional age which brought together, on the concrete economic level, the materials marking the high point in liberal possibilities for the next half-century. These possibilities were grounded not only in the intensified political consciousness which transformed the liberalism of this social group from a general attitude toward life and society into a definite fighting political doctrine,[16] but also in the fact that during these early years of high capitalism the greatest possible numbers of middle-class people participated in the individualistic forms of economic activity which supported liberal politics. For in the 60's the rise of giant corporations in the industrial system had only just begun: the iron and chemical industries which were to constitute the backbone of industrial monopoly and the banking operations which were to supply the element of financial monopoly were equally new. Since this decade did not yet witness the process of the concentration of capital, the pattern of small individually owned and operated enterprises remained the order of the day, even within the most modern spheres of industry.[17] The social and political power of liberalism was strengthened by a new entrepreneurial group, for the rapid industrialization did not yet exclude the small and medium-sized independent producer.

Equally important for the liberal conjuncture was the fact that in the 60's the forces of the older bourgeoisie were still in the political lists, spurred by the economic pressure of modern industry to a new political consciousness. These forces were primarily those of handicraft and retail trade—the petty bourgeoisie—and of the peasantry. The handicraftsmen of the towns were suffering a severe internal crisis but were not crushed by large-scale industry until the 70's; the retail merchants were actually increasing in numbers, since available goods had multiplied but were not yet accompanied by the standardization and the great sales organizations which were to squeeze this social group to the wall.[18] Unlike its social counterparts in the towns, the German peasantry's economic existence was not fundamentally threatened in this period, but it too was undergoing a radical transformation which was destroying its old patriarchal, self-sufficient way of life and integrating it into the capitalistic money economy of the nation.[19] In general, all these groups were losing their traditional character as estates and under the influence of the prevailing economic motivations were developing into economic middle classes whose specific destinies were for the time held in abeyance. Thus, just as the intellectual orbits of a declining political idealism and of an ascending political positivism crossed during the 60's, so did the economic paths of the old and new middle classes. On both levels this coincidence made for a quantitatively strong liberalism, and hence the liberal parties and societies were the predominant political associations among the German people during the whole decade.

But the social history of the liberal middle class in this period produced an important qualification of its political influence. The growing concentration on immediate interests transformed the character of the middle-class participants. Especially was this true of the new entrepreneurial bourgeoisie: their whole pattern of thought and action was changed in the development from early to high capitalism, which was accompanied by the passing of the generation of economic leaders who had been raised in the idealistic traditions of the early century and the accession of a new generation which had undergone a more realistic education.[20] This generation took over at a time when enterprises were increasing in number, competition was stiffening, the tempo of life was becoming ever more dynamic, the relative classlessness of the previous social structure was yielding to the growing extremities of wealth. The bourgeoisie developed in response to these influences. The representative of early capitalism had been "open to the whole world, affirming the progress of technic, liberal in the sense that he wanted to burst outmoded bonds but, yet always subjected in action and desire to the 'common good,' liberal also in the clerical sense but yet pious, upright, and patriarchal, satisfied with the profit of a moderate capital, demanding Victorian (*Biedermeiersche*) moderation in business and in mode of living." His successor, the representative of high capitalism, was "no longer solid in the sense of the previous age: he used means self-evident only to the following age to gain first place in the competition; he was more realistic in conduct and more rationalistic in business thinking . . . not bound to moderation or the striving for the *juste milieu* but rather to a never-ending hunt for an ever-increasing capital which was to supply power, fame, honor, and good living." [21] The transition can be summed up as that from the *"Buerger"* to the *"Bourgeois,"* with all the loss of communal feeling and all the concentration upon individual self-seeking therein implied.[22] Hence the development in the social pattern from early to high capitalism had its political counterpart in the change from "early liberalism" to "liberalism." What had been a general attitude toward life, derived from an idealistic and humanistic philosophy and yielding a general responsibility toward the reformation of the entire community in its light, now became a definite party doctrine, justifying class demands by a new emphasis on the free-trade principles and seeking fearfully a middle way between the old hostility toward aristocratic conservatism and a new terror of proletarian democracy.[23]

Although the "socialization of parties," i.e. the orientation of political parties toward "social power-politics" did not become the exclusively dominant force until after 1880, this process was already underway by the 60's. The middle classes still maintained connections with the older liberal ideals, but the pursuit of economic interests was already strong enough to shift the primary focus of political concern from liberal parliamentarianism to liberal nationalism. Wilhelm Kiesselbach, of a Bremen merchant family, declared in 1860: "The further the German bourgeoisie has concretely developed, the more concrete freedom it has achieved through its real power, the greater force has the idea of political unity gained." [24] The national idea became in this period both the expression and the instrument for the material forces which were socializing party life. For at the same time as the idea of the liberal community was being weakened by the concentration on purely economic activities, the consciousness of the individual's economic dependence upon public support was growing with the integration of modern economic life and with such striking concomitants as the financial crash of 1857.

The petty bourgeoisie too suffered from an internal conflict which frustrated successful political action. Revolutionary tradition and current economic pressure pushed this group into politically articulate opposition in alliance with the bourgeoisie against the existing regime, but its political force was sapped by its position as a declining class, its defensive concentration upon its own threatened interests, and its resulting inability to draw up a constructive political program in terms of the whole society.[25] Moreover, the fact that the peril to its economic existence came from the new capitalism drove the petty bourgeoisie ultimately into conflict with the entrepreneurial bourgeoisie. The quick rise of industrialism during the 50's fed a political division within the liberal camp based upon a growing economic and social division within the middle classes. A striking prevue of this split was staged during December 1857 in Hamburg, where representatives of small business protested bitterly against the financial assistance that had been granted by the Austrian and Hamburg governments to the great banking and merchant houses. They complained in this connection about the patriciate of upper bourgeoisie which ruled Hamburg and intimated that the bankruptcy of its enterprises would tend to promote the general welfare since it would pave the way to the desired society of many small, independent properties.[26]

If this attitude had been unequivocal, an alternate tactic might have been carried through by the petty bourgeoisie—political alliance with the working class. But the industrial development of Germany had already advanced to the point where the existence of a proletariat was beginning to call forth independent socialist organizations and where the bourgeoisie was so conscious of the threat from this quarter that a grand alliance of the three classes was no longer possible even on the lowest common denominator of political democracy. The petty bourgeoisie was not unequivocal on the question of its political ally, and when, during the 60's, the great attempt at coalition with the working class was made, the lower middle classes showed themselves to be neatly and decisively split: the southern components participated in this effort while the northern elements staked all on the alliance with the main body of the bourgeoisie. The strength of the petty bourgeoisie was thereby dissipated and both lines of action failed, leaving Germany with no political ideal save that embodied in the principle of national monarchy to bridge the growing cleavage in the corps of the society. The liberal parties during the 60's developed from the direction to the reflection of the social composition of their followings. The mantle of intellectual predominance through which the advanced standards of a pan-European culture were imposed upon an unprepared society passed from the liberal into the socialist movement.

The force of these general structural conditions was such that all the important liberal organizations went through the same historical pattern during the 60's. Pressure groups and parties alike, each began as a common front of moderates and radicals against conservative authority when the regency of William in Prussia (1858) and the defeat of Austria in Italy (1859) weakened the powers of reaction, and each ultimately fell again into the characteristic division between compromising moderates, uncertain dualists, and doctrinaire radicals when the consolidation of monarchy under Bismarck revived not only its military force but its association with liberal policy.

The Pressure Groups

A whole galaxy of societies were founded in Germany to agitate among the most varied vocations and avocations for liberal and national reform. Of these, two in particular seem fit objects for analysis, because of the generality both of their goals and their influence. The Congress of German Economists and the Political Union were the outstanding pressure groups in their respective fields.

The Congress of German Economists

It was a portent of the age that the first liberal organization on a national level to be founded in Germany was one devoted to economic interests. The free-trade doctrine which inspired it was a part of the general liberal theory of the time. The doctrine started by reflecting this theory but gradually, during the 60's, began to influence its development: The Congress of German Economists furnishes an outstanding example of this reversal. In Germany the early partisans of laissez-faire were writers and parliamentarians who became convinced of the absolute justice of the free-trade dogma as part of their philosophical liberalism and only subsequently did they find the interested groups to support them.[27] Liberalism before 1848 had risen independently of free-trade ideas, and the doctrinal association of the two theories was a work of propaganda along abstract lines. John Prince-Smith, who before 1848 had been almost the sole exponent of the Manchester School in Germany, deliberately decided to impregnate liberalism with the free-trade doctrine after he had failed to obtain an adequate response at Frankfurt. Although Prince-Smith was himself fundamentally unpolitical and a moderate in those political views which he did hold, the doctrinaire character of his economic theory dictated his choice of the political radicals as initial targets of his propaganda.[28] In analogy with their politics his economics referred free exchange to the laws of nature and made it an ordinance of Providence upon which all human progress depended.[29] During the 50's laissez-faire ideas had an increasingly favorable reception. The merger of economic and political liberalism paved the way for the shift from the tactic of bringing about economic change through political reform to one of using economic means and pressures for political change. This shift resulted in part from the frustration of direct political action, but even more from the growing recognition that economic and social support could be brought to the liberal movement only with the development of a prominent economic facet in the idea of liberty. The increasing assertion of free-trade interests by the north German centers for foreign commerce and the progressive, grain-exporting agriculture of the north-east, and the susceptibility of handicraft to a program of economic liberty as the basis for a free cooperative movement supplied the material for the new tactic.

Out of this union of political and economic considerations came the foundation of the Congress of German Economists in 1858 as a national organization designed to exercise pressure upon the conservative governments in behalf of economic liberty. The alliance of bourgeois and lower middle-class spokesmen who presided over its foundation secured the initial primacy of laissez-faire as part of the general liberal ideal. Viktor Boehmert, who occupied a particularly strategic position as contact-man between the commercial interests and the handicraft interests, issued the first call for such an organization. In May 1857, in his capacity as editor of the *Bremen Commercial Gazette* and vice-syndic of the Bremen Chamber of Commerce, Boehmert issued an appeal for the founding of an association of German political economists on a program of freedom of enterprise, tariff reform, and freer movement in transport, banking operations, and currency.[30] In September of the same year, as participant in the International Welfare Congress on handicraft and labor problems, Boehmert pressed for support of his project. Hermann Schulze-Delitzsch, the political radical who headed the cooperative movement, was enthusiastic over the project, and under his sponsorship the German delegation, representing mainly lower middle-class interests, was enlisted into Boehmert's cause. The first meeting of the Congress of German Economists—at Gotha in September 1858—was set up by the spokesmen for the petty bourgeoisie—by Schulze-Delitzsch and the working committees of the Central Association for the Welfare of the Working Classes[31] and of the International Welfare Organization, in which Boehmert was an active participant.[32] The program submitted to the meeting of the Congress showed the influence of this group, for to the topics of tariff reform and reform of commercial law was added the discussion of the cooperative system in Germany.

The development of the Congress took a direction which was to become decisive for the whole liberal movement. At the beginning the politicians who led it were dominated by the idea of drawing the economic interests into the orbit of their liberal politics. Bennigsen wrote to Boehmert in August 1858:

> Your notion of the task of the first meeting of the German Economists has my full approval. Only by treating immediately the important questions which have to some extent been prepared in reality for solution will it be possible to call forth and maintain a lively interest in the circles of practical men.[33]

At the founding meeting in September Bennigsen met with a small group of politician-participants, and the result of their consultation was a formal statement on the integral relationship between the political and the economic movement.

> The national idea has sought to move from the world of ideas to the earth, . . . to bind the demands of the nation with the economic needs of the individual and of the whole, with the autonomous cooperation of the interested groups and not simply from a leadership coming down from above. [This is] a new connection of politically like-minded people, the beginnings of a new party formation, not only doctrinaire and idealistic but practical and rooted in the world of reality.[34]

But the Congress became increasingly dominated by the specific economic interests of the free-trading bourgeoisie, and in the same measure it tended to attach itself to the empirical political power of the Prussian state, to which it was drawn by the association of interests represented in the German Customs Union. The free-trade group which dominated the organization was overwhelmingly north-German in origin and sympathy, and the conflict between free-trade and protectionism within the ranks of the Congress became at the same time a struggle between the northern pro-Prussian and the southern anti-Prussian views on the political unification of Germany.[35] The closest political ties forged by the free-trade Congress were ultimately with the moderate wing of the Prussian Progressives and with the Prussian Old Liberals to the right of it.[36] Karl Braun, the Nassau parliamentarian and the future National Liberal whose political life was directed by the twin dogmas of free trade and the Prussian solution of the German question, became the perennial chairman of the Congress from 1859. The chief spokesman of the Congress in the Prussian diet was Otto Michaelis, future National Liberal and Bismarck's subordinate in the Federal Chancellor's Office after 1867. Even more revealing was the growing tie-in between the Congress and Bismarck's commercial adviser Rudolf von Delbrueck, who invited the politicians of the Congress to positive cooperation with the Prussian government's free-trade policy in the midst of the constitutional conflict. In return, Michaelis paid positive tribute to the economic role of the government in a speech before the Prussian diet during 1865. "What must we thank that we feel secure in this way today? We must thank the trade policy which has been strictly followed during the past three years." [37]

The concern with material interests and with political institutions which could best further them immediately meant the subordination of the political movement. In 1864 the *Economic Quarterly,* organ of the Congress, declared frankly: "Economic relationships are the purpose of political rights. Out of this purpose begins the movement which, in the struggle for the means, appears as political life." [38] Consequently, although the Congress tended to eschew political discussions in its annual sessions for fear of driving the south Germans out of the organization entirely, it was prepared to rally with alacrity to Bismarck after his announcement of plans for a customs parliament and his victory over Austria. Boehmert, writing in August 1866, announced this conversion openly through the columns of the *Prussian Annals*. He dismissed as futile the former aspirations of the Prussian liberals for a peaceful development to a national German state and enthusiastically welcomed Bismarck's violent policy toward that end. He openly confessed, moreover, that the desire for quick economic results, however attained, had long since disaffected the German bourgeoisie from political liberalism and oriented it toward rapprochement with Bismarck.

Whoever will not now recognize the force of facts and will turn away, grumbling, from the results attained without his cooperation must in general renounce the pursuit of politics and the introduction of his ideas into political life; he must leave the ordering of conditions to pure power while this power is still inclined to draw the German people into collaboration and to take account of the wishes of the people.

The economy is in itself the sworn enemy of war, revolution, and policies of violence, but it is also most quickly ready to accept given conditions and to develop its activity freshly and joyously on the basis of accomplished facts. It has never been in as principled an opposition to Bismarck as abstract politics and constitutional doctrine have been, since it owes its security to the most important item of commercial progress in the past decades—the conclusion of the Prussian-French trade treaty and the revival of the Customs Union on the basis of a liberal tariff. It was often observed even before the beginning of the war that Bismarck, because of this security as well as because of his foreign policy in general, enjoyed a certain popularity amongst the more important shippers and merchants with extended overseas connections and was held to be the man who was still most capable of building a firm state structure from the chaos of our misery of medium and small states. His preference for foreign policy exerted itself particularly also through the willing and swift protection given to the threatened interests of individual German merchants . . . Although men found themselves in sharpest opposition to Bismarck's internal policy and considered his connection with the feudal party to be an error of his political career, yet on the other hand they expected from him progress in the question of power and unity and were ready to forgive him much if he would only realize the idea of the German State, on which particularly all non-Prussian patriots must lay much greater weight than on the solution of the question of the Prussian budget and army, which had achieved such significance only because of the immaturity of the Prussian and German conditions and was to be satisfactorily solved only through the German question.[39]

Thus did the spokesman for the commercial middle class anticipate by a month the analogous movement of the political moderates out of the Prussian Progressive Party toward collaboration with Bismarck.

The change in the attitude of the Congress toward politics was an expression of its growing class consciousness. Not only was the organization's *Economic Quarterly* used by Prince-Smith in 1864 to proclaim Ricardo's iron law of wages against both socialism and state regulation but the majority of the free-traders came to oppose profit-sharing and to deny that freedom of association could serve any useful function.[40] By the end of the 60's it was obvious that in the course of the decade the composition of the leadership had changed profoundly. Schulze-Delitzsch, who opposed both the opportunism and the upper-bourgeois emphasis of the majority, castigated the Congress bitterly for precisely these traits in a letter to Boehmert during 1872:

> What has become of the life of our Congress! What a contemptible decline from the principles of science! What a humiliation in the service and the pay of the vulgar interests of the stock exchange! . . . I should like to attend [the annual meeting of the Congress] if we—even only in the minority—could form a closed phalanx there against the intrusion of the money-changers into the temple.[41]

But Schulze-Delitzsch was to learn that the organization itself, and not merely a clique, had left him behind. Boehmert, like Schulze-Delitzsch a charter member and accounted by him as one of the principled old guard, replied to these strictures in terms which may stand as the epitome of the new bourgeoisie.

> I do not stand personally any closer to these men than you and have often enough quarrelled with one or another of them, but their criticism, their healthy common sense, their rich observation of life and of the conditions of life have, wholly apart from their practical activity, performed better services for economic enlightenment than the most learned works and academic lectures of the professors. And the stock exchange is in my eyes as important an organ and instrument of

prosperity as the smaller markets and the people's banks and the co-operatives. In large cities like Berlin men live today under the pressure of the stock exchange and with aversion to its operations. But we must guard against such personal emotional impressions. In goods exchanges and especially in solid industrial exchanges such as we have here and in solid commercial and industrial big business the matter looks much different. I assert that men must know and respect the exchanges. . . . I stand in this fresh life and I feel that the future of our science belongs to it and not to the wisdom of the classroom. . . . According to my conviction the Congress of Economists will rise again. I shall not leave it even should I always remain in the minority, because the lack truly lies not in its organization but only in the fact that the old friends no longer come to it.[42]

The National Union

The formation and early activities of the German National Union marked the transitional stage through which the German middle class went from the awareness of their economic interests and power in the Congress of German Economists to mobilization for actual political struggle in the liberal parties of the 60's. It was an institution for political pressure, dedicated to organizing the German bourgeoisie on a national scale and using the demand for national unity as its rallying cry. Since the National Union sought to gather to itself the middle classes as participants and the masses as supporters, the idea of national unity provided a convenient framework within which moderates and radicals could fight together for political influence upon or against the regime. Because the Union was a pressure organization for German unification rather than a frankly political party, the various political tendencies which were included within it were attenuated through their reduction to a national common denominator. And since there was a far-reaching personal identity between the liberal politicians of Germany and the leadership of the National Union the influence of the latter helped to complicate the German politics of the period by giving to every issue a national as well as a constitutional dimension. Yet the fundamental political pattern of the age was so pervasive that it broke through the Union as completely as it did through the other liberal organizations. Despite the national idiom peculiar to the Union the political divisions which fragmented the liberal parties during the 60's were worked out first within its framework.

The appeal for a National Union was issued on August 14, 1859 by a group of Prussians, north-west Germans, and southern liberals who identified themselves explicitly as an alliance of the "Democratic" and the "Constitutional" parties and proposed that party tendencies be submerged in the common neutral demand for national unity.

> We expect that all German patriots, whether they belong to the democratic or the constitutional party, will place national independence and unity higher than the demands of party and will work together harmoniously and perseveringly for the achievement of a strong German constitution.[43]

Despite the consummation of the united front, however, the characteristic attitudes of the different parties that composed it made their appearance at the very birth of the organization. The occasion for its foundation consisted in the coincidence of two events: the dawn of a "New Era" in Prussia, inaugurated by the regency of the future William I and by the appointment of more forward-looking ministers like the East Prussian liberal aristocrat Rudolf von Auerswald, during October and November 1858, and the Austro-French-Piedmontese war of April-June 1859. The concatenation of the two events encouraged the revival of liberal activity in all camps and gave it a national direction. The reaction of the moderates was to emphasize the primacy of foreign policy in the form of an alliance with Austria against France and to limit the liberal movement to pressure upon established government for official action. They were, consequently, divided on the feasibility of founding a popularly based political organization. The old moderates by and large opposed such a move. Max Duncker warned that no steps which involved the masses should be taken lest it arouse memories of the Frankfurt Pre-Parliament of 1848.[44] The Badener Ludwig Haeusser wrote: "That France wants to dominate Europe overshadows my concern with Austrian and Bavarian priests." [45] The Rhenish historian Heinrich von Sybel gave open expression to the dilemma of the moderates, who would push governments toward a constitutional and national policy but feared the possible escape of the popular means of pressure from this limited function.

> I truly agree with you . . . that it is a question today of existence, of arms and armaments, and that against it all other questions . . . have in themselves only secondary value. . . . It is a question of existence that when it [war with France] breaks out Prussia should have the greatest possible chance to have the military forces of the Customs Union at its disposition. If I think it through, I see two ways to this. On the one hand, one might take Cavour as a model, take up emphatically the interests and rights of the population, demand from Austria the execution of Articles 13 and 16 of the Act of Federation, come out formally for the Hessian Constitution, get into contact with the Hanoverian, Baden, and Wurtemburgian opposition. One need not therefore be revolutionary; one need only support the first stirrings loudly, like a real Whig. I shall on my part not press for it, but on the contrary rejoice if such upheavals are spared us. But if this path is not desired, then I wish that the possible is done, which is the only thing left—secure the good will of the government and work for alliances instead of federal reforms . . . which can finally be brought about only through revolution.

Unable at that point to decide between the two alternatives, Sybel contented himself with leaving the problem in the hands of the Prussian state, noting that if only Prussia develops "martial force" she will achieve leadership, whatever the form or the constitution, whether by unity with people or with governments.[46]

So it was from the left, from a coalition of radicals and new moderates, that the initiative for the National Union came. A meeting of "German democrats" from central and south-western Germany in Eisenach on July 17, 1859, and a convention of moderate liberals and democrats from north-western Germany held in Hanover on July 19, set the stage for the new organization. Under the leadership of Schulze-Delitzsch and Bennigsen respectively, these groups issued independent but similar declarations which announced compromise programs in behalf of national unity. These programs looked to both a strong central government—a plank involving Prussian leadership—and a German National Assembly—a plank involving independent popular political activity.

Only a greater concentration of military and political power, bound up with a German parliament, can bring about the satisfaction of the political spirit in Germany, a rich development of its internal forces and a powerful representation and defense of its interests against foreign powers.[47]

The two groups decided to proceed together. They co-opted Prussian liberals from both the moderate and radical camps, and under these auspices the National Union was founded on September 26, 1859 in Frankfurt.

The history of the National Union from its foundation until its demise on October 19, 1867 was a long and futile struggle to contain the various social and political groups to which it made its appeal. The problem of the Union was to frame an organization and a program which could include political moderates and political radicals, pro-Prussians and federalists, bourgeoisie and masses. These divisions, apparently independent of one another, were actually related, for the moderates tended to depend primarily upon the order and power of the Prussian state and to call for middle-class influence upon it, while the radicals were hostile to the conservative Prussian monarchy and looked to a comprehensive popular movement as the instrument of national unification. The National Union tried to steer a middle course amidst these tensions. Its Executive Committee included the anti-Prussian radical Fedor Streit—the Executive Director of the organization—the Prussian radical Schulze-Delitzsch, and moderates like Viktor von Unruh and A. L. von Rochau, editor of the official organ—the *National Union Weekly*. Rudolf von Bennigsen, President of the Union, held the balance between both tendencies. In its programs the Union attempted to straddle both the political and the social issues. Down to 1862 its political resolutions called both for the assumption of national leadership by the existing Prussian government and for the recognition of the Frankfurt Constitution of 1849 as the "expression" of the German people's claims to a national state.[48] The Union's social views were similarly latitudinarian. On the one hand its *Weekly* maintained that the middle classes constituted the decisive factor in the contemporary social structure of Germany and that the bourgeoisie was the real bearer of the national political movement since upon "its productive activity . . . depends everything else in the Fatherland." [49] On the other hand, the organization sought the support of all classes: Schulze-Delitzsch beamed his publicity in behalf of the National Union during this period to the "whole people" indiscriminately; Bennigsen insisted that the Union viewed national activity "coming from the circles of trade and industry" only as "a part-payment or preparation"; and in April 1862 the Executive Committee financed the visit of twelve German workers to the World Exposition in London.[50]

During the year 1862, however, two events occurred which strained both these balances to the breaking point. The conservative realignment of the Prussian ministry which ended the New Era frustrated the expectations of cooperation with the authorities, and demands of workers' associations for entrance into the National Union put to the test its overlapping appeals to the middle class for leadership and to all classes for participation. The response of the National Union to these pressures was to upset the policies of balance within the political and social fields and to replace them with an attempt at balance between its political and social positions: the organization opted for the democratic solution in politics and the bourgeois solution in the social question.

Between 1862 and 1866, the official policy of the National Union consisted in open conflict with the Prussian government, the assignment of political initiative to the Prussian and German people, and the univocal emphasis upon the activation of the Frankfurt Constitution of 1849 as the sole valid means to national unity. Under the pressure of the constitutional conflict in Prussia, which seemed to bar the way equally to liberal and national reforms under governmental auspices, moderates and radicals alike moved politically to the left toward populism. Unruh announced that "the only possible ally for Prussia is the German people." [51] Miquel coined the slogan, "people's program against cabinet's program." [52] The Union did not explicitly jettison the plank calling for Prussian leadership, but in the general assembly's resolutions of 1863 and 1864 the issue was soft-pedalled and until 1867 the Union identified "Prussia" with its people rather than with its government. A liberal solution of the Prussian domestic crisis was made a precondition to any endorsement of Prussian national policy.[53]

At the same time as the National Union was assigning the decisive role in German politics to the "people" it was giving a social definition of "people" which would secure middle-class control over their activity. The social question came to the fore during the fall of 1862 in the practical and inescapable question of workers' admission to the Union. The context from which this demand arose made it more than a purely organizational question, for it was part of a program aiming at independent political activity by the working class. During the spring of 1862 Bennigsen had refused, on behalf of the National Union, to finance a national workers' congress. The agitation for such a congress continued through the summer and fall, and when, on October 2, 1862 a Leipzig labor meeting requested the lowering of membership dues in the National Union and provision for easier methods of payment, this resolution was coupled with others calling for the immediate convocation of the national workers' congress and for the institution of universal suffrage in Prussia. Clearly, the workers were applying for membership in the National Union with the view toward directing it to fight for labor interests. During the next five months the Executive Committee debated the problem, and on February 1, 1863 it decided to reject the request. This decision was confirmed by the general assembly in 1863 and again in 1864. This resolution by the Union, which was supported by Schulze-Delitzsch, sought to avoid a break with the labor groups: workers were to consider themselves "honorary members" of the National Union, and regular members were to work with the workers' organizations as individuals. The fact remained, however, that all official connections were denied and that the spokesmen for the Union insisted upon both the general beneficence of the laissez-faire economy and its requirements of bourgeois political leadership.[54]

The attempt of the National Union to combine radicalism with moderation amidst the political and social tensions of the 60's resulted in the dissolution of the organization. From its high point of more than 25,000 members, attracted by the balanced program of its early phase the Union declined to a membership of under 18,000 in 1864 and around 1,000 in 1867. Moreover, where its early success was based upon active proselytizing among bourgeoisie, liberal land owners, intellectuals, and lower middle classes, its effective public operations were paralyzed from 1864 on by internal crises.[55] The loss of support was attributable primarily to the successive withdrawals of democratic populists from the left and politically concessive bourgeoisie from the right.

The first serious attack upon the integrity of the National Union was delivered by the radicals. They waged the struggle on two levels: on the practical issue of worker participation and on the theoretical issue of the relationship between the ideals of unity and freedom which lay behind the problem of Prussia. For the radicals, these two issues were but two sides of a single coin—the conflict of ideals, uniform in both their political and social aspects, against interests, uniform too in their compromise with political and social power.

The first defection from the left had only an indirect effect upon the National Union. In February 1863 the Leipzig workers' committee, disappointed by the adverse decision of the Union's Executive Committee, turned to Ferdinand Lassalle, and in April the socialist General German Workers' Union was formed under his leadership. These workers had not belonged to the National Union, and in any case their small numbers— 4,600 in the year 1864 and 9,400 at the end of 1865[56]—scarcely signified a powerful counter-attraction. The indirect effect of this development, however, was considerable. It turned a considerable portion of the Union's publicity from the blending of divisions in a popular front to divisive polemics against Lassalle, socialism, and social reform. More important, it started a chain of events which ended with the secession of the political democrats from the National Union itself.

In May 1863 the Federation of German Workers' Unions was formed as a democratic counter-organization to the Lassalle group by Ludwig Sonnemann, editor of the *Frankfurt News*. It was on the issue of the policy to be adopted toward this labor grouping that the conflict between the anti-Prussian democrats and the pro-Prussian liberals was joined. The struggle was postponed for a time because of Sonnemann's conviction that the time for political action by the workers had not yet come. He ran the organization at first as a representation of the spiritual and economic interests of labor to the exclusion of politics. Consequently, although most of the leading personalities in the new body were non-Prussian democrats, both Schulze-Delitzsch and even the moderates of the National Union welcomed its appearance.[57] The attitudes of the two groups toward it, however, were fundamentally different. The National Union supported Sonnemann's organization with words and money primarily as a defense against Lassallean social democracy.[58] The south German radicals, on the other hand, looked to it as the basis for the creation of a great German People's Party which would unite workers and liberal bourgeoisie under a democratic program.

After the death of Lassalle in August 1864, they began working toward this end by moving for a merger of the Federation with his social democratic worker organizations of the north. Sonnemann held off from immediate participation in this agitation because he feared that the Lassalle group would disturb the balance between workers and bourgeoisie which he was trying to establish, but the issue reached into the inner councils of the National Union through the persons of the executive secretary, Streit, who had already espoused worker participation in the earlier debate of February 1863, and the Badener Ludwig Eckhardt, who was both a member of the National Union and a leader in the movement for the People's Party. The crisis came to a head in the Union's general assembly of October 1864. The social question was touched on in the continued refusal of the convention to lower dues, but the main debate took the form of the general theoretical issue implied in the problem of Prussian national leadership. This problem had been trenchantly breached during the same year in the influential pamphlet, *The Cardinal Sin of the National Union,* written by the Rhenish democrat of 1848 fame, Jakob Venedey. Venedey had not only, under the influence of the Prussian constitutional conflict equated the advocacy of Prussian leadership by the leaders of the National Union with support of reactionary particularism but had used the argument as a takeoff for a discussion on the fundamental basis of political action:

> *Realpolitik* is nothing but German political twaddle so long as the leaders of the National Union are not really, actually, called upon to lead German politics. So long as they are only called upon to lead the spirit of the people to the great goal of German unity, . . . their task is to pursue *Idealpolitik!* . . . Whoever knows history knows that John Handen [Hampden], Cromwell, O'Connell and Cobden, Franklin and Washington, Luther and Stein were *Idealpolitiker* who defended their principle so long as it was unsuccessful in reality, until they finally achieved the power to be *Realpolitiker*.[59]

It was in this tradition of the old idealistic German radicalism that Eckhardt, as leader of the left-wing opposition within the National Union, sublimated his social program for a coalition of middle and working classes to a crusade for the rejection of a Prussian central power and for a revolutionary agitation on behalf of the fundamental rights of man (*Grundrechte*).

This attack was resisted not only by moderates like Miquel but also by the Prussian radical Schulze-Delitzsch. Miquel argued that "in all great questions the German and the Prussian interests coincide." [60] Schulze-Delitzsch, who once again opposed any change in the dues,[61] also spoke at length on the necessity of Prussian hegemony. Although he spoke of the Prussian people rather than the government—"dynasties change, peoples are eternal, and momentary mis-government cannot alter their historic destiny"—his main argument was that free institutions could survive only if they were served by power: "a parliament without power behind it, without executive force, is completely futile . . . With parliament alone nothing is and nothing ensues." [62]

That the issue was not simply one of anti-Prussians and pro-Prussians is clear from the circumstance that even the concessions to the democrats in the Union resolution of 1864, which omitted all reference to Prussian leadership, could not hold them within the organization. In April 1865 Streit and Eckhardt both withdrew. Essentially, the leading group in the National

Union espoused a policy of harnessing to the ideal of constitutional freedom the leading powers in state and society, moralized by their sense of national mission. This policy took the alternative forms of the moderates' preference for an alliance of the bourgeoisie with a traditional Prussia modulated by popular pressure into a *Rechtsstaat* or the Prussian radicals' idea of the combined bourgeoisie and lower middle class operating through a Prussia renovated into a *Volksstaat*. Against this, the anti-Prussian democrats advocated an alliance of middle and working classes under an uncompromising program of political freedom, regardless of any consideration for the existing balance of economic or political power. Eckhardt now founded a *German Weekly* and devoted his full time to agitation for his dream of a People's Party. In confirmation of the related policies which had driven him from the National Union, Eckhardt's program combined an anti-Prussian plank on the primacy of rights over power with a pro-labor plank on universal suffrage and social legislation by the state for the worker. He insisted that democracy and the workers' party belonged together in the struggle against a Caesarism which used the nationality principle and the liberal bourgeoisie, but he remained part of German middle-class political liberalism. He represented an alternative to the policy of the *"Gothaer"* of the north whom he now considered his chief opponents. His appeal was for middle-class leadership of the popular forces of democracy: "The bourgeoisie must now stand the test. Today it can still seize the movement and lead it; if it is fearful today, if it is only a cowardly bourgeoisie, then it will itself be responsible if the flood breaks out and washes over it." [63] With the foundation of the German People's Party in September 1865 the split to the left was consummated.

Nor was the Union's desperate adherence to a policy of balance any more satisfactory, in the long run, to the interest-conscious bourgeoisie on its right wing. If its leaders' social moderation and respect for Prussia alienated the democrats its principled political liberalism offended the moderates. As the Prussian internal conflict drove the left toward radicalism after 1862, so did Bismarck's national policy drive the right ever more toward reconciliation with authority after 1864. In October

1865, on the eve of the annual meeting of the general assembly, the moderates, led by the business interests of northern and western Germany, unleashed a campaign to press the Union toward compromise with the Prussian government. The Commercial and Industrial Association for Rhineland and Westphalia, in the first number of its organ, *Customs Union: Journal for Trade and Industry,* disclaimed politics in favor of "material interests," which it represented as "the basis of spiritual and moral education, and of political maturity and freedom." [64] What this position implied for politics was made explicit by both Boehmert and Unruh, who urged Bennigsen to reverse the radical trend of the Union's resolutions. Boehmert, agent for the Bremen area, gave an ominous summary of the views prevalent in that port city:

> From many competent judges of our political situation whom I in the main have cause to consider kindred spirits, I even hear the view that a dissolution of the National Union would be no great misfortune. . . . I fear, and the facts confirm it, that we gain nothing by an uncertain attitude, by constant concessions to the south, but rather gradually lose our last foothold both in the south and the north . . .[65]

Boehmert was equally forthright in his recognition of the fundamental values involved and in his choice among them:

> The times are serious enough so that a choice between unity and freedom is necessary. . . . We shall be actually defenseless in the next European conflict if Prussia does not protect us, and we must strengthen this power, however hard it may strike us to strengthen even temporarily anti-liberal tendencies . . . Prussia's representatives have at the moment greater duties toward the future of their state than to tend to mere liberalism.[66]

In response to this pressure the resolution of the Union's general assembly, enacted on October 28, 1865, restored the plank on Prussian leadership to prominence in the program, without, however, withdrawing either its opposition to Bismarck or its demand for the convocation of a national assembly.[67]

But just as the resolutions of 1863 and 1864 had not mollified the left, so did the resolution of 1865 fail to pacify the right.[68] The break came on April 9, 1866, when the Prussian delegate at the German diet submitted Bismarck's proposal for federal reform, with the institution of a German parliament its central point. This was a formal fulfillment of the moderate liberal program and introduced the crisis from the right within the National Union. The Bremen branch immediately and unanimously voted to accept Bismarck's program.[69] When, on April 27, the leaders of the National Union circularized the agents of the Union for the ascertainment of the membership's opinion on the issue the majority of the responses likewise favored agitation by the organization in behalf of Bismarck's proposal. This informal referendum revealed the disintegration which had already sapped the structure of the Union, primarily through the withdrawal of the radicals, for only an eighth of the agents responded at all and by far the greater part of these represented the right-wing groups of the north, like Bremen, Osnabrueck, and Brunswick.[70]

Thus the former balance within the membership was destroyed and what was left of the National Union, composed of moderate bourgeoisie, was no longer represented by the mediating position to which the leadership of the organization still clung. Miquel had already turned to Bismarck and had withdrawn from active participation in the Union during 1865,[71] but the majority of the executive committee, led by Bennigsen and Schulze-Delitzsch, continued to resist blandishment. On April 15, Bennigsen had declared his refusal to endorse Bismarck's plan, grounding his position on a general mistrust of the intentions of the Prussian Minister-president: "A parliament without real rights is a sorry thing, even in a positive, existing state. But a parliament without rights and without a great movement of the nation in the very midst of the attempt first to found the German state can easily turn out to be much more unfortunate than that of 1848." [72] The decisive meeting of the executive committee of the National Union on May 13 and 14, 1866 likewise refused its endorsement, despite the results of the poll of the membership.[73]

But if the leaders thus kept enough of the intellectual liberal tradition to preserve, for the time being, their detachment above the enticement of the quick practical results embodied in Bismarck's program, yet their capacity for action was paralyzed by the emerging contradiction between the elements in their position and by the falling away of their following. The resolution accepted by the executive committee on May 14 called not for opposition to Bismarck's project but rather for the adoption of a wait-and-see attitude. It recommended that the endorsement be delayed until Bismarck submitted guarantees by adhering to the constitution in the conduct of the Prussian government and by filling out his general proposal for federal reform, which, "in view of its indefinite content and the system of the government of its origin," is "not fitted to gain the trust of the German people and the ardent participation necessary to overcome the natural difficulties of the task . . ." [74]

The signals of the approaching Austro-Prussian War which filled the German political atmosphere during May and early June 1866 completed the confusion of the Union's leadership. The Union's combination of preference for the Prussian state and aversion to the Prussian government on grounds of national mission could scarcely stand the test of civil war waged by a Prussian government for ostensibly national purposes. The Union stood paralyzed before their dilemma. Its *Weekly* fulminated against Bismarck but preached passive abstention in the coming war.[75] Its president, Bennigsen, insisted still that the Union's policy was "the precise opposite of the Berlin policy," but at the same time he admonished that the Union must be ready to join the Prussian side should Bismarck fall. Caught between these two fires, he could only predict gloomily the absorption of the National Union, as a "middle party," by the "extremes." [76] The Union's leading radical, Schulze-Delitzsch, gave a radical exhibition of its inner contradictions: he opposed the war policy of the Prussian government, and yet he maintained that Prussia must not be positively resisted, for the popular basis of the "Prussian state" must necessarily turn its participation in the war, "under any government," into a "people's war" for the "realization of the principle of nationality." [77]

The basis for the balanced position which the leaders of the National Union strove to maintain had actually disappeared. The Prussian state, whose power they had wanted to use, was now using their program, while the German people, who were to provide the motive force under the direction of the liberal middle classes, had fallen away, whether through indignation against or admiration for the state. In the weeks that followed the opening of the German war the inescapable fact of their isolation was impressed upon them. On August 3, Unruh emphasized this fact in a letter to Bennigsen:

> It will hardly be denied that the efficacy of the National Union has been a very small one for some years and has had almost no influence upon the course of events, . . . even with its own members. . . . If the Union is not to dissolve, be it deliberately or automatically, it must show that it has learned now to gain power and influence.[78]

With the failure of its self-appointed mission of gathering the German people behind the liberal leadership of a united middle class, the role of the National Union was done. The political framework of Germany had been created by Bismarck's Prussia, and the heads of the National Union had now to take up their positions within this structure. But this was a function of political parties, of which the Union now became a mere reflection. When the Prussian liberals, previously organized in the Progressive Party, split, during September 1866, into a group that sought to adapt itself to the new focus of power and another that fell back upon a purely oppositional policy, it sounded the death knell of the National Union. The leaders of that organization, bereft of their following, fled into the prepared molds of party life. In March 1867, the north German moderates, led by Benningsen, went into the new National Liberal Party and played a leading role in the development of its compromise policy during the constituent Reichstag which met from February to April of that year. At the close of the *Reichstag,* in April, the Prussian radicals, led by Benningsen's old comrade-in-arms, Schulze-Delitzsch, resigned from the Union in protest. On October 19th the organization decreed its own dissolution. In a final speech on that day Bennigsen put the seal of permanence on the division:

> In the year 1859 representatives of the various liberal tendencies met and buried their old conflict. The bond is now torn; the parties which were united then oppose each other now vigorously and decisively. It will be asked whether it is possible in this way to achieve new liberal

goals. Many hope for a reunion. I do not share this wish, this opinion . . . In the year 1859 that fusion of the liberal and the democratic party was the precondition of the least measure of progress; today its renewal would hinder advancement. The events of 1866 have sprung this connection; we cannot and, I say, we do not want to mend it. Another and healthier relationship must be created henceforward between the right and left wings of liberalism.[79]

Both in policy and in composition the liberal middle classes had split and with this cleavage gave the *coup de grace* to the organization which had dedicated itself to organizing them as the political power of the land.

The Parties

The history of the liberal political parties in Germany during the 1860's was of a piece with that of the pressure organizations. There was, to be sure, a division of labor between the two kinds of institutions. The agitation of the pressure organizations was indirect: they sought to mobilize a social weight behind proposals for action in specific fields within the existing political system or for action on a new national level above the existing political system. The parties attacked directly: they constituted themselves the spearhead of the liberal movement and grappled with the dominant conservatism for the possession of the actual instruments of political power. Nevertheless, the same social process and the same political destiny comprehended them both. In some cases, like Lassalle's General German Workers' Union and the German People's Party, distinctions between pressure organization and political party scarcely existed. Where they did, a far-reaching personal identity in their leadership and an overlapping group identity in their following subjected the two sets of institutions to analogous experiences. In party and pressure groups alike the autonomous estate of political intellectuals was forced to witness the dissipation of the social support upon which it had staked its ideals and the subsequent divisions of the political liberals themselves. The consequences, however, differed. The defeat of the pressure bodies meant that the liberals lost the offensive; the defeat of the parties meant that they lost the game.

Conflict and defeat were not the universal lot of the liberal parties. Baden became the model for the cooperation of prince and moderate liberals in a program which liberalized the institutions of state in preparation for national unification. Beginning in April 1860 Grand Duke Frederick I appointed outstanding moderates like August Lamey, Julius Jolly, and Robert von Mohl to authoritative posts in his government, which worked thereafter in close conjunction with a diet majority of similar political orientation. The concrete results of this collaboration were embodied in a far-reaching administrative reform which assigned essential functions to new organs of local and district self-government under bureaucratic supervision and limited the administration by the enhanced scope and independence of the judiciary. Even in Baden, however, the attempt to establish a parliamentary government through the practice of a political ministerial responsibility failed; the political rights of the diet remained limited by the independence of a princely government whose members could be individually impeached for misgovernment but not politically controlled by the representatives of the people.[80]

But if this pattern of limited cooperation was possible it was not typical or authoritative. The leading themes in the history of German liberalism during the 60's were those of conflict and division. This last chapter in the struggle to implant the ideal of individual freedom in the reality of the German state-system was, in the main, the story of three parties. The German Progressive Party of Prussia claimed to be "the executive of the National Union in Prussia" and was actually the authoritative model throughout Germany for the union of moderates and radicals on the basis of the sovereignty of "law (Recht)." To the right of the Progressives, the German National Liberal Party embodied the rupture in the unity of the progressive opposition and signalized the continuing efficacy of the traditional association between the ideal of freedom and the authoritarian state. To the left of the Progressives, the German People's Party closed the drama when, toward the end of the decade, it tried to apply the pure ideal of democratic freedom, social and political, class-less and uncompromising—and was condemned to political isola-tion.

The Progressive Party

The German Progressive Party in Prussia was the prime instru-ment of the Prussian middle class in its constitutional struggle for the liberalization of the Prussian state. The detailed course of the Prussian constitutional conflict has been described too often to bear repetition here.[81] It will suffice simply to set the stage for what is of special relevance—the Progressives' reaction to the conflict.

The favorable conditions for domestic reform which were in-augurated with the institution of the New Era ministry in Novem-ber 1858 and the start of an eight-year liberal domination of the Prussian lower chamber in the December elections of that year produced little but disappointment. The ministry's own politi-cal heterogeneity, the distractions of the Franco-Austrian crisis, the resistance of the House of Lords, and the beginnings of fric-tion with the diet over the introduction of an army reform bill in February 1860—all these factors helped frustrate the good intentions of the progressive aristocrats in the government and spur the impatience of the deputies. Increasingly the army re-form became the focal issue in the liberal parliamentarians' fight against the regime of bureaucratic omnipotence which was the essence of what they called the Prussian "police state." The mili-tary reform aroused the bitter opposition of the deputies not so much because of the increased expenditure which it required as through its provisions for the extension of active army service from two to three years and for the distribution of active militia (the first levy of the *Landwehr*) between the regular reserve and the inactive militia (the second levy of the *Landwehr*). For the Regent and the government the reform was necessary to increase and modernize the army. To the liberals it was a means of in-tensifying royal control over conscripts and of removing the militia from civilian—and particularly middle-class—influence. Until March 1862 the lower chamber voted the additional funds for the military reorganization through extraordinary credits valid for one year only. From that point on it signified its intention to withhold such funds until the government conceded at least a two-year term of service. Caught between the determination of the king and the opposition of the Chamber, the New Era ministry was revamped toward the right in March, when it lost its more liberal members, and still again in September, when it lost its more accommodating conservatives and received Bismarck as prime minister. With this appointment the struggle over the army developed into the larger constitutional conflict over the respective rights of monarch and popular representation in the budget. Bismarck asserted his theory of the constitutional "gap"—i.e. in the absence of constitutional provision for disagreement between government and diet on the budget the king has the right to carry on his government with previously legislated tax levies—and for the next four years he ruled Prussia without a budget. During these years the opposition between the government dominated by Bismarck and the Chamber dominated by the Progressives remained at fever-pitch. Not only was the original and most sacred right of representative assemblies continuously flouted but the traditional and holiest of liberal values was brought into contumely. Bismarck's famous dictum that "the great questions of the age are decided by blood and iron" was made to the budget committee in September 1862, and it was followed in January by Bismarck's cool declaration to the Chamber that where there is a constitutional gap "whoever has power in his hands may proceed as he will." [82] This deliberate subordination of law (*Recht*) to power brought into the fray everything the liberals had ever stood for.

The German Progressive Party in Prussia was founded during the period of transition between cooperation with and opposition against the government. On June 6, 1861 the constituent meeting of the new party was held by a group composed predominantly of liberal deputies who had been growing more and more restive under the policy of unreserved collaboration, pursued by the Old Liberal parliamentary leaders *vis-à-vis* the New Era ministry. The Progressive movement began as a radical emphasis upon a moderate program, and this pattern was to remain characteristic of the party throughout its history. It was born of impatience with the "moderation" of the "means" employed by the New Era ministry and it was staffed by an imposing array of democrats and young moderates; but the program of the new Party abjured "opposition in principle to the present government," proclaimed its "unswerving loyalty to the king," announced its "conviction that the constitution is the firm bond which unites prince and people," and demanded "the strict and consistent realization of the constitutional *Rechtsstaat*" within the framework of the existing charter.[83] From the start to the close of the political conflict of the 60's, the Progressives fought under the banner of a *Recht* which they identified with the established constitutional law of the land, and they demanded only its faithful application by government and administration. Specifically, they called for an equal and independent administration of justice, the juridical responsibility of ministers, local self-government, separation of church and state, equality of religions, secular education, freedom of the press, economic liberty, retention of the militia, two-year military service, German unity "under a liberal banner," and the recognition of the legislative rights of the popular representation.[84]

The Progressives' subscription to the *Rechtsstaat* as their supreme political ideal meant that they fought not for the actual domination of the state but for the security of universally applicable private and civil liberties against bureaucratic and aristocratic encroachment. For this, the political dualism formally stipulated in the Prussian constitution of 1850 provided a sufficient guarantee, in the eyes of the Progressives, through its attribution of budget rights to the elective chamber and its provision for juridical ministerial responsibility. The refusal of the Progressives to claim either a change in the three-class voting system or the political responsibility of the government to the diet or the constitutional responsibility of the military was clear testimony that they defined political freedom not in the positive sense of parliamentary control over the state but in the negative sense of parliamentary checks against the undue exercise of authority by the state. Insofar as they did aim at a positive participation of the citizens in the political process they tended to think of it as contributory to a larger political order which would secure the application of state power within the due limits of law.

The Progressives' radical emphasis upon a moderate program was appropriate to the alliance of social forces which they were trying to achieve. They aimed at a coalition of the Prussian masses and the bourgeoisie, but in such wise that the categorical mode of the opposition was beamed at the masses while the substance of the program was tailored to the needs of the middle class. Thus it was that radical populists like Waldeck and Schulze-Delitzsch could become the authoritative leaders in a party whose policy, according to a contemporary, "corresponded to the ruling views and mood" of "the bourgeoisie." [85]

Within the common front of liberals dominated by the Progressive Party, however, the various tendencies retained their specific identities. These tendencies expressed themselves overtly in the structure and the history of the liberal front in Prussia. Structurally, this front was made up of three distinct groups. On the left of the Progressives were the radicals, led by von Hoverbeck, Waldeck, Schulze-Delitzsch, Jacoby, Franz Ziegler, Julius Frese and Rudolf Virchow. In the center of the Progressives were the new moderates like Twesten, Lasker, Theodor Mommsen, and Max von Forckenbeck. On the right wing of the party was a small group of moderates, represented by Otto Michaelis and Julius Faucher, who were particularly close to the Congress of German Economists. This Progressive right, weak in itself, was reinforced by its general agreement in policy with an influential group of moderates loosely organized as the so-called Bockum-Dolff group in the left center of the Prussian lower Chamber, just to the right of the Progressives and through most of the conflict in coalition with them. These three kinds of liberals led more than a subjective existence within the united struggle against the government between 1861 and 1866. They served characteristically different functions in that struggle. The open clash between the liberals and the Prussian government involved two distinct, albeit connected, issues—the army reorganization that dominated politics until September 1862 and the constitutional conflict concerning the budget rights of the representative Chamber that grew out of it and became the primary problem thereafter.[86] As long as the army issue, which appeared negotiable, dominated the scene the moderates led the liberal coalition; when the budget issue, which involved an irreconcilable constitutional conflict, became the bone of contention, the radicals took over the leadership of the alliance.[87] The center group in the Progressive Party retained their readiness to negotiate on the military question but they insisted, too, upon the sanctity of the budget right; thus they carried the thread of continuity between the two phases of the struggle, provided the communication between the two wings of the movement, and performed the crucial function of keeping the liberal front together.

Behind this overt specialization of labor lay the fundamental tripartite division in the German approach to liberty, which now reappeared upon the political scene. The divergent attitudes toward the concrete issues of the Prussian conflict were manifestations of the compromise mentality, the radical negation, and the eclectic dualism which even now, because of the common program against the government, could find no direct political expression. The form which the division took was the old dispute over the relationship of political principle—whatever its substantive content—to political reality, to which there was now added a conscious dimension of social or class interest.

For the moderates, whose most articulate spokesmen were the political scientist Rudolf von Gneist and the historian Heinrich von Sybel of the Bockum-Dolff parliamentary group, the conflict was to secure the civil rights due the middle class within the monarchical state. Their position was not so much one of principled opposition against the government as it was against the predominant aristocratic influence in the government.[88] They cooperated with the radicals because they endorsed that part of the idea of *Recht* which would guarantee citizens of substance against the undue interference of bureaucracy and privilege and the undue exclusion from public posts, but they acknowledged that "power interests should be primary for every state." [89] Their mistrust of the "dogmatic" politics of the radicals was centered precisely around the latter's approach, which exalted the constitutional principles of *Recht* as the exclusive canon of political action and neglected "the great power questions of the state." [90] Hence the moderates' policy in the conflict emphasized the army issue and minimized the constitutional issue because they looked for a compromise which would satisfy the concrete requirements of the middle class from the state while contributing to the military and political force of the state.[91] This moderate attitude found its natural focus in the issue of the national guard (*Landwehr*), now reputed a bourgeois stronghold. It was led by elected officers who were usually the notables of small cities. The proposed reorganization meant that this middle-class force was to be integrated into the regular army and subordinated to the military aristocracy.[92] Gneist analyzed the social meaning of the threatened institution with startling candor:

> People's army is only the equal arming of the social classes, thus the connection of property and civil calling with the exercise of arms. In an English militia, which includes distinguished lords and rabble, the connecting members of a people's army are lacking. Just as little were the sans-culottes a people's army, for those richest in property and education belong to the people above all. . . . Also our standing army of permanent officials and minors cannot represent the Prussian people in arms. . . . The *Landwehr* is indeed something different, when it gathers the whole adult population in their natural social structure according to property, education, and profession into army units in which the unpaid officer and non-commissioned officer represents not only the royal office but also his own property and in which the good habits of the soldier instinctively become one with the good habits of the citizen.[93]

In a speech to the House of Deputies on May 7, 1863, Gneist spelled out even more bluntly this middle-class stake in the *Landwehr* when he defined it as "the reconciliation and union of property with the armed power of the state. . . . Over against the arming of the non-owning classes, [it is] the systematic arming of the mature, the propertied classes, the classes which are called by their interests, their professions, and their most pressing political demands to the maintenance not only of internal order but especially of constitutional rights." [94]

The political radicals abjured both revolutionary means and democratic programs, and consequently their position too was distinguished by their characteristic emphasis and approach rather than by their substantive goals. Leopold von Hoverbeck defined the radical attitude as a mean between surrender to the government and "radical excesses." [95] Schulze-Delitzsch spelled this out to mean a defensive posture against governmental aggression and in favor of the traditional German notion of freedom as the essential harmony between popular liberty and monarchical authority.

> It has not been bloody struggles between the dynasty and the people, as in England and France, which have introduced the modern state to us but struggles of the people with and for the throne and Fatherland which have ripened the people to freedom. . . . We wish to maintain this character of our political development as much as possible, in the interests of all.[96]

The characteristic stress of the radicals upon the budget rights of the lower House was their way of concentrating upon political rather than civil rights within the doctrinal limits of the common liberal program. The Progressives' electoral appeal of September 12, 1863, which was written under radical auspices, categorically declared that "the most important right which the individual is given by the constitution" was the right "to give his vote for the election of the representatives of the people." [97] Behind this radical tendency to define the *Rechtsstaat* in terms of the positive political rights of the popular assembly in the state was the interpretation of the liberal struggle against the government as the middle-class leadership of a classless society for the assertion of a universal principle of freedom applicable to the whole people. Thus Schulze-Delitzsch explicitly denied the notion of a class struggle between "workers and employers." He claimed that the liberals "arouse and cultivate more and more the moral and intellectual forces of our workers . . . and will not fail to go hand-in-hand with them toward the pursuit of conditions of real human dignity for all classes of our people." [98]

In their effort to hold these divergent social groups together under an essentially moderate program, the radicals were driven to an ever more rigid and abstract insistence upon the principle of *Recht*. What they could not advance in the way of democratic substantive demands they had to compensate for in the formal intensity of their limited doctrine. Hence they reverted to the wonted radical formula which asserted the primacy of principle over concession. Schulze-Delitzsch explicitly connected his concern for constitutional *Recht* with his appeal to a united people:

> Someone has spoken about the power question: *Recht* is power, if there are men who assert it right. If we stand firm and if the people stand behind us with its whole moral concern for the constitution, then there is no cause for worry.[99]

Julius Frese, a left-wing Progressive who ultimately broke away with Jacoby to the German People's Party, gave a memorable formulation to this pattern of Progressive radicalism in an open letter against Karl Twesten during October 1865. "If it were true," he wrote, "that the support of an annexationist policy by force conditioned 'the power and future of the Prussian state,' then to my mind it would be better for the Prussian state to go under today rather than tomorrow; for this policy contradicts all principles of popular rights and popular freedom." *Recht,* Frese continued, is an indivisible whole, and one cannot make *"Rechtspolitik"* within Prussia and *"Unrechtspolitik"* in Germany; the same groups who now combine these policies deserted the Prussian National Assembly in 1848-49, have believed in the possibility of compromising the constitutional conflict, and are now in the process of going over to Bismarck. The inescapable choice is: "For a politics of power or for a politics of *Recht*." [100]

The Progressive Center perpetuated the both-and political approach of the German dualistic tradition. This group was composed of men whose early education had been infused with the intellectual radicalism of the pre-1848 era and whose later development had been dominated by the material and positivistic influences of the 50's. The political behavior of these new moderates of the left was directed by the continuing interplay of both attitudes. They cooperated with the other moderate groups in the persistent application of the military question as a means of reconciliation with the government,[101] and they shared with the radicals the concern with the budget rights of the assembly as the crux of political freedom. Behind this intermediate tactic lay the fundamental tendency to balance social interest and political principle. Their concern for the former led these new moderates to the latter as its practical guarantee. Hence their inclination to emphasize the tangible civil liberties of enterprising citizens, to transact with the government for economic benefits, and to "consider the power position of our state . . . not only in Prussian but in German interests," went hand in hand with their insistence that "civil and personal freedom . . . only gains real security with political freedom, whose positive nature consists in the free activity of the citizens in the service of the state." [102] Thus this group defined the *Rechtsstaat* as a legal order compounded of an active monarchical government which produced concrete advantages for the individual and of the indefeasible constitutional powers of a popular representation which produced the principles pragmatically required to secure such beneficent policies by government. In social terms, the bourgeois self-consciousness of these new moderates extended beyond the sphere of civil liberties into the demand for a predominant middle-class influence in framing the policies of the monarchical state. It was this group pre-eminently that Hermann Baumgarten meant when he described the position of the Progressive Party as representative of "the bourgeoisie," which,

> consciously proud of its intelligence, its industry, its riches, and its almost unanimous will, wanted to achieve the position in public life which, as it did not doubt, was due it. It had the feeling that it essentially carried the state with its labor: what was fairer than that this state be essentially ruled according to bourgeois points of view.[103]

Karl Twesten, the outstanding member of the group, gave the classic formulation to the interpretation of the *Rechtsstaat* as the expression in constitutional principle of the practical partnership between middle-class and monarchy.

> . . . The transfer of an essential part of the work of the state to the personal performance of independent citizens is the only means of making the state healthy and strong. In the middle classes self-reliance and participation in the state grows with their material rise. . . . A genuine constitutional system is the only form of government which in modern states can count on permanence and guarantee a moderate, constant progress.

For Twesten it was only this "existing parliamentary constitution" which could preserve "a firm structure of unchanging and guaranteed relationships of law." [104]

This center group faithfully reflected the combination of interests and principle in the Germany of the 60's. It is hardly surprising, consequently, that the destinies of liberal coalition which they held together and of the German liberalism which they epitomized should henceforward have lain in their hands.

The National Liberal Party

The foundation of the National Liberal Party on June 12, 1867 gave permanent institutional form to the division of the moderate from the radical wing of the liberal movement in Germany. The history of the origins of the new party recapitulated the general history of the movement, for it was constituted through the characteristic reactions of the three main types of the German approach to freedom when they were confronted with the renewed association of the monarchical state with the policies of a concrete, limited liberalism. The new party was organized by the union of groups who peeled off from the united liberal front in successive layers—the old moderates who made their peace with Bismarck upon his mere announcement of a German policy, and the new moderates who moved from reluctant opposition to reluctant collaboration in response to the *fait accompli* of Prussian military victory and the constitutional liberal promise of the government's indemnity bill. With these defections, the upper reaches of the German intellectual and economic middle class gave up the attempt to control the state through the assertion of constitutional principle and settled for the material benefits of government-sponsored liberal reform. The radicals in the Progressive Party were left impotent in their defense of a classless political ideal and ultimately reduced to dependence upon restricted sections of the commercial and petty bourgeoisie.

The first to break away were the two moderate groups inherently most disposed to compromise with the authorities—the economically oriented liberals who were becoming increasingly uneasy about the practical consequences of the political conflict and the Old Liberals who were always ready to infiltrate their ideal of an ordered freedom into the order of the state. Throughout the year 1865 Michaelis and Faucher, the contact men of the Congress of German Economists who led the right wing of the Progressive Party, spoke in terms recognizant of the power needs of the state and of the consequent necessity to reconcile government and parliament.[105] Rudolf von Delbrueck, Bismarck's free-trading assistant for commercial affairs, recognized in Michaelis "too governmental a nature to find pleasure for long in negative opposition," [106] and Lasker echoed this judgment when he characterized the Progressives led by Michaelis as "deputies . . . who announced a preponderant interest in economic questions and who had in the free-trade system even during the conflict a very strong and positive common bond with governmental policy and its personal representatives." [107] The Michaelis group did not formally secede from the parliamentary party until August 1866, but their internal disaffection was of much older vintage, for they were fundamentally averse to the policy of conflict with the government. Their political philosophy, as formulated during 1866 by Michaelis, integrated their utilitarian conception of politics into the traditional moderate penchant for the Prussian state as the ideal embodiment of practical liberty.

> The rights of the people are not a medal which is packed in a box of legal deductions and sealed up with negative votes. The rights of the people which are entrusted to us are a lever for the promotion of the good of the people and for the promotion of the Prussian state. . . . The rights of the people are furthered by the use which we make of them. . . . As the lower house we must act as a factor of this state for this state.[108]

But it was from the Old Liberals that the first overt rupture of the liberal front came. The experience of the Revolution of 1848 had left this branch of German liberalism with nationalism as its supreme political value, for the Prussian Union attempt to which they subscribed taught them that the historical state could liberalize itself when this liberalism was enclosed in a national organization. Consequently, their opposition to the Prussian government began to weaken from 1864, with Bismarck's adoption of a forward policy in Schleswig-Holstein. When, in April 1866, Bismarck instructed the Prussian delegate at the German diet to propose a federal reform which would include a national representative assembly, the Old Liberals found this sufficient to withdraw from the liberal opposition and went over to the government. On April 26, 1866, the Halle Old Liberals, under the leadership of Rudolf Haym, formally proclaimed its "unconditional support" of all steps which the Bismarckian government would take for "the honor of Prussia," and it grounded its conversion in its "profound faith in the power of the national idea." [109] By May these Old Liberals were looking forward to detaching a section of the Progressives and forming a new patriotic party.[110] By June 1 they were electioneering against the Progressives in the name of "The Committee of the national-liberal Party"—a party which was then more a future projection than a present reality. Their fundamental political attitude was frankly that "no liberal reservation" can detract from "the supreme political duty" of faith and sacrifice to one's own state, for the state "can only grant justice and freedom to its citizens if first its existence is secured." For these Old Liberals the national aims of the conservative government justified it even in the name of freedom itself: through our commitment of "the national will and conscience" on the Prussian side "we seize the one great lever through which the question of power is raised to the level of the interests of freedom and of the people—the constituent German parliament." [111]

The real meaning of the Old Liberal position was spelled out by Hermann Baumgarten, who began to agitate from May on for "a complete, fundamental transformation in our political thinking as in our political action." He proclaimed the political bankruptcy both of intellectual liberalism and of the bourgeoisie. The intellectuals must give up the doctrine of *"Recht"* which served only to "create an ideal state according to the excessive wishes of our whole unpolitical nature," and they must place themselves "before all on the basis of facts."

For Prussian power a favorable star shone; for Prussian freedom a contrary wind blew; [the national party] had not the sense to seek the former and give up the latter. . . . Complete freedom depends only on complete power.[112]

This weakness of liberalism rested, moreover, on the permanent political impotence of the bourgeoisie. He paid tribute to its economic importance and to its industrial and academic intelligence. He insisted that "all modern states . . . will have to grant an important influence to bourgeois forces" and that "its interests and tendencies will have to be considered above all by every wise statesman." Nevertheless, "for genuine political action the middle class is . . . little fitted." "The bourgeois is created for work and not for rule. The ablest forces of the bourgeoisie have worked themselves up from the bottom. . . . Such a career . . . gives character, freedom, and purity of soul. But whoever has risen so is in a sense too good for politics." [113]

For Baumgarten the two targets were indissolubly intertwined: intellectual liberalism was the unrealistic expression of the bourgeoisie's invalid claims to political power. Consequently, his deliberate renunciation of political liberalism was accompanied by the recommendation that liberals and middle classes alike give up their ambitions for political predominance, accept the existing order of politics, and learn to see in the state rather than in their own desires the source of their real blessings.

> As soon as German liberalism comes out for the great deeds which it now acknowledges . . . there can be no doubt that the next decade will bring us the German state which has become as pressing for our science, art, and morality as for our political development and national power-position . . . I am of the firm conviction that a satisfactory solution of our political problems will come only when liberalism ceases to be primarily opposition.[114]

Baumgarten went so far in his surrender of liberal doctrine as to demand support for the Prussian government in domestic as well as national issues. Indeed, even the nobility were to be recognized as an essential part of the state.[115] Baumgarten had formally transferred the liberal as well as the national function of his political ethic into the charge of the established authorities.

On July 3, 1866 the Austro-Prussian War was decided at Koeniggratz, and the way was opened for the Prussian unification of Germany. In response to this event a second regional group of liberals prepared to go over to cooperation with Bismarck. The liberals of the occupied north-German states met during July to announce publicly their acceptance of the Prussian victory and their approval of Bismarck's plans for a north German constitution.[116] The importance of these meetings lay in the participation of representatives from the center as well as from the right of the liberal movement. Led by Bennigsen, the non-Prussian dualists departed from their close connection with the Prussian Progressive Party while that party was still intact, and thereby they anticipated its split. The "New Prussians" could take the lead in collaboration because they had not had the embittering experience of the constitutional conflict with the Prussian government and because their own tradition of opposition to the local dynasties led them to see in the Prussian dispossession of the princes a concrete example of the inherent liberalizing character of national unification. By December the Hanoverians had organized a "Central Election Committee of the National Liberal Party" and were campaigning throughout the conquered territories on a program which called for a German parliament to act "at the side" of the king of Prussia with the functions of creating "the unified organization and leadership of the army and navy indispensable for the security and power-position of Germany" and attracting the southern states into the union.[117] The partnership of Johannes Miquel and Bennigsen in the leadership of this national liberal group symbolized the coming alliance of moderates and dualists against the radicals. Both men recognized that German unity had been achieved "exclusively through the greater power of the Prussian state without the cooperation of the German people" and that the German nation could hardly ask "to get parliamentarianism and the whole complex of freedoms granted by grace from the Prussian Crown and the German Richelieu." Both men, consequently, joined in preaching collaboration as the politics of the possible. And yet, within this common policy, a cardinal distinction between them remained in evidence, epitomizing the future segregation of right and left wings within the National Liberal Party. Miquel's enthusiasm for national unity and the external power it brought was so intense that he accepted the limitations upon popular rights without visible regret as the necessary consequence of the primacy of foreign policy. Bennigsen, on the other hand, took the new line only reluctantly and tried to view it as simply a detour toward the long-range goal of predominant liberal influence in the state:

> If our party becomes so strong in the parliament and in the Prussian lower house that the government can count on no majority without it, its leadership would have to be indeed a very unskillful one if it cannot secure reasonable concessions in internal administration and legislation as compensation for its support of the government in German and foreign affairs.[118]

The dualists within the Prussian Progressive Party came ultimately to the same conclusion, but theirs was a more gradual and more tortuous road. In this group the recognition of the material advantages of national unification, under whatever auspices, remained in conflict with their recognition of the necessity of parliamentary rights to secure practical advantages of any kind. It was this internal debate between the material and principled elements of liberalism that made the decision of this group decisive for the fate of the Progressive and the foundation of the National Liberal Parties.

The new moderates of the Progressive Party stood proof both against Bismarck's blandishments of April and May and against the outbreak of war in July of 1866. True, they wavered, for men like Twesten and Unruh evinced a desire for reconciliation with the government, but on the issue of the budget right of the assembly they refused to yield, not only because it would mean "the surrender of our standpoint of *Recht*" but because it would in practice deprive the representatives of "disposition over the resources of the country." [119] The Progressive Center, then, refused to use the war crisis to press for their maximum program of reform, but they did go along with a united Progressive Party in the refusal to vote war credits. What the government could not accomplish through the external use of force, however, it did bring about through the internal crisis of conscience which its national and liberal program initiated within the Progressive camp. The resistance of the dualists was broken by two events which made their inner dilemma impossible to bear any longer. The election of July 3, which brought a re-sounding defeat to the Progressive Party, showed that the people—and particularly the middle classes—whose interests this group felt they represented were no longer behind their policy of opposition. Moreover, it threw the Progressives into dependence upon the moderates and Catholics on their right. And secondly, Bismarck's proposal for an indemnity, inserted into the address of the Crown to the new diet on August 5, held out the promise of faithful constitutional government.[120] These developments intensified the dualists' highly developed sense for the demands of empirical politics at the same time as their constitutional idealism was mollified by the opening of possibilities for its realization in the future.

The rift between the dualists and the radicals was opened immediately upon the convocation of the diet in the intra-party debate on the answer to the Crown address, and it was made irrevocable by the internecine struggle on the indemnity bill shortly thereafter. Both Waldeck, for the radicals, and Twesten, for the dualists, submitted draft answers to the Crown,[121] the former wholly oppositional in tone and omitting all reference to the indemnity proposal, the latter conciliatory, emphasizing the national question, promising cooperation in the establishment of the projected North German Confederation, and assuring the passage of the indemnity bill in return for a guaranteed budget right. The majority of the Progressive deputies supported Waldeck, but when the dualists and moderates in the party refused to go along the radicals gave in. They raised no objections when Forckenbeck, the President of the House, replied to the Crown in language which omitted the reference to the budget right as the principle of parliamentary power and the recommendation of the Frankfurt Constitution of 1849 as the basis of a united Germany.[122]

On the concrete test of the indemnity bill, however, no such compromise was possible, for the government submitted, along with the indemnity, a request for an extraordinary credit to set up a military and naval war chest. Since this would make the government independent of the diet it involved the issue of the constitutional conflict all over again. The radicals insisted on the preservation of the undiminished principle of parliamentary rights and would accept an indemnity bill only if it were accompanied by the simultaneous submission of a regular budget to the diet. For the right wing of the party, Michaelis proposed to separate the military from the budget issue; he advocated the approval of the indemnity and the war chest and the indefinite postponement of the latter. The dualists of the center pursued a difficult intermediate line: they would vote the indemnity bill and use this approval as a counter in the subsequent continuation of the fight for parliamentary rights *vis-à-vis* the war chest. They acknowledged this policy to be a surrender, but they conceived it only as a tactical surrender, a detour which compelled different practical means to the same constitutional goals. Lasker asked rhetorically: "Do the conditions still exist which force us to continue this conflict in the previous way or can we remain in the opposition and in defense of our rights without carrying over this method of fighting, i.e. this formal conflict, into the new age?" Like his colleagues, he chose the latter alternative.[123] Twesten later summarized their position in terms of the recognition "that only in the agreement of the representative body and the government could something be achieved, and the people announced that it wanted to see something achieved," but he too drew the line at Michaelis' policy of surrendering the budget right for the future. "We must be careful not to endanger the future through temporary yielding; when it comes to the point where we must approve an unconstitutional principle against our previous conviction and principles, . . . then there is no stopping place and we work into the hands of absolutism." [124]

The implications of the dualists' position was spelled out most clearly by Ludwig Bamberger, who was not at this time a member of the Prussian Diet but was intimately connected with the Lasker-Forckenbeck group. In a series of articles which he wrote during the fall of 1866 under the revealing title of *Old Parties and New Conditions* he tackled frankly the problem of reconciling liberal convictions to present concessions. Bamberger rejected the uncritical and total submission of the "power politicians" as well as "the deluded rejection" of actuality.

> The problem lies in the evaluation of the principles which make up the content of the facts and in the separation of that which we cannot help but accept from . . . that which we, uncorrupted by its success, have to reject as eternally inadmissable and reprehensible.[125]

Hence it was not a question for Bamberger of the ultimate surrender of liberty. "We still know that there is no salvation without knowledge, no knowledge without law; and more than ever we are convinced that it is not a matter of any principled denial of a sacred article of faith." [126] The point was rather the choice of given means for the execution of that faith.

> It is worth the trouble to investigate the question of who in the end is the more truly devoted to freedom; the democracy which now goes about in sackcloth and ashes or that which lives in the faith that what has happened can lead to a salutary result. It is worth the trouble to ask whether those who perceive a success even where it has come through against their counsel and against their authority are not more freely and more selflessly devoted to a good cause than those who must themselves triumph in order to rejoice. . . . Is it so sinful to believe that Europe must either irresistibly retrogress or must go forward to the final inevitable conclusion which follows from the assumptions of human dignity and human freedom? And this assumed, is it sinful to believe that Europe will not be able to fight out this great battle before Germany is in the position to throw the whole force of its arms and its spirit into the scale? And this assumed, is it so sinful to believe that, in order to enter into this struggle, the German nation must have found the unity of its will and of its movement as an indispensable pre-condition? . . . It depends upon the future to justify us. . . . If you are not for unity in our sense, so we are not in the least against freedom in your sense. If events had brought a German federated republic we should have welcomed it heartily and hardly demanded that you make the leader of Prussian policy its president . . . And so then, since you have now actually nothing better to offer us, grant the beginning of unity, as bad as you hold it to be, its elbow-room and give us a chance to earn a place in the sun. . . . There is no question of abjuring freedom and still less of singing hosannas to the god of the battalions; the Prussian representatives have only done what they could not leave undone, and the necessity which they obeyed was not their work but the work of the entire people.[127]

Thus for Bamberger cooperation with the Prussian government in its national campaign was the only possible policy for freedom under the circumstances. "Is not unity itself a piece of freedom?" he asked on another occasion.[128] Hence he now saw the fight for freedom as the task within the North German Confederation. That this fight had to be transferred from Prussia, Bamberger explained frankly on the grounds that the power of the government was superior to the power of the people and that, consequently, the bargain which the moderates concluded in the indemnity bill was the best they could do to ward off black reaction and the complete destruction of the constitution.[129]

On the basis of this kind of thinking, then, the group for whom Bamberger wrote worked out their middle line to mean a compromise of the liberal principle in Prussia for the sole purpose of establishing a united Germany in which liberal principles could then be the more easily applied. But, as Adolph Cohn wrote, this meant a reversal of their former scale of values: instead of freedom before unity, it must now be unity before freedom. And this, in turn, meant the adoption of a traditional conception of freedom within the state. "Men wish to be forced to their salvation." [130] Hence the dualists decided to vote the indemnity bill, the war chest, and the regular budget for 1867, on the assumption that this approval would help to set up the unification of northern Germany and therewith a new arena for the conflict. Despite the efforts of the radicals to preserve the integrity of the Progressive Party by releasing its members from party discipline on this issue, the difference in political approach was so categorical that Twesten and Michaelis withdrew from the parliamentary party on August 18 and were followed shortly thereafter by the bulk of the members from the center and the right of the party. Until November this "Twesten-Michaelis group" conceived of itself as simply the vanguard of the whole Progressive Party in the establishment of a new line for the specific questions of national policy which would permit it to resume its struggle for genuine constitutional government in the German parliament. The program of the group, consequently, proclaimed the dual principle of cooperation with the Prussian government in foreign affairs and decisive opposition in domestic affairs.[131]

This precarious balance, however, proved impossible to maintain. During the months that followed the dualists drifted ever further from the radical Progressives and ever closer to the moderates. The decisive influence in this drift was the shadow of the impending constitutional assembly for the North German Confederation. Since the dualists considered this to be a part of the national question upon which there must be compromise with the government they tended increasingly to subordinate their demands for parliamentary rights under the necessities of present collaboration and to restrict the sphere of decisive opposition to practical civil liberties.[132] Twesten expressed this priority of values when he declared, on November 5, that "as long as the police and the courts are in the hands of the government and their officials, so long is political freedom, the authority and the power of parliament, precarious." [133] The radicals, in contrast, continued to emphasize the budget right in Prussia and showed themselves relatively indifferent to the coming Confederation. On November 16, the Twesten-Michaelis group declared itself to be the parliamentary section of an independent "National Party" and they campaigned as such for the constituent assembly. Whereas the Progressives were resolved upon the rejection of the Bismarckian draft constitution *en bloc,* because it was unilateral in origins and insufficient in the rights which it attributed to parliament, the National Party decided to accept the draft as the framework of deliberation and to work for liberal amendments within it. On the basis of this compromise program moderates flocked into the new party which the dualists led,[134] and the result of the coalition was a notable triumph in the elections of February 1867. On March 1, 1867 the National Liberal Party was formally constituted by the merger of the new Prussian party with the analogously-composed national liberal group from the north-German states under the leadership of Bennigsen and Miquel.

Bismarck's consummation of north-German unity and his offer of a representative constitution as its cement proved an irresistible temptation to the practical susceptibilities of the dualists, but this did not mean the surrender of their political individuality. Dualists and moderates retained their specific identities within the National Liberal Party, and this distinction prepared

the way for future divisions and future compromises. The ultimate balance of forces within the party was revealed at its inception, for on the very day of its constitution Twesten, supported by Lasker and Forckenbeck, proposed that the organization take a definite stand on the budget issue: the provisions
of the Prussian constitution on this matter should be the standard
for the north-German constitution, and the acceptance of this
demand by the government should be made a *sine qua non* for
the approval of the draft as a whole. After a bitter struggle,
which occasioned a complaint by Forckenbeck on the lack of
political character implicit in the compromising nature of the
Hanoverians, the majority resolved that it would not thus bind
itself.[135] The Twesten group submitted, but the anomalous composition of the party was confirmed. The backgrounds of the
founding deputies reflected this composition: besides the group
from the Progressive Center, the assemblage included Prussian
Old Liberals of varying stripe, like Sybel, Count Maximilian von
Schwerin, Gustav Freytag, and Wilhelm Lette, non-Prussian moderates like Miquel and Friedrich Oetker, and representatives of
practical interests like the economist Michaelis, the shipper H. H.
Meier, and the industrialist Henckel.[136] The latter three groups,
which formed a compact majority on the right, set the limitations to the action of the party, and within these limitations the
left-wing section supplied reforms which the government would
accept. This was the pattern which the party followed in the
formulation of its fundamental program in June 1867. Twesten
submitted the draft of the program, a draft which called for
new means—i.e. positive popular and representative participation in the legislation and administration of state—as the only
way of realizing the old liberal claims. The moderates in the
party then toned this down until the final version emphasized
rather that internal liberty was dependent upon the completion
of national unity.[137]

The dualist leaders on the left wing of the National Liberal Party had thought that by their approval of the north-
German constitution they were merely "setting up a scaffolding,
the development of which may be left to the future" and through
their success in imposing juridical responsibility upon the Chan-

cellor and in limiting the military budget to an interim period of four years' validity they had hoped that they would "be able to satisfy the burning need for certain indispensable rights as soon as we have brought the structure safely under shelter." [138] But in the new German state as in their new party, their acceptance of the framework meant the acceptance of its consequences —"a work which has come out of compromises among various circumstances and interests but which does not correspond to the hopes and demands which many men have wished to see realized. . . ." [139]

The German People's Party

Between 1865 and 1870, during the very period when the liberal movement in northern Germany was breaking apart on the issue of constitutional principle, a group of southern and central German liberals strove to create a national party on the openly radical program of federal democracy. Where the north-German Progressives strove to unite bourgeoisie and masses on the basis of a particular appeal to the middle classes the south-German democrats were striving to unite middle classes and masses on the basis of a particular appeal to the labor leaders. And yet both attempts suffered similar fates. For both, the solution of the German problem from above removed the cohesive element from their political program and the growth of class consciousness from below interposed a decisive social cleavage into their vision of an ideal political unity. Just as the Progressive Party split to the right in 1867 with the formation of the definitely bourgeois National Liberal Party, the German People's Party split to the left in 1870 with the formation of the Social Democratic Workers' Party. In the south as in the north the radicalism that would unite the German people against their governments was condemned to the impotence of regional parties and the limitations of a lower middle-class clientele.

The German People's Party manifested the attempt to apply the revolutionary ideals of 1848 in their logical purity to the Germany of the 60's. Its main area of operations lay in the states of Baden, Wuerttemberg, and Saxony—states in which the traditional social structure of small-scale entrepreneurs, artisans, and independent peasants was most persistent and the pattern of radical politics most familiar. Its program was founded upon a definition of *Recht* in terms of an undiluted federal equality directed particularly against compromise with Prussian power in national affairs and a political and social equality directed particularly against bourgeois predominance in domestic affairs. The history of the party consisted in the successive undermining of these basic planks from without and from within. In 1865 and 1866 it was oriented primarily toward the national issue, and the Prussian victory over Austria made this orientation politically meaningless. After an interim of confusion the party sought, from 1868 to 1870, to reorganize on the basis of the social issue, and this attempt was condemned to failure by the movement of its working-class components out of the framework of classless democracy into an independent proletarian socialism.

The priority of the national question in the early history of the People's Party was evident in its very origins. The initiative for the new party was taken by the radical Badeners under Ludwig Eckhardt, who agitated for a political democracy with the positive goals of a German federal republic and a far-reaching program of social reforms for the workers. Both the leadership and the policies of these men, however, were jettisoned by the founding conventions of the party during September and December 1865. The majority of the delegates were intellectuals whose conception of freedom did not go beyond an adherence to the formal principles of political democracy and an extreme aversion to Prussian leadership. The program which was formulated in December endorsed universal suffrage but rejected state intervention in social matters and advocated the broadest possible federal liberty for the particular states in a united Germany.[140] Party leadership passed from Eckhardt to Karl Mayer, and the party's headquarters and official journal were transferred from Baden to Wuerttemberg (Stuttgart), where there was no memory of the risings of May 1849 and subsequent suppressions to exacerbate the extremism of the left. The dominant group at this time took their political and social assumptions, by and large, from the democratic lower middle classes; they were old-fashioned democratic liberals who believed that the role of the state was to represent and protect the equal natural rights of its constituent individuals and who found in anti-Prussian federalism the chief mode of expression for their non-revolutionary and non-social radicalism.

It was into this party of middle-class democrats that the anti-Lassalle labor organizations whose strength lay outside of northern Germany began to move during 1866. The occasion for the union was the Austro-Prussian crisis and the basis of it was a common view of the national question. Workers' meetings in Saxony during April and May passed resolutions calling for the immediate convocation of a German parliament based on universal suffrage, a *levee en masse* to support this parliament, and the unequivocal condemnation of the Prussian policy of conquest. Bebel proposed this last resolution and Liebknecht spoke for it.[141] On May 20, the People's Party called a mass meeting at Frankfurt to consider the national question, and here the representatives of the workers participated significantly for the first time. The resolutions of the Frankfurt meeting resembled in general those of the Saxon assemblies, with the important difference that the revolutionary implications of the latter were subdued in favor of formulations calling for the legal introduction of the *levee en masse* by the governments, cooperation of the middle states with Austria against Prussia, and the founding of German unity on a basis of the self-determination of the individual states. Despite the comparative moderation of this program the leaders of the young working-class movement led their followers into the party on the basis of the common definition of democracy in terms of opposition to Prussia. Bebel not only approved the program but helped compose it. When the executive committee of the anti-Lassallean Federation of German Workers' Unions met on June 10, Bebel persuaded Ludwig Sonnemann, the leader of the Federation, to depart from his former policy of political neutrality and to join the People's Party. Then, on August 19, 1866, Bebel and Liebknecht sponsored the formation of the Saxon People's Party as a branch of the German People's Party. This action was taken under the immediate impression of the Prussian victory and the occupation of

Saxony. The overwhelming majority of the delegates at the founding convention were worker representatives from the Workers' Educational Unions, and they were led by Bebel and Liebknecht into the People's Party on the basis of its Frankfurt resolutions. The program set forth the usual demands for the democratization of all public bodies and the creation of a popular militia, while the social planks, under the conscious restraint of Bebel and Liebknecht, omitted any mention of class opposition and were limited to innocuous proposals for freedom of labor, the improvement of the conditions of the workers, support of producers' cooperatives, and reconciliation of the differences between capital and labor. The reason for this moderation lay in the overriding concern with the national question, for the sake of which Bebel and Liebknecht wished to maintain unity with the middle-class leaders of the Party. Their purpose was to fight the situation created by the war and to annul it by the convocation of a German parliament including German Austria.[142]

Despite this immediate reaction, which was actually the climax of the preceding period, the Prussian victory and the creation of the north-German confederation marked a fundamental turning-point in the history of the German People's Party. The period which followed, from mid-1866 until September 1868, was one of confused and tortuous striving to find a footing on the shifting ground. In the course of this interval the dominant issue on which unity was sought changed perforce from the political to the social question. Political democracy was no longer a satisfactory point of union since the north-German confederation was already established on the basis of universal suffrage, and whatever its failings in respect to democracy were, the attraction was gone from the plank which had formed the great rallying cry of the alliance between workers and the lower middle class. What remained was the national issue, but it was precisely here that the changed situation dissolved the former basis of the coalition. With the first step in the realization of German unity, the national question which as an abstraction had provided a neutral matrix for political demands no longer fulfilled that function. The issues which had been subordinated under national ideas came forth on their own. It was Johann Baptiste von Schweitzer, head of Lassalle's General German Workers' Union, who sounded the keynote of the period to come, when he wrote in 1866 that "the freedom question, this greatest and noblest of all questions of human society, can find its solution no longer in direct but only in indirect ways—through the material interests of the fourth estate; the political movement in Europe is decayed and senile and must give way more and more to the social-political movements of the working class." [143] This was a sign of the times. Socially-minded politicians like Jacoby, Sonnemann, Bebel and Liebknecht became the most active agents of the People's Party from the latter part of 1866. The social issue gradually became its paramount concern.

Concentrated agitation for the refounding of the People's Party on the basis of the social issue began early in 1868 and met with a temporary but unstable success. The primary target of this activity was the labor movement, which middle-class politicians like Sonnemann and working-class organizers like Bebel and Liebknecht agreed must furnish the mass support of any democratic politics. The arena of the agitation was provided by the Federation of German Workers' Unions, which was still at this time a cross-section of German radicalism: it included some Educational Unions connected with the Prussian Progressive Party, but the bulk of them were divided between Sonnemann on the one hand and Bebel and Liebknecht on the other. Although these leaders were all members of the People's Party their political aims were no longer the same. Sonnemann wanted to make the Federation the core of the People's Party while Bebel and Liebknecht now thought in terms of an autonomous social democratic movement which would be allied with the People's Party. [144] At the Nuremberg Congress of the Federation the majority endorsed Bebel's resolution which made the program of the First International the program of the Federation. The Progressive Unions seceded, but the delegates from the People's Party voted for the Bebel program under Sonnemann's urging, in order to prevent an open break. This was still possible because the First International's program of 1867 was not yet openly socialist: it emphasized that the conquest of political freedom was the first and necessary condition for the social emancipation of the workers and went no further towards socialization than the demand for the nationalization of the means of transportation and communication.[145] This decision of Sonnemann's was endorsed at the People's Party's Stuttgart Congress of September 20, 1868, which marked the high point of its unity with the workers' movement.

> It [the German People's Party] recognizes that the political and social questions are indivisible—that is, that the economic emancipation of the working classes and the realization of political freedom are mutually conditioning.[146]

The Congress called for unlimited freedom of association, gratuitous education, encouragement of cooperatives, worker protective legislation, the ten-hour day, and the extension of factory inspection.[147] On the strength of this program the workers' Federation retained their connection with the Party, but there were ominous portents in the self-imposed absence of Bebel and Liebknecht for the sake of party unity and in the acceptance of the program by the Wuerttemberg democrats only on the narrowly practical grounds of the party's need for working-class support and on the assumption that the party and labor movement would pursue their common political goals together and their diverse social goals independently.[148]

The dissolution of this precarious unity followed within a year. The Brussels meeting of the First International, from September 6th to the 12th, 1868, had formally approved the principle of the socialization of all landed property, and the subsequent endorsement of this plank by both Schweitzer's General German Workers' Union and the Bebel-Liebknecht Federation of German Workers' Unions initiated an open and bitter competition of the two organizations for the possession of the German labor movement on an independent socialist basis. In this struggle Bebel and Liebknecht found their connection with the middle-class democracy to be a liability, and in August 1869 they convoked the German workers' congress at Eisenach which became the constituent convention of the Social Democratic Workers' Party. The Federation of German Worker's Unions convened at the close of the Eisenach congress and dissolved itself. Therewith the labor organization which had been founded by the German liberals to combat the exclusive workers' movement went itself over into the socialist camp.

But if Sonnemann's and Jacoby's maximum policy of merging the workers' movement with the People's Party was fatally undermined by the formation of the socialist party, the minimum goal of political cooperation seemed still possible of attainment. Indeed, Julius Frese's *Democratic Correspondence* and Karl Mayer's *Stuttgart Observer* actually welcomed the new organization and declared that it provided a sound basis for combined action on the democratic political principles which were common to both parties.[149] The expression of such convictions was possible because of the moderate character of the founding program of the Social Democratic Workers' Party. Not only was "the establishment of the free democratic state" the first plank in its platform, but its immediate demands emphasized political reforms in this sense, with the social note entering only in the mild proposals for progressive income and inheritance taxes and for state support of producers' cooperatives. Even the longer-range principles were cautiously phrased: while "the economic dependence of workers on capitalists" was pronounced to be at the root of every kind of slavery, political freedom was still declared to be "the most indispensable precondition for the economic emancipation of the working classes," the struggle for the emancipation of the workers was announced as "a fight . . . for equal rights and equal duties," and the destruction of the "present form of production" was defined in the innocuous formula of securing "the full yield of his labor for every worker." [150]

In the months that followed, however, even this last hope of democratic unity was smashed. In September 1869 the Basel Congress of the First International raised the socialization of landed property from an approved principle to programmatic status, and this move unleashed the latent hostility in the moderate wing of the People's Party. The main protagonist was Julius Frese who, in a series of articles against the Basel resolution in Karl Mayer's *Stuttgart Observer,* reasserted the absolute ideality of the radical principle of freedom and therewith completed the isolation of his party. He declared that democracy begins with the individual and his natural rights, including his right to property, and is completed with the federal state which respects these rights; communism starts with the state and is completed by despotism; the German social democrats endorsed communism at Basel, and hence there could be no cooperation with them; the workers might be drawn from the People's Party by a diversity of interests but they would ultimately return to it on the ground of its essentially ethical function of emancipating the oppressed in all classes of society.[151] The socialists' response was to accept frankly the notion of a division between an ideal political liberty and real social interests and to declare open war upon the People's Party. In a series of articles during February and March 1870 Bebel accused the People's Party of a complete incapacity to understand the social problem. He attributed to the Populists the assumption that "political freedom is really all that man can demand," and he indicated that for his own social democracy political freedom was "not an end but a means to an end"—that is, to "the creation of economic equality." [152] The Stuttgart Congress of the Social Democratic Workers' Party of June 1870 put the seal of political action upon this battle of words by adopting the Basel resolution of the International into its own program and rejecting cooperation with the People's Party in future elections.

Toward the end of August, in 1870, Guido Weiss, one of the few northern organizers of the People's Party, wrote a fitting epitaph for the German radicalism that had held itself above the national and social temptations of the decisive 60's: "The concept of our party has become so pure that it is losing all corporeality . . . I see no more light before us." [153]

Epilogue

After 1871 the initiative in the struggle for political freedom passed from the hands of the liberal middle class that had waged it for a century. The pattern which had been established during the settlement of the German problem between 1866 and 1871 was hardened into permanent institutional forms, and the liberal movement, bereft of direct possibilities of development, adapted itself to routine activity within the given constitutional and political framework. The German Constitution of 1871, grounded in the initiative of the Prussian monarchy, validated by agreement with the local dynasties and the independent cities, and buttressed by the free gift of an elective Reichstag with subordinate legislative functions, organized the new nation along lines which extended the tradition of the state in Germany to the national level. The primacy of the independent princely authority in government was maintained, and this primacy continued to be based both on its control over the means of power and on its capacity to ally itself with liberal institutions of limited efficacy. The constitution of the national state in this wonted design removed the last area of flexibility from German political life and drove the center of opposition to the established system into outlying confessional and social fields. The claims of society against the state were henceforward to be represented, in different ways, predominantly by political Catholicism and political socialism. Political liberalism, which had fought frontally in the main arena over the forms of the state and had been defeated, was calcified into an institutionalized party existence. It became compatible with the recently constitutionalized Germany and pressed only for certain policies from it.

It is hardly surprising, then, to find that the pattern of liberal politics for the half-century of the Empire's duration scarcely changed at all from its structure and posture in 1870. Moderates, radicals, and dualists preserved their identities by organizing in separate party molds which stifled their further development. They continued to be dominated more by their respective approaches to politics than by substantive political goals, for their activity consisted primarily in the characteristic responses which they made to issues presented by governmental initiative.

The organ of the moderates was the National Liberal Party, from which the dualists split off during 1880 and 1881. Representing the entrepreneurial and nationalistic bourgeoisie, the National Liberals pursued to the bitter end the path of compromise upon which they had embarked in 1866. Until 1879 they collaborated with Bismarck in the enactment of the practical liberal legislation which established the economic and juridical individualism requisite for citizens' unity in the new Germany, and then they followed him one step further in supporting his policies of tariff protection and anti-socialism during the 80's. The decision to proceed from this to actual coalition with the Conservatives, initiated in the Cartel of 1887 and continued intermittently throughout the life of the Empire, represented but a natural further accommodation. In the Wilhelminian era, the National Liberals' wholehearted support for the imperialism, militarism, and interest legislation which were the stock-in-trade of government policy made the party one of the pillars of the existing regime. Behind this approach were a frank dedication to the material requirements of German industry and a predilection for influence upon the governors of the state rather than for parliamentary control of it. Their subscription to the ideal of national solidarity gave moral cover to a state whose chief function was conceived to be the dispensation of material benefits through the use of power. The National Liberals thus led important sections of the German bourgeoisie into a political alliance with the authoritarian state and a social alliance with the landed aristocracy whereby the bourgeoisie gave their support to the established order in exchange for protection against competition and against social democracy.

The juristic theory which doubled for the official political philosophy of the Empire during the last third of the 19th century corresponded more to the National Liberal mentality than to the views of any other single group. Rudolf Gneist's doctrine of the *Rechtsstaat,* from which all oppositional elements had now been removed, set the tone for the adaptation of the old liberal political ideal to cover the legal reality of the new national state.

Taking the social class conflict as his starting-point, Gneist refused to society any essential role in the sovereignty of the state. He included in this *dementi* the political parties and ideals of western constitutionalism, which he deemed destructive expressions of society. He set the state over society, made it completely independent of society, and assigned to it the decisive role in controlling the class struggle. In constitutionalism he saw the middle-class ambitions for domination of the state which he condemned as thoroughly inimical to the *Rechtsstaat*. The concept of *Rechtsstaat*, that barometer of 19th-century liberalism, was no longer defined in terms of a state which permitted to the individual rights apart from the state. It became now simply the kind of state whose power was articulated in legal modes of action—that is, in measures which conformed to general rules. The rights which it permitted—private, civil, or political—were all gauged by their function in preserving this true nature of the state. "Society can find the personal freedom, the moral and spiritual development of the individual, only in permanent subordination to a constant higher power." [1] *Recht* thus became a formal attribute of *Staat*. With the National Liberals, the formula which had successively resolved the problems of spiritual and material liberty within the existing order came to include political liberty as well. The moderate conception of freedom had come full circle.

The political radicals, too, invested themselves in a party form which perpetuated their characteristic attitudes and closed them off from further essential development after 1870. The southern German People's Party remained restricted in its influence to the Frankfurt and Wuerttemberg areas. The burden of political radicalism on the national level was borne by the Progressives— the Liberal People's Party, as they called themselves through most of the period. Despite the formal incorporation of a social plank into their platform from 1884 on, fundamentally the Progressives continued the pattern of political behavior, which they had adopted during the 60's, of insisting categorically upon guarantees of individual liberties in the policies sponsored by the government within the constitutional system. The impact of increasing practical pressures upon this pattern was to harden the doctrinaire approach into a rigid dogmatism and at the same time to moderate the substance of the dogma. Under Eugen Richter, who ruled dictatorially over the Party from 1875 until his death in 1906, this combination took two forms: popular freedom was defined more and more in terms of an economic laissez-faire uncompromisingly oriented against both paternalism and socialism, and the political tactic appropriate to this policy was vested more and more in the negative criticism of measures proposed from either direction. Implacable opponent of protection, of welfare legislation, of army increases, and, most characteristically, of government budgets, Eugen Richter became the symbol of a Progressive Party that was still trying to make an absolute liberal ideal square with the growing immediacy of the middle-class' concern for their material interests. And after Richter's death it was scarcely inconsistent with this pattern for the Progressives to add elements simultaneously to both sides of the combination. To its formal radicalism it added an overt campaign against the three-class Prussian suffrage. To its moderate policies it added its membership in the governmental Buelow-Block against the Centrists and the Social Democrats and its approval of army increases in exchange for control over their extent. In the last years of the Imperial regime the Progressives found their due place in the German political picture when they joined in an intermittently operative coalition with the Catholic Center and the Social Democracy and became the one member of the alliance that went along with but never initiated its sporadic opposition to official policy.

Between the National Liberals and the Progressives the dualists still wandered uncertainly, frustrated by the failure of their dreams for liberal unity. They embodied the only flexibility left in the liberal movement, but they too were forced to take a separate institutional form which perpetuated their distinctive attitude. Originally a self-conscious grouping within the National Liberal Party, they organized themselves into an independent party formation which as "The Secession" split from the left wing of the National Liberals in 1881 and joined the Progressives in 1884, and as the Liberal Association split from the right wing of the Progressives in 1893 to lead an autonomous political existence until 1910. Behind this wavering course lay the dualists' typical striving to maintain a balance between the demands of practical effectiveness and the requirements of the liberal conscience. During the 70's they grew increasingly restive in a National Liberal Party whose support of Bismarck failed to drive him beyond the enactment of the purely material aspects of individual freedom. The issue of free trade which was the immediate occasion of their secession in 1881 was not simply a question of economic interests. It symbolized the practical consequences of the disregard for liberal principle which had already troubled the dualists in the issues of the Septennate, the Press Law, and the *Kulturkampf* of the preceding decade. But after they joined the Progressives they were similarly maintained in the self-consciousness of their specific political identity by Richter's dogmatically critical approach to questions of national interest on which they were ever ready to bargain. When they withdrew in 1893 it was to accept the government's proposal for an army increase in exchange for the concession of the two-year service rule. Seeking a mean between principles and interests, the dualists wanted, during the Empire as on the eve of it, to collaborate in the politics of nationalism in order to wrest from it the force required for the liberalization of the state. By 1910, however, the political mobility of this group ended: it merged into a united Progressive Party and accommodated itself to the current rules of party politics until the fall of the regime.

But if the dualistic tendency followed the moderate and the radical in the adaptation of its political activity to the institutional stagnation of the Empire, the same cannot be said of its theory. Unlike the two more extreme wings of the liberal movement, whose single-minded dedication to policies of creeping compromise and defensive principle, respectively, left no scope for further theorizing, the instability of the equilibrium in liberal dualism spurred political and social thought. Eduard Lasker foreshadowed this development at the very beginning of the Empire, when he indicated that the relationship between ideal principle and empirical fact which had just been established was neither satisfactory in itself nor capable of further growth. Principles which are not embodied in practice are useless, wrote

Lasker, and the older liberal principles are no longer capable of getting themselves embodied.

> What the previously developed ideas could establish with certainty about the state is already applied; these theories and principles do not lead further and are scorned; new sources of knowledge are not yet discovered or have not yet been made productive.[2]

Lasker suggested, as the only possible course of action, an immersion into the world of concrete experience for the purpose of collecting the knowledge which would be required for new political principles and ideals appropriate to actual possibilities.

It was from this kind of thinking, which plumbed experience for ideals which could then form experience, that a new intellectual liberalism took its rise during the 1890's, and it was hardly a coincidence that this revival of intellectual politics was associated with the school of liberal dualism. Intellectually oriented politicians like Friedrich Naumann and Theodor Barth were at one time members of the Liberal Association, while political professors, like Max Weber, Hugo Preuss, and Theodor Mommsen had points of contact with it. This renewed intellectual liberalism, like its forbear in the early 19th century, strove to infuse with moral principles a state and a society whose institutions they deemed to be bound by narrow considerations of self-interest. But unlike the earlier effort to root the pure ideal of freedom in an amoral reality the new version of dualism attempted to balance realistic and ethical motifs within the ideal itself. From the industrial facts of the society they derived a social ethic and from the power conflicts of the national states they derived the ethic of democratic community. These moral impulses they attached to the older ideal of individual freedom for the purpose of intensifying its ethical validity and its practical effectiveness simultaneously. As Naumann wrote in his *Democracy and Empire,* which epitomized the new intellectual tendency: "The liberal principle will not be victorious without the liberalism of the masses . . . Liberalism will feel it a blessing, when it thinks its old principles through to their conclusions, to be able to face the new age freely and joyously."[3] Thus the ideal became a national, socially minded democracy with a realistic orientation. Freedom would be realized by a people's state, unified by the

Emperor, equalizing economic benefits at home and asserting the national interest powerfully abroad.

The revival of intellectual liberalism remained, like the pre-March original, a purely intellectual phenomenon as long as the Empire lasted. Not only was the political and constitutional structure of Germany as a whole too inflexible to receive it but even the liberal parties were closed against it. Almost without exception the intellectuals could only stand outside the parties and carp at them for their materialism, their phrase-mongering, and their impotence.[4] The Liberal Association itself, whose general approach was most akin to the new thinking, proved impervious to it: Theodor Barth angrily resigned in 1908 to form a splinter Democratic Association, and even Naumann, the political contact-man for the intellectuals, used the Liberal Association only as a convenient base from which to work for a new party formation. The organizational and practical considerations which had gradually frozen the intellectual idealists out of political life after 1848 kept them out still.

It was not until the collapse of November 1918 broke the institutional crust of German politics that the intellectual liberals could make their way back into the political arena. During the period of fluidity that marked the German revolution the organizational structure of the parties and the political structure of the state opened momentarily and permitted a decisive intervention by these democratic professors and publicists. Theodor Wolff, the editor of the *Berlin Daily,* and the sociologist Alfred Weber took the initiative in the founding of the German Democratic Party, and they were soon joined in this attempt at a new departure in liberal politics by Naumann, Preuss, and Max Weber. This group also provided the democratic framework of the Weimar Republic: Preuss wrote the basic draft of the constitution, Max Weber participated decisively in its elaboration, and Naumann supplied its underlying theory with his notion of a "people's state" in which the sovereign political freedom of the people (*Volk*) would synthesize the individual liberty of the western tradition with the social liberty of the new eastern collectivism. But this final attempt by the liberal intellectuals to transcend the actual divisions of German politics and society through the ideal of freedom proved to be an epilogue rather than a new beginning. If the intellectuals had anticipated the development of a people still corporately oriented in 1848 and 1849 they lagged behind a people already dominated by class fears and nationalist hatreds in 1918 and 1919. The authoritarian state had fallen into eclipse, but the wonted traditions, attitudes, and institutions that had been formed in reference to it gradually resumed their accustomed sway and cut across the liberalizing tendencies of both the Democratic Party which the intellectuals created and the democratic republic which they sponsored.

The history of the Democratic Party during the Weimar Republic was dominated by two persistent developments: the hegemony of the old-line politicians and the evaporation of popular support. After 1919 the party structure which had been inherited from the Progressives and a section of the National Liberals was re-knit, and the organization pushed the intellectual interlopers out of the party leadership. To the democratic youth of the Weimar era, the Party apparatus was both rigid and anachronistic. It seemed "entangled in the narrow net of political responsibilities, [in] 'necessary considerations as to the reactions of the electorate,' " and rooted in "the ground of naked facts." Its leadership, consequently, appeared "so slow, . . . so much behind the time," "all fat and satisfied, immovable and without real enthusiasm." [5] Hence the old patterns of liberal politics reasserted themselves. The political passivity which had characterized political liberals through the Empire continued into the Republic. The tension between the nationalism which led the Democrats to reject the Versailles Treaty in June 1919, the commercial interests which formed their right-wing clientele, and the social policies which the left wing deemed an essential ingredient of freedom in the 20th century produced a stalemate which favored the resumption of habitual political routines. Not only did the Party continue to be at odds within itself but the traditional division within the political liberal movement was perpetuated with the rise of the German People's Party as the heir of National Liberalism. And to put the finishing touch on the recapitulation of Imperial liberalism the People's Party itself grew a left wing under Gustav Stresemann and the Berlin law professor, Wilhelm Kahl, which, as an unofficial grouping under the reminiscent title of the Liberal Association, tried in vain to create a united liberal party.

But even more important than this persistence of character was the resumption of the quantitative trend toward the weakening of liberal influence in parliament. The intensified awareness of middle-class interests under the threats of inflation and socialism combined with the intransigence of frustrated nationalism to hollow out the middle of the political spectrum. The political polarization which was the destiny of the Weimar Republic struck precisely at those parties whose origins lay in the assertion of political principle *vis-à-vis* the state, and the order of their decline was proportionate to the emphasis upon political principle which was associated with them. The Democratic Party was the first to go, falling from more than 5½ million votes and 75 Reichstag seats in January 1919 to some 336,000 votes and two seats in November 1932. Its clientele passed to the German People's Party and, characteristically for the era, to the Economic Party which rose to national predominance around 1924 on a frank appeal to the social interests of the petty bourgeoisie. The party of moderate liberalism was next on the political block. The German People's Party, which gained its high of almost 4 million votes and 65 seats in 1920, declined to 660,000 votes and 11 seats in November 1932, with the German National People's Party the chief beneficiary. But even this organ of traditional conservative nationalism paid for its past dedication to established political order: of more than 6 million votes and 103 seats in December 1924 but 3 million votes and 52 seats still remained to it in November 1932.[6] Its receiver was the National Socialist Workers' Party, whose electoral support balanced, during 1932, the 13 million Social Democratic and Communist votes. Behind the tendency toward the extremes was a popular revulsion against the traditional institutions and values of the state, in both their liberal and their conservative forms. Whether by radical reaction against government or moderate pressure upon it the liberals had created their political ideals in reference to the state, while the conservatives, modernized by their subscription to formal notions of law and their conversion to nationalism, still invested their ideals of hierarchy and authority in the wonted instruments of political power. It was highly symbolic that when the Democratic Party reorganized itself in 1930 in the defensive attempt to stave off its demise, the new name which was chosen to signify the common framework of its diverse claims to political democracy, individual initiative, social justice, and the assertion of national interests was the German State Party. It was equally symbolic that this old magical rallying cry of "the State" failed now either to secure the liberal unity for which it was employed or to stem the drift of voters away from the political liberalism which it was to justify.

And so, for almost the whole duration of the Weimar Republic the Social Democracy and the Catholic Center were left to carry the liberal democracy which the intellectuals had prepared. Despite some loss in voting strength from 1930 on—particularly by the socialists to the communists—both parties retained a solid core of popular support to the end of the Republic. The Social Democrats were, from start to finish, the wholehearted defenders of the Republic, while the Centrists, handicapped by serious internal divisions between their democratic and their conservative wings, gave it a steady, albeit more passive, support until its final crisis. But both parties, and with them the Republic, were ultimately weakened because the political freedom for which they became responsible was for them a condition of other, social goals rather than a goal in itself. For the Social Democrats this weakness took the form of the continuous fratricidal struggle with the Communists, whose use of socialism against democracy seriously limited the Social Democratic influence upon the working class and nullified it upon the middle classes. For the Center Party, the primacy of the clerical interest meant that the Party tended to follow rather than to direct the trend of opinion on the political issues that were more marginal to it. The result was the growing preponderance of its right wing and the development of its policies through the "constitutional dictatorship" of Bruening to the endorsement of the Nazi Enabling Act of March 1933. In the final analysis, it may be said that these parties operated toward their further ends on the assumption of a political freedom that was not yet actually secured in Germany. They were diverted by class divisions and religious divisions from the thorough-going reorganization of the state in the direction of democracy. The fear of bolshevism and the fear of a secular unitary state preserved traditional pillars of authority—the army, the bureaucracy, and the oligarchic structure of industry and agriculture—that stymied the spread of a democratic conscious-ness and opened the portals of government to National Socialism.

And what of the German attitude toward freedom today? In many ways the pre-Nazi patterns have simply been resumed by the German Federal Republic in Bonn.[7] The burdens of de-mocracy are still borne primarily by the Catholic party and the socialists. The political democrats (now organized in the Free Democratic Party) are still divided between a principled liberal group under Reinhold Mayer, a power-minded nationalist group under Thomas Dehler, and the moderate compromisers still in the government. Moreover, its decline from 12% of the popular vote in the federal elections of 1949 to 9.5% in the elections of 1953 might well indicate a revival of the trend toward the de-population of the party. Beyond the structure of parties, simi-larly, older institutions and habits remain prominent. If the Junkers have disappeared and the military influence is in at least a temporary eclipse, bureaucracy and industrialism have completely recuperated their wonted forms. Observers are in general agreed that democracy in Germany is still not so much a matter of active faith as a system of formal law and that its current liberal interpretation is the effect of Allied power, eco-nomic prosperity, and anti-totalitarian resentment operating in a political vacuum.

But one fundamental pattern has been broken, and in this rup-ture lies the possibility of a new concept of freedom. The Nazis smashed the age-old association of liberty with the authoritarian state. From the 16th century to the 20th, as this study has at-tempted to show, the political history of Germany had been dominated by the successive absorptions of the various claims to human freedom piecemeal into the structure of monarchical government without undermining the independent authority of that government. Starting from the identification of princely power with the chartered rights of the Imperial aristocracy and progressing through the gradual orientation of princely institutions and policies toward the more modern and generalized forms of liberty in spiritual, economic, social, constitutional, and national activities, the state in Germany had become both the actual organization and the ideal symbol for the compatible integration of these areas of individual freedom into the established order of political government and social hierarchy. It was against this expanding structure of traditional authority in the spheres of freedom that the German liberal movement had broken into its characteristic divisions during the 19th century. Certainly the distinction between moderates who looked for compromise, radicals who strove for sweeping reorganization, and a center group which could opt for either according to the circumstances had not been peculiar to German liberalism. What had been peculiar to it, however, was the diversion of these attitudes from political programs to fundamental approaches toward life. Where liberals in the western nations had been concerned primarily with the problem of the best kind of liberal politics, the German liberals had tended to focus and ultimately to split on the prior problem of the very possibility of liberal politics. The western liberals took for granted the malleability of a reality which for the Germans remained formidably resistant. The consequent preoccupation with the relationship between ideals and existence as a philosophical as well as a political issue had not only intensified the political divisions among German parties but had brought about a total investment in the approach rather than the substance of politics. The moderates pursued compromise unto an alliance with Franz von Papen and the cabinet of barons. The radicals pursed *Recht* unto a policy of categorical negation and isolation. The liberals of the center pursued balance unto a dualism of bewildered vacillation. The social reality that had pushed the German liberals into this formal posturing in politics was the peculiar speed of commercial and industrial transformation in central Europe, for the kind of individualized society which could feed them positive political sustenance enjoyed but a brief span of influence between the epochs dominated by conservative corporativism and collectivist large-scale organization. But even more important had been the political reality of the authoritarian state which broke up the total force of modern man's claims to freedom into separate stages and, one by one, satisfied the practical side of them.

It was this primal association between freedom and the traditional state that the Nazis destroyed. The political rights of the people, the civil rights of the individual, and even the remnants of the old *Libertaet* which had been perpetuated in the federal structure of the Second Empire and the Republic—all these were totally and publicly integrated into the racial people and its Nazi Party. The task of this people and this Party was proclaimed to be the foundation of a new kind of state which would realize categorically different values from the old. Despite the wide-spread rejection of the Nazi experience in postwar Germany, one condition that has carried over is the bankruptcy of the state as a liberalizing institution. Dominant now is an attitude which views the state as a morally neutral, purely utilitarian organization of public power. The prevalent notion that the "juristic state *(Justizstaat)*" has replaced the "state of law *(Rechtsstaat)*" [8] and the current disenchantment of even such a traditional bastion as the bureaucracy with the moral and political ideals customarily attributed to the state in Germany[9] are indications of the new devaluation of the state. If this is indeed the general attitude, then the central strand in the German political tradition has been cut and all possibilities lie open for the future.

Notes

Introduction

1. Friedrich Meinecke, *Weltbuergertum und Nationalstaat* (Munich and Berlin, 1907); Ernst Troeltsch, "The Ideas of Natural Law and Humanity in World Politics," Eng. tr. in Otto Gierke, *Natural Law and the Theory of Society, 1500-1800* (Cambridge, 1934), I, 201-222; Hajo Holborn, "Der deutsche Idealismus in sozialgeschichtlicher Beleuchtung," in *Historische Zeitschrift*, vol. 174 (1952), 359-384.

2. Felix Gilbert, "Political Thought of the Renaissance and Reformation," in *Huntington Library Quarterly*, IV (1941), 456-458; Otto Hintze, "Die Epochen der Kirchenregiment," in *Historische und Politische Aufsaetze* (2nd ed., Berlin, n.d.), III, 109-112.

Chapter I. Society and Politics

1. Note the salutary warning against the assumption that royal decrees became *ipso facto* operative regulations, in *Acta Borussica: Die Getreide-handelspolitik* (Berlin, 1910), III, 40.

2. In terms of proportion of population engaged, estimated at 4:1 in 1800. J. Kuczynski, *Die Bewegung der deutschen Wirtschaft von 1800 bis 1946* (2nd ed., Meisenheim, 1948), p. 16.

3. Reinhold Koser, "Staat und Gesellschaft zur Hoehezeit des Absolutismus," in *Die Kultur der Gegenwart* (Berlin, 1908), part II, section II, vol. I, 247-248.

4. Ernst Meier, *Preussen und die franzoesische Revolution* (Leipzig, 1908), p. 26.

5. Gustav Schmoller, *Deutsches Staedtewesen im aelterer Zeit* (Bonn and Leipzig, 1922), p. 243; R. Koser, *Staat und Gesellschaft,* p. 252. In eastern Germany the subordination of the towns dates from the 15th century. See F. L. Carsten, *The Origins of Prussia* (Oxford, 1954), pp. 137-148.

6. Severinus von Monzambano (Samuel von Pufendorf), *Ueber die Verfassung des deutschen Reiches* (Berlin, 1922, Ger. tr. by Harry Bresslau), p. 35.

7. Friedrich Luetge, *Deutsche Sozial- und Wirtschaftsgeschichte* (Heidelberg, 1952), pp. 205-206.

8. *Acta Borussica: Getreidehandelspolitik,* II, 257-259; III, 128-162. Some of the Baltic towns never recovered from the economic crisis of the 15th century. F. Carsten, *op. cit.,* p. 135.

9. Richard Schroeder, *Lehrbuch der deutschen Rechtsgeschichte* (6th ed., Berlin, 1922), p. 941; O. Hintze, "Epochen der Kirchenregiment," in *Historische und Politische Aufsaetze,* III, 122-123.

10. Hans Wolff, *Die Weltanschauung der deutschen Aufklaerung in geschichtlicher Entwicklung* (Bern, 1949), pp. 16-17.

11. Territorial, or state-wide, diets continued to exist in Mecklenburg, Hesse, Saxony, and Brunswick. In Wuerttemberg, where the territorial estates attained the height of their influence, the dominant aristocracy was a burgher

oligarchy rather than the landed nobility, since in this area the latter group tended to be autonomous Imperial Knights.

12. The status of kingship which might have sharpened princely self-consciousness *vis-à-vis* the nobility into a categorical division was, down to the end of the Old Regime, limited in Germany to the King of Prussia from 1701 and the special case of the Elector of Hanover, who was King not only of but in England from 1714.

13. S. Pufendorf, *Verfassung*, pp. 32-33.

14. Bruno Gebhardt, *Handbuch der deutschen Geschichte* (7th ed., Berlin, 1931), II, 189-190.

15. R. Schroeder, *Lehrbuch*, p. 961.

16. Moritz Ritter, *Deutsche Geschichte im Zeitalter der Gegenreformation und des Dreissigjaehrigen Krieges* (Stuttgart, 1889), I, 33-36.

17. S. Pufendorf, *Verfassung*, pp. 58, 62.

18. Guenther Franz, *Der deutsche Bauernkrieg* (Munich and Berlin, 1933), pp. 134-135, 469; F. Luetge, *op. cit.*, p. 159.

19. E.g. Petitions of the Baltringer Villages, February 16, 1525, in G. Franz, *Bauernkrieg: Aktenband*, pp. 150-151, and their famous Twelve Articles, in G. Franz, *Bauernkrieg*, pp. 197-199.

20. *Ibid.*, pp. 259-263.

21. Indictment of Hans Vischer of Sterzing [Austria], April 27, 1526, in G. Franz, *Bauernkrieg: Aktenband*, p. 336; letter of Wilhelm Truchsess, Baron of Waldburg, to Duke George of Saxony, March 14, 1526, in *ibid.*, p. 386.

22. Reinhold Koser, *Koenig Friedrich der Grosse* (3rd ed., Stuttgart and Berlin, 1904), I, 212.

23. Frederick to Joseph, April 14, 1778, in *Oeuvres de Frederic le Grand* (Berlin, 1847), VI, 186.

24. Frederick's Project for a League to be formed among the Princes of Germany, in *ibid.*, VI, 211-214.

25. R. Koser, *Friedrich der Grosse*, II, 617-618.

26. J. W. Goethe, *Werke* (Leipzig, 1909-1912), V, 34.

27. R. Koser, *Friedrich der Grosse*, II, 613.

28. Thus the coincidence of commoners in the high bureaucracy with the decisive epoch of state-building in the reign of the Prussian King Frederick William I (1713-1740).

29. Karl Biedermann, *Deutschland im 18. Jahrhundert* (Leipzig, 1854), I, 92.

30. "I am led by two principles: the one is honor, the other the interest of the state which Heaven has charged me with governing." Friedrich Meinecke, *Die Idee der Staatsraeson in der neueren Geschichte* (Munich and Berlin, 1924), p. 351.

31. *Ibid.*, pp. 346-347.

32. "Essai sur les formes de gouvernement et sur les devoirs des souverains," in *Oeuvres de Frederic le Grand*, IX, 196, 200.

33. *Ibid.*, IX, 197.

34. *Ibid.*, IX, 201-207.

35. *Ibid.*, IX, 208.

36. "Miroir des princes," in *ibid.*, IX, 6.

37. "Essai sur les formes de gouvernement," in *ibid.*, IX, 208.

38. "You are so strongly bound with your *patrie*, without knowing it, that you can neither isolate nor separate yourself from it without regretting

your fault . . . Patriotism is not a thing of reason—it really exists . . . Here are the bonds which should unite you to society: the interest of the persons you should love, yours and that of the government, which, indissolubly united, compose what is called the general good of the whole community." "Lettres sur l'amour de la patrie," in *ibid.*, IX, 220.

39. "Essai sur les formes de gouvernement," in *ibid.*, IX, 200.

40. "Lettres sur l'amour de la patrie," in *ibid.*, IX, 238-239.

41. *Ibid.*, IX, 224-225; "Dissertation sur les raisons d'etablir ou d'abroger les lois," in *ibid.*, IX, 12.

42. *Allgemeines Landrecht fuer die Preussischen Staaten* (2nd ed., Berlin, 1794), I, 12-14.

43. Wilhelm Dilthey, "Studien zur Geschichte des deutschen Geistes," in *Gesammelte Schriften* (Leipzig and Berlin, 1927), III, 183.

44. "Essai sur les formes de gouvernement," in *Oeuvres de Frederic le Grand, IX*, 205-206.

45. "Dialogue de morale a l'usage de la jeune noblesse" and "Lettre sur l'education," in *ibid.*, IX, 101-127.

46. "Lettres sur l'amour de la patrie," in *ibid.*, IX, 216.

47. *Acta Borussica: Getreidehandelspolitik*, IV, 154.

48. Wilhelm Treue, "Adam Smith in Deutschland. Zum Problem des 'Politischen Professors' zwischen 1776 und 1810," in *Deutschland und Europa* (Duesseldorf, 1951), pp. 101-135.

49. *Acta Borussica: Getreidenhandelspolitik*, IV, 163; E. Meier, *Preussen und die franzoesische Revolution*, p. 150.

50. Max Lehmann, *Freiherr vom Stein* (Leipzig, 1902), I, 17-22, 31-38; Leopold von Ranke, *Denkwuerdigkeiten des Staatskanzlers Fuersten von Hardenberg* (Leipzig, 1877), I, 13-16.

51. "Perhaps more strongly than in other countries was the higher official-dom in Prussia seized by the individualistic economic ideas of the age. . . . Among the Prussian ministers and chamber presidents of that period there was hardly one who had not also been an estate owner." *Acta Borussica: Getreidehandelspolitik*, IV, 154.

52. *Acta Borussica: Getreidehandelspolitik*, I, 380-382.

53. The career of this enterprise shows the contradictory nature of Prus-sian state policy, which both led the way in the promotion of a commercial, capitalistic agriculture and refused to provide for the conditions necessary to it. Founded in 1770, the company never realized the 15% return antici-pated by Frederick, in part because of the small quantities of grain permitted for export. From 1779 the company showed a constant loss, and it folded in 1786. An Oder Trading Company, projected by Frederick on the same basis, did not even obtain a sufficient financial backing to get started. *Acta Borussica: Getreidehandelspolitik*, IV, 14-23.

54. This distinction is made by the German 19th century economist Roscher. See Theodor von der Goltz, *Geschichte der deutschen Landwirt-schaft* (Stuttgart and Berlin, 1902), I, 299.

55. *Ibid.*, I, 375-377.

56. Georg Friedrich Knapp, *Die Bauernbefreiung und der Ursprung der Landarbeiter in den aelteren Theilen Preussens* (2nd ed., Munich and Leip-zig, 1927), I, 49-64.

57. *Ibid.*, I, 84-85; T. von der Goltz, *op. cit.*, I, 434-435.

58. *Allgemeines Landrecht fuer die Preussischen Staaten*, II, 342-343.

59. T. von der Goltz, *op. cit.*, I, 425-427; G. Knapp, *op. cit.*, I, 92-93.

60. See Leo Balet, *Die Verbuergerlichung der deutschen Kunst, Literatur, und Musik im 18. Jahrhundert* (Leipzig, 1936).

61. Walter Diamont, *Studien zur Wirtschaftsgeschichte der Staedte im Pommern, der Kur- und Neumark unter Friedrich dem Grossen und seinen Nachfolgern bis 1806* (Berlin, 1913), pp. 5-6.

62. Gustav Schmoller, *Umrisse und Untersuchungen zur Verfassungs-, Verwaltungs-, und Wirtschaftsgeschichte* (Leipzig, 1898), p. 555.

63. Werner Sombart, *Der Bourgeois* (Munich and Leipzig, 1913), p. 183.

64. G. Schmoller, *Deutsches Staedtewesen*, pp. 305-322.

65. *Ibid.*, pp. 323-324, 340, 371-372; R. Koser, *Staat und Gesellschaft*, p. 352.

66. The emigres who came to Germany—and particularly to central and eastern Germany—usually had little capital. Hintze has pointed out that the older colonies of French and Jews in Berlin had no opportunity to utilize their business capacity until Frederick II put capital at their disposal. See *Acta Borussica: Seidenindustrie* (Berlin, 1892), III, 296.

67. The argument for the liberal meaning of mercantilism is made by the whole group of official Prussian historians participant in the Acta Borussica. It is most explicit in Gustav Schmoller, *The Mercantile System and its Historical Significance* (New York, 1931).

68. W. Sombart, *Der Bourgeois*, pp. 112-113; K. Biedermann, *Deutschland im 18. Jahrhundert*, I, 277-281.

69. Max Lehmann, *Freiherr vom Stein*, I, 64-67.

70. On the artificiality of the Prussian economy, see Mirabeau's *De la monarchie prussienne sous Frederic le Grand* (London, 1788), V, 338-342.

71. G. Schmoller, "Das brandenburgisch-preussische Innungswesen von 1640 bis 1800," in *Umrisse und Untersuchungen*, pp. 314-456 *passim*.

72. Compare *Acta Borussica: Wollindustrie* (Berlin, 1933), pp. 167-193, with *Acta Borussica: Seidenindustrie*, III, 282-311.

73. H. Mirabeau, *La monarchie prussienne*, IV, 228; E. von Meier, *op. cit.*, 46.

74. K. Biedermann, *Deutschland im 18. Jahrhundert*, I, 302; G. Schmoller, *Deutsches Staedtewesen*, pp. 280-289.

75. *Acta Borussica: Getreidehandelspolitik*, III, 8-12; *Acta Borussica: Seidenindustrie*, III, 295-296.

76. G. Schmoller, *Deutsches Staedtewesen*, pp. 371-373.

77. *Acta Borussica: Wollindustrie*, pp. 181-184.

78. K. Biedermann, *Deutschland im 18. Jahrhundert*, I, 112-116.

79. Fritz Valjavec, *Die Entstehung der politischen Stroemungen in Deutschland, 1770-1815* (Munich, 1951), pp. 89-122.

80. *Ibid.*, pp. 100, 123-124.

Chapter II. Constitutional and Political Theory

1. Carlo Antoni, *Der Kampf wider die Vernunft: Zur Entstehungsgeschichte des deutschen Freiheitsgedankens* (Stuttgart, 1951), pp. 89-103, 159-200.

2. Otto Gierke, *Natural Law and the Theory of Society* (Cambridge, 1934, Eng. tr. by Ernest Barker), I, 36-37.

3. Otto Gierke, *The Development of Political Theory* (New York, 1939, Eng. tr. by Bernard Freyd), pp. 166-167, 245.

4. Erik Wolf, *Grosse Rechtsdenker der deutschen Geistesgeschichte* (3rd ed., Tuebingen, 1951), pp. 195-196.

5. K. Biedermann, *op. cit.*, I, 13-19; O. Gierke, *Development*, pp. 159-160.

6. Thus in Seckendorf's *Teutscher Fuersten-Staat* (1656). See Horst Kraemer, "Der deutsche Kleinstaat des 17. Jahrhunderts im Spiegel von Seckendorff's 'Teutschem Fürstenstaat,'" in *Zeitschrift des Vereins fuer Thueringische Geschichte und Altertumskunde* (1922/4), XXV, 16-64.

7. E. Wolf, *Grosse Rechtsdenker*, pp. 233-239.

8. S. Pufendorf, *Ueber die Verfassung*, pp. 5, 85, 106. Italics mine.

9. *Ibid.*, p. 94.

10. *Ibid.*, pp. 85-94.

11. *Ibid.*, pp. 114-115.

12. *Ibid.*, pp. 115-118.

13. Samuel Pufendorf, *De Jure Naturae et Gentium Libri Octo* (Oxford, 1934, Eng. tr. by C. H. and W. A. Oldfather), II, 1012.

14. J. C. Bluntschli, *Geschichte der neueren Statswissenschaft, Allgemeines Statsrecht und Politik* (3rd ed., Munich and Leipzig, 1881), pp. 150-151.

15. Samuel Pufendorf, *Elementorum Jurisprudentiae Universalis Libri Duo* (Oxford, 1931, Eng. Tr. by W. A. Oldfather), II, 19.

16. *Ibid.*, II, 7-20, 58, 71, 168.

17. *Ibid.*, II, 14.

18. S. Pufendorf, *De Jure Naturae*, II, 1010-1011.

19. *Ibid.*, II, 1015-1016, 1055-1056.

20. *Ibid.*, II, 1118.

21. S. Pufendorf, *Elementorum*, II, 289.

22. S. Pufendorf, *De Jure Naturae*, II, 1064.

23. *Ibid.*, II, 1063.

24. *Ibid.*, II, 1070.

25. *Ibid.*, II, 1074-1076.

26. *Ibid.*, II, 1077.

27. *Ibid.*, II, 1110.

28. *Ibid.*, II, 1105-1110; S. Pufendorf, *Elementorum*, II, 288.

29. S. Pufendorf, *De Jure Naturae*, II, 1111.

30. Quoted in J. C. Bluntschli, *op. cit.*, p. 222.

31. Thus: "Any action or inaction of the human understanding, insofar as it has to do with the concept of a thing," is not subject to the will of the prince. "No one should have to speak differently of his knowledge than he thinks." "Civil society has not arisen or been made because of the worship of God, it does not encourage piety, and it has not invented the worship of God; it does not need it as an instrument to rule subjects." "A Christian prince . . . cannot force his own subjects to his religion—not a single one, let alone all of them." *Kurze Lehrsaetze vom Recht eines christlichen Fuersten in Religionssachen* (1724), quoted in *ibid.*, pp. 227-229.

32. *Ibid.*, p. 227.

33. Private property, for example, was for Locke an inviolable natural right, for Thomasius a mere acquired right, subject therefore to the will of the state.

34. *Ibid.*

35. *Ibid.*, pp. 230-231. Even these sects, however, were not to be persecuted or tried penally by the prince; they were rather to be exiled, with all their property.

36. O. Gierke, *Natural Law*, II, 288-289, 296, 338; J. Bluntschli, *op. cit.*, pp. 225, 231-236.

37. *Ibid.*, pp. 237-244.

38. A detailed analysis of these works—*Vernunft-Lehre* (1692) and *Sitten-Lehre* (1692-96)—is given by H. Wolff, *Die Weltanschauung der deutschen Aufklaerung*, pp. 29-47.

39. Peter Klassen, *Die Grundlagen des aufgeklaerten Absolutismus* (Jena, 1929), pp. 89-100.

40. Although much of his philosophical scaffolding was rejected by the following generation, the main tenets of his political theory were spread by his Halle students who became important members of the Prussian administration and particularly by the writings of Frederick the Great until these tenets became the dominant theory of the Prussian state in the second half of the 18th century. See Wilhelm Dilthey, "Das Allgemeine Landrecht," in *Gesammelte Schriften* (Leipzig and Berlin, 1936), XII, 154-199, *passim*.

41. For this incompatibility see Werner Frauendienst, *Christian Wolff als Staatsdenker* (Berlin, 1927), pp. 92-95.

42. Christian Wolff, *Institutions du Droit de la Nature et des Gens* (Leyden, 1772, 1st Latin ed. 1750), II, 142; O. Gierke, *Natural Law*, II, 308.

43. O. Gierke, *Natural Law*, II, 294.

44. W. Frauendienst, *Christian Wolff*, p. 139.

45. O. Gierke, *Natural Law*, I, 175, 185.

46. C. Wolff, *Institutions*, II, 143-154.

47. *Ibid.*, II, 180.

48. W. Frauendienst, *Christian Wolff*, pp. 100-103.

49. C. Wolff, *Institutions*, II, 165-168, 180.

50. *Ibid.*, II, 156-168; W. Frauendienst, Christian *Wolff*, pp. 130-168; J. Bluntschli, *Geschichte des allgemeinen Statsrechts*, p. 221.

51. C. *Wolff*, Institutions, II, 139.

52. *Ibid.*, II, 141.

53. *Ibid.*, I, 20-25; Wilhelm Dilthey, *op. cit.*, XII, 158-160, 168, 178-181.

54. C. Wolff, *Institutions*, I, 24, 33, 52-53; *Ibid.*, II, 88.

55. *Ibid.*, I, 27; *Ibid.*, II, 158, 179.

56. W. Frauendienst, *Christian Wolff*, p. 126.

57. *Ibid.*, pp. 117-119.

58. C. Wolff, *Institutions*, II, 164-167.

59. C. Antoni, *op. cit.*, pp. 223, 248, 278-281.

60. [Friedrich Carl von Moser] *Der Herr and der Diener, geschildert mit patriotischer Freyheit* (Frankfurt/M., 1759), pp. 4, 11, 60, 87.

61. Quoted in F. Valjavec, *Politische Stroemungen*, pp. 139-140.

62. O. Gierke, *Natural Law*, II, 292, 352-353, 360.

63. *Ibid.*, I, 148; *Ibid.*, II, 345-346.

64. F. Valjavec, *Politische Stroemungen*, pp. 135-137, 142.

65. See Carl Friedrich Bahrdt, *Geschichte seines Lebens, seiner Meinungen und Schicksale, von ihm selbst geschrieben* (4 vols., Berlin, 1790) for his absorption in religion and neglect of politics.

66. Carl Friedrich Bahrdt, *Geschichte und Tagebuch meines Gefaengnisses*

nebst geheimen Urkunden und Aufschluessen ueber Deutsche Union (Berlin, 1790), appendix pp. 34, 42, 55-62.

67. E. Heinemann, *Zur Geschichte der Staatsanschauungen in Deutschland waehrend des XVIII. Jahrhunderts vor der franzoesischen Revolution* (Brunswick, 1915), pp. 71-81.

68. Waldemar Wenck, *Deutschland vor hundert Jahren* (Leipzig, 1887), I, 12-13.

69. *Ibid.*, I, 39-40.

70. F. Moser, *Herr und Diener*, pp. 45, 61, 101-106.

71. O. Gierke, *Natural Law*, I, 155.

72. F. Valjavec, *Politische Stroemungen*, pp. 100-105.

73. August Ludwig Schloezer, *Allgemeines Statsrecht und Stats-Verfassungslehre* (Goettingen, 1793), pp. 74-75, 96, 100-101.

74. *Ibid.*, p. 114.

75. *Ibid.*, pp. 105-107.

76. *Ibid.*, pp. 145-146.

77. *Ibid.*, pp. 99, 157.

78. *Ibid.*, pp. 114-115, 150.

79. *Ibid.*, pp. 63-71.

80. *Ibid.*, pp. 106-107.

81. *Ibid.*, pp. 153-154.

82. *Ibid.*, pp. 107, 162-168.

83. Justus Moeser, "Der jetzige Hang zu allgemeinen Gesetzen und Verordnungen ist der gemeinen Freiheit gefaehrlich," in *Gesellschaft und Staat: Eine Auswahl aus seinen Schriften* (Munich, 1921), pp. 159-164.

84. Justus Moeser, "Osnabrueckische Geschichte. Allgemeine Einleitung," in *ibid.*, pp. 81-86.

85. J. Moeser, "Der Staat mit einer Pyramide verglichen," in *ibid.*, p. 167; Wolfgang Samtleben, *Die Idee einer altgermanischen Volksfreiheit im vormaerzlichen deutschen Liberalismus* (Hamburg, 1935), p. 15.

Second Section. The Assumptions.

Introduction

1. See especially the recent Fritz Valjavec, *Die Entstehung der politischen Stroemunger in Deutschland, 1770-1815* (Munich, 1951), and Jacques Droz, *L'Allemagne et la Revolution francaise* (Paris, 1949), which covers the period from 1789 to 1801.

2. *Ibid.*, pp. 111-150; F. Valjavec, *op. cit.*, pp. 146-254.

Chapter III. The Philosophical Bases

1. For a critical discussion of Kant which emphasizes his confusion of his own distinctions, see Wilhelm Metzger, *Gesellschaft, Recht, und Staat in der Ethik des deutschen Idealismus* (Heidelberg, 1917), pp. 45-111.

2. R. Aris, *History of Political Thought in Germany from 1789-1815* (London, 1936), pp. 94, 121; O. Gierke, *Natural Law*, I, 134-135, 153; J. Droz, *L'Allemagne et la Revolution francaise*, pp. 48-49.

3. "Fragmente aus dem Nachlass," in G. Hartenstein, ed., *Immanuel Kant's Saemmtliche Werke* (Leipzig, 1868), VIII, 624.

4. Ernst Cassirer, *Kants Leben und Lehre* (Berlin, 1918), p. 435.

5. Immanuel Kant, *Foundations of the Metaphysics of Morals,* in Lewis White Beck, ed., *Immanuel Kant: Critique of Practical Reason and Other Writings in Moral Philosophy* (Chicago, 1949), p. 63.

6. None of Kant's writings in this period was dedicated wholly to politics, but he dealt with the subject at some length in his *Idea for a Universal History With a Cosmopolitan Intent* (1784), and briefly in his *What Is Orientation in Thinking?* (1786).

7. Immanuel Kant, *Idea for a Universal History With a Cosmopolitan Intent,* translated in Carl J. Friedrich, ed., *The Philosophy of Kant: Immanuel Kant's Moral and Political Writings* (New York, 1949), p. 118.

8. *Ibid.,* p. 121.

9. *Ibid.,* p. 122.

10. Immanuel Kant, *What Is Enlightenment?,* translated in Lewis White Beck, ed., *op. cit.,* p. 291. It was on this point that Kant asserted his admiration for Frederick the Great.

11. *Ibid.,* pp. 291-292.

12. I. Kant, *Idea for a Universal History,* p. 128.

13. Immanuel Kant, *What Is Orientation in Thinking?,* in L. W. Beck, ed., *op. cit.,* pp. 304-305.

14. I. Kant, *Idea for a Universal History,* p. 119.

15. *Ibid.,* pp. 121-122.

16. I. Kant, *What Is Enlightenment?,* p. 286.

17. I. Kant, *Idea for a Universal History,* p. 123.

18. I. Kant, *What Is Enlightenment?,* pp. 287-288. The reversal is not quite so neat as it seems. By "private" in this context, Kant meant not personal but vocational—that is, reason was privately exercised by men in their capacity as holders of civil posts or offices, and publicly exercised by men in their capacity as thinkers communicating with a reading public. The personal right to think was impossible for Kant without the right of public communication. See his *What Is Orientation in Thinking?,* p. 303.

19. I. Kant, *What Is Enlightenment?,* p. 291.

20. *Ibid.*

21. I. Kant, *Idea for a Universal History,* p. 128. Here Kant talks of the folly of interfering with "civic freedom" and with the citizen's "seeking his welfare in any way he chooses" in economic life.

22. I. Kant, *What Is Enlightenment?,* p. 292.

23. *Ibid.,* p. 290.

24. *Ibid.,* pp. 289-290.

25. I. Kant, "Rezensionen von J. G. Herders Ideen zur Philosophie der Geschichte der Menschheit" (1785), in Ernst Cassirer, ed., *Immanuel Kants Werke* (11 vols., Berlin, 1912-1922), IV, 200. Hereafter cited as *Werke.*

26. I. Kant, *Mutmasslicher Anfang der Menschengeschichte* (1786), in *Werke,* IV, 334.

27. *Ibid.,* IV, 336.

28. I. Kant, *Idea for a Universal History, passim* but esp. p. 127.

29. *Ibid.,* p. 120. Kant's italics.

30. *Ibid.,* pp. 116-117.

31. Thus Kant simply assumed the bare existence of freedom of the will

in the course of his discussion. The grounds of his refusal to give it any definition was obvious from his indifferent opening clause: "No matter what conception one may form of the freedom of the will in metaphysics . . ." Clearly he was viewing the problem as one of knowledge and not of morality. *Ibid.*, p. 116.

32. Kant made this double concern explicit when he wrote: "Just as, on the one hand, we limit reason, lest in leaving the guiding thread of empirical conditions it should go straying into the *transcendent*, . . . so, on the other hand, we limit the law of the purely empirical employment of the understanding, lest it should presume to decide as to the possibility of things in general, and should declare the *intelligible* to be impossible. . . ." *Critique of Pure Reason* (London, 1933, Eng. tr. of 2nd ed. by Norman Kemp Smith), p. 481, Kant's italics.

33. *Ibid.*, pp. 485-486.
34. *Ibid.*, p. 320.
35. *Ibid.*, pp. 632-633.
36. *Ibid.*, p. 481.
37. *Ibid.*, p. 556.
38. *Ibid.*, p. 479, Kant's italics.
39. *Ibid.*, p. 629.
40. *Ibid.*, pp. 638-643.
41. *Ibid.*, p. 633.
42. *Ibid.*, pp. 637-638.
43. *Ibid.*, p. 312. Kant's italics.
44. Immanuel Kant, *Foundations of the Metaphysics of Morals,* in L. W. Beck, ed., *op. cit.,* pp. 51-52.
45. For this point see Beck's introduction in *op. cit.,* p. 17.
46. "Thus the question, 'How is a categorical imperative possible?' can be answered to this extent: We can cite the only presupposition under which it is alone possible. This is the idea of freedom . . . But how this presupposition is itself possible can never be discerned by any human reason . . . To presuppose the freedom of the will is not only quite possible . . . but it is also unconditionally necessary that a rational being conscious of his causality through reason and thus conscious of a will different from desires should practically presuppose it." I. Kant, *Foundations of the Metaphysics of Morals,* p. 115; "The concept of freedom, insofar as its reality is proved by an apodictic law of practical reason, is the keystone of the whole architecture of the system of pure reason and even of speculative reason. All other concepts (those of God and immortality) which, as mere ideas, are unsupported by anything in speculative reason now attach themselves to the concept of freedom and gain, with it and through it, stability and objective reality." I. Kant, *Critique of Practical Reason,* in L. W. Beck, ed., *op. cit.,* p. 118.
47. I. Kant, *Foundations of the Metaphysics of Morals,* pp. 101-102. "Therefore a free will and a will under moral laws is identical."
48. *Ibid.*, p. 102.
49. *Ibid.*, p. 80.
50. *Ibid.*, p. 87.
51. *Ibid.*, p. 93.
52. *Ibid.*, p. 91.
53. *Ibid.*, pp. 88-89.

54. *Ibid.,* p. 93.

55. Immanuel Kant, *Critique of Practical Reason,* in L. Beck, *op. cit.,* pp. 176-179.

56. *vid. supra,* p. 93-94.

57. *vid. supra,* p. 97.

58. I. Kant, *Der Streit der Fakultaeten* (1798), in Ernst Cassirer, ed., *Immanuel Kants Werke* (Berlin, 1916), VII, 401.

59. *Ibid.,* VII, 398-400.

60. *Ibid.,* VII, 397.

61. *Ibid.,* VII, 398; K. Vorlaender, "Kants Stellung zur franzoesischen Revolution," in *Philosophische Abhandlungen fuer Hermann Cohen* (Berlin, 1912), pp. 249-250.

62. E. Cassirer, *Kant,* p. 391.

63. Kant to Biester, May 18, 1794, in *Werke,* X, 240-241; Kant to Frederick William II, October 1794 (?), in preface of *Streit der Fakultaeten,* in *Werke,* VII, 320. For the mental reservation which Kant later claimed to be implicit in his promise and which justified for him the declarations for academic freedom in his *Streit der Fakultaeten* (after the censorious minister Woellner had fallen and Frederick William II had died), see *ibid.,* VII, 320 note.

64. *Ibid.,* VII, 405 and note.

65. Immanuel Kant, *Critique of Aesthetic Judgment* (Oxford, 1911, translated by James Creed Meredith), p. 4. This volume includes the introduction and the first part of the *Critique of Judgment.*

66. *Ibid.,* p. 39.

67. *Ibid.,* p. 14. Kant's italics.

68. *Ibid.,* p. 38.

69. This analysis of Kant's doctrine of judgment refers only to his teleological judgment. His ideas on aesthetic judgment are omitted as irrelevant to his political theory.

70. Immanuel Kant, *Critique of Teleological Judgment* (Oxford, 1928, translated by James Creed Meredith), pp. 3-5, 24, 28-31. This volume contains the second part of Kant's *Critique of Judgment.*

71. I. Kant, Introduction to *Critique of Judgment,* p. 18.

72. I. Kant, *Critique of Teleological Judgment,* pp. 38-40.

73. ". . . the final end of creation is such a constitution of the world as harmonizes with what we can only definitely specify according to laws, namely with the final end of our pure practical reason . . . Now, by virtue of the moral law which enjoins this final end upon us, we have reason for assuming from a practical point of view, that is for the direction of our energies towards the realization of that end, that it is possible, or, in other words, practicable. Consequently, we are also justified in assuming a nature of things harmonizing with such a possibility . . ." *Ibid.,* p. 124.

74. Kant did not, in the *Critique of Judgment,* explicitly develop the concept of the natural analogy in the moral world which he had presented in the ethical writings of the 80's. But it is clearly assumed in his concept of "a moral teleology," produced by a "practical reflective judgment" which ascribes "a final end . . . to creation from a practical point of view" and which dovetails with the physical teleology and its system of natural ends up to finality. *Ibid.,* p. 126.

75. *Ibid.*, p. 97.

76. *Ibid.*, p. 99.

77. *Ibid.*, p. 109.

78. *Ibid.*, p. 108.

79. *Ibid.*, p. 109.

80. *Ibid.*, pp. 20-22.

81. *Ibid.*, p. 23, note 1.

82. Immanuel Kant, *Religion Within the Limits of Reason Alone,* in Carl J. Friedrich, ed., *op. cit.,* p. 404.

83. *Ibid.*, p. 407.

84. *Ibid.*, pp. 404-409.

85. *Ibid.*, pp. 408-409.

86. *Ibid.*, pp. 416-417.

87. *Ibid.*, pp. 416, 429.

88. *Ibid.*, pp. 415-416.

89. *Ibid.*, p. 416.

90. *vid. supra,* p.

91. *Ibid.*, pp. 416-421.

92. *Ibid.*, pp. 421-422. Italics mine.

93. *Ibid.*, p. 422.

94. Indeed, Kant went so far as to claim that even if a law were such that the people at the moment could not be conceived as consenting to it if asked, so long as "there is a mere possibility that a people might consent" to it, the law should be considered just. *Ibid.*

95. *Ibid.*, p. 425.

96. Kant's well-known dictum that "the freedom of the pen is the sole shield of the rights of the people" (*ibid.*, p. 427) expresses Kant's intention perfectly, since it defends a civil liberty in terms of its function of bringing abuses to the attention of the ruler. See too his argument that the ruler's respect for the law of reason will inculcate a similar respect for the law in his people and thereby avoid a revolution against the existing constitutional order which reason thus upholds. *Ibid.*, p. 429.

97. I. Kant, *Streit,* in *Werke,* VII, 404.

98. Immanuel Kant, *Perpetual Peace: A Philosophical Sketch,* in L. W. Beck, *op. cit.,* pp. 331, 340.

99. *Ibid.*, pp. 322-339.

100. Immanuel Kant, *Die Metaphysik der Sitten in zwei Teilen,* in *Werke,* VII, 143.

101. *Ibid.*, VII, 148; I. Kant, *Perpetual Peace,* p. 313.

102. I. Kant, *Metaphysik der Sitten,* in *Werke,* VII, 120-121.

103. I. Kant, *Perpetual Peace,* pp. 312-314.

104. I. Kant, *Metaphysik der Sitten,* in *Werke,* VII, 119-124.

105. *Ibid.*, VII, 149; I. Kant, *Perpetual Peace,* p. 315.

106. I. Kant, *Streit der Fakultaeten,* in *Werke,* VII, 399-400, note.

107. *Ibid.*, VII, 404; I. Kant, *Perpetual Peace,* pp. 315, 332, 334.

108. *Ibid.*, pp. 312-315.

109. *Ibid.*, p. 327.

110. I. Kant, *Metaphysik der Sitten,* in *Werke,* VII, 146.

111. *Ibid.*, VII, 125.

112. *Ibid.*, VII, 120-121, 126-129, 149.

113. *Ibid.*, VII, 125-127, 148-150, 179-180.

114. *Ibid.*, VII, 179; I. Kant, *Streit der Fakultaeten,* in *Werke,* VII, 400 note, 404.

115. *Ibid.*, VII, 405, note.

116. *Ibid.*, VII, 402, 404-406.

117. *Ibid.*, VII, 404.

118. I. Kant, *Metaphysik der Sitten,* in *Werke,* VII, 179-180; I. Kant, *Perpetual Peace,* pp. 312-313 note.

119. I. Kant, *Streit der Fakultaeten,* in *Werke,* VII, 400 and note, 404.

120. *Ibid.*, VII, 404-406.

121. See R. Aris, *op. cit.,* p. 91 and O. Gierke, *Natural Law,* II, #16, note 249.

122. I. Kant, *Perpetual Peace,* p. 313 note.

123. I. Kant, *Metaphysik der Sitten,* in *Werke,* VII, 129-130.

124. For a brilliant discussion of these points, see Herbert Marcuse, *Reason and Revolution: Hegel and the Rise of Social Theory* (New York, 1941).

125. Georg Wilhelm Friedrich Hegel, *The Philosophy of History* (New York, 1944, tr. by J. Sibree), p. 19. Italics his.

126. *Ibid.*, pp. 22-23.

127. G. Hegel, "Ueber die wissenschaftlichen Behandlungsarten des Naturrechts, seine Stelle in der praktischen Philosophie, und sein Verhaeltnis zu den positiven Rechtswissenschaften," in Hermann Glockner, ed., *Georg Wilhelm Friedrich Hegel: Saemtliche Werke* (Stuttgart, 1927), I, 459-473.

128. *Ibid.*, I, 474-476.

129. *Ibid.*, I, 478-480, 525.

130. G. W. F. Hegel, *The Phenomenology of Mind* (New York, 1931, tr. by J. B. Baillie), pp. 599-610.

131. G. Hegel, "Ueber die wissenschaftlichen Behandlungsarten des Naturrechts," in *Werke,* I, 509-515.

132. T. M. Knox, ed., *Hegel's Philosophy of Right* (Oxford, 1942), p. 20.

133. G. Hegel, "Ueber die wissenschaftlichen Behandlungsarten des Naturrechts," in *Werke,* I, 532-535; Georg Wilhelm Friedrich Hegel, *Die Verfassung des Deutschen Reichs* (new ed., Stuttgart, 1935). pp. 4-5.

134. On this point see H. Marcuse, *Reason and Revolution,* pp. 162-164.

135. "Hence the ethical order is freedom or the absolute will as what is objective, a circle of necessity whose moments are the ethical powers which regulate the life of individuals. To these powers individuals are related as accidents to substance, and it is in individuals that these powers are represented, have the shape of appearance, and become actualized. . . . Since the laws and institutions of the ethical order make up the concept of freedom, they are the substance or universal essence of individuals. . . . Whether the individual exists or not is all one to the objective ethical order. It alone is permanent and is the power regulating the life of individuals." *Hegel's Philosophy of Right,* pp. 105, 259.

136. G. Hegel, "Ueber die wissenschaftlichen Behandlungsarten des Naturrechts," in *Werke,* I, 531-533; G. Hegel, *Phenomenology of Mind,* p. 497; G. Hegel, *The Philosophy of History,* p. 53.

137. *Hegel's Philosophy of Right,* p. 122.

138. *Ibid.*, pp. 122-123, 134.

139. G. Hegel, *Phenomenology of Mind,* p. 489.

140. *Hegel's Philosophy of Right,* pp. 130-131, 270.

141. *Ibid.*, pp. 152-155, 278.

142. Thus on the one hand: "For Truth is the Unity of the universal and the subjective will; and the Universal is to be found in the State, in its laws, its universal and rational arrangements." G. Hegel, *Philosophy of History*, p. 39. But on the other hand: "the State is the actually existing, realized moral life. For it is the Unity of the universal, essential Will, with that of the individual." *Ibid.*, p. 38.

143. G. Hegel, *Phenomenology of Mind*, pp. 519-520.

144. G. Hegel, *Philosophy of History*, p. 38.

145. "In considering freedom, the starting-point must not be . . . the single self-consciousness, but only the essence of self-consciousness; for whether man knows it or not, this essence is externally realized as a self-subsistent power in which single individuals are only moments. The march of God in the world, that is what the state is. The basis of the state is the power of reason actualizing itself as will." *Hegel's Philosophy of Right*, p. 279.

146. *Ibid.*, pp. 280, 161.

147. *Ibid.*, p. 280.

148. G. Hegel, *Philosophy of History*, pp. 43-46.

149. *Hegel's Philosophy of Right*, pp. 281, 163.

150. *Ibid.*, pp. 163-164.

151. *Ibid.*, p. 282.

152. *Ibid.*, p. 176.

153. *Ibid.*, pp. 175, 286.

154. *Ibid.*, pp. 179-183.

155. *Ibid.*, p. 197.

156. *Ibid.*

157. *Ibid.*, p. 292.

158. *Ibid.*, p. 197.

159. *Ibid.*, p. 198.

160. *Ibid.*

161. *Ibid.*, pp. 198-201.

162. This essay, which Hegel worked on from 1799 to 1802, was not published until 1893. Its relevance here, then, consists not in its literal influence upon 19th-century German liberalism but in its revelation of the kind of thinking which followed from Hegelian assumptions. The best edition is: Georg Wilhelm Friedrich Hegel, *Die Verfassung des Deutschen Reichs* (Stuttgart, 1935), edited by Georg Mollat.

163. *Ibid.*, pp. 6-11.

164. *Ibid.*, p. 58.

165. *Ibid.*, p. 73.

166. *Ibid.*, pp. 63-64, 75.

167. *Ibid.*, pp. 78-79.

168. *Ibid.*, pp. 83-84.

169. *Ibid.*, pp. 112-113.

170. *Ibid.*, pp. 23-24, 116-117.

171. *Ibid.*, p. 113.

172. "But that a monarch is at the same time the state power, or that he has the supreme power, or that a state exists at all—these are synonymous." *Ibid.*, p. 46, note.

173. *Ibid.*, pp. 21, 46.

174. *Ibid.*, pp. 23-26.

175. Thus Hegel's main concrete proposal for change in the German constitution was—aside from giving real diplomatic and military powers to the Emperor—limited to the addition of representation of territorial estates in the Reichstag. *Ibid.*, pp. 118-119.

176. *Ibid.*, p. 121.

Chapter IV. The Politics of Reform

1. "At the beginning of the 1820's hardly anything essential had been changed in the general structure of the German economy; it was still the same as it had been in 1750 or 1800 . . ." Werner Sombart, *Die Deutsche Volkswirtschaft im neunzehnten Jahrhundert und im Anfang des 20. Jahrhunderts* (7th ed., Berlin, 1927), p. 79.

2. Excepting Scharnhorst of Prussia and Brauer of Baden the leading reform statesmen in Germany were full-blooded aristocrats.

3. Henri Brunschwig, *La crise de l'etat prussien a la fin du XVIIIe siecle et la genese de la mentalite romantique* (Paris, 1947) is an impressive attempt to substantiate the hypothesis of a fundamental crisis not only in the Prussian state but in the German economy, society, and culture as a whole, but its evidence does not add up to its far-reaching conclusions. See Gerhard Ritter's review in *American Historical Review,* Vol. 53 (1948), pp. 817-818.

4. Sombart's figure is quite apt. "It was like a kind of premature spring. Like the first warm days in March, when what follows is not yet spring but still a genuinely perceptible post-winter period." W. Sombart, *Die deutsche Volkswirtschaft,* p. 77.

5. Ibid., pp. 75-79; H. Brunschwig, *La crise de l'etat prussien,* pp. 121-175, *passim;* M. Doeberl, *Entwicklungsgeschichte Bayerns* (3rd ed., Munich, 1928), II, 391-392; Rolf Gustav Haebler, *Ein Staat Wird Aufgebaut: Badische Geschichte 1789-1818* (Baden-Baden, 1948), pp. 18-19; Erwin Hoelzle, *Wuerttemberg im Zeitalter Napoleons und der Deutschen Erhebung* (Stuttgart and Berlin, 1937), p. 59.

6. See Hans Rothfels, *Ostraum, Preussentum, and Reichsgedanke* (Leipzig, 1935), pp. 150-162.

7. Similar factors were at play in West Prussia, for which the Baltic grain trade was likewise important, but the liberal demands here did not have the authoritative advocates or the general influence of the East Prussians'.

8. There were also local movements toward urban self-administration in Koenigsberg and Danzig in the years immediately preceding the reform period, but they too were fruitless until Stein took them up in his city ordinance of 1808.

9. H. A. L. Fisher, *Studies in Napoleonic Statesmanship: Germany* (Oxford, 1903), pp. 378-381.

10. Fritz Valjavec, *Die Entstehung der politischen Stroemungen in Deutschland, 1770-1815* (Munich, 1951), pp. 346-353; Heinrich Heffter, *Die Deutsche Selbstverwaltung im 19. Jahrhundert* (Stuttgart, 1950), pp. 104-108.

11. M. Doeberl, *op. cit.,* II, 452-530; R. Haebler, *op. cit.,* pp. 91-158; E. Hoelzle, *op. cit.,* pp. 52-130.

12. *Vid. supra,* Chapter 1.

13. Quoted in Otto Hintze, *Die Hohenzollern und ihr Werk* (Berlin, 1915), p. 427.

14. The only reform of consequence that was actually executed was the emancipation of peasants on the royal domains. For the classic discussion of the pre-reform period, see Otto Hintze, "Preussische Reformbestrebungen vor 1806," in *Historische und Politische Aufsaetze* (Berlin, n.d.), III, 29-59.

15. Stein's most authoritative biographer insists repeatedly upon this characterization. Gerhard Ritter, *Stein: eine politische Biographie* (Stuttgart and Berlin, 1931), I, 7-8, 147-148.

16. *Ibid.*, I, 179-183.

17. Franz Schnabel, *Deutsche Geschichte im neunzehnten Jahrhundert* (3rd ed., Freiburg, 1947), I, 322-324, 341, 362-363.

18. Erich Botzenhart, ed., *Freiherr vom Stein: Briefwechsel, Denkschriften und Aufzeichnungen* (Berlin, 1936), II, 583.

19. Hans Thimme, ed., *Freiherr vom Stein: Staatschriften und politische Briefe* (Munich, 1921), p. 36.

20. E. Botzenhart, ed., *Stein: Briefwechsel*, II, 583.

21. "The preponderance of one estate over its co-citizens is injurious, a disturbance of the social order and such preponderance should be abolished." H. Thimme, ed., *Stein: Staatschsriften*, p. 49.

22. "Certain privileges *(Vorzuege)*" are attributed to the nobility in Stein's comments on a projected representative body in *ibid.*, p. 52; the nobility was and would remain the primary estate in the Prussian state. E. Botzenhart, ed., *Stein: Briefwechsel*, II, 588. But at other times he declared that the great mass of property-owners had an independence which the notables lacked, and he suggested that the institutions of the state be directed to the situation of this mass. H. Thimme, *Stein: Staatschriften*, p. 50. Indeed he even specified "the lower middle class *(Mittelstand)* and the peasantry" to be the morally highest estate and suggested that it be given "the prospect of great advantages," i.e. "the extension of its activity." *Ibid.*, pp. 58-59.

23. *Ibid.*, pp. 2, 39-40.

24. E. Botzenhart, ed., *Stein: Briefwechsel*, II, p. 584; H. Thimme, ed., *Stein: Staatschriften*, p. 68.

25. E. Botzenhart, ed., *Stein: Briefwechsel*, II, 220-222; *ibid.*, II, 232-233; *ibid.*, II, 304; *ibid.*, II, 447; *ibid.*, III, 195; *ibid.*, III, 327-329; *ibid.*, III, 498; *ibid.*, III, 526.

26. *Ibid.*, II, 313; *ibid.*, III, 525.

27. *Ibid.*, II, 460-461; *ibid.*, II, 569-570.

28. *Ibid.*, II, 313.

29. *Ibid.*, II, 570.

30. *Ibid.*, II, 449, 451; *ibid.*, III, 506; *ibid.*, II, 357, 361-362.

31. *Ibid.*, II, 511.

32. *Ibid.*, II, 483, 487; *ibid.*, IV, 21.

33. *Ibid.*, IV, 405-409.

34. *Ibid.*, II, 448, 497.

35. *Ibid.*, II, 313; H. Thimme, *Stein: Staatsschriften*, p. 50.

36. E. Botzenhart, ed., *Stein: Briefwechsel*, IV, 471, 529.

37. *Ibid.*, II, 40.

38. *Ibid.*, II, 232.

39. *Ibid.*, II, 483.

40. *Ibid.*, II, 588.

41. *Ibid.*, III, 507.

42. *Ibid.*, II, 583.

43. *Ibid.*, II, 302-303, 497; H. Thimme, *Staatsschriften*, pp. 11-12.

44. *Ibid.*, pp. 7-8; E. Botzenhart, *Stein: Briefwechsel*, II, 220, 303-304, 383.

45. *Ibid.*, II, 225, 585.

46. Stein's edict for a far-reaching county self-administration and his introduction of a general income tax in East and West Prussia were left in abeyance after his resignation.

47. The preamble to the edict which simultaneously enacted peasant liberation and equality of economic opportunity for all classes frankly confessed its *raison d'être* to be the vacuum in the state which was left by the weakening of government authority and which could be filled only by individual activity. Moreover, the radical self-administration characterizing the city ordinance of 1808 is in part at least to be attributed to Stein's collaborator, J. G. Frey.

48. Johannes Ziekursch, *Das Ergebnis der friderizianischen Staedteverwaltung und die Staedteordnung Steins Am Beispiel der Schlesischen Staedte dargestellt* (Jena, 1908), pp. 148, 190-196.

49. E. Botzenhart, ed., *Stein: Briefwechsel*, II, 583-585.

50. *Ibid.*, II, 222.

51. *Ibid.*, IV, 623.

52. *Ibid.*, II, 363-365.

53. *Ibid.*, II, 564.

54. The evidence of such specific agreement and cooperation, despite an increasing personal antipathy, is abundant: The consultations and mutual support by Stein and Hardenberg in pressing for administrative reform during November and December 1806 (Leopold von Ranke, *Denkwuerdigkeiten des Staatskanzlers Fuersten von Hardenberg vom Jahre 1806 bis zum Jahre 1813* (Leipzig, 1877), pp. 48-49); Stein's inspiration of portions of the Hardenberg-Altenstein "Riga Memorandum" of September 1807 (*ibid.*, p. 124); their general agreement on the principle of this memorandum and of the reform in general (E. Botzenhart, ed., *Stein: Briefwechsel*, II, 274; *ibid.*, II, 313, 318); the insistence of each upon the other's appointment to the post of chief minister in 1807 and 1808; Stein's loyal support of Hardenberg against all detractors during 1810 and 1811 (*ibid.*, III, 419-471 *passim*); finally, their cooperation in the enactment of the edict of May 1815 for the establishment of a representative system in Prussia (L. von Ranke, *Hardenberg, 1806-1813,* p. 124).

55. *Ibid.*, p. 247; E. Botzenhart, ed., *Stein: Briefwechsel*, III, 505 and IV, 400-402.

56. Walter Simon, *The Failure of the Prussian Reform Movement, 1807-1819* (Ithaca, 1955), pp. 56-87.

57. For these uniform judgments of Hardenberg, see Ernst Walter Zeeden, *Hardenberg und der Gedanke einer Volksvertretung in Preussen 1807-1812* (Berlin, 1940), esp. pp. 29-30, 157-163; F. Schnabel, *Deutsche Geschichte im 19. Jahrhundert,* I, 458-459; Friedrich Meinecke, *Das Zeitalter der deutschen Erhebung* (Leipzig, n.d., new ed., 1st ed. 1906), pp. 98-101.

58. K. Hardenberg, "Ueber die Widersprueche des Schatz-Collegii," in Leopold von Ranke, ed., *Actenstuecke zu den Denkwuerdigkeiten des Fuer-*

sten von Hardenberg (Leipzig, 1877), pp. 19-21; E. Zeeden, *Hardenberg*, pp. 30-32.

59. Leopold von Ranke, *Denkwuerdigkeiten des Staatskanzlers Fuersten von Hardenberg bis zum Jahre 1806* (Leipzig, 1877), p. xi.

60. Hardenberg's draft for a new German constitution, in L. Ranke, ed., *Actenstuecke*, pp. 294-300.

61. Hardenberg's memorandum of October 1 (app.), 1806, in George Winter, ed., *Die Reorganisation des Preussischen Staates unter Stein und Hardenberg* (Leipzig, 1931), I, 62-67; Hardenberg's memorandum of March 3, 1807, in L. Ranke, ed., *Actenstuecke*, pp. 447-467.

62. "Riga Memorandum," in G. Winter, ed., *Die Reorganisation des Preussischen Staates*, I, 305-306.

63. *Ibid.*

64. *Ibid.*, I, 313.

65. *Ibid.*, I, 313-316. Thus Hardenberg specified that elections were to take place "not by estate but from all the estates of the communities." *Ibid.*, I, 318.

66. E. Zeeden, *Hardenberg und der Gedanke einer Volksvertretung*, p. 96.

67. "Riga Memorandum," in G. Winter, ed., *Die Reorganisation des Preussischen Staates*, I, 314-315, 323-325.

68. *Ibid.*, I, 319.

69. *Ibid.*, I, 316-317, 331-334.

70. *Ibid.*, I, 335-336.

71. L. von Ranke, *Hardenberg 1806-1813*, p. 224.

72. G. Winter, ed., *Die Reorganisation des Preussischen Staates*, I, 318. Hardenberg also made vague mention of "representatives of the nation" to whom yearly budgets were to be "officially submitted," but he asserted no more about them save this bare indication of their existence. *Ibid.*, I, 341; E. Zeeden, *Hardenberg und der Gedanke einer Volksvertretung*, pp. 45-46 and p. 46, note 24.

73. G. Winter, ed., *Die Reorganisation des Preussischen Staates*, I, 318.

74. Hardenberg's concentration of all branches of government under himself as "State Chancellor," although it proved temporary, was an earnest of this development.

75. W. Simon, *op. cit.*, pp. 81-82; E. Zeeden, *Hardenberg und der Gedanke einer Volksvertretung*, pp. 96-97.

76. *Ibid.*, pp. 90-91; L. von Ranke, *Hardenberg 1806-1813*, pp. 217-221.

77. "Concentration in one administration must take place because we do not want to perpetuate provincialism but to introduce nationalism [i.e. Prussian nationalism]. The greatest difficulty lies in the settlement between the provinces, but it seems very possible to effect this by an assembly of deputies from these provinces under purposeful leadership . . . Let the king give the state a constitution, a consultative representation whose members he at first appoints and lay the condition of the nation and the finances before it yearly. Let him secure the execution of the financial plans . . . from attacks and inconsistent execution and let him seek to convince every rational person among the people that the drain upon their forces fulfils, the purpose for which they are used." Hardenberg's "Financial Plan According to More Recent Considerations," published in full in E. Botzenhart, ed., *Stein: Briefwechsel*, III, 712-717.

78. Hardenberg's Speech to the Notables, February 24, 1811, in L. von Ranke, *Hardenberg 1806-1813*, pp. 246-248; E. Zeeden, *Hardenberg und der Gedanke einer Volksvertretung*, pp. 117-121.

79. *Ibid.*, pp. 125-129.

80. This development was sealed by the Declaration of May 29, 1816, which excepted smaller peasant holdings from regularization into private property.

81. W. Simon, *op. cit.*, pp. 83-84.

82. *Ibid.*, pp. 97-98; F. Meinecke, *Das Zeitalter der deutschen Erhebung*, p. 166.

83. On Hardenberg's "moderate" political attitude, which prevented his identification with the levellers, see W. Simon, *op. cit.*, p. 85.

84. L. von Ranke, ed., *Actenstuecke*, pp. 15-20.

85. L. von Ranke, *Hardenberg 1806-1813*, p. 240.

86. "Riga Memorandum," in G. Winter, ed., *Die Reorganisation des Preussischen Staates*, I, 314-315.

87. They were repealed in 1814.

88. See F. Schnabel, *Deutsche Geschichte im 19. Jahrhundert*, pp. 462-463.

89. F. v. Coelln, *Neue Feuerbraende* (Amsterdam and Coelln, 1808), VI, part 16, pp. 118-119.

90. *Ibid.*, VI, part 16, p. 101.

91. *Ibid.*, I, part 1, p. 87; I, part 2, pp. 45, 61; I, part 3, p. 127; II, part 6, pp. 16-23.

92. *Ibid.*, II, part 4, pp. 108-109; VI, part 16, pp. 102-103, 124.

93. H. H. I. von Held, *Ueber und wider die vertrauten Briefe und neuen Feuerbraende des preussischen Kriegsrathes von Coelln* (Berlin (?), 1808), pp. 10, 61, 63.

94. See programs in E. Zeeden, *Hardenberg*, pp. 48-83, esp. pp. 82-83.

95. F. Valjavec, *op. cit.*, pp. 389-391.

96. S. A. Kaehler, *Wilhelm v. Humboldt und der Staat* (Munich and Berlin, 1927), pp. 10-15; Friedrich Meinecke, "Wilhelm von Humboldt und der deutsche Staat," in *Die Neue Rundschau*, XXXI (1920), 892.

97. Johann-Albrecht von Rantzau, *Wilhelm von Humboldt: Der Weg seiner geistigen Entwicklung* (Munich, 1939), p. 79. Kaehler even uses the terms "enjoyment" and "egoism" to sum up Humboldt's basic attitude. S. Kaehler, *op. cit.*, pp. 27-28, 211-215.

98. His *Ideas for an Attempt to Determine the Limits of the Power of the State* (*Ideen zu einem Versuch die Grenzen der Wirksamkeit des Staates zu bestimmen*), written in 1792.

99. Humboldt published only two small sections from it—and those not particularly characteristic—as articles during his lifetime. The work was first published as a whole in 1851. See S. Kaehler, *op. cit.*, pp. 146-148, and p. 448, note 1.

100. Thus Humboldt's basic principle: "True reason can desire no other condition for man than one in which not only does every individual enjoy the most unlimited freedom to develop himself from himself in his particularity but also does physical nature receive no other form from human hands but what every individual, limited only by his force and his right, gives to it from his own free will according to the standard of his need and inclination." Wilhelm von Humboldt, *Ideen zu einem Versuch die Grenzen der Wirksamkeit des Staates zu bestimmen* (Wuppertal, 1947), p. 26. That this

freedom is primarily spiritual freedom is implicit in Humboldt's reiterated emphasis upon its internality (*ibid., passim,* and explicit in *ibid.,* p. 33). See also, F. Meinecke, "Wilhelm von Humboldt und der deutsche Staat," in *op. cit.,* XXXI, 893.

101. W. Humboldt, *Ideen,* pp. 27-45. Kaehler describes the work as "philosophical anarchism." S. Kaehler, *op. cit.,* p. 138.

102. W. Humboldt, *Ideen,* pp. 17, 48-49, 59-61.

103. *Ibid.,* pp. 157-161.

104. *Ibid.,* p. 21.

105. *Ibid.,* pp. 32-33.

106. *Ibid.,* p. 160.

107. *Ibid.,* pp. 22-23, 47-49.

108. *Ibid.,* pp. 165-166; S. Kaehler, *op. cit.,* p. 146.

109. F. Meinecke, "Humboldt und der deutsche Staat," in *op. cit.,* XXXI, 896-897; S. Kaehler, *op. cit.,* pp. 227-228; J. A. Rantzau, *op. cit.,* pp. 78-81.

110. S. Kaehler, *op. cit.,* pp. 215-238.

111. Thus Humboldt in 1808: "I love Germany with my deepest soul, and there is mixed in my love even a materialism which often makes feelings less pure and noble but therefore only the more powerful. The misfortune of the age binds me still closer to it, and since I am firmly convinced that precisely this misfortune should be the motive for individuals to strive more courageously, to feel himself more for all, so I should like to see whether the same feeling rules others and to contribute to spreading it." Quoted in F. Meinecke, "Humboldt und der deutsche Staat," in *op. cit.,* XXXI, 896.

112. *Ibid.,* XXXI, 897.

113. J. A. Rantzau, *op. cit.,* pp. 80-81.

114. Humboldt's memoranda during his period of activity as educational reformer were all concerned with problems of his office, with the possible exception of his proposals for administrative reorganization which immediately preceded his resignation. Bruno Gebhardt, ed., *Wilhelm von Humboldts Politische Denkschriften* (Berlin, 1903), I, 16-302 *passim.*

115. *Ibid.,* I, 254, 258.

116. *Ibid.,* I, 54.

117. Censorship of non-political writings was a function of his office, but he voluntarily accepted the responsibility for political censorship as well. See Humboldt's letter to Goltz, March 7, 1809, in *ibid.,* I, 37-38.

118. See Humboldt's letters to Dohna, March 7, 1809 and April 1, 1809, and his memorandum censoring a book by Friedrich Buchholz, a radical publicist, in *ibid.,* I., 38-40, 45-48, 42-45.

119. Humboldt's "Draft of a Decree concerning the Change and Simplification of the Censorship Authorities," March 1809, in *ibid.,* I, 55-72.

120. Most of the educational reforms sponsored by Humboldt were enacted after he had left office, e.g. the Gymnasium Constitution of 1812.

121. Humboldt's Report of the Section for Religion and Education, Dec. 1, 1809, in *ibid.,* I, 200, 205.

122. W. Humboldt, *Ideen,* pp. 59-63.

123. S. Kaehler, *op. cit.,* p. 231; W. Humboldt, "Ueber die innere und aeussere Organisation der hoeheren wissenschaftlichen Anstalten in Berlin," in B. Gebhardt, ed., *op. cit.,* I, 251-252, 258.

124. *Ibid.,* I, 252-253.

125. *Ibid.,* I, 255.

126. Humboldt's Memorandum, May 9, 1810, in *ibid.*, I, 270-271.

127. "Prussia should now gain a moral power instead of the political power it formerly possessed." Quoted in S. Kaehler, *op. cit.*, p. 232.

128. *Ibid.* Humboldt's policies toward the new University of Berlin—the opening of it to competition with the other German universities and the appointments of the patriots Fichte and Schleiermacher—were expressions of this idea.

Chapter V. National Liberation

1. See Friedrich Meinecke, *Weltbuergertum und Nationalstaat* (2nd ed., Munich and Berlin, 1911), pp. 319-321.

2. F. Schnabel, *Deutsche Geschichte*, I, 493. In western Germany, Westphalia demonstrated the complete absence of popular enthusiasm by delaying compliance with military conscription, and even at the end of the war the ranks of the national guard (*Landwehr*) in that section were far from filled. Friedrich Meinecke, *Das Leben des Generalfeldmarschalls Herman von Boyen* (Stuttgart, 1896) I, 347. Even in the heart of Prussia, chief seat of the popular response, the institution of a local militia (*Landsturm*) was a total failure precisely because it depended upon a local and popular initiative which was lacking. *Ibid.*, I, 284, 288-290.

3. Particularly in Prussia were the enlistments for the volunteer detachments (*Jaeger*) and the performance of the national guard impressive. These results were attributable in the first instance to the co-operation of the bourgeois academic youth and in the second to the loyal response of other sections of the population. But in neither case was the fact or threat of compulsion without influence. F. Schnabel, *Deutsche Geschichte*, I, 490-493.

4. See G. Ritter, *Stein*, II ,168-172; *Aus den Papieren des Ministers und Burggrafen von Marienburg Theodor von Schoen* (Berlin, 1883), VI, 43-45, 51-55.

5. F. Schnabel, *Deutsche Geschichte*, I, 503; F. Meinecke, *Boyen*, I, 283, 287-288; William O. Shanahan, *Prussian Military Reforms, 1786-1813* (New York, 1945), p. 205.

6. For the discontinuity between nationalism and the Prussian reform, see W. Simon, *op. cit.*, 229-230.

7. German idealism is the label generally used to cover the whole of the main tendency in German intellectual development during the half century from 1770 to 1820. Within it, the distinction is commonly made between classical idealism, which prevailed into the 1790's under Goethe and Schiller, and romantic idealism, which then developed from it and achieved preeminence under Hoelderlin, Novalis, the Schlegels and the Grimms. In the years spanning the turn of the century the relay-point of the two stages was still much in evidence: Fichte, Hegel, and Wilhelm von Humboldt, for example, were essentially classical idealists—men who strove to appreciate the diversity and fullness of life but to endow it with a total form—who were influenced by their contacts with the romantics—men who sought to express the boundless striving of the ultimate individualities in life.

8. Heinrich Ritter von Srbik, *Deutsche Einheit* (Munich, 1935), I, 169-171, 176-177, 186, 192-193.

9. Friedrich Meinecke, *Weltbuergertum und Nationalstaat*, pp. 76-92.

10. R. Aris, *History of Political Thought in Germany,* pp. 294-304.

11. H. Srbik, *Deutsche Einheit,* I, 178.

12. Eugene N. Anderson, *Nationalism and the Cultural Crisis in Prussia, 1806-1815* (New York, 1939), pp. 144-145.

13. *Ibid.,* pp. 136, 139-140, 146-147.

14. Fichte was the son of a Saxon rural weaver, Arndt of an emancipated serf under Swedish rule but of German stock.

15. Fichte's importance is that of a case-study rather than an historical force because his actual political influence—aside from the field of education—was slight, despite his turn to publicistic activity after 1799.

16. Not only did Fichte expressly align his philosophy as a liberating force with the work of the French Revolution ("As that nation [the French] emancipated man from external chains, my system frees him from the bonds of the thing-in-itself, of the external influence, and establishes him as an independent being"), but he insisted that the "great thought" with which "my soul is afire" was to solve the political task set by Kant in his idea of the just constitution. Fichte's letter of 1795 and 1793 quoted in E. Anderson, *op. cit.,* pp. 26-27. Consequently, Fichte's first writings were political.

17. See Fichte's introduction to his *System der Rechtslehre,* in J. H. Fichte, ed., *Johann Gottlieb Fichte's Nachgelassene Werke* (Bonn, 1834), II, 500-507, and to the third section of his *Staatslehre,* in J. H. Fichte, ed., *Johann Gottlieb Fichte's Saemmtliche Werke* (Berlin, 1845), IV, 430-435. On this point, see also R. Aris, *op. cit.,* 348-349 and F. Meinecke, *Weltbuergertum und Nationalstaat,* pp. 118-127.

18. His *Zurueckforderung der Denkfreiheit von den Fuersten Europens, die sie bisher unterdrueckten,* his *Beitraege zur Berichtigung der Urtheile des Publicums ueber die franzoesische Revolution* (both publishd in 1793), and on the fringes of politics but important for his political assumptions, *Einige Vorlesungen ueber die Bestimmung des Gelehrten* (1794). Used here are the editions in J. G. Fichte, *Saemmtliche Werke,* VI, 3-346.

19. J. G. Fichte, *Beitraege zur Berichtigung der Urtheile des Publicums,* in *Saemmtliche Werke,* VI, 44.

20. J. G. Fichte, *Zurueckforderung der Denkfreiheit,* in *Saemmtliche Werke,* VI, 7.

21. J. G. Fichte, *Beitraege zur Berichtigung der Urtheile des Publicums,* in *Saemmtliche Werke,* VI, 86-89; F. G. Fichte, *Die Bestimmung der Gelehrten,* in *Saemmtliche Werke,* VI, 296-300.

22. J. G. Fichte, *Beitraege,* in *Saemmtliche Werke,* VI, 160, 170-179.

23. J. G. Fichte, *Zurueckforderung der Denkfreiheit,* in *Saemmtliche Werke,* VI, 15-17.

24. J. G. Fichte, *Beitraege,* in *Saemmtliche Werke,* VI, 117-125, 147-151.

25. *Ibid.,* VI, 94.

26. *Ibid.,* VI, 135-136. Fichte graphically pictorialized his idea as a series of concentric circles showing the scope of various kinds of authority. The largest, indicating ubiquitous validity, was assigned to conscience, and then followed, in order of diminution, the spheres of natural law, contracts, and finally—smallest of all—that of the civil contract, or the state, the only sphere which bears no relationship to the supreme moral law. See *ibid.,* VI, 131-133.

27. This assumption runs all through the works of the early 1790's. It is particularly striking, perhaps, in Fichte's assertion that man cannot be given the culture necessary to freedom by any other men or by the state—

"no one *is* cultivated, but every individual *as such* must *cultivate* himself" —and in his conclusion that "man *can do* what he *should* do; and if he says: I *can* not, he *wills* not to do it." *Ibid.*, VI, 90, 73. Italics his.

28. J. G. Fichte, *Beitraege*, in *Saemmtliche Werke*, VI, 128-131; J. G. Fichte, *Bestimmung der Gelehrten*, in *Saemmtliche Werke*, VI, 306.

29. J. G. Fichte, *Bestimmung der Gelehrten*, in *Saemmtliche Werke*, VI, 320-323.

30. J. G. Fichte, *Beitraege*, in *Saemmtliche Werke*, VI, 149-150 and note.

31. J. G. Fichte, *Grundlage des Naturrechts nach Principien der Wissenschaftslehre*, in *Saemmtliche Werke*, III, 54.

32. Thus Fichte now denied that freedom of thought was a "right," since activities which did not take place in the sensory world had no status in law. *Ibid.*, III, 112.

33. *Ibid.*, III, 17-23.

34. *Ibid.*, III, 30-85.

35. *Ibid.*, III, 111-113.

36. *Ibid.*, III, 86-89.

37. *Ibid.*, III, 94-110.

38. *Ibid.*, III, 52.

39. *Ibid.*, III, 113-149.

40. Both the Property Contract and the Protective Contract were now for Fichte parts of the Civil Contract. *Ibid.*, III, 191-202.

41. This was expressed in Fichte's anomalous formula: "Everything is included in it [the state], but only partly." By this Fichte meant to show that the individual maintains a part of his rights apart from the state but that everything that he gives up to the common will of society goes over to the state. *Ibid.*, III, 204-205.

42. Thus Fichte rejected democracy in the sense of the exercise of political power by the community on this very ground. *Ibid.*, III, 158-159.

43. *Ibid.*, III, 168-177.

44. ". . . since the administrator of the public power makes himself responsible for justice and security in this contract, he must necessarily stipulate for himself the power and the free use thereof which appears necessary and on any occasion will appear necessary to him for this purpose: and it must be granted to him. The right must be granted to him of determining what should be contributed by each individual to the furthering of the purpose of the state and to proceed with this power entirely according to his best knowledge and conviction . . . Thus the power of the state must be subjected to his free disposition, without any limitation, as this follows from the concept of a state power." *Ibid.*, III, 165-166.

45. *Ibid.*, III, 160-161.

46. *Ibid.*, III, 109-110.

47. *Ibid.*, III, 197-201.

48. *Ibid.*, III, 211-212.

49. *Ibid.*, III, 212-213.

50. *Ibid.*, III, 204-205 and note 213-215; Fichte, *Der Geschlossene Handelsstaat*, in *Saemmtliche Werke*, III, 397-403.

51. Since Fichte insisted on the irrelevancy of freedom of thought and conscience as pertinent to morality rather than politics and since he emphasized that external freedom could be real only under guarantee by the state, he could not at this stage of the discussion specify precisely what inhered

in the "part" of the individual's external rights which were apart from the state.

52. J. G. Fichte, *Grundlage des Naturrechts, in Saemmtliche Werke,* III, 149.

53. "Reason is One, and its representation in the sensory world is also only One; humanity is a single organized and organizing whole of Reason. It was divided into several members independent of one another; only the natural institution of the state abolishes this independence for the time being and merges individual quantities into a whole until morality reorganizes the whole species into One." *Ibid.,* III, 203.

54. "What the individual does not contribute to the purpose of the state, in respect to this is he completely free; not woven into the whole of the state, he remains an individual, a free person dependent only upon himself. It is just this freedom which is assured to him by the state power and for which he entered into the civil contract. Humanity separates itself from its civil status *(Buergethume)* in order to raise itself with absolute freedom to morality." *Ibid.,* III, 206.

55. J. G. Fichte, *Der Geschlossene Handelsstaat, in Saemmtliche Werke,* III, 512-513.

56. In the context of his discussion of international law. J. G. Fichte, *Grundlage des Naturrechts, in Saemmtliche Werke,* III, 371; R. Aris, *op. cit.,* p. 119.

57. J. G. Fichte, *Der Geschlossene Handelsstaat, in Saemmtliche Werke,* III, 590, 512; F. Meinecke, *Weltbuergertum und Nationalstaat,* p. 96 and note 3.

58. For the gradual growth of Fichte's nationalism in this period see *ibid.,* pp. 96-107.

59. This was the basic theme of Fichte's *Grundzuege des gegenwaertigen Zeitalters* (1804).

60. J. G. Fichte, *Ueber Macchiavelli als Schriftsteller* in *Nachgelassene Werke,* III, 420, 428.

61. J. G. Fichte, *Der Patriotismus und sein Gegenteil* in *Nachgelassene Werke,* III, 226-229.

62. "The peoples are indeed not a property of the prince . . . The prince belongs to his nation as wholly and completely as it belongs to him . . ." J. G. Fichte, *Ueber Macchiavelli,* in *Nachgelassene Werke,* III, 426.

63. *Ibid.*

64. J. G. Fichte, Der Patriotismus, in *Nachgelassene Werke,* III, 229.

65. J. G. Fichte, *Ueber Macchiavelli,* in *Nachgelassene Werke,* III, 423.

66. Arthur Liebert, ed., *Fichtes Reden an die deutsche Nation* (Berlin, 1912), 10-13.

67. The individual "is a member in the eternal chain of a general spiritual life, is under a higher social order." *Ibid.,* p. 39. A nation is "the whole of the men in society, living together and continuously producing themselves out of themselves naturally and spiritually, who together stand under a certain particular law of the development of the divine out of them. It is the community of this particular law which, in the eternal world and therefore also in the temporal, binds this aggregate into a natural and self-penetrated whole." *Ibid.,* p. 135.

68. *Ibid.,* pp. 124-125.

69. *Ibid.,* p. 21, 38.

70. *Ibid.*, pp. 138-140. ". . . The state as the mere government of the ordinary peaceful course of advancing human life is nothing primal or being-for-itself . . ." *Ibid.*, 146.

71. *Ibid.*, pp. 103-104.

72. *Ibid.*, p. 140.

73. Language became the fundamental characteristic of nationality for Fichte precisely because it was the vehicle through which the philosophical grasp of transcendental total Being became effective in life. *Ibid.*, pp. 74-93.

74. "The faith of the noble man in the eternal duration of his efficacy even on this earth is based upon the hope for the eternal duration of the nation from which he has himself developed and of its particularity . . . This particularity is the eternal to which he entrusts the eternity of himself and his activity, the eternal order of things in which he lays his own eternal being." *Ibid.*, p. 136.

75. The state as such tends to limit "the natural freedom of the individual as much as possible; freedom exists only for the higher national purpose lying beyond the state and only when the state is governed by the national point of view does it expand itself to include liberty as its end. *Ibid.*, pp. 138-139.

76. The nationally-minded state is the "highest regent of human affairs, . . . the trustee, responsible to God and to its conscience alone, of the immature," with "the perfect right even to compel the latter to their salvation." *Ibid.*, p. 197.

77. *Ibid.*, p. 136. Thus his characterization of the ancient Germans: "Freedom was to them that they remain just Germans, that they continue to decide their affairs independently and originally according to their own spirit, that they also progress according to this spirit, and that they implant this independence in their posterity." *Ibid.*, p. 144.

78. *Ibid.*, pp. 151-153, 199. But Fichte did understand abstractly the logical conclusion of his nationalist doctrine. He stated in general that the natural extent of a state coincided with that of the nation. *Ibid.*, p. 223-224.

79. *Ibid.*, pp. 107, 152.

80. *Ibid.*, pp. 147-148, 199-200.

81. In his *Rechtslehre* of 1812 and his *Staatslehre* of 1813.

82. J. G. Fichte, *Rechtslehre*, in *Nachgelassene Werke*, II, 524-528, 536-538; J. G. Fichte, *Staatslehre*, in *Saemmtliche Werke*, IV, 431-433.

83. *Ibid.*, IV, chapter "On the Concept of the True War," 400-430.

84. *Ibid.*, IV, 432-436; J. G. Fichte, *Rechtslehre*, in *Nachgelassene Werke*, II, 504-518.

85. "There is no natural law in the sense of a legal condition outside the state. All law is state law." *Ibid.*, II, 499.

86. *Ibid.*, II, 517.

87. *Ibid.*, II, 539-542; J. G. Fichte, *Staatslehre*, in *Nachgelassene Werke*, II, 437-438.

88. Fitchte's doctrine of the "Lord of Force (*Zwingherr*)," ibid., II, 437-442, 451-452. "No one in the state can have another will than that which the sovereign will has. This will, which should rule like an overpowering natural force, must be furnished with a power against which all other power disappears to nothing." J. G. Fichte, *Rechtslehre*, in *Nachgelassene Werke*, II, 628.

89. *Ibid.*, II, 632-633.

90. "The claim of the state . . . goes unto a definite negative and positive product of his [the individual's] freedom. The negative product which the state demands is that no one disturb the rights of others; the positive, labor for the maintenance of himself and the state. Wholly free, on the contrary, remains for him the spirit with which he delivers this product and with which he penetrates it . . . Everyone will obey, and for that he is due no thanks. But he can obey as a compelled slave . . . or as a free man in accordance with his own will. The latter is the spirit of obedience which remains left to him." *Ibid.*, II, 538.

91. "The path of the convocation of the people by the ephorate, or of revolutions, is, before a total transformation of the human species takes place, certainly to be viewed as getting instead of one evil another, and usually a greater. . . . Therefore the only thing from which improvement may be looked for is the progress of education to understanding and morality . . . So long as the government is not good the majority will ever be bad . . . A good majority arises from good government, and therefore not good government from a good majority." *Ibid.*, II, 634-635.

92. *Ibid.*, II, 635-636; J. G. Fichte, *Staatslehre*, in *Saemmtliche Werke*, IV, 450-458.

93. J. G. Fichte, *Rede an seine Zuhoerer* (February 19, 1813), in *Saemmtliche Werke*, IV, 607-609.

94. F. Meinecke, *Weltbuergertum und Nationalstaat*, pp. 94-95 and note 2, p. 94.

95. Hans Kohn, "Arndt and the Character of German Nationalism," in *American Historical Review* (1949), LIV, 789.

96. It is true that Arndt did not develop into a *German* nationalist until 1806 (E. Anderson, *op. cit.*, 79-82), but the central position of the nation in his thinking was already apparent in his first major work, the *Germanien und Europa* of 1802.

97. E. M. Arndt, *Geist der Zeit*, I, in August Leffson und Wilhelm Steffens, eds., *Arndts Werke: Auswahl in zwoelf Teilen* (Berlin, n.d.), VI, 54-57, 200-201; E. M. Arndt, *Geist der Zeit*, II, in *ibid.*, VII, 110-111, 120-123, 125-128.

98. *Ibid.*, VII, 111, 118-121.

99. E. M. Arndt, *Geist der Zeit*, III, in *Werke*, VIII, 165.

100. E. M. Arndt, *Geist der Zeit*, II, in *Werke*, VII, 85.

101. Thus Arndt speaks of "the indelible right to be a great, free, and bold nation." *Ibid.*, VII, 117.

102. "Citizen, who stands in a totality! First feel yourself a man; . . . the courage, force and virtue through which the individual becomes glorious, also glorifies the nation . . . Man has disappeared, and the suffering citizen cannot move the machine [of the state] . . . When every individual feels himself glorious, the nation worthy, the law holy, the fatherland eternal, the princes noble—then . . . the world is saved." E. M. Arndt, *Geist der Zeit*, I, in *Werke*, VI, 201-202. And again: "I insist on . . . the highest, indelible right of man—to use my own will . . . Fortune decides about the beginnings, but what the bold and free man wills and consummates, this rules and maintains the world." E. M. Arndt, *Geist der Zeit*, II, in *Werke*, VII, 128.

103. *Ibid.*, VII, 87; E. Anderson, *op. cit.*, 86.

104. "Without the nation there is no humanity and without the free citizen there is no free man. The noblest spirits are only born from the whole nation. Where there is nothing free and high-flying in the group then is it no longer produced in the individuals." E. M. Arndt, *Geist der Zeit*, I, in *Werke*, VI, 107.

105. E. M. Arndt, *Geist der Zeit*, III, in *Werke*, VIII, 108.

106. Thus his identification of "paternal (*vaeterliche*) government" with the nation. E. M. Arndt, *Der Bauernstand*, in *Werke*, X, 62.

107. *Ibid.*, X, 73-74; E. M. Arndt, *Geist der Zeit*, II, in *Werke*, VII, 33-34.

108. *Ibid.*, VII, 157-159.

109. E. M. Arndt, *Geist der Zeit*, I, in *Werke*, VI, 196.

110. E. M. Arndt, *Geist der Zeit*, II, in *Werke*, VII, 105.

111. E. M. Arndt, *Der Bauernstand*, in *Werke*, X, 36.

112. H. Kohn, *op. cit.*, in *AHR*, LIV, 789-790, 795-796.

113. "The state constitution must become a work of art in which everything precisely and rigorously meshes together." *Ibid.*, X, 37.

114. E. M. Arndt, *Geist der Zeit*, I, in *Werke*, VI, 59-66, 166-175; E. M. Arndt, *Geist der Zeit*, II, in *Werke*, VII, 163-164.

115. E. M. Arndt, *Geist der Zeit*, III, in *Werke*, VIII, 174-180.

116. *Ibid.*, VIII, 174.

117. E. M. Arndt, *Der Bauernstand*, in *Werke*, X, 110.

118. E. M. Arndt, *Geist der Zeit*, II, in *Werke*, VII, 170-171.

119. Arndt claimed that he would be satisfied with any constitution which maintained national independence. E. M. Arndt, *Geist der Zeit*, III, in *Werke*, VIII, 179.

120. E. M. Arndt, *Geist der Zeit*, II, in *Werke*, VII, 17.

121. E. M. Arndt, *Geist der Zeit*, III, in *Werke*, VIII, 148; E. M. Arndt, *Der Bauernstand*, in *Werke*, X, 74.

122. *Ibid.*, X, 75-78; H. Kohn, *op. cit.*, in *AHR*, LIV, 799.

123. E. M. Arndt, *Geist der Zeit*, III, in *Werke*, VIII, 146.

124. *Ibid.*, VIII, 147; E. M. Arndt, *Geist der Zeit*, II, in *Werke*, VII, 172.

125. *Ibid.*

126. For Arndt's rejection of the traditional arguments for the German *Libertaet* supposedly represented by particularism, see E. M. Arndt, *Geist der Zeit*, III, in *Werke*, VIII, 133-142.

127. See F. Meinecke, *Zeitalter der deutschen Erhebung*, pp. 117-118; E. Anderson, *op. cit.*, pp. 186-187.

128. E. Anderson, *op. cit.*, p. 160.

129. F. Meinecke, *Boyen*, I, 186-187.

130. *Ibid.*, I, 191-192.

131. Hans Delbrueck, *Das Leben des Feldmarschalls Grafen Neidhardt von Gneisenau* (2nd ed., Berlin, 1894), I, 134-135; E. Anderson, *op. cit.*, p. 183.

132. Carl von Clausewitz, "Die Deutschen und die Franzoesen," in H. Rothfels, ed., *Clausewitz' Politische Schriften und Briefe* (Munich, 1922), pp. 35-51.

133. C. Clausewitz, *Politische Schriften*, pp. 75-76.

134. "I believe and profess that a people has nothing higher to respect than the dignity and freedom of its existence." *Ibid.*, p. 85.

135. *Ibid.*

136. *Ibid.*, p. 74.

137. *Ibid.*, p. 114. Such a policy is safe for constituted government because

"the government that itself calls forth this storm remains its master." *Ibid.*, p. 115.

138. A. W. A. Veithardt von Gneisenau, *Denkschriften zum Volksaufstand von 1808 und 1811* (Berlin, 1936), pp. 12-13, 27-30.

139. Text in E. Botzenhart, ed., *Stein: Briefwechsel*, II, 545-546.

140. E. Botzenhart, ed., *Stein: Briefwechsel*, II, 546. In Boyen's September proposal for a Prussian national representation which formed the background for the joint petition he justified such an institution by claiming that it would "produce that general enthusiasm which not only checks petty egoism . . . but commands respect abroad." F. Meinecke, *Boyen*, I, 200.

141. A. Gneisenau, *Denkschriften*, p. 16. See Gerhard Ritter, *Staatskunst und Kriegshandwerk* (Munich, 1954), I, 97-100.

142. For the mixture of modernity and tradition in the military laws see F. Meinecke, *Boyen*, I, 411-412.

143. Of the Protective Committees (*Schutzdeputationen*), its administrative authorities. These were abolished in 1813 only a few months after their inception under the pressure of official opposition outside the reform group.

144. *Ibid.*, I, 400-407.

145. C. Clausewitz, *Politische Schriften*, pp. 2-119, *passim*.

146. "A free constitution and a simply ordered administration will make it their [the German peoples'] desire to live with us under common laws . . . If one has encouraged the German nation to happy hopes of a beneficent reform of the state through proclamations and deeds there can be no doubt that a great part of it will raise the shield for our cause against our oppressor." A. Gneisenau, *Denkschriften*, pp. 12-13. The connection of national German projects with the practical need of the Prussian state for popular support was even more baldly exposed by Scharnhorst when during 1813 he recommended to Stein an appeal to the Saxon estates on the grounds that it was absolutely necessary for the prosecution of the war "to draw the peoples into the concern since certain success cannot be expected from the standing armies alone." E. Botzenhart, ed., *Stein: Briefwechsel*, IV, 300.

147. A. Gneisenau, *Denkschriften*, p. 16.

148. *Ibid.*, p. 19. See also Gneisenau's letter of May 2, 1809: "Poor German nation, which goes down only because of its princes." Karl Griewank, ed., *Gneisenau: Ein Leben in Briefen* (Leipzig, 1939), p. 109.

149. E. Botzenhart, ed., *Stein: Briefwechsel*, III, 210, 247, 251-253.

150. *Ibid.*, III, 56, 115, 133-135, 151.

151. *Ibid.*, III, 195, 300.

152. *Ibid.*, III, 148-149.

153. *Ibid.*, III, 319-330, 442-443, 450-451.

154. Thus: "I have but one Fatherland and that is Germany; and since by its old constitution I belong only to it and to no particular part of it, so am I also submitted with my whole soul only to it and not to a part of it. To me the dynasties are, in this moment of great developments, wholly indifferent; my wish is that Germany become great and strong, in order to attain again its independence and its nationality and to assert its position between France and Russia . . ." *Ibid.*, IV, 166-167. See Wilhelm Mommsen, *Stein, Ranke, Bismarck* (Munich, 1954), pp. 20-25.

155. E. Botzenhart, ed., *Stein: Briefwechsel*, III, 463.

156. *Ibid.*, III, 147-149, 156-172; *ibid.*, IV, 27-28, 50-51, 89-90, 156-157.

157. ". . . They have never been sovereigns but members and subjects of

the Emperor and the Empire." *Ibid.*, IV, 51. See also *ibid.*, III, 148-149, 171-172; IV, 26, 50, 156-157.

158. *Ibid.*, IV, 178, 203-204.

159. *Ibid.*, IV, 156-157, 167.

160. *Ibid.*, IV, 144.

161. *Ibid.*, IV, 26-27.

162. Thus in asking Tsar Alexander to bestow upon Germany a constitution which would give large unitary powers to Austria and Prussia and which would abolish princely sovereignty, Stein felt that this was sufficient to bring about the natural combination of assuring both "to the nation its independence and to the individual his civil liberty." *Ibid.*, IV, 400-404.

163. This shift is embodied in the distinct differences in Stein's memoranda before and after December 1813, when the treaties with the states of the Rhenish Confederation showed him that he would have to deal with the sovereign princes in forming the new Germany. See *ibid.*, IV, 501.

164. *Ibid.*, IV, 501-502, 508-509, 529-530, 595, 599-600.

165. *Ibid.*, IV, 502, 595, 599.

166. *Ibid.*, IV, 471.

167. *Ibid.*, IV, 598-600, 643.

168. For the analysis of this amorphous pamphleteering see Karl Wolff, *Die deutsche Publizistik in der Zeit der Freiheitskaempfe und des Wiener Kongresses, 1813-1815* (Plauen, 1934).

169. *Ibid.*, p. 23.

170. *Ibid.*, pp. 42-43.

171. *Ibid.*, pp. 7, 45, 53.

172. Even those few who recommended bodies which would be, in fact, of the modern parliamentary type not only did not perceive the distinction between their proposals and the estate system as such but watered down the logical ramifications of their ideas to the point that for practical purposes they were scarcely distinguishable from the projects for reformed assemblies of estates. *Ibid.*, pp. 54-55.

173. *Ibid.*, pp. 45-48.

174. S. Kaehler, *Humboldt*, pp. 261-265.

175. F. Meinecke, "Humboldt und der deutsche Staat," in *Neue Rundschau* (1920), XXXI, 897-898.

176. From Humboldt's letters to his wife, quoted in S. Kaehler, *op. cit.*, pp. 276-277.

177. *Ibid.*, pp. 277-278.

178. F. Meinecke, "Humboldt und der deutsche Staat," in *op. cit.*, XXXI, 899-900.

179. Humboldt's memorandum of December 1813 in Bruno Gebhardt, ed., *Wilhelm von Humboldts Politische Denkschriften* (Berlin, 1903), II, 96-98.

180. *Ibid.*, II, 99-104; Humboldt's Draft of a German Federal Constitution, November 1814, in *ibid.*, II, 236-242. For Humboldt the Prussian state particularly was the political embodiment of German nationality and he looked to the moral conquest of Germany by Prussia. S. Kaehler, *op. cit.*, 277-278.

181. W. Humboldt, *Politische Denkschriften*, II, 108-112, 258-261.

182. "All members of the federation bind themselves to grant to every one of their subjects the following inviolable rights, as rights which every German must enjoy." *Ibid.*, II, 269. See too his argument to Gentz in January 1814 that the opposition of the princes to the unification could be discounted

because "their subjects and representative estates would be wholeheartedly for the new system." *Ibid.*, II, 113.

183. *Ibid.*, II, 109-110, 236, 258.

184. Particularly in his *Das Preussische Volk und Heer im Jahre 1813*, *Werke*, XI, 24-28.

185. *Ibid.*, XI, 28.

186. *Ibid.*, XI, 32-33.

187. Thus his essay, *Ueber kuenftige staendische Verfassungen in Deutschland* (1814), in *Werke*, XI, 83-131.

188. *Ibid.*, XI, 88.

189. *Ibid.*, XI, 95, 121.

190. *Ibid.*, XI, 99.

191. *Ibid.*, XI, 106.

192. *Ibid.*

193. *Ibid.*, XI, 114, 118-119.

194. *Ibid.*, XI, 102-106.

195. *Ibid.*, XI, 106-107.

196. Hans A. Muenster, *Geschichte der deutschen Presse* (Leipzig, 1941), p. 79.

197. "Inner righteousness is unusable for the world if it cannot make itself effective through force and unity; mere violence will triumph until it raises itself to power." Joseph von Goerres, *Ueber den Fall Teutschlands und seine Wiedergeburt*, in Wilhelm Schellberg, ed., *Josef von Goerres' Ausgewaehlte Werke und Briefe* (Munich, 1911), I, 462.

198. *Ibid.*, I, 466.

199. *Ibid.*, I, 466-470.

200. *Ibid.*, 468.

201. Foreword of the *Rheinische Merkur*, in *ibid.*, I, 481-483.

202. J. Goerres, "Der Landsturm jenseits des Rheines," in *ibid.*, I, 524-528.

203. Literally, "the spokesmen (*Stimmfuehrer*) of their peoples." J. Goerres, "Die kuenftige teutsche Verfassung," in *ibid.*, I, 567.

204. *Ibid.*, I, 568-569.

205. *Ibid.*, I, 567. Goerres' views on the constitution of the Imperial Diet (*Reichstag*) were not entirely clear. Usually he seemed to think of it as an assemblage of princes whose counterweight would come from the assemblies in their states rather than from a national representative body, but he did demand that deputies of the people be called to the Congress of Vienna (K. Wolff, *op. cit.*, p. 36), that the subsequent constituent German Diet include not only statesmen but historians, in whatever group they be found (J. Goerres, "Der teutsche Reichstag," in *Ausgewaehlte Werke*, I, 581-585), and occasionally that the permanent German Diet include popular representatives (K. Wolff, *op. cit.*, 73).

206. J. Goerres, "Die kuenftige teutsche Verfassung," in *Ausgewaehlte Werke*, I, 574.

207. *Ibid.*, I, 574-575, 567.

208. *Ibid.*, I, 570-573.

209. E. M. Arndt, *Ueber kuenftige staendische Verfassungen in Deutschland*, in *Werke*, XI, 87, 94.

210. *Ibid.*, XI, 98.

211. *Ibid.*, XI, 108, 121.

212. *Ibid.*, XI, 106.

213. *Ibid.,* XI, 128.
214. *Ibid.,* XI, 111, 121.
215. *Ibid.,* XI, 118-119, 122-126.
216. J. Goerres, "Die kuenftige teutsche Verfassung," in *Ausgewaehlte Werke,* I, 564.
217. *Ibid.,* I, 567.
218. *Ibid.,* I, 568.
219. *Ibid.,* I, 566.
220. *Ibid.,* I, 570.
221. "It is thus ordered in such a way that the national constitution and the constitution of every region within the national association are modelled reciprocally upon each other and the same basic law which is valid for the whole also rules the individual parts; then will they also support and maintain each other, and each will find his guarantee in the other. Thus the princes, in reference to the higher power representing as estates the whole nation, will have to grant below to their own estates the same freedom which they take for themselves among their colleagues and are thereby held by their own advantage from undermining the fundamental pillars of the nation through selfish caprice. Conversely, they will be able to demand from their subjects the same obedience which they perform to their superior power and when they lead the excessive freedom in their own area back to the golden mean it must result in the advantage of the whole and the more precise internal union of its parts." *Ibid.,* I, 575-576.

Chapter VI. Post-Liberation Politics

1. Arndt in his *Geist der Zeit* (1818), IV, in *Werke,* IX, 12-100; Goerres in his *Teutschland und die Revolution* (1819), in *Ausgewaehlte Werke,* I, 656-677.
2. Quoted in Fritz Hartung, *Studien zur Geschichte der preussischen Verwaltung,* III: *Zur Geschichte des Beamtentums in 19. und 20. Jahrhundert* (Berlin, 1948), p. 14.
3. See Walter Simon, *The Failure of the Prussian Reform Movement, 1807-1819* (Ithaca, 1955), pp. 197-229; Paul Haake, *Der preussische Verfassungskampf ver hundert Jahren* (Munich and Berlin, 1921); Heinrich von Treitschke, *Deutsche Geschichte im neunzehnten Jahrhundert* (8th ed., Leipzig, 1917-1919), II, 181-295, 551-628; III, 29-47, 68-131, 198-254.
4. P. Haake, *op. cit.,* pp. 63-64.
5. For the liberal apathy outside of government circles, see the account of the pulse-taking by special royal commissioners during 1817, in H. Treitschke, *Deutsche Geschichte,* II, 288-293.
6. Hardenberg to Zerboni, Feb. 5, 1817, quoted in P. Haake, *op. cit.,* p. 79.
7. Hardenberg's Memorandum of October 10, 1820, published by Alfred Stern in *Forschungen zur deutschen Geschichte,* XXVI (1886), p. 328.
8. See Hardenberg's speeches of Mar. 30 and July 7, 1817, in H. Treitschke, *Deutsche Geschichte,* II, 198, 287-288.
9. Hardenberg's constitutional drafts of May 1819, published in Alfred Stern, *Geschichte Europas* (Berlin, 1894), I, 649-653; and of August 1819, published in H. Treitschke, *Deutsche Geschichte,* II, 637-639.

10. W. Humboldt, "Denkschrift ueber Staendische Verfassung" (Oct., 1819), in Bruno Gebhardt, ed., *Politische Denkschriften* (Berlin, 1904), III, part 2, pp. 398-399.

11. W. Humboldt, "Ueber die Karlsbader Beschluesse. II," in *ibid.*, III, part 2, pp. 362-379.

12. H. Treitschke, *Deutsche Geschichte*, III, 68.

13. *Ibid.*, III, 78.

14. Hardenberg to Buelow, Feb. 12, 1816, in H. Oncken and F. Saemisch, eds., *Vorgeschichte und Begruendung des Deutschen Zollvereins, 1815-1834* (Berlin, 1934), I, 34.

15. Hardenberg to the Reichenbach Cotton Manufacturers, May 15, 1815, and Hardenberg to the Factory Owners of Rheydt, Suechteln, . . . , June 3, 1818, in *ibid.*, I, 26-29, 80.

16. This was the tendency of the innovations, but the inevitable concessions to tradition which characterized all Prussian reforms in this era must be kept in mind as qualifications of this tendency. Thus not only were the old Prussian distinctions between rural and urban taxation maintained but inequalities of taxation were perpetuated by the enactment of a classified tax as the basic personal levy.

17. *Ibid.*, III, 112.

18. Hardenberg's Memorandum of October 10, 1820, in *Forschungen*, XXVI, 328-332.

19. H. Treitschke, *Deutsche Geschichte*, III, 114.

20. See the documentary collection edited by F. Saemisch and H. Oncken, *op. cit.* and in the analysis based largely upon it; Arnold H. Price, *The Evolution of the Zollverein* (Ann Arbor, 1949), pp. 121-158.

21. The memoranda on the military constitution of the German Confederation (1817), on the geographical connection of the eastern with the western half of the Prussian state (1817), and on the district governments (1818). These are paraphrased in H. von Treitschke, "Aus den Papieren des Staatsministers von Motz," in *Historische und Politische Aufsaetze* (Leipzig, 1897), IV, 338-342.

22. Motz advanced these views not only in his memorandum on district governments in 1818 (*ibid.*, IV, 341) but also during the visitations by the representatives of the first constitutional commission during the previous year. H. Treitschke, *Deutsche Geschichte*, II, 288.

23. The memorandum on the importance of customs and trade treaties concluded by Prussia and the south German states, paraphrased in H. von Treitschke, "Aus den Papieren des Staatsministers von Motz," in *Historische und Politische Aufsaetze*, IV, 351-353.

24. Motz' memorandum of June 1829, quoted in *ibid.*, IV, 352-353.

25. ". . . It [the constitution of 1818] was for a great part of the Bavarian people, especially in Old Bavaria . . . , a pure gift of the king." "The liberal bourgeoisie (*Buergertum*)" was involved "only indirectly, through men who were close to the king and who had a popular and enlightened orientation." Eugen Franz, *Bayerische Verfassungskaempfe von der Staendekammer zum Landtag* (Munich, 1926), pp. 3-4.

26. Quoted in M. Doeberl, *Entwicklungsgeschichte Bayerns* (3rd ed., Munich, 1928), II, 579.

27. *Verfassungs-Urkunde des Koenigsreichs Baiern* (Munich, 1818).

28. H. Treitschke, *Deutsche Geschichte*, II, 351-352; E. Franz, *op. cit.*, pp. 5-8, 11, 13-21, 31-52.

29. Schnabel's characterization in *Deutsche Geschichte*, II, 226.

30. The mediatized nobility consisted of the formerly independent Imperial aristocracy, both secular and ecclesiastical, whose territories Napoleon put under the sovereignty of neighboring princes in 1803.

31. On the liberal, even democratic, forms of this aristocratic constitutionalism, see Rolf G. Haebler, *Ein Staat Wird Aufgebaut: Badische Geschichte, 1789-1818* (Baden-Baden, 1948), pp. 255-256.

32. See the analysis of Reinhard's *Die Bundesakte ueber Ob, Wann und Wie Deutscher Landstaende* in *ibid.*, pp. 271-272.

33. *Die Landstaendische Vertassungs-Urkunde fuer das Grossherzogthum Baden* (Karlsruhe, 1819).

34. See the Electoral Ordinance of Dec. 23, 1818 which was appended to the constitution. In *ibid.*, pp. 26-57.

35. Erwin Hoelzle, *Wuerttemberg im Zeitalter Napoleons und der Deutschen Erhebung* (Stuttgart, 1937), pp. 178-183.

36. Both Heinrich Kessler and Friedrich List, for example, wrote of a primitive Wuerttemberg law that had priority both in time and in validity over the good old law of the reactionaries and was identifiable with the rights of freedom conferred by God upon every man. *Ibid.*, p. 229.

37. "Just as the freedom of the individual is all the greater the more society leaves him to care for his private welfare, so does his freedom vary directly with the freedom of corporations." Friedrich List, "Ueber die Verfassung und Verwaltung der Korporationen," in Erwin V. Beckerath, Karl Goeser, et al., eds., *Friedrich List: Schriften, Reden, Briefe* (Berlin, 1932), I, 310.

38. On the one hand: "According to the essence of the state sovereignty in all states comes from the people." On the other: "The influence of the ruler upon the government of the state remains unlimited so long as he wills the best and the right." Friedrich List, "Ueber die wuerttembergische Verfassung," in *ibid.*, I, 359, 374. His view was that the active power of governing in the state was best delegated to an hereditary and independent ruler whose acts must be endorsed by a representative body which checks on violations of rights.

39. "Since the force of the state is nothing else but the force of the individual in the state and since each individual can develop his forces only in the degree that he enjoys rational freedom, the state must possess all the more force the more the freedom of corporations helps the development of the forces of the individual." F. List, "Ueber die Korporationen," in *ibid.*, I, 310.

40. F. List, "Ueber die wuerttembergische Verfassung," in *ibid.*, I, 365-366.

41. C. Weinheimer, ed., *Das Staatsgrundgesetz des Koenigreichs Wuerttemberg an der Hand der Verfassungsurkunde vom 25, September 1819 und mit den spaeteren Landes- und Reichsgesetzen* (Stuttgart, 1879).

42. F. List, "Der Kampf um die wuerttembergische Verfassung," in *op. cit.*, I, 475-478.

43. *Ibid.*, I, 474-475; E. Hoelzle, *op. cit.*, pp. 268-269.

44. See especially Franz Schnabel, *Ludwig von Liebenstein* (Karlsruhe, 1927) and Reinhold Hoehn, *Verfassungskampf und Heereseid* (Leipzig, 1938), pp. 17-30.

45. Rotteck's chief works, with one notable exception, were rooted in

the restoration period. Not only his influential publicistic writings, like the *Ueber stehende Heere und Nationalmiliz* (1816) and the *Ideen ueber Landstaende* (1819), but also systematic works such as his *Allgemeine Geschichte* (10 vols., Freiburg, 1812-1827), his continuation of J. C. Aretin's *Staatsrecht der konstitutionellen Monarchie* (2 vols., Altenburg, 1824-1828, of which vol. II, part 2 was written by Rotteck), and his *Lehrbuch des Vernunftrechts und der Staatswissenschaften* (4 vols., Stuttgart, 1829-1934). Only the famous *Staats-Lexikon* (15 vols., Altona, 1834-1843), which he edited in collaboration with Karl Welcker, stems from the subsequent period and shows evidence of a different kind of conditioning. On this point and in general for a useful analysis of Rotteck's political ideas, see Karl Schib, *Die staatsrechtlichen Grundlagen der Politik Karl von Rottecks* (Mulhouse, 1927).

46. The existence, if not the meaning, of this gap is endorsed by commentators of every stripe. Even so conservative and anti-Rotteckian an analyst as Adelbert Wahl noted that Rotteck's assertion of the doctrine of popular sovereignty did not prevent him from supplying so many qualifications as to leave actual sovereignty floating in his writings nebulously between people and prince. See A. Wahl, "Beitraege zur deutschen Parteigeschichte," in *Historische Zeitschrift*, CIV (1910), 571-584.

47. Robert von Mohl, *Die Geschichte und Literatur der Staatswissenschaften* (Erlangen, 1856), II, 562.

48. Carl von Rotteck, *Allgemeine Geschichte* (2nd ed., Freiburg, n.d.), I, 80-87.

49. *Ibid.,* I, 348.

50. *Ibid.,* I, 356-358.

51. See his insistence upon the addition of "the subjective possibility . . . i.e. my choice—thought of as free—of good or evil," to the strict Kantian prescription of the categorical imperative. Carl von Rotteck, *Lehrbuch des Vernunftrechts und der Staatswissenschaften* (Stuttgart, 1829), I, 5-6. By insisting that Kant's rigorous divorce of inner and outer, reason and sense, as the grounds of freedom and dependence, was false and by insisting rather that subjective freedom of choice amongst objects of sense as well as reason was decisive ("self-determination through sense is not less conceivable than through reason"), Rotteck prepared the way for discovering the antinomies of liberty within the realm of experience itself.

52. The counterpart of Rotteck's transposition of metaphysical dualisms into the physical world was his distancing of metaphysical monisms from this physical world. Thus not only did he insist upon the radical distinctions between realms of morality and of justice (*Recht*) (*ibid.,* I, 37-43) and assign the moral law to practical reason and the law of justice to speculative reason (*ibid.,* I, 47), but he replaced the substance of Kant's delicately etched picture of parallel moral and legal societies as inner and outer sides of a single system with the cruder disjunction between morality as the precepts incumbent upon the isolated individual and justice as those incumbent upon men in society. *Ibid.,* I, 24.

53. Thus the distinctions between internal and external law; within the latter, the distinction between absolute and hypothetical law, embodied most immediately in the absolute (or natural) and hypothetical private law pertinent to the individual in society; within the hypothetical law the distinctions among private, social, public, and international law, essentially reducible, however, to the cardinal division between a private law independ-

ent of all authority and a public law produced and conditioned by the state. This peculiar method of analysis, in which every situation was broken down into a normative and an existential component, only to have the analytical process immediately repeated on the existential sub-situation, with the old normative component becoming a mere abstract ideal outside reality, was characteristic of Rotteck's procedure. It helps explain the very remarkable performance wherein Rotteck could dualize any given circumstance and guarantee the perpetuation of the duality by immediately removing the ideal aspect out of reality into the realm of abstraction where it could not unify reality but could only lend a pale support to the normative components resulting from further analysis. *Ibid.*, I, *passim*, but especially 92-99.

54. *Ibid.*, II, 75.

55. *Ibid.*, II, 41-42.

56. J. C. von Aretin and Karl von Rotteck, *Staatsrecht der konstitutionellen Monarchie* (Altenburg, 1828), vol. II, part 2, p. 160.

57. C. Rotteck, *Lehrbuch des Vernunftrechts*, I, 267-289.

58. Karl Schib, *Die staatsrechtlichen Grundlagen der Politik Karl v. Rottecks* (Mulhouse, 1927), pp. 88-99.

59. C. Rotteck, *Lehrbuch des Vernunftrechts*, II, 53-54, 65-66.

60. *Ibid.*, II, 102-103.

61. *Ibid.*, II, 45-170, *passim*, but especially p. 66.

62. *Ibid.*, II, 47-53.

63. "But through the mutual guarantee of rights for the members of the state, external freedom, the primary basis of the happiness which all strive for, is not yet achieved." *Ibid.*, II, 61. The hallmarks of the state, for Rotteck, consisted not only in law but also in "security," but by this term so dear to the individualists of the 19th century he sketched out an infinitely elastic sphere for positive state action—collective assistance in warding off or overcoming the effects of the hostility of nature, "bad luck," or even the individual's own ignorance and inexperience. *Ibid.*, II, 61-62.

64. References to the "ideal" nature and role of the social contract, general will, and unified political power in actual states abound throughout the section on constitutional doctrine. *Ibid.*, II, 85 ff.

65. *Ibid.*, II, 81-86. He admitted the possibility of a contract between people and government *after* the establishment and appointment of the latter, but this was not a true rulership contract. *Ibid.*, II, 90.

66. *Ibid.*, II, 88.

67. *Ibid.*, II, 88, 192.

68. *Ibid.*, II, 194.

69. In Rotteck's candid concession: "But as unshakable and ineradicable as the *legal* claim of democracy is, equally undeniable is the *political* necessity . . . of its limitation through some kind of artificial—monarchical or aristocratic or even mixed—form." *Ibid.*, II, 193. Rotteck was thinking specifically of German conditions to which he must adapt himself. See K. Schib, *Rotteck*, p. 60.

70. K. Rotteck, *Lehrbuch*, II, 193.

71. *Ibid.*, II, 200-201.

72. *Ibid.*, II, 92, 218-221.

73. *Ibid.*, II, 196-197, 215-217.

74. *Ibid.*, II, 118-121.

75. *Ibid.*, II, 121-127.

76. *Ibid.*, II, 209-221.

77. *Ibid.*, I, 25.

78. *Ibid.*, II, 69-71. And again, ". . . the inequality of material law stemming necessarily from the equality of formal law." *Ibid.*, II, 144.

79. Passive suffrage denotes the legal capacity to be elected, active suffrage the legal capacity to be a voter or elector.

80. J. Aretin and K. Rotteck, *Staatsrecht der konstitutionellen Monarchie*, Vol. II, part 2, pp. 163, 171.

81. *Ibid.*, II, 2, p. 172.

82. *Ibid.*, II, 2, p. 175.

83. *Ibid.*, II, 2, pp. 176-180 and his *Lehrbuch des Vernunftrechts*, II, 143.

84. *Ibid.*, II, 103.

85. *Ibid.*, II, 104.

86. *Ibid.*, II, 110.

87. Likewise in the last extremity of the violated individual, where no appeal is possible, "fundamentally every condition *de jure* (*Rechtszustand*) ceases and only a *de facto* (*faktischer*) one exists." For this argument as a whole see *ibid.*, II, 105-112.

88. Even Robert von Mohl, who first developed the concept into a doctrine, not only read it into theorists back as far as Grotius but even included conservatives like Hegel in the list of its protagonists. Robert von Mohl, *Die Geschichte und Literatur der Staatswissenschaften* (Erlangen, 1855), I, 227-251. On this point too see Reimund Asanger, *Beitraege zur Lehre vom Rechtsstaat im 19. Jahrhundert* (Bochum, 1938), p. 25, note 148. Most recently Schnabel's discussion of the *Rechtsstaat* has had the same latitudinarian quality. F. Schnabel, *Deutsche Geschichte*, I, 104-107.

89. Best summary of present scholarly position on this in R. Asanger, *op. cit.*, pp. 1-3.

90. Published as *Die Elemente der Staatskunst* (3 vols., Berlin, 1809).

91. A. Mueller, *Elemente der Staatskunst*, I, 1-35; Carl Theodor Welcker, *Die letzte Gruende von Recht, Staat, und Strafe* (Giessen, 1813), pp. iii-v, 3-4.

92. A. Mueller, *Elemente der Staatskunst*, I, 66.

93. *Ibid.*, I, 55.

94. Thus fundamental law (*Recht*) was the dialectical product and governor of the antithetical relationship between a particular living fact and a general abstract norm—that is, between the will of the sovereign and the written law (*Gesetz*)—while the authority of the state was similarly a simultaneous product and governor of the conflict between the freedom of individuals and the "general liberty." *Ibid.*, I, 73, 252-258.

95. *Ibid.*, I, 43-52, 265-266.

96. Welcker scorned the familiar typology of states, such as monarchy, aristocracy, democracy, in favor of "despotism," "theocracy," and *"Rechtsstaat,"* to correspond with the successive dominance of sense, faith, and reason in the history of man.

97. C. Welcker, *Die letzte Gruende*, 92-95, 102-108. Welcker added freedom of public opinion as a third constitutional right, but its function was similar to individual petition. In addition, Welcker admitted that as a social right, it was an insufficient guarantee for individual liberty. *Ibid.*, pp. 94-95. The distribution of political power was a mere matter of expedience rather than of fundamental or constitutional law. *Ibid.*, p. 107.

98. *Ibid.*, pp. 95, 100.

99. *Ibid.*, p. 99.

100. *Ibid.*, p. 101.

101. *Ibid.*, p. 99.

102. F. Schnabel, *Deutsche Geschichte*, II, 108, 383; R. Asanger, *op. cit.*, p. 10; Franz Neumann, "The Concept of Political Freedom," in *Columbia Law Review*, LIII (1953), pp. 910-911.

103. The climax of Stahl's restatement ran familiarly: "This is the concept of the *Rechtsstaat* . . . It means in general not the aim and content of the state but only the disposition [*Charakter*] and method [Art] of realizing them." The customary reference is from the 3rd edition of Stahl's political philosophy, published as *Die Staatslehre und die Principien des Staatsrechts* (3rd ed., Heidelberg, 1856), pp. 136-138. It already appears in substance, however, in the 2nd edition, published as *Die Philosophie des Rechts nach geschichtlichem Ansicht* (Heidelberg, 1837). See vol. II, part 2, pp. 1-21 for the corresponding chapter minus the *Rechtsstaat*.

104. Jordan exercised most of his actual political influence in the state of Hesse, where he lived from 1821, but the theoretical views which he applied there had already been developed through his academic and political experiences in Bavaria, where he remained until 1820, and particularly in Heidelberg (Baden), where he studied in 1820 and 1821.

105. Their chief political works during the Restoration period were Karl Heinrich Ludwig Poelitz, *Die Staatswissenschaften im Licht unsrer Zeit* (2nd ed., 4 vols., Leipzig, 1827, 1st ed., 1823), and Silvester Jordan, *Versuche ueber allgemeines Staatsrecht* (Marburg, 1828). For recent monographs on these men see Peter Pohle, *System der Staats-und Nationalerziehung bei Karl Heinrich Ludwig Poelitz und ihre philosophischen Grundanschauungen* (Muenster, 1936) and Werner Kaiser, *Sylvester Jordan: seine Staatsauffassung und sein Einfluss auf die kurhessische Verfassungsurkunde vom 5. Januar 1831* (Dresden, 1936).

106. K. Poelitz, *Die Staatswissenschaften*, I, 40-54, 75-79, 146-152; S. Jordan, *Versuche*, pp. 15-54.

107. Particularly in Jordan, who devoted two important sections of his book to the relations between "the idea of the state" and "actual states." See sections 3 and 4 of his *Versuche*.

108. K. Poelitz, *Die Staatswissenschaften*, I, 115; S. Jordan, *Versuche*, pp. 56-57.

109. Thus Poelitz started from the proposition that the state was purely "an institution dispensing law (*Rechtsanstalt*)"; he then allowed for an "extension of the purpose of the state" by attempting to syllogize along the lines that since morality and welfare were the purpose of humanity and since law (*Recht*) was ultimately a social instrument toward these ends the state as an institution dispensing this law was bound to participate in the "approach of all its citizens" to the ethical and material goals of humanity. (K. Poelitz, *Die Staatswissenschaften*, I, 153-155). He wound up by throwing overboard the use of *Recht* as an undistributed middle, reversing himself to assert point-blank that the purposes of government could not be comprehended by a mere institution dispensing law (*Rechtsanstalt*) and that they must include both "law (*Recht*)" and "welfare (*Wohlfahrt*)." *Ibid.*, II, 453. Jordan accomplished the same amendment to the rule of law by reversing the terms of this loose logic. For him the state had a duty to act in the fields of culture, moral and religious training, and material welfare because

these were necessary to fit men for living under the rule of law. S. Jordan, *Versuche,* pp. 130-131. But Jordan was frank enough to admit that his extension of the state's activity was a necessary adaptation to the actual conditions of social life rather than an essential aspect of the state. They "are not its immediate purpose but only the natural and necessary consequence of its being realized." *Ibid.,* pp. 116.

110. *Ibid.,* p. 166.

111. *Ibid.,* pp. 169-173; K. Poelitz, *Die Staatswissenschaften,* I, 192-193. The influence of the contemporary constitutional struggles was obvious in Jordan's formulation: the best form of the state "in general" was the variable one which at a certain time and in reference to a certain people acted most conformably with the fundamental law (S. Jordan, *Versuche,* pp. 164-176), but the "relatively" best form of the state "in particular reference to Germany" was "representative or constitutional monarchy." *Ibid.,* pp. 176-185.

112. K. Poelitz, *Die Staatswissenschaften,* I, 185-187; S. Jordan, *Versuche,* pp. 170-171.

113. *Ibid.,* pp. 58-62.

114. Robert von Mohl, *Die Polizei-Wissenschaft nach den Grundsaetzen des Rechtsstaates* (3rd ed., Tuebingen, 1866, 1st ed. 1832), I, 3-19, Mohl's first extensive discussion of the *Rechtsstaat,* argues the concept exclusively in terms of purpose. See too Robert von Mohl, *Encyklopaedie der Staatswissenschaften* (Tuebingen, 1859), pp. 326, 333-335.

115. In his doctoral dissertation, Robertus Mohl, *Discrimens Ordinum Provincialium et Constitutionis Repraesentativae* (Tuebingen, 1821). Mohl analyzed the traditional corporate and the modern constitutional types of the representative system for the precise purpose of explicating, in the concluding chapter, the south German constitutions. (Pp. 36-45.)

116. R. Mohl, *Encyklopaedie,* pp. 329-330.

117. R. Mohl, *Polizei-Wissenschaft,* I, 19.

118. *Ibid.,* I, 20-27.

119. Explicitly in *ibid.,* I, 5, note 1.

120. *Ibid.,* I, 8-9.

121. *Ibid.,* I, 17.

122. *Ibid.,* I, 4.

123. R. Mohl, *Encyklopaedie,* p. 326.

124. R. Mohl, *Polizei-Wissenschaft,* I, 11-12.

125. This is the general tenor of his *Polizei-Wissenschaft nach den Grundsaetzen des Rechtsstates.*

126. Robert von Mohl, *Die Geschichte und Literatur der Staatswissenschaften* (Erlangen, 1855), I, 109.

127. E.g. for the unpolitical character of the patriotic "German Societies," see Friedrich Meinecke, *Die Deutschen Gesellschaften und der Hoffmannsche Bund* (Stuttgart, 1891), pp. 12-13, 26-31.

128. Materials for analysis of Student Unions is to be found primarily in Hermann Haupt and Paul Wentzcke, ed., *Quellen und Dartstellungen zur Geschichte der deutschen Burschenschaft und der deutschen Einheitsdewegung* (17 vols., Heidelberg, 1910-1940).

129. This combination appears clearly in the circular sent out by the Student Assembly held at Jena in April, 1818. "For what are the universities but the popular training institutions in which the spirit of the people is reflected in a clear and unmuddied way? On which estate other than ours

can the obligation be binding to purify and extend the spirit more and more when it might be impure in the individual?" Published in Georg Heer, ed., "Die aeltesten Urkunden zur Geschichte der allgemeinen deutschen Burschenschaft," in *Quellen und Darstellungen*, XIII, 121.

130. "The one side saw the Student Union as a Christian German brotherhood for the furthering of morality, patriotism, and the good and the beautiful in general among the students beyond the period of student life and through the students in the people. The others saw it as the best form for establishing the general will of all the students . . . , but as a purpose in itself and subordinated to no other goal and limited to the period and the affairs of student life. The one side saw it as an outgrowth of the highest ideas of freedom, equality, and justice, the others as a continuation of the traditional associational conditions and therefore dependent on and conditioned by the previous situation of student life." F. J. Frommann, extract from his unpublished reminiscences of 1819, quoted in Paul Wentzcke, *Geschichte der Deutschen Burschenschaft* (Heidelberg, 1919), I, 298-299.

131. In the universities of Halle, Breslau, Leipzig.

132. Especially at Giessen and Heidelberg. The decisive role of Jena in the national movement consisted largely in its combination of both tendencies. *Ibid.*, I, 157-158.

133. It is so characterized in Georg Heer, *Geschichte der Deutschen Burschenschaft* (Heidelberg, 1927), II, 8-9.

134. Karl Hase, quoted in *ibid.*, II, 135. For confirming analyses by the student unionists Ferdinand Herbst and Heinrich Riemann see *ibid.*, II, 133-134.

135. Published in full in Georg Heer, ed., "Aelteste Urkunden . . .", in *Quellen und Darstellungen*, XIII, 121-122.

136. *Ibid.*, XIII, 123-124.

137. On this phase, see G. Heer, *Geschichte der Deutschen Burschenschaft*, II, 1-148, esp. 8-12, 101-120, 131-138, and H. Fraenkel, "Politische Gedanken und Stroemungen in der Burschenschaft um 1821 bis 1824," in *Quellen und Dartstellungen*, III, 277-300.

138. Resolution of assembly of Germanist Student Unionists at Stuttgart in December, 1832, quoted in G. Heer, *Geschichte der Deutschen Burschenschaft*, II, 282.

139. Most decisively in Heidelberg and Giessen. For the use of the Germanist Student Unions in the Frankfurt uprising of 1833 see *ibid.*, II, 291-302.

140. On this point see *ibid.*, II, 330-334.

141. Quoted in *ibid.*, II, 282.

142. For Karl Follen and his group, see contemporary documents and analysis in Johannes Wit, genannt von Doerring, *Fragmente aus meinem Leben und meiner Zeit* (vols. I and III (1), Leipzig, 1830 and 1828). See too later monographs: Hermann Haupt, *Karl Follen und die Giessener Schwarzen* (Giessen, 1907); Richard Preziger, *Die politischen Ideen des Karl Follen* (Stuttgart, 1912); Josephine Blesch, *Studien ueber Johannes Wit genannt v. Doerring und seine Denkwuerdigkeiten nebst einem Exkurs ueber die liberalen Stroemungen von 1815-1819* (Berlin and Leipzig, 1917); and H. Fraenkel, "Politische Gedanken und Stroemungen in der Burschenschaft um 1821 bis 1824," in *Quellen und Darstellungen*, III, 241-309.

143. Constitution of the Giessen Blacks, quoted in H. Haupt, *Karl Follen*, p. 12.

144. Karl Follen, quoted in R. Pregizer, *Karl Follen*, p. 43.

145. For his generic natural rights construction see Follen's general theoretical essay, written in 1819 and published as an appendix in J. Wit, *Fragmente*, III (1), pp. 331-344. For analysis of this see R. Pregizer, *Follen*, pp. 20-32.

146. Quoted in H. Fraenkel, "Politische Gedanken und Stroemungen," in *Quellen*, III, 281.

147. Karl Follen, *Politische Aufsetze aus dem Jahre 1819*, published in J. Wit, *Fragmente*, III (1), p. 331.

148. Quoted in P. Wentzcke, *Geschichte der Deutschen Burschenschaft*, I, 306; J. Blesch, *Johannes Wit*, p. 94; H. Haupt, *Karl Follen*, p. 130.

149. Karl Follen, quoted in J. Wit, *Fragmente*, I, 27.

150. The formulation of Christian Sartorius, a member of the group. See H. Haupt, *Karl Follen*, p. 130.

151. ". . . whoever willed this [i.e. the ideal] unconditionally must also will the republican form of state unconditionally." Robert Wesselhoeft's analysis of Karl Follen, quoted in J. Wit, *Fragmente*, I, 26-27.

152. Karl Follen to F. J. Wit, October 20, 1820, published in *ibid.*, III (1), pp. 149-150. See also Follen's reported statement that "it is not enough for a man to will the same things as we, or to bring them about in the same way. . . . He must will to belong wholly to us." Quoted in J. Blesch, *Johannes Wit*, p. 95.

153. "Necessity is inexorable: the extreme of ultra-despotism produced that of ultra-liberalism; the former is the elemental cause, the latter the necessary consequence; the stronger the action the more violent the reaction. . . . We are in no way revolutionaries, but only counter-revolutionaries, for we oppose with all our power the revolutionary measures of government." Karl Follen, *Politische Aufsaetze aus dem Jahre 1819*, in J. Wit, *Fragmente*, III (1), p. 343-344.

154. The pastor F. L. Weidig exercised an important influence upon Follen's radicalization during 1818.

155. Karl Follen, *Das Grosse Lied*, published (albeit not in full) in *ibid.*, I, 430-448.

156. *The Works of Charles Follen* (Boston, 1841), III, 8.

157. *Ibid.*, III, 222-227.

158. This analysis of Karl Follen's theory is based primarily on his *Politische Aufsaetze aus dem Jahre 1819*, in J. Wit, *Fragmente*, III (1), pp. 331-344. On this point see esp. pp. 331-334.

159. *Ibid.*, III (1), pp. 336-337.

160. *Ibid.*, III (1), p. 333.

161. *Ibid.*, III (1), p. 337.

162. *Ibid.*, III (1), p. 336.

163. *Ibid.*, III (1), p. 338.

164. *Ibid.*, III (1), pp. 338-339.

165. Karl Follen, *Das Grosse Lied*, in *ibid.*, I, 440.

166. R. Pregizer, *Karl Follen*, p. 29. The other qualification was that of physical fitness, a demand taken over from the ancient German tribal constitutions.

167. *Ibid.*, pp. 44-45.

Chapter VII. The Rise of the Liberal Intellectuals

1. Thus the commutation of compulsory labor and tithes for the peasants, provision for public and oral court procedure, repeal of censorship, and a local government ordinance in the direction of self-administration.

2. Arnold H. Price, *Evolution of the Zollverein* (Ann Arbor, 1949), pp. 171-191, 239-253.

3. Thus many of the ministers instrumental in the negotiations leading to the customs union—like Berstett of Baden, Du Thil of Hesse, Marschall von Bieberstein of Nassau, and Bernstorff of Prussia—were partisans of both political suppression and economic liberalism. *Ibid.*, p. 255.

4. This was the affair of the seven professors at the University of Goettingen who were fired for public protest against the unilateral abolition of the Hanoverian constitution by the new ruler, Ernest, Duke of Cumberland. For the impact on the intellectuals and its absence on the populace see H. Treitschke, *Deutsche Geschichte, IV,* 666-670.

5. The best discussion of both the German Catholic and the Illuminati movements is in the unpublished dissertation by Catherine M. Holden, *A Decade of Dissent in Germany: an Historical Study of the Society of Protestant Friends and the German-Catholic Church, 1840-1848* (Yale University Diss., New Haven, 1954).

6. Ernst Kaeber, *Berlin 1848* (Berlin, 1948), pp. 20-21.

7. Karl Ackermann, *Gustav von Struve* (Mannhein, 1914), pp. 24-65.

8. Hans Rosenberg, "Theologischer Rationalismus und vormaerzlicher Vulgaerliberalismus," in *Historische Zeitschrift,* CXLI (1930), 532-533.

9. Jacques Droz, *Le liberalisme rhenan, 1815-1848* (Paris, 1940), pp. 252-265.

10. Oscar Hammon, "The Spectre of Communism in the 1840's," in *Journal of the History of Ideas,* XIV (1953), 404-420; R. Stadelmann, *Soziale und politische Geschichte der Revolution von 1848* (Munich, 1948), pp. 17-18.

11. J. Droz, *Liberalisme rhenan,* pp. 266-272.

12. R. Hinton Thomas, *Liberalism, Nationalism and the German Intellectuals, 1822-1847* (Cambridge, 1951), pp. 81-119.

13. Eduard Schulze, *Gervinus als politischer Journalist* (Leipzig, 1930), pp. 45-53.

14. Thus the proportion of urban population in Prussia increased only from 25.6% to 26.7% in the period 1834-1849. P. Benaerts, *Les Origines de la grand Industrie allemande* (Paris, 1932), p. 152.

15. Friedrich Luetge, *Deutsche Sozial—und Wirtschaftsgeschichte* (Berlin, 1952), p. 341; Werner Sombart, *Die deutsche Volkswirtschaft im 19. Jahrhundert* (Berlin, 1927), p. 79.

16. A. Sartorius von Waltershausen, *Deutsche Wirtschaftsgeschichte, 1815-1914* (Jena, 1920), pp. 71-74.

17. P. Benaerts, *op. cit.,* pp. 536-546.

18. *Ibid.,* p. 306.

19. A. Sartorius von Waltershausen, *op. cit.,* p. 92. For absolute increases in the production of specific industries see *ibid.,* 85-92.

20. By 1850 Germany, with 6000 kilometers of railroad lines was the second

leading European country in this respect, ranking behind the United Kingdom only. Pierre Benaerts, *op. cit.*, p. 631.

21. F. Luetge, pp. 319-329, and R. Stadelmann, *Soziale und politische Geschichte*, pp. 22-29.

22. P. Benaerts, *op. cit.*, p. 376.

23. Thus the increase of masters and journeymen in Germany from 30.8 per thousand of population in 1816 to 59 per thousand in 1861. F. Luetge, *op. cit.*, p. 341. See also *ibid.*, pp. 333-335 and P. Benaerts, *op. cit.*, pp. 394-399.

24. R. Stadelmann, *Soziale und politische Geschichte der Revolution*, p. 26.

25. See the description of the pre-1848 Hanseatic merchant in Percy Ernst Schramm, *Hamburg, Deutschland, und die Welt* (Munich, 1943), p. 541.

26. A. Sartorius von Waltershausen, *op. cit.*, pp. 79-81.

27. R. Stadelmann, *Soziale und politische Geschichte der Revolution*, pp. 26-27.

28. E.g. F. Schnabel, *Deutsche Geschichte*, II, 196-197; Hansgeorge Schroth, *Welt- und Staatsideen des deutschen Liberalismus in der Zeit der Einheits und Freiheitskaempfe, 1859-1866* (Berlin, 1931), p. 12; Friedrich Meinecke, "Drei Generationen deutscher Gelehrtenpolitik," in *Staat und Persoenlichkeit* (Berlin, 1935), p. 137.

29. F. Schnabel, *Deutsche Geschichte*, II, 176-177.

30. Koppel S. Pinson, *Modern Germany* (New York, 1954), p. 66.

31. Herbert Strauss, "Zur sozial- und ideengeschichtlichen Einordnung Arnold Ruges," in *Schweizer Beitraege zur Allgemeinen Geschichte*, XII (1954), pp. 163-165.

32. G. Mayer, "Die Anfaenge des politischen Radikalismus im vormaezlichen Preussen," in *Zeitschrift fuer Politik*, VI (1913), pp. 59-65.

33. Ruge's Journal, Oct. 1837, in Paul Nerrlich, ed., *Arnold Ruges Briefwechsel und Tagebuchblatter aus den Jahren 1825-1880* (Berlin, 1886), I, 75.

34. Thus Boerne's Paris letters of March 4 and March 5, and March 9, 1833 in Ludwig Boerne, *Gesammelte Schriften* (Rybnik, 1884), 72-79.

35. Hans Zehntner, *Das Staatslexikon von Rotteck und Welcker* (Jena, 1929), pp. 10-23.

36. This development was most explicit, perhaps, in Ruge, who appealed first to "the being of the State" in its existing form against "the non-being of obscurantism"—i.e. pietism—and subsequently, when the authorities failed to oppose his religious opponents, to "the first liberal movement," which he saw growing out of a clerical conflict. Ruge to Strauss, Mar. 16, 1839 and Ruge to the Weidmann Publications, June 4, 1840, in Arnold Ruge, *Briefwechsel*, I, 165, 208. See also G. Mayer, "Die Junghegelianer und der preussische Staat," in *Historische Zeitschrift*, CXXI (1920), pp. 414-418.

37. H. Rosenberg, "Theologischer Rationalismus und vormaerzlicher Vulgarliberalismus," in *ibid.*, CXLI (1930), pp. 530-531.

38. F. Schnabel, *Deutsche Geschichte im 19. Jahrhundert*, IV, 190-198; Ludwig Bergstraesser, ed., *Der politische Katholizismus* (Munich, 1921), I, 8-12.

39. Orthodox Catholic liberalism stemmed primarily from the conflict of the Prussian government with the Archbishop of Cologne in 1827, on the issue of mixed marriages. The dissenting German Catholic movement had

its origins in a rationalistic objection to the exhibition of a sacred coat as a miraculous relic during 1844 in Trier.

40. Thus the prospectus for a Catholic Rhenish paper in 1844 insisted that "the Catholic Church is essentially conservative . . . and teaches loyalty and constant devotion," and asserted that it would apply not only this principle but also "the defence of the interests of the Catholic confession, and at the same time the development of civil liberty." Programm einer politischen Zeitung am Rhein," in *ibid.*, I, 99-100.

41. Friedrich C. Sell, *Die Tragoedie des deutschen Liberalismus* (Stuttgart, 1953), p. 106.

42. George Buechner, *Der Hessische Landbote* (Zuerich, 1945, new ed.), p. 63.

43. Walter Neher, *Arnold Ruge als Politiker und politischer Schriftsteller* (Heidelberg, 1933), pp. 85-87.

44. Ruge to Prutz, Jan. 25, 1843, in Paul Nerrlich, ed., *Arnold Ruges Briefwechsel*, I, 296-297.

45. Ruge to Havm, July 16, 1841, in *ibid.*, I, 232-233.

46. Ruge to Stahr, Feb. 23, 1843, in *ibid.*, I, 298-300.

47. F. Sell, *op. cit.*, p. 106.

48. J. Droz, *Liberalisme rhenane*, pp. 265-276.

49. P. A. Pfizer, *Briefwechsel zweier Deutschen: Ziel und Aufgaben des Deutschen Liberalismus* (new ed., Berlin, 1911), prefaces of 1st and 2nd editions, pp. 3-11.

50. Gustav v. Struve, *Kritische Geschichte des allgemeinen Staatsrechts* (Mannheim, 1847), preface; Karl Ackermann, *Struve*, pp. 54-55.

51. "In this front of the governed until 1848 that was still united which in other politically more progressive countries was already differentiated by party and theory. Democratic and liberal tendencies, republican and corporate (*staendische*) motives, romantic and rational conceptions, free trade and pro-guild arguments were all interwoven." R. Stadelmann, *Soziale und politische Geschichte*, p. 31.

52. Ludwig Bergstraesser, "Die parteipolitische Lage beim Zusammentritt des Vorparlaments," in *Zeitschrift fuer Politik*, VI (1913), pp. 594-614.

53. Karl Ackermann, *Gustav v. Struve* (Mannheim, 1914), pp. 41-42.

54. G. Mayer, "Die Junghegelianer und der preussische Staat," in *op. cit.*, pp. 418-425.

55. H. Rosenberg, "Theologischer Rationalismus," in *op. cit.*, p. 528. See too Arnold Ruge's call for the king to introduce "the most complete democracy" and characterizing the Prussian era of reform as "nothing but democratization." Letter to Rosenkranz, April 1842, in A. Ruge, *Briefwechsel*, I, 272. There was indeed an article on "Democracy" in the *Staats-Lexikon* of Rotteck and Welcker which defined it as "the rule of the people" and maintained that the development of humanity was in the direction of the equal inclusion of all individuals in the sovereign people. But the author, Wilhelm Schulz, set this discussion in the Tocquevillian terms of the wave of the future and indicated that it would inevitably be realized when cultural conditions for it were ripe. Carl von Rotteck and Carl Welcker, eds., *Staats-Lexikon* (Altona, 1837), IV, 241-252.

56. Emil Gerber, *Der staatstheoretische Begriff der Repraesentation in Deutschland zwischen Wiener Kongress und Maerzrevolution* (Neunkirchen-Saar, 1929).

57. The famous controversy between Meinecke and Brandenburg on the nature of the pre-March "party system" was fruitless precisely because of this over-interpretation of the movement in terms of "liberalism" vs. "democracy" by both men. See their articles in the *Historische Zeitschrift* CXVIII and CIX (1917 and 1919).

58. On this transfer, see Hajo Holborn, "Der deutsche Idealismus in sozialgeschichtlicher Beleuchtung," in *Historische Zeitschrift*, CLXXIV (1952), esp. pp. 368-379.

59. F. C. Dahlmann, *Die Politik, auf den Grund und das Maass der gegebenen Zustaende zurueckgefuehrt* (vol. I, Goettingen, 1835). Only one volume was published.

60. *Ibid.*, pp. 1-2.

61. *Ibid.*, pp. 5-7.

62. *Ibid.*, p. 6.

63. *Ibid.*, pp. 6-7.

64. *Ibid.*, pp. 77-79.

65. *Ibid.*, pp. 9, 80.

66. *Ibid.*, pp. 80-81.

67. *Ibid.*, p. 108.

68. *Ibid.*, p. 113.

69. *Ibid.*, pp. 97-108.

70. *Ibid.*, pp. 121-129.

71. *Ibid.*, pp. 120-121.

72. *Ibid.*, pp. 113-114, 122.

73. *Ibid.*, pp. 120-121.

74. *Ibid.*, pp. 114-119.

75. *Ibid.*, pp. 173-181.

76. See his letters of October 7, 1838; April 15, 1839; March 19, 1840, in Eduard Ippel, ed., *Briefwechsel Zwischen Jacob und Wilhelm Grimm, Dahlmann, und Gervinus* (Berlin, 1885), I, 259, 321-322, 383-385.

77. Dahlmann to W. Grimm, October 7, 1839, in *ibid.*, I, 342-343; F. Dahlmann, *Politik*, pp. 176-177.

78. *Ibid.*, p. 181.

79. Mevissen quoted in P. Benaerts, *op. cit.*, p. 641.

80. Mevissen quoted in J. Droz, *Liberalisme Rhenan*, pp. 251, 269, 275, note.

81. David Hansemann, "Denkschrift ueber Preussens Lage und Politik," December 31, 1830, and "Denkschrift ueber Preussens Lage und Politik," August/September 1840, published in Joseph Hansen, ed., *Rheinische Briefe und Akten zur Geschichte der politischen Bewegung, 1830-1850* (Bonn, 1919), I, 11-81, 191-269.

82. Ibid., I, 15, 19, 35.

83. *Ibid.*, I, 21-22, 39, 51, 218, 260.

84. *Ibid.*, I, 74-75.

85. *Ibid.*, I, 224, 266-267.

86. *Ibid.*, I, 218.

87. *Ibid.*, I, 59-60, 241.

88. *Ibid.*, I, 235.

89. *Ibid.*, I, 239-240.

90. *Ibid.*, I, 221, 267.

91. *Ibid.*, I, 76-81.

92. Thus: "I hold it to be worth something that German common feeling maintains our cause which has been betrayed on all sides." Dahlmann to W. Grimm, August 21, 1838, in E. Ippel, *Briefwechsel*, I, 224. See too Dahlmann to W. Grimm, October 7, 1839, in *ibid.*, I, 342-343.

93. F. Dahlmann, *Die Politik*, pp. 4-5.

94. Beckerath to Camphausen, April 10, 1846, quoted in J. Droz, *Liberalisme rhenan*, p. 355.

95. "Deutsche Briefe," in Felix Gilbert, ed., *Johann Gustav Droysen: Politische Shriften* (Munich and Berlin, 1933), pp. 27-28; "Die politische Stellung Preussens," in *ibid.*, pp. 30-65.

96. Carl von Rotteck and Carl Welcker, eds., *Staats-Lexikon* (Altona, 1834), I, xxi.

97. *Ibid.*, I, xxiv-xxv.

98. *Ibid.*, I, xxiii.

99. *Ibid.*, I, xxxii.

100. *Ibid.*, I, xxx.

101. Especially his articles on "Abgeordnete" in vol. I, "Civilrecht" and "Constitution" in vol. III, "Demokratisches Prinzip" in vol. IV, "Naturrecht" in vol. XI of the *Staats-Lexikon*.

102. See chapter VI, pp. 246-252.

103. C. Rotteck, "Constitution," in *Staats-Lexikon*, III, 786.

104. C. Rotteck, "Demokatisches Prinzip," in *ibid.*, IV, 254-259.

105. C. Rotteck, "Vorwort," in *ibid.*, I, xxv; "Constitution," in *ibid.*, III, 774.

106. C. Rotteck, "Civilrecht," in *ibid.*, III, 511; K. Schib, *Rotteck*, p. 32.

107. Thus Rotteck in a speech after the Hambach Festival of 1832: "I want unity only with freedom and rather freedom without unity than unity without freedom . . . I want no unity under the wings of the Prussian or Austrian eagle." Quoted in K. Schib, *Rotteck*, p. 92.

108. "The representation of the whole people . . . is alone capable of making a *Rechts-Staat* out of a power state (*Gewalts-Staat*)." C. Rotteck, "Constitution," in *Staats-Lexikon*, III, 773. See too his "Vorwort," in *ibid.*, I, ix, xii, xxi, and "Demokratisches Prinzip," in *ibid.*, IV, 259.

109. Pfizer explicitly excluded the conservative position from consideration. P. Pfizer, *Briefwechsel*, p. 41.

110. *Ibid.*, pp. 17-21, 25-36, 39-49.

111. *Ibid.*, pp. 21-25, 36-39, 49-54.

112. *Ibid.*, pp. 120, 222, 275.

113. *Ibid.*, pp. 113-114.

114. *Ibid.*, p. 119.

115. *Ibid.*, pp. 146-150.

116. *Ibid.*, p. 274.

117. *Ibid.*, p. 134.

118. *Ibid.*, pp. 135, 138, 144-145.

119. *Ibid.*, pp. 207-216.

120. *Ibid.*, pp. 270-271.

121. *Ibid.*, pp. 271, 279-281.

122. P. Pfizer, *Ziel und Aufgaben des Deutschen Liberalismus* (new ed., Berlin, 1911), pp. 341-342.

123. *Ibid.*, pp. 337-338.

124. *Ibid.,* p. 344.

125. *Ibid.,* pp. 347-349.

126. *Ibid.,* pp. 352-357.

127. P. A. Pfizer, *Gedanken ueber Recht, Staat, und Kirche* (2 vols., Stuttgart, 1842). See section, "Das Vaterland," in *ibid.,* II, 145-356.

128. *Ibid.,* I, 175, 256-259.

129. Georg Gervinus, "Prospectus," in E. Ippel, ed., *Briefwechsel,* II, 536.

130. Karl Marx, "Theses on Feuerbach" (1845), in V. Adoratsky, ed., *Karl Marx: Selected Works* (New York, 1936), I, 473.

131. Ruge to Fleischer, Nov. 23, 1844, in P. Nerrlich, ed., *Ruges Briefwechsel,* I, 377.

132. Ruge to Ludwig Ruge, Mar. 30, 1845, in *ibid.,* I, 394; Ruge to Prutz, Jan. 14, 1846, in *ibid.,* I, 408.

133. Georg Herwegh, *Einundzwanzig Bogen aus der Schweiz* (Zuerich, 1843), pp. 12-13.

134. "Die eine und ganze Freiheit!" in *ibid.*

135. Gustav v. Struve, *Grundzuege der Staatswissenschaft* (4 vols., Mannheim, 1847-1848).

136. *Ibid.,* I, 27-52.

137. *Ibid.,* I, 7, 101-120.

138. *Ibid.,* I, 103-105; *ibid.,* II, 1-13.

139. *Ibid.,* II, 180-203.

140. *Ibid.,* II, 276-279.

141. *Ibid.,* IV, 233, 250-252.

142. *Ibid.,* III, 40-41.

143. Compare Jacoby's justification of constitutionalism in terms of Prussian law and tradition in his *Vier Fragen* (1841), published in Johann Jacoby, *Gesammelte Schriften und Reden* (2nd ed., Hamburg, 1877), I, 116-148, with his increasing resentment against government and emphasis upon the opinions of "the people" in his *Preussen im Jahre 1845,* published in *ibid.,* I, 290-208. See too Herwegh's revelation of similar disillusion in his "Preussen seit der Einsetzung Arndts bis zur Absetzung Bauers," in *Zweiundzwanzig Bogen,* pp. 1-32.

144. K. A. Brueggemann's speech of July, 1831, published in appendix of Veit Valentin, *Das Hambacher Nationalfest* (Berlin, 1932), p. 86.

145. Ruge to Fleischer, May 27, 1845, in *Ruges Briefwechsel,* I, 397.

146. G. Struve, *Grundzuege der Staatswissenschaft,* II, 232.

147. G. Mayer, "Die Anfaenge des politischen Radikalismus imvormaerzlichen Preussen," in *Zeitschrift fuer Politik,* VI, 59-65.

148. Ruge to Fleischer, Aug. 15, 1845, in *Briefwechsel,* I, 398.

149. Ruge to Fleischer, May 27, 1845, in *ibid.,* I, 396.

150. Ruge to Prutz, Jan. 14, 1846, in *ibid.,* I, 408.

151. I.e. graduated income tax, the right to work, adjustment of relations between labor and capital.

152. Ruge to Fleischer, July 9, 1844, in *Ruges Briefwechsel,* I, 361.

153. Ruge to Prutz, Jan. 14, 1846, in *ibid.,* I, 409.

154. *Ibid.*

155. Appeal to the Hambach Festival, in Karl Obermann, ed., *Einheit und Freiheit: die deutsche Geschichte von 1815 bis 1849 in zeitgenoessischen Dokumenten* (Berlin, 1950), pp. 116-117.

156. Siebenpfeiffer quoted in *ibid.*, pp. 113-114, 119.

157. Wirth quoted in Veit Valentin, *Das Hambacher Nationalfest*, pp. 44-45.

158. Thus Wirth: "At the moment when German popular sovereignty is instituted in its fundamental rights, at that very moment is the most integrated league of nations born." Quoted in *ibid.*, p. 42.

159. J. G. A. Wirth, *Die politische Reform Deutschlands* (Strasburg, 1832), pp. 1-3.

160. J. Wirth, *Deutsche Tribune*, Feb. 3, 1832, in K. Obermann, ed., *op. cit.*, p. 110.

161. J. Wirth, *Politische Reform*, pp. 16-18, 29.

162. The analysis of the revolution will only be tentatively sketched here. The voluminous literature on its political history, topped by Veit Valentin, *Geschichte der deutschen Revolution von 1848-49* (2 vols., Berlin 1930-31) and Erich Brandenburg, *Die Reichsgruendung* (Leipzig, 1916), I, 176-343, makes a detailed account superfluous, while the incipient stage of its social historiography, recently opened up in Rudolf Stadelmann's *Soziale und politische Geschichte der Revolution von 1848* (Munich, 1948) and Theodore S. Hammerow's "History and the German Revolution of 1848," in the American Historical Review, LX (1954), pp. 27-44 (an anticipation of his forthcoming book, based upon his excellent dissertation on *Social Conflict and Adjustment in the German Revolution of 1848-9* (Yale University, New Haven, 1952), make any attempt at definitive synthesis premature.

163. R. Stadelmann, *op. cit.*, pp. 78-80.

164. P. Benaerts, *Les Origines de la grande Industrie allemande* (Paris, 1932), pp. 547-548.

165. See supra, pp. 284-287.

166. Oscar J. Hammon, "Economic and Social Factors in the Prussian Rhineland in 1848," in *American Historical Review*, LIV (1949), pp. 835-838; Ernst Kaeber, *Berlin 1848* (Berlin, 1948), pp. 94-95.

167. Quoted in R. Stadelmann, *op. cit.*, p. 74.

168. P. Benaerts, *op. cit.*, p. 548.

169. Heinrich von Gagern's inaugural speech, May 19, 1848, in *Stenographischer Bericht ueber die Verhandlungen der deutschen constituirenden Nationalversammlung 24 Frankfurt am Main* (Frankfurt, 1848), I, 17.

170. O. Hammen, *op. cit.*, p. 838; R. Stadelmann, *op. cit.*, pp. 98-99.

171. Herbert A. Strauss, *Staat, Buerger, Mensch: die Debatten der deutschen Nationalversammlung 1848/9 ueber die Grundrechte* (Aarau, 1947), passim.

172. O. Hammon, *op. cit.*, pp. 837-838.

173. P. Benaerts, *op. cit.*, pp. 548-552, 591-592; Ludwig Bergstraesser, ed., *Die Verfassung des deutschen Reiches vom Jahre 1849* (Bonn, 1913), pp. 87-89.

174. E. Kaeber, *op. cit.*, pp. 168-172; H. Srbik, *Deutsche Einheit*, I, 363.

175. R. Stadelmann, *op. cit.*, pp. 174-178.

176. Otto Hintze, *Die Hohenzollern und ihr Werk* (Berlin, 1915), pp. 547-549.

177. See the collation of the Frankfurt, Union, and Erfurt constitutional drafts in L. Bergstraesser, ed., *Die Verfassung des deutschen Reiches, passim.*

178. A. L. von Rochau and G. Oelsner-Monmerque, *Das Erfurter Parlament und der Berliner Fuersten-Congress* (Leipzig, 1850), pp. 71-73.

179. See F. T. Vischer's letter to D. F. Strauss from Stuttgart, June 12,

1849, in Adolf Rapp, ed., *Briefwechsel zwischen Vischer and Strauss* (Stuttgart, 1952), I, 228-229, for the disgust of this member of the Rump Parliament with both the "princes" and the "people" and for the impotent conclusion: "I cannot remain, but neither can I resign nor stay away without resigning."

Chapter VIII. The Decline of the Liberal Intellectuals

1. H. Srbik, *Deutsche Einheit*, II, 92-98.
2. P. Benaerts, *op. cit.*, p. 190.
3. *Ibid.*, pp. 192-194.
4. Particularly in Austria, where the "Bach System" imposed a centralized prefectorial administration, dominated by bourgeois bureaucrats, upon the traditional local estates. In Prussia the feudal camarilla was much stronger, e.g. its influence upon the definitive establishment of the House of Lords and the restoration of the former Junker domination of local rural administration. But the failure to return to the nobles patrimonial justice in the countryside and patrimonial rights over the mediatized towns, the bureaucratic influence upon the city ordinances of 1853 and 1856, and the lethargy of the restored county and provincial diets attested to the limitations upon the feudal revival. H. Heffter, *Deutsche Selbstverwaltung im 19. Jahrhundert* (Stuttgart, 1950), pp. 326-343.
5. *Ibid.*, pp. 344-349.
6. W. Sombart, *Die deutsche Volkswirtschaft im 19. Jahrhundert* (Berlin, 1927), p. 84.
7. *Ibid.*, p. 85.
8. Georg Bernhard, *Meister und Dilettanten am Kapitalismus im Reich der Hohenzollern* (Amsterdam, 1936), pp. 55-61.
9. A. Sartorius von Waltershausen, *Deutsche Wirtschaftsgeschichte 1815-1914* (Jena, 1920), pp. 184-185.
10. Eugene N. Anderson, *The Social and Political Conflict in Prussia 1858-1864* (Lincoln, 1954), pp. 11-13, 283-284.
11. *Nationalzeitung, quoted in O. Stillich, Der Liberalismus* (Berlin, 1911), p. 36.
12. *Bremer Handelsblatt,* July 11, 1857, quoted in E. Anderson, *Social and Political Conflict*, p. 149.
13. For natural science see Frederic Lilge, *The Abuse of Learning: the Failure of the German University* (New York, 1948), pp. 57-83; for social science, Robert von Mohl, "Gesellschaftswissenschaft und Staatswissenschaft," in *Zeitschrift fuer die gesammte Staatswissenschaft*, VII (1851), pp. 3-71; for the new economics, Charles Gide and Charles Rist, *Histoire des doctrines economiques* (1st ed., Paris, 1909), II, 437-446, 479-509; for the new science of administration, Lorenz von Stein, *Die Verwaltungslehre* (Stuttgart, 1865).
14. H. Heffter, *op. cit.*, pp. 351-352; E. Anderson, *Social and Political Conflict*, pp. 286-287. The role of the political professor within these notables did, however, decline. *Ibid.*, pp. 293-294.
15. For Twesten's development, see Julius Heyderhoff, "Karl Twestens Wendung zur Politik und seine erste politische Broschure," in *Historische Zeitschrift*, CXXVI (1922), 242-251.
16. For Twesten's pamphlet, see ibid., CXXVI, 251-268 and Karl Twesten,

"Woran uns gelegen ist," in Hans Rosenberg, *Die national politische Publizistik Deutschlands vom Eintritt der neuen Aera in Preussen bis zum Ausbruch des deutschen Krieges* (Muenchen und Berlin, 1935), I, 17-18.

17. [Karl Twesten] *Was uns noch retten kann* (Berlin, 1861), pp. 23-25, 88.

18. *Ibid.*, pp. 25, 65-88.

19. *Ibid.*, pp. 62-63; C. Twesten, *Machiavelli* (1866), in Rud. Virchow and Fr. v. Holtzendorff, *Sammlung gemeinverstaendlicher wissenschaftlicher Vortraege* (Berlin, 1868/9), Heft 49, pp. 22-23.

20. C. Twesten, "Der preussische Beamtenstaat," in *Preussische Jahrbuecher,* XVIII (1866), pp. 136, 139, 144.

21. *Ibid.*, XVIII, 146.

22. Paul Wentzcke, "*Glaubensbekenntnisse eines politischen Jugend.* Beitraege zum Lebensbild Ludwig Aegidis und Eduard Laskers," in *Deutsche Staat und deutsche Parteiem* (Munich and Berlin, 1922), pp. 90-94.

23. Ernst Feder, ed., *Bismarcks Grosses Spiel: Die Geheimen Tagebuecher Ludwig Bambergers* (Frankfurt/M., 1932), p. 16.

24. Collected in Eduard Lasker, *Zur Verfassungsgeschichte Preussens* (Leipzig, 1874).

25. *Ibid.*, pp. 182, 197.

26. *Ibid.*, pp. 208-209.

27. Lasker's speech of Mar. 12, 1867 in the North German Constituent *Reichstag* in E. Bezold, ed., *Materialien der Deutschen Reichs-Verfassung* (Berlin, 1873), I, 512-516.

28. August Ludwig von Rochau, *Grundsaetze der Realpolitik angewendet auf die staatliche Zustaende Deutschlands* (new ed., Stuttgart, 1859), p. 2.

29. *Ibid.*, pp. 2-3.

30. *Ibid.*, p. 4.

31. *Ibid.*, pp. 10-15.

32. *Ibid.*, pp. 21-25.

33. *Ibid.*, pp. 29, 44.

34. *Ibid.*, p. 157.

35. The best analysis of Gneist is in H. Heffter, *op. cit.*, pp. 372-403.

36. Rudolf Gneist, "Das Repraesentativ-System in England. Eine historische Skizze," in *Vier Abhandlungen ueber das Constitutionelle Princip* (Leipzig, 1864), pp. 87-181.

37. *Ibid.*, pp. 89-90.

38. *Ibid.*, pp. 179-180.

39. Hans Rosenberg, *Rudolf Haym und die Anfaenge des klassischen Liberalismus* (Munich and Berlin, 1933), pp. 181-182.

40. See Felix Gilbert, *Johann Gustav Droysen und die preussisch-deutsche Frage* (Munich and Berlin, 1931, pp. 121-131.

41. J. Droysen, "Preussen und das System der Grossmaechte," in *Politische Schriften,* pp. 212-213, 229.

42. J. Droysen, "Zur Characteristik der Europaeischen Krisis," in *ibid.*, p. 323.

43. *Ibid.*, pp. 322-327.

44. *Ibid.*, p. 333.

45. *Ibid.*, pp. 308, 335.

46. *Ibid.*, p. 335.

47. *Ibid.*, pp. 340-341.

48. For the political philosophy of the *Prussian Annals,* see Otto West-

phal, *Welt- und Staatsauffassung des deutschen Liberalismus* (Munich and Berlin, 1913) and Hansgeorg Schroth, *Welt- und Staatsideen des deutschen Liberalismus in der Zeit der Einheits- und Freiheitskaempfe,* 1859-1866 (Berlin, 1931), pp. 75-90.

49. Haym to Dahlmann, Nov. 10, 1850, and Haym to Gervinus, Dec. 31, 1850, in Hans Rosenberg, ed., *Ausgewaehlter Briefwechsel Rudolf Hayms* (Berlin and Leipzig, 1930), pp. 116, 121-123.

50. Haym to Treitschke, Sept. 28, 1861, in *ibid.,* pp. 202-204.

51. Haym to Schroder, Mar. 7, 1866, and Haym to Duncker, April 18, 1866 in *ibid.,* pp. 242-244.

52. "Erklaerung" of 66 Halle Liberals, April 26, 1866, in *ibid.,* pp. 244-246.

53. Haym's "Zur Wahl," June 1, 1866 and his "Zum 30. Juni," end of June 1866, in *ibid.,* pp. 249-250, 253.

54. Treitschke's letters of Nov. 22, 1851; Dec. 15, 1851; Nov. 27, 1853, in Max Cornicelius, ed., *Heinrich von Treitschkes Briefe* (Leipzig, 1912), I, 101, 103, 196.

55. Walter Bussmann, *Treitschke: sein Welts- und Geschichtsbild* (Goettingen, 1952), pp. 32-61 for the notion of "conviction" in Treitschke; pp. 136-149 for the idealism which his aesthetics brought to his world-view. See too letters of Nov. 27, 1853; May 28, 1954; Feb. 5, 1855; Aug. 12, 1855; Sept. 2, 1855, in *Treitschkes Briefe,* I, 296, 232, 279-280, 306, 312.

56. Letter of Feb. 5, 1855, in *ibid.,* I, 280.

57. Letters of Oct. 18, 1848; Nov. 17, 1848; Nov. 23, 1848; Dec. 2, 1848; Jan. 31, 1849, in *ibid.,* I, 27, 32, 34, 36, 45-46.

58. Letters of Mar. 25, 1855; Aug. 12, 1855; Feb. 10, 1856, in *ibid.,* I, 296, 308-309, 338-339.

59. Letter of Mar. 25, 1855, in *ibid.,* I, 295-296.

60. Letter of Nov. 22, 1855, in *ibid.,* I, 101.

61. Letter of Feb. 17, 1856, in *ibid.,* I, 349.

62. Letter of Nov. 19, 1854, in *ibid.,* I, 262.

63. *Ibid.,* I, 260-261.

64. Letter of Mar. 1, 1857, in *ibid.,* I, 407-408.

65. Letter of Mar. 23, 1865, in *ibid.,* II, 388-389.

66. "Die Freiheit," in Heinrich von Treitschke, *Historische und Politische Aufsaetze* (4th ed., Leipzig, 1871), III, 16.

67. *Ibid.,* III, 8-13.

68. *Ibid.,* III, 19.

69. *Ibid.,* III, 33.

70. *Ibid.,* III, 10-12, 15-16.

71. *Ibid.,* III, 8-9, 23.

72. "Bundesstaat und Einheitsstaat," in *ibid.,* II, 77-241, esp. 233-234.

73. W. Bussmann, *op. cit.,* pp. 217-261.

74. ". . . Positive law is in this case incompatible with the interests of the Fatherland, so it must be abolished." Letter of May 25, 1865, in *Treitschkes Briefe,* II, 399.

75. H. Treitschke, "Bundesstaat und Einheitsstaat," in *op. cit.,* II, 194-195.

76. *Ibid.,* II, 239-240.

77. W. Bussmann, *op. cit.,* pp. 301-338.

78. See Hermann Baumgarten, "Der deutsche Liberalismus: eine Selbstkritik," in *Preussische Jahrbuecher XVIII* (1866).

79. "Das constitutionelle Koenigthum in Deutschland" (1869-1871), in H. Treitschke, *op. cit.*, II, 622-625.

80. H. Heffter, *op. cit.*, pp. 352-353.

81. Gervinus to Haym, Dec. 7, 1850, in H. Rosenberg, ed., *Briefwechsel Hayms,* pp. 121-123.

82. G. G. Gervinus, *Einleitung in die Geschichte des neunzehnten Jahrhunderts* (Leipzig, 1853), pp. 165-181.

83. R. Mohl, "Gesellschafts-Wissenschaften und Staats-Wissenschaften," in *Zeitschrift fuer die gesammten Staatswissenschaft,* VII (1851), pp. 7, 24-27, 33-35, 48-49, 67-71.

84. Robert von Mohl, *Staatsrecht, Voelkerrecht, und Politik* (Tuebingen, 1860), I, 395.

85. *Ibid.*, I, 416-417.

86. *Ibid.*, I, 393, 400-401.

87. *Ibid.*, I, 403-404.

88. Thus Dr. Ludwig Kugelmann's analysis of Liebknecht during 1868/9 as a "republican on the French model" into whom "the socialist element has been drilled through the accident of personal associations." In Gustav Mayer, *Friedrich Engels* (The Hague, 1934), II, 162, 542. For Bebel's development, see his *Aus Meinem Leben* (8th ed., Berlin and Stuttgart, 1933), esp. pp. 113-116, 149-158.

89. Lassalle's speech of November 1848, quoted in Hermann Oncken, *Lassalle* (Stuttgart, 1904), p. 65.

90. Lassalle to Marx, Oct. 24, 1849, in Franz Mehring, ed., *Briefe von Ferdinand Lassalle an Karl Marx und Friedrich Engels* (Stuttgart, 1902), p. 7.

91. Lassalle to Marx, July 19, 1851, in *ibid.*, p. 38.

92. Lassalle to Marx, June 24, 1852, in *ibid.*, p. 54.

93. Lassalle to Marx, April 26, 1857, in *ibid.*, p. 109.

94. Lassalle to Marx, Mar. 6, 1859, in *ibid.*, pp. 132-141; H. Oncken, *Lassalle,* pp. 121-131.

95. Lassalle to Marx, Mar. 12, 1860, in *Briefe,* p. 249.

96. F. Lassalle, *Der Italienische Krieg und die Aufgabe Preussens* (Berlin, 1859), *passim;* Lassalle to Marx, May 1859, in *Briefe,* pp. 150, 181-182.

97. "The substantive idea of our theme is . . . none other than the transition from an old legal condition into a new." Ferdinand Lassalle, *Das System der erworbenen Rechte: eine Versoehnung des positiven Rechts und der Rechtsphilosophie,* in Erich Blum, ed., *Ferdinand Lassalle's Gesamtwerke* (Leipzig, 1901), IV, 35.

98. E.g. *Ibid.*, IV, 270-273.

99. *Ibid.*, IV, 35-46, 144-145.

100. *Ibid.*, IV, 157, 272.

101. *Ibid.*, IV, 52-53; Lassalle to Franz Duncker, quoted in H. Oncken, *Lassalle,* p. 166.

102. Lassalle to Marx, Feb. 1860, in *Briefe von Lassalle an Marx,* p. 227.

103. G. Mayer, *Engels,* II, 101-102; H. Oncken, *Lassalle,* p. 201.

104. Ferdinand Lassale, "Ueber Verfassungswesen," in *Gesamtwerke,* I, 45.

105. *Ibid.*, I, 51.

106. *Ibid.*, I, 62.

107. *Ibid.*, I, 68.

108. Ferdinand Lassalle, "Arbeiterprogramm," in *ibid.*, I, 187. This title was given the speech by Lassalle later. The original heading was "Ueber den

besonderen Zusammenhang der gegenwaertigen Geschichtsperiode mit der Idee des Arbeiterstandes." The change is revealing.

109. *Ibid.*, I, 188.

110. *Ibid.*, I, 187.

111. *Ibid.*, I, 188-197.

112. *Ibid.*, I, 95-100.

113. Frdinand Lassalle, "Macht und Recht: Offenes Sendschreiben," in *ibid.*, I, 103.

114. Ferdinand Lassalle, "Offenes Antwortschreiben an das Zentral-Komitee zur Berufung eines Allgemeinen Deutschen Arbeitervereins zu Leipzig," in *ibid.*, I, 1-7.

115. *Ibid.*, I, 7-14.

116. *Ibid.*, I, 24, 31.

117. Quoted in introduction of Gustav Mayer, *Bismarck und Lassalle: ihr Briefwechsel und ihre Gespraeche* (Berlin, 1928), pp. 15-17.

118. Ferdinand Lassalle, "Herr Bastiat-Schulze von Delitzsch, der oekonomische Julian," (1864), in *Gesamtwerke*, III, 3.

119. *Ibid.*, III, 251.

120. Lassalle to Bismarck, June 8, 1863, in *Bismarck and Lassalle: Briefwechsel*, p. 60.

121. Lassalle to Bismarck, Jan. 13, 1864, in *ibid.*, p. 81; F. Lassalle, "Offenes Antworschreiben," in *Gesamtwerke*, I, 37.

122. F. Lassalle, "Herr Bastiat-Schulze," in *ibid.*, III, 249-251.

123. Ludwig Dehio, "Die preussische Demokratie und der Krieg von 1866," in *Forschungen zur Brandenburgischen und Preussischen Geschichte*, XXXIX (1927), p. 232.

124. Carl Rodbertus, *Mein Verhalten in dem Conflict zwischen Krone und Volk* (1849), in Moritz Wirth, ed., *Kleine Schriften von Dr. Carl Rodbertus-Jagetzow* (Berlin, 1890), pp. 181-212 *passim*.

125. L. Dehio, "Die preussische Demokratie," in *Forschungen*, XXXIX, 233.

126. B. Dammermann, "Lothar Bucher in England," in *Archiv fuer Politik und Geschichte*, VIII, 217.

127. Rodbertus, von Berg, und Bucher, *Deklaration*, in Rodbertus, *Kleine Schriften*, pp. 269-272; Rodbertus, von Berg, und Bucher, *Seid Deutsch! ein Mahnwort*, in *ibid.*, pp. 283-286.

128. Rodbertus, von Berg, und Bucher, *Was Sonst? ein deutsches Program*, in *ibid.*, pp. 307-308, 317.

129. Carl Rodbertus, *Offener Brief an das Comite des Deutschen Arbeitervereins zu Leipzig*, in *ibid.*, pp. 333-334.

130. *Ibid.*, p. 335.

131. Rodbertus to Ziegler, in L. Dehio, "Die preussische Demokratie," in *Forschungen*, XXXIX, 259.

132. Rodbertus to Ziegler, May 16, 1866, in *ibid.*, XXXIX, 246.

133. Rodbertus to Ziegler, May 20 (app.), 1866, in *ibid.*, XXXIX, 250-251.

134. C. Gide and C. Rist, *op. cit.*, II, 484-496; C. Rodbertus, *Offener Brief*, in *Kleine Schriften*, pp. 332-333.

135. C. Gide and C. Rist, *op. cit.*, II, 483.

136. Letters of Vischer to Strauss, May 25, 1851; Mar. 29, 1852; April 22, 1852, in A. Rapp, ed., *Briefwechsel zwischen Strauss und Vischer*, II, 12; 32; 36.

137. Vischer to Strauss, Dec. 19, 1866, in *ibid.*, II, 235.

138. L. Dehio, "Benedikt Waldeck," in *Historische Zeitschrift*, Vol. 136 (1927), pp. 51-54.

139. H. B. Oppenheim, *Benedikt Franz Leo Waldeck, der Fuehrer der preussischen Demokratie* (Berlin, 1873), p. 14.

140. Sybel to Baumgarten, May 23, 1862 and April 7, 1863, in J. Heyderhoff, ed., *Deutsche Liberalismus im Zeitalter Bismarcks* (Berlin, 1925),I, 93, 141; Twesten to —, Sept. 27, 1862, in *ibid.*, I, 116-117; Twesten to Lipke, April 27, 1863, in *ibid.*, I, 146-147.

141. Waldeck quoted in W. Schunke, *Freihaendler*, pp. 22-23.

142. Waldeck's speech of Mar. 9, 1867 in E. Bezold, ed., *Materialien der Deutschen Reichs-Verfassung* (Berlin, 1873), I, 103-105.

143. *Ibid.*, I, 100.

144. See the "Appeal of the Prussian Democracy," Nov. 5, 1858, by Jacoby and the Koenigsberg "Democrats," in Felix Salomon, *Die deutsche Parteiprogramme* (Berlin, 1907), I, 41-42.

145. Jacoby's speech of May 6, 1867, quoted in *Deutsche Allgemeine Biographie*, XIII (Leipzig, 1881), 628.

146. G. Mayer, "Die Trennung der proletarischen und buergerlichen Demokratie in Deutschland, 1863-1870," in *Archiv fuer die Geschichte des Sozialismus und der Arbeiterbewegung*, II, (1911), pp. 29-30.

147. Johann Jacoby, *The Object of the Labor Movement* (Eng. tr., New York, 1898). This was a speech delivered in January 1870. See too *Deutsche Allgemeine Biographie*, XIII, 629.

148. The National Liberal Karl Braun, (1867) quoted in *ibid.*

149. Schulze-Delitzsch's speech of Mar. 12, 1867 in the North German Constituent *Reichstag*, in E. Bezold, ed., *Materialien*, I, 213-214.

150. Schulze-Delitzsch's speech of Mar. 19, 1867, in *ibid.*, I, 415-416; "Schreiben an die Wahlmaenner des III. Wahlbezirks in Berlin vom 28. February 1861," in F. Thorwart, ed., *Hermann Schulze-Delitzsch's Schriften und Reden* (Berlin, 1910), II, 14-15; "Tischrede auf die Arbeiter bei dem Deutschen Abgeordnetentag," in *ibid.*, II, 211.

151. H. Schulze-Delitzsch, "Soziale Rechten und Pflichten," in *ibid.*, II, 249-260.

152. H. Schulze-Delitzsch, "Deutschlands Arbeiter," in *ibid.*, II, 219.

153. E.g. H. Schulze-Delitzsch, "Arbeit und Bildung" (Feb., 1861), in *ibid.*, II, 4-11.

154. *Ibid.*, V, 183-186.

155. "Rede, gehalten in der Arbeiterversammulung zu Berlin am 2. November 1862," in *ibid.*, II, 24-25.

156. *Ibid.*, V, 186-187.

157. Speech of Schulze-Delitzsch of Mar. 28, 1867 in E. Bezold, ed., *Materialien*, I, 63.

158. Speech of Schulze-Delitzsch of Mar. 12, 1867 in *ibid.*, I, 219-220; "Zur deutschen Frage," in H. Schulze-Delitzsch, *Schriften und Reden*, III, 225.

159. *Ibid.*, III, 227, 236-237; *ibid.*, V, 157.

160. See F. Rachfahl, "Eugen Richter und der Linksliberalismus," in *Zeitschrift fuer Politik*, V (1912), 265-374.

161. E.g., His *Geschichte der Social-demokratischen Partei in Deutschland* (Berlin, 1865); *Die Fortschrittspartei und die Sozial demokratie* (Berlin, 1878); *Die Irrlehren der Sozial demokratie* (Berlin, 1890); *Sozial Demokratische Zukunftsbilder* (Berlin, 1891).

Chapter IX. The Rise and Decline of Institutional Liberalism

1. E. Anderson, *Social and Political Conflict*, pp. 283-339.

2. Johannes Ziekursch, *Politische Geschichte des neuen Kaiserreiches* (Frankfurt am Main, 1925), I, 61.

3. *Ibid.*, I, 56-59, 62.

4. G. Mayer, "Die Trennung der proletarischen und buergerlichen Demockratie," in *Archiv fuer die Geschichte der Sozialismus*, II (1992), p. 23.

5. Thus letters from Widenmann to Hoelder, January 30, 1861, in J. Heyderhoff, ed., *Deutscher Liberalismus im Zeitalter Bismarcks* (Berlin, 1925), I, 56-57; Bluntschli to Sybel, August 15, 1862, in *ibid.*, I, 110-111; Sybel to Gneist, July 3, 1863, in *ibid.*, I, 160; Schulze-Delitzsch to Freytag, July 12/14, 1863, in *ibid.*, I, 160-162.

6. Hoverbeck to Witt, June 27, 1865, in *ibid.*, I, 251-252.

7. Sybel to Baumgarten, April 7, 1863, in *ibid.*, I, 141.

8. Sybel to Baumgarten, June 17, 1863, in *ibid.*, I, 155-156.

9. Sybel to Baumgarten, May 25, 1863, in *ibid.*, I, 152-153.

10. Twesten to Lipke, September 9, 1862, in *ibid.*, I, 116-117.

11. Schulze-Delitzsch to Freytag, July 12/14, 1863, in *ibid.*, I, 160-162.

12. Sybel to Baumgarten, June 11, 1862, in *ibid.*, I, 98.

13. Percy Ernst Schramm, *Hamburg, Deutschland, und die Welt* (Muenchen, 1943), pp. 579-580.

14. *Ibid.*, pp. 487-491.

15. Karl Lamprecht, *Deutsche Geschichte der juengsten Vergangenheit und Gegenwart* (Berlin, 1912), I, 455; II, 170-172; P. Schramm, *Hamburg, Deutschland, und die Welt*, p. 611.

16. *Ibid.*, pp. 613-614.

17. W. Sombart, *Die deutsche Volkswirtschaft im 19. Jahrhundort*, pp. 85-86; K. Lamprecht, *Deutsche Geschichte*, I, 227.

18. *Ibid.*, I, 331-340, 353-355.

19. *Ibid.*, I, 391-399.

20. For this crucial turn in the economic bourgeoisie, see P. Schramm, *Hamburg, Deutschland, und die Welt*, pp. 479-614.

21. *Ibid.*, pp. 541-542.

22. *Ibid.*, p. 575.

23. *Ibid.*, pp. 608-613.

24. Quoted in *ibid.*, p. 521.

25. K. Lamprecht, *Deutsche Geschichte*, II, 17-18.

26. P. Schramm, *Hamburg, Deutschland, und die Welt*, pp. 565-566.

27. W. Lotz, *Die Ideen der deutschen Handelspolitik von 1860 bis 1891* (Leipzig, 1892), p. 14.

28. J. Becker, *Das deutsche Manchestertum*, pp. 33-34.

29. *Ibid.*, pp. 77-78.

30. W. Lotz, *Die Ideen der deutschen Handelspolitik*, p. 19; Hermann Oncken, *Rudolf von Bennigsen* (Stuttgart, 1910), I, 314.

31. A Prussian organization established with official sanction in 1844 to work for the amelioration of the artisan and working classes by nonrevolutionary methods.

32. H. Oncken, *Bennigsen*, I, 314-315; F. Thorwart, *Schulze-Delitzsch's*

Schriften und Reden, V. 95-100. Boehmert's own interests at this time are revealed in the fact that his two published works during the 50's were concerned with the artisan problem: *Briefe zweier Handwerker* (1854) and *Freiheit der Arbeit* (1858).

33. Quoted in H. Oncken, *Bennigsen*, I, 315.

34. *Ibid.*, I, 316-317.

35. Werner Schunke, *Die preussischen Freihaendler und die Entstehung der Nationalliberalen Partei* (Erfurt, 1916), p. 2.

36. *Ibid.*, pp. 6-7.

37. *Ibid.*, pp. 5-6.

38. *Ibid.*, p. 7.

39. Viktor Boehmert, "Deutschlands wirthschaftliche Neugestaltung," in the *Preussische Jahrbuecher*, XVIII (1866), 270-271.

40. J. Becker, *op. cit.*, pp. 88-96.

41. F. Thorwart, ed. *Schulze-Delitzsch's Schriften und Reden*, V. 329 note.

42. *Ibid.*, V, 329-331.

43. Felix Salomon, *Die deutsche Parteiprogramme* (Berlin, 1907), I, 40-41.

44. Duncker to Haeusser, May 20, 1859, in *Deutscher Liberalismus*, I, 38.

45. Haeusser to Duncker, May 14, 1859, in *ibid.*, I, 36.

46. Sybel to Baumgarten, Feb. 22 (?), 1860, in *ibid.*, I, 48-49.

47. H. Oncken, *Bennigsen*, I, 323-325.

48. *Ibid.*, I, 435.

49. "Wochenschrift des Nationalvereins," Aug. 30, 1861, in Hans Rosenberg, *Die nationalpolitische Publizistik Deutschlands vom Eintritt der neuen Aera in Preussen bis zum Ausbruch des deutschen Krieges* (Munich and Berlin, 1935), I, 353; E. Anderson, *Social and Political Conflict*, p. 331.

50. *Ibid.*; H. Schulze-Delitzsch, "Erstes Flugblatt des Deutschen Nationalvereins," in *Schriften und Reden*, III, 157; Bennigsen to Boehmert, April 21, 1861, in H. Oncken, *Bennigsen*, I, 499-500; Hermann Oncken, "Der Nationalverein und die Anfaenge der deutschen Arbeiterbewegung, 1862-3," in *Archiv fuer die Geschichte des Sozialismus und der Arbeiterbewegung*, II (1911), p. 121.

51. H. Oncken, *Bennigsen*, I, 537-538.

52. Hans Herzfeld, *Johannes von Miquel* (Detmold, 1938), I, 22.

53. Thus the 1864 resolution: "In re the bearer of the central power, the whole nation represented in parliament has to decide. . . . So long as the anti-liberal and un-German direction of the governments in the particular states, especially in Prussia, continues, the execution of the Frankfurt Constitution is impossible," in H. Oncken, *Bennigsen*, I, 651.

54. H. Oncken, "Der Nationalverein . . . ," in *Archiv*, II, 121-127; F. Thorwart, *Schulze-Delitzsch*, V, 183-187; "Wochenblatt des Nationalvereins," April 6, 1865, in H. Rosenberg, *Nationalpolitische Publizistik*, II, 879.

55. H. Oncken, *Bennigsen*, I, 466-469, 648-649.

56. H. Oncken, *Lassalle*, pp. 393-394.

57. Gustav Mayer, "Die Trennung der proletarischen und der buergerlichen Demokratie," in *Archiv fuer die Geschichte des Sozialismus*, II, 11.

58. Schulze-Delitzsch to Bennigsen, August 3, 1865, in H. Oncken, *Rudolf von Bennigsen*, I, 669-670.

59. Jakob Venedey, "Das Grunduebel im National Verein," in H. Rosenberg, *Nationalpolitische Publizistik*, II, 816-817.

60. H. Oncken, *Bennigsen*, I, 652.

61. Schulze-Delitzsch's speech to the National Union, October 1864, in *Schriften und Reden*, III, 223-224, note 1.

62. H. Schulze-Delitzsch, "Zur deutschen Frage," in *ibid.*, III, 230, 236.

63. H. Rosenberg, *Nationalpolitische Publizistik*, II, 969-972; G. Mayer, "Die Trennung der proletarischen und der buergerlichen Demokratie," in *Archiv fuer die Geschichte des Sozialismus*, II, 10, 13-14.

64. "Zollverein: Zeitschrift fuer Handel und Gewerbe," Oct. 1865, in H. Rosenberg, *Nationalpolitische Publizistik*, II, 963.

65. Boehmert to Bennigsen, Oct. 25, 1865, in H. Oncken, *Bennigsen*, I, 676-677.

66. *Ibid.*, I, 677; Unruh to Bennigsen, Oct. 26, 1865, in *ibid.*, I, 677-680.

67. *Ibid.*, I, 681-683.

68. Thus the *Customs Union* of April 18, 1866: "We hold the unification of Germany for such a worthy good, in both ideal and material respects, that we would even accept a despotic government for it." In H. Rosenberg, *Nationalpolitische Publizistik*, II, 965.

69. Boehmert to Bennigsen, April 12, 1866, in H. Oncken, *Bennigsen*, I, 693.

70. *Ibid.*, I, 695-698.

71. H. Herzfeld, *Johannes von Miquel*, I, 23.

72. Bennigsen to Boehmert, April 15, 1866, in H. Oncken, *Bennigsen*, I, 694-695.

73. *Ibid.*, I, 708.

74. *Ibid.*, I, 708-709.

75. "Wochenblatt des Nationalvereins," in H. Rosenberg, *Nationalpolitische Publizistik*, II, 967.

76. Bennigsen's speech of June 6, 1866 to the Hanoverian Diet, in H. Oncken, *Bennigsen*, I, 725-727.

77. H. Schulze-Delitzsch, "Gegen den Preussisch-Oesterreichischen Krieg," in *Schriften und Reden*, III, 284-295; Schulze-Delitzsch to Muellensiefen, June 20, 1866, in *ibid.*, III, 299.

78. Unruh to Bennigsen, August 3, 1866, in H. Oncken, *Bennigsen*, I, 746.

79. Bennigsen's speech, October 19, 1867, in *ibid.*, II, 78-79.

80. H. Heffter, *op. cit.*, pp. 415-423.

81. Thus E. Anderson, *Social and Political Conflict in Prussia;* H. Heffter, *Deutsche Selbstverwaltung*, pp. 427-445; F. Loewenthal, *Der preussische Verfassungsstreit* (Altenberg, 1914); L. Dehio, "Die Taktik der Opposition waehrend des Konflikts," in *Historische Zeitschrift*, CXL (1929), pp. 279-347; Kurt Kaminski, *Verfassung und Verfassungskonflikt im Preussen, 1862-1866* (Koenigsberg and Berlin, 1938); Gordon A. Craig, *The Politics of the Prussian Army, 1640-1945* (New York and Oxford, 1956), pp. 136-179.

82. Erich Eyck, *Bismarck* (Zurich, 1941), I, 429, 461.

83. Programs of January 13, June 6, and September 29, 1861, in F. Salomon, *Deutsche Parteiprogramme*, I, 42-49.

84. *Ibid.;* C. Twesten, "Der preussische Beamtenstaat," in *Preussische Jahrbuecher*, XVIII (1866), pp. 136-147.

85. Hermann Baumgarten, "Der deutsche Liberalismus," in *Preussische Jahrbuecher*, XVIII, 592.

86. Rudolf von Gneist, *Die Militaervorlage von 1892 und der preussische Verfassungskonflikt von 1862 bis 1866* (Berlin, 1893), pp. 88-89.

87. L. Dehio, "Benedikt Waldeck," in *Historische Zeitschrift*, vol. 136 (1927), pp. 52-53.

88. Johannes Ziekursch, *Politische Geschichte des neuen Kaiserreiches* (Frankfurt a/M, 1925), I, 69.

89. Sybel to Droysen, June 19, 1864, in *Deutscher Liberalismus*, I, 228.

90. Sybel to Baumgarten, April 7, 1863, and July 3, 1865, in *ibid.*, I, 141, 252.

91. For Gneist's deliberate effort to use the military question as a means of reconciling the liberals and the government see Rudolf Gneist, *Die Lage der preussischen Heeresorganisation am 29 September 1862 nebst einem Zusatz ueber die Landwehr* (Berlin, 1862), pp. 4-5, 21-25.

92. Eckart Kehr, "Zur Genesis des koeniglichen preussischen Reserveoffiziers," in *Die Gesellschaft*, II (1928), 496.

93. Rudolf Gneist, *Die Lage der Preussischen Heeresorganisation*, pp. 27-28. But for the skepticism of the Old Liberals toward the national guard, see G. Craig, op. cit., p. 143, note 3, and Gerhard Ritter, *Staatskunst und Kriegshandwerk* (Munich, 1954), I, 166-167.

94. In H. Rosenberg, *Nationalpolitische Publizistik Deutschlands*, II, 498-499.

95. Hoverbeck to Haeusser, Feb. 15, 1863, in *Deutscher Liberalismus*, I, 132-133.

96. Schulze-Delitzsch's speech to Prussian Chamber, October 7, 1862, in *Schriften und Reden*, IV, 146.

97. F. Salomon, *Deutsche Parteiprogramme*, I, 60-61.

98. Schulze-Delitzsch's speech to the Prussian Chamber, May 4, 1865, in *Schriften und Reden*, IV, 301-302.

99. Schulze-Delitzsch's speech of October 7, 1862, in *ibid.*, IV, 147.

100. Frese's open letter in *Waechter: Wochenschrift fuer Minden-Ravensberg*, October 11, 1865, in *Deutscher Liberalismus*, I, 260-262.

101. Thus the Stavenhagen-Sybel-Schubert-Twesten compromise proposal of September, 1862 and Lasker's mediating tactics of November, 1865. See R. Gneist, *Die Militaervorlage von 1892*, pp. 57-58; Sybel to Baumgarten, April 7, 1863, in *Deutscher Liberalismus*, I, 141; Lasker to Oppenheim, Nov. 24, 1865 and Twesten to Lipke, Dec. 17, 1865, in *ibid.*, I, 266, 267.

102. E. Lasker, *Zur Verfassungsgeschichte Preussens*, p. 197; W. Schunke, *Die preussische Freihaendler*, pp. 9, 15, 19; Twesten's open letter to a convention of liberal deputies, September 1865, in *Deutscher Liberalismus*, I, 257; C. Twesten, "Der preussische Beamtenstaat," in *Preussische Jahrbuecher*, XVIII, 147.

103. Hermann Baumgarten, "Der deutsche Liberalismus," in *ibid.*, XVIII, 592.

104. C. Twesten, "Der preussische Beamtenstaat," in *ibid.*, XVIII, 147.

105. W. Schunke, *Die preussische Freihaendler*, pp. 23-40.

106. Rudolf von Delbrueck, *Lebenserinnerungen* (Leipzig, 1905), II, 227.

107. Lasker, quoted in W. Schunke, *Die preussische Freihaendler*, p. 50.

108. Michaelis quoted in Martin Spahn, "Zur Entstehung der nationalliberalen Partei," in *Zeitschrift fuer Politik*, I (1908), 443-444.

109. "Erklaerung," in *Ausgewaehlte Briefwechsel Rudolf Hayms*, p. 245.

110. Haym to Schrader, May 16, 1866, in *Deutscher Liberalismus*, I, 285-287.

111. "Zur Wahl," in *Hayms Briefwechsel*, pp. 249-251.

112. Baumgarten to Sybel, May 11 and May 15/16, 1866, Baumgarten to Treitschke, Aug. 10, 1866, in *Deutscher Liberalismus*, I, 281-283, 289-290, 342; Hermann Baumgarten, "Partei oder Vaterland? Ein Wort an die norddeutschen Liberalen," in H. Rosenberg, *Nationalpolitisches Publizistik*, II, 939-940; Hermann Baumgarten, "Der deutsche Liberalismus," in *Preussische Jahrbuecher*, XVIII, 589-590, 608-610.

113. *Ibid.*, XVIII, 471-472.

114. *Ibid.*, XVIII, 626-627.

115. *Ibid.*, XVIII, 625.

116. H. Oncken, *Bennigsen*, I, 737-739.

117. *Ibid.*, II, 14-15.

118. H. Herzfeld, *Miquel*, I, 52-53; Bennigsen to Rochau, Dec. 29, 1866, in H. Oncken, *Bennigsen*, II, 13.

119. From the Twesten papers, in *Deutscher Liberalismus*, I, 499; Twesten quoted in M. Spahn, "Zur Entstehung der nationalliberalen Partei," in *Zeitschrift fuer Politik*, I, 395.

120. The provision on indemnity which Bismarck forced into the Crown address against conservative opposition was a request for parliamentary approval of governmental expenditures made during the budget-less period of the conflict and was accompanied by the royal recognition that in general expenditures of state have a legal basis only in legislation enacted yearly by agreement of king and Diet.

121. Twesten to Lipke, Aug. 10, 1866, in *Deutscher Liberalismus*, I, 341.

122. Felix Rachfahl, "Eugen Richter und der Linksliberalismus im neuen Reich," in *Zeitschrift fuer Politik*, V (1912), pp. 269-271; M. Spahn, *op. cit.*, I, 414-422.

123. Quoted in *ibid.*, I, 429.

124. *Ibid.*, I, 400; W. Schunke, *op. cit.*, p. 54.

125. Ludwig Bamberger, *Gesammelte Schriften* (Berlin, 1913), III, 299.

126. *Ibid.*, III, 304.

127. *Ibid.*, III, 306-310.

128. In M. Spahn, "Zur Entstehung der nationalliberalen Partei," in *Zeitschrift fuer Politik*, I, 409.

129. L. Bamberger, *Gesammelte Schriften*, III, 311-315.

130. Cohn to Lasker, Sept. 6, 1866, in *Deutscher Liberalismus*, I, 345.

131. Program of Sept. 28, 1866, in F. Salomon, *Deutsche Parteiprogramme*, I, 75-76.

132. *Ibid.*

133. In M. Spahn, *op. cit.*, I, 445.

134. Baumgarten to Treitschke, Oct. 26, 1866, in *Deutscher Liberalismus*, I, 352; Forckenbeck to Sybel, Dec. 19, 1866, in *ibid.*, I, 360.

135. W. Schunke, *Die preussischen Freihaendler*, p. 82; H. Herzfeld, *Johannes von Miquel*, I, 57-58.

136. H. Oncken, *Rudolf von Bennigsen*, II, 26-27.

137. Compare Twesten's draft in *Deutscher Liberalismus*, I, 500-503, with the final program of June 12, 1867, in F. Salomon, *Deutsche Parteiprogramme*, I, 77-83.

138. Twesten's speech to the North German Constituent Reichstag, Mar. 9, 1866, in E. Bezold, *Materialien*, I, 77-78; Lasker's speech of Mar. 21, 1867, in *ibid.*, I, 512.

139. Twesten's speech of April 9, 1867, in *ibid.*, I, 656-658.

140. G. Mayer, "Die Trennung der proletarischen und buergerlichen Demokratie," in *Archiv fuer die Geschichte des Sozialismus*, II, 17-20.

141. Franz Mehring, *Geschichte der deutschen Sozialdemokratie* (Stuttgart, 1898), II, 177-179.

142. *Ibid.*, II, 192-193.

143. Quoted in G. Mayer, "Die Trennung der proletarischen und buergerlichen Demokratie," in *Archiv fuer die Geschichte des Sozialismus*, II, 28-29.

144. August Bebel, *Aus meinem Leben* (8th ed., Berlin and Stuttgart, 1933), pp. 130-131.

145. F. Mehring, *op. cit.*, II, 207.

146. F. Salomon, *Deutsche Parteiprogramme*, I, 89.

147. *Ibid.*, I, 90.

148. G. Mayer, "Die Trennung der proletarischen und der buergerlichen Demokratie," in *Archiv*, II, 40-42.

149. *Ibid.*, II, 46.

150. F. Salomon, *Die deutsche Parteiprogramme*, I, 86-88.

151. *Ibid.*, II, 54-55.

152. August Bebel, *Unsere Ziele* (6th ed., Leipzig, 1877), pp. 16-17.

153. Weiss to Jacoby, August 27, 1870, in G. Mayer, "Die Trennung der proletarischen und buergerlichen Demokratie," in *Archiv*, II, 65.

Epilogue

1. Rudolf Gneist, *Der Rechtsstaat* (Berlin, 1872), p. 12.

2. Eduard Lasker, *Ueber Welt- und Staatsweisheit* (Berlin, 1873), pp. 35-36.

3. Friedrich Naumann, *Demokratie und Kaisertum* (4th ed., Berlin, 1905), pp. 16-31.

4. Max Weber, "Der Nationalstaat und die Volkswirtschaftspolitik," in *Gesammelte Politische Schriften* (Munich, 1921), p. 27; Hugo Preuss, "Zum sechzigsten Geburtstag Theodor Barths," in *Staat, Recht, und Freiheit* (Tuebingen, 1926), p. 552; Theodor Barth, "Die politische Aufgabe der Freisinnigen Vereinigung," in *Die Nation* X (1893), p. 537; *Die Neue Rundschau*, XXI, part 1 (1910), pp. 273-275; XXI, part 2, p. 443; XXIII, part 2 (1912), p. 733; XXV, part 1 (1914), pp. 431-432; Oskar Stillich, *Die politische Parteien in Deutschland: Der Liberalismus* (Leipzig, 1911), pp. 330-331.

5. Lilo Linke, *Restless Days* (New York, 1935), pp. 265, 292-293, 338.

6. See the convenient tables of Reichstag elections in Koppel S. Pinson, *Modern Germany* (New York, 1954), pp. 574-575.

7. Hajo Holborn, "Achievements and Prospects of German Democracy," in *Political Science Quarterly*, LXX (1955), p. 429.

8. *Ibid.*, LXX, 430.

9. John H. Herz, "German Officialdom Revisited," in *World Politics*, VII (1954), pp. 65-67.

Select Bibliography

This book is essentially a study in thematic history, and since the theme of political freedom has roots and ramifications in the most varied fields of German history a complete bibliography of the subject is hardly possible. Moreover, the chronological scope of the study has entailed a further selection even from those sources and commentaries that bear more or less directly upon the theme. An attempt at a definitive bibliography of the field, then, would hardly be in order here. Nor does it seem feasible simply to list all the works that have been used, since what is relevant to the host of individual figures and what is relevant from the more general literature are more easily ascertainable by reference to the table of contents, index, and footnotes, where the initial citations are given in full. It has seemed advisable, therefore, to limit this bibliography to two kinds of material which are not readily located elsewhere—collections of sources and recent secondary writing.

General

Most immediately related to the historical analysis of political freedom in Germany are the several histories of German liberalism. Because they deal more directly with the movement than with the problem, their temporal concentration is in the 19th century, when the movement was crystallized, and their substantive emphasis is upon the detailed internal development of programs, organizations, and policies. The old standard works, Oskar Klein-Hattingen, *Geschichte des deutschen Liberalismus* (2 vols., Berlin, 1911) and Oskar Stillich, *Der Liberalismus* (Leipzig, 1911) have been supplemented and revised recently by the following:

A. Source Collections

Federico Federici, ed., *Der deutsche Liberalismus: die Entwicklung einer politischen Idee von Immanuel Kant bis Thomas Mann* (Zurich, 1946). An anthology.

B. Recent Literature

Heinrich Heffter, *Die deutsche Selbstverwaltung im 19. Jahrhundert* (Stuttgart, 1950).

Rudolf Olden, *History of Liberty in Germany* (London, 1946).

Frederick C. Sell, *Die Tragoedie des deutschen Liberalismus* (Stuttgart, 1953).

I. The Tradition: the Old Regime

The literature reflects the historical fact that the overt expressions of liberty in the Germany of this period were localized in particular figures, issues, and periods. The analysis of these must be pieced together from works in various fields.

A. Source Collections

Acta Borussica, especially the volumes on *Seidenindustrie* (3 vols., Berlin, 1892), *Getreidehandel* (3 vols., Berlin, 1896-1910), and *Wollindustrie* (Berlin, 1933). Each work includes an excellent commentary.

B. Recent Literature

Carlo Antoni, *Der Kampf wider die Vernunft: Zur Entstehungsgeschichte des deutschen Freiheitsgedankens* (Ger. tr., Stuttgart, 1951). On the organicist writers of the latter 18th century.

Leo Balet, *Die Verbuergerlichung der deutschen Kunst, Literatur, und Musik im 18. Jahrhundert* (Leipzig, 1936).

Heinrich Bechtel, *Wirtschaftsgeschichte Deutschlands* (2 vols., Frankfurt/M., 1941, 1952). To the end of the 18th century.

F. L. Carsten, *The Origins of Prussia* (Oxford, 1954).

Hajo Holborn, "Der deutsche Idealismus in sozialgeschichtlicher Beleuchtung," in *Historische Zeitschrift,* vol. 174 (1952).

Friedrich Luetge, *Deutsche Sozial- und Wirtschaftsgeschichte* (Heidelberg, 1952).

Fritz Valjavec, *Die Entstehung der politischen Stroemungen in Deutschland, 1770-1815* (Munich, 1951).

Erik Wolf, *Grosse Rechtsdenker der deutschen Geistesgeschichte* (3rd ed., Tuebingen, 1951).

Hans Wolff, *Die Weltanschauung der deutschen Aufklaerung in geschichtlicher Entwicklung* (Bern, 1949).

II. The Assumptions: The Era of the French Revolution (1789-1830)

A. Source Collections

Herman Haupt and Paul Wentzcke, eds., *Quellen und Darstellungen zur Geschichte der deutschen Burschenschaft und der deutschen Einheitsbewegung* (17 vols., Heidelberg, 1910-1940).

H. Oncken and F. Saemisch, eds., *Vorgeschichte und Begruendung des deutschen Zollvereins* (Berlin, 1934).

Georg Winter, ed., *Die Reorganisation des preussischen Staates unter Stein und Hardenberg* (Leipzig, 1931). Only one volume has appeared.

B. Recent Literature

Eugene N. Anderson, *Nationalism and the Cultural Crisis in Prussia, 1806-1815* (New York, 1939).

R. Aris, *History of Political Thought in Germany from 1789-1815* (London, 1936).

Reimund Asanger, *Beitraege zur Lehre vom Rechtsstaat im 19. Jahrhundert* (Bochum, 1938).

Henri Brunschwig, *La crise de l'état prussien a la fin du XVIII siècle et la genèse de la mentalité romantique* (Paris, 1947).

Gordon A. Craig, *The Politics of the Prussian Army, 1660-1945* (Oxford, 1955).

Jacques Droz, *L'Allemagne et la Revolution française* (Paris, 1949). To 1803.

Fritz Hartung, *Studien zur Geschichte der preussischen Verwaltung* (vol. III, Berlin, 1948).

Hans Kohn, "Arndt and the Character of German Nationalism," in *American Historical Review* (1949), LIV.

Herbert Marcuse, *Reason and Revolution: Hegel and the Rise of Social Theory* (New York, 1941).

Wilhelm Mommsen, *Stein, Ranke, Bismarck* (Munich, 1954).

Johann-Albrecht von Rantzau, *Wilhelm von Humboldt: Der Weg seiner geistigen Entwicklung* (Munich, 1939).

Gerhard Ritter, *Staatskunst und Kriegshandwerk* (vol. I, Munich, 1954).

William O. Shanahan, *Prussian Military Reforms, 1786-1813* (New York, 1945).

Walter Simon, *The Failure of the Prussian Reform Movement, 1807-1819* (Ithaca, 1955).

Fritz Valjavec (*vid. supra*).

Karl Wolff, *Die deutsche Publizistik in der Zeit der Freiheits-kaempfe und des Wiener Kongresses, 1813-1815* (Plauen, 1934).

Ernst Walter Zeeden, *Hardenberg und der Gedanke einer Volks-vertretung in Preussen, 1807-1812* (Berlin, 1940).

III. The Movement: 1830-1870

Since this period was the hey-day of German liberalism, sources and authorities are legion. What follows is highly selected.

A. Source Collections

Ludwig Bergstraesser, ed., *Der politische Katholizismus* (Munich, 1921).

E. Bezold, ed., *Materialien der Deutschen Reichs-Verfassung* (Berlin, 1873).

Joseph Hansen, ed., *Rheinische Briefe und Akten zur Geschichte der politischen Bewegung, 1830-1850* (Bonn, 1919).

J. Heyderhoff, ed., *Deutscher Liberalismus im Zeitalter Bismarcks* (vol. I, Berlin, 1925).

Wilhelm Mommsen, ed., *Deutsche Parteiprogramme; eine Aus-wahl vom Vormaerz bis zur Gegenwart* (Munich, 1951).

Karl Obermann, ed., *Einheit und Freiheit: die deutsche Ge-schichte von 1815 bis 1849 in zeitgenoessischen Dokumenten* (Berlin, 1950).

Adolph Rapp, ed., *Briefwechsel zwischen Vischer und Strauss* (2 vols., Stuttgart, 1952).

Hans Rosenberg, *Die nationalpolitische Publizistik Deutschlands vom Eintritt der neuen Aera in Preussen bis zum Ausbruch des deutschen Krieges* (2 vols., Munich and Berlin, 1955).

Carl von Rotteck and Carl Welcker, eds., *Staats-Lexikon* (15 vols., Altona, 1834-1843).

Felix Salomon, *Die deutsche Parteiprogramme* (2 vols., Berlin, 1907).

Wolfgang Treue, ed., *Deutsche Parteiprogramme, 1861-1954* (Goettingen, 1955).

B. Recent Literature

Eugene N. Anderson, *The Social and Political Conflict in Prussia, 1859-1864* (Lincoln, 1864). With appendix volume on the Prussian elections of 1862 and 1863.

Georg Bernhard, *Meister und Dilettanten am Kapitalismus im Reich der Hohenzollern* (Amsterdam, 1936).

Walter Bussmann, *Treitschke: sein Welts- und Geschichtsbild* (Goettingen, 1952).

Jacques Droz, *Le liberalisme rhénan, 1815-1848* (Paris, 1940).

Theodore S. Hammerow, "History and the German Revolution of 1848," in *American Historical Review*, LX (1954).

Oscar J. Hammon, "Economic and Social Factors in the Prussian Rhineland in 1848," in *ibid.*, LIV (1949).

Hans Herzfeld, *Johannes von Miquel* (2 vols., Detmold, 1938).

Ernst Kaeber, *Berlin 1848* (Berlin, 1948).

Kurt Kaminski, *Verfassung und Verfassungskonflikt im Preussen, 1862-66* (Koenigsberg and Berlin, 1938).

Frederic Lilge, *The Abuse of Learning: the Failure of the German University* (New York, 1948).

Koppel S. Pinson, *Modern Germany* (New York, 1954).

Percy Ernst Schramm, *Hamburg, Deutschland, und die Welt* (Munich, 1943).

Rudolf Stadelmann, *Soziale und politische Geschichte der Revolution von 1848* (Munich, 1948).

Herbert A. Strauss, *Staat, Buerger, Mensch: die Debatten der deutschen Nationalversammlung 1848/9 ueber die Grundrechte* (Aarau, 1947).

R. Hinton Thomas, *Liberalism, Nationalism, and the German Intellectuals, 1822-1847* (Cambridge, 1951).

Index

Achenwall, G. A., 47
Althusius, Johannes, 48
America, 71
Aristocracy, 36, 75, 288, 303, 459; and freedom, 8-34, 45, 162; in Wolff, 70; in Kant, 123; in Hegel, 135; in Reform era, 141, 142, 143-144, 145-147; in Stein, 154-155, 485; in Hardenberg, 158, 162-165; in Arndt, 195-196; in post-Liberation era, 218-220, 226-227, 232-233, 235, 237, 241; in Dahlmann, 308; in post-revolutionary era, 342, 343-344
Army, 243; Prussian National Guard (*Landwehr*), 175-176, 201, 429, 434, 490, 526; Prussian Militia (*Landsturm*), 175, 201, 429, 490; in Liberation era, 197; in Prussian Conflict era, 429-430, 432-433
Arndt, Ernst Moritz, 178, 208, 216; his nationalism, 192-196, 210-211, 213-214
Artisans, 35, 142, 283, 285, 288, 291-292, 303, 330-331, 335, 395, 451
Auerswald, Rudolf von, 414
Austria, 195, 204, 335, 336, 337, 341, 342, 343, 407, 414, 452, 453

Baden, 83, 143, 145, 280, 283, 296, 325, 330, 331, 336, 338, 339, 428, 450-451; post-Liberation constitution, 229, 231, 233-237, 241-244
Bahrdt, Carl Friedrich, 74
Bamberger, Ludwig, 339, 348, 352, 445-447
Barth, Theodor, 463-464
Bauer, Bruno, 297
Bauer, Edgar, 297, 326
Baumgarten, Hermann, 370, 400, 437, 440-441
Bavaria, 143, 144, 344; post-Liberation constitution, 229, 231-233
Bebel, August, 373, 452-456, 457
Beckerath, Hermann, 314
Bennigsen, Rudolf von, 348, 409, 415, 416, 417, 418, 424, 425, 426-427, 442-443, 448
Berg, Philipp von, 386
Beyme, Karl Friederich, 146
Berlin, 38, 279, 283, 331, 336, 399
Besold, C. B., 47
Bismarck, Prince Otto von, 276, 341, 351, 362-363, 383, 386, 387, 407, 411, 412, 423-425, 430, 438, 443, 444, 448
Blum, Robert, 296
Bockum-Dolff Group, 432, 433
Bodin, Jean, 49
Boehmert, Viktor, 408, 411-413, 423
Boerne, Ludwig, 280, 298
Bourgeoisie, 296, 303, 312-313, 334, 336, 379-380, 382, 389, 397, 398, 400-405, 410, 416-417, 422, 432, 437, 440-441, 459
Boyen, Hermann von, 196, 201
Brandes, Ernst, 148
Brauer, Johann Nicolaus, 484
Braun, Karl, 410
Bremen, 408, 423-424
Bruck, Karl, 343
Brunswick, 229, 280, 424, 471
Bucher, Lothar, 378, 385-387
Buechner, Georg, 296, 298
Bureaucracy, 8-9, 46, 85, 143-144, 156, 232, 234, 296, 342, 343-345; and burghers, 19-20, 34-36, 42; and aristocracy, 22-28, 30, 144-147; and freedom, 45, 141, 146-147, 217-229, 288, 398, 473
Burghers, 10-11, 143, 154; and state-building, 19-20, 34, 472; and middle classes, 34-41, 44-45, 294, 310, 404; and intellectuals, 41-44, 294

Camphausen, Ludolf, 310
Capitalism, 341; agrarian, 29-31, 142, 162, 289-290, 291; commercial and industrial, 37-41, 279, 290-291, 296, 345-346, 402
Cassirer, Ernst, 88
Center Party, 461, 467
Charles, Grand Duke of Baden, 234-235
Chemnitz, Bogislaw (Hippolytus a Lapide), 51
Churches, 11, 159, 293; Lutheran, 4, 5, 49, 60, 69, 177; Catholic, 279, 284, 296, 298, 511-512; Illuminati, 279, 284, 298, 349
Clausewitz, Karl von, 196, 198, 199-200, 201
Coelln, Friedrich von, 166-167
Cohn, Adolph, 447
Communism, 326, 332, 457, 467
Congress of German Economists

(*Kongress der deutschen Volks-wirte*), 407-413, 439
Conring, Hermann, 47, 51
Constitutions, 280, 297, 343-344, 378-379; projected in Prussia, 217-229; southern, 229-241; German of 1849, 335, 338, 339, 416, 417, 444; Prussian of 1848, 337; Prussian of 1848 revised (1850), 338, 431; North German of 1867, 449; German of 1871, 458
Cosmopolitanism, 4, 174, 177, 327-328
Cotta von Cottendorf, Johann, 73, 239
Customs Union (*Zollverein*), 227-229, 276, 281, 289, 342

Dahlmann, Friedrich, 279, 281, 283; political theory, 305-309, 313-314, 339
Danzig, 11, 484
Dehler, Thomas, 468
Delbrueck, Rudolf von, 343, 410, 439
Democracy, 301-303, 316-317, 327, 331, 334-335, 362, 369, 374, 378, 380, 382-383, 384, 386-388, 389, 392-393, 420, 422, 450-457
Democratic Association, 464
Diets, Territorial (*Landtagen*), 10, 14, 153, 161, 162, 164-165, 226, 233, 236, 238, 242-243, 280, 283, 286, 344-345, 372, 429-430, 471-472
Droysen, J. G., 314, 359-361
Duncker, Max, 414

East Prussia, 142, 143, 175, 279, 282, 291, 294
Eckhardt, Ludwig, 420, 421, 422, 451
Elbing, 38
Engels, Friedrich, 375, 378
England, 71, 142, 145, 297
Erfurt Parliament, 339
Ernest, Duke of Gotha, 19
Ernest II, Duke of Saxony-Coburg-Gotha, 344
Estates, Territorial (*Landstaenden*), 10, 14, 57-58, 75, 78, 79, 135, 148, 153-154, 156-157, 162, 206, 208, 225-226, 231, 238, 239, 308

Faucher, Julius, 432, 439
Federation of German Workers' Unions, 419, 452-453, 454, 455
Feuerbach, Ludwig, 297, 349
Fichte, Johann Gottlieb, 173, 196; individualism in, 179-182; State in, 182-187; nationalism in, 187-192
First International, 454-455, 456-457

Follen, August, 267
Follen, Karl, 264; political ideas, 266-272
Forckenbeck, Max von, 432, 444, 449
France, 12, 84, 143-144, 157, 177, 194, 216, 414
Frankfurt am Main, 38, 280, 336
Frankfurt Parliament, 333, 340, 342
Frederick I, Grand Duke of Baden, 428
Frederick I, King of Wuerttemberg, 238
Frederick II ("the Great"), King of Prussia, 22, 27, 30, 32, 33, 71, 166, 474; and the League of Princes, 18-19; his enlightened absolutism, 22-26
Frederick III, Elector of Brandenburg, 60
Frederick William ("the Great Elector"), of Brandenburg, 22
Frederick William I, King of Prussia, 22, 32, 472
Frederick William II, King of Prussia, 30
Frederick William III, King of Prussia, 146, 219
Frederick William IV, King of Prussia, 282, 298, 338
Free Democratic Party (*Freie Demokratische Partei*), 468
Freedom (and Liberty), 14, 20, 26-27, 30, 86, 347-348, 350-351; German and European, 3-5; *Libertaet* and *Freiheit*, 6-7, 215, 305; aristocratic and princely, 14-19, 33-34, 145-146, 196; and the State, 21-22, 34, 36-37, 39-41, 45, 70, 80, 84, 206-207, 367-370, 435, 466-467, 468-470; in Frederick "the Great," 24-25; and the burghers, 41-45; in Pufendorf, 54-56, 59; in Thomasius, 59-66; in Wolff, 66-67, 69-70; in 18th century intellectuals, 71-72; in Schloezer, 77-79; in Moeser, 79-80; moderate, 84-85, 138, 139-173, 216-217, 275-276, 302-303, 303-314, 332, 334, 354-370, 411-412, 416, 422-424, 432-434, 438-443, 448-449, 459-460; radical, 84-85, 166-167, 216-217, 252, 261-272, 275-276, 279, 301, 302-303, 322-329, 332, 334, 335-336, 371-397, 416, 419, 421-422, 432-436, 444, 450-457, 460-461; dualist, 84-85, 213, 216-217, 229-261, 275-276, 303, 314-322, 339-340, 348-354, 416, 424-427, 432, 436-438, 442, 443-448, 448-450, 461-464; in Kant, 87-

89, 90-95, 100-104, 105, 108-109, 114-124; in Hegel, 127-129, 132-133, 135-138; in Stein, 148, 149-151, 153-155, 204-206; in Hardenberg, 157-160, 165; in Humboldt, 167-173; in Fichte, 179-184, 189-190; in Arndt, 193-194, 196, 209-210, 213-214; in Goerres, 214-215
Frese, Julius, 432, 436, 456-457
Frey, J. G., 486
Freytag, Gustav, 449
Fromman, F. J., 508

Gagern, Heinrich von, 333, 339
German Confederation, 216, 219, 227, 228, 281, 283, 313, 331, 342, 344
German Democratic Party (Deutsche Demokratische Partei), 464-467
German Empire (1871-1918), 364, 458-464
German Federal Republic, 468-470
German National People's Party, 466
German People's Party (Deutsche Volkspartei, 1865-1910), 392, 399, 420, 427, 428-429, 436, 450-457
German People's Party (Deutsche Volkspartei, 1919-1933), 465-466
German State Party, 467
Germany and Europe, 4-5, 12-14, 39-40, 49-50, 228-229, 237, 293, 469; and the French Revolution, 83-84, 139-140. See also appropriate subject-heading
General German Workers' Union, 419, 427, 454, 455
Gervinus, Georg, 318, 364, 371
Glassbrenner, Adolf, 284
Gneisenau, Neithardt von, 196, 197, 198, 200, 201-202, 220
Gneist, Rudolf von, 352, 356-358, 433-434, 459-460
Goerres, Josef, 208, 216; political ideas, 211-215
Goethe, Johann Wolfgang, 19
Gotha Congress, 339; Gotha Party, 361, 365, 367, 422
Goettingen University, 22, 26, 27, 77, 148, 279, 309
Grotius, Hugo, 49

Haeusser, Ludwig, 414
Halle University, 22, 73, 476
Hamann, Georg, 72
Hambach Festival, 280, 328
Hamburg, 29, 38, 406
Hanover, 17, 229, 279, 280, 283, 309, 339, 342, 343, 344, 472

Hansa, 11
Hansemann, David, 294; political ideas, 310-313
Hardenberg, Prince Karl August von, 27, 147, 166, 338; ideas in reform period, 155-165; policies in post-Liberation period, 219-228
Haym, Rudolf, 361-363, 370, 440
Hecker, Friedrich, 284, 332
Hegel, Georg Wilhelm Friedrich, 85, 86, 297, 304, 323, 377; and liberalism, 125-126, 129, 135-136; presuppositions, 126-129; political theory, 129-138
Heine, Heinrich, 280, 298, 300
Heinitz, Friedrich Anton von, 27
Held, Friedrich, 284
Held, H. H. von, 167
Henckel, Guido, 449
Herder, J. G., 72, 74, 192
Hertzberg, Ewald Friedrich von, 83-84
Herwegh, Georg, 279, 323-324
Hess, Moses, 299
Hesse-Darmstadt, 227, 229, 342
Hesse-Kassel, 279, 280, 342, 471
Hobbes, Thomas, 49, 53, 54, 55
Holborn, Hajo, 4
Holland, 29, 38
Holy Roman Empire, 6, 7, 14-16, 36, 46-48, 71, 146, 174, 177, 234, 239; in Chemnitz and Conring, 51; in Pufendorf, 51-52; in Moeser, 79-80; in Hegel, 136; in Fichte, 191; in Arndt, 196
Hoverbeck, Leopold von, 400, 432, 435
Huguenots, 38, 474
Humboldt, Wilhelm von, 220; pre-reform ideas, 167-170; reform ideas, 170-173; nationalism in, 208-210; in post-Liberation period, 221-223

Individualism, 27-28, 79, 147, 173, 178, 236, 237-238, 252; in Pufendorf, 53-54; in Thomasius, 65-66; in Wolff, 66-67, 69; in Kant, 91, 93-95, 100-102, 103, 111, 112-115, 121, 124; in Hegel, 129-132, 138; in Humboldt, 167-169, 173; in Fichte, 179-184; in Arndt, 192-193; in Rotteck, 250-251; and Rechtsstaat, 260-261; in Dahlmann, 308; in Lassalle, 382-383; in Schulze-Delitzsch, 394-395
Intellectuals, 8-9, 35-36, 71-72, 75, 141, 167, 173, 211, 216-217, 276, 463-465; burghers and middle classes, 41-44;

idea of freedom in old regime, 44-45, 71-72; and the French Revolution, 83-84, 139; and nationalism, 176, 206-208; and radicalism, 268; in pre-March period, 279-340; in post-March period, 347, 393, 398, 401, 406, 440-441
Itzstein, Adam von, 296

Jacoby, Johann, 296, 391-393, 432, 436, 454, 456
James I, of England, 49
Jews, 38, 160, 181, 474
Jolly, Julius, 428
Jordan, Sylvester, 236-258
Joseph II, of Austria, 18, 22, 71, 244
Jus Episcopale, 49
Justi, J. H. G. von, 73

Kahl, Wilhelm, 466
Kant, Immanuel, 27, 50, 66, 85, 86, 244-245, 256, 297, 323; and liberalism, 86-87, 124-125; on the problem of freedom, 87-89; early political theory, 89-95, 103-104; early presuppositions, 95-103; later political theory, 104-105, 111-124; later presuppositions, 105-111
Karl August, Duke of Weimar, 22
Karl Friedrich, Duke of Baden, 22, 33
Karl Wilhelm Ferdinand, Duke of Brunswick, 22
Kiesselbach, Wilhelm, 405
Kinkel, Gottfried, 339
Kleist, Heinrich von, 178
Knights, Imperial, 15-16, 148, 234
Koenigsberg, 11, 38, 399, 484
Koenigsberg University, 26, 27
Kraus, Christian Jakob, 27
Krefeld, 38
Kugelmann, Ludwig, 520

Lamey, August, 428
Lasker, Eduard, 348, 352-353, 432, 439, 445, 449, 462-463
Lassalle, Ferdinand, 419, 420, 427; political ideas, 373-383
Leibniz, Gottfried Wilhelm, 50, 61, 66, 69, 70
Leipzig, 283, 399, 419
Lerchenfeld, Alexander von, 232
Lette, Wilhelm, 449
Liberal Association (*Freisinnige Vereinigung*), 461-462, 463-464
Liberalism, 42, 77, 84, 86, 211, 275-470; economic, 26-27, 142, 159, 218-219, 224, 227-229, 288-289, 310-312, 342-343, 346, 397, 407-413; bureaucratic, 27-28, 144-145, 160, 217-229, 280-281, 282-283, 342-344, 356, 428; political, 27, 217, 219, 272, 333, 336-337, 339-340, 341, 357-358, 375-376, 398, 422, 458, 464, 467; constitutional, 71-80, 229-261, 286, 314-322, 331, 361-362, 384, 389-391, 431-432; social, 27, 324, 357-358, 464; and nationalism, 192, 276-277, 364; "classical," 282, 284-285, 295, 297, 303, 358-370
Libertaet, 6, 14, 51, 146, 196, 210, 217, 369, 470
Liebenstein, Ludwig von, 243
Liebknecht, Wilhelm, 373, 452-456, 520
List, Friedrich, 239, 297
Locke, John, 53, 59, 251
Louis, Prince of Bavaria, 232
Lower Middle Class, 378, 379, 380, 396, 399, 401, 403, 405-406, 409, 438, 450, 485
Ludewig, J. P., 47
Luebeck, 344
Luther, Martin, 61

Maassen, Karl von, 219
Magdeburg, 38
Mannheim, 284
Manteuffel, Otto von, 339, 343
Marx, Karl, 285, 296, 297, 299, 322, 326, 374, 375, 377
Maskov, J. J., 47
Mathy, Karl, 295-296, 339
Mayer, Karl, 451, 456
Mayer, Reinhold, 468
Mecklenburg, 472
Meier, H. H., 499
Meinecke, Friedrich, 4
Mencken, A. L., 146
Mercantilism, 38-41, 474; Cameralism, 30-31, 73
Metternich, Prince Clemens von, 241
Mevissen, Gustav, 285, 294, 300, 310
Michaelis, Otto, 410, 432, 439, 445, 448
Middle Classes, 4, 20, 83, 145, 232, 285, 288, 292-293, 341, 386, 393-397, 400, 402, 404-405, 414, 416, 417, 422, 434, 450. See also Bourgeoisie, Burghers, Intellectuals, Lower Middle Class
Miquel, Johannes, 348, 417, 421, 424, 442, 448, 449
Mirabeau, Honoré de, 40

Moeser, Justus, 40, 48, 72, 74, 192; political theory, 79-80
Mohl, Robert von, 231, 242, 256, 258-261, 317, 371-373, 428
Mommsen, Theodor, 361, 432, 463
Montesquieu, Charles de, 71
Montgelas, Maximilian von, 144, 231-232
Moser, Friedrich Carl von, 72-73, 75-76
Motz, Friedrich von, 219, 227-228
Mueller, Adam, 253-255

Napoleon I, 198, 202, 244
Napoleon III, 385
Nassau, 229
National Liberal Party, 348, 426, 428, 438-450, 459-462, 465
National Socialist Workers' Party, 466, 470
National Union (*Nationalverein*), 354, 395, 413-427, 428
Nationalism, 4, 84-85, 192, 276-277, 405; in Hegel, 132-133, 136-138; in Stein, 148, 150, 202-206; in Humboldt, 169, 170, 208-210; in the Liberation era, 174-215; in Fichte, 178-179, 187-192; in Arndt, 192-196; 210-211; in Goerres, 211-215; in the moderates, 313-314, 362-363, 364, 366-370, 413-414, 422-424, 439-440; in the dualists, 317-322, 424-427, 446-447; in the radicals, 327-329, 376, 386-387, 396, 413-414, 452-453
Natural Law (and Natural Rights), 47, 49-50, 71, 72, 76, 79, 80, 147, 282, 297, 303, 322, 323, 389, 393; in Pufendorf, 53-54; in Thomasius, 62-64; in Wolff, 66-67, 69; in Fichte, 191; in Rotteck, 245; in Follen, 266-267
Naumann, Freidrich, 463-464
Nebenius, Karl, 236-237
Nettelbladt, D., 73
Niebuhr, B. G., 217
North German Confederation (1867), 391, 444, 447, 448

Oetker, Friedrich, 449
Oldenburg, 343
Oldendorp, Johannes, 48
Old Liberals, 344, 363, 410, 430, 439-441, 449, 526
Old Regime, 5-80
Oppenheim, H. B., 348, 351

Palatinate, 280, 283, 338
Peasantry, 8-10, 35, 83, 142, 285, 288, 292, 303, 330, 346, 403, 451, 485, 486; revolt of 1525, 10, 16-17, 284; in 18th century, 31-33; liberation, 143, 148-149, 152, 154, 160, 162, 291-293, 330-331, 336, 338, 485
Pfizer, Paul, 300; political ideas, 317-322
Pfordten, Ludwig von der, 344
Poelitz, Karl, 256-258
Preuss, Hugo, 464
Prince-Smith, John, 407-408
Princes, 5-6, 8-9, 11-14, 18-19, 46, 47-49, 71, 75, 136-137, 149, 190-191, 195, 202, 204-205, 209-210, 428, 458; and aristocracy, 14-19, 22-23; agricultural policies, 29-34; and towns, 36-37; and freedom, 45, 212-215; and constitutions, 229-242, 321, 333, 335
Progressive Party (*Fortschrittspartei*, also *Freisinnige Volkspartei*), 375, 378, 379, 380-381, 386, 387, 390, 392, 393, 397, 399, 400, 410, 412, 428, 429-438, 439-440, 443-448, 450, 454, 460-462, 465
Prussia, 29-30, 83-84, 129, 175, 195, 216-217, 275-276, 309-313, 325, 335, 336, 337, 452; in the old regime, 13, 18, 26-27, 472; Law Code of 1794, 27, 32-33, 76; industrial policies, 40-41; in Reform era, 145-173; in Liberation era, 196-202, 204, 205, 209; in post-Liberation era, 217-229, 230, 232; in pre-March era, 282-283, 285, 286, 288, 298; in Revolution of 1848, 338-340; in post-revolutionary era, 342, 343, 360-361, 369-370, 380, 390, 396, 410, 414, 415, 416; in Conflict era, 350, 392, 417-418, 423-426, 429-438, 442, 446-447
Prussian Union, 276, 339-340
Puetter, J. S., 27, 47
Pufendorf, Samuel, 15, 50, 67, 71; constitutional theory, 50-52; political theory, 52-59

Radowitz, Josef von, 338
Realpolitik, 354, 387, 396, 421
Rechtsstaat, 65, 230, 231, 242, 252-261, 317, 351, 353, 358, 372, 378, 392, 395, 422, 431, 435, 437, 459-460, 470, 505, 506
Reformation, 5, 9, 11-12, 42, 48, 49, 174

Rehberg, August Wilhelm, 148
Reichensperger, August, 298
Reichensperger, Peter, 298
Reitzenstein, Sigismund von, 144-145
Republicanism, 74, 301, 332, 371, 389
Revolution, French: of 1789, 5, 9, 77, 80, 83-84, 86, 139, 141, 145, 146, 156, 177, 198, 210, 244; in Kant, 104-105, 111; of 1830, 278, 280; of 1848, 331
Revolution, German: of 1848, 125, 284, 301, 310, 329-340, 341, 365, 374, 393, 439; of 1918, 125, 464
Rhenish Confederation, 84, 143-144
Rhineland, 83, 143, 279, 282, 285, 291, 294, 309-310, 331, 423
Richter, Eugen, 393, 396-397, 461
Rochau, A. L. von, 348, 353-356, 416
Rodbertus, Karl, 384-388
Ronge, Johann, 298
Rotteck, Karl, 230, 231, 236, 281, 297, 322; in post-Liberation era, 241-252, 283; in pre-March era, 301, 303, 315-317
Rousseau, Jean-Jacques, 87, 244, 251
Ruge, Arnold, 294, 297, 299, 323, 326-327, 511
Ruhr, 290, 388
Russia, 341

Saxe-Weimar, 229
Saxony, 17, 38, 40, 83, 280, 338, 339, 343-344, 450-451, 452, 471
Scharnhorst, G. J. D. von, 196, 201, 484
Schlegel, Friedrich, 177
Schleiermacher, Friedrich, 177-178
Schloezer, A. L. von, 27, 43, 48, 73, 74; political theory, 76-79
Schoen, Theodor von, 167
Schroetter, Friedrich von, 142
Schubart, Christian, 43
Schulze-Delitzsch, Hermann, 401, 409, 412, 415, 416, 417, 418, 421, 424, 425, 426, 432, 435, 436; political ideas, 393-396
Schurz, Karl, 339
Schwarzenburg, Prince Felix, 343
Schweitzer, J. B. von, 454
Schwerin, Maximilian von, 449
Seckendorf, V. L. von, 48
Siebenpfeiffer, P. J., 279, 328
Silesia, 290; weavers' rising, 83, 283
Smith, Adam, 26, 27, 30
Social Democratic Party, 388, 450, 456-457, 461, 467, 468

Socialism, 338, 373-384, 386, 387, 393, 406, 451, 455-456, 457, 458, 467
Sonnemann, Ludwig, 419-420, 452, 454, 456
Sovereignty, 7, 15-16, 47, 49, 70, 79, 428; in Frederick the Great, 23-24; burghers' role in, 34; in Pufendorf, 52-59; in Wolff, 67-69; in Kant, 120-121; in Fichte, 190-191
Stahl, Friedrich Julius, 256
State, 4, 8, 49-50, 205-206, 208, 276-277, 411, 466-470; Frederician, 26; in Pufendorf, 56, 59; in Thomasius, 61-66; in Wolff, 69; in Schloezer, 77-79; in Moeser, 79-80; in Kant, 115-116, 123-124; in Hegel, 132-134, 138; in Reform era, 143; in Stein, 148-153; in Hardenberg, 156-160, 165; in Humboldt, 168, 170-173; in Fichte, 182-186, 188, 190-191; in Arndt, 194; in Rotteck, 246-249; in Rechtsstaat, 257-261, 460; in radicalism, 268; in moderates, 304-305; in Dahlmann, 305-306; in Mevissen, 310; in Hansemann, 312-313; in Gneist, 358; in Droysen, 359-361; in Treitschke, 266; in Mohl, 372; in Lassalle, 382-383; in Bucher, 383. See also Freedom
States, Ecclesiastical, 15-16
States, Territorial, 5-7, 8-9, 12-14, 46-47, 140, 155, 230, 276; formation, 19-20; enlightened absolutism in, 21-45, 49-50; in Pufendorf, 52-53; in Schloezer, 79; in Moeser, 79; in Hegel, 136; in Fichte, 191; in Stein, 203
Stein, Baron Karl vom, 27, 147, 155, 156, 166, 297, 388; political ideas in Reform era, 147-155; political ideas in Liberation era, 202-206
Stein, Lorenz, 299, 387
Stettin, 11
Stirner, Max, 297
Stolberg, Friedrich von, 74
Strauss, David Friedrich, 297, 331
Streit, Fedor, 416, 421
Stresemann, Gustav, 465
Struensee, Karl August von, 27, 146
Struve, Gustav, 284, 301, 332, 339; political ideas, 324-325
Student Unions (Burschenschaften), 85, 217, 261-272, 280; the Blacks (die Schwarzen), 262, 266-267; Arminians, 265; Germanists, 265-266, 508

Stueve, Johann, 344
Sweden, 29, 71
Sybel, Heinrich von, 400, 414-415, 433, 449

Thaer, Albrecht, 142
Thirty Years' War, 11, 29, 48, 50, 51
Thomasius, Christian, 50, 67; political theory, 59-66
Towns, 10-11, 35-51, 471; self-administration, 149, 152-153, 239, 484
Treitschke, Heinrich von, 363-370
Troeltsch, Ernst, 4
Twesten, Karl, 349-351, 432, 437-438, 443, 444, 445, 448, 449

Uhland, Ludwig, 318
Unruh, Viktor von, 416, 417, 423, 426, 443

Venedey, Jakob, 420-421
Vienna, 38, 336; Congress of, 216, 218, 219
Vincke, Georg von, 296
Virchow, Rudolf, 432
Vischer, Friedrich Theodor, 318, 388-389

Waldeck, Benedikt, 389-391, 401, 432, 444
Weber, Alfred, 464
Weber, Max, 463-464
Weidig, F. L., 509
Weishaupt, Adam, 74

Weiss, Guido, 457
Weimar Republic, 464-468
Welcker, Karl Theodor, 253-256, 281, 283, 297, 315, 317, 318
Wesselhoeft, Robert, 268
Westphalia, Kingdom of, 143, 144, 490
Westphalia, Treaties of, 49
William I, King of Prussia, 407, 414
William I, King of Wuerttemberg, 238
Winckelmann, J. J., 72
Winter, Ludwig, 243, 296
Wirth, J. A., 279, 328-329
Wolff, Christian, 50, 71, 87; political theory, 66-70
Wolff, Theodor, 464
Workers, 335, 336, 338, 375, 376, 379, 380, 386, 395-396, 397, 399, 401, 406, 417, 418, 419-420, 422, 450, 451-453, 454
Wuerttemberg, 143, 450-451, 471-472; in post-Liberation period, 229, 231, 237-241, 256

Young Germany, 279, 284-285, 294, 296, 297, 298
Young Hegelians, 279, 282, 284-285, 296, 297, 301, 303, 325
Youth League, 264

Zehntner, Georg von, 232
Ziegler, Franz, 432